PENNSYLVANIA CONSOLIDATED STATUTES

TITLE 18
CRIMES
AND OFFENSES

2020 EDITION

Revised on January 3, 2020
By West Hartford Legal Publishing

PENNSYLVANIA
LEGISLATURE

4

DETAILED TABLE OF CONTENTS

TITLE 18

CRIMES AND OFFENSES

Chapter 57. Wiretapping and Electronic Surveillance

Subchapter A. General Provisions

Subchapter B. Wire, Electronic or Oral Communication

Subchapter C. Stored Wire and Electronic Communications and Transactional Records Access

15

TITLE 18
CRIMES AND OFFENSES

Enactment. Unless otherwise noted, the provisions of Title 18 were added December 6, 1972, P.L.1482, No.334, effective in six months.

Special Provisions in Appendix. See sections 2, 3 and 4 of Act 334 of 1972 in the appendix to this title for special provisions relating to offenses committed prior to the effective date of this title, severability and applicability of Statutory Construction Act.

PART I PRELIMINARY PROVISIONS

Enactment. Part I was added December 6, 1972, P.L.1482, No.334, effective in six months.

CHAPTER 1 GENERAL PROVISIONS

109. When prosecution barred by former prosecution for the same offense.

110. When prosecution barred by former prosecution for different offense.

111. When prosecution barred by former prosecution in another jurisdiction.

112. Former prosecution before court lacking jurisdiction or when fraudulently procured by the defendant.

Enactment. Chapter 1 was added December 6, 1972, P.L.1482, No.334, effective in six months.

§ 101. Short title of title.

This title shall be known and may be cited as the "Crimes Code."

§ 102. Territorial applicability.

(a) General rule.--Except as otherwise provided in this section, a person may be convicted under the law of this Commonwealth of an offense committed by his own conduct or the conduct of another for which he is legally accountable if either:

(1) the conduct which is an element of the offense or the result which is such an element occurs within this Commonwealth;

(2) conduct occurring outside this Commonwealth is sufficient under the law of this Commonwealth to constitute an attempt to commit an offense within this Commonwealth;

(3) conduct occurring outside this Commonwealth is sufficient under the law of this Commonwealth to constitute a conspiracy to commit an offense within this Commonwealth and an overt act in furtherance of such conspiracy occurs within this Commonwealth;

(4) conduct occurring within this Commonwealth establishes complicity in the commission of, or an attempt, solicitation or conspiracy to commit, an offense in another jurisdiction which also is an offense under the law of this Commonwealth;

(5) the offense consists of the omission to perform a legal duty imposed by the law of this Commonwealth with respect to domicile, residence or a relationship to a person, thing or transaction in this Commonwealth; or

(6) the offense is based on a statute of this Commonwealth which expressly prohibits conduct outside this Commonwealth when the conduct bears a reasonable relation to a legitimate interest of this Commonwealth and the actor knows or should know that his conduct is likely to affect that interest.

(b) Exception.--Paragraph (a)(1) of this section does not apply when causing a particular result is an element of an offense and the result is caused by conduct occurring outside this Commonwealth which would not constitute an offense if the result had occurred there, unless the actor intentionally or knowingly caused the result within this Commonwealth.

(c) Homicide.--When the offense is homicide or homicide of an unborn child, either the death of the victim, including an unborn child, or the bodily impact causing death constitutes a "result" within the meaning of paragraph (a)(1) of this section, and if the body of a homicide victim, including an unborn child, is found within this Commonwealth, it is presumed that such result occurred within this Commonwealth.

(d) Air space.--This Commonwealth includes the land and water and the air space above such land and water with respect to which the Commonwealth has legislative jurisdiction.

(Oct. 2, 1997, P.L.379, No.44, eff. 180 days)

1997 Amendment. Act 44 amended subsec. (c).

Cross References. Section 102 is referred to in sections 910, 7602 of this title.

§ 103. Definitions.

Subject to additional definitions contained in subsequent provisions of this title which are applicable to specific provisions of this part, the following words and phrases when used in this title shall have, unless the context clearly indicates otherwise, the meanings given to them in this section:

"Act" or **"action."** A bodily movement whether voluntary or involuntary.

"Actor." Includes, where relevant, a person guilty of an omission.

"Acted." Includes, where relevant, "omitted to act."

"Cohabit." To live together under the representation or appearance of being married.

"Conduct." An action or omission and its accompanying state of mind, or, where relevant, a series of acts and omissions.

"Court." Includes (when exercising criminal or quasi-criminal jurisdiction pursuant to 42 Pa.C.S. § 1515 (relating to jurisdiction and venue)) a magisterial district judge.

"Element of an offense." Such conduct or such attendant circumstances or such a result of conduct as:

(1) is included in the description of the forbidden conduct in the definition of the offense;

(2) establishes the required kind of culpability;

(3) negatives an excuse or justification for such conduct;

(4) negatives a defense under the statute of limitation; or

(5) establishes jurisdiction or venue.

"Fiduciary." Includes trustee, guardian, executor, administrator, receiver and any person carrying on fiduciary functions on behalf of a corporation or other organization which is a fiduciary.

"Intentionally." The meaning specified in section 302 of this title (relating to general requirements of culpability) and equivalent terms such as "with intent," "designed" or "with design" have the same meaning.

"Judge." Includes (when exercising criminal or quasi-criminal jurisdiction pursuant to 42 Pa.C.S. § 1515 (relating to jurisdiction and venue)) a magisterial district judge.

"Knowingly." The meaning specified in section 302 of this title (relating to general requirements of culpability) and equivalent terms such as "knowing" or "with knowledge" have the same meaning.

"Material element of an offense." An element that does not relate exclusively to the statute of limitations, jurisdiction, venue or to any other matter similarly unconnected with:

(1) the harm or evil incident to conduct, sought to be prevented by the law defining the offense; or

(2) the existence of a justification or excuse for such conduct.

"Negligently." The meaning specified in section 302 of this title (relating to general requirements of culpability) and equivalent terms such as "negligence" or "with negligence" have the same meaning.

"Omission." A failure to act.

"Police officer." The term shall include the sheriff of a county of the second class and deputy sheriffs of a county of the second class who have successfully completed the requirements under the act of June 18, 1974 (P.L.359, No.120), referred to as the Municipal Police Education and Training Law.

"Purposely" or **"with purpose."** Intentionally.

"Reasonably believes" or **"reasonable belief."** A belief which the actor is not reckless or negligent in holding.

"Recklessly." The meaning specified in section 302 of this title (relating to general requirements of culpability) and equivalent terms such as "recklessness" or "with recklessness" have the same meaning.

"Statute." Includes the Constitution of Pennsylvania and a local law or ordinance of a political subdivision.

"Whoever." Includes any person.

(Apr. 28, 1978, P.L.202, No.53, eff. 60 days; Nov. 22, 1995, P.L.621, No.66, eff. 60 days; Nov. 30, 2004, P.L.1618, No.207, eff. 60 days)

2004 Amendment. Act 207 amended the defs. of "court" and "judge." See section 29 of Act 207 in the appendix to this title for special provisions relating to construction of law.

1995 Amendment. Act 66 added the def. of "police officer."

1978 Amendment. Act 53 amended the intro. par. and added the defs. of "court" and "judge."

References in Text. The act of June 18, 1974 (P.L.359, No.120), referred to as the Municipal Police Education and Training Law, referred to in the def. of "police officer," was repealed by the act of December 19, 1996 (P.L.1158, No.177). The subject matter is now contained in Subchapter D of Chapter 21 of Title 53 (Municipalities Generally).

§ 104. Purposes.

The general purposes of this title are:

(1) To forbid and prevent conduct that unjustifiably inflicts or threatens substantial harm to individual or public interest.

(2) To safeguard conduct that is without fault from condemnation as criminal.

(3) To safeguard offenders against excessive, disproportionate or arbitrary punishment.

(4) To give fair warning of the nature of the conduct declared to constitute an offense, and of the sentences that may be imposed on conviction of an offense.

(5) To differentiate on reasonable grounds between serious and minor offenses, and to differentiate among offenders with a view to a just individualization in their treatment.

§ 105. Principles of construction.

The provisions of this title shall be construed according to the fair import of their terms but when the language is susceptible of differing constructions it shall be interpreted to further the general purposes stated in this title and the special purposes of the particular provision involved. The discretionary powers conferred by this title shall be exercised in accordance with the criteria stated in this title and, in so far as such criteria are not decisive, to further the general purposes stated in this title.

§ 106. Classes of offenses.

(a) General rule.--An offense defined by this title for which a sentence of death or of imprisonment is authorized constitutes a crime. The classes of crime are:

(1) Murder of the first degree, of the second degree or of the third degree, first degree murder of an unborn child, second degree murder of an unborn child or third degree murder of an unborn child.

(2) Felony of the first degree.

(3) Felony of the second degree.

(4) Felony of the third degree.

(5) Misdemeanor of the first degree.

(6) Misdemeanor of the second degree.

(7) Misdemeanor of the third degree.

(b) Classification of crimes.--

(1) A crime is a murder of the first degree, of the second degree or of the third degree if it is so designated in this title or if a person convicted of criminal homicide may be sentenced in accordance with the provisions of section 1102 (relating to sentence for murder and murder of an unborn child). A crime is first degree murder of an unborn child, second degree murder of an unborn child or third degree murder of an unborn child if it is so designated in this title or if a person convicted of criminal homicide of an unborn child may be sentenced in accordance with the provisions of section 1102.

(2) A crime is a felony of the first degree if it is so designated in this title or if a person convicted thereof may be sentenced to a term of imprisonment, the maximum of which is more than ten years.

(3) A crime is a felony of the second degree if it is so designated in this title or if a person convicted thereof may be sentenced to a term of imprisonment, the maximum of which is not more than ten years.

(4) A crime is a felony of the third degree if it is so designated in this title or if a person convicted thereof may be sentenced to a term of imprisonment, the maximum of which is not more than seven years.

(5) A crime declared to be a felony, without specification of degree, is of the third degree.

(6) A crime is a misdemeanor of the first degree if it is so designated in this title or if a person convicted thereof may be sentenced to a term of imprisonment, the maximum of which is not more than five years.

(7) A crime is a misdemeanor of the second degree if it is so designated in this title or if a person convicted thereof may be sentenced to a term of imprisonment, the maximum of which is not more than two years.

(8) A crime is a misdemeanor of the third degree if it is so designated in this title or if a person convicted thereof may be sentenced to a term of imprisonment, the maximum of which is not more than one year.

(9) A crime declared to be a misdemeanor, without specification of degree, is of the third degree.

(c) Summary offenses.--An offense defined by this title constitutes a summary offense if:

(1) it is so designated in this title, or in a statute other than this title; or

(2) if a person convicted thereof may be sentenced to a term of imprisonment, the maximum of which is not more than 90 days.

(d) Other crimes.--Any offense declared by law to constitute a crime, without specification of the class thereof, is a misdemeanor of the second degree, if the maximum sentence does not make it a felony under this section.

(e) Section applicable to other statutes.--An offense hereafter defined by any statute other than this title shall be classified as provided in this section.

(Mar. 26, 1974, P.L.213, No.46, eff. imd.; Oct. 2, 1997, P.L.379, No.44, eff. 180 days)

1997 Amendment. Act 44 amended subsecs. (a)(1) and (b)(1).

Cross References. Section 106 is referred to in sections 305, 2710, 2717, 3311 of this title; sections 1725.3, 1725.5, 9762 of Title 42 (Judiciary and Judicial Procedure).

§ 107. Application of preliminary provisions.

(a) General rule.--The provisions of Part I of this title (relating to preliminary provisions) are applicable to offenses defined by this title or by any other statute.

(b) Common law crimes abolished.--No conduct constitutes a crime unless it is a crime under this title or another statute of this Commonwealth.

(c) Exceptions.--This section does not affect the power of a court to declare forfeitures or to punish for contempt or to employ any sanction authorized by law for the enforcement of an order or a civil judgment or decree, nor does it bar, suspend, or otherwise affect any right of liability to damages, penalty, forfeiture or other remedy authorized by law to be recovered or enforced in a civil action, regardless of whether the conduct involved in such civil action or matter constitutes an offense defined in this title.

§ 108. Time limitations.

(a) General rule.--Except as set forth in subsection (b), a prosecution for any offense under this title must be commenced within the period, if any, limited by Chapter 55 of Title 42 (relating to limitation of time).

(b) Offenses against unborn child.--

(1) A prosecution for criminal homicide of an unborn child may be commenced at any time.

(2) A prosecution for an offense under section 2606 (relating to aggravated assault of unborn child) must be commenced within five years after it is committed.

(Mar. 26, 1974, P.L.213, No.46, eff. imd.; July 9, 1976, P.L.586, No.142; Apr. 28, 1978, P.L.83, No.38, eff. 60 days; Oct. 5, 1980, P.L.693, No.142, eff. 60 days; Oct. 2, 1997, P.L.379, No.44, eff. 180 days)

1980 Repeal. Act 142 repealed Act 38 of 1978, which amended subsec. (a), prior to the effective date of the repeal of former section 108 by Act 142 of 1976.

1976 Amendment. Act 142 added present section 108 and repealed former section 108, which related to the same subject matter, effective 60 days from the date of final enactment of the act of April 28, 1978 (P.L.202, No.53).

§ 109. When prosecution barred by former prosecution for the same offense.

When a prosecution is for a violation of the same provision of the statutes and is based upon the same facts as a former prosecution, it is barred by such former prosecution under the following circumstances:

(1) The former prosecution resulted in an acquittal. There is an acquittal if the prosecution resulted in a finding of not guilty by the trier of fact or in a determination that there was insufficient evidence to warrant a conviction. A finding of guilty of a lesser included offense is an acquittal of the greater inclusive offense, although the conviction is subsequently set aside.

(2) The former prosecution was terminated, after the indictment had been found, by a final order or judgment for the defendant, which has not been set aside, reversed, or vacated and which necessarily required a determination inconsistent with a fact or a legal proposition that must be established for conviction of the offense.

(3) The former prosecution resulted in a conviction. There is a conviction if the prosecution resulted in a judgment of conviction which has not been reversed or vacated, a verdict of guilty which has not been set aside and which is capable of supporting a judgment, or a plea of guilty accepted by the court. In the latter two cases failure to enter judgment must be for a reason other than a motion of the defendant.

(4) The former prosecution was improperly terminated after the first witness was sworn but before a verdict, or after a plea of guilty was accepted by the court.

Cross References. Section 109 is referred to in sections 110, 111, 112 of this title.

§ 110. When prosecution barred by former prosecution for different offense.

Although a prosecution is for a violation of a different provision of the statutes than a former prosecution or is based on different facts, it is barred by such former prosecution under the following circumstances:

(1) The former prosecution resulted in an acquittal or in a conviction as defined in section 109 of this title (relating to when prosecution barred by former prosecution for the same offense) and the subsequent prosecution is for:

(i) any offense of which the defendant could have been convicted on the first prosecution;

(ii) any offense based on the same conduct or arising from the same criminal episode, if such offense was known to the appropriate prosecuting officer at the time of the commencement of the first trial and occurred within the same judicial district as the former prosecution unless the court ordered a separate trial of the charge of such offense; or

(iii) the same conduct, unless:

(A) the offense of which the defendant was formerly convicted or acquitted and the offense for which he is subsequently prosecuted each requires proof of a fact not required by the other and the law defining each of such offenses is intended to prevent a substantially different harm or evil; or

(B) the second offense was not consummated when the former trial began.

(2) The former prosecution was terminated, after the indictment was found, by an acquittal or by a final order or judgment for the defendant which has not been set aside, reversed or vacated and which acquittal, final order or judgment necessarily required a determination inconsistent with a fact which must be established for conviction of the second offense.

(3) The former prosecution was improperly terminated, as improper termination is defined in section 109 of this title (relating to when prosecution barred by former prosecution for the same offense) and the subsequent prosecution is for an offense of which the defendant could have been convicted had the former prosecution not been improperly terminated.

(June 28, 2002, P.L.481, No.82, eff. 60 days)

2002 Amendment. Act 82 amended par. (1)(ii).

Cross References. Section 110 is referred to in section 112 of this title.

§ 111. When prosecution barred by former prosecution in another jurisdiction.

When conduct constitutes an offense within the concurrent jurisdiction of this Commonwealth and of the United States or another state, a prosecution in any such other jurisdiction is a bar to a subsequent prosecution in this Commonwealth under the following circumstances:

(1) The first prosecution resulted in an acquittal or in a conviction as defined in section 109 of this title (relating to when prosecution barred by former prosecution for the same offense) and the subsequent prosecution is based on the same conduct unless:

(i) the offense of which the defendant was formerly convicted or acquitted and the offense for which he is subsequently prosecuted each requires proof of a fact not required by the other and the law defining each of such offenses is intended to prevent a substantially different harm or evil; or

(ii) the second offense was not consummated when the former trial began.

(2) The former prosecution was terminated, after the indictment was found, by an acquittal or by a final order or judgment for the defendant which has not been set aside, reversed or vacated and which acquittal, final order or judgment necessarily required a determination inconsistent with a fact which must be established for conviction of the offense of which the defendant is subsequently prosecuted.

Cross References. Section 111 is referred to in section 112 of this title.

§ 112. Former prosecution before court lacking jurisdiction or when fraudulently procured by the defendant.

A prosecution is not a bar within the meaning of section 109 of this title (relating to when prosecution barred by former prosecution for the same offense) through section 111 of this title (relating to when prosecution barred by former prosecution in another jurisdiction) under any of the following circumstances:

(1) The former prosecution was before a court which lacked jurisdiction over the defendant or the offense.

(2) The former prosecution was procured by the defendant without the knowledge of the appropriate prosecuting officer and with the purpose of avoiding the sentence which might otherwise be imposed.

(3) The former prosecution resulted in a judgment of conviction which was held invalid in a subsequent proceeding on a writ of habeas corpus, coram nobis or similar process.

CHAPTER 3
CULPABILITY

Enactment. Chapter 3 was added December 6, 1972, P.L.1482, No.334, effective in six months.

Cross References. Chapter 3 is referred to in section 2607 of this title.

§ 301. Requirement of voluntary act.

(a) General rule.--A person is not guilty of an offense unless his liability is based on conduct which includes a voluntary act or the omission to perform an act of which he is physically capable.

(b) Omission as basis of liability.--Liability for the commission of an offense may not be based on an omission unaccompanied by action unless:

(1) the omission is expressly made sufficient by the law defining the offense; or

(2) a duty to perform the omitted act is otherwise imposed by law.

(c) Possession as an act.--Possession is an act, within the meaning of this section, if the possessor knowingly procured or received the thing possessed or was aware of his control thereof for a sufficient period to have been able to terminate his possession.

Cross References. Section 301 is referred to in section 305 of this title.

§ 302. General requirements of culpability.

(a) Minimum requirements of culpability.--Except as provided in section 305 of this title (relating to limitations on scope of culpability requirements), a person is not guilty of an offense unless he acted intentionally, knowingly, recklessly or negligently, as the law may require, with respect to each material element of the offense.

(b) Kinds of culpability defined.--

(1) A person acts intentionally with respect to a material element of an offense when:

(i) if the element involves the nature of his conduct or a result thereof, it is his conscious object to engage in conduct of that nature or to cause such a result; and

(ii) if the element involves the attendant circumstances, he is aware of the existence of such circumstances or he believes or hopes that they exist.

(2) A person acts knowingly with respect to a material element of an offense when:

(i) if the element involves the nature of his conduct or the attendant circumstances, he is aware that his conduct is of that nature or that such circumstances exist; and

(ii) if the element involves a result of his conduct, he is aware that it is practically certain that his conduct will cause such a result.

(3) A person acts recklessly with respect to a material element of an offense when he consciously disregards a substantial and unjustifiable risk that the material element exists or will result from his conduct. The risk must be of such a nature and degree that, considering the nature and intent of the actor's conduct and the circumstances known to him, its disregard involves a gross deviation from the standard of conduct that a reasonable person would observe in the actor's situation.

(4) A person acts negligently with respect to a material element of an offense when he should be aware of a substantial and unjustifiable risk that the material element exists or will result from his conduct. The risk must be of such a nature and degree that the actor's failure to perceive it, considering the nature and intent of his conduct and the circumstances known to him, involves a gross deviation from the standard of care that a reasonable person would observe in the actor's situation.

(c) Culpability required unless otherwise provided.--When the culpability sufficient to establish a material element of an offense is not prescribed by law, such element is established if a person acts intentionally, knowingly or recklessly with respect thereto.

(d) Prescribed culpability requirement applies to all material elements.--When the law defining an offense prescribes the kind of culpability that is sufficient for the commission of an offense, without distinguishing among the material elements thereof, such provision shall apply to all the material elements of the offense, unless a contrary purpose plainly appears.

24

(e) Substitutes for negligence, recklessness and knowledge.--When the law provides that negligence suffices to establish an element of an offense, such element also is established if a person acts intentionally or knowingly. When acting knowingly suffices to establish an element, such element also is established if a person acts intentionally.

(f) Requirement of intent satisfied if intent is conditional.--When a particular intent is an element of an offense, the element is established although such intent is conditional, unless the condition negatives the harm or evil sought to be prevented by the law defining the offense.

(g) Requirement of willfulness satisfied by acting knowingly.--A requirement that an offense be committed willfully is satisfied if a person acts knowingly with respect to the material elements of the offense, unless a purpose to impose further requirements appears.

(h) Culpability as to illegality of conduct.--Neither knowledge nor recklessness or negligence as to whether conduct constitutes an offense or as to the existence, meaning or application of the law determining the elements of an offense is an element of such offense, unless the definition of the offense or this title so provides.

Cross References. Section 302 is referred to in sections 103, 305 of this title; section 6303 of Title 23 (Domestic Relations).

§ 303. Causal relationship between conduct and result.

(a) General rule.--Conduct is the cause of a result when:

(1) it is an antecedent but for which the result in question would not have occurred; and

(2) the relationship between the conduct and result satisfies any additional causal requirements imposed by this title or by the law defining the offense.

(b) Divergence between result designed or contemplated and actual result.--When intentionally or knowingly causing a particular result is an element of an offense, the element is not established if the actual result is not within the intent or the contemplation of the actor unless:

(1) the actual result differs from that designed or contemplated as the case may be, only in the respect that a different person or different property is injured or affected or that

the injury or harm designed or contemplated would have been more serious or more extensive than that caused; or

(2) the actual result involves the same kind of injury or harm as that designed or contemplated and is not too remote or accidental in its occurrence to have a bearing on the actor's liability or on the gravity of his offense.

(c) Divergence between probable and actual result.--When recklessly or negligently causing a particular result is an element of an offense, the element is not established if the actual result is not within the risk of which the actor is aware or, in the case of negligence, of which he should be aware unless:

(1) the actual result differs from the probable result only in the respect that a different person or different property is injured or affected or that the probable injury or harm would have been more serious or more extensive than that caused; or

(2) the actual result involves the same kind of injury or harm as the probable result and is not too remote or accidental in its occurrence to have a bearing on the liability of the actor or on the gravity of his offense.

(d) Absolute liability.--When causing a particular result is a material element of an offense for which absolute liability is imposed by law, the element is not established unless the actual result is a probable consequence of the conduct of the actor.

Cross References. Section 303 is referred to in section 2607 of this title.

§ 304. Ignorance or mistake.

Ignorance or mistake as to a matter of fact, for which there is reasonable explanation or excuse, is a defense if:

(1) the ignorance or mistake negatives the intent, knowledge, belief, recklessness, or negligence required to establish a material element of the offense; or

(2) the law provides that the state of mind established by such ignorance or mistake constitutes a defense.

§ 305. Limitations on scope of culpability requirements.

(a) When culpability requirements are inapplicable to summary offenses and to offenses defined by other statutes.--The requirements of culpability prescribed by section 301 of this title (relating to requirement of voluntary act) and section 302 of this title (relating to general requirements of culpability) do not apply to:

(1) summary offenses, unless the requirement involved is included in the definition of the offense or the court determines that its application is consistent with effective enforcement of the law defining the offense; or

(2) offenses defined by statutes other than this title, in so far as a legislative purpose to impose absolute liability for such offenses or with respect to any material element thereof plainly appears.

(b) Effect of absolute liability in reducing grade of offense to summary offense.--Notwithstanding any other provision of existing law and unless a subsequent statute otherwise provides:

(1) when absolute liability is imposed with respect to any material element of an offense defined by a statute other than this title and a conviction is based upon such liability, the offense constitutes a summary offense; and

(2) although absolute liability is imposed by law with respect to one or more of the material elements of an offense defined by a statute other than this title, the culpable commission of the offense may be charged and proved, in which event negligence with respect to such elements constitutes sufficient culpability and the classification of the offense and the sentence that may be imposed therefor upon conviction are determined by section 106 of this title (relating to classes of offenses) and Chapter 11 of this title (relating to authorized disposition of offenders).

Cross References. Section 305 is referred to in section 302 of this title.

§ 306. Liability for conduct of another; complicity.

(a) General rule.--A person is guilty of an offense if it is committed by his own conduct or by the conduct of another person for which he is legally accountable, or both.

(b) Conduct of another.--A person is legally accountable for the conduct of another person when:

(1) acting with the kind of culpability that is sufficient for the commission of the offense, he causes an innocent or irresponsible person to engage in such conduct;

(2) he is made accountable for the conduct of such other person by this title or by the law defining the offense; or

(3) he is an accomplice of such other person in the commission of the offense.

(c) Accomplice defined.--A person is an accomplice of another person in the commission of an offense if:

(1) with the intent of promoting or facilitating the commission of the offense, he:

(i) solicits such other person to commit it; or

(ii) aids or agrees or attempts to aid such other person in planning or committing it; or

(2) his conduct is expressly declared by law to establish his complicity.

(d) Culpability of accomplice.--When causing a particular result is an element of an offense, an accomplice in the conduct causing such result is an accomplice in the commission of that offense, if he acts with the kind of culpability, if any, with respect to that result that is sufficient for the commission of the offense.

(e) Status of actor.--In any prosecution for an offense in which criminal liability of the defendant is based upon the conduct of another person pursuant to this section, it is no defense that the offense in question, as defined, can be committed only by a particular class or classes of persons, and the defendant, not belonging to such class or classes, is for that reason legally incapable of committing the offense in an individual capacity.

(f) Exceptions.--Unless otherwise provided by this title or by the law defining the offense, a person is not an accomplice in an offense committed by another person if:

(1) he is a victim of that offense;

(2) the offense is so defined that his conduct is inevitably incident to its commission; or

(3) he terminates his complicity prior to the commission of the offense and:

(i) wholly deprives it of effectiveness in the commission of the offense; or

(ii) gives timely warning to the law enforcement authorities or otherwise makes proper effort to prevent the commission of the offense.

(g) Prosecution of accomplice only.--An accomplice may be convicted on proof of the commission of the offense and of his complicity therein, though the person claimed to have committed the offense has not been prosecuted or convicted or has been convicted of a different offense or degree of offense or has an immunity to prosecution or conviction or has been acquitted.

Cross References. Section 306 is referred to in sections 904, 3218, 6111 of this title; section 9711 of Title 42 (Judiciary and Judicial Procedure).

§ 307. Liability of organizations and certain related persons.

(a) Corporations generally.--A corporation may be convicted of the commission of an offense if:

(1) the offense is a summary offense or the offense is defined by a statute other than this title in which a legislative purpose to impose liability on corporations plainly appears and the conduct is performed by an agent of the corporation acting in behalf of the corporation within the scope of his office or employment, except that if the law defining the offense designates the agents for whose conduct the corporation is accountable or the circumstances under which it is accountable, such provisions shall apply;

(2) the offense consists of an omission to discharge a specific duty of affirmative performance imposed on corporations by law; or

(3) the commission of the offense was authorized, requested, commanded, performed or recklessly tolerated by the board of directors or by a high managerial agent acting in behalf of the corporation within the scope of his office or employment.

(b) Corporations, absolute liability.-- When absolute liability is imposed for the commission of an offense, a legislative purpose to impose liability on a corporation shall be assumed, unless the contrary plainly appears.

(c) Unincorporated associations.--An unincorporated association may be convicted of the commission of an offense if:

(1) the offense is defined by a statute other than this title which expressly provides for the liability of such an association and the conduct is performed by an agent of the association acting in behalf of the association within the scope of his office or employment, except that if the law defining the offense designates the agents for whose conduct the association is accountable or the circumstances under which it is accountable, such provisions shall apply; or

(2) the offense consists of an omission to discharge a specific duty of affirmative performance imposed on associations by law.

(d) Defenses.--In any prosecution of a corporation or an unincorporated association for the commission of an offense included within the terms of paragraph (a)(1) or paragraph (c)(1) of this section, other than an offense for which absolute liability has been imposed, it shall be a defense if the defendant proves by a preponderance of evidence that the high managerial agent having supervisory responsibility over the subject matter of the offense employed due diligence to prevent its commission. This subsection shall not apply if it is plainly inconsistent with the legislative purpose in defining the particular offense.

(e) Persons acting or under a duty to act for organizations.--

(1) A person is legally accountable for any conduct he performs or causes to be performed in the name of a corporation or an unincorporated association or in its behalf to the same extent as if it were performed in his own name or behalf.

(2) Whenever a duty to act is imposed by law upon a corporation or an unincorporated association, any agent of the corporation or association having primary responsibility for the discharge of the duty is legally accountable for a reckless omission to perform the required act to the same extent as if the duty were imposed by law directly upon himself.

(3) When a person is convicted of an offense by reason of his legal accountability for the conduct of a corporation or an unincorporated association, he is subject to the sentence authorized by law when a natural person is convicted of an offense of the grade and the degree involved.

(f) Definitions.--As used in this section the following words and phrases shall have the meanings given to them in this subsection:

"Agent." Any director, officer, servant, employee or other person authorized to act in behalf of the corporation or association and, in the case of an unincorporated association, a member of such association.

"Corporation." Does not include an entity organized as or by a governmental agency for the execution of a governmental program.

"High managerial agent." An officer of a corporation or an unincorporated association, or, in the case of a partnership, a partner, or any other agent of a corporation or association having duties of such responsibility that his conduct may fairly be assumed to represent the policy of the corporation or association.

Cross References. Section 307 is referred to in section 6305 of this title.

§ 308. Intoxication or drugged condition.

Neither voluntary intoxication nor voluntary drugged condition is a defense to a criminal charge, nor may evidence of such conditions be introduced to negative the element of intent of the offense, except that evidence of such intoxication or drugged condition of the defendant may be offered by the defendant whenever it is relevant to reduce murder from a higher degree to a lower degree of murder.

(Apr. 7, 1976, P.L.72, No.32, eff. imd.)

§ 309. Duress.

(a) General rule.--It is a defense that the actor engaged in the conduct charged to constitute an offense because he was coerced to do so by the use of, or a threat to use, unlawful force against his person or the person of another, which a person of reasonable firmness in his situation would have been unable to resist.

(b) Exception.--The defense provided by subsection (a) of this section is unavailable if the actor recklessly placed himself in a situation in which it was probable that he would be subjected to duress. The defense is also unavailable if he was negligent in placing himself in such a situation, whenever negligence suffices to establish culpability for the offense charged.

Cross References. Section 309 is referred to in section 9711 of Title 42 (Judiciary and Judicial Procedure).

§ 310. Military orders.

It is a defense that the actor, in engaging in the conduct charged to constitute an offense, does no more than execute an order of his superior in the armed services which he does not know and cannot reasonably be expected to know to be unlawful.

§ 311. Consent.

(a) General rule.--The consent of the victim to conduct charged to constitute an offense or to the result thereof is a defense if such consent negatives an element of the offense or precludes the infliction of the harm or evil sought to be prevented by the law defining the offense.

(b) Consent to bodily injury.--When conduct is charged to constitute an offense because it causes or threatens bodily injury, consent to such conduct or to the infliction of such injury is a defense if:

(1) the conduct and the injury are reasonably foreseeable hazards of joint participation in a lawful athletic contest or competitive sport; or

(2) the consent establishes a justification for the conduct under Chapter 5 of this title (relating to general principles of justification).

(c) Ineffective consent.--Unless otherwise provided by this title or by the law defining the offense, assent does not constitute consent if:

(1) it is given by a person who is legally incapacitated to authorize the conduct charged to constitute the offense;

(2) it is given by a person who by reason of youth, mental disease or defect or intoxication is manifestly unable or known by the actor to be unable to make a reasonable judgment as to the nature or harmfulness of the conduct charged to constitute the offense;

(3) it is given by a person whose improvident consent is sought to be prevented by the law defining the offense; or

(4) it is induced by force, duress or deception of a kind sought to be prevented by the law defining the offense.

(Apr. 16, 1992, P.L.108, No.24, eff. 60 days)

1992 Amendment. Act 24 amended subsec. (c).

Cross References. Section 311 is referred to in sections 2607, 2718 of this title.

§ 312. De minimis infractions.

(a) General rule.--The court shall dismiss a prosecution if, having regard to the nature of the conduct charged to constitute an offense and the nature of the attendant circumstances, it finds that the conduct of the defendant:

(1) was within a customary license or tolerance, neither expressly negatived by the person whose interest was infringed nor inconsistent with the purpose of the law defining the offense;

(2) did not actually cause or threaten the harm or evil sought to be prevented by the law defining the offense or did so only to an extent too trivial to warrant the condemnation of conviction; or

(3) presents such other extenuations that it cannot reasonably be regarded as envisaged by the General Assembly or other authority in forbidding the offense.

(b) Written statement.--The court shall not dismiss a prosecution under this section without filing a written statement of its reasons, except that if the attorney for the Commonwealth is the moving party for such dismissal no such written statement need be filed.

(June 22, 1978, P.L.494, No.73, eff. 60 days)

1978 Amendment. Act 73 amended subsec. (b).

§ 313. Entrapment.

(a) General rule.--A public law enforcement official or a person acting in cooperation with such an official perpetrates an entrapment if for the purpose of obtaining evidence of the commission of an offense, he induces or encourages another person to engage in conduct constituting such offense by either:

(1) making knowingly false representations designed to induce the belief that such conduct is not prohibited; or

(2) employing methods of persuasion or inducement which create a substantial risk that such an offense will be committed by persons other than those who are ready to commit it.

(b) Burden of proof.--Except as provided in subsection (c) of this section, a person prosecuted for an offense shall be acquitted if he proves by a preponderance of evidence that his conduct occurred in response to an entrapment.

(c) Exception.--The defense afforded by this section is unavailable when causing or threatening bodily injury is an element of the offense charged and the prosecution is based on conduct causing or threatening such injury to a person other than the person perpetrating the entrapment.

§ 314. Guilty but mentally ill.

(a) General rule.--A person who timely offers a defense of insanity in accordance with the Rules of Criminal Procedure may be found "guilty but mentally ill" at trial if the trier of facts finds, beyond a reasonable doubt, that the person is guilty of an offense, was mentally ill at the time of the commission of the offense and was not legally insane at the time of the commission of the offense.

(b) Plea of guilty but mentally ill.--A person who waives his right to trial may plead guilty but mentally ill. No plea of guilty but mentally ill may be accepted by the trial judge until he has examined all reports prepared pursuant to the Rules of Criminal Procedure, has held a hearing on the sole issue of the defendant's mental illness at which either party may present evidence and is satisfied that the defendant was mentally ill at the time of the offense to which the plea is entered. If the trial judge refuses to accept a plea of guilty but mentally ill, the defendant shall be permitted to withdraw his plea. A defendant whose plea is not accepted by the court shall be entitled to a jury trial, except that if a defendant subsequently waives his right to a jury trial, the judge who presided at the hearing on mental illness shall not preside at the trial.

(c) Definitions.--For the purposes of this section and 42 Pa.C.S. § 9727 (relating to disposition of persons found guilty but mentally ill):

(1) "Mentally ill." One who as a result of mental disease or defect, lacks substantial capacity either to appreciate the wrongfulness of his conduct or to conform his conduct to the requirements of the law.

(2) "Legal insanity." At the time of the commission of the act, the defendant was laboring under such a defect of reason, from disease of the mind, as not to know the nature and quality of the act he was doing or, if he did know it, that he did not know he was doing what was wrong.

(d) Common law M'Naghten's Rule preserved.--Nothing in this section shall be deemed to repeal or otherwise abrogate the common law defense of insanity (M'Naghten's Rule) in effect in this Commonwealth on the effective date of this section.

(Dec. 15, 1982, P.L.1262, No.286, eff. 90 days)

1982 Amendment. Act 286 added section 314. Section 4 of Act 286 provided that Act 286 shall apply to all indictments or informations filed on or after the effective date of Act 286.

Cross References. Section 314 is referred to in section 9727 of Title 42 (Judiciary and Judicial Procedure).

§ 315. Insanity.

(a) General rule.--The mental soundness of an actor engaged in conduct charged to constitute an offense shall only be a defense to the charged offense when the actor proves by a preponderance of evidence that the actor was legally insane at the time of the commission of the offense.

(b) **Definition.**--For purposes of this section, the phrase "legally insane" means that, at the time of the commission of the offense, the actor was laboring under such a defect of reason, from disease of the mind, as not to know the nature and quality of the act he was doing or, if the actor did know the quality of the act, that he did not know that what he was doing was wrong.

(Dec. 15, 1982, P.L.1262, No.286, eff. 90 days)

1982 Amendment. Act 286 added section 315. Section 4 of Act 286 provided that Act 286 shall apply to all indictments or informations filed on or after the effective date of Act 286.

CHAPTER 5 GENERAL PRINCIPLES OF JUSTIFICATION

Enactment. Chapter 5 was added December 6, 1972, P.L.1482, No.334, effective in six months.

Cross References. Chapter 5 is referred to in sections 311, 908.1, 2503, 2507, 2605, 2608 of this title; section 711 of Title 51 (Military Affairs).

§ 501. Definitions.

Subject to additional definitions contained in subsequent provisions of this chapter which are applicable to specific provisions of this chapter, the following words and phrases, when used in this chapter shall have, unless the context clearly indicates otherwise, the meanings given to them in this section:

"Believes" or **"belief."** Means "reasonably believes" or "reasonable belief."

"Correctional institution." Any penal institution, penitentiary, State farm, reformatory, prison, jail, house of correction, or other institution for the incarceration or custody of persons under sentence for offenses or awaiting trial or sentence for offenses.

"Corrections officer." A full-time employee assigned to the Department of Corrections whose principal duty is the care, custody and control of inmates of a penal or correctional institution operated by the Department of Corrections.

"Deadly force." Force which, under the circumstances in which it is used, is readily capable of causing death or serious bodily injury.

"Dwelling." Any building or structure, including any attached porch, deck or patio, though movable or temporary, or a portion thereof, which is for the time being the home or place of lodging of the actor.

"Peace officer." Any person who by virtue of his office or public employment is vested by law with a duty to maintain public order or to make arrests for offenses, whether that duty extends to all offenses or is limited to specific offenses, or any person on active State duty pursuant to 51 Pa.C.S. § 508 (relating to active duty for emergency). The term "peace officer" shall also include any member of any park police department of any county of the third class.

"Residence." A dwelling in which a person resides, either temporarily or permanently, or visits as an invited guest.

"Unlawful force." Force, including confinement, which is employed without the consent of the person against whom it is directed and the employment of which constitutes an offense or actionable tort or would constitute such offense or tort except for a defense (such as the absence of intent, negligence, or mental capacity; duress; youth; or diplomatic status) not amounting to a privilege to use the force. Assent constitutes consent, within the meaning of this section, whether or not it otherwise is legally effective, except assent to the infliction of death or serious bodily injury.

"Vehicle." A conveyance of any kind, whether or not motorized, that is designed to transport people or property.

(July 6, 1984, P.L.647, No.134, eff. 90 days; July 17, 2007, P.L.139, No.41, eff. 60 days; June 28, 2011, P.L.48, No.10, eff. 60 days)

2011 Amendment. See the preamble to Act 10 in the appendix to this title for special provisions relating to legislative findings.

Cross References. Section 501 is referred to in sections 2507, 2702.1 of this title; section 9719.1 of Title 42 (Judiciary and Judicial Procedure).

§ 502. Justification a defense.

In any prosecution based on conduct which is justifiable under this chapter, justification is a defense.

§ 503. Justification generally.

(a) General rule.--Conduct which the actor believes to be necessary to avoid a harm or evil to himself or to another is justifiable if:

(1) the harm or evil sought to be avoided by such conduct is greater than that sought to be prevented by the law defining the offense charged;

(2) neither this title nor other law defining the offense provides exceptions or defenses dealing with the specific situation involved; and

(3) a legislative purpose to exclude the justification claimed does not otherwise plainly appear.

(b) Choice of evils.--When the actor was reckless or negligent in bringing about the situation requiring a choice of harms or evils or in appraising the necessity for his conduct, the justification afforded by this section is unavailable in a prosecution for any offense for which recklessness or negligence, as the case may be, suffices to establish culpability.

§ 504. Execution of public duty.

(a) General rule.--Except as provided in subsection (b) of this section, conduct is justifiable when it is required or authorized by any law of the following:

(1) The law defining the duties or functions of a public officer or the assistance to be rendered to such officer in the performance of his duties.

(2) The law governing the execution of legal process.

(3) The judgment or order of a competent court or tribunal.

(4) The law governing the armed services or the lawful conduct of war.

(5) Any other provision of law imposing a public duty.

(b) Exceptions.--The other sections of this chapter apply to:

(1) The use of force upon or toward the person of another for any of the purposes dealt with in such sections.

(2) The use of deadly force for any purpose, unless the use of such force is otherwise expressly authorized by law or occurs in the lawful conduct of war.

(c) Requisite state of mind.--The justification afforded by subsection (a) of this section applies:

(1) when the actor believes his conduct to be required or authorized by the judgment or direction of a competent court or tribunal or in the lawful execution of legal process, notwithstanding lack of jurisdiction of the court or defect in the legal process; and

(2) when the actor believes his conduct to be required or authorized to assist a public officer in the performance of his duties, notwithstanding that the officer exceeded his legal authority.

§ 505. Use of force in self-protection.

(a) Use of force justifiable for protection of the person.--The use of force upon or toward another person is justifiable when the actor believes that such force is immediately necessary for the purpose of protecting himself against the use of unlawful force by such other person on the present occasion.

(b) Limitations on justifying necessity for use of force.--

(1) The use of force is not justifiable under this section:

(i) to resist an arrest which the actor knows is being made by a peace officer, although the arrest is unlawful; or

(ii) to resist force used by the occupier or possessor of property or by another person on his behalf, where the actor knows that the person using the force is doing so under a claim of right to protect the property, except that this limitation shall not apply if:

(A) the actor is a public officer acting in the performance of his duties or a person lawfully assisting him therein or a person making or assisting in a lawful arrest;

(B) the actor has been unlawfully dispossessed of the property and is making a reentry or recaption justified by section 507 of this title (relating to use of force for the protection of property); or

(C) the actor believes that such force is necessary to protect himself against death or serious bodily injury.

(2) The use of deadly force is not justifiable under this section unless the actor believes that such force is necessary to protect himself against death, serious bodily injury, kidnapping or sexual intercourse compelled by force or threat; nor is it justifiable if:

(i) the actor, with the intent of causing death or serious bodily injury, provoked the use of force against himself in the same encounter; or

(ii) the actor knows that he can avoid the necessity of using such force with complete safety by retreating, except the actor is not obliged to retreat from his dwelling or place of work, unless he was the initial aggressor or is assailed in his place of work by another person whose place of work the actor knows it to be.

(2.1) Except as otherwise provided in paragraph (2.2), an actor is presumed to have a reasonable belief that deadly force is immediately necessary to protect himself against death, serious bodily injury, kidnapping or sexual intercourse compelled by force or threat if both of the following conditions exist:

(i) The person against whom the force is used is in the process of unlawfully and forcefully entering, or has unlawfully and forcefully entered and is present within, a dwelling, residence or occupied vehicle; or the person against whom the force is used is or is attempting to unlawfully and forcefully remove another against that other's will from the dwelling, residence or occupied vehicle.

(ii) The actor knows or has reason to believe that the unlawful and forceful entry or act is occurring or has occurred.

(2.2) The presumption set forth in paragraph (2.1) does not apply if:

(i) the person against whom the force is used has the right to be in or is a lawful resident of the dwelling, residence or vehicle, such as an owner or lessee;

(ii) the person sought to be removed is a child or grandchild or is otherwise in the lawful custody or under the lawful guardianship of the person against whom the protective force is used;

(iii) the actor is engaged in a criminal activity or is using the dwelling, residence or

occupied vehicle to further a criminal activity; or

(iv) the person against whom the force is used is a peace officer acting in the performance of his official duties and the actor using force knew or reasonably should have known that the person was a peace officer.

(2.3) An actor who is not engaged in a criminal activity, who is not in illegal possession of a firearm and who is attacked in any place where the actor would have a duty to retreat under paragraph (2)(ii) has no duty to retreat and has the right to stand his ground and use force, including deadly force, if:

(i) the actor has a right to be in the place where he was attacked;

(ii) the actor believes it is immediately necessary to do so to protect himself against death, serious bodily injury, kidnapping or sexual intercourse by force or threat; and

(iii) the person against whom the force is used displays or otherwise uses:

(A) a firearm or replica of a firearm as defined in 42 Pa.C.S. § 9712 (relating to sentences for offenses committed with firearms); or

(B) any other weapon readily or apparently capable of lethal use.

(2.4) The exception to the duty to retreat set forth under paragraph (2.3) does not apply if the person against whom the force is used is a peace officer acting in the performance of his official duties and the actor using force knew or reasonably should have known that the person was a peace officer.

(2.5) Unless one of the exceptions under paragraph (2.2) applies, a person who unlawfully and by force enters or attempts to enter an actor's dwelling, residence or occupied vehicle or removes or attempts to remove another against that other's will from the actor's dwelling, residence or occupied vehicle is presumed to be doing so with the intent to commit:

(i) an act resulting in death or serious bodily injury; or

(ii) kidnapping or sexual intercourse by force or threat.

(2.6) A public officer justified in using force in the performance of his duties or a person justified in using force in his assistance or a person justified in using force in making an arrest or preventing an escape is not obliged to desist from efforts to perform such duty, effect such arrest or prevent such escape because of resistance or threatened resistance by or on behalf of the person against whom such action is directed.

(3) Except as otherwise required by this subsection, a person employing protective force may estimate the necessity thereof under the circumstances as he believes them to be when the force is used, without retreating, surrendering possession, doing any other act which he has no legal duty to do or abstaining from any lawful action.

(c) Use of confinement as protective force.--The justification afforded by this section extends to the use of confinement as protective force only if the actor takes all reasonable measures to terminate the confinement as soon as he knows that he safely can, unless the person confined has been arrested on a charge of crime.

(d) Definition.--As used in this section, the term "criminal activity" means conduct which is a misdemeanor or felony, is not justifiable under this chapter and is related to the confrontation between an actor and the person against whom force is used.

(June 28, 2011, P.L.48, No.10, eff. 60 days)

2011 Amendment. Act 10 amended subsec. (b) and added subsec. (d). See the preamble to Act 10 in the appendix to this title for special provisions relating to legislative findings.

Cross References. Section 505 is referred to in section 506 of this title; section 6304 of Title 23 (Domestic Relations); section 8340.2 of Title 42 (Judiciary and Judicial Procedure).

§ 506. Use of force for the protection of other persons.

(a) General rule.--The use of force upon or toward the person of another is justifiable to protect a third person when:

(1) the actor would be justified under section 505 (relating to use of force in self-protection) in using such force to protect himself against the injury he believes to be threatened to the person whom he seeks to protect;

(2) under the circumstances as the actor believes them to be, the person whom he seeks to protect would be justified in using such protective force; and

(3) the actor believes that his intervention is necessary for the protection of such other person.

(b) Exception.--Notwithstanding subsection (a), the actor is not obliged to retreat to any greater extent than the person whom he seeks to protect.

(June 28, 2011, P.L.48, No.10, eff. 60 days)

2011 Amendment. See the preamble to Act 10 in the appendix to this title for special provisions relating to legislative findings.

Cross References. Section 506 is referred to in section 6304 of Title 23 (Domestic Relations); section 8340.2 of Title 42 (Judiciary and Judicial Procedure).

§ 507. Use of force for the protection of property.

(a) Use of force justifiable for protection of property.--The use of force upon or toward the person of another is justifiable when the actor believes that such force is immediately necessary:

(1) to prevent or terminate an unlawful entry or other trespass upon land or a trespass against or the unlawful carrying away of tangible movable property, if such land or movable property is, or is believed by the actor to be, in his possession or in the possession of another person for whose protection he acts; or

(2) to effect an entry or reentry upon land or to retake tangible movable property, if:

(i) the actor believes that he or the person by whose authority he acts or a person from whom he or such other person derives title was unlawfully dispossessed of such land or movable property and is entitled to possession; and

(ii) (A) the force is used immediately or on fresh pursuit after such dispossession; or

(B) the actor believes that the person against whom he uses force has no claim of right to the possession of the property and, in the case of land, the circumstances, as the actor believes them to be, are of such urgency that it would be an exceptional hardship to postpone the entry or reentry until a court order is obtained.

(b) Meaning of possession.--For the purpose of subsection (a) of this section:

(1) A person who has parted with the custody of property to another who refuses to restore it to him is no longer in possession, unless the property is movable and was and still is located on land in his possession.

33

(2) A person who has been dispossessed of land does not regain possession thereof merely by setting foot thereon.

(3) A person who has a license to use or occupy real property is deemed to be in possession thereof except against the licensor acting under claim of right.

(c) Limitations on justifiable use of force.--

(1) The use of force is justifiable under this section only if the actor first requests the person against whom such force is used to desist from his interference with the property, unless the actor believes that:

(i) such request would be useless;

(ii) it would be dangerous to himself or another person to make the request; or

(iii) substantial harm will be done to the physical condition of the property which is sought to be protected before the request can effectively be made.

(2) The use of force to prevent or terminate a trespass is not justifiable under this section if the actor knows that the exclusion of the trespasser will expose him to substantial danger of serious bodily injury.

(3) The use of force to prevent an entry or reentry upon land or the recaption of movable property is not justifiable under this section, although the actor believes that such reentry or caption is unlawful, if:

(i) the reentry or recaption is made by or on behalf of a person who was actually dispossessed of the property; and

(ii) it is otherwise justifiable under subsection (a)(2).

(4) (i) The use of deadly force is justifiable under this section if:

(A) there has been an entry into the actor's dwelling;

(B) the actor neither believes nor has reason to believe that the entry is lawful; and

(C) the actor neither believes nor has reason to believe that force less than deadly force would be adequate to terminate the entry.

(ii) If the conditions of justification provided in subparagraph (i) have not been met, the use of deadly force is not justifiable under this section unless the actor believes that:

(A) the person against whom the force is used is attempting to dispossess him of his dwelling otherwise than under a claim of right to its possession; or

(B) such force is necessary to prevent the commission of a felony in the dwelling.

(d) Use of confinement as protective force.--The justification afforded by this section extends to the use of confinement as protective force only if the actor takes all reasonable measures to terminate the confinement as soon as he knows that he can do so with safety to the property, unless the person confined has been arrested on a charge of crime.

(e) Use of device to protect property.-- The justification afforded by this section extends to the use of a device for the purpose of protecting property only if:

(1) the device is not designed to cause or known to create a substantial risk of causing death or serious bodily injury;

(2) the use of the particular device to protect the property from entry or trespass is reasonable under the circumstances, as the actor believes them to be; and

(3) the device is one customarily used for such a purpose or reasonable care is taken to make known to probable intruders the fact that it is used.

(f) Use of force to pass wrongful obstructor.--The use of force to pass a person whom the actor believes to be intentionally or knowingly and unjustifiably obstructing the actor from going to a place to which he may lawfully go is justifiable, if:

(1) the actor believes that the person against whom he uses force has no claim of right to obstruct the actor;

(2) the actor is not being obstructed from entry or movement on land which he knows to be in the possession or custody of the person obstructing him, or in the possession or custody of another person by whose authority the obstructor acts, unless the circumstances, as the actor believes them to be, are of such urgency that it would not be reasonable to postpone the entry or movement on such land until a court order is obtained; and

(3) the force used is not greater than it would be justifiable if the person obstructing the actor were using force against him to prevent his passage.

(Dec. 19, 1980, P.L.1310, No.235, eff. imd.)

1980 Amendment. Act 235 amended subsec. (c).

Cross References. Section 507 is referred to in section 505 of this title; section 8340.2 of Title 42 (Judiciary and Judicial Procedure).

§ 508. Use of force in law enforcement.

(a) Peace officer's use of force in making arrest.--

(1) A peace officer, or any person whom he has summoned or directed to assist him, need not retreat or desist from efforts to make a lawful arrest because of resistance or threatened resistance to the arrest. He is justified in the use of any force which he believes to be necessary to effect the arrest and of any force which he believes to be necessary to defend himself or another from bodily harm while making the arrest. However, he is justified in using deadly force only when he believes that such force is necessary to prevent death or serious bodily injury to himself or such other person, or when he believes both that:

(i) such force is necessary to prevent the arrest from being defeated by resistance or escape; and

(ii) the person to be arrested has committed or attempted a forcible felony or is attempting to escape and possesses a deadly weapon, or otherwise indicates that he will endanger human life or inflict serious bodily injury unless arrested without delay.

(2) A peace officer making an arrest pursuant to an invalid warrant is justified in the use of any force which he would be justified in using if the warrant were valid, unless he knows that the warrant is invalid.

(b) Private person's use of force in making arrest.--

(1) A private person who makes, or assists another private person in making a lawful arrest is justified in the use of any force which he would be justified in using if he were summoned or directed by a peace officer to make such arrest, except that he is justified in the use of deadly force only when he believes that such force is necessary to prevent death or serious bodily injury to himself or another.

(2) A private person who is summoned or directed by a peace officer to assist in making an arrest which is unlawful, is justified in the use of any force which he would be justified in using if the arrest were lawful, unless he knows that the arrest is unlawful.

(3) A private person who assists another private person in effecting an unlawful arrest, or who, not being summoned, assists a peace officer in effecting an unlawful arrest, is justified in using any force which he would be justified in using if the arrest were lawful, if:

(i) he believes the arrest is lawful; and

(ii) the arrest would be lawful if the facts were as he believes them to be.

(c) Use of force regarding escape.--

(1) A peace officer, corrections officer or other person who has an arrested or convicted person in his custody is justified in the use of such force to prevent the escape of the person from custody as the officer or other person would be justified in using under subsection (a) if the officer or other person were arresting the person.

(2) A peace officer or corrections officer is justified in the use of such force, including deadly force, which the officer believes to be necessary to prevent the escape from a correctional institution of a person whom the officer believes to be lawfully detained in such institution under sentence for an offense or awaiting trial or commitment for an offense.

(3) A corrections officer is justified in the use of such force, which the officer believes to be necessary to defend himself or another from bodily harm during the pursuit of the escaped person. However, the officer is justified in using deadly force only when the officer believes that such force is necessary to prevent death or serious bodily injury to himself or another or when the officer believes that:

(i) such force is necessary to prevent the apprehension from being defeated by resistance; and

(ii) the escaped person has been convicted of committing or attempting to commit a forcible felony, possesses a deadly weapon or otherwise indicates that he will endanger human life or inflict serious bodily injury unless apprehended without delay.

(d) Use of force to prevent suicide or the commission of crime.--

(1) The use of force upon or toward the person of another is justifiable when the actor believes that such force is immediately necessary to prevent such other person from committing suicide, inflicting serious bodily injury upon himself, committing or consummating the commission of a crime involving or threatening bodily injury, damage to or loss of property or a breach of the peace, except that:

(i) Any limitations imposed by the other provisions of this chapter on the justifiable use of force in self-protection, for the protection of others, the protection of property, the effectuation of an arrest or the prevention of an escape from custody shall apply notwithstanding the criminality of the conduct against which such force is used.

(ii) The use of deadly force is not in any event justifiable under this subsection unless:

(A) the actor believes that there is a substantial risk that the person whom he seeks to prevent from committing a crime will cause death or serious bodily injury to another unless the commission or the consummation of the crime is prevented and that the use of such force presents no substantial risk of injury to innocent persons; or

(B) the actor believes that the use of such force is necessary to suppress a riot or mutiny after the rioters or mutineers have been ordered to disperse and warned, in any particular manner that the law may require, that such force will be used if they do not obey.

(2) The justification afforded by this subsection extends to the use of confinement as preventive force only if the actor takes all reasonable measures to terminate the confinement as soon as he knows that he safely can, unless the person confined has been arrested on a charge of crime.

(July 17, 2007, P.L.139, No.41, eff. 60 days)

2007 Amendment. Act 41 amended subsec. (c).

Cross References. Section 508 is referred to in section 8340.2 of Title 42 (Judiciary and Judicial Procedure).

§ 509. Use of force by persons with special responsibility for care, discipline or safety of others.

The use of force upon or toward the person of another is justifiable if:

(1) The actor is the parent or guardian or other person similarly responsible for the general care and supervision of a minor or a person acting at the request of such parent, guardian or other responsible person and:

(i) the force is used for the purpose of safeguarding or promoting the welfare of the minor, including the preventing or punishment of his misconduct; and

(ii) the force used is not designed to cause or known to create a substantial risk of causing death, serious bodily injury, disfigurement, extreme pain or mental distress or gross degradation.

(2) The actor is a teacher or person otherwise entrusted with the care or supervision for a special purpose of a minor and:

(i) the actor believes that the force used is necessary to further such special purpose, including the maintenance of reasonable discipline in a school, class or other group, and that the use of such force is consistent with the welfare of the minor; and

(ii) the degree of force, if it had been used by the parent or guardian of the minor, would not be unjustifiable under paragraph (1)(ii).

(3) The actor is the guardian or other person similarly responsible for the general care and supervision of an incapacitated, mentally ill or mentally retarded person; and:

(i) the force is used for the purpose of safeguarding or promoting the welfare of the incapacitated, mentally ill or mentally retarded person, including the prevention of his misconduct, and there is no reasonable alternative to the use of such force; and

(ii) the force used is not designed to cause or known to create a substantial risk of causing death, bodily injury, disfigurement, unnecessary pain, mental distress, or humiliation.

(4) The actor is a doctor or other therapist or a person assisting him at his direction; and:

(i) the force is used for the purpose of administering a recognized form of treatment not prohibited by law of this Commonwealth which the actor believes to be adapted to promoting the physical or mental health of the patient; and

(ii) the treatment is administered with the consent of the patient, or, if the patient is a minor or an incapacitated person with the consent of his parent or guardian or other person legally competent to consent in his behalf, or the treatment is administered in an emergency when the actor believes that no one competent to consent can be consulted and that a reasonable person, wishing to safeguard the welfare of the patient, would consent.

(5) The actor is a warden or other authorized official of a correctional institution; and:

(i) he believes that the force used is necessary for the purpose of enforcing the lawful rules or procedures of the institution, unless his belief in the lawfulness of the rule or procedure sought to be enforced is erroneous and his error is due to ignorance or mistake as to the provisions of this title, any other provision of the criminal law or the law governing the administration of the institution;

(ii) the nature or degree of force used is not forbidden by law; and

(iii) if deadly force is used, its use is otherwise justifiable under this chapter.

(6) The actor is a person responsible for the safety of a vessel or an aircraft or a person acting at his direction; and:

(i) he believes that the force used is necessary to prevent interference with the operation of the vessel or aircraft or obstruction of the execution of a lawful order, unless his belief in the lawfulness of the order is erroneous and his error is due to ignorance or mistake as to the law defining his authority; and

(ii) if deadly force is used, its use is otherwise justifiable under this chapter.

(7) The actor is a person who is authorized or required by law to maintain order or decorum in a vehicle, train or other carrier or in a place where others are assembled; and:

(i) he believes that the force used is necessary for such purpose; and

(ii) the force used is not designed to cause death, or known to create a substantial risk of causing death, bodily injury, or extreme mental distress.

(Oct. 21, 1988, P.L.1000, No.115, eff. imd.; Apr. 16, 1992, P.L.108, No.24, eff. 60 days)

Cross References. Section 509 is referred to in section 8340.2 of Title 42 (Judiciary and Judicial Procedure).

§ 510. Justification in property crimes.

Conduct involving the appropriation, seizure or destruction of, damage to, intrusion on or interference with property is justifiable under circumstances which would establish a defense of privilege in a civil action based thereon, unless:

(1) this title or the law defining the offense deals with the specific situation involved; or

(2) a legislative purpose to exclude the justification claimed otherwise plainly appears.

CHAPTER 7 RESPONSIBILITY (Reserved)

Enactment. Chapter 7 (Reserved) was added December 6, 1972, P.L.1482, No.334, effective in six months.

CHAPTER 9 INCHOATE CRIMES

Sec.
901. Criminal attempt.
902. Criminal solicitation.
903. Criminal conspiracy.
904. Incapacity, irresponsibility or immunity of party to solicitation or conspiracy.
905. Grading of criminal attempt, solicitation and conspiracy.
906. Multiple convictions of inchoate crimes barred.
907. Possessing instruments of crime.
908. Prohibited offensive weapons.
908.1. Use or possession of electric or electronic incapacitation device.
909. Manufacture, distribution or possession of master keys for motor vehicles.
910. Manufacture, distribution, use or possession of devices for theft of telecommunications services.
911. Corrupt organizations.
912. Possession of weapon on school property.
913. Possession of firearm or other dangerous weapon in court facility.

Enactment. Chapter 9 was added December 6, 1972, P.L.1482, No.334, effective in six months.

Cross References. Chapter 9 is referred to in section 3218 of this title.

§ 901. Criminal attempt.

(a) Definition of attempt.--A person commits an attempt when, with intent to commit a specific crime, he does any act which constitutes a substantial step toward the commission of that crime.

(b) Impossibility.--It shall not be a defense to a charge of attempt that because of a misapprehension of the circumstances it would have been impossible for the accused to commit the crime attempted.

(c) Renunciation.--

(1) In any prosecution for an attempt to commit a crime, it is a defense that, under circumstances manifesting a voluntary and complete renunciation of his criminal intent, the defendant avoided the commission of the crime attempted by abandoning his criminal effort

and, if the mere abandonment was insufficient to accomplish such avoidance, by taking further and affirmative steps which prevented the commission thereof.

(2) A renunciation is not "voluntary and complete" within the meaning of this subsection if it is motivated in whole or part by:

(i) a belief that circumstances exist which increase the probability of detection or apprehension of the defendant or another participant in the criminal enterprise, or which render more difficult the accomplishment of the criminal purpose; or

(ii) a decision to postpone the criminal conduct until another time or to transfer the criminal effort to another victim or another but similar objective.

Cross References. Section 901 is referred to in section 5702 of this title; sections 5552, 6302 of Title 42 (Judiciary and Judicial Procedure).

§ 902. Criminal solicitation.

(a) Definition of solicitation.--A person is guilty of solicitation to commit a crime if with the intent of promoting or facilitating its commission he commands, encourages or requests another person to engage in specific conduct which would constitute such crime or an attempt to commit such crime or which would establish his complicity in its commission or attempted commission.

(b) Renunciation.--It is a defense that the actor, after soliciting another person to commit a crime, persuaded him not to do so or otherwise prevented the commission of the crime, under circumstances manifesting a complete and voluntary renunciation of his criminal intent.

Cross References. Section 902 is referred to in section 5702 of this title; section 3304 of Title 5 (Athletics and Sports); sections 5552, 6302 of Title 42 (Judiciary and Judicial Procedure).

§ 903. Criminal conspiracy.

(a) Definition of conspiracy.--A person is guilty of conspiracy with another person or persons to commit a crime if with the intent of promoting or facilitating its commission he:

(1) agrees with such other person or persons that they or one or more of them will engage in conduct which constitutes such crime or an attempt or solicitation to commit such crime; or

(2) agrees to aid such other person or persons in the planning or commission of such crime or of an attempt or solicitation to commit such crime.

(b) Scope of conspiratorial relationship.--If a person guilty of conspiracy, as defined by subsection (a) of this section, knows that a person with whom he conspires to commit a crime has conspired with another person or persons to commit the same crime, he is guilty of conspiring with such other person or persons, to commit such crime whether or not he knows their identity.

(c) Conspiracy with multiple criminal objectives.--If a person conspires to commit a number of crimes, he is guilty of only one conspiracy so long as such multiple crimes are the object of the same agreement or continuous conspiratorial relationship.

(d) Joinder and venue in conspiracy prosecutions.--

(1) Subject to the provisions of paragraph (2) of this subsection, two or more persons charged with criminal conspiracy may be prosecuted jointly if:

(i) they are charged with conspiring with one another; or

(ii) the conspiracies alleged, whether they have the same or different parties, are so related that they constitute different aspects of a scheme of organized criminal conduct.

(2) In any joint prosecution under paragraph (1) of this subsection:

(i) no defendant shall be charged with a conspiracy in any county other than one in which he entered into such conspiracy or in which an overt act pursuant to such conspiracy was done by him or by a person with whom he conspired;

(ii) neither the liability of any defendant nor the admissibility against him of evidence of acts or declarations of another shall be enlarged by such joinder; and

(iii) the court shall order a severance or take a special verdict as to any defendant who so requests, if it deems it necessary or appropriate to promote the fair determination of his guilt or innocence, and shall take any other proper measures to protect the fairness of the trial.

(e) Overt act.--No person may be convicted of conspiracy to commit a crime unless an overt act in pursuance of such conspiracy is alleged and proved to have been done by him or by a person with whom he conspired.

(f) Renunciation.--It is a defense that the actor, after conspiring to commit a crime, thwarted the success of the conspiracy, under circumstances manifesting a complete and voluntary renunciation of his criminal intent.

(g) Duration of conspiracy.--For purposes of 42 Pa.C.S. § 5552(d) (relating to commission of offense):

(1) conspiracy is a continuing course of conduct which terminates when the crime or crimes which are its object are committed or the agreement that they be committed is abandoned by the defendant and by those with whom he conspired;

(2) such abandonment is presumed if neither the defendant nor anyone with whom he conspired does any overt act in pursuance of the conspiracy during the applicable period of limitation; and

(3) if an individual abandons the agreement, the conspiracy is terminated as to him only if and when he advises those with whom he conspired of his abandonment or he informs the law enforcement authorities of the existence of the conspiracy and of his participation therein.

(Apr. 28, 1978, P.L.202, No.53, eff. 60 days)

1978 Amendment. Act 53 amended subsec. (g).

Cross References. Section 903 is referred to in sections 4120, 5702 of this title; sections 5552, 6302 of Title 42 (Judiciary and Judicial Procedure).

§ 904. Incapacity, irresponsibility or immunity of party to solicitation or conspiracy.

(a) General rule.--Except as provided in subsection (b) of this section, it is immaterial to the liability of a person who solicits or conspires with another to commit a crime that:

(1) he or the person whom he solicits or with whom he conspires does not occupy a particular position or have a particular characteristic which is an element of such crime, if he believes that one of them does; or

(2) the person whom he solicits or with whom he conspires is irresponsible or has an immunity to prosecution or conviction for the commission of the crime.

(b) Exception.--It is a defense to a charge of solicitation or conspiracy to commit a crime that if the criminal object were achieved, the actor would not be guilty of a crime under the law defining the offense or as an accomplice under section 306(e) of this title (relating to status of actor) or section 306(f)(1) or (2) of this title (relating to exceptions).

§ 905. Grading of criminal attempt, solicitation and conspiracy.

(a) Grading.--Except as otherwise provided in this title, attempt, solicitation and conspiracy are crimes of the same grade and degree as the most serious offense which is attempted or solicited or is an object of the conspiracy.

(b) Mitigation.--If the particular conduct charged to constitute a criminal attempt, solicitation or conspiracy is so inherently unlikely to result or culminate in the commission of a crime that neither such conduct nor the actor presents a public danger warranting the grading of such offense under this section, the court may dismiss the prosecution.

(Mar. 26, 1974, P.L.213, No.46, eff. imd.; Mar. 9, 1995, 1st Sp.Sess., P.L.964, No.3, eff. 60 days)

§ 906. Multiple convictions of inchoate crimes barred.

A person may not be convicted of more than one of the inchoate crimes of criminal attempt, criminal solicitation or criminal conspiracy for conduct designed to commit or to culminate in the commission of the same crime.

(Dec. 11, 1986, P.L.1517, No.164, eff. 60 days)

§ 907. Possessing instruments of crime.

(a) Criminal instruments generally.--A person commits a misdemeanor of the first degree if he possesses any instrument of crime with intent to employ it criminally.

(b) Possession of weapon.--A person commits a misdemeanor of the first degree if he possesses a firearm or other weapon concealed upon his person with intent to employ it criminally.

(c) Unlawful body armor.--A person commits a felony of the third degree if in the course of the commission of a felony or in the attempt to commit a felony he uses or wears body armor or has in his control, custody or possession any body armor.

(d) Definitions.--As used in this section, the following words and phrases shall have the meanings given to them in this subsection:

"Body armor." Any protective covering for the body, or parts thereof, made of any polyaramid fiber or any resin-treated glass fiber cloth or any material or combination of materials made or designed to prevent, resist, deflect or deter the penetration thereof by ammunition, knife, cutting or piercing instrument or any other weapon.

"Instrument of crime." Any of the following:

(1) Anything specially made or specially adapted for criminal use.

(2) Anything used for criminal purposes and possessed by the actor under circumstances not manifestly appropriate for lawful uses it may have.

"Weapon." Anything readily capable of lethal use and possessed under circumstances not manifestly appropriate for lawful uses which it may have. The term includes a firearm which is not loaded or lacks a clip or other component to render it immediately operable, and components which can readily be assembled into a weapon.

(July 6, 1995, P.L.238, No.27, eff. 60 days; July 11, 1996, P.L.552, No.98, eff. 60 days)

1996 Amendment. Act 98 overlooked the amendment by Act 27 of 1995, but the amendments do not conflict in substance and have both been given effect in setting forth the text of section 907.

Cross References. Section 907 is referred to in sections 912, 2718 of this title; section 6102 of Title 23 (Domestic Relations).

§ 908. Prohibited offensive weapons.

(a) Offense defined.--A person commits a misdemeanor of the first degree if, except as authorized by law, he makes repairs, sells, or otherwise deals in, uses, or possesses any offensive weapon.

(b) Exceptions.--

(1) It is a defense under this section for the defendant to prove by a preponderance of evidence that he possessed or dealt with the weapon solely as a curio or in a dramatic performance, or that, with the exception of a bomb, grenade or incendiary device, he complied with the National Firearms Act (26 U.S.C. § 5801 et seq.), or that he possessed it briefly in consequence of having found it or taken it from an aggressor, or under circumstances similarly negating any intent or

likelihood that the weapon would be used unlawfully.

(2) This section does not apply to police forensic firearms experts or police forensic firearms laboratories. Also exempt from this section are forensic firearms experts or forensic firearms laboratories operating in the ordinary course of business and engaged in lawful operation who notify in writing, on an annual basis, the chief or head of any police force or police department of a city, and, elsewhere, the sheriff of a county in which they are located, of the possession, type and use of offensive weapons.

(3) This section shall not apply to any person who makes, repairs, sells or otherwise deals in, uses or possesses any firearm for purposes not prohibited by the laws of this Commonwealth.

(c) Definitions.--As used in this section, the following words and phrases shall have the meanings given to them in this subsection:

"Firearm." Any weapon which is designed to or may readily be converted to expel any projectile by the action of an explosive or the frame or receiver of any such weapon.

"Offensive weapons." Any bomb, grenade, machine gun, sawed-off shotgun with a barrel less than 18 inches, firearm specially made or specially adapted for concealment or silent discharge, any blackjack, sandbag, metal knuckles, dagger, knife, razor or cutting instrument, the blade of which is exposed in an automatic way by switch, push-button, spring mechanism, or otherwise, any stun gun, stun baton, taser or other electronic or electric weapon or other implement for the infliction of serious bodily injury which serves no common lawful purpose.

(d) Exemptions.--The use and possession of blackjacks by the following persons in the course of their duties are exempt from this section:

(1) Police officers, as defined by and who meet the requirements of the act of June 18, 1974 (P.L.359, No.120), referred to as the Municipal Police Education and Training Law.

(2) Police officers of first class cities who have successfully completed training which is substantially equivalent to the program under the Municipal Police Education and Training Law.

(3) Pennsylvania State Police officers.

(4) Sheriffs and deputy sheriffs of the various counties who have satisfactorily met the requirements of the Municipal Police Education and Training Law.

(5) Police officers employed by the Commonwealth who have satisfactorily met the requirements of the Municipal Police Education and Training Law.

(6) Deputy sheriffs with adequate training as determined by the Pennsylvania Commission on Crime and Delinquency.

(7) Liquor Control Board agents who have satisfactorily met the requirements of the Municipal Police Education and Training Law.

(Dec. 20, 1983, P.L.291, No.78, eff. imd.; July 6, 1984, P.L.647, No.134, eff. 90 days; July 11, 1985, P.L.235, No.58, eff. 60 days; Oct. 4, 1994, P.L.571, No.84, eff. 60 days; Nov. 6, 2002, P.L.1096, No.132, eff. 60 days)

2002 Amendment. Act 132 amended subsec. (c).

References in Text. The act of June 18, 1974 (P.L.359, No.120), referred to as the Municipal Police Education and Training Law, referred to in subsection (d)(1), was repealed by the act of December 19, 1996 (P.L.1158, No.177). The subject matter is now contained in Subchapter D of Chapter 21 of Title 53 (Municipalities Generally).

Cross References. Section 908 is referred to in section 6105 of this title; section 3304 of Title 5 (Athletics and Sports).

§ 908.1. Use or possession of electric or electronic incapacitation device.

(a) Offense defined.--Except as set forth in subsection (b), a person commits an offense if the person does any of the following:

(1) Uses an electric or electronic incapacitation device on another person for an unlawful purpose.

(2) Possesses, with intent to violate paragraph (1), an electric or electronic incapacitation device.

(b) Self defense.--A person may possess and use an electric or electronic incapacitation device in the exercise of reasonable force in defense of the person or the person's property pursuant to Chapter 5 (relating to general principles of justification) if the electric or electronic incapacitation device is labeled with or accompanied by clearly written instructions as to its use and the damages involved in its use.

(c) Prohibited possession.--No person prohibited from possessing a firearm pursuant to section 6105 (relating to persons not to possess, use, manufacture, control, sell or transfer firearms) may possess or use an electric or electronic incapacitation device.

(d) Grading.--An offense under subsection (a) shall constitute a felony of the second degree if the actor acted with the intent to commit a felony. Otherwise any offense under this section is graded as a misdemeanor of the first degree.

(e) Exceptions.--Nothing in this section shall prohibit the possession or use by, or the sale or furnishing of any electric or electronic incapacitation device to, a law enforcement agency, peace officer, employee of a correctional institution, county jail or prison or detention center, the National Guard or reserves or a member of the National Guard or reserves for use in their official duties.

(f) Definition.--As used in this section, the term "electric or electronic incapacitation device" means a portable device which is designed or intended by the manufacturer to be used, offensively or defensively, to temporarily immobilize or incapacitate persons by means of electric pulse or current, including devices operating by means of carbon dioxide propellant. The term does not include cattle prods, electric fences or other electric devices when used in agricultural, animal husbandry or food production activities.

(Nov. 6, 2002, P.L.1096, No.132, eff. 60 days)

2002 Amendment. Act 132 added section 908.1.

§ 909. Manufacture, distribution or possession of master keys for motor vehicles.

(a) Offense defined.--A person commits a misdemeanor of the first degree if he manufactures, distributes, or possesses any motor vehicle master key.

(b) Exception.--Subsection (a) of this section shall not apply to:

(1) The introduction, manufacture for introduction, transportation, distribution, sale or possession in commerce in this Commonwealth of motor vehicle master keys for use in the ordinary course of business by any commercial or professional locksmith, common carrier, contract carrier, motor vehicle fleet owner, new or used car dealer, rental car agency, car manufacturer, automobile club or association

operating in more than one state or an affiliate thereof, or any department, agency, or instrumentality of:

(i) the Commonwealth of Pennsylvania, the United States, any state, the District of Columbia, or any possession of the United States; or

(ii) any political subdivision of any entity specified in subparagraph (i) of this paragraph.

(2) The shipment, transportation, or delivery for shipment in commerce in this Commonwealth of motor vehicle master keys in the ordinary course of business by any common carrier or contract carrier.

(c) Definition.--As used in this section "master key" means any key adapted to fit the ignition switch, trunk or door of two or more motor vehicles, the ignition switches, trunks or doors of which are designed to be operated by keys.

§ 910. Manufacture, distribution, use or possession of devices for theft of telecommunications services.

(a) Offense defined.--Any person commits an offense if he:

(1) makes, distributes, possesses, uses or assembles an unlawful telecommunication device or modifies, alters, programs or reprograms a telecommunication device designed, adapted or which can be used:

(i) for commission of a theft of telecommunication service or to disrupt, transmit, decrypt, acquire or facilitate the disruption, transmission, decryption or acquisition of any telecommunication service without the consent of the telecommunication service provider; or

(ii) to conceal or to assist another to conceal from any telecommunication service provider or from any lawful authority the existence or place of origin or of destination of any telecommunication; or

(2) sells, possesses, distributes, gives or otherwise transfers to another or offers, promotes or advertises for sale any:

(i) unlawful telecommunication device, or plans or instructions for making or assembling the same, under circumstances evidencing an intent to use or employ such unlawful telecommunication device, or to allow the same to be used or employed for a purpose described in paragraph (1), or knowing or having reason to believe that the same is intended to be so used, or that the aforesaid plans or instructions are intended to be used for making or

assembling such unlawful telecommunication device; or

(ii) material, including hardware, cables, tools, data, computer software or other information or equipment, knowing that the purchaser or a third person intends to use the material in the manufacture of an unlawful telecommunication device.

(b) Grading.--

(1) Except for violations of this section as provided for in paragraph (2) or (3), an offense under this section is a misdemeanor of the first degree.

(2) An offense under this section is a felony of the third degree if:

(i) the defendant has been convicted previously under this section or convicted of any similar crime in this or any Federal or other state jurisdiction; or

(ii) the violation of this section involves at least ten, but not more than 50, unlawful telecommunication devices.

(3) An offense under this section is a felony of the second degree if:

(i) the defendant has been convicted previously on two or more occasions for offenses under this section or for any similar crime in this or any Federal or other state jurisdiction; or

(ii) the violation of this section involves more than 50 unlawful telecommunication devices.

(4) For purposes of grading an offense based upon a prior conviction under this section or for any similar crime pursuant to paragraphs (2)(i) and (3)(i), a prior conviction shall consist of convictions upon separate indictments or criminal complaints for offenses under this section or any similar crime in this or any Federal or other state jurisdiction.

(5) As provided for in paragraphs (2)(i) and (3)(i), in grading an offense under this section based upon a prior conviction, the term "any similar crime" shall include, but not be limited to, offenses involving theft of service or fraud, including violations of the Cable Communications Policy Act of 1984 (Public Law 98-549, 98 Stat. 2779).

(b.1) Separate offenses.--For purposes of all criminal penalties or fines established for violations of this section, the prohibited activity established herein as it applies to each unlawful telecommunication device shall be deemed a separate offense.

(b.2) Fines.--For purposes of imposing fines upon conviction of a defendant for an offense under this section, all fines shall be imposed in accordance with section 1101 (relating to fines).

(c) Restitution.--The court shall, in addition to any other sentence authorized by law, sentence a person convicted of violating this section to make restitution under section 1106 (relating to restitution for injuries to person or property) or 42 Pa.C.S. § 9721(c) (relating to sentencing generally).

(c.1) Forfeiture of unlawful telecommunication devices.--Upon conviction of a defendant under this section, the court may, in addition to any other sentence authorized by law, direct that the defendant forfeit any unlawful telecommunication devices in the defendant's possession or control which were involved in the violation for which the defendant was convicted. The forfeiture shall be conducted in accordance with 42 Pa.C.S. §§ 5803 (relating to asset forfeiture), 5805 (relating to forfeiture procedure), 5806 (relating to motion for return of property), 5807 (relating to restrictions on use), 5807.1 (relating to prohibition on adoptive seizures) and 5808 (relating to exceptions).

(c.2) Venue.--An offense under subsection (a) may be deemed to have been committed at either place where the defendant manufactures or assembles an unlawful telecommunication device or assists others in doing so or the places where the unlawful telecommunication device is sold or delivered to a purchaser, in accordance with section 102 (relating to territorial applicability). It shall be no defense to a violation of subsection (a) that some of the acts constituting the offense occurred outside of this Commonwealth.

(d) Civil action.--

(1) Any person aggrieved by a violation of this section may bring a civil action in any court of competent jurisdiction.

(2) The court may:

(i) grant preliminary and final injunctions to prevent or restrain violations of this section;

(ii) at any time while an action is pending, order the impounding, on such terms as it deems reasonable, of any unlawful telecommunication device that is in the custody or control of the violator and that the court has reasonable cause to believe was involved in the alleged violation of this section;

(iii) award damages as described in subsection (d.1);

(iv) in its discretion, award reasonable attorney fees and costs, including, but not limited to, costs for investigation, testing and expert witness fees, to an aggrieved party who prevails; or

(v) as part of a final judgment or decree finding a violation of this section, order the remedial modification or destruction of any unlawful telecommunication device involved in the violation that is in the custody or control of the violator or has been impounded under subparagraph (ii).

(d.1) Types of damages recoverable.-- Damages awarded by a court under this section shall be computed as either of the following:

(1) Upon his election of such damages at any time before final judgment is entered, the complaining party may recover the actual damages suffered by him as a result of the violation of this section and any profits of the violator that are attributable to the violation and are not taken into account in computing the actual damages. In determining the violator's profits, the complaining party shall be required to prove only the violator's gross revenue, and the violator shall be required to prove his deductible expenses and the elements of profit attributable to factors other than the violation.

(2) Upon election by the complaining party at any time before final judgment is entered, that party may recover in lieu of actual damages an award of statutory damages of between $250 to $10,000 for each unlawful telecommunication device involved in the action, with the amount of statutory damages to be determined by the court, not the jury, as the court considers just. In any case where the court finds that any of the violations of this section were committed willfully and for purposes of commercial advantage or private financial gain, the court in its discretion may increase the award of statutory damages by an amount of not more than $50,000 for each unlawful telecommunication device involved in the action.

(3) For purposes of all civil remedies established for violations of this section, the prohibited activity established in this section applies to each unlawful telecommunication device and shall be deemed a separate violation.

(e) Definitions.--As used in this section, the following words and phrases shall have the meanings given to them in this subsection:

"Manufacture of an unlawful telecommunication device." To produce or assemble an unlawful telecommunication device or to modify, alter, program or reprogram a telecommunication device to be capable of acquiring, disrupting, receiving, transmitting, decrypting or facilitating the acquisition, disruption, receipt, transmission or decryption of a telecommunication service without the consent of the telecommunication service provider or to knowingly assist others in those activities.

"Telecommunication device." Any type of instrument, device, machine or equipment which is capable of transmitting, acquiring, decrypting or receiving any telephonic, electronic, data, Internet access, audio, video, microwave or radio transmissions, signals, communications or services, including the receipt, acquisition, transmission or decryption of all such communications, transmissions, signals or services over any cable television, telephone, satellite, microwave, radio or wireless distribution system or facility, or any part, accessory or components thereof, including any computer circuit, security module, smart card, software, computer chip, electronic mechanism or other component, accessory or part which is capable of facilitating the transmission, decryption, acquisition or reception of all such communications, transmissions, signals or services.

"Telecommunication service." The meaning given to it in section 3926 (relating to theft of services) and also any service provided by any radio, telephone, cable television, satellite, microwave or wireless distribution system or facility, including, but not limited to, any and all electronic, data, video, audio, Internet access, telephonic, microwave and radio communications, transmissions, signals and services.

"Telecommunication service provider." The meaning given to it in section 3926 (relating to theft of services) and includes any person or entity providing any telecommunication service, including, but not limited to, any person or entity owning or operating any cable television, satellite, telephone, wireless, microwave or radio distribution system or facility.

"Unlawful telecommunication device." The meaning given to it in section 3926 (relating to theft of services) and includes any telecommunication device which is capable of or has been altered, designed, modified, programmed or reprogrammed, alone or in conjunction with another telecommunication device or devices so as to be capable of facilitating the disruption, acquisition, receipt, transmission or decryption of a telecommunication service without the consent or knowledge of the telecommunication service provider. In addition to the examples listed in section 3926, the term includes, but is not limited to, any device, technology, product, service, equipment, computer software or component or part thereof, primarily distributed, sold, designed, assembled, manufactured, modified, programmed, reprogrammed or used for the purpose of providing unauthorized disruption of, decryption of, access to or acquisition of any telecommunication service provided by any cable television, satellite, telephone, wireless, microwave or radio distribution system or facility.

(July 20, 1974, P.L.539, No.185; June 13, 1995, P.L.52, No.8, eff. 60 days; June 22, 2000, P.L.469, No.64, eff. 60 days; Dec. 20, 2000, P.L.831, No.116, eff. imd.; June 29, 2017, P.L.247, No.13, eff. July 1, 2017)

2017 Amendment. Act 13 amended subsec. (c.1).

2000 Amendment. Act 116 reenacted section 910.

Cross References. Section 910 is referred to in section 5708 of this title; section 5803 of Title 42 (Judiciary and Judicial Procedure).

§ 911. Corrupt organizations.

(a) **Findings of fact.**--The General Assembly finds that:

(1) organized crime is a highly sophisticated, diversified, and widespread phenomenon which annually drains billions of dollars from the national economy by various patterns of unlawful conduct including the illegal use of force, fraud, and corruption;

(2) organized crime exists on a large scale within the Commonwealth of Pennsylvania, engaging in the same patterns of unlawful conduct which characterize its activities nationally;

(3) the vast amounts of money and power accumulated by organized crime are increasingly used to infiltrate and corrupt legitimate businesses operating within the Commonwealth, together with all of the

techniques of violence, intimidation, and other forms of unlawful conduct through which such money and power are derived;

(4) in furtherance of such infiltration and corruption, organized crime utilizes and applies to its unlawful purposes laws of the Commonwealth of Pennsylvania conferring and relating to the privilege of engaging in various types of business and designed to insure that such businesses are conducted in furtherance of the public interest and the general economic welfare of the Commonwealth;

(5) such infiltration and corruption provide an outlet for illegally obtained capital, harm innocent investors, entrepreneurs, merchants and consumers, interfere with free competition, and thereby constitute a substantial danger to the economic and general welfare of the Commonwealth of Pennsylvania; and

(6) in order to successfully resist and eliminate this situation, it is necessary to provide new remedies and procedures.

(b) Prohibited activities.--

(1) It shall be unlawful for any person who has received any income derived, directly or indirectly, from a pattern of racketeering activity in which such person participated as a principal, to use or invest, directly or indirectly, any part of such income, or the proceeds of such income, in the acquisition of any interest in, or the establishment or operation of, any enterprise: Provided, however, That a purchase of securities on the open market for purposes of investment, and without the intention of controlling or participating in the control of the issuer, or of assisting another to do so, shall not be unlawful under this subsection if the securities of the issue held by the purchaser, the members of his immediate family, and his or their accomplices in any pattern of racketeering activity after such purchase, do not amount in the aggregate to 1% of the outstanding securities of any one class, and do not confer, either in law or in fact, the power to elect one or more directors of the issuer: Provided, further, That if, in any proceeding involving an alleged investment in violation of this subsection, it is established that over half of the defendant's aggregate income for a period of two or more years immediately preceding such investment was derived from a pattern of racketeering activity, a rebuttable presumption shall arise that such investment included income derived from such pattern of racketeering activity.

(2) It shall be unlawful for any person through a pattern of racketeering activity to acquire or maintain, directly or indirectly, any interest in or control of any enterprise.

(3) It shall be unlawful for any person employed by or associated with any enterprise to conduct or participate, directly or indirectly, in the conduct of such enterprise's affairs through a pattern of racketeering activity.

(4) It shall be unlawful for any person to conspire to violate any of the provisions of paragraphs (1), (2) or (3) of this subsection.

(c) **Grading.**--Whoever violates any provision of subsection (b) of this section is guilty of a felony of the first degree. A violation of this subsection shall be deemed to continue so long as the person who committed the violation continues to receive any benefit from the violation.

(d) Civil remedies.--

(1) The several courts of common pleas, and the Commonwealth Court, shall have jurisdiction to prevent and restrain violations of subsection (b) of this section by issuing appropriate orders, including but not limited to:

(i) ordering any person to divest himself of any interest direct or indirect, in the enterprise; imposing reasonable restrictions on the future activities or investments of any person, including but not limited to, prohibiting any person from engaging in the same type of endeavor as the enterprise engaged in; and

(ii) making due provision for the rights of innocent persons, ordering the dissolution of the enterprise, ordering the denial, suspension or revocation of charters of domestic corporations, certificates of authority authorizing foreign corporations to do business within the Commonwealth of Pennsylvania, licenses, permits, or prior approval granted to any enterprise by any department or agency of the Commonwealth of Pennsylvania; or prohibiting the enterprise from engaging in any business.

(2) In any proceeding under this subsection, the court shall proceed as soon as practicable to the hearing and determination thereof. Pending final determination, the court may enter preliminary or special injunctions, or take such other actions, including the acceptance of satisfactory performance bonds, as it may deem proper.

(3) A final judgment or decree rendered in favor of the Commonwealth of Pennsylvania in any criminal proceeding under this section

shall estop the defendant from denying the essential allegations of the criminal offense in any subsequent civil proceeding under this subsection.

(4) Proceedings under this subsection, at pretrial, trial and appellate levels, shall be governed by the Pennsylvania Rules of Civil Procedure and all other rules and procedures relating to civil actions, except to the extent inconsistent with the provisions of this section.

(e) Enforcement.--

(1) The Attorney General shall have the power and duty to enforce the provisions of this section, including the authority to issue civil investigative demands pursuant to subsection (f), institute proceedings under subsection (d), and to take such actions as may be necessary to ascertain and investigate alleged violations of this section.

(2) The Attorney General and the district attorneys of the several counties shall have concurrent authority to institute criminal proceedings under the provisions of this section.

(3) Nothing contained in this subsection shall be construed to limit the regulatory or investigative authority of any department or agency of the Commonwealth whose functions might relate to persons, enterprises, or matters falling within the scope of this section.

(f) Civil investigative demand.--

(1) Whenever the Attorney General has reason to believe that any person or enterprise may be in possession, custody, or control of any documentary material relevant to a racketeering investigation, he may issue in writing, and cause to be served upon such person or enterprise, a civil investigative demand requiring the production of such material for examination.

(2) Each such demand shall:

(i) state the nature of the conduct constituting the alleged racketeering violation which is under investigation, the provision of law applicable thereto and the connection between the documentary material demanded and the conduct under investigation;

(ii) describe the class or classes of documentary material to be produced thereunder with such definiteness and certainty as to permit such material to be fairly identified;

(iii) state that the demand is returnable forthwith or prescribe a return date which will provide a reasonable period of time within which the material so demanded may be assembled and made available for inspection and copying or reproduction;

(iv) identify a racketeering investigator to whom such material shall be made available; and

(v) contain the following statement printed conspicuously at the top of the demand: "You have the right to seek the assistance of any attorney and he may represent you in all phases of the racketeering investigation of which this civil investigative demand is a part."

(3) No such demand shall:

(i) contain any requirement which would be held to be unreasonable if contained in a subpoena duces tecum issued by any court in connection with a grand jury investigation of such alleged racketeering violation; or

(ii) require the production of any documentary evidence which would be privileged from disclosure if demanded by a subpoena duces tecum issued by any court in connection with a grand jury investigation of such alleged racketeering violation.

(4) Service of any such demand or any petition filed under this subsection shall be made in the manner prescribed by the Pennsylvania Rules of Civil Procedure for service of writs and complaints.

(5) A verified return by the individual serving any such demand or petition setting forth the manner of such service shall be prima facie proof of such service. In the case of service by registered or certified mail, such return shall be accompanied by the return post office receipt of delivery of such demand.

(6) (i) Any party upon whom any demand issued under this subsection has been duly served shall make such material available for inspection and copying or reproduction to the racketeering investigator designated therein at the principal place of business of such party, or at such other place as such investigator and such party thereafter may agree or as the court may direct pursuant to this subsection, on the return date specified in such demand. Such party may upon agreement of the investigator substitute copies of all or any part of such material for the originals thereof.

(ii) The racketeering investigator to whom any documentary material is so delivered shall take physical possession thereof, and shall be responsible for the use made thereof and for its return pursuant to this subsection. The investigator may cause the preparation of such copies of such documentary material as may be required for official use. While in the possession of the investigator, no material so produced shall be available for examination, without the consent of the party who produced such material, by any individual other than the Attorney General or any racketeering investigator. Under such reasonable terms and conditions as the Attorney General shall prescribe, documentary material while in the possession of the investigator shall be available for examination by the party who produced such material or any duly authorized representatives of such party.

(iii) Upon completion of:

(A) the racketeering investigation for which any documentary material was produced under this subsection; and

(B) any case or proceeding arising from such investigation;

the investigator shall return to the party who produced such material all such material other than copies thereof made pursuant to this subsection which have not passed into the control of any court or grand jury through introduction into the record of such case or proceeding.

(iv) When any documentary material has been produced by any party under this subsection for use in any racketeering investigation, and no case or proceeding arising therefrom has been instituted within a reasonable time after completion of the examination and analysis of all evidence assembled in the course of such investigation, such party shall be entitled, upon written demand made upon the Attorney General, to the return of all documentary material, other than copies thereof made pursuant to this subsection, so produced by such party.

(7) Whenever any person or enterprise fails to comply with any civil investigative demand duly served upon him under this subsection or whenever satisfactory copying or reproduction of any such material cannot be done and such party refuses to surrender such material, the Attorney General may file, in the court of common pleas for any county in which such party resides or transacts business, and serve upon such party a petition for an order of such court for the enforcement of this subsection, except that if such person transacts business in more than one county such petition shall be filed in the county in which party maintains his or its principal place of business.

(8) Within 20 days after the service of any such demand upon any person or enterprise, or at any time before the return date specified in the demand, whichever period is shorter, such party may file, in the court of common pleas of the county within which such party resides or transacts business, and serve upon the Attorney General a petition for an order of such court modifying or setting aside such demand. The time allowed for compliance with the demand in whole or in part as deemed proper and ordered by the court shall not run during the pendency of such petition in the court. Such petition shall specify each ground upon which the petitioner relies in seeking such relief, and may be based upon any failure of such demand to comply with the provisions of this subsection or upon any constitutional or other legal right or privilege of such party.

(9) At any time during which the Attorney General is in custody or control of any documentary material delivered by any party in compliance with any such demand, such party may file, in the court of common pleas of the county within which such documentary material was delivered, and serve upon the Attorney General a petition for an order of such court requiring the performance of any duty imposed by this subsection.

(10) Whenever any petition is filed in any court of common pleas under this subsection, such court shall have jurisdiction to hear and determine the matter so presented, and, after a hearing at which all parties are represented, to enter such order or orders as may be required to carry into effect the provisions of this subsection.

(g) **Immunity.**--Whenever any individual refuses, on the basis of his privilege against self-incrimination, to comply with a civil investigative demand issued pursuant to subsection (f) or to testify or produce other information in any proceeding under subsection (d), the Attorney General may invoke the provisions of 42 Pa.C.S. § 5947 (relating to immunity of witnesses).

(h) **Definitions.**--As used in this section:

(1) "Racketeering activity" means all of the following:

(i) An act which is indictable under any of the following provisions of this title:

Chapter 25 (relating to criminal homicide)

Section 2706 (relating to terroristic threats)

Chapter 29 (relating to kidnapping)

Chapter 30 (relating to human trafficking)

Chapter 33 (relating to arson, criminal mischief and other property destruction)

Chapter 37 (relating to robbery)

Chapter 39 (relating to theft and related offenses)

Section 4108 (relating to commercial bribery and breach of duty to act disinterestedly)

Section 4109 (relating to rigging publicly exhibited contest)

Section 4117 (relating to insurance fraud)

Chapter 47 (relating to bribery and corrupt influence)

Chapter 49 (relating to falsification and intimidation)

Section 5111 (relating to dealing in proceeds of unlawful activities)

Section 5512 (relating to lotteries, etc.)

Section 5513 (relating to gambling devices, gambling, etc.)

Section 5514 (relating to pool selling and bookmaking)

Chapter 59 (relating to public indecency).

(ii) An offense indictable under section 13 of the act of April 14, 1972 (P.L.233, No.64), known as The Controlled Substance, Drug, Device and Cosmetic Act (relating to the sale and dispensing of narcotic drugs).

(iii) A conspiracy to commit any of the offenses set forth in subparagraph (i), (ii) and (v).

(iv) The collection of any money or other property in full or partial satisfaction of a debt which arose as the result of the lending of money or other property at a rate of interest exceeding 25% per annum or the equivalent rate for a longer or shorter period, where not otherwise authorized by law.

(v) An offense indictable under 4 Pa.C.S. Pt. II (relating to gaming).

An act which otherwise would be considered racketeering activity by reason of the application of this paragraph, shall not be excluded from its application solely because the operative acts took place outside the jurisdiction of this Commonwealth, if such acts would have been in violation of the law of the jurisdiction in which they occurred.

(2) "Person" means any individual or entity capable of holding a legal or beneficial interest in property.

(3) "Enterprise" means any individual, partnership, corporation, association or other legal entity, and any union or group of individuals associated in fact although not a legal entity, engaged in commerce and includes legitimate as well as illegitimate entities and governmental entities.

(4) "Pattern of racketeering activity" refers to a course of conduct requiring two or more acts of racketeering activity one of which occurred after the effective date of this section.

(5) "Racketeering investigator" means an attorney, investigator or investigative body so designated in writing by the Attorney General and charged with the duty of enforcing or carrying into effect the provisions of this section.

(6) "Racketeering investigation" means any inquiry conducted by any racketeering investigator for the purpose of ascertaining whether any person has been involved in any violation of this section or of any order, judgment, or decree of any court duly entered in any case or proceeding arising under this section.

(7) "Documentary material" means any book, paper, record, recording, tape, report, memorandum, written communication, or other document relating to the business affairs of any person or enterprise.

(8) "Organized crime" means any person or combination of persons engaging in or having the purpose of engaging in conduct which violates any provision of subsection (b) and also includes "organized crime" as defined in section 5702 (relating to definitions).

(Dec. 30, 1974, P.L.1044, No.341, eff. imd.; Apr. 28, 1978, P.L.202, No.53, eff. 60 days; Oct. 5, 1980, P.L.693, No.142, eff. 60 days; Feb. 7, 1990, P.L.11, No.6, eff. 60 days; June 19, 1996, P.L.342, No.55, eff. imd.; Nov. 1, 2006, P.L.1243, No.135, eff. imd.; Nov. 9, 2006, P.L.1340, No.139, eff. 60 days; Nov. 29, 2006, P.L.1481, No.168, eff. 60 days; July 2, 2014, P.L.945, No.105, eff. 60 days)

2014 Amendment. Act 105 amended subsec. (h)(1)(i) and carried without amendment subsec. (h)(1) last sentence.

1996 Amendment. Act 55 amended subsec. (h)(1) and (3) and added subsec. (h)(8).

1990 Amendment. Act 6 amended subsec. (h).

1980 Amendment. Act 142 amended subsec. (g).

Cross References. Section 911 is referred to in sections 5708, 6105 of this title; section

5552 of Title 42 (Judiciary and Judicial Procedure).

§ 912. Possession of weapon on school property.

(a) Definition.--Notwithstanding the definition of "weapon" in section 907 (relating to possessing instruments of crime), "weapon" for purposes of this section shall include but not be limited to any knife, cutting instrument, cutting tool, nun-chuck stick, firearm, shotgun, rifle and any other tool, instrument or implement capable of inflicting serious bodily injury.

(b) Offense defined.--A person commits a misdemeanor of the first degree if he possesses a weapon in the buildings of, on the grounds of, or in any conveyance providing transportation to or from any elementary or secondary publicly-funded educational institution, any elementary or secondary private school licensed by the Department of Education or any elementary or secondary parochial school.

(c) Defense.--It shall be a defense that the weapon is possessed and used in conjunction with a lawful supervised school activity or course or is possessed for other lawful purpose.

(Oct. 16, 1980, P.L.978, No.167, eff. 60 days)

1980 Amendment. Act 167 added section 912.

Cross References. Section 912 is referred to in section 6105 of this title.

§ 913. Possession of firearm or other dangerous weapon in court facility.

(a) Offense defined.--A person commits an offense if he:

(1) knowingly possesses a firearm or other dangerous weapon in a court facility or knowingly causes a firearm or other dangerous weapon to be present in a court facility; or

(2) knowingly possesses a firearm or other dangerous weapon in a court facility with the intent that the firearm or other dangerous weapon be used in the commission of a crime or knowingly causes a firearm or other dangerous weapon to be present in a court facility with the intent that the firearm or other dangerous weapon be used in the commission of a crime.

(b) Grading.--

(1) Except as otherwise provided in paragraph (3), an offense under subsection (a)(1) is a misdemeanor of the third degree.

(2) An offense under subsection (a)(2) is a misdemeanor of the first degree.

(3) An offense under subsection (a)(1) is a summary offense if the person was carrying a firearm under section 6106(b) (relating to firearms not to be carried without a license) or 6109 (relating to licenses) and failed to check the firearm under subsection (e) prior to entering the court facility.

(c) Exceptions.--Subsection (a) shall not apply to:

(1) The lawful performance of official duties by an officer, agent or employee of the United States, the Commonwealth or a political subdivision who is authorized by law to engage in or supervise the prevention, detection, investigation or prosecution of any violation of law.

(2) The lawful performance of official duties by a court official.

(3) The carrying of rifles and shotguns by instructors and participants in a course of instruction provided by the Pennsylvania Game Commission under 34 Pa.C.S. § 2704 (relating to eligibility for license).

(4) Associations of veteran soldiers and their auxiliaries or members of organized armed forces of the United States or the Commonwealth, including reserve components, when engaged in the performance of ceremonial duties with county approval.

(5) The carrying of a dangerous weapon or firearm unloaded and in a secure wrapper by an attorney who seeks to employ the dangerous weapon or firearm as an exhibit or as a demonstration and who possesses written authorization from the court to bring the dangerous weapon or firearm into the court facility.

(d) Posting of notice.--Notice of the provisions of subsections (a) and (e) shall be posted conspicuously at each public entrance to each courthouse or other building containing a court facility and each court facility, and no person shall be convicted of an offense under subsection (a)(1) with respect to a court facility if the notice was not so posted at each public entrance to the courthouse or other building containing a court facility and at the court facility unless the person had actual notice of the provisions of subsection (a).

(e) Facilities for checking firearms or other dangerous weapons.--Each county shall make available at or within the building containing a court facility by July 1, 2002, lockers or similar facilities at no charge or cost for the temporary checking of firearms by persons carrying firearms under section 6106(b) or 6109 or for the checking of other dangerous weapons that are not otherwise prohibited by law. Any individual checking a firearm, dangerous weapon or an item deemed to be a dangerous weapon at a court facility must be issued a receipt. Notice of the location of the facility shall be posted as required under subsection (d).

(f) Definitions.--As used in this section, the following words and phrases shall have the meanings given to them in this subsection:

"Court facility." The courtroom of a court of record; a courtroom of a community court; the courtroom of a magisterial district judge; a courtroom of the Philadelphia Municipal Court; a courtroom of the Pittsburgh Magistrates Court; a courtroom of the Traffic Court of Philadelphia; judge's chambers; witness rooms; jury deliberation rooms; attorney conference rooms; prisoner holding cells; offices of court clerks, the district attorney, the sheriff and probation and parole officers; and any adjoining corridors.

"Dangerous weapon." A bomb, any explosive or incendiary device or material when possessed with intent to use or to provide such material to commit any offense, graded as a misdemeanor of the third degree or higher, grenade, blackjack, sandbag, metal knuckles, dagger, knife (the blade of which is exposed in an automatic way by switch, push-button, spring mechanism or otherwise) or other implement for the infliction of serious bodily injury which serves no common lawful purpose.

"Firearm." Any weapon, including a starter gun, which will or is designed to expel a projectile or projectiles by the action of an explosion, expansion of gas or escape of gas. The term does not include any device designed or used exclusively for the firing of stud cartridges, explosive rivets or similar industrial ammunition.

(June 13, 1995, 1st Sp.Sess., P.L.1024, No.17, eff. 120 days; Nov. 22, 1995, P.L.621, No.66, eff. imd.; Dec. 15, 1999, P.L.915, No.59, eff. 60 days; Nov. 30, 2004, P.L.1618, No.207, eff. 60 days; Feb. 25, 2014, P.L.33, No.16, eff. 60 days)

2014 Amendment. Act 16 amended subsec. (f).

2004 Amendment. See section 29 of Act 207 in the appendix to this title for special provisions relating to construction of law.

1999 Amendment. Act 59 amended subsec. (e).

1995 Amendments. Act 17, 1st Sp.Sess., added section 913 and Act 66 amended subsecs. (c) and (e). See the preamble to Act 17, 1st Sp.Sess., in the appendix to this title for special provisions relating to legislative purpose.

CHAPTER 11 AUTHORIZED DISPOSITION OF OFFENDERS

Enactment. Chapter 11 was added December 6, 1972, P.L.1482, No.334, effective in six months.

Cross References. Chapter 11 is referred to in section 305 of this title.

§ 1101. Fines.

A person who has been convicted of an offense may be sentenced to pay a fine not exceeding:

(1) $50,000, when the conviction is of murder or attempted murder.

(2) $25,000, when the conviction is of a felony of the first or second degree.

(3) $15,000, when the conviction is of a felony of the third degree.

(4) $10,000, when the conviction is of a misdemeanor of the first degree.

(5) $5,000, when the conviction is of a misdemeanor of the second degree.

(6) $2,500, when the conviction is of a misdemeanor of the third degree.

(7) $300, when the conviction is of a summary offense for which no higher fine is established.

(8) Any higher amount equal to double the pecuniary gain derived from the offense by the offender.

(9) Any higher or lower amount specifically authorized by statute.

(Mar. 22, 1974, P.L.210, No.44, eff. imd.; Apr. 28, 1978, P.L.202, No.53, eff. 60 days; Mar. 25, 1988, P.L.262, No.31, eff. 60 days; Mar. 9, 1995, 1st Sp.Sess., P.L.964, No.3, eff. 60 days; Mar. 15, 1995, 1st Sp.Sess., P.L.970, No.5, eff. 60 days)

1995 Amendments. Act 5, 1st Sp.Sess., overlooked the amendment by Act 3, 1st Sp.Sess., but the amendments do not conflict in substance and both have been given effect in setting forth the text of section 1101.

Cross References. Section 1101 is referred to in sections 910, 3308 of this title; section 1571 of Title 75 (Vehicles).

§ 1102. Sentence for murder, murder of unborn child and murder of law enforcement officer.

(a) First degree.--

(1) Except as provided under section 1102.1 (relating to sentence of persons under the age of 18 for murder, murder of an unborn child and murder of a law enforcement officer), a person who has been convicted of a murder of the first degree or of murder of a law enforcement officer of the first degree shall be sentenced to death or to a term of life imprisonment in accordance with 42 Pa.C.S. § 9711 (relating to sentencing procedure for murder of the first degree).

(2) The sentence for a person who has been convicted of first degree murder of an unborn child shall be the same as the sentence for murder of the first degree, except that the death penalty shall not be imposed. This paragraph shall not affect the determination of an aggravating circumstance under 42 Pa.C.S. §

9711(d)(17) for the killing of a pregnant woman.

(b) Second degree.--Except as provided under section 1102.1, a person who has been convicted of murder of the second degree, of second degree murder of an unborn child or of second degree murder of a law enforcement officer shall be sentenced to a term of life imprisonment.

(c) Attempt, solicitation and conspiracy.--Notwithstanding section 1103(1) (relating to sentence of imprisonment for felony), a person who has been convicted of attempt, solicitation or conspiracy to commit murder, murder of an unborn child or murder of a law enforcement officer where serious bodily injury results may be sentenced to a term of imprisonment which shall be fixed by the court at not more than 40 years. Where serious bodily injury does not result, the person may be sentenced to a term of imprisonment which shall be fixed by the court at not more than 20 years.

(d) Third degree.--Notwithstanding section 1103, a person who has been convicted of murder of the third degree or of third degree murder of an unborn child shall be sentenced to a term which shall be fixed by the court at not more than 40 years.

(Mar. 26, 1974, P.L.213, No.46, eff. imd.; Mar. 9, 1995, 1st Sp.Sess., P.L.964, No.3, eff. 60 days; Mar. 15, 1995, 1st Sp.Sess., P.L.970, No.5, eff. 60 days; Oct. 2, 1997, P.L.379, No.44, eff. 180 days; Oct. 17, 2008, P.L.1628, No.131, eff. 60 days; Oct. 25, 2012, P.L.1655, No.204, eff. imd.)

2012 Amendment. Act 204 amended subsecs. (a)(1) and (b).

2008 Amendment. Act 131 amended the section heading and subsecs. (a), (b) and (c).

Cross References. Section 1102 is referred to in sections 106, 2604 of this title.

§ 1102.1. Sentence of persons under the age of 18 for murder, murder of an unborn child and murder of a law enforcement officer.

(a) First degree murder.--A person who has been convicted after June 24, 2012, of a murder of the first degree, first degree murder of an unborn child or murder of a law enforcement officer of the first degree and who was under the age of 18 at the time of the commission of the offense shall be sentenced as follows:

(1) A person who at the time of the commission of the offense was 15 years of age or older shall be sentenced to a term of life imprisonment without parole, or a term of imprisonment, the minimum of which shall be at least 35 years to life.

(2) A person who at the time of the commission of the offense was under 15 years of age shall be sentenced to a term of life imprisonment without parole, or a term of imprisonment, the minimum of which shall be at least 25 years to life.

(b) Notice.--Reasonable notice to the defendant of the Commonwealth's intention to seek a sentence of life imprisonment without parole under subsection (a) shall be provided after conviction and before sentencing.

(c) Second degree murder.--A person who has been convicted after June 24, 2012, of a murder of the second degree, second degree murder of an unborn child or murder of a law enforcement officer of the second degree and who was under the age of 18 at the time of the commission of the offense shall be sentenced as follows:

(1) A person who at the time of the commission of the offense was 15 years of age or older shall be sentenced to a term of imprisonment the minimum of which shall be at least 30 years to life.

(2) A person who at the time of the commission of the offense was under 15 years of age shall be sentenced to a term of imprisonment the minimum of which shall be at least 20 years to life.

(d) Findings.--In determining whether to impose a sentence of life without parole under subsection (a), the court shall consider and make findings on the record regarding the following:

(1) The impact of the offense on each victim, including oral and written victim impact statements made or submitted by family members of the victim detailing the physical, psychological and economic effects of the crime on the victim and the victim's family. A victim impact statement may include comment on the sentence of the defendant.

(2) The impact of the offense on the community.

(3) The threat to the safety of the public or any individual posed by the defendant.

(4) The nature and circumstances of the offense committed by the defendant.

(5) The degree of the defendant's culpability.

(6) Guidelines for sentencing and resentencing adopted by the Pennsylvania Commission on Sentencing.

(7) Age-related characteristics of the defendant, including:

(i) Age.

(ii) Mental capacity.

(iii) Maturity.

(iv) The degree of criminal sophistication exhibited by the defendant.

(v) The nature and extent of any prior delinquent or criminal history, including the success or failure of any previous attempts by the court to rehabilitate the defendant.

(vi) Probation or institutional reports.

(vii) Other relevant factors.

(e) Minimum sentence.--Nothing under this section shall prevent the sentencing court from imposing a minimum sentence greater than that provided in this section. Sentencing guidelines promulgated by the Pennsylvania Commission on Sentencing may not supersede the mandatory minimum sentences provided under this section.

(f) Appeal by Commonwealth.--If a sentencing court refuses to apply this section where applicable, the Commonwealth shall have the right to appellate review of the action of the sentencing court. The appellate court shall vacate the sentence and remand the case to the sentencing court for imposition of a sentence in accordance with this section if it finds that the sentence was imposed in violation of this section.

(Oct. 25, 2012, P.L.1655, No.204, eff. imd.)

2012 Amendment. Act 204 added section 1102.1.

Cross References. Section 1102.1 is referred to in section 1102 of this title; section 6139 of Title 61 (Prisons and Parole).

§ 1103. Sentence of imprisonment for felony.

Except as provided in 42 Pa.C.S. § 9714 (relating to sentences for second and subsequent offenses), a person who has been convicted of a felony may be sentenced to imprisonment as follows:

(1) In the case of a felony of the first degree, for a term which shall be fixed by the court at not more than 20 years.

(2) In the case of a felony of the second degree, for a term which shall be fixed by the court at not more than ten years.

(3) In the case of a felony of the third degree, for a term which shall be fixed by the court at not more than seven years.

(Oct. 11, 1995, 1st Sp.Sess., P.L.1058, No.21, eff. 60 days)

Cross References. Section 1103 is referred to in sections 1102, 2702.1, 3121, 3123 of this title; sections 9714, 9718.2 of Title 42 (Judiciary and Judicial Procedure); section 1571 of Title 75 (Vehicles).

§ 1104. Sentence of imprisonment for misdemeanors.

A person who has been convicted of a misdemeanor may be sentenced to imprisonment for a definite term which shall be fixed by the court and shall be not more than:

(1) Five years in the case of a misdemeanor of the first degree.

(2) Two years in the case of a misdemeanor of the second degree.

(3) One year in the case of a misdemeanor of the third degree.

Cross References. Section 1104 is referred to in section 1571 of Title 75 (Vehicles).

§ 1105. Sentence of imprisonment for summary offenses.

A person who has been convicted of a summary offense may be sentenced to imprisonment for a term which shall be fixed by the court at not more than 90 days.

§ 1106. Restitution for injuries to person or property.

(a) General rule.--Upon conviction for any crime wherein:

(1) property of a victim has been stolen, converted or otherwise unlawfully obtained, or its value substantially decreased as a direct result of the crime; or

(2) the victim, if an individual, suffered personal injury directly resulting from the crime,

the offender shall be sentenced to make restitution in addition to the punishment prescribed therefor.

(b) Condition of probation or parole.-- Whenever restitution has been ordered pursuant to subsection (a) and the offender has been placed on probation or parole, the offender's compliance with such order may be made a condition of such probation or parole.

(c) Mandatory restitution.--

(1) The court shall order full restitution:

(i) Regardless of the current financial resources of the defendant, so as to provide the victim with the fullest compensation for the loss. The court shall not reduce a restitution award by any amount that the victim has received from the Crime Victim's Compensation Board or other government agency but shall order the defendant to pay any restitution ordered for loss previously compensated by the board to the Crime Victim's Compensation Fund or other designated account when the claim involves a government agency in addition to or in place of the board. The court shall not reduce a restitution award by any amount that the victim has received from an insurance company but shall order the defendant to pay any restitution ordered for loss previously compensated by an insurance company to the insurance company.

(ii) If restitution to more than one victim is set at the same time, the court shall set priorities of payment. However, when establishing priorities, the court shall order payment in the following order:

(A) Any individual.

(A.1) Any affected government agency.

(B) The Crime Victim's Compensation Board.

(C) Any other government agency which has provided reimbursement to the victim as a result of the defendant's criminal conduct.

(D) Any insurance company which has provided reimbursement to the victim as a result of the defendant's criminal conduct.

(E) Any estate or testamentary trust.

(F) Any business entity organized as a nonprofit or not-for-profit entity.

(G) Any other business entity.

(2) At the time of sentencing the court shall specify the amount and method of restitution. In determining the amount and method of restitution, the court:

(i) Shall consider the extent of injury suffered by the victim, the victim's request for restitution as presented to the district attorney in accordance with paragraph (4) and such other matters as it deems appropriate.

(ii) May order restitution in a lump sum, by monthly installments or according to such other schedule as it deems just.

(iii) Shall not order incarceration of a defendant for failure to pay restitution if the failure results from the offender's inability to pay.

(iv) Shall consider any other preexisting orders imposed on the defendant, including, but not limited to, orders imposed under this title or any other title.

(v) (Deleted by amendment).

(3) The court may, at any time or upon the recommendation of the district attorney that is based on information received from the victim and the probation section of the county or other agent designated by the county commissioners of the county with the approval of the president judge to collect restitution, alter or amend any order of restitution made pursuant to paragraph (2), provided, however, that the court states its reasons and conclusions as a matter of record for any change or amendment to any previous order.

(4) (i) It shall be the responsibility of the district attorneys of the respective counties to make a recommendation to the court at or prior to the time of sentencing as to the amount of restitution to be ordered. This recommendation shall be based upon information solicited by the district attorney and received from the victim.

(ii) Where the district attorney has solicited information from the victims as provided in subparagraph (i) and has received no response, the district attorney shall, based on other available information, make a recommendation to the court for restitution.

(iii) The district attorney may, as appropriate, recommend to the court that the restitution order be altered or amended as provided in paragraph (3).

(d) Limitations on district justices.--Restitution ordered by a magisterial district judge shall be limited to the return of the actual property or its undisputed dollar amount or, where the claim for restitution does not exceed the civil jurisdictional limit specified in 42 Pa.C.S. § 1515(a)(3) (relating to jurisdiction) and is disputed as to amount, the magisterial district judge shall determine and order the dollar amount of restitution to be made.

(e) Restitution payments and records.--Restitution, when ordered by a judge, shall be made by the offender to the probation section of the county in which he was convicted or to another agent designated by the county commissioners with the approval of the president judge of the county to collect restitution according to the order of the court or, when ordered by a magisterial district judge, shall be made to the magisterial district judge. The probation section or other agent designated by the county commissioners of the county with the approval of the president judge to collect restitution and the magisterial district judge shall maintain records of the restitution order and its satisfaction and shall forward to the victim the property or payments made pursuant to the restitution order.

(f) Noncompliance with restitution order.--Whenever the offender shall fail to make restitution as provided in the order of a judge, the probation section or other agent designated by the county commissioners of the county with the approval of the president judge to collect restitution shall notify the court within 20 days of such failure. Whenever the offender shall fail to make restitution within 20 days to a magisterial district judge, as ordered, the magisterial district judge shall declare the offender in contempt and forward the case to the court of common pleas. Upon such notice of failure to make restitution, or upon receipt of the contempt decision from a magisterial district judge, the court shall order a hearing to determine if the offender is in contempt of court or has violated his probation or parole.

(g) Preservation of private remedies.--No judgment or order of restitution shall debar the victim, by appropriate action, to recover from the offender as otherwise provided by law, provided that any civil award shall be reduced by the amount paid under the criminal judgment.

(h) Definitions.--As used in this section, the following words and phrases shall have the meanings given to them in this subsection:

"Affected government agency." The Commonwealth, a political subdivision or local authority that has sustained injury to property.

"Business entity." A domestic or foreign:

(1) business corporation;

(2) nonprofit corporation;

(3) general partnership;

(4) limited partnership;

(5) limited liability company;

(6) unincorporated nonprofit association;

(7) professional association; or

(8) business trust, common law business trust or statutory trust.

"Crime." Any offense punishable under this title or by a magisterial district judge.

"Injury to property." Loss of real or personal property, including negotiable instruments, or decrease in its value, directly resulting from the crime.

"Insurance company." An entity that compensates a victim for loss under an insurance contract.

"Insurance contract." A contract governed by the insurance laws of the state in which it was issued or a plan of benefits sponsored by an employer or employee organization.

"Offender." Any person who has been found guilty of any crime.

"Personal injury." Actual bodily harm, including pregnancy, directly resulting from the crime.

"Property." Any real or personal property, including currency and negotiable instruments, of the victim.

"Restitution." The return of the property of the victim or payments in cash or the equivalent thereof pursuant to an order of the court.

"Victim." As defined in section 103 of the act of November 24, 1998 (P.L.882, No.111), known as the Crime Victims Act. The term includes an affected government agency, the Crime Victim's Compensation Fund, if compensation has been paid by the Crime Victim's Compensation Fund to the victim, any insurance company that has compensated the victim for loss under an insurance contract and any business entity.

(June 18, 1976, P.L.394, No.86, eff. 60 days; Apr. 28, 1978, P.L.202, No.53, eff. 60 days; May 3, 1995, 1st Sp.Sess., P.L.999, No.12, eff. 60 days; Dec. 3, 1998, P.L.933, No.121, eff. imd.; Nov. 30, 2004, P.L.1618, No.207, eff. 60 days; Oct. 24, 2018, P.L.891, No.145, eff. imd.)

2018 Amendment. Act 145 amended subsecs. (a), (b), (c)(1), (g) and (h).

2004 Amendment. Act 207 amended subsecs. (d), (e) and (f) and the def. of "crime" in subsec. (h). See sections 28 and 29 of Act 207 in the appendix to this title for special provisions relating to applicability and construction of law.

1998 Amendment. Act 121 amended subsecs. (a), (c), (e) and (f).

1995 Amendment. Act 12, 1st Sp.Sess., amended subsec. (c) and the def. of "victim" in subsec. (h)

1978 Amendment. Act 53 amended subsecs. (d), (e), (f) and (h).

1976 Amendment. Act 86 added section 1106.

Cross References. Section 1106 is referred to in sections 910, 3020, 3926, 4116 of this title; sections 8316.1, 9728, 9738 of Title 42 (Judiciary and Judicial Procedure); section 6126 of Title 75 (Vehicles).

§ 1107. Restitution for theft of timber.

Any person convicted for the theft of standing timber under section 3921 (relating to theft by unlawful taking or disposition) shall, in addition to any other sentence imposed, be sentenced to pay the owner of the timber restitution in an amount twice the value of the timber taken.

(Oct. 11, 1984, P.L.892, No.173, eff. imd.)

1984 Amendment. Act 173 added section 1107.

Cross References. Section 1107 is referred to in section 8311 of Title 42 (Judiciary and Judicial Procedure).

§ 1107.1. Restitution for identity theft.

(a) General rule.--The court shall, in addition to any other restitution sentence or order authorized by law, sentence a person convicted of a violation of section 4106 (relating to access device fraud) or 4120 (relating to identity theft) to make restitution for all reasonable expenses incurred by the victim or on the victim's behalf:

(1) to investigate theft of the victim's identity;

(2) to bring or defend civil or criminal actions related to theft of the victim's identity; or

(3) to take other efforts to correct the victim's credit record or negative credit reports related to theft of the victim's identity.

(b) Types of expenses.--The types of expenses recoverable under this section include, but are not limited to:

(1) fees for professional services by attorneys or accountants;

(2) fees and costs imposed by credit bureaus, associated with efforts to correct the victim's credit record, incurred in private investigations or associated with contesting unwarranted debt collections; and

(3) court costs and filing fees.

(Sept. 18, 2009, P.L.391, No.42, eff. 60 days)

2009 Amendment. Act 42 added section 1107.1.

§ 1108. District attorneys' standing and interest in prisoner litigation.

The district attorney shall receive written notice of, and shall have automatic standing and a legal interest in, any proceeding which may involve the release or nonadmission of county prisoners, delinquents or detainees due to the fact, duration or other conditions of custody. In addition to the district attorney's rights in such a proceeding, the district attorney may seek any equitable relief necessary to protect the district attorney's interest in the continued institutional custody and admission of county prisoners, delinquents or detainees.

(Mar. 25, 1988, P.L.262, No.31, eff. 60 days)

1988 Amendment. Act 31 added section 1108.

§ 1109. Costs.

In addition to any other sentence imposed, the court may order an offender to pay the cost of any reward paid for the apprehension and conviction of the offender.

(Sept. 26, 1995, 1st Sp.Sess., P.L.1056, No.20, eff. 60 days)

1995 Amendment. Act 20, 1st Sp.Sess., added section 1109. Section 4 of Act 20 provided that section 1109 shall apply to sentences imposed on or after the effective date of Act 20.

§ 1110. Restitution for cleanup of clandestine laboratories.

(a) General rule.--When any person is convicted of an offense under The Controlled Substance, Drug, Device and Cosmetic Act involving the manufacture of a controlled substance, the court shall order the person to make restitution for the costs incurred in the cleanup, including labor costs, equipment and supplies, of any clandestine laboratory used by the person to manufacture the controlled substance.

(b) Definitions.--As used in this section, the following words and phrases shall have the meanings given to them in this subsection:

"Clandestine laboratory." A location or site, including buildings or vehicles, in which glassware, heating devices, precursors or related reagents or solvents which are intended to be used or are used to unlawfully manufacture a controlled substance are located.

"Cleanup." Actions necessary to contain, collect, control, identify, analyze, disassemble, treat, remove or otherwise disperse all substances and materials in a clandestine laboratory, including those found to be hazardous waste and any contamination caused by those substances or materials.

"The Controlled Substance, Drug, Device and Cosmetic Act." The act of April 14, 1972 (P.L.233, No.64), known as The Controlled Substance, Drug, Device and Cosmetic Act.

(Nov. 19, 2004, P.L.848, No.109, eff. 60 days)

2004 Amendment. Act 109 added section 1110.

Cross References. Section 1110 is referred to in section 7508.2 of this title.

§ 1111. Accelerated Rehabilitative Disposition prohibited.

The attorney for the Commonwealth may not recommend and the court may not authorize placement on Accelerated Rehabilitative Disposition for a violation of any offense set forth in any of the following if the victim was, at the time of the commission of the offense, under 18 years of age:

(1) Section 3121 (relating to rape).

(2) Section 3123 (relating to involuntary deviate sexual intercourse).

(3) Section 3125 (relating to aggravated indecent assault).

(June 28, 2018, P.L.364, No.50, eff. 60 days)

2018 Amendment. Act 50 added section 1111.

CHAPTER 13
AUTHORITY OF COURT IN SENTENCING
(Transferred)

G. Pennsylvania Commission on
Sentencing (Repealed or
    Transferred)

Transfer Note. Chapter 13 was renumbered and transferred to Chapter 97 of Title 42 (Judiciary and Judicial Procedure) October 5, 1980, P.L.693, No.142, effective in 60 days.

Prior Provisions. The number and heading of Chapter 13 were added December 6, 1972, P.L.1482, No.334. Unless otherwise noted, the remaining provisions of Chapter 13 were added December 30, 1974, P.L.1052, No.345.

SUBCHAPTER A
GENERAL PROVISIONS
(Transferred)

Transfer Note. Subchapter A (§ 1301) was renumbered and transferred to Subchapter A of Chapter 97 of Title 42 (Judiciary and Judicial Procedure) October 5, 1980, P.L.693, No.142, effective in 60 days.

SUBCHAPTER B
SENTENCING AUTHORITY
(Transferred)

Transfer Note. Subchapter B (§§ 1311 & 1312) was renumbered and transferred to Subchapter B of Chapter 97 of Title 42 (Judiciary and Judicial Procedure) October 5, 1980, P.L.693, No.142, effective in 60 days.

SUBCHAPTER C
SENTENCING ALTERNATIVES
(Transferred)

Transfer Note. Subchapter C (§§ 1321 - 1326) was renumbered and transferred to Subchapter C of Chapter 97 of Title 42 (Judiciary and Judicial Procedure) October 5, 1980, P.L.693, No.142, effective in 60 days.

SUBCHAPTER D
INFORMATIONAL BASIS OF
SENTENCE
(Transferred)

Transfer Note. Subchapter D (§§ 1331 - 1337) was renumbered and transferred to Subchapter D of Chapter 97 of Title 42 (Judiciary and Judicial Procedure) October 5, 1980, P.L.693, No.142, effective in 60 days.

SUBCHAPTER E
IMPOSITION OF SENTENCE
(Transferred)

Transfer Note. Subchapter E (§§ 1351 - 1362) was renumbered and transferred to Subchapter E of Chapter 97 of Title 42 (Judiciary and Judicial Procedure) October 5, 1980, P.L.693, No.142, effective in 60 days.

SUBCHAPTER F
FURTHER JUDICIAL ACTION
(Transferred)

Transfer Note. Subchapter F (§§ 1371 & 1372) was renumbered and transferred to Subchapter F of Chapter 97 of Title 42 (Judiciary and Judicial Procedure) October 5, 1980, P.L.693, No.142, effective in 60 days.

SUBCHAPTER G
PENNSYLVANIA COMMISSION ON
SENTENCING
(Repealed or Transferred)

Repeal and Transfer Note. Subchapter G (§§ 1381 - 1386) was repealed except for section 1386 which was renumbered 9781 and transferred to Subchapter G of Chapter 97 of Title 42 (Judiciary and Judicial Procedure) October 5, 1980, P.L.693, No.142, effective in 60 days. The subject matter of former sections 1381 through 1385 is now contained in Subchapter F of Chapter 21 of Title 42.

Prior Provisions. Subchapter G was added November 26, 1978, P.L.1316, No.319, effective January 1, 1979. Former Subchapter G, which related to sentencing council, was added December 30, 1974, P.L.1052, No.345, and repealed November 26, 1978, P.L.1316, No.319, effective January 1, 1979.

PART II DEFINITION OF SPECIFIC OFFENSES

Article
A. Offenses Against Existence or Stability of Government
B. Offenses Involving Danger to the Person
C. Offenses Against Property
D. Offenses Against the Family
E. Offenses Against Public Administration
F. Offenses Against Public Order and Decency
G. Miscellaneous Offenses

Enactment. Part II was added December 6, 1972, P.L.1482, No.334, effective in six months.

ARTICLE A OFFENSES AGAINST EXISTENCE OR STABILITY OF GOVERNMENT

Chapter
21. Offenses Against the Flag

CHAPTER 21 OFFENSES AGAINST THE FLAG

Sec.
2101. Display of flag at public meetings.
2102. Desecration of flag.
2103. Insults to national or Commonwealth flag.

Enactment. Chapter 21 was added December 6, 1972, P.L.1482, No.334, effective in six months.

§ 2101. Display of flag at public meetings.

(a) Offense defined.--A person is guilty of a summary offense if, being directly or indirectly in charge of any public gathering, in any place, he fails at such gathering to display publicly and visibly the flag of the United States reasonably clean and in good repair.

(b) Exceptions.--

(1) Subsection (a) of this section does not apply to gatherings for religious worship.

(2) The provisions of subsection (a) of this section do not prohibit the exhibition of torn, soiled or worn flags of the United States which have historical significance when exhibited in conjunction with the type of flag required by subsection (a) of this section.

§ 2102. Desecration of flag.

(a) Offense defined.--A person is guilty of a misdemeanor of the third degree if, in any manner, he:

(1) for exhibition or display places any marks, writing or design of any nature or any advertisement upon any flag;

(2) exposes to public view any such marked or defiled flag;

(3) manufactures, sells, exposes for sale, gives away, or has in his possession for any of such purposes any article which uses the flag for the purposes of advertisement, sale or trade; or

(4) publicly or privately mutilates, defaces, defiles, or tramples upon, or casts contempt in any manner upon any flag.

(b) Exception.--Subsection (a) of this section does not apply:

(1) To any act permitted by the statutes of the United States, or by the regulations of the armed forces of the United States.

(2) In a case where the government of the United States has granted the use of such flag, standard, color, or ensign as a trademark.

(3) To any writing or instrument, or stationery for use in correspondence on any of which shall be printed, painted, or placed said flag, disconnected from any advertisement for the purpose of sale or trade.

(4) To any patriotic or political demonstration or decorations.

(c) Definition.--As used in this section the word "flag" shall include any flag, standard, color, ensign or any picture or representation of any thereof, made of any substance or represented on any substance and of any size, purporting to be a flag, standard, color or ensign of the United States or of the Commonwealth, or a picture or a representation of any thereof, upon which shall be shown the colors or any color, or any combination of colors, or either the stars or the stripes, or the stars and the stripes, in any number of either thereof, or anything which the person seeing the same, may reasonably believe the same to represent the flag, colors, standard or ensign of the United States or of the Commonwealth.

§ 2103. Insults to national or Commonwealth flag.

A person is guilty of a misdemeanor of the second degree if he maliciously takes down, defiles, injures, removes or in any manner damages, insults, or destroys any American flag or the flag of the Commonwealth which is displayed anywhere.

ARTICLE B OFFENSES INVOLVING DANGER TO THE PERSON

CHAPTER 23 GENERAL PROVISIONS

Enactment. Chapter 23 was added December 6, 1972, P.L.1482, No.334, effective in six months.

§ 2301. Definitions.

Subject to additional definitions contained in subsequent provisions of this article which are applicable to specific chapters or other provisions of this article, the following words and phrases, when used in this article shall have, unless the context clearly indicates otherwise, the meanings given to them in this section:

"Bodily injury." Impairment of physical condition or substantial pain.

"Deadly weapon." Any firearm, whether loaded or unloaded, or any device designed as a weapon and capable of producing death or serious bodily injury, or any other device or instrumentality which, in the manner in which it is used or intended to be used, is calculated or likely to produce death or serious bodily injury.

"Serious bodily injury." Bodily injury which creates a substantial risk of death or which causes serious, permanent disfigurement, or protracted loss or impairment of the function of any bodily member or organ.

"Serious provocation." Conduct sufficient to excite an intense passion in a reasonable person.

Cross References. Section 2301 is referred to in sections 2602, 3101, 3505, 5106, 5131 of this title; section 6338.1 of Title 23 (Domestic Relations); sections 6302, 6355 of Title 42 (Judiciary and Judicial Procedure); sections 3326, 3327 of Title 75 (Vehicles).

CHAPTER 25 CRIMINAL HOMICIDE

Enactment. Chapter 25 was added December 6, 1972, P.L.1482, No.334, effective in six months.

Cross References. Chapter 25 is referred to in sections 911, 2602, 3502 of this title; section 5432 of Title 20 (Decedents, Estates and Fiduciaries); sections 2511, 3103, 5329, 6344 of Title 23 (Domestic Relations); sections 5750, 5985.1, 5993, 6302 of Title 42 (Judiciary and Judicial Procedure).

§ 2501. Criminal homicide.

(a) Offense defined.--A person is guilty of criminal homicide if he intentionally, knowingly, recklessly or negligently causes the death of another human being.

(b) Classification.--Criminal homicide shall be classified as murder, voluntary manslaughter, or involuntary manslaughter.

Cross References. Section 2501 is referred to in section 5708 of this title; section 4503 of Title 42 (Judiciary and Judicial Procedure).

§ 2502. Murder.

(a) Murder of the first degree.--A criminal homicide constitutes murder of the first degree when it is committed by an intentional killing.

(b) Murder of the second degree.--A criminal homicide constitutes murder of the second degree when it is committed while defendant was engaged as a principal or an accomplice in the perpetration of a felony.

(c) Murder of the third degree.--All other kinds of murder shall be murder of the third degree. Murder of the third degree is a felony of the first degree.

(d) Definitions.--As used in this section the following words and phrases shall have the meanings given to them in this subsection:

"Fireman." Includes any employee or member of a municipal fire department or volunteer fire company.

"Hijacking." Any unlawful or unauthorized seizure or exercise of control, by force or violence or threat of force or violence.

"Intentional killing." Killing by means of poison, or by lying in wait, or by any other kind of willful, deliberate and premeditated killing.

"Perpetration of a felony." The act of the defendant in engaging in or being an accomplice in the commission of, or an attempt to commit, or flight after committing, or attempting to commit robbery, rape, or deviate sexual intercourse by force or threat of force, arson, burglary or kidnapping.

"Principal." A person who is the actor or perpetrator of the crime.

(Mar. 26, 1974, P.L.213, No.46, eff. imd.; Apr. 28, 1978, P.L.84, No.39, eff. 60 days)

Cross References. Section 2502 is referred to in sections 2506, 2507, 2602, 5702, 5708, 6105 of this title; section 3304 of Title 5 (Athletics and Sports); section 5329 of Title 23 (Domestic Relations); sections 1515, 5551, 9711.1, 9718, 9802 of Title 42 (Judiciary and Judicial Procedure); sections 3903, 4103, 6124, 7122 of Title 61 (Prisons and Parole).

§ 2503. Voluntary manslaughter.

(a) General rule.--A person who kills an individual without lawful justification commits voluntary manslaughter if at the time of the killing he is acting under a sudden and intense passion resulting from serious provocation by:

(1) the individual killed; or

(2) another whom the actor endeavors to kill, but he negligently or accidentally causes the death of the individual killed.

(b) Unreasonable belief killing justifiable.--A person who intentionally or knowingly kills an individual commits voluntary manslaughter if at the time of the killing he believes the circumstances to be such that, if they existed, would justify the killing under Chapter 5 of this title (relating to general principles of justification), but his belief is unreasonable.

(c) Grading.--Voluntary manslaughter is a felony of the first degree.

(Nov. 17, 1995, 1st Sp.Sess., P.L.1144, No.36, eff. 60 days)

1995 Amendment. Act 36, 1st Sp.Sess., amended subsec. (c).

Cross References. Section 2503 is referred to in sections 5702, 5708, 6105 of this title; sections 1515, 9711, 9802 of Title 42 (Judiciary and Judicial Procedure); sections 3903, 4103, 7122 of Title 61 (Prisons and Parole).

§ 2504. Involuntary manslaughter.

(a) General rule.--A person is guilty of involuntary manslaughter when as a direct result of the doing of an unlawful act in a reckless or grossly negligent manner, or the doing of a lawful act in a reckless or grossly negligent manner, he causes the death of another person.

(b) Grading.--Involuntary manslaughter is a misdemeanor of the first degree. Where the victim is under 12 years of age and is in the care, custody or control of the person who caused the death, involuntary manslaughter is a felony of the second degree.

(July 6, 1995, P.L.251, No.31, eff. 60 days)

Cross References. Section 2504 is referred to in sections 2711, 6105 of this title; section 1611 of Title 75 (Vehicles).

§ 2505. Causing or aiding suicide.

(a) Causing suicide as criminal homicide.--A person may be convicted of criminal homicide for causing another to commit suicide only if he intentionally causes such suicide by force, duress or deception.

(b) Aiding or soliciting suicide as an independent offense.--A person who intentionally aids or solicits another to commit suicide is guilty of a felony of the second degree if his conduct causes such suicide or an attempted suicide, and otherwise of a misdemeanor of the second degree.

§ 2506. Drug delivery resulting in death.

(a) Offense defined.--A person commits a felony of the first degree if the person intentionally administers, dispenses, delivers, gives, prescribes, sells or distributes any controlled substance or counterfeit controlled substance in violation of section 13(a)(14) or (30) of the act of April 14, 1972 (P.L.233, No.64), known as The Controlled Substance, Drug, Device and Cosmetic Act, and another person dies as a result of using the substance.

(b) Penalty.--

(1) A person convicted under subsection (a) shall be sentenced to a term of imprisonment which shall be fixed by the court at not more than 40 years.

(2) Paragraph (1) shall not apply to a person convicted under section 2502(c) (relating to murder) when the victim is less than 13 years of age and the conduct arises out of the same criminal act.

(c) Proof of sentencing.--(Deleted by amendment).

(d) Authority of court in sentencing.--(Deleted by amendment).

(e) Appeal by Commonwealth.--(Deleted by amendment).

(f) Forfeiture.--Assets against which a forfeiture petition has been filed and is pending or against which the Commonwealth has indicated an intention to file a forfeiture petition shall not be subject to a fine. Nothing in this section shall prevent a fine from being imposed on assets which have been subject to an unsuccessful forfeiture petition.

(Dec. 22, 1989, P.L.773, No.109, eff. imd.; Feb. 18, 1998, P.L.102, No.19, eff. 60 days; July 7, 2011, P.L.220, No.40, eff. 60 days; June 18, 2014, P.L.741, No.56, eff. 60 days)

2014 Amendment. Act 56 amended subsec. (b).

Cross References. Section 2506 is referred to in sections 3308, 5702 of this title; section 9714 of Title 42 (Judiciary and Judicial Procedure); sections 3903, 4103 of Title 61 (Prisons and Parole).

§ 2507. Criminal homicide of law enforcement officer.

(a) Murder of a law enforcement officer of the first degree.--A person commits murder of a law enforcement officer of the first degree who intentionally kills a law enforcement officer while in the performance of duty knowing the victim is a law enforcement officer.

(b) Murder of a law enforcement officer of the second degree.--A person commits murder of a law enforcement officer of the second degree who engages as a principal or an accomplice in the perpetration of a felony during which a law enforcement officer is killed while in the performance of duty.

(c) Manslaughter of a law enforcement officer in the first degree.--A person commits a felony in the first degree who does any of the following:

(1) Without lawful justification kills a law enforcement officer while in the performance of duty and with knowledge that the victim was a law enforcement officer, if at the time of the killing:

(i) the person is acting under a sudden and intense passion resulting from serious provocation by the victim killed; or

(ii) the person is acting under a sudden and intense passion resulting from serious provocation by another individual whom the actor endeavors to kill, but the person negligently or accidentally causes the death of the victim.

(2) Intentionally or knowingly kills a law enforcement officer while in the performance of duty and with knowledge that the victim was a law enforcement officer, if at the time of the killing the person believes the circumstances to be such that, if they existed, would justify the killing under Chapter 5 (relating to general principles of justification), but his belief is unreasonable.

(d) Manslaughter of a law enforcement officer in the second degree.--A person commits a felony of the second degree who, as a direct result of the doing of an unlawful or lawful act in a reckless or grossly negligent manner, causes the death of a law enforcement officer while in the performance of duty and the person knew or should have known the victim was a law enforcement officer.

(e) **Definitions.**--As used in this section, the following words and phrases shall have the meanings given to them in this subsection:

"Law enforcement officer." This term shall have the same meaning as the term "peace officer" is given under section 501 (relating to definitions).

"Perpetration of a felony." As defined under section 2502(d) (relating to murder).

(Oct. 17, 2008, P.L.1628, No.131, eff. 60 days)

2008 Amendment. Act 131 added section 2507.

Cross References. Section 2507 is referred to in section 9714 of Title 42 (Judiciary and Judicial Procedure).

CHAPTER 26
CRIMES AGAINST UNBORN CHILD

Enactment. Chapter 26 was added October 2, 1997, P.L.379, No.44, effective in 180 days.

§ 2601. Short title of chapter.

This chapter shall be known and may be cited as the Crimes Against the Unborn Child Act.

§ 2602. Definitions.

The following words and phrases when used in this chapter shall have the meanings given to them in this section unless the context clearly indicates otherwise:

"Abortion." As defined in section 3203 (relating to definitions).

"Intentional killing." Killing by means of poison, or by lying in wait, or by any other kind of willful, deliberate and premeditated killing.

"Murder." As used in this chapter, the term includes the same element of malice which is required to prove murder under Chapter 25 (relating to criminal homicide).

"Perpetration of a felony." As defined in section 2502(d) (relating to murder).

"Principal." As defined in section 2502(d) (relating to murder).

"Serious bodily injury." Bodily injury which creates a substantial risk of death or which causes serious, permanent disfigurement or protracted loss or impairment of the function of any bodily member or organ.

"Serious provocation." As defined in section 2301 (relating to definitions).

"Unborn child." As defined in section 3203 (relating to definitions).

§ 2603. Criminal homicide of unborn child.

(a) **Offense defined.**--An individual commits criminal homicide of an unborn child if the individual intentionally, knowingly, recklessly or negligently causes the death of an unborn child in violation of section 2604 (relating to murder of unborn child) or 2605 (relating to voluntary manslaughter of unborn child).

(b) **Classification.**--Criminal homicide of an unborn child shall be classified as murder of an unborn child or voluntary manslaughter of an unborn child.

§ 2604. Murder of unborn child.

(a) First degree murder of unborn child.--

(1) A criminal homicide of an unborn child constitutes first degree murder of an unborn child when it is committed by an intentional killing.

(2) The penalty for first degree murder of an unborn child shall be imposed in accordance with section 1102(a)(2) (relating to sentence for murder and murder of an unborn child).

(b) Second degree murder of unborn child.--

(1) A criminal homicide of an unborn child constitutes second degree murder of an unborn child when it is committed while the defendant was engaged as a principal or an accomplice in the perpetration of a felony.

(2) The penalty for second degree murder of an unborn child shall be the same as for murder of the second degree.

(c) Third degree murder of unborn child.--

(1) All other kinds of murder of an unborn child shall be third degree murder of an unborn child.

(2) The penalty for third degree murder of an unborn child is the same as the penalty for murder of the third degree.

Cross References. Section 2604 is referred to in section 2603 of this title; section 9714 of Title 42 (Judiciary and Judicial Procedure).

§ 2605. Voluntary manslaughter of unborn child.

(a) Offense defined.--A person who kills an unborn child without lawful justification commits voluntary manslaughter of an unborn child if at the time of the killing he is acting under a sudden and intense passion resulting from serious provocation by:

(1) the mother of the unborn child whom the actor endeavors to kill, but he negligently or accidentally causes the death of the unborn child; or

(2) another whom the actor endeavors to kill, but he negligently or accidentally causes the death of the unborn child.

(b) Unreasonable belief killing justifiable.--A person who intentionally or knowingly kills an unborn child commits voluntary manslaughter of an unborn child if at the time of the killing he believes the circumstances to be such that, if they existed, would justify the killing under Chapter 5 (relating to general principles of justification) but his belief is unreasonable.

(c) Penalty.--The penalty for voluntary manslaughter of an unborn child shall be the same as the penalty for voluntary manslaughter.

Cross References. Section 2605 is referred to in section 2603 of this title.

§ 2606. Aggravated assault of unborn child.

(a) Offense.--A person commits aggravated assault of an unborn child if he attempts to cause serious bodily injury to the unborn child or causes such injury intentionally, knowingly or recklessly under circumstances manifesting extreme indifference to the life of the unborn child.

(b) Grading.--Aggravated assault of an unborn child is a felony of the first degree.

Cross References. Section 2606 is referred to in section 108 of this title; section 9714 of Title 42 (Judiciary and Judicial Procedure).

§ 2607. Culpability.

In any criminal prosecution pursuant to this chapter, the provisions of Chapter 3 (relating to culpability) shall apply, except that:

(1) The term "different person" as used in section 303(b) and (c) (relating to causal relationship between conduct and result) shall also include an unborn child.

(2) The term "victim" as used in section 311 (relating to consent) shall not include the mother of the unborn child.

§ 2608. Nonliability and defenses.

(a) Nonliability.--Nothing in this chapter shall impose criminal liability:

(1) For acts committed during any abortion or attempted abortion, whether lawful or unlawful, in which the pregnant woman cooperated or consented.

(2) For the consensual or good faith performance of medical practice, including medical procedures, diagnostic testing or therapeutic treatment, the use of an intrauterine device or birth control pill to inhibit or prevent ovulation, fertilization or the implantation of a fertilized ovum within the uterus.

(3) Upon the pregnant woman in regard to crimes against her unborn child.

(b) Defenses.--In any prosecution pursuant to this chapter, it shall be a defense that:

(1) The use of force that caused death or serious bodily injury to the unborn child would have been justified pursuant to Chapter 5 (relating to general principles of justification) if it caused death or serious bodily injury to the mother.

(2) Death or serious bodily injury to the unborn child was caused by the use of force which would have been justified pursuant to Chapter 5 if the same level of force was used upon or toward the mother.

§ 2609. Construction.

The provisions of this chapter shall not be construed to prohibit the prosecution of an offender under any other provision of law.

CHAPTER 27 ASSAULT

Sec.
2701. Simple assault.
2702. Aggravated assault.
2702.1. Assault of law enforcement officer.

2703. Assault by prisoner.

2703.1. Aggravated harassment by prisoner.

2704. Assault by life prisoner.

2705. Recklessly endangering another person.

2706. Terroristic threats.

2707. Propulsion of missiles into an occupied vehicle or onto a roadway.

2707.1. Discharge of a firearm into an occupied structure.

2707.2. Paintball guns and paintball markers.

2708. Use of tear or noxious gas in labor disputes.

2709. Harassment.

2709.1. Stalking.

2710. Ethnic intimidation.

2711. Probable cause arrests in domestic violence cases.

2712. Assault on sports official.

2713. Neglect of care-dependent person.

2713.1. Abuse of care-dependent person.

2714. Unauthorized administration of intoxicant.

2715. Threat to use weapons of mass destruction.

2716. Weapons of mass destruction.

2717. Terrorism.

2718. Strangulation.

Enactment. Chapter 27 was added December 6, 1972, P.L.1482, No.334, effective in six months.

Cross References. Chapter 27 is referred to in sections 3104, 3502 of this title; section 3103 of Title 23 (Domestic Relations); sections 5750, 5985.1, 5993 of Title 42 (Judiciary and Judicial Procedure).

§ 2701. Simple assault.

(a) Offense defined.--Except as provided under section 2702 (relating to aggravated assault), a person is guilty of assault if he:

(1) attempts to cause or intentionally, knowingly or recklessly causes bodily injury to another;

(2) negligently causes bodily injury to another with a deadly weapon;

(3) attempts by physical menace to put another in fear of imminent serious bodily injury; or

(4) conceals or attempts to conceal a hypodermic needle on his person and intentionally or knowingly penetrates a law enforcement officer or an officer or an employee of a correctional institution, county jail or prison, detention facility or mental hospital during the course of an arrest or any search of the person.

(b) Grading.--Simple assault is a misdemeanor of the second degree unless committed:

(1) in a fight or scuffle entered into by mutual consent, in which case it is a misdemeanor of the third degree; or

(2) against a child under 12 years of age by a person 18 years of age or older, in which case it is a misdemeanor of the first degree.

(Dec. 19, 1988, P.L.1275, No.158, eff. 60 days; June 22, 2001, P.L.605, No.48, eff. 60 days; Dec. 9, 2002, P.L.1391, No.172, eff. 60 days; Dec. 18, 2013, P.L.1198, No.118, eff. Jan. 1, 2014)

2013 Amendment. Act 118 amended subsecs. (a) and (b)(2).

Cross References. Section 2701 is referred to in sections 2709.1, 2711, 2712, 6105.1, of this title; section 6711 of Title 23 (Domestic Relations); section 9720.8 of Title 42 (Judiciary and Judicial Procedure; section 2303 of Title 44 (Law and Justice); sections 4503, 4601 of Title 61 (Prisons and Parole).

§ 2702. Aggravated assault.

(a) Offense defined.--A person is guilty of aggravated assault if he:

(1) attempts to cause serious bodily injury to another, or causes such injury intentionally, knowingly or recklessly under circumstances manifesting extreme indifference to the value of human life;

(2) attempts to cause or intentionally, knowingly or recklessly causes serious bodily injury to any of the officers, agents, employees or other persons enumerated in subsection (c) or to an employee of an agency, company or other entity engaged in public transportation, while in the performance of duty;

(3) attempts to cause or intentionally or knowingly causes bodily injury to any of the officers, agents, employees or other persons enumerated in subsection (c), in the performance of duty;

(4) attempts to cause or intentionally or knowingly causes bodily injury to another with a deadly weapon;

(5) attempts to cause or intentionally or knowingly causes bodily injury to a teaching staff member, school board member or other employee, including a student employee, of any

elementary or secondary publicly-funded educational institution, any elementary or secondary private school licensed by the Department of Education or any elementary or secondary parochial school while acting in the scope of his or her employment or because of his or her employment relationship to the school;

(6) attempts by physical menace to put any of the officers, agents, employees or other persons enumerated in subsection (c), while in the performance of duty, in fear of imminent serious bodily injury;

(7) uses tear or noxious gas as defined in section 2708(b) (relating to use of tear or noxious gas in labor disputes) or uses an electric or electronic incapacitation device against any officer, employee or other person enumerated in subsection (c) while acting in the scope of his employment;

(8) attempts to cause or intentionally, knowingly or recklessly causes bodily injury to a child less than six years of age, by a person 18 years of age or older; or

(9) attempts to cause or intentionally, knowingly or recklessly causes serious bodily injury to a child less than 13 years of age, by a person 18 years of age or older.

(b) Grading.--Aggravated assault under subsection (a)(1), (2) and (9) is a felony of the first degree. Aggravated assault under subsection (a)(3), (4), (5), (6), (7) and (8) is a felony of the second degree.

(c) Officers, employees, etc., enumerated.--The officers, agents, employees and other persons referred to in subsection (a) shall be as follows:

(1) Police officer.

(2) Firefighter.

(3) County adult probation or parole officer.

(4) County juvenile probation or parole officer.

(5) An agent of the Pennsylvania Board of Probation and Parole.

(6) Sheriff.

(7) Deputy sheriff.

(8) Liquor control enforcement agent.

(9) Officer or employee of a correctional institution, county jail or prison, juvenile detention center or any other facility to which the person has been ordered by the court pursuant to a petition alleging delinquency under 42 Pa.C.S. Ch. 63 (relating to juvenile matters).

(10) Judge of any court in the unified judicial system.

(11) The Attorney General.

(12) A deputy attorney general.

(13) A district attorney.

(14) An assistant district attorney.

(15) A public defender.

(16) An assistant public defender.

(17) A Federal law enforcement official.

(18) A State law enforcement official.

(19) A local law enforcement official.

(20) Any person employed to assist or who assists any Federal, State or local law enforcement official.

(21) Emergency medical services personnel.

(22) Parking enforcement officer.

(23) A magisterial district judge.

(24) A constable.

(25) A deputy constable.

(26) A psychiatric aide.

(27) A teaching staff member, a school board member or other employee, including a student employee, of any elementary or secondary publicly funded educational institution, any elementary or secondary private school licensed by the Department of Education or any elementary or secondary parochial school while acting in the scope of his or her employment or because of his or her employment relationship to the school.

(28) Governor.

(29) Lieutenant Governor.

(30) Auditor General.

(31) State Treasurer.

(32) Member of the General Assembly.

(33) An employee of the Department of Environmental Protection.

(34) An individual engaged in the private detective business as defined in section 2(a) and (b) of the act of August 21, 1953 (P.L.1273, No.361), known as The Private Detective Act of 1953.

(35) An employee or agent of a county children and youth social service agency or of the legal representative of such agency.

(36) A public utility employee or an employee of an electric cooperative.

(37) A wildlife conservation officer or deputy wildlife conservation officer of the Pennsylvania Game Commission.

(38) A waterways conservation officer or deputy waterways conservation officer of the Pennsylvania Fish and Boat Commission.

(d) **Definitions.**--As used in this section, the following words and phrases shall have the meanings given to them in this subsection:

"Electric or electronic incapacitation device." A portable device which is designed or intended by the manufacturer to be used, offensively or defensively, to temporarily immobilize or incapacitate persons by means of electric pulse or current, including devices operated by means of carbon dioxide propellant. The term does not include cattle prods, electric fences or other electric devices when used in agricultural, animal husbandry or food production activities.

"Emergency medical services personnel." The term includes, but is not limited to, doctors, residents, interns, registered nurses, licensed practical nurses, nurse aides, ambulance attendants and operators, paramedics, emergency medical technicians and members of a hospital security force while working within the scope of their employment.

(Oct. 1, 1980, P.L.689, No.139, eff. 60 days; Oct. 16, 1980, P.L.978, No.167, eff. 60 days; Dec. 11, 1986, P.L.1517, No.164, eff. 60 days; Feb. 2, 1990, P.L.6, No.4, eff. 60 days; July 6, 1995, P.L.238, No.27, eff. 60 days; Feb. 23, 1996, P.L.17, No.7, eff. 60 days; July 2, 1996, P.L.478, No.75, eff. 60 days; Dec. 21, 1998, P.L.1245, No.159, eff. 60 days; Nov. 6, 2002, P.L.1096, No.132, eff. 60 days; Nov. 29, 2004, P.L.1349, No.173, eff. 60 days; Nov. 30, 2004, P.L.1618, No.207, eff. 60 days; Oct. 24, 2012, P.L.1205, No.150, eff. 60 days; Dec. 18, 2013, P.L.1198, No.118, eff. Jan. 1, 2014)

2013 Amendment. Act 118 amended subsecs. (a)(6) and (7) and (b) and added subsec. (a)(8) and (9).

2012 Amendment. Act 150 amended subsec. (c).

2004 Amendments. See section 29 of Act 207 in the appendix to this title for special provisions relating to construction of law.

Cross References. Section 2702 is referred to in sections 2701, 2703, 2709.1, 2711, 5702, 5708, 6105 of this title; sections 2511, 5329, 6344, 6711 of Title 23 (Domestic Relations); section 904 of Title 30 (Fish); section 905.1 of Title 34 (Game); sections 5551, 5552, 6302, 6307, 6308, 6336, 6355, 9714, 9717, 9718, 9719, 9720.8, 9802 of Title 42 (Judiciary and Judicial Procedure); section 702 of Title 54 (Names); section 7122 of Title 61 (Prisons and Parole).

§ 2702.1. Assault of law enforcement officer.

(a) **Assault of a law enforcement officer in the first degree.**--A person commits a felony of the first degree who attempts to cause or intentionally or knowingly causes bodily injury to a law enforcement officer, while in the performance of duty and with knowledge that the victim is a law enforcement officer, by discharging a firearm.

(b) **Penalties.**--Notwithstanding section 1103(1) (relating to sentence of imprisonment for felony), a person convicted under subsection (a) shall be sentenced to a term of imprisonment fixed by the court at not more than 40 years.

(c) **Definitions.**--As used in this section, the following words and phrases shall have the meanings given to them in this subsection:

"Law enforcement officer." The term shall have the same meaning as the term "peace officer" is given under section 501 (relating to definitions).

"Firearm." As defined under 42 Pa.C.S. § 9712(e) (relating to sentences for offenses committed with firearms).

(Oct. 17, 2008, P.L.1628, No.131, eff. 60 days)

2008 Amendment. Act 131 added section 2702.1.

Cross References. Section 2702.1 is referred to in section 905.1 of Title 34 (Game); sections 9714, 9719.1 of Title 42 (Judiciary and Judicial Procedure).

§ 2703. Assault by prisoner.

(a) **Offense defined.**--A person who is confined in or committed to any local or county detention facility, jail or prison or any State penal or correctional institution or other State penal or correctional facility located in this Commonwealth is guilty of a felony of the second degree if he, while so confined or committed or while undergoing transportation to or from such an institution or facility in or to which he was confined or committed intentionally or knowingly, commits an assault upon another with a deadly weapon or instrument, or by any means or force likely to produce serious bodily injury. A person is guilty of this offense if he intentionally or knowingly causes another to come into contact with blood, seminal fluid, saliva, urine or feces by throwing, tossing, spitting or expelling such fluid or material when, at the time of the offense, the person knew, had reason to know, should have known or believed such fluid or material to have been obtained from an individual, including the person charged under this section, infected by a communicable disease, including, but not limited to, human immunodeficiency virus (HIV) or hepatitis B.

(b) Consecutive sentences.--The court shall order that any sentence imposed for a violation of subsection (a), or any sentence imposed for a violation of section 2702(a) (relating to aggravated assault) where the victim is a detention facility or correctional facility employee, be served consecutively with the person's current sentence.

(Dec. 10, 1974, P.L.810, No.268; Feb. 18, 1998, P.L.102, No.19, eff. imd.)

Cross References. Section 2703 is referred to in section 6105 of this title; section 9802 of Title 42 (Judiciary and Judicial Procedure); section 7122 of Title 61 (Prisons and Parole).

§ 2703.1. Aggravated harassment by prisoner.

A person who is confined in or committed to any local or county detention facility, jail or prison or any State penal or correctional institution or other State penal or correctional facility located in this Commonwealth commits a felony of the third degree if he, while so confined or committed or while undergoing transportation to or from such an institution or facility in or to which he was confined or committed, intentionally or knowingly causes or attempts to cause another to come into contact with blood, seminal fluid, saliva, urine or feces by throwing, tossing, spitting or expelling such fluid or material.

(Feb. 18, 1998, P.L.102, No.19, eff. imd.)

1998 Amendment. Act 19 added section 2703.1.

§ 2704. Assault by life prisoner.

Every person who has been sentenced to death or life imprisonment in any penal institution located in this Commonwealth, and whose sentence has not been commuted, who commits an aggravated assault with a deadly weapon or instrument upon another, or by any means of force likely to produce serious bodily injury, is guilty of a crime, the penalty for which shall be the same as the penalty for murder of the second degree. A person is guilty of this offense if he intentionally or knowingly causes another to come into contact with blood, seminal fluid, saliva, urine or feces by throwing, tossing, spitting or expelling such fluid or material when, at the time of the offense, the person knew, had reason to know, should have known or believed such fluid or material to have been obtained from an individual, including the person charged under this section, infected by a communicable disease, including, but not limited to, human immunodeficiency virus (HIV) or hepatitis B.

(Mar. 26, 1974, P.L.213, No.46, eff. imd.; Feb. 18, 1998, P.L.102, No.19, eff. imd.)

Cross References. Section 2704 is referred to in section 6105 of this title; section 9802 of Title 42 (Judiciary and Judicial Procedure); section 7122 of Title 61 (Prisons and Parole).

§ 2705. Recklessly endangering another person.

A person commits a misdemeanor of the second degree if he recklessly engages in conduct which places or may place another person in danger of death or serious bodily injury.

Cross References. Section 2705 is referred to in sections 2709.1, 2711 of this title; section 6711 of Title 23 (Domestic Relations).

§ 2706. Terroristic threats.

(a) Offense defined.--A person commits the crime of terroristic threats if the person communicates, either directly or indirectly, a threat to:

(1) commit any crime of violence with intent to terrorize another;

(2) cause evacuation of a building, place of assembly or facility of public transportation; or

(3) otherwise cause serious public inconvenience, or cause terror or serious public inconvenience with reckless disregard of the risk of causing such terror or inconvenience.

(b) Restitution.--A person convicted of violating this section shall, in addition to any other sentence imposed or restitution ordered under 42 Pa.C.S. § 9721(c) (relating to sentencing generally), be sentenced to pay restitution in an amount equal to the cost of the evacuation, including, but not limited to, fire and police response; emergency medical service or emergency preparedness response; and transportation of an individual from the building, place of assembly or facility.

(c) Preservation of private remedies.-- No judgment or order of restitution shall debar a person, by appropriate action, to recover from the offender as otherwise provided by law, provided that any civil award shall be reduced by the amount paid under the criminal judgment.

(d) Grading.--An offense under subsection (a) constitutes a misdemeanor of the first degree unless the threat causes the occupants of the building, place of assembly or facility of public transportation to be diverted from their normal or customary operations, in which case the offense constitutes a felony of the third degree.

(e) Definition.--As used in this section, the term "communicates" means conveys in person or by written or electronic means, including telephone, electronic mail, Internet, facsimile, telex and similar transmissions.

(June 18, 1998, P.L.534, No.76, eff. 60 days; Dec. 15, 1999, P.L.915, No.59, eff. 60 days; June 28, 2002, P.L.481, No.82, eff. 60 days)

2002 Amendment. Act 82 amended subsecs. (b), (c) and (d).

1999 Amendment. Act 59 amended subsec. (a) and added subsecs. (d) and (e).

Cross References. Section 2706 is referred to in sections 911, 2711, 5708 of this title; section 5329 of Title 23 (Domestic Relations); section 5552 of Title 42 (Judiciary and Judicial Procedure); section 1532 of Title 75 (Vehicles).

§ 2707. Propulsion of missiles into an occupied vehicle or onto a roadway.

(a) Occupied vehicles.--Whoever intentionally throws, shoots or propels a rock, stone, brick, or piece of iron, steel or other like metal, or any deadly or dangerous missile, or fire bomb, into a vehicle or instrumentality of public transportation that is occupied by one or more persons commits a misdemeanor of the first degree.

(b) Roadways.--Whoever intentionally throws, shoots, drops or causes to be propelled any solid object, from an overpass or any other location adjacent to or on a roadway, onto or toward said roadway shall be guilty of a misdemeanor of the second degree.

(July 16, 1975, P.L.62, No.37; Dec. 21, 1998, P.L.1103, No.149, eff. 60 days)

1998 Amendment. Act 149 amended subsec. (b).

§ 2707.1. Discharge of a firearm into an occupied structure.

(a) Offense defined.--A person commits an offense if he knowingly, intentionally or recklessly discharges a firearm from any location into an occupied structure.

(b) Grading.--An offense under this section shall be a felony of the third degree.

(c) Defense.--It is a defense to prosecution under this section that:

(1) the person discharging the firearm was a law enforcement officer engaged in the performance of his official law enforcement duties; or

(2) the person discharging the firearm was engaged in a hunting activity; and

(i) the discharge of the firearm took place from a location where the hunting activity is lawful; and

(ii) the passage of the projectile from the firearm into the occupied structure was not intentional, knowing or reckless.

(d) Definitions.--As used in this section, the following words and phrases shall have the meanings given to them in this subsection:

"Firearm." Any weapon which is designed to or may readily be converted to expel any projectile by the action of an explosion or the frame or receiver of any such weapon.

"Occupied structure." Any structure, vehicle or place adapted for overnight accommodation of persons or for carrying on business therein, whether or not a person is actually present.

(Dec. 20, 2000, P.L.831, No.116, eff. 60 days)

2000 Amendment. Act 116 added section 2707.1.

§ 2707.2. Paintball guns and paintball markers.

(a) Unlawful carrying in vehicle.--

(1) (Deleted by amendment).

(1.1) Except as set forth in paragraph (2), an individual may not carry a paintball gun or a paintball marker in a vehicle on a highway unless all of the following apply:

(i) The paintball gun or paintball marker is empty of encapsulated gelatin paintballs.

(ii) The propellant source on the paintball gun or paintball marker is disconnected, disabled or turned off.

(iii) The paintballs are stored in a separate and closed container.

(iv) The paintball gun or paintball marker is:

(A) in a secure wrapper;

(B) has a barrel-blocking device installed; or

(C) is not readily or directly accessible from the passenger compartment of the vehicle.

(2) Paragraph (1.1) does not apply to a commercial paintball field, range or course where passengers are being transported by the commercial field, range or course operator to and from designated player areas.

(a.1) Unlawful discharge of paintball gun or paintball marker.--An individual may not discharge or fire a paintball gun or paintball marker at a person who is not participating in paintball games or paintball-related recreational activities.

(b) Penalty.--A person who violates this section commits a summary offense.

(c) Definitions.--As used in this section, the following words and phrases shall have the meanings given to them in this subsection:

"Barrel-blocking device." A device which captures or prevents the discharge of an encapsulated gelatin paintball from a paintball gun or paintball marker and meets the specifications of the American Society for Testing Materials (ASTM) F2271-03 (Standard Specification for Paintball Marker Barrel Blocking Devices) or its successor.

"Paintball gun." A device designed and manufactured to propel, by gas or air, an encapsulated gelatin paintball.

"Paintball marker." A device designed and manufactured to propel, by gas or air, an encapsulated gelatin paintball.

(Nov. 21, 2001, P.L.846, No.87, eff. 60 days; Dec. 22, 2005, P.L.449, No.85, eff. 60 days)

Cross References. Section 2707.2 is referred to in section 6304 of this title.

§ 2708. Use of tear or noxious gas in labor disputes.

(a) Offense defined.--A person other than a duly constituted officer of the law is guilty of a misdemeanor of the first degree if he uses or directs the use of tear or noxious gas against any person involved in a labor dispute.

(b) Definition.--As used in this section, the term "tear or noxious gas" means any liquid or gaseous substance that, when dispersed in the atmosphere, blinds the eyes with tears or irritates or injures other organs and tissues of the human body or causes nausea, including, but not limited to, red pepper spray.

(Nov. 6, 2002, P.L.1096, No.132, eff. 60 days)

Cross References. Section 2708 is referred to in section 2702 of this title.

§ 2709. Harassment.

(a) Offense defined.--A person commits the crime of harassment when, with intent to harass, annoy or alarm another, the person:

(1) strikes, shoves, kicks or otherwise subjects the other person to physical contact, or attempts or threatens to do the same;

(2) follows the other person in or about a public place or places;

(3) engages in a course of conduct or repeatedly commits acts which serve no legitimate purpose;

(4) communicates to or about such other person any lewd, lascivious, threatening or obscene words, language, drawings or caricatures;

(5) communicates repeatedly in an anonymous manner;

(6) communicates repeatedly at extremely inconvenient hours; or

(7) communicates repeatedly in a manner other than specified in paragraphs (4), (5) and (6).

(a.1) Cyber harassment of a child.--

(1) A person commits the crime of cyber harassment of a child if, with intent to harass, annoy or alarm, the person engages in a continuing course of conduct of making any of the following by electronic means directly to a child or by publication through an electronic social media service:

(i) seriously disparaging statement or opinion about the child's physical characteristics, sexuality, sexual activity or mental or physical health or condition; or

(ii) threat to inflict harm.

(2) (i) If a juvenile is charged with a violation of paragraph (1), the judicial authority with jurisdiction over the violation shall give first consideration to referring the juvenile charged with the violation to a diversionary program under Pa.R.J.C.P. No. 312 (relating to Informal Adjustment) or No. 370 (relating to Consent Decree). As part of the diversionary program, the judicial authority may order the juvenile to participate in an educational

program which includes the legal and nonlegal consequences of cyber harassment.

(ii) If the person successfully completes the diversionary program, the juvenile's records of the charge of violating paragraph (1) shall be expunged as provided for under section 9123 (relating to juvenile records).

(b) **Stalking.**--(Deleted by amendment).

(b.1) Venue.--

(1) An offense committed under this section may be deemed to have been committed at either the place at which the communication or communications were made or at the place where the communication or communications were received.

(2) Acts indicating a course of conduct which occur in more than one jurisdiction may be used by any other jurisdiction in which an act occurred as evidence of a continuing pattern of conduct or a course of conduct.

(3) In addition to paragraphs (1) and (2), an offense under subsection (a.1) may be deemed to have been committed at the place where the child who is the subject of the communication resides.

(c) Grading.--

(1) Except as provided under paragraph (3), an offense under subsection (a)(1), (2) or (3) shall constitute a summary offense.

(2) An offense under subsection (a)(4), (5), (6) or (7) or (a.1) shall constitute a misdemeanor of the third degree.

(3) The grading of an offense under subsection (a)(1), (2) or (3) shall be enhanced one degree if the person has previously violated an order issued under 23 Pa.C.S. § 6108 (relating to relief) involving the same victim, family or household member.

(d) **False reports.**--A person who knowingly gives false information to any law enforcement officer with the intent to implicate another under this section commits an offense under section 4906 (relating to false reports to law enforcement authorities).

(e) **Application of section.**--This section shall not apply to constitutionally protected activity.

(e.1) Course of conduct.--(Deleted by amendment).

(f) **Definitions.**--As used in this section, the following words and phrases shall have the meanings given to them in this subsection:

"**Communicates.**" Conveys a message without intent of legitimate communication or address by oral, nonverbal, written or electronic means, including telephone, electronic mail, Internet, facsimile, telex, wireless communication or similar transmission.

"**Course of conduct.**" A pattern of actions composed of more than one act over a period of time, however short, evidencing a continuity of conduct. The term includes lewd, lascivious, threatening or obscene words, language, drawings, caricatures or actions, either in person or anonymously. Acts indicating a course of conduct which occur in more than one jurisdiction may be used by any other jurisdiction in which an act occurred as evidence of a continuing pattern of conduct or a course of conduct.

"**Emotional distress.**" A temporary or permanent state of mental anguish.

"**Family or household member.**" Spouses or persons who have been spouses, persons living as spouses or who lived as spouses, parents and children, other persons related by consanguinity or affinity, current or former sexual or intimate partners or persons who share biological parenthood.

"**Seriously disparaging statement or opinion.**" A statement or opinion which is intended to and under the circumstances is reasonably likely to cause substantial emotional distress to a child of the victim's age and which produces some physical manifestation of the distress.

(June 23, 1993, P.L.124, No.28, eff. imd.; Oct. 2, 1997, P.L.379, No.44, eff. 60 days; Dec. 15, 1999, P.L.915, No.59, eff. 60 days; Dec. 9, 2002, P.L.1759, No.218, eff. 60 days; Nov. 27, 2013, P.L.1061, No.91, eff. 60 days; July 10, 2015, P.L.140, No.26, eff. 60 days; Nov. 4, 2015, P.L.224, No.59, eff. 60 days)

2015 Amendments. Act 26 amended subsecs. (c)(2) and (f) and added subsecs. (a.1) and (b.1)(3) and Act 59 amended subsec. (e). See the preamble to Act 59 of 2015 in the appendix to this title for special provisions relating to legislative intent.

2013 Amendment. Act 91 amended subsec. (c) and added the def. of "family or household member" in subsec. (f).

2002 Amendment. See sections 9 and 10 of Act 218 in the appendix to this title for special provisions relating to references to section 2709 and references to section 5504.

Cross References. Section 2709 is referred to in sections 4954, 4955, 5708 of this title; section 3304 of Title 5 (Athletics and Sports); sections 6108, 6711 of Title 23 (Domestic Relations); sections 3573, 62A03 of Title 42 (Judiciary and Judicial Procedure).

§ 2709.1. Stalking.

(a) Offense defined.--A person commits the crime of stalking when the person either:

(1) engages in a course of conduct or repeatedly commits acts toward another person, including following the person without proper authority, under circumstances which demonstrate either an intent to place such other person in reasonable fear of bodily injury or to cause substantial emotional distress to such other person; or

(2) engages in a course of conduct or repeatedly communicates to another person under circumstances which demonstrate or communicate either an intent to place such other person in reasonable fear of bodily injury or to cause substantial emotional distress to such other person.

(b) Venue.--

(1) An offense committed under this section may be deemed to have been committed at either the place at which the communication or communications were made or at the place where the communication or communications were received.

(2) Acts indicating a course of conduct which occur in more than one jurisdiction may be used by any other jurisdiction in which an act occurred as evidence of a continuing pattern of conduct or a course of conduct.

(c) Grading.--

(1) Except as otherwise provided for in paragraph (2), a first offense under this section shall constitute a misdemeanor of the first degree.

(2) A second or subsequent offense under this section or a first offense under subsection (a) if the person has been previously convicted of a crime of violence involving the same victim, family or household member, including, but not limited to, a violation of section 2701 (relating to simple assault), 2702 (relating to aggravated assault), 2705 (relating to recklessly endangering another person), 2901 (relating to kidnapping), 3121 (relating to rape) or 3123 (relating to involuntary deviate sexual intercourse), an order issued under section 4954 (relating to protective orders) or an order issued under 23 Pa.C.S. § 6108 (relating to relief) shall constitute a felony of the third degree.

(d) False reports.--A person who knowingly gives false information to any law enforcement officer with the intent to implicate another under this section commits an offense under section 4906 (relating to false reports to law enforcement authorities).

(e) Application of section.--This section shall not apply to constitutionally protected activity.

(f) Definitions.--As used in this section, the following words and phrases shall have the meanings given to them in this subsection:

"Communicates." To convey a message without intent of legitimate communication or address by oral, nonverbal, written or electronic means, including telephone, electronic mail, Internet, facsimile, telex, wireless communication or similar transmission.

"Course of conduct." A pattern of actions composed of more than one act over a period of time, however short, evidencing a continuity of conduct. The term includes lewd, lascivious, threatening or obscene words, language, drawings, caricatures or actions, either in person or anonymously. Acts indicating a course of conduct which occur in more than one jurisdiction may be used by any other jurisdiction in which an act occurred as evidence of a continuing pattern of conduct or a course of conduct.

"Emotional distress." A temporary or permanent state of mental anguish.

"Family or household member." Spouses or persons who have been spouses, persons living as spouses or who lived as spouses, parents and children, other persons related by consanguinity or affinity, current or former sexual or intimate partners or persons who share biological parenthood.

(Dec. 9, 2002, P.L.1759, No.218, eff. 60 days; Nov. 4, 2015, P.L.224, No.59, eff. 60 days)

2015 Amendment. Act 59 amended subsec. (e). See the preamble to Act 59 of 2015 in the appendix to this title for special provisions relating to legislative intent.

2002 Amendment. Act 218 added section 2709.1. See sections 9 and 10 of Act 218 in the appendix to this title for special provisions relating to references to section 2709 and references to section 5504.

Cross References. Section 2709.1 is referred to in sections 2711, 2718, 3133, 4954, 4955, 5708, 6105 of this title; section 3304 of

Title 5 (Athletics and Sports); sections 5329, 6108, 6344, 6702, 6704, 6711 of Title 23 (Domestic Relations); section 62A03 of Title 42 (Judiciary and Judicial Procedure).

§ 2710. Ethnic intimidation.

(a) Offense defined.--A person commits the offense of ethnic intimidation if, with malicious intention toward the race, color, religion or national origin of another individual or group of individuals, he commits an offense under any other provision of this article or under Chapter 33 (relating to arson, criminal mischief and other property destruction) exclusive of section 3307 (relating to institutional vandalism) or under section 3503 (relating to criminal trespass) with respect to such individual or his or her property or with respect to one or more members of such group or to their property.

(b) Grading.--An offense under this section shall be classified as a misdemeanor of the third degree if the other offense is classified as a summary offense. Otherwise, an offense under this section shall be classified one degree higher in the classification specified in section 106 (relating to classes of offenses) than the classification of the other offense.

(c) Definition.--As used in this section "malicious intention" means the intention to commit any act, the commission of which is a necessary element of any offense referred to in subsection (a) motivated by hatred toward the race, color, religion or national origin of another individual or group of individuals.

(June 18, 1982, P.L.537, No.154, eff. imd.; Dec. 3, 2002, P.L.1176, No.143, eff. imd.; Dec. 9, 2002, P.L.1759, No.218, eff. 60 days)

2008 Effectuation of Declaration of Unconstitutionality. The Legislative Reference Bureau effectuated the 2007 unconstitutionality.

2007 Unconstitutionality. Act 143 of 2002 was declared unconstitutional. Marcavage v. Rendell, 936 A.2d 188 (Pa. Commonwealth 2007).

2002 Amendments. Act 143 amended the entire section and Act 218 amended subsec. (a). Act 218 overlooked the amendment by Act 143, but the amendments do not conflict in substance and both have been given effect in setting forth the text of subsec. (a).

1982 Amendment. See section 2 of Act 154 of 1982 in the appendix to this title for special provisions relating to right of action for injunction, damages or other relief.

Effective Date. After December 2, 2002, and before February 7, 2003, section 2710 will reflect only the amendment by Act 143, as follows:

§ 2710. Ethnic intimidation.

(a) Offense defined.--A person commits the offense of ethnic intimidation if, with malicious intention toward the actual or perceived race, color, religion, national origin, ancestry, mental or physical disability, sexual orientation, gender or gender identity of another individual or group of individuals, he commits an offense under any other provision of this article or under Chapter 33 (relating to arson, criminal mischief and other property destruction) exclusive of section 3307 (relating to institutional vandalism) or under section 3503 (relating to criminal trespass) or under section 5504 (relating to harassment by communication or address) with respect to such individual or his or her property or with respect to one or more members of such group or to their property.

(b) Grading.--An offense under this section shall be classified as a misdemeanor of the third degree if the other offense is classified as a summary offense. Otherwise, an offense under this section shall be classified one degree higher in the classification specified in section 106 (relating to classes of offenses) than the classification of the other offense.

(c) Definition.--As used in this section "malicious intention" means the intention to commit any act, the commission of which is a necessary element of any offense referred to in subsection (a) motivated by hatred toward the actual or perceived race, color, religion or national origin, ancestry, mental or physical disability, sexual orientation, gender or gender identity of another individual or group of individuals.

Cross References. Section 2710 is referred to in section 8309 of Title 42 (Judiciary and Judicial Procedure).

§ 2711. Probable cause arrests in domestic violence cases.

(a) General rule.--A police officer shall have the same right of arrest without a warrant as in a felony whenever he has probable cause to believe the defendant has violated section 2504 (relating to involuntary manslaughter), 2701 (relating to simple assault), 2702(a)(3), (4) and (5) (relating to aggravated assault),

2705 (relating to recklessly endangering another person), 2706 (relating to terroristic threats), 2709.1 (relating to stalking) or 2718 (relating to strangulation) against a family or household member although the offense did not take place in the presence of the police officer. A police officer may not arrest a person pursuant to this section without first observing recent physical injury to the victim or other corroborative evidence. For the purposes of this subsection, the term "family or household member" has the meaning given that term in 23 Pa.C.S. § 6102 (relating to definitions).

(b) **Seizure of weapons.**--The arresting police officer shall seize all weapons used by the defendant in the commission of the alleged offense.

(c) Bail.--

(1) A defendant arrested pursuant to this section shall be afforded a preliminary arraignment by the proper issuing authority without unnecessary delay. In no case shall the arresting officer release the defendant from custody rather than taking the defendant before the issuing authority.

(2) In determining whether to admit the defendant to bail, the issuing authority shall consider whether the defendant poses a threat of danger to the victim. In making a determination whether the defendant poses a threat of danger to the victim in cases under this section, the issuing authority may use a pretrial risk assessment tool as set forth in subsection (c.1). If the issuing authority makes such a determination, it shall require as a condition of bail that the defendant shall refrain from entering the residence or household of the victim and the victim's place of employment and shall refrain from committing any further criminal conduct against the victim and shall so notify the defendant thereof at the time the defendant is admitted to bail. Such condition shall expire at the time of the preliminary hearing or upon the entry or the denial of the protection of abuse order by the court, whichever occurs first. A violation of this condition may be punishable by the revocation of any form of pretrial release or the forfeiture of bail and the issuance of a bench warrant for the defendant's arrest or remanding him to custody or a modification of the terms of the bail. The defendant shall be provided a hearing on this matter.

(c.1) **Pretrial risk assessment tool.**--The president judge of a court of common pleas may adopt a pretrial risk assessment tool for use by the court of common pleas or by the Philadelphia Municipal Court, the Pittsburgh Magistrates Court or magisterial district judges when acting as the issuing authority in cases under this section. The issuing authority may use the pretrial risk assessment tool to aid in determining whether the defendant poses a threat of danger to the victim. However, the pretrial risk assessment tool may not be the only means of determining whether to admit the defendant to bail. Nothing in this subsection shall be construed to conflict with the issuing authority's ability to determine whether to admit the defendant to bail under the Pennsylvania Rules of Criminal Procedure.

(c.2) **Pennsylvania Commission on Sentencing.**--The following apply to the Pennsylvania Commission on Sentencing:

(1) The commission shall develop a model pretrial risk assessment tool which may be used by the issuing authority in cases under this section, as set forth in subsection (c.1).

(2) Subject to any inconsistent rule of court, in order to ensure that the model pretrial risk assessment tool or other pretrial risk assessment tool adopted under this section is effective, accurate and free from racial or economic bias, prior to the adoption of the tool, the commission shall publish a report of validation using information from cases from the judicial district where the tool is to be utilized. The report shall be updated every two years.

(d) **Notice of rights.**--Upon responding to a domestic violence case, the police officer shall, orally or in writing, notify the victim of the availability of a shelter, including its telephone number, or other services in the community. Said notice shall include the following statement: "If you are the victim of domestic violence, you have the right to go to court and file a petition requesting an order for protection from domestic abuse pursuant to 23 Pa.C.S. Ch. 61 (relating to protection from abuse) which could include the following:

(1) An order restraining the abuser from further acts of abuse.

(2) An order directing the abuser to leave your household.

(3) An order preventing the abuser from entering your residence, school, business or place of employment.

(4) An order awarding you or the other parent temporary custody of or temporary visitation with your child or children.

(5) An order directing the abuser to pay support to you and the minor children if the abuser has a legal obligation to do so."

(Feb. 15, 1986, P.L.27, No.10, eff. 60 days; Dec. 19, 1990, P.L.1240, No.206, eff. 90 days; Dec. 20, 2000, P.L.728, No.101, eff. 60 days; Dec. 9, 2002, P.L.1759, No.218, eff. 60 days; Apr. 16, 2018, P.L.89, No.14)

2018 Amendment. Act 14 amended subsecs. (a) and (c)(2) and added subsecs. (c.1) and (c.2), effective in 60 days as to subsecs. (a), (c)(2), (c.1) and (c.2)(1) and two years as to subsec. (c.2)(2).

2002 Amendment. Act 218 amended subsec. (a).

1990 Amendment. Act 206 amended subsec. (d).

Cross References. Section 2711 is referred to in section 6108.7 of Title 23 (Domestic Relations).

§ 2712. Assault on sports official.

(a) Offense defined.--A person who violates section 2701 (relating to simple assault), where the victim is a sports official who was assaulted during a sports event or was assaulted as a result of his or her official acts as a sports official, is guilty of assault on a sports official.

(b) Grading.--Assault on a sports official is a misdemeanor of the first degree.

(c) Definitions.--As used in this section, the following words and phrases shall have the meanings given to them in this subsection:

"Sports event." Any interscholastic athletic activity in a junior high school, high school, college or university in this Commonwealth or any other organized athletic activity in this Commonwealth, including a professional or semiprofessional event.

"Sports official." A person at a sports event who enforces the rules of the event, such as an umpire or referee, or a person who supervises the participants, such as a coach. The term includes a trainer, team attendant, game manager, athletic director, assistant athletic director, president, dean, headmaster, principal and assistant principal of a school, college or university.

(Feb. 14, 1990, P.L.54, No.7, eff. imd.)

1990 Amendment. Act 7 added section 2712.

§ 2713. Neglect of care-dependent person.

(a) Offense defined.--A caretaker is guilty of neglect of a care-dependent person if he:

(1) Intentionally, knowingly or recklessly causes bodily injury, serious bodily injury or death by failing to provide treatment, care, goods or services necessary to preserve the health, safety or welfare of a care-dependent person for whom he is responsible to provide care.

(2) Intentionally or knowingly uses a physical restraint or chemical restraint or medication on a care-dependent person, or isolates a care-dependent person contrary to law or regulation, such that bodily injury, serious bodily injury or death results.

(3) Intentionally, knowingly or recklessly endangers the welfare of a care-dependent person for whom he is responsible by failing to provide treatment, care, goods or services necessary to preserve the health, safety or welfare of the care-dependent person.

(b) Penalty.--

(1) A violation of subsection (a)(1) constitutes a misdemeanor of the first degree if the victim suffers bodily injury.

(2) A violation of subsection (a)(1) constitutes a felony of the first degree if the victim suffers serious bodily injury or death.

(3) A violation of subsection (a)(2) constitutes a misdemeanor of the first degree if the victim suffers bodily injury.

(4) A violation of subsection (a)(2) constitutes a felony of the first degree if the victim suffers serious bodily injury or death.

(5) A violation of subsection (a)(3) constitutes a misdemeanor of the second degree, except that where there is a course of conduct of endangering the welfare of a care-dependent person, the offense constitutes a felony of the third degree.

(c) Report during investigation.--When in the course of conducting any regulatory or investigative responsibility, the Department of Aging, the Department of Health or the Department of Public Welfare has a reasonable cause to believe that a care-dependent person or care-dependent persons residing in a facility have suffered bodily injury or been unlawfully restrained in violation of subsection (a)(1) or (2), a report shall be made immediately to the local law enforcement agency or to the Office of Attorney General.

(d) Enforcement.--

(1) The district attorneys of the several counties shall have authority to investigate and to institute criminal proceedings for any violations of this section.

(2) In addition to the authority conferred upon the Attorney General under the act of October 15, 1980 (P.L.950, No.164), known as the Commonwealth Attorneys Act, the Attorney General shall have the authority to investigate and institute criminal proceedings for any violation of this section. A person charged with a violation of this section by the Attorney General shall not have standing to challenge the authority of the Attorney General to investigate or prosecute the case, and, if any such challenge is made, the challenge shall be dismissed and no relief shall be available in the courts of this Commonwealth to the person making the challenge.

(e) **Treatment in conformance with care-dependent person's right to accept or refuse services.**--A caretaker or any other individual or facility may offer an affirmative defense to charges filed pursuant to this section if the caretaker, individual or facility can demonstrate through a preponderance of the evidence that the alleged violations result directly from:

(1) the caretaker's, individual's or facility's lawful compliance with a care-dependent person's living will as provided in 20 Pa.C.S. Ch. 54 (relating to health care);

(2) the caretaker's, individual's or facility's lawful compliance with the care-dependent person's written, signed and witnessed instructions, executed when the care-dependent person is competent as to the treatment he wishes to receive;

(3) the caretaker's, individual's or facility's lawful compliance with the direction of the care-dependent person's:

(i) agent acting pursuant to a lawful durable power of attorney under 20 Pa.C.S. Ch. 56 (relating to powers of attorney), within the scope of that power; or

(ii) health care agent acting pursuant to a health care power of attorney under 20 Pa.C.S. Ch. 54 Subch. C (relating to health care agents and representatives), within the scope of that power;

(4) the caretaker's, individual's or facility's lawful compliance with a "Do Not Resuscitate" order written and signed by the care-dependent person's attending physician; or

(5) the caretaker's, individual's or facility's lawful compliance with the direction of the care-dependent person's health care representative under 20 Pa.C.S. § 5461 (relating to decisions by health care representative), provided the care-dependent person has an end-stage medical condition or is permanently unconscious as these terms are defined in 20 Pa.C.S. § 5422 (relating to definitions) as determined and documented in the person's medical record by the person's attending physician.

(e.1) **Reckless conduct.**--For purposes of this section, a person acts recklessly when the person consciously disregards a substantial and unjustifiable risk to the care-dependent person.

(f) **Definitions.**--As used in this section, the following words and phrases shall have the meanings given to them in this subsection:

"**Care-dependent person.**" Any adult who, due to physical or cognitive disability or impairment, requires assistance to meet his needs for food, shelter, clothing, personal care or health care.

"**Caretaker.**" Any person who:

(1) is an owner, operator, manager or employee of any of the following licensed or unlicensed entities:

(i) A nursing home, personal care home, assisted living facility, private care residence or domiciliary care home.

(ii) A community residential facility or intermediate care facility for a person with mental disabilities.

(iii) An adult daily living center.

(iv) A home health service provider.

(v) A health care facility as defined in section 802.1 of the act of July 19, 1979 (P.L.130, No.48), known as the Health Care Facilities Act;

(2) provides care to a care-dependent person in the settings described under paragraph (1);

(3) has an obligation to care for a care-dependent person for monetary consideration in the settings described under paragraph (1);

(4) is an adult who resides with a care-dependent person and who has a legal duty to provide care or who has voluntarily assumed an obligation to provide care because of a familial relationship, contract or court order; or

(5) is an adult who does not reside with a care-dependent person but who has a legal duty

to provide care or who has affirmatively assumed a responsibility for care, or who has responsibility by contract or court order.

"Legal entity." An individual, partnership, unincorporated association, corporation or governing authority.

"Person." A natural person, corporation, partnership, unincorporated association or other business entity.

"Private care residence." A private residence:

(1) in which the owner of the residence or the legal entity responsible for the operation of the residence, for monetary consideration, provides or assists with or arranges for the provision of food, room, shelter, clothing, personal care or health care in the residence, for a period exceeding 24 hours, to fewer than four care-dependent persons who are not relatives of the owner; and

(2) (i) that is not required to be licensed as a long-term care nursing facility, as defined in section 802.1 of the Health Care Facilities Act; and

(ii) that is not identified in paragraph (1) of the definition of "caretaker."

(July 6, 1995, P.L.242, No.28, eff. 60 days; June 25, 1997, P.L.284, No.26, eff. 60 days; June 18, 1998, P.L.503, No.70, eff. 60 days; Nov. 29, 2006, P.L.1484, No.169, eff. 60 days; June 28, 2018, P.L.371, No.53, eff. 60 days)

2018 Amendment. Act 53 amended subsecs. (a) and (b) and the def. of "caretaker" in subsec. (f) and added subsec. (e.1) and the defs. of "legal entity" and "private care residence" in subsec. (f).

2006 Amendment. Act 169 amended subsec. (e).

1998 Amendment. Act 70 amended subsec. (d)(2).

1997 Amendment. Act 26 amended subsec. (f).

1995 Amendment. Act 28 added section 2713.

References in Text. The Department of Public Welfare, referred to in this section, was redesignated as the Department of Human Services by Act 132 of 2014.

Cross References. Section 2713 is referred to in sections 2713.1, 4120 of this title; section 5461 of Title 20 (Decedents, Estates and Fiduciaries); section 5552 of Title 42 (Judiciary and Judicial Procedure).

§ 2713.1. Abuse of care-dependent person.

(a) Offense defined.--A caretaker is guilty of abuse of a care-dependent person if the caretaker:

(1) With the intent to harass, annoy or alarm a care-dependent person:

(i) strikes, shoves, kicks or otherwise subjects or attempts to subject a care-dependent person to or threatens a care-dependent person with physical contact;

(ii) engages in a course of conduct or repeatedly commits acts that serve no legitimate purpose;

(iii) communicates to a care-dependent person any lewd, lascivious, threatening or obscene words, language, drawings or caricatures; or

(iv) communicates repeatedly with the care-dependent person at extremely inconvenient hours.

(2) Commits an offense under section 2709.1 (relating to stalking) against a care-dependent person.

(b) Penalty.--

(1) A violation of subsection (a)(1) constitutes a misdemeanor of the first degree.

(2) A violation of subsection (a)(2) constitutes a felony of the third degree.

(c) Report during investigation.--When, in the course of conducting a regulatory or investigative responsibility, the Department of Aging, the Department of Health or the Department of Human Services has reasonable cause to believe that a caretaker has engaged in conduct in violation of this section or section 2713 (relating to neglect of care-dependent person), a report shall be made immediately to the local law enforcement agency or to the Office of Attorney General.

(d) Enforcement.--

(1) The district attorneys of the several counties shall have authority to investigate and institute criminal proceedings for a violation of this section or section 2713.

(2) In addition to the authority conferred upon the Attorney General under the act of October 15, 1980 (P.L.950, No.164), known as the Commonwealth Attorneys Act, the Attorney General shall have the authority to investigate and institute criminal proceedings for a violation of this section. A person charged with a violation of this section by the Attorney General shall not have standing to challenge the authority of the Attorney General to investigate

or prosecute the case, and, if the challenge is made, the challenge shall be dismissed and no relief shall be available in the courts of this Commonwealth to the person making the challenge.

(e) **Definitions.**--As used in this section, the following words and phrases shall have the meanings given to them in this subsection:

"Care-dependent person." The term shall have the same meaning given to it under section 2713.

"Caretaker." The term shall have the same meaning given to it under section 2713.

"Person." The term shall have the same meaning given to it under section 2713.

(June 28, 2018, P.L.371, No.53, eff. 60 days)

2018 Amendment. Act 53 added section 2713.1.

§ 2714. Unauthorized administration of intoxicant.

A person commits a felony of the third degree when, with the intent to commit an offense under section 3121(a)(4) (relating to rape), 3123(a)(4) (relating to involuntary deviate sexual intercourse), 3125(5) (relating to aggravated indecent assault) or 3126(a)(5) (relating to indecent assault), he or she substantially impairs the complainant's power to appraise or control his or her conduct by administering, without the knowledge of the complainant, drugs or other intoxicants.

(Dec. 19, 1997, P.L.621, No.65, eff. 60 days)

1997 Amendment. Act 65 added section 2714.

§ 2715. Threat to use weapons of mass destruction.

(a) **Offense defined.**--A person who intentionally:

(1) (Deleted by amendment).

(2) (Deleted by amendment).

(3) reports without factual basis of knowledge the existence or potential existence of a weapon of mass destruction; or

(4) threatens by any means the placement or setting of a weapon of mass destruction;

commits an offense under this section. A separate offense shall occur for each report or threat to place or set a weapon of mass destruction.

(b) **Penalty.**--An offense under this section shall be graded as follows:

(1) Except as set forth in paragraph (2), a misdemeanor of the first degree.

(2) If the report or threat causes the occupants of a building, place of assembly or facility of public transportation to be diverted from their normal or customary operations, a felony of the third degree.

(3) A felony of the second degree if the offense occurs during a declared state of emergency and the report or threat causes disruption to the operations of any person, business entity or governmental agency where the weapon of mass destruction is reported to exist or threatened to be placed or set.

(c) **Emergency response costs.**--A person convicted of violating this section shall, in addition to any other sentence imposed or restitution ordered under 42 Pa.C.S. § 9721(c) (relating to sentencing generally), be sentenced to pay restitution in an amount equal to the cost of the evacuation, including, but not limited to, fire and police response; emergency medical service or emergency preparedness response; and transportation of an individual from the building, place of assembly or facility.

(c.1) **Preservation of private remedies.**-- No judgment or order of restitution shall debar a person, by appropriate action, to recover from the offender as otherwise provided by law, provided that any civil award shall be reduced by the amount paid under the criminal judgment.

(c.2) Application of section.--(Deleted by amendment).

(d) **Definitions.**--As used in this section, the following words and phrases shall have the meanings given to them in this subsection:

"Biological agent." A natural or genetically engineered pathogen, toxin, virus, bacteria, prion, fungus or microorganism which causes infections, disease or bodily harm.

"Bomb." An explosive device used for unlawful purposes.

"Chemical agent." Any of the following:

(1) A nerve agent, including tabun (GA), sarin (GB), soman (GD), GF and VX.

(2) A choking agent, including phosgene (CG) and diphosgene (DP).

(3) A blood agent, including hydrogen cyanide (AC), cyanogen chloride (CK) and arsine (SA).

(4) A blister agent. This paragraph includes:

(i) Mustard (H).

(ii) Sulfur mustard (HD).

(iii) HN-1.

(iv) HN-2.

(v) Sulfur mustard (HN-3).

(vi) An arsenical, such as lewisite (L).

(vii) An urticant, such as CX.

(viii) An incapacitating agent, such as B2.

(5) Any other chemical element or compound which causes death or bodily harm.

"Nuclear agent." A radioactive material.

"Weapon of mass destruction." A bomb, biological agent, chemical agent or nuclear agent.

(Dec. 20, 2000, P.L.728, No.101, eff. 60 days; June 28, 2002, P.L.481, No.82, eff. 60 days; Nov. 4, 2015, P.L.224, No.59, eff. 60 days)

2015 Amendment. Act 59 deleted subsec. (c.2). See the preamble to Act 59 of 2015 in the appendix to this title for special provisions relating to legislative intent.

§ 2716. Weapons of mass destruction.

(a) Unlawful possession or manufacture.--A person commits an offense if the person, without lawful authority to do so, intentionally, knowingly or recklessly possesses or manufactures a weapon of mass destruction.

(b) Use.--A person commits an offense if the person, without lawful authority to do so, intentionally, knowingly or recklessly sells, purchases, transports or causes another to transport, delivers or causes to be delivered or uses a weapon of mass destruction and if such action causes any of the following:

(1) Illness or injury to another individual.

(2) Damage to or disruption of a water or food supply or public natural resources, including waterways, State forests and parks, surface water, groundwater and wildlife.

(3) Evacuation of a building, place of assembly or facility of public transportation.

(c) Grading.--

(1) A first offense under subsection (a) constitutes a felony of the second degree. A subsequent offense under subsection (a) constitutes a felony of the first degree.

(2) An offense under subsection (b)(1) constitutes a felony of the first degree. If the offense results in the death of an individual, the defendant shall be sentenced to life imprisonment.

(3) An offense under subsection (b)(2) or (3) constitutes a felony of the first degree.

(d) Restitution.--A person convicted of violating this section shall, in addition to any other sentence imposed or restitution ordered under 42 Pa.C.S. § 9721(c) (relating to sentencing generally), be sentenced to pay restitution in an amount equal to the cost of the evacuation, including, but not limited to, fire and police response; emergency medical service or emergency preparedness response; and transportation of an individual from the building, place of assembly or facility.

(e) Preservation of private remedies.-- No judgment or order of restitution shall debar a person, by appropriate action, to recover from the offender as otherwise provided by law, provided that any civil award shall be reduced by the amount paid under the criminal judgment.

(f) Possession.--For purposes of this section, an individual shall not be deemed to be in possession of an agent if the individual is naturally exposed to or innocently infected or contaminated with the agent.

(g) Enforcement.--

(1) In addition to the authority conferred upon the Attorney General under sections 205 and 206 of the act of October 15, 1980 (P.L.950, No.164), known as the Commonwealth Attorneys Act, the Attorney General has the authority to investigate and to institute criminal proceedings for a violation of this section committed:

(i) anywhere in this Commonwealth;

(ii) in different counties; or

(iii) in this Commonwealth and another jurisdiction.

(2) Each district attorney has the authority to investigate and to institute criminal proceedings for a violation of this section.

(h) Jurisdiction.--No person charged with a violation of this section shall have standing to challenge the authority of the Attorney General under subsection (g)(1). If a challenge is made in violation of this subsection, the challenge shall be dismissed, and no relief shall be available in the courts of this Commonwealth to the person making the challenge.

(i) Definitions.--As used in this section, the following words and phrases shall have the meanings given to them in this subsection:

"Biological agent." A natural or genetically engineered pathogen, toxin, virus, bacteria, prion, fungus or microorganism which causes infections, disease or bodily harm.

"Bomb." An explosive device used for unlawful purposes.

"Chemical agent." Any of the following:

(1) A nerve agent, including tabun (GA), sarin (GB), soman (GD), GF and VX.

(2) A choking agent, including phosgene (CG) and diphosgene (DP).

(3) A blood agent, including hydrogen cyanide (AC), cyanogen chloride (CK) and arsine (SA).

(4) A blister agent. This paragraph includes:

(i) Mustard (H).

(ii) Sulfur mustard (HD).

(iii) HN-1.

(iv) HN-2.

(v) Nitrogen mustard (HN-3).

(vi) An arsenical, such as lewisite (L).

(vii) An urticant, such as CX.

(viii) An incapacitating agent, such as B2.

(5) Any other chemical element or compound which causes death or bodily harm.

"Nuclear agent." A radioactive material.

"Weapon of mass destruction." A biological agent, bomb, chemical agent or nuclear agent.

(June 28, 2002, P.L.481, No.82, eff. 60 days)

2002 Amendment. Act 82 added section 2716.

Cross References. Section 2716 is referred to in sections 5708, 6105 of this title; section 9714 of Title 42 (Judiciary and Judicial Procedure).

§ 2717. Terrorism.

(a) **General rule.**--A person is guilty of terrorism if he commits a violent offense intending to do any of the following:

(1) Intimidate or coerce a civilian population.

(2) Influence the policy of a government by intimidation or coercion.

(3) Affect the conduct of a government.

(b) Grading and penalty.--

(1) If the violent offense is a misdemeanor or a felony of the third or second degree, an offense under this section shall be classified one degree higher than the classification of the violent offense specified in section 106 (relating to classes of offenses).

(2) If the violent offense is a felony of the first degree, a person convicted of an offense under this section shall be sentenced to a term of imprisonment fixed by the court at not more than 40 years and may be sentenced to pay a fine of not more than $100,000.

(b.1) **Forfeiture.**--Each foreign or domestic asset related to terrorism, including the following, shall be subject to forfeiture under 42 Pa.C.S. §§ 5803 (relating to asset forfeiture), 5805 (relating to forfeiture procedure), 5806 (relating to motion for return of property), 5807 (relating to restrictions on use), 5807.1 (relating to prohibition on adoptive seizures) and 5808 (relating to exceptions) and no property right shall exist in the asset:

(1) Each foreign or domestic asset:

(i) Of an individual, entity or organization engaged in planning or perpetrating an act in this Commonwealth which violates this section and each foreign or domestic asset affording a person a source of influence over the entity or organization.

(ii) Acquired or maintained by a person with the intent and for the purpose of supporting, planning, conducting or concealing an act in this Commonwealth which violates this section.

(iii) Derived from, involved in or used or intended to be used to commit an act in this Commonwealth which violates this section.

(2) Each asset within this Commonwealth:

(i) Of an individual, entity or organization engaged in planning or perpetrating an act which violates this section.

(ii) Acquired or maintained with the intent and for the purpose of supporting, planning, conducting or concealing an act which violates this section.

(iii) Derived from, involved in or used or intended to be used to commit an act which violates this section.

(c) **Definitions.**--As used in this section, the following words and phrases shall have the meanings given to them in this subsection:

"Dangerous to human life or property." A violent act or an act which is intended to or likely to cause death, serious bodily injury or mass destruction.

"Mass destruction." An act which is intended to or likely to destroy or cause serious damage to transportation-related infrastructure or facilities, energy-related infrastructure or facilities, public or private buildings, places of public accommodation or public works under circumstances evincing depraved indifference to human life or property.

"Violent offense." An offense under this part, including an attempt, conspiracy or solicitation to commit any such offense, which is punishable by imprisonment of more than one year and involves an act dangerous to human life or property.

(July 7, 2006, P.L.342, No.71, eff. 60 days; June 29, 2017, P.L.247, No.13, eff. July 1, 2017)

2017 Amendment. Act 13 added subsec. (b.1).

2006 Amendment. Act 71 added section 2717.

Cross References. Section 2717 is referred to in sections 5803, 9714 of Title 42 (Judiciary and Judicial Procedure).

§ 2718. Strangulation.

(a) Offense defined.--A person commits the offense of strangulation if the person knowingly or intentionally impedes the breathing or circulation of the blood of another person by:

(1) applying pressure to the throat or neck; or

(2) blocking the nose and mouth of the person.

(b) Physical injury.--Infliction of a physical injury to a victim shall not be an element of the offense. The lack of physical injury to a victim shall not be a defense in a prosecution under this section.

(c) Affirmative defense.--It shall be an affirmative defense to a charge under this section that the victim consented to the defendant's actions as provided under section 311 (relating to consent).

(d) Grading.--

(1) Except as provided in paragraph (2) or (3), a violation of this section shall constitute a misdemeanor of the second degree.

(2) A violation of this section shall constitute a felony of the second degree if committed:

(i) against a family or household member as defined in 23 Pa.C.S. § 6102 (relating to definitions);

(ii) by a caretaker against a care-dependent person; or

(iii) in conjunction with sexual violence as defined in 42 Pa.C.S. § 62A03 (relating to definitions) or conduct constituting a crime under section 2709.1 (relating to stalking) or Subchapter B of Chapter 30 (relating to prosecution of human trafficking).

(3) A violation of this section shall constitute a felony of the first degree if:

(i) at the time of commission of the offense, the defendant is subject to an active protection from abuse order under 23 Pa.C.S. Ch. 61 (relating to protection from abuse) or a sexual violence or intimidation protection order under 42 Pa.C.S. Ch. 62A (relating to protection of victims of sexual violence or intimidation) that covers the victim;

(ii) the defendant uses an instrument of crime as defined in section 907 (relating to possessing instruments of crime) in commission of the offense under this section; or

(iii) the defendant has previously been convicted of an offense under paragraph (2) or a substantially similar offense in another jurisdiction.

(e) Definitions.--As used in this section, the following words and phrases shall have the meanings given to them in this subsection unless the context clearly indicates otherwise:

"Care-dependent person." An adult who, due to physical or cognitive disability or impairment, requires assistance to meet his needs for food, shelter, clothing, personal care or health care.

"Caretaker." Any person who:

(1) Is an owner, operator, manager or employee of any of the following:

(i) A nursing home, personal care home, assisted living facility, private care residence or domiciliary home.

(ii) A community residential facility or intermediate care facility for a person with mental disabilities.

(iii) An adult daily living center.

(iv) A home health service provider whether licensed or unlicensed.

(v) An entity licensed under the act of July 19, 1979 (P.L.130, No.48), known as the Health Care Facilities Act.

(2) Provides care to a care-dependent person in the settings described under paragraph (1).

(3) Has an obligation to care for a care-dependent person for monetary consideration in the settings described under paragraph (1).

(4) Is an adult who resides with a care-dependent person and who has a legal duty to provide care or who has voluntarily assumed an obligation to provide care because of a familial relationship, contract or court order.

(5) Is an adult who does not reside with a care-dependent person but who has a legal duty

to provide care or who has affirmatively assumed a responsibility for care or who has responsibility by contract or court order.

"Legal entity." An individual, partnership, unincorporated association, corporation or governing authority.

"Private care residence."

(1) A private residence:

(i) in which the owner of the residence or the legal entity responsible for the operation of the residence, for monetary consideration, provides or assists with or arranges for the provision of food, room, shelter, clothing, personal care or health care in the residence, for a period exceeding 24 hours, to fewer than four care-dependent persons who are not relatives of the owner; and

(ii) which is not required to be licensed as a long-term care nursing facility, as defined in section 802.1 of the Health Care Facilities Act.

(2) The term does not include:

(i) Domiciliary care as defined in section 2202-A of the act of April 9, 1929 (P.L.177, No.175), known as The Administrative Code of 1929.

(ii) A facility which provides residential care for fewer than four care-dependent adults and which is regulated by the Department of Human Services.

(Oct. 26, 2016, P.L.888, No.111, eff. 60 days)

2016 Amendment. Act 111 added section 2718.

Cross References. Section 2718 is referred to in section 2711 of this title.

CHAPTER 28 ANTIHAZING

Enactment. Chapter 28 was added October 19, 2018, P.L.535, No.80, effective in 30 days. Act 80 of 2018 shall be referred to as the "Timothy J. Piazza Antihazing Law."

Special Provisions in Appendix. See section 6 of Act 80 of 2018 in the appendix to this title for special provisions relating to continuation of prior law.

Applicability. The addition of Chapter 28 shall apply to causes of action which accrue on or after the effective date of section 7 of Act 80 of 2018.

§ 2801. Definitions.

The following words and phrases when used in this chapter shall have the meanings given to them in this section unless the context clearly indicates otherwise:

"911 call." A transmission of information via a telecommunications device to a public safety answering point for the initial reporting of police, fire, medical or other emergency situations.

"Alcoholic liquid." A substance containing liquor, spirit, wine, beer, malt or brewed beverage or any combination thereof.

"Bodily injury." The term has the same meaning as given to that term in section 2301 (relating to definitions).

"Campus security officer." An employee of an institution of higher education charged with maintaining the safety and security of the property of the institution and the individuals on the property.

"Drug." A controlled substance or drug as defined in the act of April 14, 1972 (P.L.233, No.64), known as The Controlled Substance, Drug, Device and Cosmetic Act.

"Emergency services personnel." Individuals, including a trained volunteer or a member of the armed forces of the United States or the National Guard, whose official or assigned responsibilities include performing or directly supporting the performance of emergency medical and rescue services or firefighting.

"Institution of higher education" or "institution." An institution located within this Commonwealth authorized to grant an associate or higher academic degree.

"Law enforcement officer." An individual who, by virtue of the individual's office or public employment, is vested by law with a duty to maintain public order or to make arrests for offenses, whether that duty extends to all offenses or is limited to specific offenses, or an individual on active State duty under 51 Pa.C.S. § 508 (relating to active duty for emergency).

"**Minor.**" An individual younger than 18 years of age.

"**Organization.**" Any of the following:

(1) A fraternity, sorority, association, corporation, order, society, corps, club or service, social or similar group, whose members are primarily minors, students or alumni of the organization, an institution or secondary school.

(2) A national or international organization with which a fraternity or sorority or other organization as enumerated under paragraph (1) is affiliated.

"**Secondary school.**" A public or private school within this Commonwealth that provides instruction in grades 7 through 12 or a combination of grades 7 through 12.

"**Serious bodily injury.**" The term shall have the same meaning as given to that term in section 2301.

"**Student.**" An individual who attends or has applied to attend or has been admitted to an institution or secondary school.

§ 2802. Hazing.

(a) **Offense defined.**--A person commits the offense of hazing if the person intentionally, knowingly or recklessly, for the purpose of initiating, admitting or affiliating a minor or student into or with an organization, or for the purpose of continuing or enhancing a minor or student's membership or status in an organization, causes, coerces or forces a minor or student to do any of the following:

(1) Violate Federal or State criminal law.

(2) Consume any food, liquid, alcoholic liquid, drug or other substance which subjects the minor or student to a risk of emotional or physical harm.

(3) Endure brutality of a physical nature, including whipping, beating, branding, calisthenics or exposure to the elements.

(4) Endure brutality of a mental nature, including activity adversely affecting the mental health or dignity of the individual, sleep deprivation, exclusion from social contact or conduct that could result in extreme embarrassment.

(5) Endure brutality of a sexual nature.

(6) Endure any other activity that creates a reasonable likelihood of bodily injury to the minor or student.

(b) Grading.--

(1) Except as provided under paragraph (2), hazing is a summary offense.

(2) Hazing shall be a misdemeanor of the third degree if it results in or creates a reasonable likelihood of bodily injury to the minor or student.

(c) **Limitation.**--Hazing shall not include reasonable and customary athletic, law enforcement or military training, contests, competitions or events.

Cross References. Section 2802 is referred to in sections 2803, 2804, 2805 of this title.

§ 2803. Aggravated hazing.

(a) **Offense defined.**--A person commits the offense of aggravated hazing if the person commits a violation of section 2802 (relating to hazing) that results in serious bodily injury or death to the minor or student and:

(1) the person acts with reckless indifference to the health and safety of the minor or student; or

(2) the person causes, coerces or forces the consumption of an alcoholic liquid or drug by the minor or student.

(b) **Grading.**--Aggravated hazing shall be a felony of the third degree.

Cross References. Section 2803 is referred to in sections 2804, 2805, 2807 of this title.

§ 2804. Organizational hazing.

(a) **Offense defined.**--An organization that intentionally, knowingly or recklessly promotes or facilitates a violation of section 2802 (relating to hazing) or 2803 (relating to aggravated hazing) commits the offense of organizational hazing and shall be subject to any of the following penalties:

(1) A fine of not more than $5,000 for each violation of section 2802.

(2) A fine of not more than $15,000 for each violation of section 2803.

(b) **Penalties.**--In addition to any other sentence imposed, if an organization commits the offense of organizational hazing, the organization shall be subject to such other relief as the court deems equitable.

Cross References. Section 2804 is referred to in section 2807 of this title.

§ 2805. Institutional hazing.

An institution which intentionally, knowingly or recklessly promotes or facilitates a violation of section 2802 (relating to hazing) or 2803 (relating to aggravated hazing) commits the offense of institutional hazing and shall be subject to any of the following penalties:

(1) A fine of not more than $5,000 for each violation of section 2802.

(2) A fine of not more than $15,000 for each violation of section 2803.

§ 2806. Defenses prohibited.

It shall not be a defense to any offense under this chapter that any of the following apply:

(1) The consent of the minor or student was sought or obtained.

(2) The conduct was sanctioned or approved by the institution, secondary school or organization.

§ 2807. Forfeiture.

Upon conviction of a defendant under section 2803 (relating to aggravated hazing) or 2804 (relating to organizational hazing) the court may, in addition to any other sentence authorized under law, direct the defendant to forfeit property which was involved in the violation for which the defendant was convicted. The forfeiture shall be conducted in accordance with 42 Pa.C.S. §§ 5803 (relating to asset forfeiture), 5805 (relating to forfeiture procedure), 5806 (relating to motion for return of property), 5807 (relating to restrictions on use), 5807.1 (relating to prohibition on adoptive seizures) and 5808 (relating to exceptions).

Cross References. Section 2807 is referred to in section 5803 of Title 42 (Judiciary and Judicial Procedure).

§ 2808. Enforcement by institution and secondary school.

(a) Antihazing policy.--

(1) Each institution and each governing board of a secondary school shall adopt a written policy against hazing and, pursuant to that policy, shall adopt rules prohibiting students or other persons associated with an organization operating under the sanction of or recognized as an organization by the institution or secondary school from engaging in hazing or an offense under this chapter.

(2) Each institution shall provide a copy of the policy, including the institution's rules, penalties and program of enforcement, to each organization within the institution. Each secondary school shall ensure that students are informed of the secondary school's policy, including the secondary school's rules, penalties and program of enforcement.

(3) Each institution and secondary school shall post the policy on the institution's or the secondary school's publicly accessible Internet website.

(b) Enforcement and penalties.--

(1) Each institution and each governing board of a secondary school shall provide a program for the enforcement of the policy required under subsection (a) and shall adopt appropriate penalties for violations of the policy to be administered by the individual or agency at the institution or secondary school responsible for the sanctioning or recognition of the organizations covered by the policy.

(2) Penalties under paragraph (1) may include any of the following:

(i) The imposition of fines.

(ii) The withholding of diplomas or transcripts pending compliance with the rules or payment of fines.

(iii) The rescission of permission for the organization to operate on campus or school property or to otherwise operate under the sanction or recognition of the institution or secondary school.

(iv) The imposition of probation, suspension, dismissal or expulsion.

(3) A penalty imposed under this section shall be in addition to a penalty imposed for violation of an offense under this chapter or the criminal laws of this Commonwealth or for violation of any other institutional or secondary school rule to which the violator may be subject.

(4) A policy adopted under this section shall apply to each act conducted on or off campus or school property if the acts are deemed to constitute hazing or any offense under this chapter.

§ 2809. Institutional reports.

(a) **Maintenance.**--An institution shall maintain a report of all violations of the institution's antihazing policy or Federal or State laws related to hazing that are reported to the institution.

(b) **Contents.**--The report shall include all of the following:

(1) The name of the subject of the report.

(2) The date when the subject was charged with a violation of the institution's

antihazing policy or Federal or State laws related to hazing.

(3) A general description of the violation, any investigation and findings by the institution and, if applicable, penalties.

(4) The date on which the matter was resolved.

(c) **Initial report.**--This section shall apply beginning with the 2018-2019 academic year. The initial report shall include information concerning violations that have been reported to the institution for the five consecutive years prior to the effective date of this section to the extent the institution has retained information concerning the violations.

(d) **Personal identifying information.**-- The report shall not include the personal identifying information of an individual.

(e) **Time.**--An institution shall post an initial report required under this section on its publicly accessible Internet website by January 15, 2019.

(f) **Update.**--An institution shall update the report biannually on January 1 and August 1 and shall post the updated report on its publicly accessible Internet website.

(g) **Duration.**--An institution shall retain reports for five years.

§ 2810. Safe harbor.

(a) **Immunity for the individual seeking medical attention for another.**--An individual shall not be prosecuted for an offense under this chapter if the individual can establish all of the following:

(1) A law enforcement officer first became aware of the individual's violation of this chapter because the individual placed a 911 call or contacted campus security, police or emergency services, based on a reasonable belief that another individual was in need of immediate medical attention to prevent death or serious bodily injury.

(2) The individual reasonably believed the individual was the first individual to make a 911 call or contact campus security, police or emergency services and report that an individual needed immediate medical attention to prevent death or serious bodily injury.

(3) The individual provided the individual's own name to the 911 operator or equivalent campus security officer, police or emergency services personnel.

(4) The individual remained with the individual needing medical assistance until a campus security officer, police or emergency services personnel arrived and the need for the individual's presence had ended.

(b) **Derivative immunity for the individual needing medical attention.**--An individual needing medical attention shall be immune under this section from prosecution for an offense under this chapter or section 6308(a) (relating to purchase, consumption, possession or transportation of liquor or malt or brewed beverages) only if another individual against whom probable cause exists to charge an offense under this chapter reported the incident and remained with the individual needing medical attention and the other individual qualifies for a safe harbor under this section.

(c) **Limitations.**--The safe harbors described under this section shall be limited as follows:

(1) This section may not bar prosecuting a person for an offense under this chapter if a law enforcement officer learns of the offense prior to and independent of the action of seeking or obtaining emergency assistance as described in subsection (a).

(2) This section shall not interfere with or prevent the investigation, arrest, charging or prosecution of an individual for a crime other than an offense under this chapter or section 6308(a).

(3) This section shall not bar the admissibility of evidence in connection with the investigation and prosecution for a crime other than an offense under this chapter or section 6308(a).

(4) This section shall not bar the admissibility of evidence in connection with the investigation and prosecution of a crime with regard to another defendant who does not independently qualify for a safe harbor under this section.

(d) **Civil immunity.**--In addition to any other applicable immunity or limitation on civil liability, a law enforcement officer, campus security officer or prosecuting attorney who, acting in good faith, charges a person who is thereafter determined to be entitled to immunity under this section shall not be subject to civil liability for the filing of the charges.

§ 2811. Civil remedies.

Nothing in this chapter precludes a civil remedy otherwise provided by law.

CHAPTER 29 KIDNAPPING

Enactment. Chapter 29 was added December 6, 1972, P.L.1482, No.334, effective in six months.

Cross References. Chapter 29 is referred to in sections 911, 3104, 3502, 5743.1 of this title; section 3103 of Title 23 (Domestic Relations); sections 5750, 5985.1, 5993 of Title 42 (Judiciary and Judicial Procedure).

§ 2901. Kidnapping.

(a) Offense defined.--Except as provided in subsection (a.1), a person is guilty of kidnapping if he unlawfully removes another a substantial distance under the circumstances from the place where he is found, or if he unlawfully confines another for a substantial period in a place of isolation, with any of the following intentions:

(1) To hold for ransom or reward, or as a shield or hostage.

(2) To facilitate commission of any felony or flight thereafter.

(3) To inflict bodily injury on or to terrorize the victim or another.

(4) To interfere with the performance by public officials of any governmental or political function.

(a.1) Kidnapping of a minor.--A person is guilty of kidnapping of a minor if he unlawfully removes a person under 18 years of age a substantial distance under the circumstances from the place where he is found, or if he unlawfully confines a person under 18 years of age for a substantial period in a place of isolation, with any of the following intentions:

(1) To hold for ransom or reward, or as a shield or hostage.

(2) To facilitate commission of any felony or flight thereafter.

(3) To inflict bodily injury on or to terrorize the victim or another.

(4) To interfere with the performance by public officials of any governmental or political function.

(b) Grading.--The following apply:

(1) Kidnapping under subsection (a) is a felony of the first degree. A removal or confinement is unlawful within the meaning of subsection (a) if it is accomplished by force, threat or deception, or, in the case of an incapacitated person, if it is accomplished without the consent of a parent, guardian or other person responsible for general supervision of his welfare.

(2) Kidnapping under subsection (a.1) is a felony of the first degree. A removal or confinement is unlawful within the meaning of subsection (a.1) if it is accomplished by force, threat or deception, or, in the case of a person under 14 years of age, if it is accomplished without consent of a parent, guardian or other person responsible for general supervision of his welfare.

(Apr. 16, 1992, P.L.108, No.24, eff. 60 days; Dec. 20, 2011, P.L.446, No.111, eff. 60 days)

Cross References. Section 2901 is referred to in sections 2709.1, 5702, 5708, 6105 of this title; section 3304 of Title 5 (Athletics and Sports); sections 5329, 6344, 6711 of Title 23 (Domestic Relations); sections 5552, 6302, 9720.2, 9799.14, 9802 of Title 42 (Judiciary and Judicial Procedure); sections 3903, 4103, 7122 of Title 61 (Prisons and Parole).

§ 2902. Unlawful restraint.

(a) Offense defined.--Except as provided under subsection (b) or (c), a person commits a misdemeanor of the first degree if he knowingly:

(1) restrains another unlawfully in circumstances exposing him to risk of serious bodily injury; or

(2) holds another in a condition of involuntary servitude.

(b) Unlawful restraint of a minor where offender is not victim's parent.--If the victim is a person under 18 years of age, a person who is not the victim's parent commits a felony of the second degree if he knowingly:

(1) restrains another unlawfully in circumstances exposing him to risk of serious bodily injury; or

(2) holds another in a condition of involuntary servitude.

(c) Unlawful restraint of minor where offender is victim's parent.--If the victim is a person under 18 years of age, a parent of the victim commits a felony of the second degree if he knowingly:

(1) restrains another unlawfully in circumstances exposing him to risk of serious bodily injury; or

(2) holds another in a condition of involuntary servitude.

(d) Definition.--As used in this section the term "parent" means a natural parent, stepparent, adoptive parent or guardian of a minor.

(Dec. 30, 1974, P.L.1120, No.361, eff. imd.; Dec. 20, 2000, P.L.721, No.98, eff. imd.; Dec. 20, 2011, P.L.446, No.111, eff. 60 days)

Cross References. Section 2902 is referred to in section 6105 of this title; sections 5329, 6344 of Title 23 (Domestic Relations); sections 9799.13, 9799.14 of Title 42 (Judiciary and Judicial Procedure).

§ 2903. False imprisonment.

(a) Offense defined.--Except as provided under subsection (b) or (c), a person commits a misdemeanor of the second degree if he knowingly restrains another unlawfully so as to interfere substantially with his liberty.

(b) False imprisonment of a minor where offender is not victim's parent.--If the victim is a person under 18 years of age, a person who is not the victim's parent commits a felony of the second degree if he knowingly restrains another unlawfully so as to interfere substantially with his liberty.

(c) False imprisonment of a minor where offender is victim's parent.--If the victim is a person under 18 years of age, a parent of the victim commits a felony of the second degree if he knowingly restrains another unlawfully so as to interfere substantially with his liberty.

(d) Definition.--As used in this section the term "parent" means a natural parent, stepparent, adoptive parent or guardian of a minor.

(Dec. 20, 2000, P.L.721, No.98, eff. imd.; Dec. 20, 2011, P.L.446, No.111, eff. 60 days)

2000 Amendment. See the preamble to Act 98 in the appendix to this title for special provisions relating to legislative intent.

Cross References. Section 2903 is referred to in sections 5329, 6102 of Title 23 (Domestic Relations); sections 9799.13, 9799.14 of Title 42 (Judiciary and Judicial Procedure); section 2303 of Title 44 (Law and Justice).

§ 2904. Interference with custody of children.

(a) Offense defined.--A person commits an offense if he knowingly or recklessly takes or entices any child under the age of 18 years from the custody of its parent, guardian or other lawful custodian, when he has no privilege to do so.

(b) Defenses.--It is a defense that:

(1) the actor believed that his action was necessary to preserve the child from danger to its welfare; or

(2) the child, being at the time not less than 14 years old, was taken away at its own instigation without enticement and without purpose to commit a criminal offense with or against the child; or

(3) the actor is the child's parent or guardian or other lawful custodian and is not acting contrary to an order entered by a court of competent jurisdiction.

(c) Grading.--The offense is a felony of the third degree unless:

(1) the actor, not being a parent or person in equivalent relation to the child, acted with knowledge that his conduct would cause serious alarm for the safety of the child, or in reckless disregard of a likelihood of causing such alarm. In such cases, the offense shall be a felony of the second degree; or

(2) the actor acted with good cause for a period of time not in excess of 24 hours; and

(i) the victim child is the subject of a valid order of custody issued by a court of this Commonwealth;

(ii) the actor has been given either partial custody or visitation rights under said order; and

(iii) the actor is a resident of this Commonwealth and does not remove the child from the Commonwealth.

In such cases, the offense shall be a misdemeanor of the second degree.

(July 9, 1984, P.L.661, No.138, eff. imd.)

1984 Amendment. Act 138 amended subsec. (c).

Cross References. Section 2904 is referred to in section 6108 of Title 23 (Domestic Relations); sections 9799.13, 9799.14 of Title 42 (Judiciary and Judicial Procedure).

§ 2905. Interference with custody of committed persons.

(a) Offense defined.--A person is guilty of a misdemeanor of the second degree if he knowingly or recklessly takes or entices any committed person away from lawful custody when he is not privileged to do so.

(b) Definition.--As used in this section, the term "committed person" means, in addition to anyone committed under judicial warrant, any orphan, neglected or delinquent child, mentally disabled person, or other dependent or incapacitated person entrusted to the custody of another by or through a recognized social agency or otherwise by authority of law.

(Apr. 16, 1992, P.L.108, No.24, eff. 60 days)

1992 Amendment. Act 24 amended subsec. (b).

§ 2906. Criminal coercion.

(a) Offense defined.--A person is guilty of criminal coercion, if, with intent unlawfully to restrict freedom of action of another to the detriment of the other, he threatens to:

(1) commit any criminal offense;

(2) accuse anyone of a criminal offense;

(3) expose any secret tending to subject any person to hatred, contempt or ridicule; or

(4) take or withhold action as an official, or cause an official to take or withhold action.

(b) Defense.--It is a defense to prosecution based on paragraphs (a)(2), (a)(3) or (a)(4) of this section that the actor believed the accusation or secret to be true or the proposed official action justified and that his intent was limited to compelling the other to behave in a way reasonably related to the circumstances which were the subject of the accusation, exposure or proposed official action, as by desisting from further misbehavior, making good a wrong done, refraining from taking any action or responsibility for which the actor believes the other disqualified.

(c) Grading.--Criminal coercion is a misdemeanor of the second degree unless the threat is to commit a felony or the intent of the actor is felonious, in which cases the offense is a misdemeanor of the first degree.

Cross References. Section 2906 is referred to in section 3012 of this title.

§ 2907. Disposition of ransom.

A person, other than a member of the family or an intermediary of the family of a person held for ransom, who knowingly receives, retains or disposes of any money or other property of another knowing that the money or other property constitutes a ransom derived from an offense under this chapter, or has reason to believe that such money or other property is ransom derived from an offense under this chapter, is guilty of a felony of the third degree.

(Dec. 30, 1974, P.L.1120, No.361, eff. imd.)

1974 Amendment. Act 361 added section 2907.

§ 2908. Missing children.

(a) Duties of law enforcement agencies.--Law enforcement agencies shall have the following duties with respect to missing children:

(1) To investigate a report of a missing child immediately upon receipt of the report regardless of the age of the missing child or the circumstances surrounding the disappearance of the child. In no case shall law enforcement agencies impose a mandatory waiting period prior to commencing the investigation of a missing child.

(2) When conducting a missing child investigation, to record all information relevant to the missing child and the circumstances surrounding the disappearance of the missing child on the appropriate law enforcement investigative report.

(3) To make an entry into the Missing Persons File through the Commonwealth Law Enforcement Assistance Network (CLEAN) in accord with Pennsylvania State Police policy and procedures immediately upon receipt of sufficient identification information on the missing child.

(3.1) To make an entry into the Unidentified Persons File through Commonwealth Law Enforcement Assistance Network (CLEAN) in accord with Pennsylvania State Police policy and procedures immediately upon:

(i) taking custody of an unidentified living child, such as an infant, or a physically or mentally disabled child; or

(ii) discovering an unidentified deceased child.

(4) To insure timely cancellation of any entry made pursuant to this section where the missing child has returned or is located.

(a.1) Unidentified deceased children.-- Law enforcement agencies and coroners shall, with respect to unidentified deceased children, have the duty to make an entry into the Unidentified Deceased Person File through the Commonwealth Law Enforcement Assistance Network (CLEAN) in accordance with Pennsylvania State Police policy and procedures immediately upon observing or receiving any descriptive information on an unidentified deceased child.

(b) Definition.--As used in this section the term "child" means a person under 18 years of age.

(May 9, 1985, P.L.31, No.14, eff. imd.; Feb. 2, 1990, P.L.6, No.4, eff. 60 days; June 25, 1992, P.L.315, No.59, eff. 60 days)

1992 Amendment. Act 59 added subsec. (a)(3.1).

1990 Amendment. Act 4 added subsec. (a.1).

1985 Amendment. Act 14 added section 2908.

Cross References. Section 2908 is referred to in section 5701 of Title 23 (Domestic Relations).

§ 2909. Concealment of whereabouts of a child.

(a) Offense defined.--A person who removes a child from the child's known place of residence with the intent to conceal the child's whereabouts from the child's parent or guardian, unless concealment is authorized by court order or is a reasonable response to domestic violence or child abuse, commits a felony of the third degree. For purposes of this subsection, the term "removes" includes personally removing the child from the child's known place of residence, causing the child to be removed from the child's known place of residence, preventing the child from returning or being returned to the child's known place of residence and, when the child's parent or guardian has a reasonable expectation that the person will return the child, failing to return the child to the child's known place of residence.

(b) Application.--A person may be convicted under subsection (a) if either of the following apply:

(1) The acts that initiated the concealment occurred in this Commonwealth.

(2) The offender or the parent or guardian from whom the child is being concealed resides in this Commonwealth.

(Feb. 2, 1990, P.L.6, No.4, eff. 60 days)

1990 Amendment. Act 4 added section 2909.

§ 2910. Luring a child into a motor vehicle or structure.

(a) Offense.--Unless the circumstances reasonably indicate that the child is in need of assistance, a person who lures or attempts to lure a child into a motor vehicle or structure without the consent, express or implied, of the child's parent or guardian commits an offense.

(a.1) Grading.--The following shall apply:

(1) Except as provided under paragraph (2), an offense under subsection (a) is a misdemeanor of the first degree.

(2) If an offense under subsection (a) involves a child under 13 years of age, the offense is a felony of the second degree.

(a.2) Mistake as to age.--If an offense under subsection (a) involves a child under 13 years of age, it shall be no defense that the defendant did not know the age of the child or reasonably believed the child to be 13 years of age or older.

(b) Affirmative defense.--It shall be an affirmative defense to a prosecution under this section that the person lured or attempted to lure the child into the structure for a lawful purpose.

(c) Definitions.--As used in this section, the following words and phrases shall have the meanings given to them in this subsection:

"Child." A person under 18 years of age.

"Motor vehicle." Every self-propelled device in, upon or by which any person or property is or may be transported or drawn on a public highway.

"Structure." A house, apartment building, shop, warehouse, barn, building, vessel, railroad car, cargo container, house car, trailer, trailer coach, camper, mine, floating home or other enclosed structure capable of holding a child, which is not open to the general public.

(Feb. 2, 1990, P.L.6, No.4, eff. 60 days;
Nov. 10, 2005, P.L.330, No.64, eff. 60 days;
Dec. 18, 2013, P.L.1194, No.116, eff. 60 days)

Cross References. Section 2910 is referred to in section 6105 of this title; section 5329 of Title 23 (Domestic Relations); section 9799.14 of Title 42 (Judiciary and Judicial Procedure).

CHAPTER 30 HUMAN TRAFFICKING

Enactment. Chapter 30 was added July 2, 2014, P.L.945, No.105, effective in 60 days.
Prior Provisions. Former Chapter 30, which related to Trafficking of Persons, was added November 9, 2006, P.L.1340, No.139, and repealed July 2, 2014, P.L.945, No.105, effective in 60 days.
Special Provisions in Appendix. See section 9 of Act 105 of 2014 in the appendix to this title for special provisions relating to application of law.
Cross References. Chapter 30 is referred to in sections 911, 3104, 5743.1 of this title; section 3103 of Title 23 (Domestic Relations); sections 5985.1, 5993 of Title 42 (Judiciary and Judicial Procedure).

SUBCHAPTER A
GENERAL PROVISIONS

Sec.
3001. Definitions.
§ 3001. Definitions.
The following words and phrases when used in this chapter shall have the meanings given to them in this section unless the context clearly indicates otherwise:

"Commission." The Pennsylvania Commission on Crime and Delinquency.
"County agency." A county children and youth social service agency established under section 405 of the act of June 24, 1937 (P.L.2017, No.396), known as the County Institution District Law, and supervised by the department under Article IX of the act of June 13, 1967 (P.L.31, No.21), known as the Human Services Code.
"Debt coercion." Exploitation of the status or condition of a debtor arising from a pledge by the debtor of the personal services of the debtor or an individual under the debtor's control as a security or payment for debt, if any of the following apply:
(1) The value of those services as reasonably assessed is not applied toward the liquidation of the debt.
(2) The length and nature of those services are not respectively limited and defined.
(3) The principal amount of the debt does not reasonably reflect the value of the items or services for which the debt was incurred.
(4) The debtor is coerced to perform sex acts as payment for the debt.
(5) The creditor controls and determines the movement, housing and services performed by the debtor until repayment of the debt.
"Department." The Department of Human Services of the Commonwealth.
"Extortion." As defined in section 3923 (relating to theft by extortion).
"Financial harm." Includes any of the following:
(1) A violation of the act of March 30, 1859 (P.L.318, No.318), entitled "An act for the better securing the Payment of the Wages of Labor in certain counties of this Commonwealth."
(2) A violation of the act of May 23, 1887 (P.L.181, No.122), entitled "An act to regulate the employment of labor."
(3) A criminal violation of the act of January 30, 1974 (P.L.13, No.6), referred to as the Loan Interest and Protection Law (Usury Law).
(4) A violation of Chapter 2 of the act of June 23, 1978 (P.L.537, No.93), known as the Seasonal Farm Labor Act.
(5) A violation of any other law of this Commonwealth governing the payment of wages for labor or services.

"Fund." The Safe Harbor for Sexually Exploited Children Fund.

"Human trafficking." Any activity in violation of section 3011 (relating to trafficking in individuals) either alone or in conjunction with an activity in violation of section 3012 (relating to involuntary servitude).

"Involuntary servitude." Labor servitude or sexual servitude.

"Labor." Work or service of economic or financial value.

"Labor servitude." Labor which is performed or provided by another individual and is induced or obtained by any of the means set forth in section 3012(b).

"Minor." An individual who is less than 18 years of age.

"Record." Information, regardless of physical form or characteristics, that documents a transaction or activity and that is created, received or retained under law or in connection with a transaction, business or activity. The term includes any of the following:

(1) A document, paper, letter, map, book, tape, photograph, film or sound recording.

(2) Information stored or maintained electronically.

(3) A data-processed or image-processed document.

"Serious harm." Any harm, whether physical or nonphysical, that is sufficiently serious, under all the surrounding circumstances, to compel a reasonable person of the same background and in the same circumstances as the victim of human trafficking to perform or to continue performing labor or a service, a commercial sex act or a performance involving sex acts in order to avoid incurring that harm.

"Service." Any act committed at the behest of, under the supervision of or for the benefit of another.

"Sex act." Any touching or exposure of the sexual or other intimate parts of any individual for the purpose of gratifying sexual desire of any individual.

"Sexual servitude." Any sex act or performance involving a sex act for which anything of value is directly or indirectly given, promised to or received by any individual or which is performed or provided by any individual and is induced or obtained from:

(1) A minor.

(2) Any other individual by any of the means set forth in section 3012(b).

"Sexually exploited child." An individual under 18 years of age who:

(1) is a victim of sexual servitude; or

(2) is a victim of an offense under 18 U.S.C. § 1591 (relating to sex trafficking of children or by force, fraud, or coercion).

"Victim of human trafficking" or **"victim."** An individual who has been subjected to human trafficking.
(Oct. 24, 2018, P.L.797, No.130, eff. 60 days)

2018 Amendment. Act 130 added the defs. of "county agency," "department," "fund" and "sexually exploited child."

Cross References. Section 3001 is referred to in section 3065 of this title; sections 5945.3, 6328, 9738 of Title 42 (Judiciary and Judicial Procedure).

SUBCHAPTER B
PROSECUTION OF HUMAN TRAFFICKING

Cross References. Subchapter B is referred to in section 2718 of this title.

§ 3011. Trafficking in individuals.

(a) Offense defined.--A person commits a felony of the second degree if the person:

(1) recruits, entices, solicits, harbors, transports, provides, obtains or maintains an individual if the person knows or recklessly

disregards that the individual will be subject to involuntary servitude; or

(2) knowingly benefits financially or receives anything of value from any act that facilitates any activity described in paragraph (1).

(b) Trafficking in minors.--A person commits a felony of the first degree if the person engages in any activity listed in subsection (a) that results in a minor's being subjected to sexual servitude.

Cross References. Section 3011 is referred to in sections 3001, 3021, 3064, 5708 of this title; sections 5551, 5552, 9720.2, 9730.3, 9799.14 of Title 42 (Judiciary and Judicial Procedure).

§ 3012. Involuntary servitude.

(a) Offense defined.--A person commits a felony of the first degree if the person knowingly, through any of the means described in subsection (b), subjects an individual to labor servitude or sexual servitude, except where the conduct is permissible under Federal or State law other than this chapter.

(b) Means of subjecting an individual to involuntary servitude.--A person may subject an individual to involuntary servitude through any of the following means:

(1) Causing or threatening to cause serious harm to any individual.

(2) Physically restraining or threatening to physically restrain another individual.

(3) Kidnapping or attempting to kidnap any individual.

(4) Abusing or threatening to abuse the legal process.

(5) Taking or retaining the individual's personal property or real property as a means of coercion.

(6) Engaging in unlawful conduct with respect to documents, as defined in section 3014 (relating to unlawful conduct regarding documents).

(7) Extortion.

(8) Fraud.

(9) Criminal coercion, as defined in section 2906 (relating to criminal coercion).

(10) Duress, through the use of or threat to use unlawful force against the person or another.

(11) Debt coercion.

(12) Facilitating or controlling the individual's access to a controlled substance.

(13) Using any scheme, plan or pattern intended to cause the individual to believe that, if the individual does not perform the labor, services, acts or performances, that individual or another individual will suffer serious harm or physical restraint.

Cross References. Section 3012 is referred to in sections 3001, 3018, 3021, 3064, 5708 of this title; sections 5551, 5552, 9720.2, 9730.3 of Title 42 (Judiciary and Judicial Procedure).

§ 3013. Patronizing a victim of sexual servitude.

(a) Offense defined.--A person commits a felony of the second degree if the person engages in any sex act or performance with another individual knowing that the act or performance is the result of the individual being a victim of human trafficking.

(b) Investigation.--An individual arrested for a violation of section 5902(e) (relating to prostitution and related offenses) may be formally detained and questioned by law enforcement personnel to determine if the individual engaged in any sex act or performance with the alleged prostitute knowing that the individual is a victim of human trafficking.

(c) Fine.--A person whose violation of this section results in a judicial disposition other than acquittal or dismissal shall also pay a fine of $500 to the court, to be distributed to the commission to fund the grant program established under section 3031 (relating to grants).

Cross References. Section 3013 is referred to in section 3064 of this title.

§ 3014. Unlawful conduct regarding documents.

A person commits a felony of the third degree if, to prevent or restrict or attempt to prevent or restrict, without lawful authority, the ability of an individual to move or travel, the person knowingly destroys, conceals, removes, confiscates or possesses an actual or purported:

(1) passport or other immigration document of an individual; or

(2) government identification document of an individual.

Cross References. Section 3014 is referred to in section 3012 of this title.

§ 3015. Nonpayment of wages.

(a) Offense defined.--A person who, in connection with, as a part of or in addition to engaging in human trafficking, willfully or with intent to defraud, fails or refuses to pay wages for or otherwise causes financial harm to an individual in connection with labor services rendered commits:

(1) A misdemeanor of the third degree if the amount owed to the individual is less than $2,000.

(2) A felony of the third degree, if:

(i) the amount owed to the individual is equal to or greater than $2,000;

(ii) the failure or refusal constitutes a second or subsequent violation of this section; or

(iii) the person falsely denies the amount due or the validity of the debt.

(b) Offenses cumulative.--A person commits a separate offense under this section for each calendar month during which the individual earned wages that the person failed to pay or was otherwise financially harmed.

§ 3016. Obstruction of justice.

A person who commits a violation of Subchapter B of Chapter 49 (relating to victim and witness intimidation) or Chapter 51 (relating to obstructing governmental operations) that in any way interferes with or prevents the enforcement of this chapter shall be subject to the same penalties that may be imposed for the offense for which the person has been charged under this chapter.

§ 3017. Violation by business entities.

(a) Penalty.--Any business entity, including a corporation or unincorporated association, limited liability partnership or company or other legal entity, that knowingly aids or participates in any violation of this chapter, shall be subject to any of the following penalties:

(1) A fine of not more than $1,000,000.

(2) Revocation of the business entity's:

(i) charter, if it is organized under the laws of this Commonwealth; or

(ii) certificate of authority to do business in this Commonwealth, if the business entity is not organized under the laws of this Commonwealth.

(3) Other relief as the court deems equitable, including forfeiture of assets or restitution as provided in this chapter.

(b) Disposition of fines.--Fines imposed under this section shall be deposited as provided in section 3031 (relating to grants).

§ 3018. Evidence and defenses to human trafficking.

(a) General rule.--Evidence of the following facts or conditions shall not constitute a defense in a prosecution for a violation under this chapter, nor shall the evidence preclude a finding of a violation under this chapter:

(1) Specific instances of past sexual conduct of the victim of human trafficking, opinion evidence of the alleged victim's past sexual conduct and reputation evidence of the alleged victim's past sexual conduct shall not be admissible in a prosecution under this chapter, except evidence of the alleged victim's past sexual conduct with the defendant shall be admissible where consent of the alleged victim is at issue and the evidence is otherwise admissible under the rules of evidence. A defendant who proposes to offer evidence of the alleged victim's past sexual conduct under this paragraph shall file a written motion and offer of proof at the time of trial. If, at the time of trial, the court determines that the motion and offer of proof are sufficient on their faces, the court shall order an in camera hearing and shall make findings on the record as to the relevance and admissibility of the proposed evidence under the standards of this paragraph.

(2) The age of the victim of human trafficking with respect to the age of consent to sex or legal age of marriage.

(b) Victim's consent to employment contract in labor servitude.--The consent of the victim of human trafficking to an employment contract, notwithstanding if there was not fraud involved in the contract's formation, shall not be a defense to labor trafficking if force or coercion as described in section 3012(b) (relating to involuntary servitude) were involved in the making of the contract.

(c) Victim's age in sexual servitude.-- Except as provided in section 3102 (relating to mistake as to age), evidence of a defendant's lack of knowledge of a person's age, or a reasonable mistake of age, is not a defense for a violation of this chapter involving the sexual servitude of a minor.

§ 3019. Victim protection during prosecution.

(a) Disclosure of name of victim of human trafficking.--Notwithstanding any other provision of law to the contrary, unless the court otherwise orders in a prosecution involving a victim of human trafficking, an officer or employee of the court may not disclose the identity of the victim of human trafficking to the public. Any record revealing the name of the victim of human trafficking shall not be open to public inspection.

(b) Affirmative defense.--An individual who is charged with any violation under section 5902 (relating to prostitution and related offenses) may offer the defense at trial that he engaged in the conduct charged because he was compelled to do so by coercion or the use of or a threat to use unlawful force against his person or the person of another, which a person of reasonable firmness in his situation would have been unable to resist.

(c) Diversionary program.--An individual who is charged with violating a trespassing, loitering, obstruction of highway, disorderly conduct or simple possession of a controlled substance statute as a direct result of being a victim of human trafficking, where the violation is his first offense, shall be given first consideration for a pretrial diversionary program by the judicial authority with jurisdiction over the violations. If the individual successfully completes the diversionary program, the court shall order that the individual's records of the charge of violating the statute shall be expunged as provided for under section 9122 (relating to expungement).

(d) Motion to vacate conviction.--

(1) An individual convicted under section 3503 (relating to criminal trespass), 5503 (relating to disorderly conduct), 5506 (relating to loitering and prowling at night time), 5507 (relating to obstructing highways and other public passages) or 5902 or an offense for simple possession of a controlled substance committed as a direct result of being a victim of human trafficking may file a motion to vacate the conviction.

(2) In order to be considered, a motion under this subsection must:

(i) Be in writing.

(ii) Be consented to by the attorney for the Commonwealth.

(iii) Describe the supporting evidence with particularity.

(iv) Include copies of any documents showing that the moving party is entitled to relief under this section.

(e) Official documentation.--No official determination or documentation is required to grant a motion under this section, but official documentation from a Federal, State or local government agency indicating that the defendant was a victim at the time of the offense creates a presumption that the defendant's participation in the offense was a direct result of being a victim.

(f) Grant of motion.--The court shall grant the motion if it finds that:

(1) The moving party was convicted of an offense described in subsection (d)(1).

(2) The conviction was obtained as a result of the moving party's having been a victim of human trafficking.

(g) Conviction vacated.--If the motion under subsection (d) is granted, the court shall vacate the conviction, strike the adjudication of guilt and order the expungement of the record of the criminal proceedings. The court shall issue an order to expunge all records and files related to the moving party's arrest, citation, investigation, charge, adjudication of guilt, criminal proceedings and probation for the offense.

§ 3020. Restitution.

In addition to the provisions of section 1106 (relating to restitution for injuries to person or property), the following shall apply:

(1) A person who violates this chapter shall be ineligible to receive restitution.

(2) The following items may be included in an order of restitution:

(i) For the period during which the victim of human trafficking was engaged in involuntary servitude, the greater of the following:

(A) The value of the victim's time during the period of involuntary servitude as guaranteed under the minimum wage and overtime provisions of the laws of this Commonwealth.

(B) The gross income or value to the defendant of the services of the victim.

(C) The amount the victim was promised or the amount an individual in the position of the victim would have reasonably expected to earn. This clause shall not apply to the amount an individual would have reasonably expected to earn in an illegal activity.

(ii) The return of property of the victim of human trafficking, cost of damage to the property or the replacement value of the property if taken, destroyed or damaged beyond repair as a result of human trafficking.

(3) Collection and distribution of restitution payments shall be governed by the

provisions of 42 Pa.C.S. §§ 9728 (relating to collection of restitution, reparation, fees, costs, fines and penalties), 9730 (relating to payment of court costs, restitution and fines) and 9730.1 (relating to collection of court costs, restitution and fines by private collection agency).

§ 3021. Asset forfeiture.

(a) General rule.--The following shall be subject to forfeiture to this Commonwealth, and no property right shall exist in them:

(1) All assets, foreign or domestic:

(i) Of an individual, entity or organization engaged in planning or perpetrating an act in this Commonwealth which violates section 3011 (relating to trafficking in individuals) or 3012 (relating to involuntary servitude).

(ii) Affording a person a source of influence over the individual, entity or organization under subparagraph (i).

(iii) Acquired or maintained by a person with the intent and for the purpose of supporting, planning, conducting or concealing an act in this Commonwealth which violates section 3011 or 3012.

(iv) Derived from, involved in or used or intended to be used to commit an act in this Commonwealth which violates section 3011 or 3012.

(2) All assets within this Commonwealth:

(i) Of an individual, entity or organization engaged in planning or perpetrating an act which violates section 3011 or 3012.

(ii) Acquired or maintained with the intent and for the purpose of supporting, planning, conducting or concealing an act which violates section 3011 or 3012.

(iii) Derived from, involved in or used or intended to be used to commit an act which violates section 3011 or 3012.

(b) Process and seizures.--

(1) Property subject to forfeiture under this section may be seized by a law enforcement agency upon process issued by any court of common pleas having jurisdiction over the property.

(2) Seizure without process may be made if:

(i) the seizure is incident to an arrest or a search under a search warrant or inspection under an administrative inspection warrant;

(ii) the property subject to seizure has been the subject of a prior judgment in favor of the Commonwealth in a criminal injunction or forfeiture proceeding under this chapter;

(iii) there is probable cause to believe that the property is dangerous to health or safety; or

(iv) there is probable cause to believe that the property has been used or is intended to be used in violation of this chapter.

(3) In the event that seizure without process occurs as provided for in paragraph (2), proceedings for the issuance of process shall be instituted promptly.

(c) Custody of property.--

(1) Property taken or detained under this section shall not be subject to replevin but is deemed to be in the custody of the law enforcement agency, the district attorney or the Attorney General subject only to the orders and decrees of the court of common pleas having jurisdiction over the forfeiture proceedings.

(2) When property is seized under this section, the law enforcement agency shall place the property under seal and either:

(i) remove the property to a place designated by it; or

(ii) require that the district attorney take custody of the property and remove it to an appropriate location for disposition in accordance with law.

(d) Transfer of property.--If property is forfeited under this section, the property shall be transferred to the custody of the district attorney if the law enforcement authority seizing the property has county or local jurisdiction, or the Attorney General if the law enforcement authority seizing the property has Statewide jurisdiction. The Attorney General or district attorney, where appropriate, may sell the property. The proceeds from a sale shall first be used to pay all proper expenses of the proceedings for forfeiture and sale, including expenses of seizure, maintenance of custody, advertising and court costs. The balance of the proceeds shall be distributed under subsection (m).

(e) Proceedings and petition.--

(1) The proceedings for the forfeiture or condemnation of property shall be in rem, in which the Commonwealth shall be the plaintiff and the property the defendant.

(2) A petition shall:

(i) be filed in the court of common pleas of the judicial district where the property is located;

(ii) be verified by oath or affirmation of an officer or citizen; and

(iii) contain the following:

(A) A description of the property seized.

(B) A statement of the time and place where seized.

(C) The owner, if known.

(D) The person or persons in possession, if known.

(E) An allegation that the property is subject to forfeiture under this section and an averment of material facts upon which forfeiture action is based.

(F) A prayer for an order of forfeiture that the property be adjudged forfeited to the Commonwealth and condemned unless cause to the contrary is shown.

(f) Service.--

(1) A copy of the petition required under subsection (e) shall be served personally or by certified mail on the owner or the person or persons in possession at the time of the seizure.

(2) The copy shall have endorsed a notice as follows:

To the claimant of the within described property:

You are required to file an answer to this petition, setting forth your title in and right to possession of the property within 30 days from the service of this notice. You are also notified that, if you fail to file the answer, a decree of forfeiture and condemnation will be entered against the property.

(3) The notice shall be signed by the district attorney, deputy district attorney or assistant district attorney or the Attorney General or a deputy attorney general.

(g) Notice.--

(1) Notice of the petition shall be given by the Commonwealth through an advertisement in only one newspaper of general circulation published in the county where the property shall have been seized, once a week for two successive weeks if:

(i) the owner of the property is unknown;

(ii) there was no person in possession of the property when seized; or

(iii) the owner or the person or persons in possession at the time of the seizure cannot be personally served or located within the jurisdiction of the court.

(2) Notwithstanding any other law to the contrary, no advertisement shall be required.

(3) The notice shall:

(i) contain a statement of the seizure of the property, a description of the property and the place and date of seizure; and

(ii) direct any claimants to the property to file a claim on or before a date given in the notice, which date shall not be less than 30 days from the date of the first publication.

(4) If no claims are filed within 30 days of publication, the property shall summarily forfeit to the Commonwealth.

(h) Unknown owner.--For purposes of this section, the owner or other person cannot be found in the jurisdiction of the court if:

(1) A copy of the petition is mailed to the last known address by certified mail and is returned without delivery.

(2) Personal service is attempted once but cannot be made at the last known address.

(3) A copy of the petition is left at the last known address.

(i) Waiver of notice.--The notice provisions of this section are automatically waived if the owner, without good cause, fails to appear in court in response to a subpoena on the underlying criminal charges. If good cause has not been demonstrated and 45 days have passed since the owner failed to appear, the property shall summarily forfeit to the Commonwealth.

(j) Hearing date.--Upon the filing of a claim for the property setting forth a right of possession, the case shall be deemed at issue, and a date and time shall be fixed for the hearing.

(k) Burden of proof.--If the Commonwealth produces evidence at the hearing under this section that the property in question was unlawfully used, possessed or otherwise subject to forfeiture under this section, the burden shall be upon the claimant to show by a preponderance of the evidence that:

(1) the claimant is the owner of the property or the holder of a chattel mortgage or contract of conditional sale thereon;

(2) the claimant lawfully acquired the property; and

(3) the property was not unlawfully used or possessed by the claimant. If it appears that the property was unlawfully used or possessed by a person other than the claimant, the claimant shall show that the unlawful use or possession was without his knowledge or consent. The absence of knowledge or consent must be reasonable under the circumstances presented.

(l) Claims of ownership.--

(1) A person may file a petition or answer the Commonwealth's petition alleging:

(i) Ownership of the property.

(ii) A right of possession to the property.

(iii) A lien or reservation of title to the property as the holder of:

(A) a chattel mortgage upon the property; or

(B) a contract of conditional sale upon the property.

(2) A public hearing shall be held, with due notice given to the district attorney or Attorney General.

(3) The court may order the property returned or delivered to the claimant upon proof by a preponderance of the evidence by the claimant that:

(i) the property was lawfully acquired, possessed and used by the claimant; or

(ii) if it appears that the property was unlawfully used by a person other than the claimant, the unlawful use was without the claimant's knowledge or consent. The absence of knowledge or consent must be reasonable under the circumstances presented.

(m) Disposition of proceeds.--Subject to subsection (d), all moneys forfeited and the proceeds from the sale of all property forfeited and seized under this section shall be paid as follows:

(1) Any law enforcement agency shall be reimbursed if it has used its own funds in the detection, investigation, apprehension and prosecution of persons for violation of sections 3011 and 3012.

(2) Any amount remaining after reimbursement under paragraph (1) shall be distributed under the following formula:

(i) Thirty percent to the office of the prosecuting attorney to be used to investigate and prosecute human trafficking cases.

(ii) Seventy percent to the commission, one-half of which shall be used to fund the grant programs established under section 3031 (relating to grants) and one-half to be used by the Office of Victims' Services within the commission to provide services to victims of human trafficking in the manner set forth in Chapter 9 of the act of November 24, 1998 (P.L.882, No.111), known as the Crime Victims Act.

(n) Assets located outside United States.--Assets of persons convicted of violations of sections 3011 and 3012 that are located outside the United States shall also be subject to forfeiture to the extent they can be retrieved by the Commonwealth.

§ 3022. Professional licenses.

(a) Suspension of professional license.-- The professional license of a licensee who in the course of a violation of this chapter knowingly employs or permits the employment of a victim of human trafficking shall be suspended for a minimum period of one year.

(b) Administrative procedure.--A suspension under subsection (a) shall be subject to 2 Pa.C.S. Chs. 5 Subch. A (relating to practice and procedure of Commonwealth agencies) and 7 Subch. A (relating to judicial review of Commonwealth agency action).

(c) Definition.--As used in this section, "licensee" shall mean an individual, corporation, partnership, limited liability company or other legal entity that holds a license issued by an administrative board or commission under the Bureau of Professional and Occupational Affairs in the Department of State.

§ 3023. Cumulative remedies.

Any remedies under this chapter shall be in addition to any other criminal penalties or forfeitures authorized under the laws of this Commonwealth.

§ 3024. Sentencing.

The Pennsylvania Commission on Sentencing, in accordance with 42 Pa.C.S. § 2154 (relating to adoption of guidelines for sentencing), shall provide for sentencing enhancements for courts to consider in cases involving trafficking in individuals and involuntary servitude.

§ 3025. Data collection.

The Pennsylvania Commission on Sentencing established in 42 Pa.C.S. § 2151.2 (relating to commission) shall collect data and other relevant information on sentences imposed under this subchapter.

References in Text. Section 2151.2, referred to in this section, was repealed.

§ 3026. Concurrent jurisdiction.

The Attorney General and the district attorneys of the several counties shall have concurrent authority to investigate and institute criminal proceedings under the provisions of this chapter.

(Oct. 24, 2018, P.L.797, No.130, eff. 60 days)

2018 Amendment. Act 130 added section 3026.

SUBCHAPTER C
PREVENTION OF HUMAN
TRAFFICKING

Sec.
§ 3031. Grants.

Subject to the availability of funds, the commission shall make grants to State agencies, units of local government and nongovernmental organizations to:

(1) Develop, expand or strengthen programs for victims of human trafficking. Such programs may include:

(i) Health services, including mental health services.

(ii) Temporary and permanent housing placement.

(iii) Legal and immigration services.

(iv) Employment placement, education and training.

(2) Ensure prevention of human trafficking, including increasing public awareness.

(3) Ensure protection of victims of human trafficking, including training of first responders.

Cross References. Section 3031 is referred to in sections 3013, 3017, 3021 of this title.

§ 3032. (Reserved).

SUBCHAPTER D
PROTECTION OF VICTIMS OF
HUMAN TRAFFICKING

Sec.
§ 3051. Civil causes of action.

(a) General rule.--

(1) An individual who is a victim of human trafficking may bring a civil action against any person that participated in the human trafficking of the individual in the court of common pleas of the county where the individual resides or where any of the alleged violations of this chapter occurred.

(2) An individual who is a victim of the sex trade may bring a civil action in the court of common pleas of the county where the individual resides against a person that:

(i) recruits, profits from or maintains the victim in any sex trade act;

(ii) abuses or causes bodily harm to the victim in any sex trade act; and

(iii) knowingly advertises or publishes advertisements for purposes of recruitment into sex trade activity.

(b) Exception.--This section shall not be construed to create liability for any person who provides goods or services to the general public and to a person who would be liable under subsection (a)(2), absent a showing that the person:

(1) knowingly markets or provides its goods or services to a person liable under subsection (a)(2);

(2) knowingly receives a higher level of compensation from a person liable under subsection (a)(2); or

(3) supervises or exercises control over a person liable under subsection (a)(2).

(c) Damages.--The court may award any of the following forms of relief:

(1) Actual damages.

(2) Compensatory damages.

(3) Punitive damages.

(4) Injunctive relief.

(5) Any other appropriate relief.

(d) Attorney fees and costs.--A prevailing plaintiff who is a victim of human trafficking shall be awarded reasonable attorney fees and costs.

(e) Treble damages.--Treble damages shall be awarded to a victim of human trafficking on proof of actual damages where the defendant's acts were willful and malicious.

(f) Joinder of actions.--In the discretion of the court:

(1) Two or more individuals may join in one action under this section as plaintiffs if their respective actions involve at least one defendant in common.

(2) Two or more persons may be joined in one action under this section as defendants if those persons may be liable to at least one plaintiff in common.

(g) Attempts at avoidance of liability.--No person may avoid liability under this section by:

(1) a conveyance of any right, title or interest in real property; or

(2) an agreement, including an indemnification agreement or hold harmless agreement, that purports to show the consent of the victim of human trafficking.

(h) Statute of limitations.--

(1) An action may be brought under this section by an individual who was the victim of human trafficking while an adult within five years of the last act against that individual that constitutes an offense under this chapter.

(2) An action may be brought under this section by an individual who was a victim of human trafficking while a minor for any offense committed against the victim while the victim was under 18 years of age until that victim reaches 30 years of age.

(i) Estoppel.--A defendant is estopped from asserting a defense of the statute of limitations when the expiration of the statute is due to intentional conduct by the defendant knowingly inducing or coercing the plaintiff to delay the filing of the action.

(j) Nondefenses.--It shall not be a defense to an action under this section that the following occurred:

(1) The victim of the sex trade and the defendant had a consensual sexual relationship.

(2) The defendant is related to the victim of the sex trade by blood or marriage.

(3) The defendant has lived with the victim of the sex trade in any formal or informal household arrangement.

(4) The victim of the sex trade was paid or otherwise compensated for sex trade activity.

(5) The victim of the sex trade engaged in sex trade activity prior to any involvement with the defendant.

(6) The victim of the sex trade continued to engage in sex trade activity following any involvement with the defendant.

(7) The victim of the sex trade made no attempt to escape, flee or otherwise terminate the contact with the defendant.

(8) The victim of the sex trade consented to engage in sex trade activity.

(9) The victim of the sex trade engaged in only a single incident of sex trade activity.

(10) There was no physical contact involved in the sex trade activity.

(11) As a condition of employment, the defendant required the victim of the sex trade to agree not to engage in prostitution.

(12) The defendant's place of business was posted with signs prohibiting prostitution or prostitution-related activities.

(13) The victim of the sex trade has been convicted or charged with prostitution or prostitution-related offenses.

(14) The victim of labor trafficking made no attempt to escape, flee or otherwise terminate the contact with the defendant.

(k) Definitions.--The following words and phrases when used in this section shall have the meanings given to them in this subsection unless the context clearly indicates otherwise:

"Sex trade." An act, which if proven beyond a reasonable doubt, could support a conviction for violation or attempted violation of Chapter 59 (relating to public indecency) or section 6312 (relating to sexual abuse of children).

"Victim of the sex trade." An individual who has:

(1) been the object of a solicitation for prostitution;

(2) been the object of a transaction in a sex act;

(3) been intended or compelled to engage in an act of prostitution;

(4) been intended or compelled to engage in a sex act;

(5) been described or depicted in material that advertises an intent or compulsion to engage in sex acts; or

(6) in the case of obscenity or child pornography, has appeared in or been described or depicted in the offending conduct or material.

§ 3052. Protection of victims.

Law enforcement agencies shall take reasonable steps necessary to identify, protect and assist victims of human trafficking.

§ 3053. Appropriate implementation for minor victims of human trafficking (Repealed).

2018 Repeal. Section 3053 was repealed October 24, 2018, P.L.797, No.130, effective in 60 days.

§ 3054. Services.

(a) Information for victims.--Subject to the availability of funding, the commission shall prepare a model informational form to be used by any person having contact with victims of human trafficking that informs victims of human trafficking, in a language they can understand, of the following:

(1) The procedure for repatriation to the country of citizenship or lawful residence of the victim of human trafficking.

(2) A directory of local service organizations for victims of human trafficking.

(3) A directory of legal services organizations that can assist victims of human trafficking in obtaining or maintaining legal immigration status.

(4) A directory of benefits for victims of human trafficking under Federal and State laws.

(b) Labor standards and working conditions.--The Department of Labor and Industry shall:

(1) Administer labor standards regarding wages, hours of work and working conditions under its jurisdiction without regard to the legal status of the individual's right to work in the United States.

(2) Report to the appropriate law enforcement agency any evidence of human trafficking that may be discovered during the course of an investigation of wages, hours of work and working conditions.

(c) Immigration certification.--

(1) The Attorney General, a district attorney or any representative of a law enforcement agency may certify in writing to the United States Department of Justice or other Federal agency, including the United States Department of Homeland Security, that:

(i) an investigation or prosecution under this chapter has begun; and

(ii) an individual who may be a victim of human trafficking is willing to cooperate or is cooperating with the investigation to enable the individual, if eligible under Federal law, to qualify for an appropriate special immigrant visa and to access available Federal benefits.

(2) Cooperation with law enforcement agencies shall not be required of a victim of human trafficking who is a minor.

(3) Certification under this subsection may be made available to the victim of human trafficking and the designated legal representative of the victim of human trafficking.

(d) Access to crime victims services.--Victims of human trafficking shall be eligible for benefits and compensation under the act of November 24, 1998 (P.L.882, No.111), known as the Crime Victims Act.

§ 3055. Victims in shelters.

(a) Voluntary placement.--Residence of a victim of human trafficking in a shelter or other facility shall be voluntary, and a victim of human trafficking may decline to stay in a shelter or other facility.

(b) Restrictions on admission.-- Admission to a shelter:

(1) shall be made without regard to race, religion, ethnic background, sexual orientation, country of origin or culture; and

(2) may not be conditioned on whether the victim of human trafficking is cooperating with a law enforcement agency in its attempts to prosecute persons under this chapter.

§ 3056. Special relief to restore victim's dignity and autonomy.

(a) General rule.--An individual who is a victim of human trafficking and has been tattooed with an identifying mark of human trafficking as a direct result of being trafficked may be eligible for special relief.

(b) Form of special relief.--

(1) An individual who is a victim of human trafficking may be reimbursed from the fund for the costs of removing or covering up a tattoo with an identifying mark.

(2) No reimbursement may be paid if the individual has incurred reimbursable expenses of less than $100, and no reimbursement may exceed $10,000 per individual.

(3) If a reimbursement paid from the fund to an individual is later recovered by an insurance settlement, civil suit settlement or restitution, the individual shall pay to the fund an amount equal to the reimbursement.

(Oct. 24, 2018, P.L.797, No.130, eff. 60 days)

2018 Amendment. Act 130 added section 3056.

SUBCHAPTER D.1
SAFE HARBOR FOR SEXUALLY EXPLOITED CHILDREN

Enactment. Subchapter D.1 was added October 24, 2018, P.L.797, No.130, effective in 60 days.

§ 3061. Statewide protocol.

The department shall develop a Statewide protocol to efficiently and effectively coordinate the provision of specialized services to sexually exploited children.

§ 3062. Specialized services for sexually exploited children.

The department shall, in conjunction with county agencies:

(1) Develop and provide specialized programs and services for sexually exploited children that address a victim's needs, including the following:

(i) Safe and stable housing.

(ii) Access to education.

(iii) Employment and life-skills training.

(iv) Comprehensive case management.

(v) Physical and behavioral health care, including trauma therapy.

(vi) Treatment for drug or alcohol dependency.

(vii) Medical and dental care.

(viii) Access to personal care items and adequate clothing.

(ix) Other needs that sexually exploited children may have as determined by the department or the county agencies.

(2) Ensure that providers of the specialized programs and services provided under paragraph (1) receive sufficient training and understand the unique circumstances surrounding the victimization of sexually exploited children.

Cross References. Section 3062 is referred to in section 3065 of this title.

§ 3063. Law enforcement training.

The Municipal Police Officers' Education and Training Commission and the Pennsylvania State Police shall provide training to appropriate law enforcement officers. The training shall include:

(1) Methods used to identify a sexually exploited child.

(2) Methods used to interview and engage with a sexually exploited child.

(3) Methods to assist victims to access specialized programs and services for a sexually exploited child.

(4) Methods to minimize trauma in the detention of a sexually exploited child.

§ 3064. Safe Harbor for Sexually Exploited Children Fund.

(a) Establishment.--

(1) The Safe Harbor for Sexually Exploited Children Fund is established in the State Treasury and shall be administered by the department.

(2) Appropriations for transfers to the fund and fines paid and interest accrued on money collected under subsection (b) shall be deposited into the fund.

(3) In addition to money that may be appropriated by the General Assembly, the department may apply for and expend Federal grants and contributions from other public, quasi-public or private sources to assist in implementing this subchapter.

(4) Money in the fund shall be used as follows:

(i) At least 50% of the fund may be expended by the department to provide victim services either directly by the department or through grants.

(ii) At least 40% of the fund may be expended to increase public awareness through an anti-demand campaign.

(iii) Not more than 10% of the fund may be expended by the department for the costs of operating and maintaining the fund.

(b) **Fines.**--Notwithstanding any law to the contrary, the fines provided by this subsection shall be in addition to any fine authorized or required by law:

(1) An individual who is convicted of an offense under section 3011 (relating to trafficking in individuals), 3012 (relating to involuntary servitude), 3013 (relating to patronizing a victim of sexual servitude) or 5902(b) or (b.1) (relating to prostitution and related offenses) shall be ordered to pay a fine of $5,000 for each offense.

(2) An individual who is convicted of an offense under section 5902(e) shall be ordered to pay a fine of $2,500 for each offense.

(3) An individual who is convicted of an offense under section 5902(e), when the individual knew or should have known the victim was under 18 years of age, shall be ordered to pay a fine of $5,000 for each offense.

§ 3065. Safe harbor for sexually exploited children.

(a) **Safe harbor.**--If it is determined by a law enforcement officer, after reasonable detention for investigative purposes, that an individual is under 18 years of age and is determined to be a sexually exploited child as defined in section 3001 (relating to definitions), the individual shall be immune from:

(1) Prosecution or adjudication as a delinquent child for a violation of sections 5507 (relating to obstructing highways and other public passages) and 5902(a) (relating to prostitution and related offenses).

(2) Revocation of an existing term of probation or parole arising from a conviction or adjudication for another offense if the revocation is based on conduct under paragraph (1).

(b) Exceptions to safe harbor.--The safe harbor under subsection (a) shall not:

(1) Interfere with or prevent an investigation, arrest, charge, prosecution, delinquency adjudication or revocation for violations other than a violation under subsection (a).

(2) Bar the admission of evidence in connection with the investigation and prosecution for a violation other than a violation under subsection (a).

(3) Bar the admission of evidence in connection with an investigation and prosecution of an individual who does not qualify for safe harbor as provided under this section.

(c) Detainment.--An individual determined to be a sexually exploited child as defined in section 3001 (relating to definitions) shall be detained no longer than necessary and only to assist the child in securing specialized services available under section 3062 (relating to specialized services for sexually exploited children) or to refer the child to a county agency if required under 42 Pa.C.S. § 6328 (relating to dependency in lieu of delinquency).

(d) Immunity.--In addition to any other immunity or limitation on civil liability, a law enforcement officer or prosecuting attorney who, acting in good faith, investigates, detains, charges or institutes delinquency proceedings against an individual who is thereafter determined to be entitled to immunity under this section shall not be subject to civil liability for the actions.

SUBCHAPTER E
MISCELLANEOUS PROVISIONS

Sec.

3071. Funding.
3072. Nonexclusivity.
§ 3071. Funding.

In addition to any money that may be appropriated from time to time by the General Assembly for its work, the commission may apply for and expend Federal grants and grants and contributions from other public, quasi-public or private sources to assist in implementing this chapter.

§ 3072. Nonexclusivity.

Remedies under this chapter are not exclusive and shall be in addition to other procedures or remedies for a violation or conduct provided for in other law.

CHAPTER 31 SEXUAL OFFENSES

Subchapter
A. General Provisions
B. Definition of Offenses
C. Loss of Property Rights

Enactment. Chapter 31 was added December 6, 1972, P.L.1482, No.334, effective in six months.

Cross References. Chapter 31 is referred to in sections 3502, 5743.1, 6301, 6318 of this title; section 3103 of Title 23 (Domestic Relations); sections 1726.1, 5750, 5920, 5985.1, 5987, 5993, 62A03, 9718.1, 9912 of Title 42 (Judiciary and Judicial Procedure); section 2303 of Title 44 (Law and Justice).

SUBCHAPTER A
GENERAL PROVISIONS

Sec.
3101. Definitions.
3102. Mistake as to age.
3103. Spouse relationships (Repealed).
3104. Evidence of victim's sexual conduct.
3105. Prompt complaint.
3106. Testimony of complainants.
3107. Resistance not required.
§ 3101. Definitions.

Subject to additional definitions contained in subsequent provisions of this chapter which are applicable to specific provisions of this chapter, the following words and phrases when used in this chapter shall have, unless the context clearly indicates otherwise, the meanings given to them in this section:

"Complainant." An alleged victim of a crime under this chapter.

"Deviate sexual intercourse." Sexual intercourse per os or per anus between human beings and any form of sexual intercourse with an animal. The term also includes penetration, however slight, of the genitals or anus of another person with a foreign object for any purpose other than good faith medical, hygienic or law enforcement procedures.

"Forcible compulsion." Compulsion by use of physical, intellectual, moral, emotional or psychological force, either express or implied. The term includes, but is not limited to, compulsion resulting in another person's death, whether the death occurred before, during or after sexual intercourse.

"Foreign object." Includes any physical object not a part of the actor's body.

"Indecent contact." Any touching of the sexual or other intimate parts of the person for the purpose of arousing or gratifying sexual desire, in any person.

"Serious bodily injury." As defined in section 2301 (relating to definitions).

"Sexual intercourse." In addition to its ordinary meaning, includes intercourse per os or per anus, with some penetration however slight; emission is not required.

(Dec. 21, 1984, P.L.1210, No.230, eff. 60 days; Feb. 2, 1990, P.L.6, No.4, eff. 60 days; Mar. 31, 1995, 1st Sp.Sess., P.L.985, No.10, eff. 60 days; Dec. 9, 2002, P.L.1350, No.162, eff. 60 days; Dec. 16, 2002, P.L.1953, No.226, eff. 60 days; Dec. 18, 2013, P.L.1163, No.105, eff. Jan. 1, 2014)

2013 Amendment. Act 105 amended the def. of "indecent contact."

2002 Amendments. Act 162 added the def. of "serious bodily injury" and Act 226 added the def. of "serious bodily injury." The amendments by Acts 162 and 226 are identical and therefore have been merged.

Cross References. Section 3101 is referred to in sections 3133, 6312 of this title; sections 5533, 6302 of Title 42 (Judiciary and Judicial Procedure).

§ 3102. Mistake as to age.

Except as otherwise provided, whenever in this chapter the criminality of conduct depends on a child being below the age of 14 years, it is no defense that the defendant did not know the age of the child or reasonably believed the child to be the age of 14 years or older. When criminality depends on the child's being below a critical age older than 14 years, it is a defense for the defendant to prove by a preponderance of the evidence that he or she reasonably believed the child to be above the critical age.

(May 18, 1976, P.L.120, No.53, eff. 30 days; Mar. 31, 1995, 1st Sp.Sess., P.L.985, No.10, eff. 60 days)

1995 Amendment. Section 18 of Act 10, 1st Sp.Sess., provided that the amendment of section 3102 shall apply to offenses committed on or after the effective date of Act 10.

Cross References. Section 3102 is referred to in section 3018 of this title.

§ 3103. Spouse relationships (Repealed).

1995 Repeal. Section 3103 was repealed March 31, 1995, 1st Sp.Sess. (P.L.985, No.10), effective in 60 days.

§ 3104. Evidence of victim's sexual conduct.

(a) General rule.--Evidence of specific instances of the alleged victim's past sexual conduct, past sexual victimization, allegations of past sexual victimization, opinion evidence of the alleged victim's past sexual conduct, and reputation evidence of the alleged victim's past sexual conduct shall not be admissible in prosecutions of any offense listed in subsection (c) except evidence of the alleged victim's past sexual conduct with the defendant where consent of the alleged victim is at issue and such evidence is otherwise admissible pursuant to the rules of evidence.

(b) Evidentiary proceedings.--A defendant who proposes to offer evidence of the alleged victim's past sexual conduct, past sexual victimization, allegations of past sexual victimization, opinion evidence of the alleged victim's past sexual conduct and reputation evidence of the alleged victim's past sexual conduct pursuant to subsection (a) shall file a written motion and offer of proof at the time of trial. If, at the time of trial, the court determines that the motion and offer of proof are sufficient on their faces, the court shall order an in camera hearing and shall make findings on the record as to the relevance and admissibility of the proposed evidence pursuant to the standards set forth in subsection (a).

(c) Applicability.--This section shall apply to prosecutions of any of the following offenses, including conspiracy, attempt or solicitation to commit any of the following offenses, enumerated in this title:

Chapter 27 (relating to assault).

Chapter 29 (relating to kidnapping).

Chapter 30 (relating to human trafficking).

Chapter 31 (relating to sexual offenses).

Section 4302 (relating to incest).

Section 4304 (relating to endangering welfare of children), if the offense involved sexual contact with the victim.

Section 6301(a)(1)(ii) (relating to corruption of minors).

Section 6312(b) (relating to sexual abuse of children).

Section 6318 (relating to unlawful contact with minor).

Section 6320 (relating to sexual exploitation of children).

(May 18, 1976, P.L.120, No.53, eff. 30 days; June 28, 2019, P.L.214, No.24, eff. 60 days)

§ 3105. Prompt complaint.

Prompt reporting to public authority is not required in a prosecution under this chapter: Provided, however, That nothing in this section shall be construed to prohibit a defendant from introducing evidence of the complainant's failure to promptly report the crime if such evidence would be admissible pursuant to the rules of evidence.

(May 18, 1976, P.L.120, No.53, eff. 30 days; Mar. 31, 1995, 1st Sp.Sess., P.L.985, No.10, eff. 60 days)

1995 Amendment. Section 18 of Act 10, 1st Sp.Sess., provided that the amendment of section 3105 shall apply to offenses committed on or after the effective date of Act 10.

§ 3106. Testimony of complainants.

The credibility of a complainant of an offense under this chapter shall be determined by the same standard as is the credibility of a complainant of any other crime. The testimony of a complainant need not be corroborated in prosecutions under this chapter. No instructions shall be given cautioning the jury to view the complainant's testimony in any other way than that in which all complainants' testimony is viewed.

(May 18, 1976, P.L.120, No.53, eff. 30 days; Mar. 31, 1995, 1st Sp.Sess., P.L.985, No.10, eff. 60 days)

1995 Amendment. Section 18 of Act 10, 1st Sp.Sess., provided that the amendment of section 3106 shall apply to offenses committed on or after the effective date of Act 10.

Prior Provisions. Former section 3106, which related to the same subject matter, was added December 6, 1972 (P.L.1482, No.334), and repealed November 21, 1973 (P.L.339, No.115), effective in 60 days.

§ 3107. Resistance not required.

The alleged victim need not resist the actor in prosecutions under this chapter: Provided, however, That nothing in this section shall be construed to prohibit a defendant from introducing evidence that the alleged victim consented to the conduct in question.

(May 18, 1976, P.L.120, No.53, eff. 30 days)

1976 Amendment. Act 53 added section 3107.

SUBCHAPTER B
DEFINITION OF OFFENSES

Sec.

3121. Rape.

3122. Statutory rape (Repealed).

3122.1. Statutory sexual assault.

3123. Involuntary deviate sexual intercourse.

3124. Voluntary deviate sexual intercourse (Repealed).

3124.1. Sexual assault.

3124.2. Institutional sexual assault.

3124.3. Sexual assault by sports official, volunteer or employee of nonprofit association.

3125. Aggravated indecent assault.

3126. Indecent assault.

3127. Indecent exposure.

3128. Spousal sexual assault (Repealed).

3129. Sexual intercourse with animal.

3130. Conduct relating to sex offenders.

3131. Unlawful dissemination of intimate image.

3132. Female mutilation.

3133. Sexual extortion.

§ 3121. Rape.

(a) Offense defined.--A person commits a felony of the first degree when the person engages in sexual intercourse with a complainant:

    (1) By forcible compulsion.

    (2) By threat of forcible compulsion that would prevent resistance by a person of reasonable resolution.

    (3) Who is unconscious or where the person knows that the complainant is unaware that the sexual intercourse is occurring.

    (4) Where the person has substantially impaired the complainant's power to appraise or control his or her conduct by administering or employing, without the knowledge of the complainant, drugs, intoxicants or other means for the purpose of preventing resistance.

    (5) Who suffers from a mental disability which renders the complainant incapable of consent.

    (6) (Deleted by amendment).

  (b) Additional penalties.--In addition to the penalty provided for by subsection (a), a person may be sentenced to an additional term not to exceed ten years' confinement and an additional amount not to exceed $100,000 where the person engages in sexual intercourse with a complainant and has substantially impaired the complainant's power to appraise or control his or her conduct by administering or employing, without the knowledge of the complainant, any substance for the purpose of preventing resistance through the inducement of euphoria, memory loss and any other effect of this substance.

  (c) Rape of a child.--A person commits the offense of rape of a child, a felony of the first degree, when the person engages in sexual intercourse with a complainant who is less than 13 years of age.

  (d) Rape of a child with serious bodily injury.--A person commits the offense of rape of a child resulting in serious bodily injury, a felony of the first degree, when the person violates this section and the complainant is under 13 years of age and suffers serious bodily injury in the course of the offense.

  (e) Sentences.--Notwithstanding the provisions of section 1103 (relating to sentence of imprisonment for felony), a person convicted of an offense under:

    (1) Subsection (c) shall be sentenced to a term of imprisonment which shall be fixed by the court at not more than 40 years.

    (2) Subsection (d) shall be sentenced up to a maximum term of life imprisonment.

(Dec. 21, 1984, P.L.1210, No.230, eff. 60 days; Mar. 31, 1995, 1st Sp.Sess., P.L.985, No.10, eff. 60 days; Dec. 19, 1997, P.L.621, No.65, eff. 60 days; Dec. 9, 2002, P.L.1350, No.162, eff. 60 days; Dec. 16, 2002, P.L.1953, No.226, eff. 60 days)

2002 Amendments. Act 226 overlooked the amendment by Act 162, but the amendments do not conflict in substance (except for the designation of the offenses in subsecs. (c) and (d) as felonies of the first degree, as to which Act 162 has been given effect) and both have been given effect in setting forth the text of section 3121.

Effective Date. After February 6, 2003, and before February 14, 2003, section 3121 will reflect only the amendment by Act 162, as follows:

Cross References. Section 3121 is referred to in sections 1111, 2709.1, 2714, 3122.1, 3124.1, 3124.2, 3124.3, 3125, 3141, 5702, 5708, 6105, 9122, 9123 of this title; section 3304 of Title 5 (Athletics and Sports); sections 4321, 5329, 6303, 6304, 6344, 6702, 6711 of Title 23 (Domestic Relations); sections 5551, 5552, 6302, 6358, 6402, 6403, 9717, 9718, 9720.2, 9730.3, 9799.12, 9799.14, 9799.17, 9799.24 of Title 42 (Judiciary and Judicial Procedure); section 7122 of Title 61 (Prisons and Parole).

  § 3122. Statutory rape (Repealed).

1995 Repeal. Section 3122 was repealed March 31, 1995 (1st Sp.Sess., P.L.985, No.10), effective in 60 days.

  § 3122.1. Statutory sexual assault.

  (a) Felony of the second degree.--Except as provided in section 3121 (relating to rape), a person commits a felony of the second degree when that person engages in sexual intercourse with a complainant to whom the person is not married who is under the age of 16 years and that person is either:

    (1) four years older but less than eight years older than the complainant; or

    (2) eight years older but less than 11 years older than the complainant.

  (b) Felony of the first degree.--A person commits a felony of the first degree when that person engages in sexual intercourse with a complainant under the age of 16 years and that person is 11 or more years older than the complainant and the complainant and the person are not married to each other.

(Mar. 31, 1995, 1st Sp.Sess., P.L.985, No.10, eff. 60 days; Dec. 20, 2011, P.L.446, No.111, eff. 60 days)

Cross References. Section 3122.1 is referred to in sections 3124.2, 3124.3, 3125, 3141, 9122 of this title; sections 4321, 5329, 6303, 6344 of Title 23 (Domestic Relations); sections 5551, 5552, 6302, 9730.3, 9799.13, 9799.14, 9802 of Title 42 (Judiciary and Judicial Procedure).

§ 3123. Involuntary deviate sexual intercourse.

(a) Offense defined.--A person commits a felony of the first degree when the person engages in deviate sexual intercourse with a complainant:

(1) by forcible compulsion;

(2) by threat of forcible compulsion that would prevent resistance by a person of reasonable resolution;

(3) who is unconscious or where the person knows that the complainant is unaware that the sexual intercourse is occurring;

(4) where the person has substantially impaired the complainant's power to appraise or control his or her conduct by administering or employing, without the knowledge of the complainant, drugs, intoxicants or other means for the purpose of preventing resistance;

(5) who suffers from a mental disability which renders him or her incapable of consent; or

(6) (Deleted by amendment).

(7) who is less than 16 years of age and the person is four or more years older than the complainant and the complainant and person are not married to each other.

(b) Involuntary deviate sexual intercourse with a child.--A person commits involuntary deviate sexual intercourse with a child, a felony of the first degree, when the person engages in deviate sexual intercourse with a complainant who is less than 13 years of age.

(c) Involuntary deviate sexual intercourse with a child with serious bodily injury.--A person commits an offense under this section with a child resulting in serious bodily injury, a felony of the first degree, when the person violates this section and the complainant is less than 13 years of age and the complainant suffers serious bodily injury in the course of the offense.

(d) Sentences.--Notwithstanding the provisions of section 1103 (relating to sentence of imprisonment for felony), a person convicted of an offense under:

(1) Subsection (b) shall be sentenced to a term of imprisonment which shall be fixed by the court at not more than 40 years.

(2) Subsection (c) shall be sentenced up to a maximum term of life imprisonment.

(e) Definition.--As used in this section, the term "forcible compulsion" includes, but is not limited to, compulsion resulting in another person's death, whether the death occurred before, during or after the sexual intercourse.

(Mar. 31, 1995, 1st Sp.Sess., P.L.985, No.10, eff. 60 days; Dec. 9, 2002, P.L.1350, No.162, eff. 60 days; Dec. 16, 2002, P.L.1953, No.226, eff. 60 days)

2002 Amendments. Act 226 overlooked the amendment by Act 162, but the amendments do not conflict in substance (except for the designation of the offenses in subsecs. (b) and (c) as felonies of the first degree, as to which Act 162 has been given effect) and both have been given effect in setting forth the text of section 3123.

Effective Date. After February 6, 2003, and before February 14, 2003, section 3123 will reflect only the amendment by Act 162, as follows:

Cross References. Section 3123 is referred to in sections 1111, 2709.1, 2714, 3124.1, 3124.2, 3124.3, 3125, 3141, 5702, 5708, 6105, 9122, 9123 of this title; sections 5329, 6303, 6304, 6344, 6711 of Title 23 (Domestic Relations); sections 5551, 5552, 6302, 6358, 6402, 6403, 9717, 9718, 9720.2, 9730.3, 9799.12, 9799.14, 9799.17, 9799.24 of Title 42 (Judiciary and Judicial Procedure); section 7122 of Title 61 (Prisons and Parole).

§ 3124. Voluntary deviate sexual intercourse (Repealed).

1995 Repeal. Section 3124 was repealed March 31, 1995 (1st Sp.Sess., P.L.985, No.10), effective in 60 days.

§ 3124.1. Sexual assault.

Except as provided in section 3121 (relating to rape) or 3123 (relating to involuntary deviate sexual intercourse), a person commits a felony of the second degree when that person engages in sexual intercourse or deviate sexual intercourse with a complainant without the complainant's consent.

(Mar. 31, 1995, 1st Sp.Sess., P.L.985, No.10, eff. 60 days)

1995 Amendment. Act 10, 1st Sp.Sess., added section 3124.1. Section 18 of Act 10, 1st Sp.Sess., provided that section 3124.1 shall apply to offenses committed on or after the effective date of Act 10.

Cross References. Section 3124.1 is referred to in sections 3124.2, 3124.3, 3125, 3141, 5702, 5708, 9122 of this title; sections 4321, 5329, 6303, 6304, 6344 of Title 23 (Domestic Relations); sections 5551, 5552, 6302, 6307, 6308, 6358, 6402, 6403, 9730.3, 9799.14, 9799.24 of Title 42 (Judiciary and Judicial Procedure).

§ 3124.2. Institutional sexual assault.

(a) General rule.--Except as provided under subsection (a.1) and in sections 3121 (relating to rape), 3122.1 (relating to statutory sexual assault), 3123 (relating to involuntary deviate sexual intercourse), 3124.1 (relating to sexual assault) and 3125 (relating to aggravated indecent assault), a person who is an employee or agent of the Department of Corrections or a county correctional authority, youth development center, youth forestry camp, State or county juvenile detention facility, other licensed residential facility serving children and youth, or mental health or mental retardation facility or institution commits a felony of the third degree when that person engages in sexual intercourse, deviate sexual intercourse or indecent contact with an inmate, detainee, patient or resident.

(a.1) Institutional sexual assault of a minor.--A person who is an employee or agent of the Department of Corrections or a county correctional authority, youth development center, youth forestry camp, State or county juvenile detention facility, other licensed residential facility serving children and youth or mental health or mental retardation facility or institution commits a felony of the third degree when that person engages in sexual intercourse, deviate sexual intercourse or indecent contact with an inmate, detainee, patient or resident who is under 18 years of age.

(a.2) Schools.--

(1) Except as provided in sections 3121, 3122.1, 3123, 3124.1 and 3125, a person who is a volunteer or an employee of a school or any other person who has direct contact with a student at a school commits a felony of the third degree when he engages in sexual intercourse, deviate sexual intercourse or indecent contact with a student of the school.

(2) As used in this subsection, the following terms shall have the meanings given to them in this paragraph:

(i) "Direct contact." Care, supervision, guidance or control.

(ii) "Employee."

(A) Includes:

(I) A teacher, a supervisor, a supervising principal, a principal, an assistant principal, a vice principal, a director of vocational education, a dental hygienist, a visiting teacher, a home and school visitor, a school counselor, a child nutrition program specialist, a school librarian, a school secretary the selection of whom is on the basis of merit as determined by eligibility lists, a school nurse, a substitute teacher, a janitor, a cafeteria worker, a bus driver, a teacher aide and any other employee who has direct contact with school students.

(II) An independent contractor who has a contract with a school for the purpose of performing a service for the school, a coach, an athletic trainer, a coach hired as an independent contractor by the Pennsylvania Interscholastic Athletic Association or an athletic trainer hired as an independent contractor by the Pennsylvania Interscholastic Athletic Association.

(B) The term does not include:

(I) A student employed at the school.

(II) An independent contractor or any employee of an independent contractor who has no direct contact with school students.

(iii) "School." A public or private school, intermediate unit or area vocational-technical school.

(iv) "Volunteer." The term does not include a school student.

(a.3) Child care.--Except as provided in sections 3121, 3122.1, 3123, 3124.1 and 3125, a person who is a volunteer or an employee of a center for children commits a felony of the third degree when he engages in sexual intercourse, deviate sexual intercourse or indecent contact with a child who is receiving services at the center.

(b) Definitions.--As used in this section, the following words and phrases shall have the meanings given to them in this subsection unless the context clearly indicates otherwise:

"Agent." A person who is assigned to work in a State or county correctional or juvenile detention facility, a youth development center, youth forestry camp, other licensed residential facility serving children and youth or mental health or mental retardation facility or institution, who is employed by any State or county agency or any person employed by an entity providing contract services to the agency.

"Center for children." Includes a child day-care center, group and family day-care home, boarding home for children, a center providing early intervention and drug and alcohol services for children or other facility which provides child-care services which are subject to approval, licensure, registration or certification by the Department of Public Welfare or a county social services agency or which are provided pursuant to a contract with the department or a county social services agency. The term does not include a youth development center, youth forestry camp, State or county juvenile detention facility and other licensed residential facility serving children and youth.

(Dec. 21, 1998, P.L.1240, No.157, eff. 60 days; May 10, 2000, P.L.38, No.12, eff. imd.; Dec. 20, 2011, P.L.446, No.111, eff. 60 days)

References in Text. The Department of Public Welfare, referred to in this section, was redesignated as the Department of Human Services by Act 132 of 2014.

Section 27 of Act 16 of 2019 provided that a reference in statute or regulation to "area vocational-technical school" shall be deemed a reference to "area career and technical school," and a reference in statute or regulation to "vocational curriculums" shall be deemed a reference to "career and technical curriculums."

Cross References. Section 3124.2 is referred to in sections 4321, 5329, 6303 of Title 23 (Domestic Relations); sections 5551, 5552, 9730.3, 9799.14 of Title 42 (Judiciary and Judicial Procedure).

§ 3124.3. Sexual assault by sports official, volunteer or employee of nonprofit association.

(a) Sports official.--Except as provided in sections 3121 (relating to rape), 3122.1 (relating to statutory sexual assault), 3123 (relating to involuntary deviate sexual intercourse), 3124.1 (relating to sexual assault) and 3125 (relating to aggravated indecent assault), a person who serves as a sports official in a sports program of a nonprofit association or a for-profit association commits a felony of the third degree when that person engages in sexual intercourse, deviate sexual intercourse or indecent contact with a child under 18 years of age who is participating in a sports program of the nonprofit association or for-profit association.

(b) Volunteer or employee of nonprofit association.--Except as provided in sections 3121, 3122.1, 3123, 3124.1 and 3125, a volunteer or an employee of a nonprofit association having direct contact with a child under 18 years of age who participates in a program or activity of the nonprofit association commits a felony of the third degree if the volunteer or employee engages in sexual intercourse, deviate sexual intercourse or indecent contact with that child.

(c) Definitions.--As used in this section, the following words and phrases shall have the meanings given to them in this subsection unless the context clearly indicates otherwise:

"**Direct contact.**" Care, supervision, guidance or control.

"**Nonprofit association.**" As defined in 42 Pa.C.S. § 8332.1 (relating to manager, coach, umpire or referee and nonprofit association negligence standard).

"**Sports official.**" A person who supervises children participating in a sports program of a nonprofit association or a for-profit association, including, but not limited to, a coach, assistant coach, athletic trainer, team attendant, game manager, instructor or a person at a sports program who enforces the rules of a sporting event sponsored by a sports program of a nonprofit association or a for-profit association, including, but not limited to, an umpire or referee, whether receiving remuneration or holding the position as a volunteer.

"**Sports program.**" As defined in 42 Pa.C.S. § 8332.1.

(June 18, 2014, P.L.741, No.56, eff. 60 days)

2014 Amendment. Act 56 added section 3124.3.

§ 3125. Aggravated indecent assault.

(a) Offenses defined.--Except as provided in sections 3121 (relating to rape), 3122.1 (relating to statutory sexual assault), 3123 (relating to involuntary deviate sexual intercourse) and 3124.1 (relating to sexual assault), a person who engages in penetration, however slight, of the genitals or anus of a complainant with a part of the person's body for any purpose other than good faith medical, hygienic or law enforcement procedures commits aggravated indecent assault if:

(1) the person does so without the complainant's consent;

(2) the person does so by forcible compulsion;

(3) the person does so by threat of forcible compulsion that would prevent resistance by a person of reasonable resolution;

(4) the complainant is unconscious or the person knows that the complainant is unaware that the penetration is occurring;

(5) the person has substantially impaired the complainant's power to appraise or control his or her conduct by administering or employing, without the knowledge of the complainant, drugs, intoxicants or other means for the purpose of preventing resistance;

(6) the complainant suffers from a mental disability which renders him or her incapable of consent;

(7) the complainant is less than 13 years of age; or

(8) the complainant is less than 16 years of age and the person is four or more years older than the complainant and the complainant and the person are not married to each other.

(b) Aggravated indecent assault of a child.--A person commits aggravated indecent assault of a child when the person violates subsection (a)(1), (2), (3), (4), (5) or (6) and the complainant is less than 13 years of age.

(c) Grading and sentences.--

(1) An offense under subsection (a) is a felony of the second degree.

(2) An offense under subsection (b) is a felony of the first degree.

(Feb. 2, 1990, P.L.6, No.4, eff. 60 days; Mar. 31, 1995, 1st Sp.Sess., P.L.985, No.10, eff. 60 days; Dec. 9, 2002, P.L.1350, No.162, eff. 60 days; Dec. 16, 2002, P.L.1953, No.226, eff. 60 days)

2002 Amendments. The amendments by Acts 162 and 226 are identical and therefore have been merged.

Prior Provisions. Former section 3125, which related to corruption of minors, was added December 6, 1972 (P.L.1482, No.334), and repealed July 1, 1978 (P.L.573, No.104), effective in 60 days.

Cross References. Section 3125 is referred to in sections 1111, 2714, 3124.2, 3124.3, 3141, 5702, 5708, 6105, 9122, 9123 of this title; sections 5329, 6303, 6304, 6344 of Title 23 (Domestic Relations); sections 5551, 5552, 6302, 6307, 6308, 6358, 6402, 6403, 9718, 9730.3, 9799.12, 9799.14, 9977.17, 9799.24 of Title 42 (Judiciary and Judicial Procedure); section 7122 of Title 61 (Prisons and Parole).

§ 3126. Indecent assault.

(a) Offense defined.--A person is guilty of indecent assault if the person has indecent contact with the complainant, causes the complainant to have indecent contact with the person or intentionally causes the complainant to come into contact with seminal fluid, urine or feces for the purpose of arousing sexual desire in the person or the complainant and:

(1) the person does so without the complainant's consent;

(2) the person does so by forcible compulsion;

(3) the person does so by threat of forcible compulsion that would prevent resistance by a person of reasonable resolution;

(4) the complainant is unconscious or the person knows that the complainant is unaware that the indecent contact is occurring;

(5) the person has substantially impaired the complainant's power to appraise or control his or her conduct by administering or employing, without the knowledge of the complainant, drugs, intoxicants or other means for the purpose of preventing resistance;

(6) the complainant suffers from a mental disability which renders the complainant incapable of consent;

(7) the complainant is less than 13 years of age; or

(8) the complainant is less than 16 years of age and the person is four or more years older than the complainant and the complainant and the person are not married to each other.

(b) Grading.--Indecent assault shall be graded as follows:

(1) An offense under subsection (a)(1) or (8) is a misdemeanor of the second degree.

(2) An offense under subsection (a)(2), (3), (4), (5) or (6) is a misdemeanor of the first degree.

(3) An offense under subsection (a)(7) is a misdemeanor of the first degree unless any of the following apply, in which case it is a felony of the third degree:

(i) It is a second or subsequent offense.

(ii) There has been a course of conduct of indecent assault by the person.

(iii) The indecent assault was committed by touching the complainant's sexual or intimate parts with sexual or intimate parts of the person.

(iv) The indecent assault is committed by touching the person's sexual or intimate parts with the complainant's sexual or intimate parts.

(May 18, 1976, P.L.120, No.53, eff. 30 days; Feb. 2, 1990, P.L.6, No.4, eff. 60 days; Mar. 31, 1995, 1st Sp.Sess., P.L.985, No.10, eff. 60 days; Nov. 23, 2005, P.L.412, No.76, eff. 60 days)

Cross References. Section 3126 is referred to in sections 2714, 3141, 9122 of this title; section 3304 of Title 5 (Athletics and Sports); sections 5329, 6303, 6304, 6344 of Title 23 (Domestic Relations); sections 5552, 6302, 6358, 6402, 6403, 9730.3, 9799.13, 9799.14, 9799.24 of Title 42 (Judiciary and Judicial Procedure); section 2303 of Title 44 (Law and Justice); section 7122 of Title 61 (Prisons and Parole).

§ 3127. Indecent exposure.

(a) Offense defined.--A person commits indecent exposure if that person exposes his or her genitals in any public place or in any place where there are present other persons under circumstances in which he or she knows or should know that this conduct is likely to offend, affront or alarm.

(b) Grading.--If the person knows or should have known that any of the persons present are less than 16 years of age, indecent exposure under subsection (a) is a misdemeanor of the first degree. Otherwise, indecent exposure under subsection (a) is a misdemeanor of the second degree.

(Mar. 31, 1995, 1st Sp.Sess., P.L.985, No.10, eff. 60 days)

1995 Amendment. Section 18 of Act 10, 1st Sp.Sess., provided that the amendment of section 3127 shall apply to offenses committed on or after the effective date of Act 10.

Cross References. Section 3127 is referred to in sections 9122, 9122.1, 9122.3 of this title; sections 5329, 6303, 6304, 6344 of Title 23 (Domestic Relations); sections 5552, 9730.3 of Title 42 (Judiciary and Judicial Procedure); section 2303 of Title 44 (Law and Justice).

§ 3128. Spousal sexual assault (Repealed).

1995 Repeal. Section 3128 was repealed March 31, 1995 (1st Sp.Sess., P.L.985, No.10), effective in 60 days.

§ 3129. Sexual intercourse with animal.

A person who engages in any form of sexual intercourse with an animal commits a misdemeanor of the second degree.

(June 18, 1999, P.L.67, No.8, eff. 60 days)

1999 Amendment. Act 8 added section 3129.

Cross References. Section 3129 is referred to in sections 9122.1, 9122.3 of this title; section 5329 of Title 23 (Domestic Relations); section 62A03 of Title 42 (Judiciary and Judicial Procedure).

§ 3130. Conduct relating to sex offenders.

(a) Offense defined.--A person commits a felony of the third degree if the person has reason to believe that a sex offender is not complying with or has not complied with the requirements of the sex offender's probation or parole, imposed by statute or court order, or with the registration requirements of 42 Pa.C.S. Ch. 97 Subch. H (relating to registration of sexual offenders) or I (relating to continued registration of sexual offenders), and the person, with the intent to assist the sex offender in eluding a law enforcement agent or agency that is seeking to find the sex offender to question the sex offender about, or to arrest the sex offender for, noncompliance with the requirements of the sex offender's probation or parole or the requirements of 42 Pa.C.S. Ch. 97 Subch. H or I:

(1) withholds information from or does not notify the law enforcement agent or agency about the sex offender's noncompliance with the requirements of parole, the requirements of 42 Pa.C.S. Ch. 97 Subch. H or I or, if known, the sex offender's whereabouts;

(2) harbors or attempts to harbor or assist another person in harboring or attempting to harbor the sex offender;

(3) conceals or attempts to conceal, or assists another person in concealing or attempting to conceal, the sex offender; or

(4) provides information to the law enforcement agent or agency regarding the sex offender which the person knows to be false.

(b) Definition.--As used in this section, the term "sex offender" means a person who is required to register with the Pennsylvania State Police pursuant to the provisions of 42 Pa.C.S. Ch. 97 Subch. H or I.

(Nov. 29, 2006, P.L.1567, No.178, eff. Jan. 1, 2007; Dec. 20, 2011, P.L.446, No.111, eff. one year; Feb. 21, 2018, P.L.27, No.10, eff. imd.; June 12, 2018, P.L.140, No.29, eff. imd.)

2018 Amendment. Act 29 reenacted section 3130.

2006 Amendment. See the preamble to Act 178 in the appendix to this title for special provisions relating to legislative intent.

Cross References. Section 3130 is referred to in section 5329 of Title 23 (Domestic Relations).

§ 3131. Unlawful dissemination of intimate image.

(a) Offense defined.--Except as provided in sections 5903 (relating to obscene and other sexual materials and performances), 6312 (relating to sexual abuse of children) and 6321 (relating to transmission of sexually explicit images by minor), a person commits the offense of unlawful dissemination of intimate image if, with intent to harass, annoy or alarm a current or former sexual or intimate partner, the person disseminates a visual depiction of the current or former sexual or intimate partner in a state of nudity or engaged in sexual conduct.

(b) Defense.--It is a defense to a prosecution under this section that the actor disseminated the visual depiction with the consent of the person depicted.

(c) Grading.--An offense under subsection (a) shall be:

(1) A misdemeanor of the first degree, when the person depicted is a minor.

(2) A misdemeanor of the second degree, when the person depicted is not a minor.

(d) Territorial applicability.--A person may be convicted under the provisions of this section if the victim or the offender is located within this Commonwealth.

(e) Nonapplicability.--Nothing in this section shall be construed to apply to a law enforcement officer engaged in the performance of the law enforcement officer's official duties.

(f) Concurrent jurisdiction to prosecute.--In addition to the authority conferred upon the Attorney General by the act of October 15, 1980 (P.L.950, No.164), known as the Commonwealth Attorneys Act, the Attorney General shall have the authority to investigate and to institute criminal proceedings for any violation of this section or any series of violations involving more than one county of this Commonwealth or another state. No person charged with a violation of this section by the Attorney General shall have standing to challenge the authority of the Attorney General to investigate or prosecute the case, and, if a challenge is made, the challenge shall be dismissed, and no relief shall be made available in the courts of this Commonwealth to the person making the challenge.

(g) Definitions.--As used in this section, the following words and phrases shall have the meanings given to them in this subsection unless the context clearly indicates otherwise:

"Law enforcement officer." Any officer of the United States, of the Commonwealth or political subdivision thereof, or of another state or subdivision thereof, who is empowered to conduct investigations of or to make arrests for offenses enumerated in this title or an equivalent crime in another jurisdiction, and any attorney authorized by law to prosecute or participate in the prosecution of such offense.

"Minor." An individual under 18 years of age.

"Nudity." As defined in section 5903(e).

"Sexual conduct." As defined in section 5903(e).

"Visual depiction." As defined in section 6321.

(July 9, 2014, P.L.1013, No.115, eff. 60 days)

2014 Amendment. Act 115 added section 3131.

Cross References. Section 3131 is referred to in section 8316.1 of Title 42 (Judiciary and Judicial Procedure).

§ 3132. Female mutilation.

(a) Offense defined.--A person commits the offense of female mutilation if the person:

(1) knowingly circumcises, excises or infibulates the whole or any part of the genitalia of a minor;

(2) is a parent of a minor and the parent knowingly consents or permits the circumcision, excision or infibulation of the whole or any part of the minor's genitalia; or

(3) knowingly removes or permits the removal of a minor from this Commonwealth for the purpose of circumcising, excising or infibulating, in whole or in part, the genitalia of the minor.

(b) Grading.--Female mutilation is a felony of the first degree.

(c) **Exception.**--The provisions of subsection (a) shall not apply if the circumcision, excision or infibulation is:

(1) necessary to the health of the minor on whom it is performed and either is performed by a physician or is performed in the presence of a physician by a person in training to become a physician in accordance with the act of October 5, 1978 (P.L.1109, No.261), known as the Osteopathic Medical Practice Act, or the act of December 20, 1985 (P.L.457, No.112), known as the Medical Practice Act of 1985; or

(2) performed on a minor in labor or who has just given birth and is performed for medical reasons connected with that labor or birth by a physician or in the presence of a physician by a person in training to become a physician in accordance with the Osteopathic Medical Practice Act or the Medical Practice Act of 1985.

(d) **Custom or consent not a defense.**--It shall not be a defense to a prosecution under this section that:

(1) the actor believed that the procedure was necessary or appropriate as a matter of custom, ritual or standard practice; or

(2) the minor upon whom the circumcision, excision or infibulation was performed consented to the procedure or that the minor's parent consented to the procedure.

(e) **Definitions.**--As used in this section, the following words and phrases shall have the meanings given to them in this subsection unless the context clearly indicates otherwise:

"**Minor.**" A natural person who is a female under 18 years of age.

"**Parent.**" The term includes a natural parent, stepparent, adoptive parent, guardian or custodian of the minor.

(June 28, 2019, P.L.210, No.21, eff. 60 days)

2019 Amendment. Act 21 added section 3132.

§ 3133. Sexual extortion.

(a) **Offense defined.**--A person commits the offense of sexual extortion if the person knowingly or intentionally coerces or causes a complainant, through any means set forth in subsection (b), to:

(1) engage in sexual conduct, the simulation of sexual conduct or a state of nudity; or

(2) make, produce, disseminate, transmit or distribute any image, video, recording or other material depicting the complainant in a state of nudity or engaging in sexual conduct or in the simulation of sexual conduct.

(b) **Means of subjecting complainant to sexual extortion.**--A person subjects a complainant to sexual extortion through any of the following means:

(1) Harming or threatening to harm the complainant or the property of the complainant, the reputation of the complainant or any other thing of value of the complainant.

(2) Making, producing, disseminating, transmitting or distributing or threatening to make, produce, disseminate, transmit or distribute any image, video, recording or other material depicting the complainant in a state of nudity or engaged in sexual conduct or in the simulation of sexual conduct.

(3) Exposing or threatening to expose any fact or piece of information that, if revealed, would tend to subject the complainant to criminal proceedings, a civil action, hatred, contempt, embarrassment or ridicule.

(4) Holding out, withholding or threatening to withhold a service, employment, position or other thing of value.

(5) Threatening to cause or causing a loss, disadvantage or injury, including a loss, disadvantage or injury to a family or household member.

(c) **Demanding property.**--A person commits the offense of sexual extortion if the person knowingly or intentionally:

(1) solicits or demands the payment of money, property or services or any other thing of value from the complainant or a family or household member of the complainant in exchange for removing from public view or preventing the disclosure of any image, video, recording or other material obtained through a violation of subsection (a)(2); or

(2) disseminates, transmits or distributes, or threatens to disseminate, transmit or distribute, an image, video, recording or other material depicting the complainant in a state of nudity or engaging in sexual conduct or the simulation of sexual conduct to another person or entity, including a commercial social networking site, and solicits or demands the payment of money, property or services or any other thing of value from the complainant or a family or household member of the complainant in exchange for removing from public view or preventing disclosure of the image, video, recording or other material.

(d) Grading.--

(1) Except as otherwise provided in paragraphs (2) and (3), a violation of this section shall constitute a misdemeanor of the first degree.

(2) A violation of this section shall constitute a felony of the third degree if the actor is at least 18 years of age and:

(i) the complainant is under 18 years of age;

(ii) the complainant has an intellectual disability; or

(iii) the actor holds a position of trust or supervisory or disciplinary power over the complainant by virtue of the actor's legal, professional or occupational status.

(3) A violation of this section shall constitute a felony of the third degree if:

(i) the violation is part of a course of conduct of sexual extortion by the actor; or

(ii) the actor was previously convicted or adjudicated delinquent of a violation of this section or of a similar offense in another jurisdiction.

(e) **Sentencing.**--The Pennsylvania Commission on Sentencing, in accordance with 42 Pa.C.S. § 2154 (relating to adoption of guidelines for sentencing), shall provide for a sentence enhancement within its guidelines for an offense under this section when at the time of the offense the complainant is under 18 years of age or has an intellectual disability or the actor holds a position of trust or supervisory or disciplinary power over the complainant by virtue of the actor's legal, professional or occupational status.

(f) Venue.--

(1) An offense committed under this section may be deemed to have been committed at either the place at which the communication was made or at the place where the communication was received.

(2) Acts indicating a course of conduct which occur in more than one jurisdiction may be used by any other jurisdiction in which an act occurred as evidence of a continuing pattern of conduct or a course of conduct.

(g) **Territorial applicability.**--A person may be convicted under the provisions of this section if the complainant or the offender is located within this Commonwealth.

(h) **Concurrent jurisdiction to prosecute.**--In addition to the authority conferred upon the Attorney General by the act of October 15, 1980 (P.L.950, No.164), known as the Commonwealth Attorneys Act, the Attorney General shall have the authority to investigate and to institute criminal proceedings for any violation of this section or any series of violations involving more than one county of this Commonwealth or another state. No person charged with a violation of this section by the Attorney General shall have standing to challenge the authority of the Attorney General to investigate or prosecute the case, and, if a challenge is made, the challenge shall be dismissed, and no relief shall be made available in the courts of this Commonwealth to the person making the challenge.

(i) **Applicability.**--Nothing in this section shall be construed to apply to:

(1) A person who acts within the legitimate and lawful course of the person's employment.

(2) Works of public interest, including commentary, satire or parody.

(j) **Definitions.**--As used in this section, the following words and phrases shall have the meanings given to them in this subsection unless the context clearly indicates otherwise:

"**Commercial social networking site.**" A business, organization or other similar entity that operates an Internet website and permits persons to become registered users for the purposes of establishing personal relationships with other users through direct or real-time communication with other users or the creation of web pages or profiles available to the public or to other users. The term does not include an electronic mail program or a message board program.

"**Course of conduct.**" A pattern of actions composed of more than one act over a period of time, however short, evidencing a continuity of conduct.

"**Disseminate.**" To cause or make an electronic or actual communication from one place or electronic communication device to two or more other persons, places or electronic communication devices.

"**Distribute.**" To sell, lend, rent, lease, give, advertise, publish or exhibit in a physical or electronic medium.

"**Family or household member.**" As defined in section 2709.1(f) (relating to stalking).

"**Intellectual disability.**" Regardless of the age of the individual, significantly subaverage general intellectual functioning that is accompanied by significant limitations in adaptive functioning in at least two of the following skill areas: communication; self-care; home living; social and interpersonal skills; use of community resources'; self-direction; functional academic skills; work; health; and safety.

"**Nudity.**" As defined in section 5903(e) (relating to obscene and other sexual materials and performances).

"**Sexual conduct.**" Any of the following:

(1) Intentional touching by the complainant or actor, either directly or through clothing, of the complainant's or actor's intimate parts. Sexual contact of the actor with himself must be in view of the complainant whom the actor knows to be present.

(2) Sexual intercourse as defined in section 3101 (relating to definitions), masturbation, sadism, masochism, bestiality, fellatio, cunnilingus or lewd exhibition of the genitals.

"**Simulation.**" Conduct engaged in that is depicted in a manner that would cause a reasonable viewer to believe was sexual conduct, even if sexual conduct did not occur.

"**Transmit.**" To cause or make an electronic or actual communication from one place or electronic communication device to another person, place or electronic communication device.

(Nov. 27, 2019, P.L.691, No.100, eff. 60 days)

2019 Amendment. Act 100 added section 3133.

SUBCHAPTER C
LOSS OF PROPERTY RIGHTS

Sec.
3141. General rule.
3142. Process and seizure (Repealed).
3143. Custody of property (Repealed).
3144. Disposal of property(Repealed).

Enactment. Subchapter C was added November 29, 2006, P.L.1567, No.178, effective January 1, 2007.

Special Provisions in Appendix. See the preamble to Act 178 of 2006 in the appendix to this title for special provisions relating to legislative intent.

§ 3141. General rule.

A person:

(1) convicted under section 3121 (relating to rape), 3122.1 (relating to statutory sexual assault), 3123 (relating to involuntary deviate sexual intercourse), 3124.1 (relating to sexual assault), 3125 (relating to aggravated indecent assault) or 3126 (relating to indecent assault); or

(2) required to register with the Pennsylvania State Police under 42 Pa.C.S. Ch. 97 Subch. H (relating to registration of sexual offenders) or I (relating to continued registration of sexual offenders);

may be required to forfeit property rights in any property or assets used to implement or facilitate commission of the crime or crimes of which the person has been convicted. The forfeiture shall be conducted in accordance with 42 Pa.C.S. §§ 5803 (relating to asset forfeiture), 5805 (relating to forfeiture procedure), 5806 (relating to motion for return of property), 5807 (relating to restrictions on use), 5807.1 (relating to prohibition on adoptive seizures) and 5808 (relating to exceptions).

(Dec. 20, 2011, P.L.446, No.111, eff. one year; June 29, 2017, P.L.247, No.13, eff. July 1, 2017; Feb. 21, 2018, P.L.27, No.10, eff. imd.; June 12, 2018, P.L.140, No.29, eff. imd.)

2018 Amendment. Act 29 reenacted section 3141.

Cross References. Section 3141 is referred to in section 5803 of Title 42 (Judiciary and Judicial Procedure).

§ 3142. Process and seizure (Repealed).

2017 Repeal. Section 3142 was repealed June 29, 2017, P.L.247, No.13, effective July 1, 2017.

§ 3143. Custody of property (Repealed).

2017 Repeal. Section 3143 was repealed June 29, 2017, P.L.247, No.13, effective July 1, 2017.

§ 3144. Disposal of property (Repealed).

2017 Repeal. Section 3144 was repealed June 29, 2017, P.L.247, No.13, effective July 1, 2017.

CHAPTER 32
ABORTION

Sec.
3201. Short title of chapter.

Enactment. Chapter 32 was added June 11, 1982, P.L.476, No.138, effective in 180 days.

§ 3201. Short title of chapter.

This chapter shall be known and may be cited as the "Abortion Control Act."

§ 3202. Legislative intent.

(a) **Rights and interests.**--It is the intention of the General Assembly of the Commonwealth of Pennsylvania to protect hereby the life and health of the woman subject to abortion and to protect the life and health of the child subject to abortion. It is the further intention of the General Assembly to foster the development of standards of professional conduct in a critical area of medical practice, to provide for development of statistical data and to protect the right of the minor woman voluntarily to decide to submit to abortion or to carry her child to term. The General Assembly finds as fact that the rights and interests furthered by this chapter are not secure in the context in which abortion is presently performed.

(b) **Conclusions.**--Reliable and convincing evidence has compelled the General Assembly to conclude and the General Assembly does hereby solemnly declare and find that:

(1) Many women now seek or are encouraged to undergo abortions without full knowledge of the development of the unborn child or of alternatives to abortion.

(2) The gestational age at which viability of an unborn child occurs has been lowering substantially and steadily as advances in neonatal medical care continue to be made.

(3) A significant number of late-term abortions result in live births, or in delivery of children who could survive if measures were taken to bring about breathing. Some physicians have been allowing these children to die or have been failing to induce breathing.

(4) Because the Commonwealth places a supreme value upon protecting human life, it is necessary that those physicians which it permits to practice medicine be held to precise standards of care in cases where their actions do or may result in the death of an unborn child.

(5) A reasonable waiting period, as contained in this chapter, is critical to the assurance that a woman elect to undergo an abortion procedure only after having the fullest opportunity to give her informed consent thereto.

(c) **Construction.**--In every relevant civil or criminal proceeding in which it is possible to do so without violating the Federal Constitution, the common and statutory law of Pennsylvania shall be construed so as to extend to the unborn the equal protection of the laws and to further the public policy of this Commonwealth encouraging childbirth over abortion.

(d) **Right of conscience.**--It is the further public policy of the Commonwealth of Pennsylvania to respect and protect the right of conscience of all persons who refuse to obtain, receive, subsidize, accept or provide abortions including those persons who are engaged in the delivery of medical services and medical care whether acting individually, corporately or in association with other persons; and to prohibit all forms of discrimination, disqualification, coercion, disability or imposition of liability or financial burden upon such persons or entities by reason of their refusing to act contrary to their conscience or conscientious convictions in refusing to obtain, receive, subsidize, accept or provide abortions.

§ 3203. Definitions.

The following words and phrases when used in this chapter shall have, unless the

114

context clearly indicates otherwise, the meanings given to them in this section:

"Abortion." The use of any means to terminate the clinically diagnosable pregnancy of a woman with knowledge that the termination by those means will, with reasonable likelihood, cause the death of the unborn child except that, for the purposes of this chapter, abortion shall not mean the use of an intrauterine device or birth control pill to inhibit or prevent ovulation, fertilization or the implantation of a fertilized ovum within the uterus.

"Born alive." When used with regard to a human being, means that the human being was completely expelled or extracted from her or his mother and after such separation breathed or showed evidence of any of the following: beating of the heart, pulsation of the umbilical cord, definite movement of voluntary muscles or any brain-wave activity.

"Complication." Includes but is not limited to hemorrhage, infection, uterine perforation, cervical laceration and retained products. The department may further define complication.

"Conscience." A sincerely held set of moral convictions arising from belief in and relation to a deity or which, though not so derived, obtains from a place in the life of its possessor parallel to that filled by a deity among adherents to religious faiths.

"Department." The Department of Health of the Commonwealth of Pennsylvania.

"Facility" or **"medical facility."** Any public or private hospital, clinic, center, medical school, medical training institution, health care facility, physician's office, infirmary, dispensary, ambulatory surgical treatment center or other institution or location wherein medical care is provided to any person.

"Fertilization" and "conception." Each term shall mean the fusion of a human spermatozoon with a human ovum.

"First trimester." The first 12 weeks of gestation.

"Gestational age." The age of the unborn child as calculated from the first day of the last menstrual period of the pregnant woman.

"Hospital." An institution licensed pursuant to the provisions of the law of this Commonwealth.

"In vitro fertilization." The purposeful fertilization of a human ovum outside the body of a living human female.

"Medical emergency." That condition which, on the basis of the physician's good faith clinical judgment, so complicates the medical condition of a pregnant woman as to necessitate the immediate abortion of her pregnancy to avert her death or for which a delay will create serious risk of substantial and irreversible impairment of major bodily function.

"Medical personnel." Any nurse, nurse's aide, medical school student, professional or any other person who furnishes, or assists in the furnishing of, medical care.

"Physician." Any person licensed to practice medicine in this Commonwealth. The term includes medical doctors and doctors of osteopathy.

"Pregnancy" and "pregnant." Each term shall mean that female reproductive condition of having a developing fetus in the body and commences with fertilization.

"Probable gestational age of the unborn child." What, in the judgment of the attending physician, will with reasonable probability be the gestational age of the unborn child at the time the abortion is planned to be performed.

"Unborn child" and "fetus." Each term shall mean an individual organism of the species homo sapiens from fertilization until live birth.

"Viability." That stage of fetal development when, in the judgment of the physician based on the particular facts of the case before him and in light of the most advanced medical technology and information available to him, there is a reasonable likelihood of sustained survival of the unborn child outside the body of his or her mother, with or without artificial support.

(Dec. 18, 1984, P.L.1057, No.207, eff. imd.; Mar. 25, 1988, P.L.262, No.31, eff. 30 days; Nov. 17, 1989, P.L.592, No.64, eff. 60 days)

1989 Amendment. Act 64 amended the defs. of "fertilization," "pregnancy" and "unborn child" and added the def. of "gestational age."

1988 Amendment. Act 31 amended the def. of "medical emergency" and added the def. of "physician."

Cross References. Section 3203 is referred to in section 2602 of this title; section 3301 of Title 40 (Insurance).

§ 3204. Medical consultation and judgment.

(a) Abortion prohibited; exceptions.-- No abortion shall be performed except by a physician after either:

(1) he determines that, in his best clinical judgment, the abortion is necessary; or

(2) he receives what he reasonably believes to be a written statement signed by another physician, hereinafter called the "referring physician," certifying that in this referring physician's best clinical judgment the abortion is necessary.

(b) Requirements.-- Except in a medical emergency where there is insufficient time before the abortion is performed, the woman upon whom the abortion is to be performed shall have a private medical consultation either with the physician who is to perform the abortion or with the referring physician. The consultation will be in a place, at a time and of a duration reasonably sufficient to enable the physician to determine whether, based on his best clinical judgment, the abortion is necessary.

(c) Factors.-- In determining in accordance with subsection (a) or (b) whether an abortion is necessary, a physician's best clinical judgment may be exercised in the light of all factors (physical, emotional, psychological, familial and the woman's age) relevant to the well-being of the woman. No abortion which is sought solely because of the sex of the unborn child shall be deemed a necessary abortion.

(d) Penalty.-- Any person who intentionally, knowingly or recklessly violates the provisions of this section commits a felony of the third degree, and any physician who violates the provisions of this section is guilty of "unprofessional conduct" and his license for the practice of medicine and surgery shall be subject to suspension or revocation in accordance with procedures provided under the act of October 5, 1978 (P.L.1109, No.261), known as the Osteopathic Medical Practice Act, the act of December 20, 1985 (P.L.457, No.112), known as the Medical Practice Act of 1985, or their successor acts.

(Mar. 25, 1988, P.L.262, No.31, eff. 30 days; Nov. 17, 1989, P.L.592, No.64, eff. 60 days)

1989 Amendment. Act 64 amended subsecs. (c) and (d).

Cross References. Section 3204 is referred to in section 3217 of this title.

§ 3205. Informed consent.

(a) General rule.-- No abortion shall be performed or induced except with the voluntary and informed consent of the woman upon whom the abortion is to be performed or induced. Except in the case of a medical emergency, consent to an abortion is voluntary and informed if and only if:

(1) At least 24 hours prior to the abortion, the physician who is to perform the abortion or the referring physician has orally informed the woman of:

(i) The nature of the proposed procedure or treatment and of those risks and alternatives to the procedure or treatment that a reasonable patient would consider material to the decision of whether or not to undergo the abortion.

(ii) The probable gestational age of the unborn child at the time the abortion is to be performed.

(iii) The medical risks associated with carrying her child to term.

(2) At least 24 hours prior to the abortion, the physician who is to perform the abortion or the referring physician, or a qualified physician assistant, health care practitioner, technician or social worker to whom the responsibility has been delegated by either physician, has informed the pregnant woman that:

(i) The department publishes printed materials which describe the unborn child and list agencies which offer alternatives to abortion and that she has a right to review the printed materials and that a copy will be provided to her free of charge if she chooses to review it.

(ii) Medical assistance benefits may be available for prenatal care, childbirth and neonatal care, and that more detailed information on the availability of such assistance is contained in the printed materials published by the department.

(iii) The father of the unborn child is liable to assist in the support of her child, even in instances where he has offered to pay for the abortion. In the case of rape, this information may be omitted.

(3) A copy of the printed materials has been provided to the pregnant woman if she chooses to view these materials.

(4) The pregnant woman certifies in writing, prior to the abortion, that the information required to be provided under paragraphs (1), (2) and (3) has been provided.

(b) Emergency.-- Where a medical emergency compels the performance of an

116

abortion, the physician shall inform the woman, prior to the abortion if possible, of the medical indications supporting his judgment that an abortion is necessary to avert her death or to avert substantial and irreversible impairment of major bodily function.

(c) Penalty.--Any physician who violates the provisions of this section is guilty of "unprofessional conduct" and his license for the practice of medicine and surgery shall be subject to suspension or revocation in accordance with procedures provided under the act of October 5, 1978 (P.L.1109, No.261), known as the Osteopathic Medical Practice Act, the act of December 20, 1985 (P.L.457, No.112), known as the Medical Practice Act of 1985, or their successor acts. Any physician who performs or induces an abortion without first obtaining the certification required by subsection (a)(4) or with knowledge or reason to know that the informed consent of the woman has not been obtained shall for the first offense be guilty of a summary offense and for each subsequent offense be guilty of a misdemeanor of the third degree. No physician shall be guilty of violating this section for failure to furnish the information required by subsection (a) if he or she can demonstrate, by a preponderance of the evidence, that he or she reasonably believed that furnishing the information would have resulted in a severely adverse effect on the physical or mental health of the patient.

(d) Limitation on civil liability.--Any physician who complies with the provisions of this section may not be held civilly liable to his patient for failure to obtain informed consent to the abortion within the meaning of that term as defined by the act of October 15, 1975 (P.L.390, No.111), known as the Health Care Services Malpractice Act.

(Mar. 25, 1988, P.L.262, No.31, eff. 30 days; Nov. 17, 1989, P.L.592, No.64, eff. 60 days)

1989 Amendment. Act 64 amended subsecs. (a) and (c).

Cross References. Section 3205 is referred to in sections 3216, 3217 of this title.

§ 3206. Parental consent.

(a) General rule.--Except in the case of a medical emergency, or except as provided in this section, if a pregnant woman is less than 18 years of age and not emancipated, or if she has been adjudged an incapacitated person under 20

Pa.C.S. § 5511 (relating to petition and hearing; independent evaluation), a physician shall not perform an abortion upon her unless, in the case of a woman who is less than 18 years of age, he first obtains the informed consent both of the pregnant woman and of one of her parents; or, in the case of a woman who is an incapacitated person, he first obtains the informed consent of her guardian. In deciding whether to grant such consent, a pregnant woman's parent or guardian shall consider only their child's or ward's best interests. In the case of a pregnancy that is the result of incest where the father is a party to the incestuous act, the pregnant woman need only obtain the consent of her mother.

(b) Unavailability of parent or guardian.--If both parents have died or are otherwise unavailable to the physician within a reasonable time and in a reasonable manner, consent of the pregnant woman's guardian or guardians shall be sufficient. If the pregnant woman's parents are divorced, consent of the parent having custody shall be sufficient. If neither any parent nor a legal guardian is available to the physician within a reasonable time and in a reasonable manner, consent of any adult person standing in loco parentis shall be sufficient.

(c) Petition to court for consent.--If both of the parents or guardians of the pregnant woman refuse to consent to the performance of an abortion or if she elects not to seek the consent of either of her parents or of her guardian, the court of common pleas of the judicial district in which the applicant resides or in which the abortion is sought shall, upon petition or motion, after an appropriate hearing, authorize a physician to perform the abortion if the court determines that the pregnant woman is mature and capable of giving informed consent to the proposed abortion, and has, in fact, given such consent.

(d) Court order.--If the court determines that the pregnant woman is not mature and capable of giving informed consent or if the pregnant woman does not claim to be mature and capable of giving informed consent, the court shall determine whether the performance of an abortion upon her would be in her best interests. If the court determines that the performance of an abortion would be in the best interests of the woman, it shall authorize a physician to perform the abortion.

(e) Representation in proceedings.--The pregnant woman may participate in proceedings in the court on her own behalf and the court may appoint a guardian ad litem to assist her. The court shall, however, advise her that she has a right to court appointed counsel, and shall provide her with such counsel unless she wishes to appear with private counsel or has knowingly and intelligently waived representation by counsel.

(f) Proceedings.--

(1) Court proceedings under this section shall be confidential and shall be given such precedence over other pending matters as will ensure that the court may reach a decision promptly and without delay in order to serve the best interests of the pregnant woman. In no case shall the court of common pleas fail to rule within three business days of the date of application. A court of common pleas which conducts proceedings under this section shall make in writing specific factual findings and legal conclusions supporting its decision and shall, upon the initial filing of the minor's petition for judicial authorization of an abortion, order a sealed record of the petition, pleadings, submissions, transcripts, exhibits, orders, evidence and any other written material to be maintained which shall include its own findings and conclusions.

(2) The application to the court of common pleas shall be accompanied by a non-notarized verification stating that the information therein is true and correct to the best of the applicant's knowledge, and the application shall set forth the following facts:

(i) The initials of the pregnant woman.

(ii) The age of the pregnant woman.

(iii) The names and addresses of each parent, guardian or, if the minor's parents are deceased and no guardian has been appointed, any other person standing in loco parentis to the minor.

(iv) That the pregnant woman has been fully informed of the risks and consequences of the abortion.

(v) Whether the pregnant woman is of sound mind and has sufficient intellectual capacity to consent to the abortion.

(vi) A prayer for relief asking the court to either grant the pregnant woman full capacity for the purpose of personal consent to the abortion, or to give judicial consent to the abortion under subsection (d) based upon a finding that the abortion is in the best interest of the pregnant woman.

(vii) That the pregnant woman is aware that any false statements made in the application are punishable by law.

(viii) The signature of the pregnant woman. Where necessary to serve the interest of justice, the orphans' court division, or, in Philadelphia, the family court division, shall refer the pregnant woman to the appropriate personnel for assistance in preparing the application.

(3) The name of the pregnant woman shall not be entered on any docket which is subject to public inspection. All persons shall be excluded from hearings under this section except the applicant and such other persons whose presence is specifically requested by the applicant or her guardian.

(4) At the hearing, the court shall hear evidence relating to the emotional development, maturity, intellect and understanding of the pregnant woman, the fact and duration of her pregnancy, the nature, possible consequences and alternatives to the abortion and any other evidence that the court may find useful in determining whether the pregnant woman should be granted full capacity for the purpose of consenting to the abortion or whether the abortion is in the best interest of the pregnant woman. The court shall also notify the pregnant woman at the hearing that it must rule on her application within three business days of the date of its filing and that, should the court fail to rule in favor of her application within the allotted time, she has the right to appeal to the Superior Court.

(g) Coercion prohibited.--Except in a medical emergency, no parent, guardian or other person standing in loco parentis shall coerce a minor or incapacitated woman to undergo an abortion. Any minor or incapacitated woman who is threatened with such coercion may apply to a court of common pleas for relief. The court shall provide the minor or incapacitated woman with counsel, give the matter expedited consideration and grant such relief as may be necessary to prevent such coercion. Should a minor be denied the financial support of her parents by reason of her refusal to undergo abortion, she shall be considered emancipated for purposes of eligibility for assistance benefits.

(h) Regulation of proceedings.--No filing fees shall be required of any woman availing herself of the procedures provided by this section. An expedited confidential appeal shall be available to any pregnant woman whom the court fails to grant an order authorizing an abortion within the time specified in this section. Any court to which an appeal is taken under this section shall give prompt and confidential attention thereto and shall rule thereon within five business days of the filing of the appeal. The Supreme Court of Pennsylvania may issue such rules as may further assure that the process provided in this section is conducted in such a manner as will ensure confidentiality and sufficient precedence over other pending matters to ensure promptness of disposition.

(i) Penalty.--Any person who performs an abortion upon a woman who is an unemancipated minor or incapacitated person to whom this section applies either with knowledge that she is a minor or incapacitated person to whom this section applies, or with reckless disregard or negligence as to whether she is a minor or incapacitated person to whom this section applies, and who intentionally, knowingly or recklessly fails to conform to any requirement of this section is guilty of "unprofessional conduct" and his license for the practice of medicine and surgery shall be suspended in accordance with procedures provided under the act of October 5, 1978 (P.L.1109, No.261), known as the Osteopathic Medical Practice Act, the act of December 20, 1985 (P.L.457, No.112), known as the Medical Practice Act of 1985, or their successor acts, for a period of at least three months. Failure to comply with the requirements of this section is prima facie evidence of failure to obtain informed consent and of interference with family relations in appropriate civil actions. The law of this Commonwealth shall not be construed to preclude the award of exemplary damages or damages for emotional distress even if unaccompanied by physical complications in any appropriate civil action relevant to violations of this section. Nothing in this section shall be construed to limit the common law rights of parents.

(Mar. 25, 1988, P.L.262, No.31, eff. 30 days; Nov. 17, 1989, P.L.592, No.64, eff. 60 days; Apr. 16, 1992, P.L.108, No.24, eff. 60 days)

1992 Amendment. Act 24 amended subsecs. (a), (g) and (i).

1989 Amendment. Act 64 amended subsec. (f)(1).

1988 Amendment. Act 31 amended subsecs. (a), (e), (f), (g), (h) and (i).

Cross References. Section 3206 is referred to in section 3215 of this title.

§ 3207. Abortion facilities.

(a) Regulations.--The department shall have power to make rules and regulations pursuant to this chapter, with respect to performance of abortions and with respect to facilities in which abortions are performed, so as to protect the health and safety of women having abortions and of premature infants aborted alive. These rules and regulations shall include, but not be limited to, procedures, staff, equipment and laboratory testing requirements for all facilities offering abortion services.

(b) Reports.--Within 30 days after the effective date of this chapter, every facility at which abortions are performed shall file, and update immediately upon any change, a report with the department, containing the following information:

(1) Name and address of the facility.

(2) Name and address of any parent, subsidiary or affiliated organizations, corporations or associations.

(3) Name and address of any parent, subsidiary or affiliated organizations, corporations or associations having contemporaneous commonality of ownership, beneficial interest, directorship or officership with any other facility.

The information contained in those reports which are filed pursuant to this subsection by facilities which receive State-appropriated funds during the 12-calendar-month period immediately preceding a request to inspect or copy such reports shall be deemed public information. Reports filed by facilities which do not receive State-appropriated funds shall only be available to law enforcement officials, the State Board of Medicine and the State Board of Osteopathic Medicine for use in the performance of their official duties. Any facility failing to comply with the provisions of this subsection shall be assessed by the department a fine of $500 for each day it is in violation hereof.

(Mar. 25, 1988, P.L.262, No.31, eff. 30 days)

1988 Amendment. Act 31 amended subsec. (b).

Cross References. Section 3207 is referred to in section 3213 of this title.

§ 3208. Printed information.

(a) General rule.--The department shall cause to be published in English, Spanish and Vietnamese, within 60 days after this chapter becomes law, and shall update on an annual basis, the following easily comprehensible printed materials:

(1) Geographically indexed materials designed to inform the woman of public and private agencies and services available to assist a woman through pregnancy, upon childbirth and while the child is dependent, including adoption agencies, which shall include a comprehensive list of the agencies available, a description of the services they offer and a description of the manner, including telephone numbers, in which they might be contacted, or, at the option of the department, printed materials including a toll-free, 24-hour a day telephone number which may be called to obtain, orally, such a list and description of agencies in the locality of the caller and of the services they offer. The materials shall provide information on the availability of medical assistance benefits for prenatal care, childbirth and neonatal care, and state that it is unlawful for any individual to coerce a woman to undergo abortion, that any physician who performs an abortion upon a woman without obtaining her informed consent or without according her a private medical consultation may be liable to her for damages in a civil action at law, that the father of a child is liable to assist in the support of that child, even in instances where the father has offered to pay for an abortion and that the law permits adoptive parents to pay costs of prenatal care, childbirth and neonatal care.

(2) Materials designed to inform the woman of the probable anatomical and physiological characteristics of the unborn child at two-week gestational increments from fertilization to full term, including pictures representing the development of unborn children at two-week gestational increments, and any relevant information on the possibility of the unborn child's survival; provided that any such pictures or drawings must contain the dimensions of the fetus and must be realistic and appropriate for the woman's stage of pregnancy. The materials shall be objective, nonjudgmental and designed to convey only accurate scientific information about the unborn child at the various gestational ages. The material shall also contain objective information describing the methods of abortion procedures commonly employed, the medical risks commonly associated with each such procedure, the possible detrimental psychological effects of abortion and the medical risks commonly associated with each such procedure and the medical risks commonly associated with carrying a child to term.

(b) Format.--The materials shall be printed in a typeface large enough to be clearly legible.

(c) Free distribution.--The materials required under this section shall be available at no cost from the department upon request and in appropriate number to any person, facility or hospital.

(Mar. 25, 1988, P.L.262, No.31, eff. 30 days; Nov. 17, 1989, P.L.592, No.64, eff. imd.)

1989 Amendment. Act 64 amended subsec. (a). See sections 7, 8 and 9 of Act 64 in the appendix to this title for special provisions relating to publication of forms and materials, applicability of reporting and distribution requirements and effective date.

§ 3208.1. Commonwealth interference prohibited.

The Commonwealth shall not interfere with the use of medically appropriate methods of contraception or the manner in which medically appropriate methods of contraception are provided.

(Nov. 17, 1989, P.L.592, No.64, eff. 60 days)

1989 Amendment. Act 64 added section 3208.1.

§ 3209. Spousal notice.

(a) Spousal notice required.--In order to further the Commonwealth's interest in promoting the integrity of the marital relationship and to protect a spouse's interests in having children within marriage and in protecting the prenatal life of that spouse's child, no physician shall perform an abortion on a married woman, except as provided in subsections (b) and (c), unless he or she has received a signed statement, which need not be notarized, from the woman upon whom the abortion is to be performed, that she has notified her spouse that she is about to undergo an abortion. The statement shall bear a notice that any false statement made therein is punishable by law.

(b) Exceptions.--The statement certifying that the notice required by subsection (a) has been given need not be furnished where the woman provides the physician a signed statement certifying at least one of the following:

(1) Her spouse is not the father of the child.

(2) Her spouse, after diligent effort, could not be located.

(3) The pregnancy is a result of spousal sexual assault as described in section 3128 (relating to spousal sexual assault), which has been reported to a law enforcement agency having the requisite jurisdiction.

(4) The woman has reason to believe that the furnishing of notice to her spouse is likely to result in the infliction of bodily injury upon her by her spouse or by another individual.

Such statement need not be notarized, but shall bear a notice that any false statements made therein are punishable by law.

(c) Medical emergency.--The requirements of subsection (a) shall not apply in case of a medical emergency.

(d) Forms.--The department shall cause to be published forms which may be utilized for purposes of providing the signed statements required by subsections (a) and (b). The department shall distribute an adequate supply of such forms to all abortion facilities in this Commonwealth.

(e) Penalty; civil action.--Any physician who violates the provisions of this section is guilty of "unprofessional conduct," and his or her license for the practice of medicine and surgery shall be subject to suspension or revocation in accordance with procedures provided under the act of October 5, 1978 (P.L.1109, No.261), known as the Osteopathic Medical Practice Act, the act of December 20, 1985 (P.L.457, No.112), known as the Medical Practice Act of 1985, or their successor acts. In addition, any physician who knowingly violates the provisions of this section shall be civilly liable to the spouse who is the father of the aborted child for any damages caused thereby and for punitive damages in the amount of $5,000, and the court shall award a prevailing plaintiff a reasonable attorney fee as part of costs.

(Nov. 17, 1989, P.L.592, No.64)

1989 Amendment. Act 64 added section 3209. See sections 7, 8 and 9 of Act 64 in the appendix to this title for special provisions relating to publication of forms and materials, applicability of reporting and distribution requirements and effective date.

Prior Provisions. Former section 3209, which related to abortion after first trimester, was added June 11, 1982 (P.L.476, No.138), and repealed March 25, 1988 (P.L.262, No.31), effective in 30 days.

References in Text. Section 3128, referred to in subsec. (b), is repealed.

§ 3210. Determination of gestational age.

(a) Requirement.--Except in the case of a medical emergency which prevents compliance with this section, no abortion shall be performed or induced unless the referring physician or the physician performing or inducing it has first made a determination of the probable gestational age of the unborn child. In making such determination, the physician shall make such inquiries of the patient and perform or cause to be performed such medical examinations and tests as a prudent physician would consider necessary to make or perform in making an accurate diagnosis with respect to gestational age. The physician who performs or induces the abortion shall report the type of inquiries made and the type of examinations and tests utilized to determine the gestational age of the unborn child and the basis for the diagnosis with respect to gestational age on forms provided by the department.

(b) Penalty.--Failure of any physician to conform to any requirement of this section constitutes "unprofessional conduct" within the meaning of the act of October 5, 1978 (P.L.1109, No.261), known as the Osteopathic Medical Practice Act, the act of December 20, 1985 (P.L.457, No.112), known as the Medical Practice Act of 1985, or their successor acts. Upon a finding by the State Board of Medicine or the State Board of Osteopathic Medicine that any physician has failed to conform to any requirement of this section, the board shall not fail to suspend that physician's license for a period of at least three months. Intentional, knowing or reckless falsification of any report required under this section is a misdemeanor of the third degree.

(Mar. 25, 1988, P.L.262, No.31, eff. 30 days; Nov. 17, 1989, P.L.592, No.64, eff. 60 days)

Cross References. Section 3210 is referred to in sections 3211, 3214 of this title.

§ 3211. Abortion on unborn child of 24 or more weeks gestational age.

(a) Prohibition.--Except as provided in subsection (b), no person shall perform or induce an abortion upon another person when the gestational age of the unborn child is 24 or more weeks.

(b) Exceptions.--

(1) It shall not be a violation of subsection (a) if an abortion is performed by a physician and that physician reasonably believes that it is necessary to prevent either the death of the pregnant woman or the substantial and irreversible impairment of a major bodily function of the woman. No abortion shall be deemed authorized under this paragraph if performed on the basis of a claim or a diagnosis that the woman will engage in conduct which would result in her death or in substantial and irreversible impairment of a major bodily function.

(2) It shall not be a violation of subsection (a) if the abortion is performed by a physician and that physician reasonably believes, after making a determination of the gestational age of the unborn child in compliance with section 3210 (relating to determination of gestational age), that the unborn child is less than 24 weeks gestational age.

(c) Abortion regulated.--Except in the case of a medical emergency which, in the reasonable medical judgment of the physician performing the abortion, prevents compliance with a particular requirement of this subsection, no abortion which is authorized under subsection (b)(1) shall be performed unless each of the following conditions is met:

(1) The physician performing the abortion certifies in writing that, based upon his medical examination of the pregnant woman and his medical judgment, the abortion is necessary to prevent either the death of the pregnant woman or the substantial and irreversible impairment of a major bodily function of the woman.

(2) Such physician's judgment with respect to the necessity for the abortion has been concurred in by one other licensed physician who certifies in writing that, based upon his or her separate personal medical examination of the pregnant woman and his or her medical judgment, the abortion is necessary to prevent either the death of the pregnant woman or the substantial and irreversible impairment of a major bodily function of the woman.

(3) The abortion is performed in a hospital.

(4) The physician terminates the pregnancy in a manner which provides the best opportunity for the unborn child to survive, unless the physician determines, in his or her good faith medical judgment, that termination of the pregnancy in that manner poses a significantly greater risk either of the death of the pregnant woman or the substantial and irreversible impairment of a major bodily function of the woman than would other available methods.

(5) The physician performing the abortion arranges for the attendance, in the same room in which the abortion is to be completed, of a second physician who shall take control of the child immediately after complete extraction from the mother and shall provide immediate medical care for the child, taking all reasonable steps necessary to preserve the child's life and health.

(d) Penalty.--Any person who violates subsection (a) commits a felony of the third degree. Any person who violates subsection (c) commits a misdemeanor of the second degree for the first offense and a misdemeanor of the first degree for subsequent offenses.

(Mar. 25, 1988, P.L.262, No.31, eff. 30 days; Nov. 17, 1989, P.L.592, No.64, eff. 60 days)

Cross References. Section 3211 is referred to in section 3214 of this title.

§ 3212. Infanticide.

(a) Status of fetus.--The law of this Commonwealth shall not be construed to imply that any human being born alive in the course of or as a result of an abortion or pregnancy termination, no matter what may be that human being's chance of survival, is not a person under the Constitution and laws of this Commonwealth.

(b) Care required.--All physicians and licensed medical personnel attending a child who is born alive during the course of an abortion or premature delivery, or after being carried to term, shall provide such child that type and degree of care and treatment which, in the good faith judgment of the physician, is commonly and customarily provided to any other person under similar conditions and circumstances. Any individual who intentionally, knowingly or recklessly violates the provisions of this subsection commits a felony of the third degree.

(c) Obligation of physician.--Whenever the physician or any other person is prevented by lack of parental or guardian consent from fulfilling his obligations under subsection (b), he shall nonetheless fulfill said obligations and immediately notify the juvenile court of the facts of the case. The juvenile court shall immediately institute an inquiry and, if it finds that the lack of parental or guardian consent is preventing treatment required under subsection (b), it shall immediately grant injunctive relief to require such treatment.

(Nov. 17, 1989, P.L.592, No.64, eff. 60 days)

1989 Amendment. Act 64 amended subsec. (b).

§ 3213. Prohibited acts.

(a) Payment for abortion.--Except in the case of a pregnancy which is not yet clinically diagnosable, any person who intends to perform or induce abortion shall, before accepting payment therefor, make or obtain a determination that the woman is pregnant. Any person who intentionally or knowingly accepts such a payment without first making or obtaining such a determination commits a misdemeanor of the second degree. Any person who makes such a determination erroneously either knowing that it is erroneous or with reckless disregard or negligence as to whether it is erroneous, and who either:

(1) thereupon or thereafter intentionally relies upon that determination in soliciting or obtaining any such payment; or

(2) intentionally conveys that determination to any person or persons with knowledge that, or with reckless disregard as to whether, that determination will be relied upon in any solicitation or obtaining of any such payment;

commits a misdemeanor of the second degree.

(b) Referral fee.--The payment or receipt of a referral fee in connection with the performance of an abortion is a misdemeanor of the first degree. For purposes of this section, "referral fee" means the transfer of anything of value between a physician who performs an abortion or an operator or employee of a clinic at which an abortion is performed and the person who advised the woman receiving the abortion to use the services of that physician or clinic.

(c) Regulations.--The department shall issue regulations to assure that prior to the performance of any abortion, including abortions performed in the first trimester of pregnancy, the maternal Rh status shall be determined and that anti-Rh sensitization prophylaxis shall be provided to each patient at risk of sensitization unless the patient refuses to accept the treatment. Except when there exists a medical emergency or, in the judgment of the physician, there exists no possibility of Rh sensitization, the intentional, knowing, or reckless failure to conform to the regulations issued pursuant to this subsection constitutes "unprofessional conduct" and his license for the practice of medicine and surgery shall be subject to suspension or revocation in accordance with procedures provided under the act of October 5, 1978 (P.L.1109, No.261), known as the Osteopathic Medical Practice Act, the act of December 20, 1985 (P.L.457, No.112), known as the Medical Practice Act of 1985, or their successor acts.

(d) Participation in abortion.--Except for a facility devoted exclusively to the performance of abortions, no medical personnel or medical facility, nor any employee, agent or student thereof, shall be required against his or its conscience to aid, abet or facilitate performance of an abortion or dispensing of an abortifacient and failure or refusal to do so shall not be a basis for any civil, criminal, administrative or disciplinary action, penalty or proceeding, nor may it be the basis for refusing to hire or admit anyone. Nothing herein shall be construed to limit the provisions of the act of October 27, 1955 (P.L.744, No.222), known as the "Pennsylvania Human Relations Act." Any person who knowingly violates the provisions of this subsection shall be civilly liable to the person thereby injured and, in addition, shall be liable to that person for punitive damages in the amount of $5,000.

(e) In vitro fertilization.--All persons conducting, or experimenting in, in vitro fertilization shall file quarterly reports with the department, which shall be available for public inspection and copying, containing the following information:

(1) Names of all persons conducting or assisting in the fertilization or experimentation process.

(2) Locations where the fertilization or experimentation is conducted.

(3) Name and address of any person, facility, agency or organization sponsoring the fertilization or experimentation except that names of any persons who are donors or recipients of sperm or eggs shall not be disclosed.

(4) Number of eggs fertilized.

(5) Number of fertilized eggs destroyed or discarded.

(6) Number of women implanted with a fertilized egg.

Any person required under this subsection to file a report, keep records or supply information, who willfully fails to file such report, keep records or supply such information or who submits a false report shall be assessed a fine by the department in the amount of $50 for each day in which that person is in violation hereof.

(f) Notice.--

(1) Except for a facility devoted exclusively to the performance of abortions, every facility performing abortions shall prominently post a notice, not less than eight and one-half inches by eleven inches in size, entitled "Right of Conscience," for the exclusive purpose of informing medical personnel, employees, agents and students of such facilities of their rights under subsection (d) and under section 5.2 of the Pennsylvania Human Relations Act. The facility shall post the notice required by this subsection in a location or locations where notices to employees, medical personnel and students are normally posted or, if notices are not normally posted, in a location or locations where the notice required by this subsection is likely to be seen by medical personnel, employees or students of the facility. The department shall prescribe a model notice which may be used by any facility, and any facility which utilizes the model notice or substantially similar language shall be deemed in compliance with this subsection.

(2) The department shall have the authority to assess a civil penalty of up to $5,000 against any facility for each violation of this subsection, giving due consideration to the appropriateness of the penalty with respect to the size of the facility, the gravity of the violation, the good faith of the facility and the history of previous violations. Civil penalties due under this subsection shall be paid to the department for deposit in the State Treasury and may be collected by the department in the appropriate court of common pleas. The department shall send a copy of its model notice to every facility which files a report under section 3207(b) (relating to abortion facilities). Failure to receive a notice shall not be a defense to any civil action brought pursuant to this subsection.

(Mar. 25, 1988, P.L.262, No.31, eff. 30 days)

1988 Amendment. Act 31 amended subsec. (c) and added subsec. (f).

§ 3214. Reporting.

(a) General rule.--For the purpose of promotion of maternal health and life by adding to the sum of medical and public health knowledge through the compilation of relevant data, and to promote the Commonwealth's interest in protection of the unborn child, a report of each abortion performed shall be made to the department on forms prescribed by it. The report forms shall not identify the individual patient by name and shall include the following information:

(1) Identification of the physician who performed the abortion, the concurring physician as required by section 3211(c)(2) (relating to abortion on unborn child of 24 or more weeks gestational age), the second physician as required by section 3211(c)(5) and the facility where the abortion was performed and of the referring physician, agency or service, if any.

(2) The county and state in which the woman resides.

(3) The woman's age.

(4) The number of prior pregnancies and prior abortions of the woman.

(5) The gestational age of the unborn child at the time of the abortion.

(6) The type of procedure performed or prescribed and the date of the abortion.

(7) Pre-existing medical conditions of the woman which would complicate pregnancy, if any, and, if known, any medical complication which resulted from the abortion itself.

(8) The basis for the medical judgment of the physician who performed the abortion that the abortion was necessary to prevent either the death of the pregnant woman or the substantial and irreversible impairment of a major bodily function of the woman, where an abortion has been performed pursuant to section 3211(b)(1).

(9) The weight of the aborted child for any abortion performed pursuant to section 3211(b)(1).

(10) Basis for any medical judgment that a medical emergency existed which excused the physician from compliance with any provision of this chapter.

(11) The information required to be reported under section 3210(a) (relating to determination of gestational age).

(12) Whether the abortion was performed upon a married woman and, if so, whether notice to her spouse was given. If no notice to her spouse was given, the report shall also indicate the reason for failure to provide notice.

(b) Completion of report.--The reports shall be completed by the hospital or other licensed facility, signed by the physician who performed the abortion and transmitted to the department within 15 days after each reporting month.

(c) Pathological examinations.--When there is an abortion performed during the first trimester of pregnancy, the tissue that is removed shall be subjected to a gross or microscopic examination, as needed, by the physician or a qualified person designated by the physician to determine if a pregnancy existed and was terminated. If the examination indicates no fetal remains, that information shall immediately be made known to the physician and sent to the department within 15 days of the analysis. When there is an abortion performed after the first trimester of pregnancy where the physician has certified the unborn child is not viable, the dead unborn child and all tissue removed at the time of the abortion shall be submitted for tissue analysis to a board eligible or certified pathologist. If the report reveals evidence of viability or live birth, the pathologist shall report such findings to the department within 15 days and a copy of the report shall also be sent to the physician performing the abortion. Intentional, knowing, reckless or negligent failure of the physician to submit such an unborn child or such tissue remains to such a pathologist for such a purpose, or intentional, knowing or reckless failure of the pathologist to report any evidence of live birth or viability to the department in the manner and within the time prescribed is a misdemeanor of the third degree.

(d) Form.--The department shall prescribe a form on which pathologists may report any evidence of absence of pregnancy, live birth or viability.

(e) Statistical reports; public availability of reports.--

(1) The department shall prepare a comprehensive annual statistical report for the General Assembly based upon the data gathered under subsections (a) and (h). Such report shall not lead to the disclosure of the identity of any person filing a report or about whom a report is filed, and shall be available for public inspection and copying.

(2) Reports filed pursuant to subsection (a) or (h) shall not be deemed public records within the meaning of that term as defined by the act of June 21, 1957 (P.L.390, No.212), referred to as the Right-to-Know Law, and shall remain confidential, except that disclosure may be made to law enforcement officials upon an order of a court of common pleas after application showing good cause therefor. The court may condition disclosure of the information upon any appropriate safeguards it may impose.

(3) Original copies of all reports filed under subsections (a), (f) and (h) shall be available to the State Board of Medicine and the State Board of Osteopathic Medicine for use in the performance of their official duties.

(4) Any person who willfully discloses any information obtained from reports filed pursuant to subsection (a) or (h), other than that disclosure authorized under paragraph (1), (2) or (3) hereof or as otherwise authorized by law, shall commit a misdemeanor of the third degree.

(f) Report by facility.--Every facility in which an abortion is performed within this Commonwealth during any quarter year shall file with the department a report showing the total number of abortions performed within the hospital or other facility during that quarter year. This report shall also show the total abortions performed in each trimester of pregnancy. Any report shall be available for public inspection and copying only if the facility receives State-appropriated funds within the 12-calendar-month period immediately preceding the filing of the report. These reports shall be submitted on a form prescribed by the department which will enable a facility to indicate whether or not it is receiving State-appropriated funds. If the facility indicates on the form that it is not receiving State-appropriated funds, the department shall regard its report as confidential unless it receives other evidence which causes it to conclude that the facility receives State-appropriated funds.

(g) Report of maternal death.--After 30 days' public notice, the department shall henceforth require that all reports of maternal deaths occurring within the Commonwealth arising from pregnancy, childbirth or intentional abortion in every case state the cause of death, the duration of the woman's pregnancy when her death occurred and whether or not the woman was under the care of a physician during her pregnancy prior to her death and shall issue such regulations as are necessary to assure that such information is reported, conducting its own investigation if necessary in order to ascertain such data. A woman shall be deemed to have been under the care of a physician prior to her death for the purpose of this chapter when she had either been examined or treated by a physician, not including any examination or treatment in connection with emergency care for complications of her pregnancy or complications of her abortion, preceding the woman's death at any time which is both 21 or more days after the time she became pregnant and within 60 days prior to her death. Known incidents of maternal mortality of nonresident women arising from induced abortion performed in this Commonwealth shall be included as incidents of maternal mortality arising from induced abortions. Incidents of maternal mortality arising from continued pregnancy or childbirth and occurring after induced abortion has been attempted but not completed, including deaths occurring after induced abortion has been attempted but not completed as the result of ectopic pregnancy, shall be included as incidents of maternal mortality arising from induced abortion. The department shall annually compile a statistical report for the General Assembly based upon the data gathered under this subsection, and all such statistical reports shall be available for public inspection and copying.

(h) Report of complications.--Every physician who is called upon to provide medical care or treatment to a woman who is in need of medical care because of a complication or complications resulting, in the good faith judgment of the physician, from having undergone an abortion or attempted abortion shall prepare a report thereof and file the report with the department within 30 days of the date of his first examination of the woman, which report shall be on forms prescribed by the department, which forms shall contain the following information, as received, and such other information except the name of the patient as the department may from time to time require:

(1) Age of patient.

(2) Number of pregnancies patient may have had prior to the abortion.

(3) Number and type of abortions patient may have had prior to this abortion.

(4) Name and address of the facility where the abortion was performed.

(5) Gestational age of the unborn child at the time of the abortion, if known.

(6) Type of abortion performed, if known.

(7) Nature of complication or complications.

(8) Medical treatment given.

(9) The nature and extent, if known, of any permanent condition caused by the complication.

(i) Penalties.--

(1) Any person required under this section to file a report, keep any records or supply any information, who willfully fails to file such report, keep such records or supply such information at the time or times required by law or regulation is guilty of "unprofessional conduct" and his license for the practice of medicine and surgery shall be subject to suspension or revocation in accordance with procedures provided under the act of October 5, 1978 (P.L.1109, No.261), known as the Osteopathic Medical Practice Act, the act of December 20, 1985 (P.L.457, No.112), known as the Medical Practice Act of 1985, or their successor acts.

(2) Any person who willfully delivers or discloses to the department any report, record or information known by him to be false commits a misdemeanor of the first degree.

(3) In addition to the above penalties, any person, organization or facility who willfully violates any of the provisions of this section requiring reporting shall upon conviction thereof:

(i) For the first time, have its license suspended for a period of six months.

(ii) For the second time, have its license suspended for a period of one year.

(iii) For the third time, have its license revoked.

(Mar. 25, 1988, P.L.262, No.31, eff. 30 days; Nov. 17, 1989, P.L.592, No.64, eff. imd.)

1989 Amendment. Act 64 amended subsec. (a). See sections 7, 8 and 9 of Act 64 in the appendix to this title for special provisions relating to publication of forms and materials, applicability of reporting and distribution requirements and effective date.

1988 Amendment. Act 31 amended subsecs. (a), (e), (f), (h) and (i).

References in Text. The act of June 21, 1957 (P.L.390, No.212), referred to as the Right-to-Know Law, referred to in subsec. (e)(2), was repealed by the act of February 14, 2008 (P.L.6, No.3), known as the Right-to-Know Law.

Cross References. Section 3214 is referred to in section 3220 of this title.

§ 3215. Publicly owned facilities; public officials and public funds.

(a) Limitations.--No hospital, clinic or other health facility owned or operated by the Commonwealth, a county, a city or other governmental entity (except the government of the United States, another state or a foreign nation) shall:

(1) Provide, induce, perform or permit its facilities to be used for the provision, inducement or performance of any abortion except where necessary to avert the death of the woman or where necessary to terminate pregnancies initiated by acts of rape or incest if reported in accordance with requirements set forth in subsection (c).

(2) Lease or sell or permit the subleasing of its facilities or property to any physician or health facility for use in the provision, inducement or performance of abortion, except abortion necessary to avert the death of the woman or to terminate pregnancies initiated by acts of rape or incest if reported in accordance with requirements set forth in subsection (c).

(3) Enter into any contract with any physician or health facility under the terms of which such physician or health facility agrees to provide, induce or perform abortions, except abortion necessary to avert the death of the woman or to terminate pregnancies initiated by acts of rape or incest if reported in accordance with requirements set forth in subsection (c).

(b) Permitted treatment.--Nothing in subsection (a) shall be construed to preclude any hospital, clinic or other health facility from providing treatment for post-abortion complications.

(c) Public funds.--No Commonwealth funds and no Federal funds which are appropriated by the Commonwealth shall be expended by any State or local government agency for the performance of abortion, except:

(1) When abortion is necessary to avert the death of the mother on certification by a physician. When such physician will perform the abortion or has a pecuniary or proprietary interest in the abortion there shall be a separate certification from a physician who has no such interest.

(2) When abortion is performed in the case of pregnancy caused by rape which, prior to the performance of the abortion, has been reported, together with the identity of the offender, if known, to a law enforcement agency having the requisite jurisdiction and has been personally reported by the victim.

(3) When abortion is performed in the case of pregnancy caused by incest which, prior to the performance of the abortion, has been personally reported by the victim to a law enforcement agency having the requisite jurisdiction, or, in the case of a minor, to the county child protective service agency and the other party to the incestuous act has been named in such report.

(d) Health plans.--No health plan for employees, funded with any Commonwealth funds, shall include coverage for abortion, except under the same conditions and requirements as provided in subsection (c). The prohibition contained herein shall not apply to health plans for which abortion coverage has been expressly bargained for in any collective bargaining agreement presently in effect, but shall be construed to preclude such coverage with respect to any future agreement.

(e) Insurance policies.--All insurers who make available health care and disability insurance policies in this Commonwealth shall make available such policies which contain an express exclusion of coverage for abortion services not necessary to avert the death of the woman or to terminate pregnancies caused by rape or incest.

(f) Public officers; ordering abortions.-- Except in the case of a medical emergency, no court, judge, executive officer, administrative agency or public employee of the Commonwealth or of any local governmental body shall have power to issue any order

127

requiring an abortion without the express voluntary consent of the woman upon whom the abortion is to be performed or shall coerce any person to have an abortion.

(g) Public officers; limiting benefits prohibited.--No court, judge, executive officer, administrative agency or public employee of the Commonwealth or of any local governmental body shall withhold, reduce or suspend or threaten to withhold, reduce or suspend any benefits to which a person would otherwise be entitled on the ground that such person chooses not to have an abortion.

(h) Penalty.--Whoever orders an abortion in violation of subsection (f) or withholds, reduces or suspends any benefits or threatens to withhold, reduce or suspend any benefits in violation of subsection (g) commits a misdemeanor of the first degree.

(i) Public funds for legal services.--No Federal or State funds which are appropriated by the Commonwealth for the provision of legal services by private agencies, and no public funds generated by collection of interest on lawyer's trust accounts, as authorized by statute previously or subsequently enacted, may be used, directly or indirectly, to:

(1) Advocate the freedom to choose abortion or the prohibition of abortion.

(2) Provide legal assistance with respect to any proceeding or litigation which seeks to procure or prevent any abortion or to procure or prevent public funding for any abortion.

(3) Provide legal assistance with respect to any proceeding or litigation which seeks to compel or prevent the performance or assistance in the performance of any abortion, or the provision of facilities for the performance of any abortion.

Nothing in this subsection shall be construed to require or prevent the expenditure of funds pursuant to a court order awarding fees for attorney's services under the Civil Rights Attorney's Fees Awards Act of 1976 (Public law 94-559, 90 Stat. 2641), nor shall this subsection be construed to prevent the use of public funds to provide court appointed counsel in any proceeding authorized under section 3206 (relating to parental consent).

(j) Required statements.--No Commonwealth agency shall make any payment from Federal or State funds appropriated by the Commonwealth for the performance of any abortion pursuant to subsection (c)(2) or (3) unless the Commonwealth agency first:

(1) receives from the physician or facility seeking payment a statement signed by the physician performing the abortion stating that, prior to performing the abortion, he obtained a non-notarized, signed statement from the pregnant woman stating that she was a victim of rape or incest, as the case may be, and that she reported the crime, including the identity of the offender, if known, to a law enforcement agency having the requisite jurisdiction or, in the case of incest where a pregnant minor is the victim, to the county child protective service agency and stating the name of the law enforcement agency or child protective service agency to which the report was made and the date such report was made;

(2) receives from the physician or facility seeking payment, the signed statement of the pregnant woman which is described in paragraph (1). The statement shall bear the notice that any false statements made therein are punishable by law and shall state that the pregnant woman is aware that false reports to law enforcement authorities are punishable by law; and

(3) verifies with the law enforcement agency or child protective service agency named in the statement of the pregnant woman whether a report of rape or incest was filed with the agency in accordance with the statement.

The Commonwealth agency shall report any evidence of false statements, of false reports to law enforcement authorities or of fraud in the procurement or attempted procurement of any payment from Federal or State funds appropriated by the Commonwealth pursuant to this section to the district attorney of appropriate jurisdiction and, where appropriate, to the Attorney General.

(Mar. 25, 1988, P.L.262, No.31, eff. 30 days; Nov. 17, 1989, P.L.592, No.64, eff. 60 days)

1989 Amendment. Act 64 amended subsec. (b).

1988 Amendment. Act 31 amended subsecs. (c) and (e) and added subsecs. (i) and (j).

Cross References. Section 3215 is referred to in section 3302 of Title 40 (Insurance).

§ 3216. Fetal experimentation.

(a) **Unborn or live child.**--Any person who knowingly performs any type of nontherapeutic experimentation or nontherapeutic medical procedure (except an abortion as defined in this chapter) upon any unborn child, or upon any child born alive during the course of an abortion, commits a felony of the third degree. "Nontherapeutic" means that which is not intended to preserve the life or health of the child upon whom it is performed.

(b) **Dead child.**--The following standards govern the procurement and use of any fetal tissue or organ which is used in animal or human transplantation, research or experimentation:

(1) No fetal tissue or organs may be procured or used without the written consent of the mother. No consideration of any kind for such consent may be offered or given. Further, if the tissue or organs are being derived from abortion, such consent shall be valid only if obtained after the decision to abort has been made.

(2) No person who provides the information required by section 3205 (relating to informed consent) shall employ the possibility of the use of aborted fetal tissue or organs as an inducement to a pregnant woman to undergo abortion except that payment for reasonable expenses occasioned by the actual retrieval, storage, preparation and transportation of the tissues is permitted.

(3) No remuneration, compensation or other consideration may be paid to any person or organization in connection with the procurement of fetal tissue or organs.

(4) All persons who participate in the procurement, use or transplantation of fetal tissue or organs, including the recipients of such tissue or organs, shall be informed as to whether the particular tissue or organ involved was procured as a result of either:

(i) stillbirth;
(ii) miscarriage;
(iii) ectopic pregnancy;
(iv) abortion; or
(v) any other means.

(5) No person who consents to the procurement or use of any fetal tissue or organ may designate the recipient of that tissue or organ, nor shall any other person or organization act to fulfill that designation.

(6) The department may assess a civil penalty upon any person who procures, sells or uses any fetal tissue or organs in violation of this section or the regulations issued thereunder. Such civil penalties may not exceed $5,000 for each separate violation. In assessing such penalties, the department shall give due consideration to the gravity of the violation, the good faith of the violator and the history of previous violations. Civil penalties due under this paragraph shall be paid to the department for deposit in the State Treasury and may be enforced by the department in the Commonwealth Court.

(c) **Construction of section.**--Nothing in this section shall be construed to condone or prohibit the performance of diagnostic tests while the unborn child is in utero or the performance of pathological examinations on an aborted child. Nor shall anything in this section be construed to condone or prohibit the performance of in vitro fertilization and accompanying embryo transfer.
(Nov. 17, 1989, P.L.592, No.64, eff. 60 days)

§ 3217. Civil penalties.

Any physician who knowingly violates any of the provisions of section 3204 (relating to medical consultation and judgment) or 3205 (relating to informed consent) shall, in addition to any other penalty prescribed in this chapter, be civilly liable to his patient for any damages caused thereby and, in addition, shall be liable to his patient for punitive damages in the amount of $5,000, and the court shall award a prevailing plaintiff a reasonable attorney fee as part of costs.
(Mar. 25, 1988, P.L.262, No.31, eff. 30 days; Nov. 17, 1989, P.L.592, No.64, eff. 60 days)

§ 3218. Criminal penalties.

(a) **Application of chapter.**--Notwithstanding any other provision of this chapter, no criminal penalty shall apply to a woman who violates any provision of this chapter solely in order to perform or induce or attempt to perform or induce an abortion upon herself. Nor shall any woman who undergoes an abortion be found guilty of having committed an offense, liability for which is defined under section 306 (relating to liability for conduct of another; complicity) or Chapter 9 (relating to inchoate crimes), by reason of having undergone such abortion.

(b) **False statement, etc.**--A person commits a misdemeanor of the second degree if, with intent to mislead a public servant in performing his official function under this chapter, such person:

(1) makes any written false statement which he does not believe to be true; or

(2) submits or invites reliance on any writing which he knows to be forged, altered or otherwise lacking in authenticity.

(c) Statements "under penalty".--A person commits a misdemeanor of the third degree if such person makes a written false statement which such person does not believe to be true on a statement submitted as required under this chapter, bearing notice to the effect that false statements made therein are punishable.

(d) Perjury provisions applicable.--Section 4902(c) through (f) (relating to perjury) apply to subsections (b) and (c).

(Mar. 25, 1988, P.L.262, No.31, eff. 30 days; Nov. 17, 1989, P.L.592, No.64, eff. 60 days)

1989 Amendment. Act 64 amended subsec. (a).

§ 3219. State Board of Medicine; State Board of Osteopathic Medicine.

(a) Enforcement.--It shall be the duty of the State Board of Medicine and the State Board of Osteopathic Medicine to vigorously enforce those provisions of this chapter, violation of which constitutes "unprofessional conduct" within the meaning of the act of October 5, 1978 (P.L.1109, No.261), known as the Osteopathic Medical Practice Act, the act of December 20, 1985 (P.L.457, No.112), known as the Medical Practice Act of 1985, or their successor acts. Each board shall have the power to conduct, and its responsibilities shall include, systematic review of all reports filed under this chapter.

(b) Penalties.--Except as otherwise herein provided, upon a finding of "unprofessional conduct" under the provisions of this chapter, the board shall, for the first such offense, prescribe such penalties as it deems appropriate; for the second such offense, suspend the license of the physician for at least 90 days; and, for the third such offense, revoke the license of the physician.

(c) Reports.--The board shall prepare and submit an annual report of its enforcement efforts under this chapter to the General Assembly, which shall contain the following items:

(1) number of violations investigated, by section of this chapter;

(2) number of physicians complained against;

(3) number of physicians investigated;

(4) penalties imposed; and

(5) such other information as any committee of the General Assembly shall require.

Such reports shall be available for public inspection and copying.

(Mar. 25, 1988, P.L.262, No.31, eff. 30 days)

§ 3220. Construction.

(a) Referral to coroner.--The provisions of section 503(3) of the act of June 29, 1953 (P.L.304, No.66), known as the "Vital Statistics Law of 1953," shall not be construed to require referral to the coroner of cases of abortions performed in compliance with this chapter.

(b) Other laws unaffected.--Apart from the provisions of subsection (a) and section 3214 (relating to reporting) nothing in this chapter shall have the effect of modifying or repealing any part of the "Vital Statistics Law of 1953" or section 5.2 of the act of October 27, 1955 (P.L.744, No.222), known as the "Pennsylvania Human Relations Act."

(c) Required statement.--When any provision of this chapter requires the furnishing or obtaining of a nonnotarized statement or verification, the furnishing or acceptance of a notarized statement or verification shall not be deemed a violation of that provision.

(Nov. 17, 1989, P.L.592, No.64, eff. 60 days)

ARTICLE C OFFENSES AGAINST PROPERTY

CHAPTER 33 ARSON, CRIMINAL MISCHIEF AND OTHER PROPERTY DESTRUCTION

Enactment. Chapter 33 was added December 6, 1972, P.L.1482, No.334, effective in six months.

Cross References. Chapter 33 is referred to in sections 911, 2710 of this title.

§ 3301. Arson and related offenses.

(a) Arson endangering persons.--

(1) A person commits a felony of the first degree if he intentionally starts a fire or causes an explosion, or if he aids, counsels, pays or agrees to pay another to cause a fire or explosion, whether on his own property or on that of another, and if:

(i) he thereby recklessly places another person in danger of death or bodily injury, including but not limited to a firefighter, police officer or other person actively engaged in fighting the fire; or

(ii) he commits the act with the purpose of destroying or damaging an inhabited building or occupied structure of another.

(2) A person who commits arson endangering persons is guilty of murder of the second degree if the fire or explosion causes the death of any person, including but not limited to a firefighter, police officer or other person actively engaged in fighting the fire, and is guilty of murder of the first degree if the fire or explosion causes the death of any person and

was set with the purpose of causing the death of another person.

(a.1) Aggravated arson.--

(1) A person commits a felony of the first degree if he intentionally starts a fire or causes an explosion, or if he aids, counsels, pays or agrees to pay another to cause a fire or explosion, whether on his own property or on that of another, and if:

(i) he thereby attempts to cause, or intentionally, knowingly or recklessly causes bodily injury to another person, including, but not limited to, a firefighter, police officer or other person actively engaged in fighting the fire; or

(ii) he commits an offense under this section which is graded as a felony when a person is present inside the property at the time of the offense.

(2) A person who commits aggravated arson is guilty of murder of the second degree if the fire or explosion causes the death of any person, including, but not limited to, a firefighter, police officer or other person actively engaged in fighting the fire.

(a.2) Arson of historic resource.--A person commits a felony of the second degree if the person, with the intent of destroying or damaging a historic resource of another, does any of the following:

(1) Intentionally starts a fire or causes an explosion, whether on the person's own property or that of another.

(2) Aids, counsels, pays or agrees to pay another to cause a fire or explosion.

(b) Sentence.--

(1) A person convicted of violating the provisions of subsection (a)(2), murder of the first degree, shall be sentenced to death or life imprisonment without right to parole; a person convicted of murder of the second degree, pursuant to subsection (a)(2), shall be sentenced to life imprisonment without right to parole. Notwithstanding provisions to the contrary, no language herein shall infringe upon the inherent powers of the Governor to commute said sentence.

(2) A person convicted under subsection (a.1) may be sentenced to a term of imprisonment which shall be fixed by the court at not more than 40 years if:

(i) bodily injury results to a firefighter, police officer or other person actively engaged in fighting the fire; or

(ii) serious bodily injury results to a civilian.

(c) Arson endangering property.--A person commits a felony of the second degree if he intentionally starts a fire or causes an explosion, whether on his own property or that of another, or if he aids, counsels, pays or agrees to pay another to cause a fire or explosion, and if:

(1) he commits the act with intent of destroying or damaging a building or unoccupied structure of another;

(2) he thereby recklessly places an inhabited building or occupied structure of another in danger of damage or destruction; or

(3) he commits the act with intent of destroying or damaging any property, whether his own or of another, to collect insurance for such loss.

(d) Reckless burning or exploding.--A person commits a felony of the third degree if he intentionally starts a fire or causes an explosion, or if he aids, counsels, pays or agrees to pay another to cause a fire or explosion, whether on his own property or on that of another, and thereby recklessly:

(1) places an uninhabited building or unoccupied structure of another in danger of damage or destruction; or

(2) places any personal property of another having a value that exceeds $5,000 or if the property is an automobile, airplane, motorcycle, motorboat or other motor-propelled vehicle in danger of damage or destruction.

(d.1) Dangerous burning.--A person commits a summary offense if he intentionally or recklessly starts a fire to endanger any person or property of another whether or not any damage to person or property actually occurs.

(e) Failure to control or report dangerous fires.--A person who knows that a fire is endangering the life or property of another and fails to take reasonable measures to put out or control the fire, when he can do so without substantial risk to himself, or to give a prompt fire alarm, commits a misdemeanor of the first degree if:

(1) he knows that he is under an official, contractual or other legal duty to control or combat the fire; or

(2) the fire was started, albeit lawfully, by him or with his assent, or on property in his custody or control.

(f) Possession of explosive or incendiary materials or devices.--A person commits a felony of the third degree if he possesses, manufactures or transports any incendiary or explosive device or material with the intent to use or to provide such device or material to commit any offense described in this chapter.

(g) Disclosure of true owner.--Law enforcement officers investigating an offense under this section may require a trustee of a passive trust or trust involving an undisclosed principal or straw party to disclose the actual owner or beneficiary of the real property in question. The name of the actual owner or beneficiary of real estate subject to a passive trust, trust involving an undisclosed principal or arrangement with a straw party when obtained under the provisions of this subsection shall not be disclosed except as an official part of an investigation and prosecution of an offense under this section. A person who refuses to disclose a name as required by this section or who discloses a name in violation of this subsection is guilty of a misdemeanor of the third degree.

(h) Limitations on liability.--The provisions of subsections (a), (b), (c), (d), (d.1) and (e) shall not be construed to establish criminal liability upon any volunteer or paid firefighter or volunteer or paid firefighting company or association if said company or association endangers a participating firefighter or real or personal property in the course of an approved, controlled fire training program or fire evolution, provided that said company or association has complied with the following:

(1) a sworn statement from the owner of any real or personal property involved in such program or evolution that there is no fire insurance policy or no lien or encumbrance exists which applies to such real or personal property;

(2) approval or permits from the appropriate local government or State officials, if necessary, to conduct such program or exercise have been received;

(3) precautions have been taken so that the program or evolution does not affect any other persons or real or personal property; and

(4) participation of firefighters in the program or exercise if voluntary.

(h.1) Prohibition on certain service.-- (Deleted by amendment).

(i) Defenses.--It is a defense to prosecution under subsections (c), (d) and (d.1) where a person is charged with destroying a vehicle, lawful title to which is vested in him, if the vehicle is free of any encumbrances, there is no insurance covering loss by fire or explosion or both on the vehicle and the person delivers to the nearest State Police station at least 48 hours in advance of the planned destruction a written sworn statement certifying that the person is the lawful titleholder, that the vehicle is free of any encumbrances and that there is no insurance covering loss by fire or explosion or both on the vehicle.

(j) Definitions.--As used in this section the following words and phrases shall have the meanings given to them in this subsection:

"Historic resource." A building or structure, including a covered bridge, which:

(1) has been in existence for more than 100 years, including partial or complete reconstruction of a building or structure originally erected at least 100 years ago; or

(2) has been listed on the National Register of Historic Places or the Pennsylvania Register of Historic Places.

"Occupied structure." Any structure, vehicle or place adapted for overnight accommodation of persons or for carrying on business therein, whether or not a person is actually present. If a building or structure is divided into separately occupied units, any unit not occupied by the actor is an occupied structure of another.

"Property of another." A building or other property, whether real or personal, in which a person other than the actor has an interest which the actor has no authority to defeat or impair, even though the actor may also have an interest in the building or property.

(Apr. 29, 1982, P.L.363, No.101, eff. 90 days; Dec. 7, 1982, P.L.811, No.227, eff. 60 days; Dec. 3, 1998, P.L.933, No.121, eff. 60 days; Nov. 29, 2006, P.L.1481, No.168, eff. 60 days; Nov. 23, 2010, P.L.1181, No.118, eff. 60 days; Feb. 25, 2014, P.L.33, No.16, eff. 60 days)

2014 Amendment. Act 16 amended subsecs. (b), (f) and (j) and added subsecs. (a.1) and (a.2).

2010 Amendment. Act 118 deleted subsec. (h.1).

1998 Amendment. Act 121 amended subsecs. (d), (h) and (i) and added subsec. (d.1).

1982 Amendment. Section 3 of Act 227 provided that, notwithstanding the provisions of

1 Pa.C.S. § 1955, the amendments to section 3301 by Act 101 are repealed.

Cross References. Section 3301 is referred to in sections 3308, 3311, 3502, 5702, 5708, 6105 of this title; sections 3103, 5329 of Title 23 (Domestic Relations); section 7713 of Title 35 (Health and Safety); sections 5552, 6307, 6308, 6336, 9714, 9802 of Title 42 (Judiciary and Judicial Procedure); section 702 of Title 54 (Names); sections 3903, 4103, 7122 of Title 61 (Prisons and Parole).

§ 3302. Causing or risking catastrophe.

(a) Causing catastrophe.--A person who causes a catastrophe by explosion, fire, flood, avalanche, collapse of building, release of poison gas, radioactive material or other harmful or destructive force or substance, or by any other means of causing potentially widespread injury or damage, including selling, dealing in or otherwise providing licenses or permits to transport hazardous materials in violation of 75 Pa.C.S. Ch. 83 (relating to hazardous materials transportation), commits a felony of the first degree if he does so intentionally or knowingly, or a felony of the second degree if he does so recklessly.

(b) Risking catastrophe.--A person is guilty of a felony of the third degree if he recklessly creates a risk of catastrophe in the employment of fire, explosives or other dangerous means listed in subsection (a) of this section.

(Apr. 30, 2002, P.L.300, No.40, eff. 60 days)

Cross References. Section 3302 is referred to in sections 3304, 3311, 5708, 6105 of this title.

§ 3303. Failure to prevent catastrophe.

A person who knowingly or recklessly fails to take reasonable measures to prevent or mitigate a catastrophe, when he can do so without substantial risk to himself, commits a misdemeanor of the second degree if:

(1) he knows that he is under an official, contractual or other legal duty to take such measures; or

(2) he did or assented to the act causing or threatening the catastrophe.

§ 3304. Criminal mischief.

(a) Offense defined.--A person is guilty of criminal mischief if he:

(1) damages tangible property of another intentionally, recklessly, or by negligence in the employment of fire, explosives, or other

dangerous means listed in section 3302(a) of this title (relating to causing or risking catastrophe);

(2) intentionally or recklessly tampers with tangible property of another so as to endanger person or property;

(3) intentionally or recklessly causes another to suffer pecuniary loss by deception or threat;

(4) intentionally defaces or otherwise damages tangible public property or tangible property of another with graffiti by use of any aerosol spray-paint can, broad-tipped indelible marker or similar marking device;

(5) intentionally damages real or personal property of another; or

(6) intentionally defaces personal, private or public property by discharging a paintball gun or paintball marker at that property.

(b) Grading.--Criminal mischief is a felony of the third degree if the actor intentionally causes pecuniary loss in excess of $5,000, or a substantial interruption or impairment of public communication, transportation, supply of water, gas or power, or other public service. It is a misdemeanor of the second degree if the actor intentionally causes pecuniary loss in excess of $1,000, or a misdemeanor of the third degree if he intentionally or recklessly causes pecuniary loss in excess of $500 or causes a loss in excess of $150 for a violation of subsection (a)(4). Otherwise criminal mischief is a summary offense.

(c) Definition.--As used in this section, the term "graffiti" means an unauthorized inscription, word, figure, mark or design which is written, marked, etched, scratched, drawn or painted.

(Apr. 21, 1994, P.L.131, No.17, eff. 60 days; Dec. 20, 1996, P.L.1522, No.198, eff. 60 days; Oct. 2, 2002, P.L.806, No.116, eff. imd.; Dec. 22, 2005, P.L.449, No.85, eff. 60 days)

2005 Amendment. Act 85 amended subsec. (a).

2002 Amendment. Act 116 amended subsec. (a) and added subsec. (c).

1996 Amendment. Act 198 amended subsec. (b).

1994 Amendment. See the preamble to Act 17 of 1994 in the appendix to this title for special provisions relating to legislative findings and declarations.

Cross References. Section 3304 is referred to in section 3311 of this title; sections 3573, 9720 of Title 42 (Judiciary and Judicial Procedure).

§ 3305. Injuring or tampering with fire apparatus, hydrants, etc.

Whoever willfully and maliciously cuts, injures, damages, or destroys or defaces any fire hydrant or any fire hose or fire engine, or other public or private fire equipment, or any apparatus appertaining to the same, commits a misdemeanor of the third degree.

(Nov. 28, 1973, P.L.370, No.131)

1973 Amendment. Act 131 added section 3305.

§ 3306. Unauthorized use or opening of fire hydrants.

Whoever opens for private usage any fire hydrant without authorization of the water authority or company having jurisdiction over such fire hydrant, commits a summary offense.

(Nov. 28, 1973, P.L.370, No.131)

1973 Amendment. Act 131 added section 3306.

§ 3307. Institutional vandalism.

(a) Offenses defined.--A person commits the offense of institutional vandalism if he knowingly desecrates, as defined in section 5509 (relating to desecration or sale of venerated objects), vandalizes, defaces or otherwise damages:

(1) any church, synagogue or other facility or place used for religious worship or other religious purposes;

(2) any cemetery, mortuary or other facility used for the purpose of burial or memorializing the dead;

(3) any school, educational facility, community center, municipal building, courthouse facility, State or local government building or vehicle or juvenile detention center;

(4) the grounds adjacent to and owned or occupied by any facility set forth in paragraph (1), (2) or (3); or

(5) any personal property located in any facility set forth in this subsection.

(a.1) Illegal possession.--A person commits the offense of institutional vandalism if, with intent to violate subsection (a), the person carries an aerosol spray-paint can, broad-tipped indelible marker or similar marking device onto property identified in subsection (a).

(b) Grading.--An offense under this section is a felony of the third degree if the act is one of desecration as defined in section 5509 or if the actor causes pecuniary loss in excess of $5,000. Pecuniary loss includes the cost of repair or replacement of the property affected. Otherwise, institutional vandalism is a misdemeanor of the second degree.

(June 18, 1982, P.L.537, No.154, eff. imd.; Dec. 20, 1983, P.L.291, No.78, eff. imd.; Oct. 3, 1988, P.L.734, No.103, eff. 60 days; Apr. 21, 1994, P.L.130, No.16, eff. 60 days; Oct. 2, 2002, P.L.806, No.116, eff. imd.)

2002 Amendment. Act 116 amended subsec. (a).

1994 Amendment. Act 16 added subsec. (a.1). See the preamble to Act 16 of 1994 in the appendix to this title for special provisions relating to legislative findings and declarations.

Special Provisions in Appendix. See section 2 of Act 154 of 1982 in the appendix to this title for special provisions relating to right of action for injunction, damages or other relief.

Cross References. Section 3307 is referred to in sections 2710, 3311 of this title; sections 8309, 9720 of Title 42 (Judiciary and Judicial Procedure).

§ 3308. Additional fine for arson committed for profit.

(a) General rule.--Any person convicted under section 2506 (relating to arson murder) or 3301 (relating to arson and related offenses) where any consideration was paid or payable, in addition to any sentence of imprisonment, shall be fined an amount double the amount of the consideration or the maximum lawful fine as provided in section 1101 (relating to fines), whichever is greater.

(b) Disposition of fines and forfeitures.--All fines collected and bail deposits forfeited under subsection (a) shall be provided to the Pennsylvania Emergency Management Agency for the Pennsylvania State Firemen's Training School also known as the Vocational Education Fire School and Fire Training and Education Programs.

(Dec. 7, 1982, P.L.811, No.227, eff. 60 days)

1982 Amendment. Act 227 added section 3308.

References in Text. Section 2506, referred to subsec. (a), did not exist when this section was added. Present section 2506

contains provisions relating to drug delivery resulting in death.

§ 3309. Agricultural vandalism.

(a) Offense defined.--A person commits the offense of agricultural vandalism if he intentionally or recklessly defaces, marks or otherwise damages the real or tangible personal property of another, where the property defaced, marked or otherwise damaged is used in agricultural activity or farming.

(b) Grading.--Agricultural vandalism is a felony of the third degree if the actor intentionally causes pecuniary loss in excess of $5,000, a misdemeanor of the first degree if the actor intentionally causes pecuniary loss in excess of $1,000 or a misdemeanor of the second degree if the actor intentionally or recklessly causes pecuniary loss in excess of $500. Pecuniary loss includes the cost of repair or replacement of the property affected. Otherwise, agricultural vandalism is a misdemeanor of the third degree.

(c) Definition.--As used in this section, the terms "agricultural activity" and "farming" include public and private research activity, records, data and data-gathering equipment related to agricultural products as well as the commercial production of agricultural crops, livestock or livestock products, poultry or poultry products, trees and timber products, milk, eggs or dairy products, or fruits or other horticultural products.

(July 13, 1988, P.L.500, No.86, eff. imd.; June 22, 2001, P.L.386, No.27, eff. imd.)

2001 Amendment. Act 27 amended subsec. (c).

1988 Amendment. Act 86 added section 3309.

Cross References. Section 3309 is referred to in sections 3311, 3503 of this title; section 2303 of Title 3 (Agriculture).

§ 3310. Agricultural crop destruction.

(a) Offenses defined.--A person commits a felony of the second degree if he intentionally and knowingly damages any field crop, vegetable or fruit plant or tree that is grown, stored or raised for scientific or commercial purposes or for any testing or research purpose in conjunction with a public or private research facility or a university or any Federal, State or local government agency.

(b) Restitution.--Any person convicted of violating this section shall, in addition to any other penalty imposed, be sentenced to pay the owner of the damaged field crops, vegetable or fruit plants or trees restitution. Restitution shall be in an amount equal to the cost of the financial damages incurred as a result of the offense, including the following:

(1) Value of the damaged crop.

(2) Disposal of the damaged crop.

(3) Cleanup of the property.

(4) Lost revenue for the aggrieved owner of the damaged crop.

(c) Exceptions.--The provisions of this section shall not apply to field crops, vegetable or fruit plants or trees damaged through research or normal commercial activity.

(June 22, 2001, P.L.386, No.27, eff. imd.; Apr. 14, 2006, P.L.81, No.27, eff. 60 days)

Cross References. Section 3310 is referred to in section 3311 of this title.

§ 3311. Ecoterrorism.

(a) General rule.--A person is guilty of ecoterrorism if the person commits a specified offense against property intending to do any of the following:

(1) Intimidate or coerce an individual lawfully:

(i) participating in an activity involving animals, plants or an activity involving natural resources; or

(ii) using an animal, plant or natural resource facility.

(2) Prevent or obstruct an individual from lawfully:

(i) participating in an activity involving animals, plants or an activity involving natural resources; or

(ii) using an animal, plant or natural resource facility.

(b) Grading and penalty.--

(1) If the specified offense against property is a summary offense, an offense under this section shall be classified as a misdemeanor of the third degree.

(2) If the specified offense against property is a misdemeanor or a felony of the third or second degree, an offense under this section shall be classified one degree higher than the classification of the specified offense against property specified in section 106 (relating to classes of offenses).

(3) If the specified offense against property is a felony of the first degree, a person convicted of an offense under this section shall be sentenced to a term of imprisonment fixed by the court at not more than 40 years and may be sentenced to pay a fine of not more than $100,000.

(c) Restitution.--Any person convicted of violating this section shall, in addition to any other penalty imposed, be sentenced to pay the owner of any damaged property which resulted from the violation restitution. Restitution shall be in an amount up to triple the value of the property damages incurred as a result of the specified offense against property. In ordering restitution pursuant to this subsection, the court shall consider as part of the value of the damaged property the market value of the property prior to the violation and the production, research, testing, replacement and development costs directly related to the property that was the subject of the specified offense.

(c.1) Immunity.--A person who exercises the right of petition or free speech under the United States Constitution or the Constitution of Pennsylvania on public property or with the permission of the landowner where the person is peaceably demonstrating or peaceably pursuing his constitutional rights shall be immune from prosecution for these actions under this section or from civil liability under 42 Pa.C.S. § 8319 (relating to ecoterrorism).

(d) Definitions.--As used in this section, the following words and phrases shall have the meanings given to them in this subsection:

"Activity involving animals or plants." A lawful activity involving the use of animals, animal parts or plants, including any of the following:

(1) Activities authorized under 30 Pa.C.S. (relating to fish) and 34 Pa.C.S. (relating to game).

(2) Activities authorized under the act of December 7, 1982 (P.L.784, No.225), known as the Dog Law.

(3) Food production, processing and preparation.

(4) Clothing manufacturing and distribution.

(5) Entertainment and recreation.

(6) Research, teaching and testing.

(7) Propagation, production, sale, use or possession of legal plants.

(8) Agricultural activity and farming as defined in section 3309 (relating to agricultural vandalism).

"Activity involving natural resources." A lawful activity involving the use of a natural resource with an economic value, including any of the following:

(1) Mining, foresting, harvesting or processing natural resources.

(2) The sale, loan or lease of products which requires the use of natural resources.

"Animal, plant or natural resource facility." A vehicle, building, structure or other premises:

(1) where an animal, plant or natural resource is lawfully housed, exhibited or offered for sale; or

(2) which is used for scientific purposes involving animals, plants or natural resources, including research, teaching and testing.

"Specified offense against property." Any of the following offenses:

Section 3301(a), (c), (d), (d.1) and (f) (relating to arson and related offenses).

Section 3302 (relating to causing or risking catastrophe).

Section 3304 (relating to criminal mischief).

Section 3307 (relating to institutional vandalism).

Section 3309 (relating to agricultural vandalism).

Section 3310 (relating to agricultural crop destruction).

Section 3502 (relating to burglary) but only if the actor commits the crime for the purpose of committing one of the other offenses listed in this definition.

Section 3503 (relating to criminal trespass) but only if the actor commits the crime for the purpose of releasing a dangerous transmissible disease or hazardous substance, as those terms are defined under 3 Pa.C.S. § 2303 (relating to definitions), threatening or terrorizing the owner or occupant of the premises, starting or causing to be started any fire upon the premises or defacing or damaging the premises.

Section 3921 (relating to theft by unlawful taking or disposition).

Section 3922 (relating to theft by deception).

Section 4101 (relating to forgery).

Section 4120 (relating to identity theft).

(Apr. 14, 2006, P.L.81, No.27, eff. 60 days; Nov. 23, 2010, P.L.1360, No.125, eff. imd.)

2010 Amendment. Act 125 amended the def. of "specified offense against property" in subsec. (d).

2006 Amendment. Act 27 added section 3311.

Cross References. Section 3311 is referred to in sections 8319, 9714 of Title 42 (Judiciary and Judicial Procedure).

§ 3312. Destruction of a survey monument.

(a) Offense defined.--

(1) A person commits a summary offense if he intentionally cuts, injures, damages, destroys, defaces or removes any survey monument or marker, other than a natural object such as a tree or stream.

(2) A person commits a misdemeanor of the second degree if he willfully or maliciously cuts, injures, damages, destroys, defaces or removes any survey monument or marker in order to call into question a boundary line.

(b) **Restitution.**--Any person convicted of violating this section shall, in addition to any other penalty imposed, be liable for the cost of the reestablishment of permanent survey monuments or markers by a professional land surveyor and all reasonable attorney fees.

(c) **Affirmative defense.**--It is an affirmative defense to any prosecution for an offense under this section that the survey monument or marker was improperly placed by a professional land surveyor.

(d) **Definitions.**--As used in this section, the following words and phrases shall have the meanings given to them in this subsection:

"Professional land surveyor." As defined under the act of May 23, 1945 (P.L.913, No.367), known as the Engineer, Land Surveyor and Geologist Registration Law.

"Survey monument or marker." Any object adopted or placed by a professional land surveyor to define the boundaries of a property, including, but not limited to, natural objects such as trees or streams, or artificial monuments such as iron pins, concrete monuments, set stones or party walls. The phrase does not include a wooden stake placed by a professional land surveyor as a temporary marker or placeholder.

(July 7, 2006, P.L.348, No.72, eff. 60 days)

2006 Amendment. Act 72 added section 3312.

§ 3313. Illegal dumping of methamphetamine waste.

(a) Offense defined.--A person commits a felony of the third degree if he intentionally, knowingly or recklessly deposits, stores or disposes on any property a precursor or reagent substance, chemical waste or debris, resulting from or used in the manufacture of methamphetamine or the preparation of a precursor or reagent substance for the manufacture of methamphetamine.

(b) Exceptions.--Subsection (a) does not apply to the disposal of waste products:

(1) by a licensed pharmaceutical company in the normal course of business; or

(2) pursuant to Federal or State laws regulating the cleanup or disposal of waste products from unlawful manufacturing of methamphetamine.

(Apr. 29, 2010, P.L.174, No.18, eff. 60 days)

2010 Amendment. Act 18 added section 3313.

CHAPTER 35 BURGLARY AND OTHER CRIMINAL INTRUSION

Sec.
3501. Definitions.
3502. Burglary.
3503. Criminal trespass.
3504. Railroad protection, railroad vandalism and interference with transportation facilities.
3505. Unlawful use of unmanned aircraft.

Enactment. Chapter 35 was added December 6, 1972, P.L.1482, No.334, effective in six months.

Cross References. Chapter 35 is referred to in sections 5985.1, 5993 of Title 42 (Judiciary and Judicial Procedure).

§ 3501. Definitions.

Subject to additional definitions contained in subsequent provisions of this chapter which are applicable to specific provisions of this chapter, the following words or phrases when used in this chapter shall have, unless the context clearly indicates otherwise, the meanings given to them in this section:

"Occupied structure." Any structure, vehicle or place adapted for overnight accommodation of persons, or for carrying on business therein, whether or not a person is actually present.

§ 3502. Burglary.

(a) Offense defined.--A person commits the offense of burglary if, with the intent to commit a crime therein, the person:

(1) (i) enters a building or occupied structure, or separately secured or occupied portion thereof, that is adapted for overnight accommodations in which at the time of the offense any person is present and the person commits, attempts or threatens to commit a bodily injury crime therein;

(ii) enters a building or occupied structure, or separately secured or occupied portion thereof that is adapted for overnight accommodations in which at the time of the offense any person is present;

(2) enters a building or occupied structure, or separately secured or occupied portion thereof that is adapted for overnight accommodations in which at the time of the offense no person is present;

(3) enters a building or occupied structure, or separately secured or occupied portion thereof that is not adapted for overnight accommodations in which at the time of the offense any person is present; or

(4) enters a building or occupied structure, or separately secured or occupied portion thereof that is not adapted for overnight accommodations in which at the time of the offense no person is present.

(b) Defense.--It is a defense to prosecution for burglary if any of the following exists at the time of the commission of the offense:

(1) The building or structure was abandoned.

(2) The premises are open to the public.

(3) The actor is licensed or privileged to enter.

(c) Grading.--

(1) Except as provided in paragraph (2), burglary is a felony of the first degree.

(2) As follows:

(i) Except under subparagraph (ii), an offense under subsection (a)(4) is a felony of the second degree.

(ii) If the actor's intent upon entering the building, structure or portion under subparagraph (i) is to commit theft of a controlled substance or designer drug as those terms are defined in section 2 of the act of April 14, 1972 (P.L.233, No.64), known as The Controlled Substance, Drug, Device and Cosmetic Act, burglary is a felony of the first degree.

(d) **Multiple convictions.**--A person may not be sentenced both for burglary and for the offense which it was his intent to commit after the burglarious entry or for an attempt to commit that offense, unless the additional offense constitutes a felony of the first or second degree.

(e) **Definitions.**--As used in this section, the following words and phrases shall have the meanings given to them in this subsection:

"Bodily injury crime." As follows:

(1) An act, attempt or threat to commit an act which would constitute a misdemeanor or felony under the following:

Chapter 25 (relating to criminal homicide).

Chapter 27 (relating to assault).

Chapter 29 (relating to kidnapping).

Chapter 31 (relating to sexual offenses).

Section 3301 (relating to arson and related offenses).

Chapter 37 (relating to robbery).

Chapter 49 Subch. B (relating to victim and witness intimidation).

(2) The term includes violations of any protective order issued as a result of an act related to domestic violence.

(Dec. 19, 1990, P.L.1196, No.201, eff. July 1, 1991; July 5, 2012, P.L.1050, No.122, eff. 60 days; Dec. 23, 2013, P.L.1264, No.131, eff. 60 days; Nov. 4, 2016, P.L.1194, No.158, eff. 60 days)

2016 Amendment. Act 158 amended subsec. (a)(1) and added subsec. (e).

2013 Amendment. Act 131 amended subsec. (c)(2). Section 3 of Act 131 provided that the amendment shall apply to offenses committed on or after the effective date of section 3.

Cross References. Section 3502 is referred to in sections 3311, 5702, 5708, 6105 of this title; sections 5552, 6307, 6308, 9714, 9720.7, 9802 of Title 42 (Judiciary and Judicial Procedure); sections 3903, 4103, 7122 of Title 61 (Prisons and Parole).

§ 3503. Criminal trespass.

(a) Buildings and occupied structures.--

(1) A person commits an offense if, knowing that he is not licensed or privileged to do so, he:

(i) enters, gains entry by subterfuge or surreptitiously remains in any building or occupied structure or separately secured or occupied portion thereof; or

(ii) breaks into any building or occupied structure or separately secured or occupied portion thereof.

(2) An offense under paragraph (1)(i) is a felony of the third degree, and an offense under paragraph (1)(ii) is a felony of the second degree.

(3) As used in this subsection:

"Breaks into." To gain entry by force, breaking, intimidation, unauthorized opening of locks, or through an opening not designed for human access.

(b) Defiant trespasser.--

(1) A person commits an offense if, knowing that he is not licensed or privileged to do so, he enters or remains in any place as to which notice against trespass is given by:

(i) actual communication to the actor;

(ii) posting in a manner prescribed by law or reasonably likely to come to the attention of intruders;

(iii) fencing or other enclosure manifestly designed to exclude intruders;

(iv) notices posted in a manner prescribed by law or reasonably likely to come to the person's attention at each entrance of school grounds that visitors are prohibited without authorization from a designated school, center or program official;

(v) an actual communication to the actor to leave school grounds as communicated by a school, center or program official, employee or agent or a law enforcement officer; or

(vi) subject to paragraph (3), the placement of identifying purple paint marks on trees or posts on the property which are:

(A) vertical lines of not less than eight inches in length and not less than one inch in width;

(B) placed so that the bottom of the mark is not less than three feet from the ground nor more than five feet from the ground; and

(C) placed at locations that are readily visible to a person approaching the property and no more than 100 feet apart.

(2) Except as provided in paragraph (1)(v), an offense under this subsection constitutes a misdemeanor of the third degree if

the offender defies an order to leave personally communicated to him by the owner of the premises or other authorized person. An offense under paragraph (1)(v) constitutes a misdemeanor of the first degree. Otherwise it is a summary offense.

(3) Paragraph (1)(vi) shall not apply in a county of the first class or a county of the second class.

(b.1) Simple trespasser.--

(1) A person commits an offense if, knowing that he is not licensed or privileged to do so, he enters or remains in any place for the purpose of:

(i) threatening or terrorizing the owner or occupant of the premises;

(ii) starting or causing to be started any fire upon the premises; or

(iii) defacing or damaging the premises.

(2) An offense under this subsection constitutes a summary offense.

(b.2) Agricultural trespasser.--

(1) A person commits an offense if knowing that he is not licensed or privileged to do so he:

(i) enters or remains on any agricultural or other open lands when such lands are posted in a manner prescribed by law or reasonably likely to come to the person's attention or are fenced or enclosed in a manner manifestly designed to exclude trespassers or to confine domestic animals; or

(ii) enters or remains on any agricultural or other open lands and defies an order not to enter or to leave that has been personally communicated to him by the owner of the lands or other authorized person.

(2) An offense under this subsection shall be graded as follows:

(i) An offense under paragraph (1)(i) constitutes a misdemeanor of the third degree and is punishable by imprisonment for a term of not more than one year and a fine of not less than $250.

(ii) An offense under paragraph (1)(ii) constitutes a misdemeanor of the second degree and is punishable by imprisonment for a term of not more than two years and a fine of not less than $500 nor more than $5,000.

(3) For the purposes of this subsection, the phrase "agricultural or other open lands" shall mean any land on which agricultural activity or farming as defined in section 3309 (relating to agricultural vandalism) is conducted or any land populated by forest trees of any size

and capable of producing timber or other wood products or any land in an agricultural security area as defined in the act of June 30, 1981 (P.L.128, No.43), known as the Agricultural Area Security Law, or any area zoned for agricultural use.

(b.3) Agricultural biosecurity area trespasser.--

(1) A person commits an offense if the person does any of the following:

(i) Enters an agricultural biosecurity area, knowing that the person is not licensed or privileged to do so.

(ii) Knowingly or recklessly fails to perform reasonable measures for biosecurity that by posted notice are required to be performed for entry to the agricultural biosecurity area.

(2) It is a defense to prosecution under paragraph (1)(ii) that:

(i) no reasonable means or method was available to perform the measures that the posted notice required to be performed for entry to the agricultural biosecurity area;

(ii) entry is made in response to a condition within the agricultural biosecurity area that the person reasonably believes to be a serious threat to human or animal health as necessitating immediate entry to the agricultural biosecurity area; or

(iii) entry is made under exigent circumstances by a law enforcement officer to:

(A) pursue and apprehend a suspect of criminal conduct reasonably believed by the officer to be present within the agricultural biosecurity area; or

(B) prevent the destruction of evidence of criminal conduct reasonably believed by the officer to be located within the agricultural biosecurity area.

(3) (i) Except as set forth in subparagraph (iii), an offense under paragraph (1)(i) constitutes a misdemeanor of the third degree.

(ii) Except as set forth in subparagraph (iii), an offense under paragraph (1)(ii) constitutes a summary offense.

(iii) If an offense under paragraph (1) causes damage to or death of an animal or plant within an agricultural biosecurity area, the offense constitutes a misdemeanor of the first degree.

(4) For purposes of this subsection, the terms "agricultural biosecurity area" and "posted notice" shall have the meanings given

to them in 3 Pa.C.S. § 2303 (relating to definitions).

(c) Defenses.--It is a defense to prosecution under this section that:

(1) a building or occupied structure involved in an offense under subsection (a) of this section was abandoned;

(2) the premises were at the time open to members of the public and the actor complied with all lawful conditions imposed on access to or remaining in the premises; or

(3) the actor reasonably believed that the owner of the premises, or other person empowered to license access thereto, would have licensed him to enter or remain.

(c.1) Applicability.--This section shall not apply to an unarmed person who enters onto posted property for the sole purpose of retrieving a hunting dog.

(d) Definition.--As used in this section, the term "school grounds" means any building of or grounds of any elementary or secondary publicly funded educational institution, any elementary or secondary private school licensed by the Department of Education, any elementary or secondary parochial school, any certified day-care center or any licensed preschool program.

(June 23, 1978, P.L.497, No.76, eff. 60 days; Oct. 27, 1995, P.L.334, No.53, eff. 60 days; Dec. 3, 1998, P.L.933, No.121, eff. imd.; Oct. 2, 2002, P.L.806, No.116, eff. imd.; Nov. 23, 2010, P.L.1360, No.125, eff. imd.; Nov. 6, 2014, P.L.2921, No.192, eff. 60 days; Nov. 27, 2019, P.L.714, No.103, eff. 60 days)

2019 Amendment. Act 103 amended subsec. (b)(1) and added subsecs. (b)(3) and (c.1).

2016Unconstitutionality. Act 192 of 2014 was declared unconstitutional. Leach v. Commonwealth, 141 A.3d 426 (Pa. 2016). The Legislative Reference Bureau effectuated the 2016 unconstitutionality.

2014 Amendment. Act 192 amended subsecs. (b.1) and (d).

2010 Amendment. Act 125 added subsec. (b.3).

2002 Amendment. Act 116 amended subsec. (b) and added subsec. (d).

1998 Amendment. Act 121 added subsec. (b.2).

1978 Amendment. Act 76 amended subsec. (a).

Cross References. Section 3503 is referred to in sections 2710, 3019, 3311, 6105 of this title; section 2303 of Title 3 (Agriculture); sections 3573, 6328 of Title 42 (Judiciary and Judicial Procedure).

§ 3504. Railroad protection, railroad vandalism and interference with transportation facilities.

(a) Damage to railroad or delay of railroad operations.--

(1) A person commits an offense if, without lawful authority or the railroad carrier's consent, he causes damage to property that he knows or reasonably should have known to be railroad property, including the railroad right-of-way or yard, or causes a delay in railroad operations by an act including, but not limited to:

(i) Knowingly, purposefully or recklessly disrupting, delaying or preventing the operation of any train, jitney, trolley or any other facility of transportation.

(ii) Driving or operating a recreational vehicle or nonrecreational vehicle, including, but not limited to, a bicycle, motorcycle, snowmobile, all-terrain vehicle, car or truck.

(iii) Knowingly, purposefully or recklessly damaging railroad property, railroad infrastructure or railroad equipment or using railroad property to access adjoining property to commit acts of vandalism, theft or other criminal acts.

(2) An offense under this subsection constitutes a misdemeanor of the third degree.

(b) Stowaways prohibited.--

(1) A person commits an offense if, without lawful authority or the railroad carrier's consent, he rides on the outside of a train or inside a passenger car, locomotive or freight car, including a box car, flatbed or container.

(2) An offense under this subsection constitutes a misdemeanor of the third degree.

(c) Definitions.--As used in this section, the following words and phrases shall have the meanings given to them in this subsection:

"Railroad." Any form of nonhighway ground transportation that runs on rails or electromagnetic guideways, including, but not limited to:

(1) Commuter or other short-haul railroad passenger service in a metropolitan or suburban area.

(2) High-speed ground transportation systems that connect metropolitan areas, but not rapid transit operations in an urban area that are

not connected to the general railroad system of transportation.

"Railroad carrier." A person, including, but not limited to, an owner or operator, providing railroad transportation.

"Railroad carrier's consent." Written or other affirmative communication of permission to be on railroad property. Consent shall not be implied.

"Railroad property." All tangible property owned, leased or operated by a railroad carrier, including a right-of-way, track, bridge, yard, shop, station, tunnel, viaduct, trestle, depot, warehouse, terminal or any other structure, appurtenance or equipment owned, leased or used in the operation of any railroad carrier, including a train, locomotive, engine, railroad car, work equipment, rolling stock or safety device. The term does not include a railroad carrier's administrative building or offices, office equipment or intangible property such as computer software or other information.

"Right-of-way." The track or roadbed owned, leased or operated by a railroad carrier which is located on either side of its tracks and which is readily recognizable to a reasonable person as being railroad property or is reasonably identified as such by fencing or appropriate signs.

"Yard." A system of parallel tracks, crossovers and switches where railroad cars are switched and made up into trains and where railroad cars, locomotives and other rolling stock are kept when not in use or when awaiting repairs.

(July 15, 2004, P.L.691, No.74, eff. 60 days)

2004 Amendment. Act 74 added section 3504.

§ 3505. Unlawful use of unmanned aircraft.

(a) Offense defined.--A person commits the offense of unlawful use of unmanned aircraft if the person uses an unmanned aircraft intentionally or knowingly to:

(1) Conduct surveillance of another person in a private place.

(2) Operate in a manner which places another person in reasonable fear of bodily injury.

(3) Deliver, provide, transmit or furnish contraband in violation of section 5123 (relating to contraband) or 61 Pa.C.S. § 5902 (relating to contraband prohibited).

(b) Grading.--The offense of unlawful use of unmanned aircraft shall be graded as follows:

(1) An offense under subsection (a)(1) or (2) is a summary offense punishable by a fine of up to $300.

(2) An offense under subsection (a)(3) is a felony of the second degree.

(c) Exceptions for law enforcement officers.--Subsection (a) shall not apply if the conduct proscribed under subsection (a) is committed by any of the following:

(1) Law enforcement officers engaged in the performance of their official law enforcement duties.

(2) Personnel of the Department of Corrections, local correctional facility, prison or jail engaged in the performance of their official duties.

(d) Other exceptions.--Subsection (a)(1) and (2) shall not apply if the conduct proscribed under subsection (a)(1) or (2) is committed by any of the following:

(1) Firefighters, as defined in section 2 of the act of December 16, 1998 (P.L.980, No.129), known as the Police Officer, Firefighter, Correction Employee and National Guard Member Child Beneficiary Education Act, or special fire police, as provided for in 35 Pa.C.S. Ch. 74 Subch. D (relating to special fire police), engaged in the performance of their official firefighting or fire police duties.

(2) Emergency medical responders, as defined in 35 Pa.C.S. § 8103 (relating to definitions), engaged in the performance of their official duties.

(3) An employee or agent of an electric, water, natural gas or other utility while engaged in the performance of the employee's or agent's official duties.

(4) An employee or agent of a government agency while engaged in the performance of the employee's or agent's official duties.

(e) Aerial data collection.--Subsection (a)(1) shall not apply if the conduct proscribed is committed by a person engaged in aerial data collection if:

(1) the person utilized the unmanned aircraft in a manner which complies with Federal Aviation Administration regulations or the unmanned aircraft is authorized by an exemption that is issued by the Federal Aviation Administration; and

(2) the person did not knowingly or intentionally conduct surveillance of another person in a private place.

(f) Definitions.--As used in this section, the following words and phrases shall have the meanings given to them in this subsection unless the context clearly indicates otherwise:

"Bodily injury." As defined in section 2301 (relating to definitions).

"Law enforcement officer." An officer of the United States, of another state or subdivision thereof, or of the Commonwealth or political subdivision thereof, who is empowered by law to conduct investigations of or to make arrests for offenses enumerated in this title or an equivalent crime in another jurisdiction and an attorney authorized by law to prosecute or participate in the prosecution of the offense.

"Private place." A place where a person has a reasonable expectation of privacy.

"Surveillance." Using or causing to be used an unmanned aircraft to observe, record or invade the privacy of another.

"Unmanned aircraft." An aircraft that is operated without the possibility of direct human intervention from within or on the aircraft.

(Oct. 12, 2018, P.L.516, No.78, eff. 90 days)

2018 Amendment. Act 78 added section 3505.

Cross References. Section 3505 is referred to in section 305 of Title 53 (Municipalities Generally).

CHAPTER 37 ROBBERY

Sec.
3701. Robbery.
3702. Robbery of motor vehicle.

Enactment. Chapter 37 was added December 6, 1972, P.L.1482, No.334, effective in six months.

Cross References. Chapter 37 is referred to in sections 911, 3502 of this title; section 3103 of Title 23 (Domestic Relations); sections 5985.1, 5993 of Title 42 (Judiciary and Judicial Procedure).

§ 3701. Robbery.
(a) Offense defined.--

(1) A person is guilty of robbery if, in the course of committing a theft, he:

(i) inflicts serious bodily injury upon another;

(ii) threatens another with or intentionally puts him in fear of immediate serious bodily injury;

(iii) commits or threatens immediately to commit any felony of the first or second degree;

(iv) inflicts bodily injury upon another or threatens another with or intentionally puts him in fear of immediate bodily injury;

(v) physically takes or removes property from the person of another by force however slight; or

(vi) takes or removes the money of a financial institution without the permission of the financial institution by making a demand of an employee of the financial institution orally or in writing with the intent to deprive the financial institution thereof.

(2) An act shall be deemed "in the course of committing a theft" if it occurs in an attempt to commit theft or in flight after the attempt or commission.

(3) For purposes of this subsection, a "financial institution" means a bank, trust company, savings trust, credit union or similar institution.

(b) Grading.--

(1) Except as provided under paragraph (2), robbery under subsection (a)(1)(iv) and (vi) is a felony of the second degree; robbery under subsection (a)(1)(v) is a felony of the third degree; otherwise, it is a felony of the first degree.

(2) If the object of a robbery under paragraph (1) is a controlled substance or designer drug as those terms are defined in section 2 of the act of April 14, 1972 (P.L.233, No.64), known as The Controlled Substance, Drug, Device and Cosmetic Act, robbery is a felony of the first degree.

(June 24, 1976, P.L.425, No.102, eff. imd.; Mar. 16, 2010, P.L.143, No.11, eff. 60 days; Dec. 23, 2013, P.L.1264, No.131, eff. 60 days)

2013 Amendment. Act 131 amended subsec. (b). Section 3 of Act 131 provided that the amendment shall apply to offenses committed on or after the effective date of section 3.

Cross References. Section 3701 is referred to in sections 5702, 5708, 6105 of this title; sections 5552, 6302, 6307, 6308, 6336, 6355, 9714, 9719, 9802 of Title 42 (Judiciary and Judicial Procedure); section 702 of Title 54 (Names); sections 3903, 4103, 7122 of Title 61 (Prisons and Parole).

§ 3702. Robbery of motor vehicle.

(a) Offense defined.--A person commits a felony of the first degree if he steals or takes a motor vehicle from another person in the presence of that person or any other person in lawful possession of the motor vehicle.

(b) Sentencing.--The Pennsylvania Commission on Sentencing, pursuant to 42 Pa.C.S. § 2154 (relating to adoption of guidelines for sentencing), shall provide for a sentencing enhancement for an offense under this section.

(June 23, 1993, P.L.124, No.28, eff. imd.)

1993 Amendment. Act 28 added section 3702.

Cross References. Section 3702 is referred to in sections 3213, 5702, 6105 of this title; section 6302 of Title 42 (Judiciary and Judicial Procedure); sections 3903, 4103 of Title 61 (Prisons and Parole).

CHAPTER 39 THEFT AND RELATED OFFENSES

Subchapter
A. General Provisions
B. Definition of Offenses

Enactment. Chapter 39 was added December 6, 1972, P.L.1482, No.334, effective in six months.

Cross References. Chapter 39 is referred to in section 911 of this title; section 2303 of Title 44 (Law and Justice); section 2905 of Title 66 (Public Utilities).

SUBCHAPTER A
GENERAL PROVISIONS

§ 3901. Definitions.

Subject to additional definitions contained in subsequent provisions of this chapter which are applicable to specific provisions of this chapter, the following words and phrases when used in this chapter shall have, unless the context clearly indicates otherwise, the meanings given to them in this section:

"Deprive."

(1) To withhold property of another permanently or for so extended a period as to appropriate a major portion of its economic value, or with intent to restore only upon payment of reward or other compensation; or

(2) to dispose of the property so as to make it unlikely that the owner will recover it.

"Financial institution." A bank, insurance company, credit union, building and loan association, investment trust or other organization held out to the public as a place of deposit of funds or medium of savings or collective investment.

"Firearm." Any weapon that is designed to or may readily be converted to expel any projectile by the action of an explosive or the frame or receiver of any such weapon.

"Government." The United States, any state, county, municipality, or other political unit, or any department, agency or subdivision of any of the foregoing, or any corporation or other association carrying out the functions of government.

"Movable property." Property the location of which can be changed, including things growing on, affixed to, or found in land, and documents although the rights represented thereby have no physical location. "Immovable property" is all other property.

"Obtain."

(1) To bring about a transfer or purported transfer of legal interest in property, whether to the obtainer or another; or

(2) in relation to labor or service, to secure performance thereof.

"Property." Anything of value, including real estate, tangible and intangible personal property, contract rights, choses-in-action and other interests in or claims to wealth, admission or transportation tickets, captured or domestic animals, food and drink, electric or other power.

"Property of another." Includes property in which any person other than the actor has an interest which the actor is not privileged to infringe, regardless of the fact that the actor also has an interest in the property and regardless of the fact that the other person might be precluded from civil recovery because the property was used in an unlawful transaction or was subject to forfeiture as contraband. Property in possession of the actor shall not be deemed property of another who has only a security interest therein, even if legal title is in the creditor pursuant to a conditional sales contract or other security agreement.

(July 17, 2007, P.L.139, No.41, eff. 60 days)

2007 Amendment. Act 41 added the def. of "firearm."

§ 3902. Consolidation of theft offenses.

Conduct denominated theft in this chapter constitutes a single offense. An accusation of theft may be supported by evidence that it was committed in any manner that would be theft under this chapter, notwithstanding the specification of a different manner in the complaint or indictment, subject only to the power of the court to ensure fair trial by granting a continuance or other appropriate relief where the conduct of the defense would be prejudiced by lack of fair notice or by surprise.

§ 3903. Grading of theft offenses.

(a) Felony of the second degree.--Theft constitutes a felony of the second degree if:

(1) The offense is committed during a manmade disaster, a natural disaster or a war-caused disaster and constitutes a violation of section 3921 (relating to theft by unlawful taking or disposition), 3925 (relating to receiving stolen property), 3928 (relating to unauthorized use of automobiles and other vehicles) or 3929 (relating to retail theft).

(2) The property stolen is a firearm.

(3) In the case of theft by receiving stolen property, the property received, retained or disposed of is a firearm.

(4) The property stolen is any amount of anhydrous ammonia.

(5) The amount involved is $100,000 or more but less than $500,000.

(a.1) Felony of the third degree.--Except as provided in subsection (a) or (a.2), theft constitutes a felony of the third degree if the amount involved exceeds $2,000, or if the property stolen is an automobile, airplane, motorcycle, motorboat or other motor-propelled vehicle, or in the case of theft by receiving stolen property, if the receiver is in the business of buying or selling stolen property.

(a.2) Felony of the first degree.--Except as provided in subsections (a) and (a.1), theft constitutes a felony of the first degree if:

(1) in the case of theft by receiving stolen property, the property received, retained or disposed of is a firearm and the receiver is in the business of buying or selling stolen property; or

(2) the amount involved is $500,000 or more.

(b) Other grades.--Theft not within subsection (a), (a.1) or (a.2), constitutes a misdemeanor of the first degree, except that if the property was not taken from the person or by threat, or in breach of fiduciary obligation, and:

(1) the amount involved was $50 or more but less than $200 the offense constitutes a misdemeanor of the second degree; or

(2) the amount involved was less than $50 the offense constitutes a misdemeanor of the third degree.

(c) Valuation.--The amount involved in a theft shall be ascertained as follows:

(1) Except as otherwise specified in this section, value means the market value of the property at the time and place of the crime, or if such cannot be satisfactorily ascertained, the cost of replacement of the property within a reasonable time after the crime.

(2) Whether or not they have been issued or delivered, certain written instruments, not including those having a readily ascertainable market value such as some public and corporate bonds and securities, shall be evaluated as follows:

(i) The value of an instrument constituting an evidence of debt, such as a check, draft or promissory note, shall be deemed the amount due or collectible thereon or thereby, such figure ordinarily being the face amount of the indebtedness less any portion thereof which has been satisfied.

(ii) The value of any other instrument which creates, releases, discharges or otherwise affects any valuable legal right, privilege or obligation shall be deemed the greatest amount of economic loss which the owner of the instrument might reasonably suffer by virtue of the loss of the instrument.

(3) When the value of property cannot be satisfactorily ascertained pursuant to the standards set forth in paragraphs (1) and (2) of this subsection its value shall be deemed to be an amount less than $50. Amounts involved in

thefts committed pursuant to one scheme or course of conduct, whether from the same person or several persons, may be aggregated in determining the grade of the offense.

(d) **Definitions.**--As used in this section, the following words and phrases shall have the meanings given to them in this subsection:

"Manmade disaster." Any industrial, nuclear or transportation accident, explosion, conflagration, power failure, natural resource shortage or other condition, except enemy action, resulting from manmade causes, such as oil spills and other injurious environmental contamination, which threatens or causes substantial damage to property, human suffering, hardship or loss of life.

"Natural disaster." Any hurricane, tornado, storm, flood, high water, wind-driven water, tidal wave, earthquake, landslide, mudslide, snowstorm, drought, fire, explosion or other catastrophe which results in substantial damage to property, hardship, suffering or possible loss of life.

"War-caused disaster." Any condition following an attack upon the United States resulting in substantial damage to property or injury to persons in the United States caused by use of bombs, missiles, shellfire, nuclear, radiological, chemical or biological means, or other weapons or overt paramilitary actions, or other conditions such as sabotage.

(June 17, 1974, P.L.356, No.118, eff. imd.; Nov. 29, 1990, P.L.608, No.154, eff. 60 days; Dec. 15, 1999, P.L.915, No.59, eff. 60 days; Nov. 23, 2004, P.L.953, No.143, eff. 60 days; June 28, 2011, P.L.48, No.10, eff. 60 days; Dec. 23, 2013, P.L.1264, No.131, eff. 60 days)

2013 Amendment. Act 131 amended subsecs. (a) and (a.2). Section 3 of Act 131 provided that the amendment shall apply to offenses committed on or after the effective date of section 3. Section 4 of Act 131 provided that the amendment shall apply to sentences imposed on or after the effective date of section 4.

2011 Amendment. Act 10 amended subsecs. (a), (a.1) and (b) and added subsec. (a.2). See the preamble to Act 10 in the appendix to this title for special provisions relating to legislative findings.

Cross References. Section 3903 is referred to in section 3926 of this title.

§ 3904. Arrest without warrant.

A law enforcement officer shall have the same right of arrest without a warrant for any grade of theft as exists or may hereafter exist in the case of the commission of a felony.

(Oct. 17, 1974, P.L.749, No.251)

1974 Amendment. Act 251 added section 3904.

SUBCHAPTER B
DEFINITION OF OFFENSES

Sec.
3921. Theft by unlawful taking or disposition.
3922. Theft by deception.
3923. Theft by extortion.
3924. Theft of property lost, mislaid, or delivered by mistake.
3925. Receiving stolen property.
3926. Theft of services.
3927. Theft by failure to make required disposition of funds received.
3928. Unauthorized use of automobiles and other vehicles.
3929. Retail theft.
3929.1. Library theft.
3929.2. Unlawful possession of retail or library theft instruments.
3929.3. Organized retail theft.
3930. Theft of trade secrets.
3931. Theft of unpublished dramas and musical compositions.
3932. Theft of leased property.
3933. Unlawful use of computer (Repealed).
3934. Theft from a motor vehicle.
3935. Theft of secondary metal (Unconstitutional).
3935.1. Theft of secondary metal.

§ 3921. Theft by unlawful taking or disposition.

(a) **Movable property.**--A person is guilty of theft if he unlawfully takes, or exercises unlawful control over, movable property of another with intent to deprive him thereof.

(b) **Immovable property.**--A person is guilty of theft if he unlawfully transfers, or exercises unlawful control over, immovable property of another or any interest therein with intent to benefit himself or another not entitled thereto.

Cross References. Section 3921 is referred to in sections 1107, 3311, 3903, 3935.1, 5708, 6105 of this title; section 5552 of Title 42 (Judiciary and Judicial Procedure).

§ 3922. Theft by deception.

(a) Offense defined.--A person is guilty of theft if he intentionally obtains or withholds property of another by deception. A person deceives if he intentionally:

(1) creates or reinforces a false impression, including false impressions as to law, value, intention or other state of mind; but deception as to a person's intention to perform a promise shall not be inferred from the fact alone that he did not subsequently perform the promise;

(2) prevents another from acquiring information which would affect his judgment of a transaction; or

(3) fails to correct a false impression which the deceiver previously created or reinforced, or which the deceiver knows to be influencing another to whom he stands in a fiduciary or confidential relationship.

(b) Exception.--The term "deceive" does not, however, include falsity as to matters having no pecuniary significance, or puffing by statements unlikely to deceive ordinary persons in the group addressed.

Cross References. Section 3922 is referred to in sections 3311, 5708 of this title; sections 5552, 9717 of Title 42 (Judiciary and Judicial Procedure).

§ 3923. Theft by extortion.

(a) Offense defined.--A person is guilty of theft if he intentionally obtains or withholds property of another by threatening to:

(1) commit another criminal offense;

(2) accuse anyone of a criminal offense;

(3) expose any secret tending to subject any person to hatred, contempt or ridicule;

(4) take or withhold action as an official, or cause an official to take or withhold action;

(5) bring about or continue a strike, boycott or other collective unofficial action, if the property is not demanded or received for the benefit of the group in whose interest the actor purports to act;

(6) testify or provide information or withhold testimony or information with respect to the legal claim or defense of another; or

(7) inflict any other harm which would not benefit the actor.

(b) Defenses.--It is a defense to prosecution based on paragraphs (a)(2), (a)(3) or (a)(4) of this section that the property obtained by threat of accusation, exposure, lawsuit or other invocation of official action was honestly claimed as restitution or indemnification for harm done in the circumstances to which such accusation, exposure, lawsuit or other official action relates, or as compensation for property or lawful services.

(June 24, 1976, P.L.425, No.102, eff. imd.)

Cross References. Section 3923 is referred to in sections 3001, 5708, 6105 of this title; section 3304 of Title 5 (Athletics and Sports); sections 5552, 9802 of Title 42 (Judiciary and Judicial Procedure); section 7122 of Title 61 (Prisons and Parole).

§ 3924. Theft of property lost, mislaid, or delivered by mistake.

A person who comes into control of property of another that he knows to have been lost, mislaid, or delivered under a mistake as to the nature or amount of the property or the identity of the recipient is guilty of theft if, with intent to deprive the owner thereof, he fails to take reasonable measures to restore the property to a person entitled to have it.

Cross References. Section 3924 is referred to in section 5552 of Title 42 (Judiciary and Judicial Procedure).

§ 3925. Receiving stolen property.

(a) Offense defined.--A person is guilty of theft if he intentionally receives, retains, or disposes of movable property of another knowing that it has been stolen, or believing that it has probably been stolen, unless the property is received, retained, or disposed with intent to restore it to the owner.

(b) Definition.--As used in this section the word "receiving" means acquiring possession, control or title, or lending on the security of the property.

Cross References. Section 3925 is referred to in sections 3903, 3929.3, 5708, 6105 of this title; section 5552 of Title 42 (Judiciary and Judicial Procedure).

§ 3926. Theft of services.

(a) Acquisition of services.--

(1) A person is guilty of theft if he intentionally obtains services for himself or for

147

another which he knows are available only for compensation, by deception or threat, by altering or tampering with the public utility meter or measuring device by which such services are delivered or by causing or permitting such altering or tampering, by making or maintaining any unauthorized connection, whether physically, electrically or inductively, to a distribution or transmission line, by attaching or maintaining the attachment of any unauthorized device to any cable, wire or other component of an electric, telephone or cable television system or to a television receiving set connected to a cable television system, by making or maintaining any unauthorized modification or alteration to any device installed by a cable television system, or by false token or other trick or artifice to avoid payment for the service.

(1.1) A person is guilty of theft if he intentionally obtains or attempts to obtain telecommunication service by the use of an unlawful telecommunication device or without the consent of the telecommunication service provider.

(3) A person is not guilty of theft of cable television service under this section who subscribes to and receives service through an authorized connection of a television receiving set at his dwelling and, within his dwelling, makes an unauthorized connection of an additional television receiving set or sets or audio system which receives only basic cable television service obtained through such authorized connection.

(4) Where compensation for service is ordinarily paid immediately upon the rendering of such service, as in the case of hotels and restaurants, refusal to pay or absconding without payment or offer to pay gives rise to a presumption that the service was obtained by deception as to intention to pay.

(b) Diversion of services.--A person is guilty of theft if, having control over the disposition of services of others to which he is not entitled, he knowingly diverts such services to his own benefit or to the benefit of another not entitled thereto.

(c) Grading.--

(1) An offense under this section constitutes a summary offense when the value of the services obtained or diverted is less than $50.

(2) When the value of the services obtained or diverted is $50 or more, the grading of the offense shall be as established in section 3903 (relating to grading of theft offenses).

(3) Amounts involved in theft of services committed pursuant to one scheme or course of conduct, whether from the same person or several persons, may be aggregated in determining the grade of the offense.

(d) Inferences.--

(1) Any person having possession of or access to the location of a public utility meter or service measuring device which has been avoided or tampered with so as to inhibit or prevent the accurate measurement of utility service and who enjoys the use of or receives the benefit from the public utility service intended to be metered or measured by the public utility meter or measuring device so avoided or tampered with may be reasonably inferred to have acted to avoid or tamper with the public utility meter or measuring device with the intent to obtain the public utility service without making full compensation therefor.

(2) Any person having possession of or access to the location of the distribution or transmission lines or other facilities of a cable television system which have been tapped, altered or tampered with or to which any unauthorized connection has been made or to which any unauthorized device has been attached or any person having possession of or access to any device installed by a cable television system to which an unauthorized modification or alteration has been made, the result of which tapping, altering, tampering, connection, attachment or modification is to avoid payment for all or any part of the cable television service for which payment is normally required, and who enjoys the use of or receives the benefit from the cable television service, may be reasonably inferred to have acted to have tapped, altered, tampered with, connected or attached to or modified cable television facilities with the intent to obtain cable television service without making full compensation therefor. This inference shall not apply to the act of a subscriber to cable television service, who receives service through an authorized connection of a television receiving set at his dwelling, in making, within his dwelling, an unauthorized connection of an additional television receiving set or sets or audio system which receives only basic cable television service obtained through such authorized connection.

148

(e) Sale or transfer of device or plan intended for acquisition or diversion.--A person is guilty of a misdemeanor of the third degree if he sells, gives or otherwise transfers to others or offers, advertises or exposes for sale to others, any device, kit, plan or other instructional procedure for the making of such device or a printed circuit, under circumstances indicating his having knowledge or reason to believe that such device, kit, plan or instructional procedure is intended for use by such others for the acquisition or diversion of services as set forth in subsections (a) and (b).

(f) Restitution.--The court may, in addition to any other sentence authorized by law, sentence a person convicted of violating this section to make restitution under section 1106 (relating to restitution for injuries to person or property) or 42 Pa.C.S. § 9721(c) (relating to sentencing generally).

(g) Civil action.--A telecommunication service provider aggrieved by a violation of this section may in a civil action in any court of competent jurisdiction obtain appropriate relief, including preliminary and other equitable or declaratory relief, compensatory and punitive damages, reasonable investigation expenses, costs of suit and attorney fees.

(h) Definitions.--As used in this section, the following words and phrases shall have the meanings given to them in this subsection:

"Service." Includes, but is not limited to, labor, professional service, transportation service, the supplying of hotel accommodations, restaurant services, entertainment, cable television service, the supplying of equipment for use and the supplying of commodities of a public utility nature such as gas, electricity, steam and water, and telephone or telecommunication service. The term "unauthorized" means that payment of full compensation for service has been avoided, or has been sought to be avoided, without the consent of the supplier of the service.

"Telecommunication service provider." A person or entity providing telecommunication service, including, but not limited to, a cellular, paging or other wireless communications company or other person or entity which, for a fee, supplies the facility, cell site, mobile telephone switching office or other equipment or telecommunication service.

"Telephone service" or "telecommunication service." Includes, but is not limited to, any service provided for a charge or compensation to facilitate the origination, transmission, emission or reception of signs, signals, data, writings, images and sounds or intelligence of any nature by telephone, including cellular telephones, wire, radio, electromagnetic, photoelectronic or photo-optical system.

"Unlawful telecommunication device." Any electronic serial number, mobile identification number, personal identification number or any telecommunication device that is capable or has been altered, modified, programmed or reprogrammed alone or in conjunction with another access device or other equipment so as to be capable of acquiring or facilitating the acquisition of a telecommunication service without the consent of the telecommunication service provider. The term includes, but is not limited to, phones altered to obtain service without the consent of the telecommunication service provider, tumbler phones, counterfeit or clone phones, tumbler microchips, counterfeit or clone microchips, scanning receivers of wireless telecommunication service of a telecommunication service provider and other instruments capable of disguising their identity or location or of gaining access to a communications system operated by a telecommunication service provider.

(Apr. 28, 1978, P.L.85, No.40, eff. 60 days; Nov. 26, 1978, P.L.1326, No.321, eff. 90 days; Dec. 21, 1984, P.L.1210, No.230, eff. imd.; June 13, 1995, P.L.52, No.8, eff. 60 days)

Cross References. Section 3926 is referred to in sections 910, 5708 of this title; section 5552 of Title 42 (Judiciary and Judicial Procedure).

§ 3927. Theft by failure to make required disposition of funds received.

(a) Offense defined.--A person who obtains property upon agreement, or subject to a known legal obligation, to make specified payments or other disposition, whether from such property or its proceeds or from his own property to be reserved in equivalent amount, is guilty of theft if he intentionally deals with the property obtained as his own and fails to make the required payment or disposition. The foregoing applies notwithstanding that it may be impossible to identify particular property as belonging to the victim at the time of the failure of the actor to make the required payment or disposition.

(b) Presumptions.--An officer or employee of the government or of a financial institution is presumed:

(1) to know any legal obligation relevant to his criminal liability under this section; and

(2) to have dealt with the property as his own if he fails to pay or account upon lawful demand, or if an audit reveals a shortage or falsification of accounts.

Cross References. Section 3927 is referred to in section 5708 of this title; section 5552 of Title 42 (Judiciary and Judicial Procedure).

§ 3928. Unauthorized use of automobiles and other vehicles.

(a) Offense defined.--A person is guilty of a misdemeanor of the second degree if he operates the automobile, airplane, motorcycle, motorboat, or other motor-propelled vehicle of another without consent of the owner.

(b) Defense.--It is a defense to prosecution under this section that the actor reasonably believed that the owner would have consented to the operation had he known of it.

Cross References. Section 3928 is referred to in section 3903 of this title; section 5552 of Title 42 (Judiciary and Judicial Procedure).

§ 3929. Retail theft.

(a) Offense defined.--A person is guilty of a retail theft if he:

(1) takes possession of, carries away, transfers or causes to be carried away or transferred, any merchandise displayed, held, stored or offered for sale by any store or other retail mercantile establishment with the intention of depriving the merchant of the possession, use or benefit of such merchandise without paying the full retail value thereof;

(2) alters, transfers or removes any label, price tag marking, indicia of value or any other markings which aid in determining value affixed to any merchandise displayed, held, stored or offered for sale in a store or other retail mercantile establishment and attempts to purchase such merchandise personally or in consort with another at less than the full retail value with the intention of depriving the merchant of the full retail value of such merchandise;

(3) transfers any merchandise displayed, held, stored or offered for sale by any store or other retail mercantile establishment from the container in or on which the same shall be displayed to any other container with intent to deprive the merchant of all or some part of the full retail value thereof; or

(4) under-rings with the intention of depriving the merchant of the full retail value of the merchandise.

(5) destroys, removes, renders inoperative or deactivates any inventory control tag, security strip or any other mechanism designed or employed to prevent an offense under this section with the intention of depriving the merchant of the possession, use or benefit of such merchandise without paying the full retail value thereof.

(b) Grading.--

(1) Retail theft constitutes a:

(i) Summary offense when the offense is a first offense and the value of the merchandise is less than $150.

(ii) Misdemeanor of the second degree when the offense is a second offense and the value of the merchandise is less than $150.

(iii) Misdemeanor of the first degree when the offense is a first or second offense and the value of the merchandise is $150 or more.

(iv) Felony of the third degree when the offense is a third or subsequent offense, regardless of the value of the merchandise.

(v) Felony of the third degree when the amount involved exceeds $1,000 or if the merchandise involved is a firearm or a motor vehicle.

(1.1) Any person who is convicted under subsection (a) of retail theft of motor fuel may, in addition to any other penalty imposed, be sentenced as follows:

(i) For a first offense, to pay a fine of not less than $100 nor more than $250.

(ii) For a second offense, to pay a fine of not less than $250 nor more than $500.

(iii) For a third or subsequent offense, to pay a fine of not less than $500, or the court may order the operating privilege of the person suspended for 30 days. A copy of the order shall be transmitted to the Department of Transportation.

(2) Amounts involved in retail thefts committed pursuant to one scheme or course of conduct, whether from the same store or retail mercantile establishment or several stores or retail mercantile establishments, may be aggregated in determining the grade of the offense.

(b.1) Calculation of prior offenses.--For the purposes of this section, in determining whether an offense is a first, second, third or subsequent offense, the court shall include a conviction, acceptance of accelerated rehabilitative disposition or other form of preliminary disposition, occurring before the sentencing on the present violation, for an offense under this section, an offense substantially similar to an offense under this section or under the prior laws of this Commonwealth or a similar offense under the statutes of any other state or of the United States.

(c) Presumptions.--Any person intentionally concealing unpurchased property of any store or other mercantile establishment, either on the premises or outside the premises of such store, shall be prima facie presumed to have so concealed such property with the intention of depriving the merchant of the possession, use or benefit of such merchandise without paying the full retail value thereof within the meaning of subsection (a), and the finding of such unpurchased property concealed, upon the person or among the belongings of such person, shall be prima facie evidence of intentional concealment, and, if such person conceals, or causes to be concealed, such unpurchased property, upon the person or among the belongings of another, such fact shall also be prima facie evidence of intentional concealment on the part of the person so concealing such property.

(c.1) Evidence.--To the extent that there is other competent evidence to substantiate the offense, the conviction shall not be avoided because the prosecution cannot produce the stolen merchandise.

(d) Detention.--A peace officer, merchant or merchant's employee or an agent under contract with a merchant, who has probable cause to believe that retail theft has occurred or is occurring on or about a store or other retail mercantile establishment and who has probable cause to believe that a specific person has committed or is committing the retail theft may detain the suspect in a reasonable manner for a reasonable time on or off the premises for all or any of the following purposes: to require the suspect to identify himself, to verify such identification, to determine whether such suspect has in his possession unpurchased merchandise taken from the mercantile establishment and, if so, to recover such merchandise, to inform a peace officer, or to institute criminal proceedings against the suspect. Such detention shall not impose civil or criminal liability upon the peace officer, merchant, employee, or agent so detaining.

(e) Reduction prohibited.--No magisterial district judge shall have the power to reduce any other charge of theft to a charge of retail theft as defined in this section.

(f) Definitions.--

"Conceal." To conceal merchandise so that, although there may be some notice of its presence, it is not visible through ordinary observation.

"Full retail value." The merchant's stated or advertised price of the merchandise.

"Merchandise." Any goods, chattels, foodstuffs or wares of any type and description, regardless of the value thereof.

"Merchant." An owner or operator of any retail mercantile establishment or any agent, employee, lessee, consignee, officer, director, franchisee or independent contractor of such owner or operator.

"Premises of a retail mercantile establishment." Includes but is not limited to, the retail mercantile establishment, any common use areas in shopping centers and all parking areas set aside by a merchant or on behalf of a merchant for the parking of vehicles for the convenience of the patrons of such retail mercantile establishment.

"Store or other retail mercantile establishment." A place where merchandise is displayed, held, stored or sold or offered to the public for sale.

"Under-ring." To cause the cash register or other sales recording device to reflect less than the full retail value of the merchandise.

(g) Fingerprinting.--Prior to the commencement of trial or entry of plea of a defendant 16 years of age or older accused of the summary offense of retail theft, the issuing authority shall order the defendant to submit within five days of such order for fingerprinting by the municipal police of the jurisdiction in which the offense allegedly was committed or the State Police. Fingerprints so obtained shall be forwarded immediately to the Pennsylvania State Police for determination as to whether or not the defendant previously has been convicted of the offense of retail theft. The results of such determination shall be forwarded to the Police Department obtaining the fingerprints if such department is the prosecutor, or to the issuing authority if the prosecutor is other than a police officer. The issuing authority shall not proceed with the trial or plea in summary cases until in receipt of the determination made by the State Police. The magisterial district judge shall use the information obtained solely for the purpose of grading the offense pursuant to subsection (b).

(Dec. 2, 1976, P.L.1230, No.272, eff. imd.; Apr. 28, 1978, P.L.202, No.53, eff. 2 years; Dec. 20, 1996, P.L.1530, No.200, eff. 60 days; June 25, 1997, P.L.377, No.42, eff. imd.; Oct. 2, 2002, P.L.806, No.116, eff. 60 days; Nov. 30, 2004, P.L.1618, No.207, eff. 60 days; Dec. 23, 2013, P.L.1264, No.131, eff. 60 days)

2013 Amendment. Act 131 amended subsec. (b)(1)(v) and added subsec. (b.1). Section 3 of Act 131 provided that the amendment of subsec. (b)(1)(v) shall apply to offenses committed on or after the effective date of section 3. Section 4 of Act 131 provided that subsec. (b.1) shall apply to sentences imposed on or after the effective date of section 4.

2004 Amendment. Act 207 amended subsecs. (e) and (g). See section 29 of Act 207 in the appendix to this title for special provisions relating to construction of law.

2002 Amendment. Act 116 amended subsec. (b).

1997 Amendment. Act 42 added subsec. (a)(5).

Cross References. Section 3929 is referred to in sections 3903, 3929.2, 3929.3, 9112 of this title; sections 3573, 5552, 8308 of Title 42 (Judiciary and Judicial Procedure).

§ 3929.1. Library theft.

(a) Offense defined.--A person is guilty of library theft if he willfully conceals on his person or among his belongings any library or museum material while still on the premises of a library or willfully and without authority removes any library or museum material from a library with the intention of converting such material to his own use.

(b) Grading.--

(1) Library theft constitutes a:

(i) Summary offense when the offense is a first offense and the value of the material is less than $150.

(ii) Misdemeanor of the second degree when the offense is a second offense and the value of the material is less than $150.

(iii) Misdemeanor of the first degree when the offense is a first or second offense and the value of the material is $150 or more.

(iv) Felony of the third degree when the offense is a third or subsequent offense, regardless of the value of the material.

(2) Amounts involved in library thefts committed pursuant to one scheme or course of conduct, whether from the same library or several libraries, may be aggregated in determining the grade of the offense.

(c) Presumption.--A person who willfully conceals any library or museum material on his person or among his belongings while still on the premises of the library or in the immediate vicinity thereof shall be prima facie presumed to have concealed the library or museum material with the intention of converting such material to his own use.

(d) Detention.--A peace officer, employee or agent of a library who has probable cause to believe that a person has committed library theft may detain such person on the premises of the library or in the immediate vicinity thereof for the following purposes:

(1) To conduct an investigation in a reasonable manner and within a reasonable length of time to determine whether such person has unlawfully concealed or removed any library or museum material.

(2) To inform a peace officer of the detention of the person or surrender that person to the custody of a peace officer.

(e) Exemption from liability.--A peace officer, employee or agent of a library who detains or causes the arrest of any person pursuant to this section shall not be held civilly or criminally liable for false arrest, false imprisonment, unlawful detention, assault, battery, slander, libel or malicious prosecution of the person detained or arrested provided the peace officer, employee or agent of the library had at the time of the detention or arrest probable cause to believe that the person committed library theft.

(f) Public display of law.--A copy of this section shall be publicly displayed in the reading rooms and other public rooms of all libraries in such number and manner as will bring this section to the attention of patrons.

(g) Prior offenses.--Prior to the commencement of trial or entry of plea of a defendant 16 years of age or older accused of the summary offense of library theft, the issuing authority shall notify the Pennsylvania State Police for determination as to whether or not the defendant previously has been convicted of the offense of library theft. The results of such determination shall be forwarded to the police department if the department is the prosecutor, or to the issuing authority if the prosecutor is other than a police officer. The issuing authority shall not proceed with the trial or plea in summary cases until in receipt of the determination made by the State Police. The magisterial district judge shall use the information obtained solely for the purpose of grading the offense pursuant to subsection (b).

(h) Fingerprinting.--Upon conviction the issuing authority shall order the defendant to submit within five days of such order for fingerprinting by the municipal police of the jurisdiction in which the offense allegedly was committed or the State Police.

(i) Definitions.--As used in this section the following words and phrases shall have the meanings given to them in this subsection:

"Conceal." To conceal library or museum material so that, although there may be some notice of its presence, it is not visible through ordinary observation.

"Library." Any public library, any library, archives or manuscript repository of educational, historical or eleemosynary institution, organization or society, any museum and any repository of public records.

"Library or museum material." Any book, plate, picture, photograph, engraving, painting, drawing, map, newspaper, magazine, pamphlet, broadside, manuscript, document, letter, public record, microfilm, sound recording, audiovisual materials in any format, magnetic or other tapes, electronic data processing records, display object, exhibit, work of art, artifact, or other documentary, written or printed materials regardless of physical form or characteristics, belonging to, on loan to, or otherwise in the custody of a library.

"Premises of a library." Includes but is not limited to the library and all parking areas set aside for the parking of vehicles for the convenience of the patrons of such library.

(Apr. 27, 1982, P.L.345, No.95, eff. imd.; Nov. 30, 2004, P.L.1618, No.207, eff. 60 days)

2004 Amendment. Act 207 amended subsec. (g). See section 29 of Act 207 in the appendix to this title for special provisions relating to construction of law.

1982 Amendment. Act 95 added section 3929.1.

Cross References. Section 3929.1 is referred to in section 3929.2 of this title; section 5552 of Title 42 (Judiciary and Judicial Procedure).

§ 3929.2. Unlawful possession of retail or library theft instruments.

(a) Offense.--A person commits a misdemeanor of the first degree if he knowingly possesses, manufactures, sells, offers for sale or distributes in any way a theft detection shielding device or a theft detection deactivation device.

(b) Definitions.--As used in this section, the following words and phrases shall have the meanings given to them in this subsection:

"Conceal." To conceal merchandise or library or museum material so that, although there may be some notice of its presence, it is not visible through ordinary observation.

"Full retail value." The merchant's stated or advertised price of the merchandise.

"Library." Any public library, any library, archives or manuscript repository of an educational, historical or eleemosynary institution, organization or society, any museum and any repository of public records.

"Library or museum material." Any book, plate, picture, photograph, engraving, painting, drawing, map, newspaper, magazine, pamphlet, broadside, manuscript, document, letter, public record, microfilm, sound recording, audiovisual materials in any format, magnetic or other tapes, electronic data processing records, display object, exhibit, work of art, artifact or other documentary, written or printed materials regardless of physical form or characteristics, belonging to, on loan to or otherwise in the custody of a library.

"Merchandise." Any goods, chattels, foodstuffs or wares of any type and description regardless of the value thereof.

"Merchant." An owner or operator of any retail mercantile establishment or any agent, employee, lessee, consignee, officer, director, franchisee or independent contractor of such owner or operator.

"Store or other retail mercantile establishment." A place where merchandise is displayed, held, stored or sold or offered to the public for sale.

"Theft detection deactivation device." Any tool, device, equipment or object designed to destroy, remove, render inoperative or

153

deactivate any inventory control tag, security strip or any other mechanism designed or employed to prevent an offense under section 3929 (relating to retail theft) or 3929.1 (relating to library theft) which is possessed, manufactured, sold or offered for sale with the intention that it be used to:

(1) deprive merchants of the possession, use or benefit of merchandise displayed, held, stored or offered for sale or lease without paying the full retail value thereof; or

(2) convert library or museum material to one's own use.

"Theft detection shielding device." Any laminated, lined or coated bag, purse, container, case, coat or similar device which is intended to be used to take possession of, carry away, transfer, cause to be carried away or transferred or conceal:

(1) any merchandise displayed, held, stored or offered for sale or lease by any store or other retail mercantile establishment with the intent to deprive merchants of the possession, use or benefit of such merchandise without paying the full retail value thereof; or

(2) any library or museum material on his person or among his belongings with the intent to convert such material to his own use.

(Apr. 17, 2002, P.L.246, No.33, eff. 60 days)

2002 Amendment. Act 33 added section 3929.2.

Cross References. Section 3929.2 is referred to in section 5552 of Title 42 (Judiciary and Judicial Procedure).

§ 3929.3. Organized retail theft.

(a) Offense defined.--A person commits organized retail theft if the person organizes, coordinates, controls, supervises, finances or manages any of the activities of an organized retail theft enterprise.

(b) Grading.--

(1) If the retail value of the stolen merchandise in the possession of or under the control of the organized retail theft enterprise is at least $5,000, but not more than $19,999, the offense is a felony of the third degree.

(2) If the retail value of the stolen merchandise in the possession of or under the control of the organized retail theft enterprise is at least $20,000, the offense is a felony of the second degree.

(c) Definitions.--The following words and phrases when used in this section shall have the meanings given to them in this subsection:

"Merchandise." Any goods, chattels, foodstuffs or wares of any type and description, regardless of the value thereof.

"Merchant." An owner or operator of a retail mercantile establishment or an agent, employee, lessee, consignee, officer, director, franchise or independent contractor of such owner or operator.

"Organized retail theft enterprise." A corporation, partnership or any other type of association, whether or not legally formed, operated for the purpose of engaging in violations of the provisions of section 3925 (relating to receiving stolen property) or 3929 (relating to retail theft).

"Retail value." A merchant's stated or advertised price of merchandise. If merchandise is not traceable to a specific merchant, the stated or advertised price of the merchandise by merchants in the same geographical region.

(June 16, 2010, P.L.212, No.33, eff. 60 days)

2010 Amendment. Act 33 added section 3929.3.

§ 3930. Theft of trade secrets.

(a) Felony of the second degree.--A person is guilty of a felony of the second degree if he:

(1) by force or violence or by putting him in fear takes from the person of another any article representing a trade secret;

(2) willfully and maliciously enters any building or other structure with intent to obtain unlawful possession of, or access to, an article representing a trade secret; or

(3) willfully and maliciously accesses any computer, computer network or computer system, whether in person or electronically, with the intent to obtain unlawful possession of, or access to, an article representing a trade secret.

(b) Felony of the third degree.--A person is guilty of a felony of the third degree if he, with intent to wrongfully deprive of, or withhold from the owner, the control of a trade secret, or with intent to wrongfully appropriate a trade secret for his use, or for the use of another:

(1) unlawfully obtains possession of, or access to, an article representing a trade secret; or

(2) having lawfully obtained possession of an article representing a trade secret, or access thereto, converts such article to his own use or that of another person, while having possession thereof or access thereto makes, or causes to be made, a copy of such article, or exhibits such article to another.

(c) Further disposition irrelevant.--The crime or crimes defined in subsections (a) and (b) of this section shall be deemed complete without regard to the further disposition, return, or intent to return, of the article representing a trade secret.

(d) Defense.--It shall be a complete defense to any prosecution under subsection (b) of this section for the defendant to show that information comprising the trade secret was rightfully known or available to him from a source other than the owner of the trade secret.

(e) Definitions.--As used in this section the following words and phrases shall have the meanings given to them in this subsection:

"Article." Any object, material, device or substance or copy thereof, including any writing, record, recording, drawing, description, sample, specimen, prototype, model, photograph, microorganism, blueprint or map.

"Computer." An electronic, magnetic, optical, hydraulic, organic or other high-speed data processing device or system which performs logic, arithmetic or memory functions and includes all input, output, processing, storage, software or communication facilities which are connected or related to the device in a system or network.

"Computer network." The interconnection of two or more computers through the usage of satellite, microwave, line or other communication medium.

"Computer system." A set of related, connected or unconnected computer equipment, devices and software.

"Copy." Any facsimile, replica, photograph or reproduction of, an article, or any note, drawing, sketch, or description made of, or from an article.

"Representing." Describing, depicting, containing, constituting, reflecting or recording.

"Trade secret." The whole or any portion or phase of any scientific or technical information, design, process, procedure, formula or improvement which is of value and has been specifically identified by the owner as of a confidential character, and which has not been published or otherwise become a matter of general public knowledge. There shall be a rebuttable presumption that scientific or technical information has not been published or otherwise become a matter of general public knowledge when the owner thereof takes measures to prevent it from becoming available to persons other than those selected by him to have access thereto for limited purposes.

(f) Construction.--Nothing in this section shall be construed to interfere with or prohibit terms or conditions in a contract or license related to a computer, a computer network or computer software.

(Oct. 16, 1996, P.L.715, No.128, eff. 60 days; June 25, 1997, P.L.284, No.26, eff. 60 days; Feb. 19, 2004, P.L.143, No.14, eff. 60 days)

2004 Amendment. Section 4 of Act 14 provided that Act 14 shall not apply to misappropriation occurring prior to the effective date of Act 14, including a continuing misappropriation that began prior to the effective date of Act 14 and which continues to occur after the effective date of Act 14.

Cross References. Section 3930 is referred to in section 5552 of Title 42 (Judiciary and Judicial Procedure).

§ 3931. Theft of unpublished dramas and musical compositions.

A person is guilty of theft if he publicly presents for profit, without the consent of the author thereof, any unpublished dramatic play or musical composition.

Cross References. Section 3931 is referred to in section 5552 of Title 42 (Judiciary and Judicial Procedure).

§ 3932. Theft of leased property.

(a) Offense defined.--A person who obtains personal property under an agreement for the lease or rental of the property is guilty of theft if he intentionally deals with the property as his own.

(b) Definition.--As used in this section:

(1) A person "deals with the property as his own" if he sells, secretes, destroys, converts to his own use or otherwise disposes of the property.

(2) A "written demand to return the property is delivered" when it is sent simultaneously by first class mail, evidenced by

a certificate of mailing, and by registered or certified mail to the address provided by the lessee.

(c) Presumption.--A person shall be prima facie presumed to have intent if he:

(1) signs the lease or rental agreement with a name other than his own and fails to return the property within the time specified in the agreement; or

(2) fails to return the property to its owner within seven days after a written demand to return the property is delivered.

(d) Exception.--This section shall not apply to secured transactions as defined in Title 13 (relating to commercial code).

(Aug. 8, 1977, P.L.184, No.49, eff. 90 days; Nov. 1, 1979, P.L.255, No.86, eff. Jan. 1, 1980; Oct. 9, 2008, P.L.1403, No.111, eff. imd.)

2008 Amendment. Act 111 amended subsecs. (b) and (c)(2).

Cross References. Section 3932 is referred to in sections 5552, 8310 of Title 42 (Judiciary and Judicial Procedure).

§ 3933. Unlawful use of computer (Repealed).

2002 Repeal. Section 3933 was repealed December 16, 2002 (P.L.1953, No.226), effective in 60 days.

§ 3934. Theft from a motor vehicle.

(a) Offense defined.--A person commits the offense of theft from a motor vehicle if he unlawfully takes or attempts to take possession of, carries away or exercises unlawful control over any movable property of another from a motor vehicle with the intent to deprive him thereof.

(b) Grading.--

(1) An offense under this section is:

(i) a misdemeanor of the third degree if the amount involved was less than $50; or

(ii) a misdemeanor of the second degree if the amount involved was $50 or more but less than $200; or

(iii) a misdemeanor of the first degree if the amount involved was greater than $200.

(2) When the offense is a third or subsequent offense within a five-year period, regardless of the amount involved and regardless of the grading of the prior offenses, an offense under this section is a felony of the third degree.

(Dec. 21, 1998, P.L.1103, No.149, eff. 60 days; June 18, 1999, P.L.67, No.8, eff. 60 days)

§ 3935. Theft of secondary metal (Unconstitutional).

2016 Unconstitutionality. Act 192 of 2014 was declared unconstitutional. Leach v. Commonwealth, 141 A.3d 426 (Pa. 2016). The Legislative Reference Bureau effectuated the 2016 unconstitutionality.

2014 Amendment. Act 192 added section 3935.

§ 3935.1. Theft of secondary metal.

(a) Offense defined.--A person commits the offense of theft of secondary metal if the person unlawfully takes or attempts to take possession of, carries away or exercises unlawful control over any secondary metal with intent to deprive the rightful owner thereof.

(b) Grading.--Except as set forth in subsection (c):

(1) An offense under this section constitutes a misdemeanor of the third degree when the value of the secondary metal unlawfully obtained is less than $50.

(2) When the value of the secondary metal unlawfully obtained is $50 or more but less than $200, the offense constitutes a misdemeanor of the second degree.

(3) When the value of the secondary metal unlawfully obtained is $200 or more but less than $1,000, the offense constitutes a misdemeanor of the first degree.

(4) When the value of the secondary metal unlawfully obtained is $1,000 or more, the offense constitutes a felony of the third degree.

(c) Third or subsequent offenses.--An offense under this section constitutes a felony of the third degree when the offense is a third or subsequent offense, regardless of the value of the secondary metal. For purposes of this subsection, a first and second offense includes a conviction, acceptance of Accelerated Rehabilitative Disposition or other form of preliminary disposition before the sentencing on the present violation for an offense under this section or section 3921 (relating to theft by unlawful taking or disposition).

(d) Definition.--As used in this section, the term "secondary metal" means wire, pipe or cable commonly used by communications, gas, water, wastewater and electrical utilities and railroads and mass transit or commuter rail agencies, copper, aluminum or other metal, or a combination of metals, that is valuable for recycling or reuse as raw material.

(June 22, 2017, P.L.213, No.8, eff. 60 days)

2017 Amendment. Act 8 added section 3935.1.

CHAPTER 41 FORGERY AND FRAUDULENT PRACTICES

Enactment. Chapter 41 was added December 6, 1972, P.L.1482, No.334, effective in six months.

Cross References. Chapter 41 is referred to in section 3575 of Title 42 (Judiciary and Judicial Procedure).

§ 4101. Forgery.

(a) Offense defined.--A person is guilty of forgery if, with intent to defraud or injure anyone, or with knowledge that he is facilitating a fraud or injury to be perpetrated by anyone, the actor:

(1) alters any writing of another without his authority;

(2) makes, completes, executes, authenticates, issues or transfers any writing so that it purports to be the act of another who did not authorize that act, or to have been executed at a time or place or in a numbered sequence other than was in fact the case, or to be a copy of an original when no such original existed; or

(3) utters any writing which he knows to be forged in a manner specified in paragraphs (1) or (2) of this subsection.

(b) Definition.--As used in this section the word "writing" includes printing or any other method of recording information, money, coins, tokens, stamps, seals, credit cards, badges, trademarks, electronic signatures and other symbols of value, right, privilege, or identification.

(c) Grading.--Forgery is a felony of the second degree if the writing is or purports to be part of an issue of money, securities, postage or revenue stamps, or other instruments issued by the government, or part of an issue of stock, bonds or other instruments representing interests in or claims against any property or enterprise. Forgery is a felony of the third degree if the writing is or purports to be a will, deed, contract, release, commercial instrument, or other document evidencing, creating, transferring, altering, terminating, or otherwise affecting legal relations. Otherwise forgery is a misdemeanor of the first degree.

(Dec. 16, 2002, P.L.1953, No.226, eff. 60 days)

2002 Amendment. Act 226 amended subsec. (b).

Cross References. Section 4101 is referred to in section 3311 of this title; section

5552 of Title 42 (Judiciary and Judicial Procedure).

§ 4102. Simulating objects of antiquity, rarity, etc.

A person commits a misdemeanor of the first degree if, with intent to defraud anyone or with knowledge that he is facilitating a fraud to be perpetrated by anyone, he makes, alters or utters any object so that it appears to have value because of antiquity, rarity, source, or authorship which it does not possess.

§ 4103. Fraudulent destruction, removal or concealment of recordable instruments.

A person commits a felony of the third degree if, with intent to deceive or injure anyone, he destroys, removes or conceals any will, deed, mortgage, security instrument or other writing for which the law provides public recording.

§ 4104. Tampering with records or identification.

(a) Writings.--A person commits a misdemeanor of the first degree if, knowing that he has no privilege to do so, he falsifies, destroys, removes or conceals any writing or record, or distinguishing mark or brand or other identification with intent to deceive or injure anyone or to conceal any wrongdoing.

(b) Personal property.--A person commits a summary offense if he knowingly buys, sells or moves in commerce any personal property from which the manufacturer's name plate, serial number or any other distinguishing number or identification mark has been removed, defaced, covered, altered or destroyed unless the alterations have been customarily made or done as an established practice in the ordinary and regular conduct of business by the original manufacturer or under specific authorization and direction from the original manufacturer. Personal property as set forth in this subsection shall not include firearms, motor vehicles or insurance company salvage recoveries.

(c) Innocent alterations.--If property subject to the provisions of this section has had its identifying marks defaced or eliminated innocently and is in the possession of its rightful owner, the owner may, notwithstanding the provisions of subsection (a) or (b), dispose of the property by sale or otherwise if he delivers to the acquirer a notarized statement that the property was innocently altered and that the person disposing of it is its rightful owner.

(Nov. 26, 1978, P.L.1316, No.319, eff. Jan. 1, 1979)

§ 4105. Bad checks.

(a) Offense defined.--

(1) A person commits an offense if he issues or passes a check or similar sight order for the payment of money, knowing that it will not be honored by the drawee.

(2) A person commits an offense if he, knowing that it will not be honored by the drawee, issues or passes a check or similar sight order for the payment of money when the drawee is located within this Commonwealth. A violation of this paragraph shall occur without regard to whether the location of the issuance or passing of the check or similar sight order is within or outside of this Commonwealth. It shall be no defense to a violation of this section that some or all of the acts constituting the offense occurred outside of this Commonwealth.

(b) Presumptions.--For the purposes of this section as well as in any prosecution for theft committed by means of a bad check, the following shall apply:

(1) An issuer is presumed to know that the check or order (other than a post-dated check or order) would not be paid, if:

(i) payment was refused because the issuer had no such account with the drawee at the time the check or order was issued; or

(ii) payment was refused by the drawee for lack of funds, upon presentation within 30 days after issue, and the issuer failed to make good within ten days after receiving notice of that refusal.

Notice of refusal may be given to the issuer orally or in writing by any person. Proof that notice was sent by registered or certified mail, regardless of whether a receipt was requested or returned, to the address printed on the check or, if none, then to the issuer's last known address, shall raise a presumption that the notice was received.

(2) A check or order stamped "NSF" or "insufficient funds" shall raise a presumption that payment was refused by the drawee for lack of funds.

(3) A check or order stamped "account closed" or "no such account" or "counterfeit" shall raise a presumption that payment was refused by the drawee because the issuer had no such account with the drawee at the time the check or order was issued.

(c) Grading.--

(1) An offense under this section is:

(i) a summary offense if the check or order is less than $200;

(ii) a misdemeanor of the third degree if the check or order is $200 or more but less than $500;

(iii) a misdemeanor of the second degree if the check or order is $500 or more but less than $1,000;

(iv) a misdemeanor of the first degree if the check or order is $1,000 or more but is less than $75,000; or

(v) a felony of the third degree if the check or order is $75,000 or more.

(2) When the offense is a third or subsequent offense within a five-year period, regardless of the amount of the check or order and regardless of the grading of the prior offenses, an offense under this section is a misdemeanor of the first degree unless the amount of the check or order involved in the third or subsequent offense is $75,000 or more, then the offense is a felony of the third degree.

(d) Venue.--An offense under subsection (a) may be deemed to have been committed at either the place where the defendant issues or passes the bad check or similar sight order for the payment of money or the place where the financial institution upon which the bad check or similar sight order for the payment of money was drawn is located.

(e) Costs.--Upon conviction under this section the sentence shall include an order for the issuer or passer to reimburse the payee or such other party as the circumstances may indicate for:

(1) The face amount of the check.

(2) Interest at the legal rate on the face amount of the check from the date of dishonor by the drawee.

(3) A service charge if written notice of the service charge was conspicuously displayed on the payee's premises when the check was issued. The service charge shall not exceed $50 unless the payee is charged fees in excess of $50 by financial institutions as a result of such bad check or similar sight order for the payment of money. If the payee is charged fees in excess of $50, then the service charge shall not exceed the actual amount of the fees.

(July 6, 1984, P.L.647, No.134, eff. 90 days; Dec. 20, 1996, P.L.1531, No.201, eff. 60 days; June 22, 2000, P.L.382, No.50, eff. 60 days; Dec. 18, 2007, P.L.462, No.70, eff. 60 days)

2007 Amendment. Act 70 amended subsec. (e).

1996 Amendment. Act 201 amended subsecs. (b) and (c).

Cross References. Section 4105 is referred to in section 6122 of Title 7 (Banks and Banking); sections 3573, 3575, 8304 of Title 42 (Judiciary and Judicial Procedure); section 2303 of Title 44 (Law and Justice).

§ 4106. Access device fraud.

(a) Offense defined.--A person commits an offense if he:

(1) uses an access device to obtain or in an attempt to obtain property or services with knowledge that:

(i) the access device is counterfeit, altered or incomplete;

(ii) the access device was issued to another person who has not authorized its use;

(iii) the access device has been revoked or canceled; or

(iv) for any other reason his use of the access device is unauthorized by the issuer or the device holder; or

(2) publishes, makes, sells, gives, or otherwise transfers to another, or offers or advertises, or aids and abets any other person to use an access device knowing that the access device is counterfeit, altered or incomplete, belongs to another person who has not authorized its use, has been revoked or canceled or for any reason is unauthorized by the issuer or the device holder; or

(3) possesses an access device knowing that it is counterfeit, altered, incomplete or belongs to another person who has not authorized its possession.

(a.1) Presumptions.--For the purpose of this section as well as in any prosecution for theft committed by the means specified in this section:

(1) An actor is presumed to know an access device is counterfeit, altered or incomplete if he has in his possession or under his control two or more counterfeit, altered or incomplete access devices.

(2) Knowledge of revocation or cancellation shall be presumed to have been received by an access device holder seven days after it has been mailed to him at the address set forth on the access device application or at a new address if a change of address has been provided to the issuer.

(b) Defenses.--It is a defense to a prosecution under subsection (a)(1)(iv) if the actor proves by a preponderance of the evidence that he had the intent and ability to meet all obligations to the issuer arising out of his use of the access device.

(c) Grading.--

(1) An offense under subsection (a)(1) falls within the following classifications depending on the value of the property or service obtained or sought to be obtained by means of the access device:

(i) if the value involved was $500 or more, the offense constitutes a felony of the third degree; or

(ii) if the value involved was $50 or more but less than $500, the offense constitutes a misdemeanor of the first degree; or

(iii) if the value involved was less than $50, the offense constitutes a misdemeanor of the second degree.

(2) Amounts involved in unlawful use of an access device pursuant to a scheme or course of conduct, whether from the same issuer or several issuers, may be aggregated in determining the classification of the offense.

(3) An offense under subsection (a)(2) constitutes a felony of the third degree.

(4) An offense under subsection (a)(3) constitutes a misdemeanor of the third degree.

(5) Each access device involved in the offense specified in subsection (a)(2) or (3) shall constitute a separate offense.

(d) Definitions.--As used in this section, the following words and phrases shall have the meanings given to them in this subsection:

"Access device." Any card, including, but not limited to, a credit card, debit card and automated teller machine card, plate, code, account number, personal identification number or other means of account access that can be used alone or in conjunction with another access device to obtain money, goods, services or anything else of value or that can be used to transfer funds.

"Altered access device." A validly issued access device which after issue is changed in any way.

"Counterfeit access device." An access device not issued by an issuer in the ordinary course of business.

"Device holder." The person or organization named on the access device to whom or for whose benefit the access device is issued by an issuer.

"Incomplete access device." An access device which does not contain all of the printed, embossed, encoded, stamped or other matter which an issuer requires to appear on a validly issued access device.

"Issuer." The business organization or financial institution which issues an access device or its duly authorized agent.

"Publishes." The communication of information to any one or more persons, either in person, by telephone, radio, other telecommunication or electronic device, television or in a writing of any kind, including without limitation a letter or memorandum, circular or handbill, newspaper or magazine article, or book.

(e) Venue.--Any offense committed under subsection (a)(1) may be deemed to have been committed at either the place where the attempt to obtain property or services is made, or at the place where the property or services were received or provided, or at the place where the lawful charges for said property or services are billed.

(July 20, 1974, P.L.539, No.185; Dec. 21, 1998, P.L.1103, No.149, eff. 60 days)

Cross References. Section 4106 is referred to in section 1107.1 of this title; section 2303 of Title 44 (Law and Justice); section 1406 of Title 66 (Public Utilities).

§ 4106.1. Unlawful device-making equipment.

(a) Offense defined.--A person commits an offense if, with intent to defraud or injure anyone or with knowledge that he may be facilitating a fraud or injury to be perpetrated by anyone, he:

(1) produces or traffics in device-making equipment; or

(2) possesses device-making equipment.

(b) Grading.--An offense under subsection (a)(1) is a felony of the third degree. An offense under subsection (a)(2) is a misdemeanor of the first degree.

(c) Definitions.--As used in this section, the following words and phrases shall have the meanings given to them in this subsection:

"Access device." Any card, including, but not limited to, a credit card, debit card and automated teller machine card, plate, code, account number, personal identification number or other means of account access that can be used alone or in conjunction with another access device to obtain money, goods, services or anything else of value or that can be used to initiate a transfer of funds.

"Device-making equipment." Any equipment, mechanism or impression designed or capable of being used for making an access device.

"Produce." Includes design, alter, authenticate, duplicate or assemble.

"Traffic." Sell, give or otherwise transfer to another or obtain control of with intent to dispose of or transfer.

(Dec. 21, 1998, P.L.1103, No.149, eff. 60 days)

1998 Amendment. Act 149 added section 4106.1.

§ 4107. Deceptive or fraudulent business practices.

(a) Offense defined.--A person commits an offense if, in the course of business, the person:

(1) uses or possesses for use a false weight or measure, or any other device for falsely determining or recording any quality or quantity;

(2) sells, offers or exposes for sale, or delivers less than the represented quantity of any commodity or service;

(3) takes or attempts to take more than the represented quantity of any commodity or service when as buyer he furnishes the weight or measure;

(4) sells, offers or exposes for sale adulterated or mislabeled commodities. As used in this paragraph, the term "adulterated" means varying from the standard of composition or quality prescribed by or pursuant to any statute providing criminal penalties for such variance or set by established commercial usage. As used in this paragraph, the term "mislabeled" means varying from the standard of trust or disclosure in labeling prescribed by or pursuant to any statute providing criminal penalties for such variance or set by established commercial usage;

(5) makes a false or misleading statement in any advertisement addressed to the public or to a substantial segment thereof for the purpose of promoting the purchase or sale of property or services;

(6) makes or induces others to rely on a false or misleading written statement for the purpose of obtaining property or credit;

(7) makes or induces others to rely on a false or misleading written statement for the purpose of promoting the sale of securities, or omits information required by law to be disclosed in written documents relating to securities;

(8) makes or induces others to rely on a false or misleading material statement to induce an investor to invest in a business venture. The offense is complete when any false or misleading material statement is communicated to an investor regardless of whether any investment is made. For purposes of grading, the "amount involved" is the amount or value of the investment solicited or paid, whichever is greater. As used in this paragraph, the following words and phrases shall mean: "Amount" as used in the definition of "material statement" includes currency values and comparative expressions of value, including, but not limited to, percentages or multiples. "Business venture" means any venture represented to an investor as one where he may receive compensation either from the sale of a product, from the investment of other investors or from any other commercial enterprise. "Compensation" means anything of value received or to be received by an investor. "Invest" means to pay, give or lend money, property, service or other thing of value for the opportunity to receive compensation. The term also includes payment for the purchase of a product. "Investment" means the money, property, service or other thing of value paid or given, or to be paid or given, for the opportunity to receive compensation. "Investor" means any natural person, partnership, corporation, limited liability company, business trust, other association, government entity, estate, trust, foundation or other entity solicited to invest in a business venture, regardless of whether any investment is made. "Material statement" means a statement about any matter which could affect an investor's decision to invest in a business venture, including, but not limited to, statements about:

(i) the existence, value, availability or marketability of a product;

(ii) the number of former or current investors, the amount of their investments or the amount of their former or current compensation;

(iii) the available pool or number of prospective investors, including those who have not yet been solicited and those who already have been solicited but have not yet made an investment;

(iv) representations of future compensation to be received by investors or prospective investors; or

(v) the source of former, current or future compensation paid or to be paid to investors or prospective investors.

"Product" means a good, a service or other tangible or intangible property of any kind;

(9) obtains or attempts to obtain property of another by false or misleading representations made through communications conducted in whole or in part by telephone involving the following:

(i) express or implied claims that the person contacted has won or is about to win a prize;

(ii) express or implied claims that the person contacted may be able to recover any losses suffered in connection with a prize promotion; or

(iii) express or implied claims regarding the value of goods or services offered in connection with a prize or a prize promotion.

As used in this paragraph, the term "prize" means anything of value offered or purportedly offered. The term "prize promotion" means an oral or written express or implied representation that a person has won, has been selected to receive or may be eligible to receive a prize or purported prize;

(10) knowingly makes a false or misleading statement in a privacy policy, published on the Internet or otherwise distributed or published, regarding the use of personal information submitted by members of the public; or

(11) does either of the following when the person is in a client relationship with a certified public accountant, public accountant or public accounting firm:

(i) provides false or misleading information to the certified public accountant, public accountant or public accounting firm in connection with performance of an attestation function for the client which results in an attestation by the certified public accountant, public accountant or public accounting firm of a materially misleading financial statement, audit, review or other document; or

(ii) fails to provide information to the certified public accountant, public accountant or public accounting firm which the person knows is material to the performance of an attestation function and which results in an attestation by the certified public accountant,

public accountant or public accounting firm of a materially misleading financial statement, audit, review or other document.

(a.1) Grading of offenses.--

(1) A violation of this section, except for subsection (a)(10), constitutes:

(i) a felony of the third degree if the amount involved exceeds $2,000;

(ii) a misdemeanor of the first degree if the amount involved is $200 or more but $2,000 or less;

(iii) a misdemeanor of the second degree if the amount involved is less than $200; or

(iv) when the amount involved cannot be satisfactorily ascertained, the offense constitutes a misdemeanor of the second degree.

(2) Amounts involved in deceptive or fraudulent business practices pursuant to one scheme or course of conduct, whether from the same person or several persons, may be aggregated in determining the grade of the offense.

(3) Where a person commits an offense under subsection (a) and the victim of the offense is 60 years of age or older, the grading of the offense shall be one grade higher than specified in paragraph (1).

(4) An offense under subsection (a)(10) shall be a summary offense and shall be punishable by a fine not less than $50 and not to exceed $500.

(a.2) Jurisdiction.--

(1) The district attorneys of the several counties shall have the authority to investigate and to institute criminal proceedings for any violation of this section.

(2) In addition to the authority conferred upon the Attorney General by the act of October 15, 1980 (P.L.950, No.164), known as the Commonwealth Attorneys Act, the Attorney General shall have the authority to investigate and to institute criminal proceedings for any violation of this section or any series of such violations involving more than one county of this Commonwealth or involving any county of this Commonwealth and another state. No person charged with a violation of this section by the Attorney General shall have standing to challenge the authority of the Attorney General to investigate or prosecute the case, and, if any such challenge is made, the challenge shall be dismissed and no relief shall be available in the courts of this Commonwealth to the person making the challenge.

(b) Defenses.--It is a defense to prosecution under this section if the defendant proves by a preponderance of the evidence that his conduct was not knowingly or recklessly deceptive.

(c) Exceptions.--Subsection (a)(10) shall not apply to the activities of:

(1) A financial institution as defined by section 509(3) of the Gramm-Leach-Bliley Act (Public Law 106-102, 15 U.S.C. § 6809(3)) or regulations adopted by agencies as designated by section 504(a) of the Gramm-Leach-Bliley Act (15 U.S.C. § 6804(a)) and subject to Title V of the Gramm-Leach-Bliley Act (15 U.S.C. § 6801 et seq.).

(2) A covered entity as defined by regulations promulgated at 45 CFR Pts. 160 (relating to general administration requirements) and 164 (relating to security and privacy) pursuant to Subtitle F of the Health Insurance Portability and Accountability Act of 1996 (Public Law 104-191, 42 U.S.C. § 1320d et seq.).

(3) A licensee or person subject to 31 Pa. Code Ch. 146a (relating to privacy of consumer financial information) or 146b (relating to privacy of consumer health information).

(Dec. 4, 1996, P.L.902, No.145, eff. 60 days; April 5, 2004, P.L.211, No.26, eff. 60 days; Nov. 30, 2004, P.L.1592, No.202, eff. 60 days; Dec. 8, 2004, P.L.1781, No.234, eff. 60 days)

2004 Amendments. Act 234 overlooked the amendment by Act 202, but the amendments do not conflict in substance and have both been given effect in setting forth the text of section 4107.

Cross References. Section 4107 is referred to in section 5552 of Title 42 (Judiciary and Judicial Procedure).

§ 4107.1. Deception relating to kosher food products.

(a) Offense defined.--A person commits a misdemeanor of the third degree if in the course of business, he knowingly sells or exposes for sale any food product represented as kosher or kosher style when such food product is not kosher, said representation having been made orally, in writing or by display on the premises of such sign, mark, insignia or simulation reasonably calculated to induce an individual to believe that said food product is kosher.

(b) Definitions.--As used in this section the following words and phrases shall have the meanings given to them in this subsection:

"Food product." Any article whether in raw or prepared form which is utilized in human consumption.

"Kosher" or "kosher style." A food product having been prepared, processed, manufactured, maintained and vended in accordance with the requisites of traditional Jewish Law.

(Oct. 4, 1978, P.L.908, No.172, eff. 15 days)

1978 Amendment. Act 172 added section 4107.1.

§ 4107.2. Deception relating to certification of minority business enterprise or women's business enterprise.

(a) Offense defined.--A person commits a felony of the third degree if, in the course of business, he:

(1) Fraudulently obtains or retains certification as a minority business enterprise or a women's business enterprise.

(2) Willfully makes a false statement, whether by affidavit, report or other representation, to an official or employee of a public body for the purpose of influencing the certification or denial of certification of any business entity as a minority business enterprise or a women's business enterprise.

(3) Willfully obstructs or impedes any agency official or employee who is investigating the qualifications of a business entity which has requested certification as a minority business enterprise or a women's business enterprise.

(4) Fraudulently obtains public moneys reserved for or allocated or available to minority business enterprises or women's business enterprises.

(b) Definitions.--As used in this section the following words and phrases shall have the meanings given to them in this subsection:

"Certification." A determination made by a public body that a business entity is a minority business enterprise or a women's business enterprise for whatever purpose.

"Control." The exclusive or ultimate and sole control of the business including, but not limited to, capital investment and all other financial, property, acquisition, contract negotiation, legal matters, officer-director-employee selection and comprehensive hiring, operating responsibility, cost-control matters, income and dividend matters, financial transactions and rights of other shareholders or joint partners. Control shall be real, substantial and continuing not pro forma. Control shall include the power to direct or cause the direction of the management and policies of the business and to make the day-to-day as well as major decisions in matters of policy, management and operations. Control shall be exemplified by possessing the requisite knowledge and expertise to run the particular business and control shall not include simple majority or absentee ownership. Further, control by a socially and economically disadvantaged individual or woman shall not be deemed to exist in any case where any nonminority owner or employee of the business is disproportionately responsible for the operation of the firm.

"Minority business enterprise." A small business concern which is:

(1) A sole proprietorship, owned and controlled by a socially and economically disadvantaged individual.

(2) A partnership or joint venture controlled by socially and economically disadvantaged individuals in which 51% of the beneficial ownership interest is held by socially and economically disadvantaged individuals.

(3) A corporation or other entity controlled by socially and economically disadvantaged individuals in which at least 51% of the voting interest and 51% of the beneficial ownership interest are held by socially and economically disadvantaged individuals.

"Public body." A department, bureau, agency, commission or other instrumentality of the Commonwealth, political subdivision, municipal authority or any wholly or partially owned government corporation which enters into contracts.

"Socially and economically disadvantaged individuals." Persons who are citizens of the United States and who are Black Americans, Hispanic Americans, Native Americans, Asian-Pacific Americans, women and other minorities or persons found to be disadvantaged by the Small Business Administration pursuant to the Small Business Act (15 U.S.C. § 631 et seq.).

"Women's business enterprise." A small business concern which is at least 51% owned and controlled by women, or, in the case of any publicly owned business, at least 51% of the stock of which is owned by one or more women and whose management and daily business operations are controlled by one or more of the women who own it.

(Dec. 21, 1984, P.L.1210, No.230, eff. 60 days)

1984 Amendment. Act 230 added section 4107.2.

§ 4108. Commercial bribery and breach of duty to act disinterestedly.

(a) Corrupt employee, agent or fiduciary.--An employee, agent or fiduciary commits a misdemeanor of the second degree when, without the consent of his employer or principal, he solicits, accepts, or agrees to accept any benefit from another person upon agreement or understanding that such benefit will influence his conduct in relation to the affairs of his employer or principal.

(b) Corrupt disinterested person.--A person who holds himself out to the public as being engaged in the business of making disinterested selection, appraisal, or criticism of commodities or services commits a misdemeanor of the second degree if he solicits, accepts or agrees to accept any benefit to influence his selection, appraisal or criticism.

(c) Solicitation.--A person commits a misdemeanor of the second degree if he confers, or offers or agrees to confer, any benefit the acceptance of which would be criminal under subsections (a) or (b) of this section.

Cross References. Section 4108 is referred to in sections 911, 5708 of this title; section 5552 of Title 42 (Judiciary and Judicial Procedure).

§ 4109. Rigging publicly exhibited contest.

(a) Offense defined.--A person commits a misdemeanor of the first degree if, with intent to prevent a publicly exhibited contest from being conducted in accordance with the rules and usages purporting to govern it, he:

(1) confers or offers or agrees to confer any benefit upon, or threatens any injury to a participant, official or other person associated with the contest or exhibition; or

(2) tampers with any person, animal or thing.

(b) Soliciting or accepting benefit for rigging.--A person commits a misdemeanor of the first degree if he knowingly solicits, accepts or agrees to accept any benefit the giving of which would be criminal under subsection (a) of this section.

(c) Participation in rigged contest.--A person commits a misdemeanor of the first degree if he knowingly engages in, sponsors, produces, judges, or otherwise participates in a publicly exhibited contest knowing that the contest is not being conducted in compliance with the rules and usages purporting to govern it, by reason of conduct which would be criminal under this section.

Cross References. Section 4109 is referred to in sections 911, 5708 of this title; sections 9318, 9323 of Title 3 (Agriculture); section 3304 of Title 5 (Athletics and Sports); section 5552 of Title 42 (Judiciary and Judicial Procedure).

§ 4110. Defrauding secured creditors.

A person commits a misdemeanor of the second degree if he destroys, removes, conceals, encumbers, transfers or otherwise deals with property subject to a security interest or after levy has been made thereon with intent to hinder enforcement of such interest.

§ 4111. Fraud in insolvency.

A person commits a misdemeanor of the second degree if, knowing that proceedings have been or are about to be instituted for the appointment of a receiver or other person entitled to administer property for the benefit of creditors, or that any other composition or liquidation for the benefit of creditors has been or is about to be made, he:

(1) destroys, removes, conceals, encumbers, transfers, or otherwise deals with any property with intent to defeat or obstruct the claim of any creditor, or otherwise to obstruct the operation of any law relating to administration of property for the benefit of creditors;

(2) knowingly falsifies any writing or record relating to the property; or

(3) knowingly misrepresents or refuses to disclose to a receiver or other person entitled to administer property for the benefit of creditors, the existence, amount or location of the property, or any other information which the actor could be legally required to furnish in relation to such administration.

§ 4112. Receiving deposits in a failing financial institution.

An officer, manager or other person directing or participating in the direction of a financial institution commits a misdemeanor of the second degree if he receives or permits the receipt of a deposit, premium payment or other investment in the institution knowing that:

(1) due to financial difficulties the institution is about to suspend operations or go into receivership or reorganization; and

(2) the person making the deposit or other payment is unaware of the precarious situation of the institution.

§ 4113. Misapplication of entrusted property and property of government or financial institutions.

(a) Offense defined.--A person commits an offense if he applies or disposes of property that has been entrusted to him as a fiduciary, or property of the government or of a financial institution, in a manner which he knows is unlawful and involves substantial risk of loss or detriment to the owner of the property or to a person for whose benefit the property was entrusted.

(b) Grading.--The offense is a misdemeanor of the second degree if the amount involved exceeds $50; otherwise it is a misdemeanor of the third degree.

Cross References. Section 4113 is referred to in section 5508.3 of Title 53 (Municipalities Generally); section 6017 of Title 64 (Public Authorities and Quasi-Public Corporations).

§ 4114. Securing execution of documents by deception.

A person commits a misdemeanor of the second degree if by deception he causes another to execute any instrument affecting or purporting to affect or likely to affect the pecuniary interest of any person.

§ 4115. Falsely impersonating persons privately employed.

A person commits a misdemeanor of the second degree if, without due authority, he pretends or holds himself out to any one as an employee of any person for the purpose of gaining access to any premises.

§ 4116. Copying; recording devices.

(a) Definitions.--As used in this section, the following words and phrases shall have the meanings given to them in this subsection:

"Manufacturer." The person or entity which authorized or caused the recording or transfer of sounds, images or a combination of sounds and images to the recorded device in issue. The term shall not include the manufacturer of the cartridge or casing itself.

"Owner." The person who owns the master phonograph record, master disc, master tape, master film or other device used for reproducing recorded sounds on phonograph records, discs, tapes, films or other articles on which sound is recorded and from which the transferred sounds are directly or indirectly derived.

"Recorded device." Any phonograph record, disc, tape, film, videotape, video cassette or other tangible article, now known or later developed, upon which sounds or images or any combination of sounds and images are recorded.

(b) Unauthorized transfer of sounds on recording devices.--It shall be unlawful for any person to:

(1) knowingly transfer or cause to be transferred, directly or indirectly by any means, any sounds recorded on a phonograph record, disc, wire, tape, film or other article on which sounds are recorded, with the intent to sell or cause to be sold, or to be used for profit through public performance, such article on which sounds are so transferred, without consent of the owner; or

(2) manufacture, distribute or wholesale any article with the knowledge that the sounds are so transferred, without consent of the owner.

(c) Exceptions.--

(1) Subsection (b) shall not apply to any person engaged in radio or television broadcasting who transfers, or causes to be transferred, any such sounds other than from the sound track of a motion picture intended for, or in connection with broadcast or telecast transmission or related uses, or for archival purposes.

(2) Subsection (b) shall not apply to motion pictures or to sound recordings fixed on or after February 15, 1972.

(d) **Manufacture, sale or rental of illegal recording or recorded devices.**--It shall be unlawful for any person to knowingly manufacture, transport, sell, resell, rent, advertise or offer for sale, resale or rental or cause the manufacture, sale, resale or rental or possess for such purpose or purposes any recorded device in violation of this section.

(d.1) Manufacture, sale or rental of a recording of a live performance without consent of the owner.--

(1) It shall be unlawful for any person to knowingly manufacture, transport, sell, resell, rent, advertise or offer for sale, resale or rental or cause the manufacture, sale, resale or rental or possess for such purpose or purposes any recording of a live performance with the knowledge that the live performance has been recorded without the consent of the owner.

(2) In the absence of a written agreement or law to the contrary, the performer or performers of a live performance are presumed to own the rights to record those sounds.

(3) For purposes of this section, a person who is authorized to maintain custody and control over business records that reflect whether or not the owner of the live performance consented to having the live performance recorded is a competent witness in a proceeding regarding the issue of consent.

(e) **Name of manufacturer on recorded device packaging.**--Every recorded device manufactured, transported, rented, sold, offered for sale or rental, or transferred or possessed for such purpose or purposes by any person shall contain on its packaging or label the true name of the manufacturer.

(f) **Confiscation of non-conforming recorded devices.**--It shall be the duty of all law enforcement officers, upon discovery, to confiscate all recorded devices that do not conform to the provisions of subsection (e). The non-conforming recorded devices shall be delivered to the district attorney of the county in which the confiscation was made. The officer confiscating the recorded devices shall provide to the person from whom the recorded devices were confiscated notice that the person may request a hearing concerning the confiscation and disposition of the devices. Thereafter, the district attorney may seek a court order for destruction of the recorded devices. The provisions of this section shall apply to any non-conforming recorded device, regardless of the requirement in subsection (d) of knowledge or intent.

(g) Grading of offenses.--

(1) Any violation of the provisions of this section involving, within any 180-day period, at least 100 devices upon which motion pictures or portions thereof have been recorded or at least 1,000 devices containing sound recordings or portions thereof is a felony of the third degree. A second or subsequent conviction is a felony of the second degree if at the time of sentencing the defendant has been convicted of another violation of this section.

(2) Any other violation of the provisions of this section not described in paragraph (1) upon a first conviction is a misdemeanor of the first degree and upon a second or subsequent conviction is a felony of the third degree if at the time of sentencing the defendant has been convicted of another violation of this section.

(h) Rights of owners and producers to damages.--

(1) Any owner of a recorded device whose work is allegedly the subject of a violation of the provisions of subsection (b), (d) or (e) shall have a cause of action for all damages resultant therefrom, including actual and punitive damages.

(2) Any lawful producer of a recorded device whose product is allegedly the subject of a violation of the provisions of subsection (b), (d) or (e) shall have a cause of action for all damages resultant therefrom, including actual and punitive damages.

(3) Upon conviction for any offense under this section, the offender may be sentenced to make restitution to any owner or lawful producer of a recorded device or any other person who suffered injury resulting from the crime. Notwithstanding any limitation in section 1106 (relating to restitution for injuries to person or property), the order of restitution may be based on the aggregate wholesale value of lawfully manufactured and authorized recorded devices corresponding to the non-conforming recorded devices involved in the offense. All other provisions of section 1106 not inconsistent with this provision shall apply to an order of restitution under this section.

(i) Forfeiture.--

(1) No property right shall exist in any property used or intended for use in the commission of a violation of this section or in any proceeds traceable to a violation of this section, and the same shall be deemed contraband and forfeited in accordance with the provisions of 42 Pa.C.S. §§ 5803 (relating to asset forfeiture), 5805 (relating to forfeiture procedure), 5806 (relating to motion for return of property), 5807 (relating to restrictions on use), 5807.1 (relating to prohibition on adoptive seizures) and 5808 (relating to exceptions).

(2) (Deleted by amendment).

(3) The provisions of this subsection shall not, in any way, limit the right of the Commonwealth to exercise any rights or remedies otherwise provided by law.

(Dec. 20, 1996, P.L.1499, No.194, eff. 60 days; June 29, 2017, P.L.247, No.13, eff. July 1, 2017)

2017 Amendment. Act 13 amended subsec. (i).

Cross References. Section 4116 is referred to in section 5803 of Title 42 (Judiciary and Judicial Procedure).

§ 4116.1. Unlawful operation of recording device in motion picture theater.

(a) Offense.--A person commits the offense of unauthorized operation of a recording device in a motion picture theater if the person operates a recording device in the theater without written authority or permission from the motion picture theater owner.

(b) Theater owner rights.--

(1) A peace officer, theater owner or an agent under contract with a theater owner who reasonably believes that an offense under the section has occurred or is occurring and who reasonably believes that a specific person has committed or is committing an offense under this section may detain the suspect in a reasonable manner for a reasonable time on or off the premises for any of the following purposes:

(i) To require the suspect to identify himself.

(ii) To verify such identification.

(iii) To determine whether the suspect has any recordings in violation of this section and, if so, to recover such recordings.

(iv) To inform a peace officer.

(v) To institute criminal proceedings against the suspect.

(2) If any person admitted to a theater in which a motion picture is to be or is being exhibited refuses or fails to give or surrender possession or to cease operation of any recording device that the person has brought into or attempts to bring into that theater, then a theater owner shall have the right to refuse further admission to that person or request that the person leave the premises.

(c) Liability.--A theater owner or an employee or agent of a theater owner who detains or causes the arrest of a person in or immediately adjacent to a motion picture theater shall not be held civilly or criminally liable in any proceeding arising out of such detention or arrest if:

(1) the person detaining or causing the arrest had, at the time thereof, reasonably

believed that the person detained or arrested had committed or attempted to commit in that person's presence an offense described in this section;

(2) the manner of the detention or arrest was reasonable;

(3) law enforcement authorities were notified within a reasonable time; and

(4) the person detained or arrested was surrendered to law enforcement authorities within a reasonable time.

(d) **Penalty.**--A first violation of this section constitutes a misdemeanor of the first degree. A second or subsequent conviction is a felony of the third degree if at the time of sentencing the defendant has been convicted of another violation of this section.

(e) **Definitions.**--As used in this section, the following words and phrases shall have the meanings given to them in this subsection:

"Motion picture theater." A premises used for the exhibition or performance of motion pictures to the general public.

"Recording device." A photographic or video camera, audio or video recorder or any other device now existing or later developed which may be used for recording or transferring sounds or images.

"Theater owner." An owner or operator and the agent, employee, consignee, lessee or officer of an owner or operator of any motion picture theater.

(Dec. 20, 1996, P.L.1499, No.194, eff. 60 days)

1996 Amendment. Act 194 added section 4116.1.

§ 4117. Insurance fraud.

(a) **Offense defined.**--A person commits an offense if the person does any of the following:

(1) Knowingly and with the intent to defraud a State or local government agency files, presents or causes to be filed with or presented to the government agency a document that contains false, incomplete or misleading information concerning any fact or thing material to the agency's determination in approving or disapproving a motor vehicle insurance rate filing, a motor vehicle insurance transaction or other motor vehicle insurance action which is required or filed in response to an agency's request.

(2) Knowingly and with the intent to defraud any insurer or self-insured, presents or causes to be presented to any insurer or self-insured any statement forming a part of, or in support of, a claim that contains any false, incomplete or misleading information concerning any fact or thing material to the claim.

(3) Knowingly and with the intent to defraud any insurer or self-insured, assists, abets, solicits or conspires with another to prepare or make any statement that is intended to be presented to any insurer or self-insured in connection with, or in support of, a claim that contains any false, incomplete or misleading information concerning any fact or thing material to the claim, including information which documents or supports an amount claimed in excess of the actual loss sustained by the claimant.

(4) Engages in unlicensed agent, broker or unauthorized insurer activity as defined by the act of May 17, 1921 (P.L.789, No.285), known as The Insurance Department Act of one thousand nine hundred and twenty-one, knowingly and with the intent to defraud an insurer, a self-insured or the public.

(5) Knowingly benefits, directly or indirectly, from the proceeds derived from a violation of this section due to the assistance, conspiracy or urging of any person.

(6) Is the owner, administrator or employee of any health care facility and knowingly allows the use of such facility by any person in furtherance of a scheme or conspiracy to violate any of the provisions of this section.

(7) Borrows or uses another person's financial responsibility or other insurance identification card or permits his financial responsibility or other insurance identification card to be used by another, knowingly and with intent to present a fraudulent claim to an insurer.

(8) If, for pecuniary gain for himself or another, he directly or indirectly solicits any person to engage, employ or retain either himself or any other person to manage, adjust or prosecute any claim or cause of action against any person for damages for negligence or, for pecuniary gain for himself or another, directly or indirectly solicits other persons to bring causes of action to recover damages for personal injuries or death, provided, however, that this paragraph shall not apply to any conduct otherwise permitted by law or by rule of the Supreme Court.

(b) Additional offenses defined.--

(1) A lawyer may not compensate or give anything of value to a nonlawyer to recommend or secure employment by a client or as a reward for having made a recommendation resulting in employment by a client; except that the lawyer may pay:

(i) the reasonable cost of advertising or written communication as permitted by the rules of professional conduct; or

(ii) the usual charges of a not-for-profit lawyer referral service or other legal service organization.

Upon a conviction of an offense provided for by this paragraph, the prosecutor shall certify such conviction to the disciplinary board of the Supreme Court for appropriate action. Such action may include a suspension or disbarment.

(2) With respect to an insurance benefit or claim covered by this section, a health care provider may not compensate or give anything of value to a person to recommend or secure the provider's service to or employment by a patient or as a reward for having made a recommendation resulting in the provider's service to or employment by a patient; except that the provider may pay the reasonable cost of advertising or written communication as permitted by rules of professional conduct. Upon a conviction of an offense provided for by this paragraph, the prosecutor shall certify such conviction to the appropriate licensing board in the Department of State which shall suspend or revoke the health care provider's license.

(3) A lawyer or health care provider may not compensate or give anything of value to a person for providing names, addresses, telephone numbers or other identifying information of individuals seeking or receiving medical or rehabilitative care for accident, sickness or disease, except to the extent a referral and receipt of compensation is permitted under applicable professional rules of conduct. A person may not knowingly transmit such referral information to a lawyer or health care professional for the purpose of receiving compensation or anything of value. Attempts to circumvent this paragraph through use of any other person, including, but not limited to, employees, agents or servants, shall also be prohibited.

(4) A person may not knowingly and with intent to defraud any insurance company, self-insured or other person file an application for insurance containing any false information or conceal for the purpose of misleading information concerning any fact material thereto.

(c) **Electronic claims submission.**--If a claim is made by means of computer billing tapes or other electronic means, it shall be a rebuttable presumption that the person knowingly made the claim if the person has advised the insurer in writing that claims will be submitted by use of computer billing tapes or other electronic means.

(d) **Grading.**--An offense under subsection (a)(1) through (8) is a felony of the third degree. An offense under subsection (b) is a misdemeanor of the first degree.

(e) **Restitution.**--The court may, in addition to any other sentence authorized by law, sentence a person convicted of violating this section to make restitution.

(f) **Immunity.**--An insurer, and any agent, servant or employee thereof acting in the course and scope of his employment, shall be immune from civil or criminal liability arising from the supply or release of written or oral information to any entity duly authorized to receive such information by Federal or State law, or by Insurance Department regulations.

(g) **Civil action.**--An insurer damaged as a result of a violation of this section may sue therefor in any court of competent jurisdiction to recover compensatory damages, which may include reasonable investigation expenses, costs of suit and attorney fees. An insurer may recover treble damages if the court determines that the defendant has engaged in a pattern of violating this section.

(h) Criminal action.--

(1) The district attorneys of the several counties shall have authority to investigate and to institute criminal proceedings for any violation of this section.

(2) In addition to the authority conferred upon the Attorney General by the act of October 15, 1980 (P.L.950, No.164), known as the Commonwealth Attorneys Act, the Attorney General shall have the authority to investigate and to institute criminal proceedings for any violation of this section or any series of such violations involving more than one county of the Commonwealth or involving any county of the Commonwealth and another state. No person charged with a violation of this section by the Attorney General shall have standing to

challenge the authority of the Attorney General to investigate or prosecute the case, and, if any such challenge is made, the challenge shall be dismissed and no relief shall be available in the courts of the Commonwealth to the person making the challenge.

(i) **Regulatory and investigative powers additional to those now existing.**--Nothing contained in this section shall be construed to limit the regulatory or investigative authority of any department or agency of the Commonwealth whose functions might relate to persons, enterprises or matters falling within the scope of this section.

(j) Violations, penalties, etc.--

(1) If a person is found by court of competent jurisdiction, pursuant to a claim initiated by a prosecuting authority, to have violated any provision of this section, the person shall be subject to civil penalties of not more than $5,000 for the first violation, $10,000 for the second violation and $15,000 for each subsequent violation. The penalty shall be paid to the prosecuting authority to be used to defray the operating expenses of investigating and prosecuting insurance fraud. The court may also award court costs and reasonable attorney fees to the prosecuting authority.

(2) Nothing in this subsection shall be construed to prohibit a prosecuting authority and the person accused of violating this section from entering into a written agreement in which that person does not admit or deny the charges but consents to payment of the civil penalty. A consent agreement may not be used in a subsequent civil or criminal proceeding, but notification thereof shall be made to the licensing authority if the person is licensed by a licensing authority of the Commonwealth so that the licensing authority may take appropriate administrative action. Penalties paid under this section shall be deposited into the Insurance Fraud Prevention Trust Fund created under the act of December 28, 1994 (P.L.1414, No.166), known as the Insurance Fraud Prevention Act.

(3) The imposition of any fine or other remedy under this section shall not preclude prosecution for a violation of the criminal laws of this Commonwealth.

(k) Insurance forms and verification of services.--

(1) All applications for insurance and all claim forms shall contain or have attached thereto the following notice:

Any person who knowingly and with intent to defraud any insurance company or other person files an application for insurance or statement of claim containing any materially false information or conceals for the purpose of misleading, information concerning any fact material thereto commits a fraudulent insurance act, which is a crime and subjects such person to criminal and civil penalties.

(2) (Repealed).

(l) **Definitions.**--As used in this section, the following words and phrases shall have the meanings given to them in this subsection:

"Insurance policy." A document setting forth the terms and conditions of a contract of insurance or agreement for the coverage of health or hospital services.

"Insurer." A company, association or exchange defined by section 101 of the act of May 17, 1921 (P.L.682, No.284), known as The Insurance Company Law of 1921; an unincorporated association of underwriting members; a hospital plan corporation; a professional health services plan corporation; a health maintenance organization; a fraternal benefit society; and a self-insured health care entity under the act of October 15, 1975 (P.L.390, No.111), known as the Health Care Services Malpractice Act.

"Person." An individual, corporation, partnership, association, joint-stock company, trust or unincorporated organization. The term includes any individual, corporation, association, partnership, reciprocal exchange, interinsurer, Lloyd's insurer, fraternal benefit society, beneficial association and any other legal entity engaged or proposing to become engaged, either directly or indirectly, in the business of insurance, including agents, brokers, adjusters and health care plans as defined in 40 Pa.C.S. Chs. 61 (relating to hospital plan corporations), 63 (relating to professional health services plan corporations), 65 (relating to fraternal benefit societies) and 67 (relating to beneficial societies) and the act of December 29, 1972 (P.L.1701, No.364), known as the Health Maintenance Organization Act. For purposes of this section, health care plans, fraternal benefit societies and beneficial societies shall be deemed to be engaged in the business of insurance.

"Self-insured." Any person who is self-insured for any risk by reason of any filing, qualification process, approval or exception granted, certified or ordered by any department or agency of the Commonwealth.

"Statement." Any oral or written presentation or other evidence of loss, injury or expense, including, but not limited to, any notice, statement, proof of loss, bill of lading, receipt for payment, invoice, account, estimate of property damages, bill for services, diagnosis, prescription, hospital or doctor records, X-ray, test result or computer-generated documents.

(Feb. 7, 1990, P.L.11, No.6, eff. 60 days; Dec. 19, 1990, P.L.1451, No.219, eff. imd.; Dec. 28, 1994, P.L.1408, No.165, eff. 60 days; July 6, 1995, P.L.242, No.28, eff. 60 days)

1995 Repeal. Act 28 repealed subsec. (k)(2).

References in Text. Chapter 65 of Title 40 (Insurance), referred to in this section, is repealed. The subject matter is now contained in Subarticle A of Article XXIV of the act of May 17, 1921 (P.L.682, No.284), known as The Insurance Company Law of 1921.

The act of December 28, 1994 (P.L.1414, No.166), known as the Insurance Fraud Protection Act, referred to in subsec. (j)(2) was repealed by the act of December 6, 2002 (P.L.1183, No.147). The subject matter is now contained in Article XI of the act of May 17, 1921 (P.L.682, No.284), known as The Insurance Company Law of 1921.

Cross References. Section 4117 is referred to in sections 911, 5708 of this title; section 3802 of Title 40 (Insurance); section 5552 of Title 42 (Judiciary and Judicial Procedure).

§ 4118. Washing vehicle titles.

A person commits a felony of the third degree if, with intent to deceive anyone or with knowledge that the person is facilitating a deception to be perpetrated by anyone concerning the true mileage of a motor vehicle, the person makes or causes to be made an application for a certificate of title for a motor vehicle which includes materially false or fictitious information.

(Mar. 21, 1996, P.L.35, No.11, eff. 60 days)

1996 Amendment. Act 11 added section 4118.

§ 4119. Trademark counterfeiting.

(a) Offense defined.--Any person who knowingly and with intent to sell or to otherwise transfer for purposes of commercial advantage or private financial gain:

(1) manufactures;

(2) sells;

(3) offers for sale;

(4) displays;

(5) advertises;

(6) distributes; or

(7) transports

any items or services bearing or identified by a counterfeit mark shall be guilty of the crime of trademark counterfeiting.

(b) (Reserved).

(c) Penalties.--

(1) Except as provided in paragraphs (2) and (3), a violation of this section constitutes a misdemeanor of the first degree.

(2) A violation of this section constitutes a felony of the third degree if:

(i) the defendant has previously been convicted under this section; or

(ii) the violation involves more than 100 but less than 1,000 items bearing a counterfeit mark or the total retail value of all items or services bearing or identified by a counterfeit mark is more than $2,000, but less than $10,000.

(3) A violation of this section constitutes a felony of the second degree if:

(i) the defendant has been previously convicted of two or more offenses under this section;

(ii) the violation involves the manufacture or production of items bearing counterfeit marks; or

(iii) the violation involves 1,000 or more items bearing a counterfeit mark or the total retail value of all items or services bearing or identified by a counterfeit mark is more than $10,000.

(d) Quantity or retail value.--The quantity or retail value of items or services shall include the aggregate quantity or retail value of all items or services the defendant manufactures, sells, offers for sale, displays, advertises, distributes or transports.

(e) Fine.--Any person convicted under this section shall be fined in accordance with existing law or an amount up to three times the retail value of the items or services bearing or identified by a counterfeit mark, whichever is greater.

(f) Seizure, forfeiture and disposition.--

(1) Any items bearing a counterfeit mark, any property constituting or derived from any proceeds obtained, directly or indirectly, as the result of an offense under this section and all personal property, including, but not limited to, any items, objects, tools, machines, equipment, instrumentalities or vehicles of any kind, used in connection with a violation of this section shall be seized by a law enforcement officer.

(2) (i) All seized personal property and property constituting or derived from any proceeds referenced in paragraph (1) shall be forfeited in accordance with 42 Pa.C.S. §§ 5803 (relating to asset forfeiture), 5805 (relating to forfeiture procedure), 5806 (relating to motion for return of property), 5807 (relating to restrictions on use), 5807.1 (relating to prohibition on adoptive seizures) and 5808 (relating to exceptions).

(ii) Upon the conclusion of all criminal and civil forfeiture proceedings, the court shall order that forfeited items bearing or consisting of a counterfeit mark be destroyed or alternatively disposed of in another manner with the written consent of the trademark owners and the prosecuting attorney responsible for the charges.

(3) (i) If a person is convicted of an offense under this section, the court shall order the person to pay restitution to the trademark owner and to any other victim of the offense.

(ii) In determining the value of the property loss involving an offense against the trademark owner, a court shall grant restitution for all amounts, including expenses incurred by the trademark owner in the investigation and prosecution of the offense as well as the disgorgement of any profits realized by a person convicted of the offense.

(g) **Evidence.**--Any Federal or State certificate of registration shall be prima facie evidence of the facts stated therein.

(h) **Remedies cumulative.**--The remedies provided for in this section shall be cumulative to the other civil and criminal remedies provided by law.

(i) **Definitions.**--As used in this section, the following words and phrases shall have the meanings given to them in this subsection:

"Counterfeit mark." A spurious mark that meets all of the following:

(1) Is applied to, used or intended to be used in connection with an item or service.

(2) Is identical with or substantially indistinguishable from a mark registered and in use in this Commonwealth, any other state or on the principal register in the United States Patent and Trademark Office, whether or not the person knew the mark was registered.

(3) The application of which is either:

(i) likely to cause confusion, to cause mistake or to deceive; or

(ii) otherwise intended to be used on or in connection with the item or service for which the mark is registered.

"Item." Any of the following:

(1) Goods.

(2) Labels.

(3) Patches.

(4) Fabric.

(5) Stickers.

(6) Wrappers.

(7) Badges.

(8) Emblems.

(9) Medallions.

(10) Charms.

(11) Boxes.

(12) Containers.

(13) Cans.

(14) Cases.

(15) Hangtags.

(16) Documentation.

(17) Packaging.

(18) Any other components of a type or nature that are designed, marketed or otherwise intended to be used on or in connection with any goods or services.

"Retail value." One of the following:

(1) The counterfeiter's regular selling price for the item or service bearing or identified by a counterfeit mark, except that it shall be the retail price of the authentic counterpart if the item or service bearing or identified by a counterfeit mark would appear to a reasonably prudent person to be authentic. If no authentic reasonably similar counterpart exists, the retail value shall be the counterfeiter's regular selling price.

(2) If the items bearing a counterfeit mark are components of a finished product, the retail value shall be treated as if each component were a finished good and valued under paragraph (1).

(Oct. 16, 1996, P.L.715, No.128, eff. 60 days; Oct. 19, 2010, P.L.517, No.74, eff. 60 days; June 29, 2017, P.L.247, No.13, eff. July 1, 2017)

2017 Amendment. Act 13 amended subsec. (f)(2)(i).

Cross References. Section 4119 is referred to in sections 5803, 5808 of Title 42 (Judiciary and Judicial Procedure).

§ 4120. Identity theft.

(a) Offense defined.--A person commits the offense of identity theft of another person if he possesses or uses, through any means, identifying information of another person without the consent of that other person to further any unlawful purpose.

(b) Separate offenses.--Each time a person possesses or uses identifying information in violation of subsection (a) constitutes a separate offense under this section. However, the total values involved in offenses under this section committed pursuant to one scheme or course of conduct, whether from the same victim or several victims, may be aggregated in determining the grade of the offense.

(c) Grading.--The offenses shall be graded as follows:

(1) Except as otherwise provided in paragraph (2), an offense under subsection (a) falls within the following classifications depending on the value of any property or services obtained by means of the identifying information:

(i) if the total value involved is less than $2,000, the offense is a misdemeanor of the first degree;

(ii) if the total value involved was $2,000 or more, the offense is a felony of the third degree;

(iii) regardless of the total value involved, if the offense is committed in furtherance of a criminal conspiracy as defined in section 903 (relating to criminal conspiracy), the offense is a felony of the third degree; or

(iv) regardless of the total value involved, if the offense is a third or subsequent offense under this section, the offense is a felony of the second degree.

(2) When a person commits an offense under subsection (a) and the victim of the offense is 60 years of age or older, a care-dependent person as defined in section 2713 (relating to neglect of care-dependent person) or an individual under 18 years of age, the grading of the offense shall be one grade higher than specified in paragraph (1).

(d) Concurrent jurisdiction to prosecute.--In addition to the authority conferred upon the Attorney General by the act of October 15, 1980 (P.L.950, No.164), known as the Commonwealth Attorneys Act, the Attorney General shall have the authority to investigate and to institute criminal proceedings for any violation of this section or any series of such violations involving more than one county of this Commonwealth or another state. No person charged with a violation of this section by the Attorney General shall have standing to challenge the authority of the Attorney General to investigate or prosecute the case, and if any such challenge is made, the challenge shall be dismissed and no relief shall be made available in the courts of this Commonwealth to the person making the challenge.

(e) Use of police reports.--A report to a law enforcement agency by a person stating that the person's identifying information has been lost or stolen or that the person's identifying information has been used without the person's consent shall be prima facie evidence that the identifying information was possessed or used without the person's consent.

(e.1) Venue.--Any offense committed under subsection (a) may be deemed to have been committed at any of the following:

(1) The place where a person possessed or used the identifying information of another without the other's consent to further any unlawful purpose.

(2) The residence of the person whose identifying information has been lost or stolen or has been used without the person's consent.

(3) The business or employment address of the person whose identifying information has been lost or stolen or has been used without the person's consent, if the identifying information at issue is associated with the person's business or employment.

(f) Definitions.--As used in this section, the following words and phrases shall have the meanings given to them in this subsection:

"Document." Any writing, including, but not limited to, birth certificate, Social Security card, driver's license, nondriver government-issued identification card, baptismal certificate, access device card, employee identification card, school identification card or other identifying information recorded by any other method, including, but not limited to, information stored on any computer, computer disc, computer printout, computer system, or part thereof, or by any other mechanical or electronic means.

"Identifying information." Any document, photographic, pictorial or computer image of another person, or any fact used to establish identity, including, but not limited to, a name, birth date, Social Security number, driver's license number, nondriver governmental identification number, telephone number, checking account number, savings account number, student identification number, employee or payroll number or electronic signature.

(May 22, 2000, P.L.102, No.21, eff. 60 days; June 19, 2002, P.L.430, No.62, eff. 60 days; Nov. 27, 2013, P.L.1080, No.97, eff. 60 days)

2013 Amendment. Act 97 amended subsec. (c)(2).

2002 Amendment. Act 62 amended subsecs. (a), (b), (c) and (f) and added subsec. (e.1).

2000 Amendment. Act 21 added section 4120.

Cross References. Section 4120 is referred to in sections 1107.1, 3311 of this title; section 8315 of Title 42 (Judiciary and Judicial Procedure).

§ 4121. Possession and use of unlawful devices.

(a) Offense defined.--A person commits an offense if:

(1) The person, with the intent to defraud another person:

(i) uses a device to access, read, obtain, memorize or store, temporarily or permanently, information encoded on the computer chip, magnetic strip or stripe or other storage mechanism of a payment card or possesses a device capable of doing so; or

(ii) places information encoded on the computer chip, magnetic strip or stripe or other storage mechanism of a payment card onto the computer chip, magnetic strip or stripe or other storage mechanism of a different card or possesses a device capable of doing so.

(2) The person knowingly possesses, sells or delivers a device which is designed to read and store in the device's internal memory information encoded on a computer chip, magnetic strip or stripe or other storage mechanism of a payment card other than for the purpose of processing the information to facilitate a financial transaction.

(b) Grading.--

(1) A first offense under subsection (a) constitutes a felony of the third degree.

(2) A second or subsequent offense under subsection (a) constitutes a felony of the second degree.

(c) Definitions.--As used in this section, the following words and phrases shall have the meanings given to them in this subsection unless the context clearly indicates otherwise:

"Payment card." A credit card, a charge card, a debit card or another card which is issued to an authorized card user to purchase or obtain goods, services, money or another thing of value.

(June 28, 2018, P.L.425, No.60, eff. 60 days)

2018 Amendment. Act 60 added section 4121.

ARTICLE D OFFENSES AGAINST THE FAMILY

Chapter
43. Offenses Against the Family

CHAPTER 43 OFFENSES AGAINST THE FAMILY

Subchapter
A. Definition of Offenses Generally
B. Nonsupport (Repealed)

Enactment. Chapter 43 was added December 6, 1972, P.L.1482, No.334, effective in six months.

SUBCHAPTER A
DEFINITION OF OFFENSES GENERALLY

Sec.
4301. Bigamy.
4302. Incest.
4303. Concealing death of child.
4304. Endangering welfare of children.
4305. Dealing in infant children.

4306. Newborn protection.

Cross References. Subchapter A is referred to in section 2101 of Title 5 (Athletics and Sports).

§ 4301. Bigamy.

(a) Bigamy.--A married person is guilty of bigamy, a misdemeanor of the second degree, if he contracts or purports to contract another marriage, unless at the time of the subsequent marriage:

(1) the actor believes that the prior spouse is dead;

(2) the actor and the prior spouse have been living apart for two consecutive years throughout which the prior spouse was not known by the actor to be alive; or

(3) a court has entered a judgment purporting to terminate or annul any prior disqualifying marriage, and the actor does not know that judgment to be invalid.

(b) Other party to bigamous marriage.--A person is guilty of bigamy if he contracts or purports to contract marriage with another knowing that the other is thereby committing bigamy.

§ 4302. Incest.

(a) General rule.--Except as provided under subsection (b), a person is guilty of incest, a felony of the second degree, if that person knowingly marries or cohabits or has sexual intercourse with an ancestor or descendant, a brother or sister of the whole or half blood or an uncle, aunt, nephew or niece of the whole blood.

(b) Incest of a minor.--A person is guilty of incest of a minor, a felony of the second degree, if that person knowingly marries, cohabits with or has sexual intercourse with a complainant who is an ancestor or descendant, a brother or sister of the whole or half blood or an uncle, aunt, nephew or niece of the whole blood and:

(1) is under the age of 13 years; or

(2) is 13 to 18 years of age and the person is four or more years older than the complainant.

(c) Relationships.--The relationships referred to in this section include blood relationships without regard to legitimacy, and relationship of parent and child by adoption.

(Nov. 17, 1989, P.L.592, No.64, eff. 60 days; Mar. 31, 1995, 1st Sp.Sess., P.L.985, No.10, eff. 60 days; Dec. 20, 2011, P.L.446, No.111, eff. 60 days)

Cross References. Section 4302 is referred to in sections 3104, 5702 of this title; section 3304 of Title 5 (Athletics and Sports); sections 4321, 5329, 6303, 6344, 6702 of Title 23 (Domestic Relations); sections 5551, 5552, 5985.1, 5993, 6358, 6402, 6403, 9718.1, 9730.3, 9799.14, 9799.24, 9802 of Title 42 (Judiciary and Judicial Procedure); section 2303 of Title 44 (Law and Justice); sections 4503, 4601 of Title 61 (Prisons and Parole).

§ 4303. Concealing death of child.

(a) Offense defined.--A person is guilty of a misdemeanor of the first degree if he or she endeavors privately, either alone or by the procurement of others, to conceal the death of his or her child, so that it may not come to light, whether it was born dead or alive or whether it was murdered or not.

(b) Procedure.--If the same indictment or information charges any person with the murder of his or her child, as well as with the offense of the concealment of the death, the jury may acquit or convict him or her of both offenses, or find him or her guilty of one and acquit him or her of the other.

(Oct. 4, 1978, P.L.909, No.173, eff. 60 days; Mar. 31, 1995, 1st Sp.Sess., P.L.985, No.10, eff. 60 days)

1995 Amendment. Section 18 of Act 10, 1st Sp.Sess., provided that the amendment of section 4303 shall apply to offenses committed on or after the effective date of Act 10.

Cross References. Section 4303 is referred to in section 2106 of Title 20 (Decedents, Estates and Fiduciaries); sections 5329, 6344 of Title 23 (Domestic Relations); section 1515 of Title 42 (Judiciary and Judicial Procedure).

§ 4304. Endangering welfare of children.

(a) Offense defined.--

(1) A parent, guardian or other person supervising the welfare of a child under 18 years of age, or a person that employs or supervises such a person, commits an offense if he knowingly endangers the welfare of the child by violating a duty of care, protection or support.

(2) A person commits an offense if the person, in an official capacity, prevents or interferes with the making of a report of suspected child abuse under 23 Pa.C.S. Ch. 63 (relating to child protective services).

(3) As used in this subsection, the term "person supervising the welfare of a child" means a person other than a parent or guardian that provides care, education, training or control of a child.

(b) Grading.--

(1) Except as provided under paragraph (2), the following apply:

(i) An offense under this section constitutes a misdemeanor of the first degree.

(ii) If the actor engaged in a course of conduct of endangering the welfare of a child, the offense constitutes a felony of the third degree.

(iii) If, in the commission of the offense under subsection (a)(1), the actor created a substantial risk of death or serious bodily injury, the offense constitutes a felony of the third degree.

(iv) If the actor's conduct under subsection (a)(1) created a substantial risk of death or serious bodily injury and was part of a course of conduct, the offense constitutes a felony of the second degree.

(2) The grading of an offense under this section shall be increased one grade if, at the time of the commission of the offense, the child was under six years of age.

(c) Counseling.--A court shall consider ordering an individual convicted of an offense under this section to undergo counseling.

(Dec. 19, 1988, P.L.1275, No.158, eff. 60 days; July 6, 1995, P.L.251, No.31, eff. 60 days; Nov. 29, 2006, P.L.1581, No.179, eff. 60 days; June 29, 2017, P.L.246, No.12, eff. 60 days)

2017 Amendment. Act 12 amended subsec. (b) and added subsec. (c).

2006 Amendment. Act 179 amended subsec. (a).

Cross References. Section 4304 is referred to in section 3104 of this title; section 3304 of Title 5 (Athletics and Sports); section 2106 of Title 20 (Decedents, Estates and Fiduciaries); sections 5329, 6340, 6344 of Title 23 (Domestic Relations); sections 5552, 5985.1, 5993, 62A03, 9718.1 of Title 42 (Judiciary and Judicial Procedure).

§ 4305. Dealing in infant children.

A person is guilty of a misdemeanor of the first degree if he deals in humanity, by trading, bartering, buying, selling, or dealing in infant children.

Cross References. Section 4305 is referred to in section 5708 of this title; section 3304 of Title 5 (Athletics and Sports); sections 2533, 5329, 6344 of Title 23 (Domestic Relations).

§ 4306. Newborn protection.

(a) General rule.--A parent of a newborn shall not be criminally liable for any violation of this title solely for leaving a newborn in the care of a hospital, a police officer at a police station pursuant to 23 Pa.C.S. Ch. 65 (relating to newborn protection) or an emergency services provider on the grounds of an entity employing the emergency services provider or otherwise providing access to the emergency services provider pursuant to 23 Pa.C.S. Ch. 65 if the following criteria are met:

(1) The parent expresses, either orally or through conduct, the intent to have the hospital, police officer or emergency services provider accept the newborn pursuant to 23 Pa.C.S. Ch. 65.

(2) The newborn is not a victim of child abuse or criminal conduct.

(a.1) Incubator.--A parent of a newborn shall not be criminally liable for any violation of this title solely for leaving a newborn in an incubator if the newborn is not a victim of child abuse or criminal conduct and the incubator is located:

(1) at a hospital;

(2) at a police station pursuant to 23 Pa.C.S. Ch. 65; or

(3) on the grounds of an entity employing the emergency services provider or otherwise providing access to the emergency services provider pursuant to 23 Pa.C.S. Ch. 65.

(b) Definitions.--As used in this section, the following words and phrases shall have the meanings given to them in this subsection unless the context clearly indicates otherwise:

"Child abuse." As defined in 23 Pa.C.S. § 6303(b.1) (relating to definitions).

"Emergency services provider." An emergency medical responder, emergency medical technician, advanced emergency medical technician or a paramedic as defined in 35 Pa.C.S. § 8103 (relating to definitions).

"Newborn." As defined in 23 Pa.C.S. § 6502 (relating to definitions).

"Police department." A public agency of a political subdivision having general police powers and charged with making arrests in connection with the enforcement of criminal or traffic laws.

"Police officer." A full-time or part-time employee assigned to criminal or traffic law enforcement duties of a police department of a county, city, borough, town or township. The term also includes a member of the State Police Force.

"Police station." The station or headquarters of a police department or a Pennsylvania State Police station or headquarters.

(Dec. 9, 2002, P.L.1549, No.201, eff. 60 days; July 2, 2014, P.L.843, No.91, eff. 60 days; Dec. 22, 2017, P.L.1219, No.68)

2017 Amendment. Section 7(2) of Act 68 provided that the addition of subsec. (a.1) shall take effect 120 days after the publication in the Pennsylvania Bulletin of the promulgation of final regulations under 23 Pa.C.S. § 6504.3(c).

2014 Amendment. Act 91 amended subsecs. (a) intro. par. and (1) and (b).

2002 Amendment. Act 201 added section 4306.

Cross References. Section 4306 is referred to in sections 6503, 6504.2 of Title 23 (Domestic Relations).

SUBCHAPTER B
NONSUPPORT
(Repealed)

1985 Repeal. Subchapter B (§§ 4321 - 4324) was added December 6, 1972 (P.L.1482, No.334), and repealed October 30, 1985 (P.L.264, No.66), effective in 90 days. The subject matter is now contained in Chapter 43 of Title 23 (Domestic Relations).

ARTICLE E
OFFENSES AGAINST PUBLIC
ADMINISTRATION

CHAPTER 45
GENERAL PROVISIONS

Enactment. Chapter 45 was added December 6, 1972, P.L.1482, No.334, effective in six months.

§ 4501. Definitions.

Subject to additional definitions contained in subsequent provisions of this article which are applicable to specific chapters or other provisions of this article, the following words and phrases, when used in this article shall have, unless the context clearly indicates otherwise, the meanings given to them in this section:

"Administrative proceeding." Any proceeding other than a judicial proceeding, the outcome of which is required to be based on a record or documentation prescribed by law, or in which law or regulation is particularized in application to individuals.

"Benefit." Gain or advantage, or anything regarded by the beneficiary as gain or advantage, including benefit to any other person or entity in whose welfare he is interested, but not an advantage promised generally to a group or class of voters as a consequence of public measures which a candidate engages to support or oppose.

"Government." Includes any branch, subdivision or agency of:
(1) the Commonwealth government;
(2) any political subdivision; or
(3) any municipal or local authority.

"Harm." Loss, disadvantage or injury, or anything so regarded by the person affected, including loss, disadvantage or injury to any other person or entity in whose welfare he is interested.

"Licensing board." Any of the following:
(1) A board or commission:
(i) which is empowered to license, certify or register individuals as members of an occupation or profession; and
(ii) of which the Commissioner of Professional and Occupational Affairs is a member.
(2) The State Board of Certified Real Estate Appraisers.
(3) The Navigation Commission for the Delaware River and its navigable tributaries.

"Official proceeding." A proceeding heard or which may be heard before any legislative, judicial, administrative or other government agency or official authorized to take evidence under oath, including any referee, hearing examiner, commissioner, notary or other person taking testimony or deposition in connection with any such proceeding.

"Party official." A person who holds an elective or appointive post in a political party in the United States by virtue of which he directs or conducts, or participates in directing or conducting party affairs at any level of responsibility.

"Pecuniary benefit." Benefit in the form of money, property, commercial interests or anything else the primary significance of which is economic gain.

"Professional or occupational license." An authorization by a licensing board to practice a profession or occupation.

(1) The term includes:

(i) an authorization that is suspended, retired, inactive or expired; and

(ii) a temporary practice permit, license, certification or registration.

(2) The term does not include an authorization that has been revoked or voluntarily surrendered.

"Public servant." Any officer or employee of government, including members of the General Assembly and judges, and any person participating as juror, advisor, consultant or otherwise, in performing a governmental function; but the term does not include witnesses.

(Mar. 22, 2010, P.L.144, No.12, eff. 60 days)

2010 Amendment. Act 12 added the defs. of "licensing board" and "professional or occupational license."

Cross References. Section 4501 is referred to in section 4958 of this title.

CHAPTER 47 BRIBERY AND CORRUPT INFLUENCE

Sec.

4701. Bribery in official and political matters.

4702. Threats and other improper influence in official and political matters.

4703. Retaliation for past official action.

Enactment. Chapter 47 was added December 6, 1972, P.L.1482, No.334, effective in six months.

Cross References. Chapter 47 is referred to in section 911 of this title; section 3575 of Title 42 (Judiciary and Judicial Procedure); section 5508.3 of Title 53 (Municipalities Generally); section 6017 of Title 64 (Public Authorities and Quasi-Public Corporations).

§ 4701. Bribery in official and political matters.

(a) **Offenses defined.**--A person is guilty of bribery, a felony of the third degree, if he offers, confers or agrees to confer upon another, or solicits, accepts or agrees to accept from another:

(1) any pecuniary benefit as consideration for the decision, opinion, recommendation, vote or other exercise of discretion as a public servant, party official or voter by the recipient;

(2) any benefit as consideration for the decision, vote, recommendation or other exercise of official discretion by the recipient in a judicial, administrative or legislative proceeding; or

(3) any benefit as consideration for a violation of a known legal duty as public servant or party official.

(b) **Defenses prohibited.**--It is no defense to prosecution under this section that a person whom the actor sought to influence was not qualified to act in the desired way whether because he had not yet assumed office, had left office, or lacked jurisdiction, or for any other reason.

Cross References. Section 4701 is referred to in section 5708 of this title; section 3304 of Title 5 (Athletics and Sports); section 5552 of Title 42 (Judiciary and Judicial Procedure).

§ 4702. Threats and other improper influence in official and political matters.

(a) **Offenses defined.**--A person commits an offense if he:

(1) threatens unlawful harm to any person with intent to influence his decision, opinion, recommendation, vote or other exercise of discretion as a public servant, party official or voter;

(2) threatens unlawful harm to any public servant with intent to influence his decision, opinion, recommendation, vote or other

exercise of discretion in a judicial or administrative proceeding; or

(3) threatens unlawful harm to any public servant or party official with intent to influence him to violate his known legal duty.

(b) **Defense prohibited.**--It is no defense to prosecution under this section that a person whom the actor sought to influence was not qualified to act in the desired way, whether because he had not yet assumed office, or lacked jurisdiction, or for any other reason.

(c) **Grading.**--An offense under this section is a misdemeanor of the second degree unless the actor threatened to commit a crime or made a threat with intent to influence a judicial or administrative proceeding, in which cases the offense is a felony of the third degree.

Cross References. Section 4702 is referred to in section 5708 of this title; section 5552 of Title 42 (Judiciary and Judicial Procedure).

§ 4703. Retaliation for past official action.

A person commits a misdemeanor of the second degree if he harms another by any unlawful act in retaliation for anything lawfully done by the latter in the capacity of public servant.

Cross References. Section 4703 is referred to in section 5552 of Title 42 (Judiciary and Judicial Procedure).

CHAPTER 49 FALSIFICATION AND INTIMIDATION

Subchapter
A. Perjury and Falsification in Official Matters
B. Victim and Witness Intimidation

Enactment. Chapter 49 was added December 6, 1972, P.L.1482, No.334, effective in six months.

Chapter Heading. The heading of Chapter 49 was amended December 4, 1980, P.L.1097, No.187, effective in 60 days.

Cross References. Chapter 49 is referred to in section 911 of this title; section 6122 of Title 23 (Domestic Relations); section 62A20 of Title 42 (Judiciary and Judicial Procedure);

section 5508.3 of Title 53 (Municipalities Generally); section 6017 of Title 64 (Public Authorities and Quasi-Public Corporations); sections 2702, 3104 of Title 71 (State Government).

SUBCHAPTER A
PERJURY AND FALSIFICATION
IN OFFICIAL MATTERS

Subchapter Heading. The heading of Subchapter A was added December 4, 1980, P.L.1097, No.187, effective in 60 days.

Cross References. Subchapter A is referred to in section 3575 of Title 42 (Judiciary and Judicial Procedure).

§ 4901. Definition.

As used in this chapter, unless a different meaning plainly is required "statement" means any representation, but includes a representation of opinion, belief or other state of mind only if the representation clearly relates to state of mind apart from or in addition to any facts which are the subject of the representation.

§ 4902. Perjury.

(a) Offense defined.--A person is guilty of perjury, a felony of the third degree, if in any official proceeding he makes a false statement under oath or equivalent affirmation, or swears or affirms the truth of a statement previously made, when the statement is material and he does not believe it to be true.

(b) Materiality.--Falsification is material, regardless of the admissibility of the statement under rules of evidence, if it could have affected the course or outcome of the proceeding. It is no defense that the declarant mistakenly believed the falsification to be immaterial. Whether a falsification is material in a given factual situation is a question of law.

(c) Irregularities no defense.--It is not a defense to prosecution under this section that the oath or affirmation was administered or taken in an irregular manner or that the declarant was not competent to make the statement. A document purporting to be made upon oath or affirmation at any time when the actor presents it as being so verified shall be deemed to have been duly sworn or affirmed.

(d) Retraction.--No person shall be guilty of an offense under this section if he retracted the falsification in the course of the proceeding in which it was made before it became manifest that the falsification was or would be exposed and before the falsification substantially affected the proceeding.

(e) Inconsistent statements.--Where the defendant made inconsistent statements under oath or equivalent affirmation, both having been made within the period of the statute of limitations, the prosecution may proceed by setting forth the inconsistent statements in a single count alleging in the alternative that one or the other was false and not believed by the defendant. In such case it shall not be necessary for the prosecution to prove which statement was false but only that one or the other was false and not believed by the defendant to be true.

(f) Corroboration.--In any prosecution under this section, except under subsection (e) of this section, falsity of a statement may not be established by the uncorroborated testimony of a single witness.

Cross References. Section 4902 is referred to in sections 3218, 4903, 4904, 5708

of this title; sections 1518, 3905 of Title 4 (Amusements); sections 916, 3304 of Title 5 (Athletics and Sports); section 1714 of Title 25 (Elections); sections 5552, 5947, 9543.1 of Title 42 (Judiciary and Judicial Procedure).

§ 4903. False swearing.

(a) False swearing in official matters.-- A person who makes a false statement under oath or equivalent affirmation, or swears or affirms the truth of such a statement previously made, when he does not believe the statement to be true is guilty of a misdemeanor of the second degree if:

(1) the falsification occurs in an official proceeding; or

(2) the falsification is intended to mislead a public servant in performing his official function.

(b) Other false swearing.--A person who makes a false statement under oath or equivalent affirmation, or swears or affirms the truth of such a statement previously made, when he does not believe the statement to be true, is guilty of a misdemeanor of the third degree, if the statement is one which is required by law to be sworn or affirmed before a notary or other person authorized to administer oaths.

(c) Perjury provisions applicable.-- Section 4902(c) through (f) of this title (relating to perjury) applies to this section.

Cross References. Section 4903 is referred to in sections 1310, 1518, 1602, 3905 of Title 4 (Amusements); section 1714 of Title 25 (Elections); section 4110 of Title 27 (Environmental Resources); sections 5552, 5947, 9543.1 of Title 42 (Judiciary and Judicial Procedure); section 2304 of Title 68 (Real and Personal Property).

§ 4904. Unsworn falsification to authorities.

(a) In general.--A person commits a misdemeanor of the second degree if, with intent to mislead a public servant in performing his official function, he:

(1) makes any written false statement which he does not believe to be true;

(2) submits or invites reliance on any writing which he knows to be forged, altered or otherwise lacking in authenticity; or

(3) submits or invites reliance on any sample, specimen, map, boundary mark, or other object which he knows to be false.

(b) Statements "under penalty".--A person commits a misdemeanor of the third degree if he makes a written false statement which he does not believe to be true, on or pursuant to a form bearing notice, authorized by law, to the effect that false statements made therein are punishable.

(c) Perjury provisions applicable.--Section 4902(c) through (f) of this title (relating to perjury) applies to this section.

(d) Penalty.--In addition to any other penalty that may be imposed, a person convicted under this section shall be sentenced to pay a fine of at least $1,000.

(Nov. 29, 2006, P.L.1481, No.168, eff. 60 days)

2006 Amendment. Act 168 added subsec. (d).

Cross References. Section 4904 is referred to in section 6116 of this title; section 2344 of Title 3 (Agriculture); sections 1518, 3905 of Title 4 (Amusements); sections 102, 134, 142, 8998 of Title 15 (Corporations and Unincorporated Associations); sections 761, 911, 3101, 3175 of Title 20 (Decedents, Estates and Fiduciaries); sections 4308.1, 5103, 5337, 6344.2, 6711 of Title 23 (Domestic Relations); section 1714 of Title 25 (Elections); section 4110 of Title 27 (Environmental Resources); section 7923 of Title 35 (Health and Safety); sections 102, 1904, 5552, 5903 of Title 42 (Judiciary and Judicial Procedure); section 101 of Title 54 (Names); section 13A08 of Title 65 (Public Officers); section 2301 of Title 71 (State Government); sections 1510, 1920.2 of Title 75 (Vehicles).

§ 4905. False alarms to agencies of public safety.

(a) Offense defined.--A person commits an offense if he knowingly causes a false alarm of fire or other emergency to be transmitted to or within any organization, official or volunteer, for dealing with emergencies involving danger to life or property.

(b) Grading.--An offense under this section is a misdemeanor of the first degree unless the transmission of the false alarm of fire or other emergency occurs during a declared state of emergency and the false alarm causes the resources of the organization to be diverted from dealing with the declared state of emergency, in which case the offense is a felony of the third degree.

(June 28, 2002, P.L.481, No.82, eff. 60 days)

Cross References. Section 4905 is referred to in section 5552 of Title 42 (Judiciary and Judicial Procedure).

§ 4906. False reports to law enforcement authorities.

(a) Falsely incriminating another.--Except as provided in subsection (c), a person who knowingly gives false information to any law enforcement officer with intent to implicate another commits a misdemeanor of the second degree.

(b) Fictitious reports.--Except as provided in subsection (c), a person commits a misdemeanor of the third degree if he:

(1) reports to law enforcement authorities an offense or other incident within their concern knowing that it did not occur; or

(2) pretends to furnish such authorities with information relating to an offense or incident when he knows he has no information relating to such offense or incident.

(c) Grading.--

(1) If the violation of subsection (a) or (b) occurs during a declared state of emergency and the false report causes the resources of the law enforcement authority to be diverted from dealing with the declared state of emergency, the offense shall be graded one step greater than that set forth in the applicable subsection.

(2) If the violation of subsection (a) or (b) relates to a false report of the theft or loss of a firearm, as defined in section 5515 (relating to prohibiting of paramilitary training), the offense shall be graded one step greater than that set forth in the applicable subsection.

(June 28, 2002, P.L.481, No.82, eff. 60 days; Oct. 17, 2008, P.L.1628, No.131, eff. 60 days)

2008 Amendment. Act 131 amended subsec. (c).

Cross References. Section 4906 is referred to in sections 2709, 2709.1, 6105 of this title; section 6106 of Title 23 (Domestic Relations); sections 5552, 62A05 of Title 42 (Judiciary and Judicial Procedure).

§ 4906.1. False reports of child abuse.

A person commits a misdemeanor of the second degree if the person intentionally or knowingly makes a false report of child abuse under 23 Pa.C.S. Ch. 63 (relating to child protective services) or intentionally or knowingly induces a child to make a false claim of child abuse under 23 Pa.C.S. Ch. 63.

(Dec. 18, 2013, P.L.1198, No.118, eff. Jan. 1, 2014)

2013 Amendment. Act 118 added section 4906.1.

Cross References. Section 4906.1 is referred to in sections 6331, 6335, 6336, 6340 of Title 23 (Domestic Relations).

§ 4907. Tampering with witnesses and informants (Repealed).

1980 Repeal. Section 4907 was repealed December 4, 1980 (P.L.1097, No.187), effective in 60 days. The subject matter is now contained in Subchapter B of this chapter.

§ 4908. Retaliation against witness or informant (Repealed).

1980 Repeal. Section 4908 was repealed December 4, 1980 (P.L.1097, No.187), effective in 60 days. The subject matter is now contained in Subchapter B of this chapter.

§ 4909. Witness or informant taking bribe.

A person commits a felony of the third degree if he solicits, accepts or agrees to accept any benefit in consideration of his doing any of the things specified in section 4952(a)(1) through (6) (relating to intimidation of witnesses or victims).

(Dec. 4, 1980, P.L.1097, No.187, eff. 60 days)

Cross References. Section 4909 is referred to in section 5708 of the title; section 5552 of Title 42 (Judiciary and Judicial Procedure).

§ 4910. Tampering with or fabricating physical evidence.

A person commits a misdemeanor of the second degree if, believing that an official proceeding or investigation is pending or about to be instituted, he:

(1) alters, destroys, conceals or removes any record, document or thing with intent to impair its verity or availability in such proceeding or investigation; or

(2) makes, presents or uses any record, document or thing knowing it to be false and with intent to mislead a public servant who is or may be engaged in such proceeding or investigation.

Cross References. Section 4910 is referred to in section 5552 of Title 42 (Judiciary and Judicial Procedure).

§ 4911. Tampering with public records or information.

(a) Offense defined.--A person commits an offense if he:

(1) knowingly makes a false entry in, or false alteration of, any record, document or thing belonging to, or received or kept by, the government for information or record, or required by law to be kept by others for information of the government;

(2) makes, presents or uses any record, document or thing knowing it to be false, and with intent that it be taken as a genuine part of information or records referred to in paragraph (1) of this subsection; or

(3) intentionally and unlawfully destroys, conceals, removes or otherwise impairs the verity or availability of any such record, document or thing.

(b) Grading.--An offense under this section is a misdemeanor of the second degree unless the intent of the actor is to defraud or injure anyone, in which case the offense is a felony of the third degree.

Cross References. Section 4911 is referred to in section 5708 of this title; section 9518 of Title 13 (Commercial Code); section 5552 of Title 42 (Judiciary and Judicial Procedure).

§ 4912. Impersonating a public servant.

A person commits a misdemeanor of the second degree if he falsely pretends to hold a position in the public service with intent to induce another to submit to such pretended official authority or otherwise to act in reliance upon that pretense to his prejudice.

Cross References. Section 4912 is referred to in section 6105 of this title; section 5552 of Title 42 (Judiciary and Judicial Procedure).

§ 4913. Impersonating a notary public or a holder of a professional or occupational license.

(a) Offense defined.--A person commits an offense if the person does any of the following:

(1) falsely pretends to hold the office of notary public within this Commonwealth or to hold a professional or occupational license issued by a licensing board; and

(2) performs any action in furtherance of this false pretense.

(b) Grading.--

(1) Except as set forth in paragraph (2) or (3), an offense under this section is a misdemeanor of the second degree.

(2) If the intent of the actor is to harm, defraud or injure anyone, an offense under this section is a misdemeanor of the first degree.

(3) If the intent of the actor is to impersonate a doctor of medicine and, in so doing, the actor provides medical advice or treatment to another person as a patient, regardless of whether or not the other person suffers harm from the medical advice or treatment, an offense under this section is a misdemeanor of the first degree.

(Mar. 21, 1996, P.L.35, No.11, eff. 60 days; Mar. 22, 2010, P.L.144, No.12, eff. 60 days; June 26, 2015, P.L.32, No.10, eff. 60 days)

2015 Amendment. Act 10 amended subsec. (b)(1) and added subsec. (b)(3).

Cross References. Section 4913 is referred to in section 323 of Title 57 (Notaries Public).

§ 4914. False identification to law enforcement authorities.

(a) Offense defined.--A person commits an offense if he furnishes law enforcement authorities with false information about his identity after being informed by a law enforcement officer who is in uniform or who has identified himself as a law enforcement officer that the person is the subject of an official investigation of a violation of law.

(b) Grading.--An offense under this section is a misdemeanor of the third degree.

(Dec. 20, 2000, P.L.972, No.133, eff. 60 days)

2000 Amendment. Act 133 added section 4914.

Cross References. Section 4914 is referred to in section 6328 of Title 42 (Judiciary and Judicial Procedure).

§ 4915. Failure to comply with registration of sexual offenders requirements (Expired).

2012 Expiration. Section 4915 expired December 20, 2012. See Act 91 of 2012.

2013 Unconstitutionality. Act 152 of 2004 was declared unconstitutional.

Commonwealth v. Neiman, 84 A.3d 603 (Pa. 2013). The unconstitutionality took effect March 17, 2014.

§ 4915.1. Failure to comply with registration requirements.

(a) Offense defined.--An individual who is subject to registration under 42 Pa.C.S. § 9799.13 (relating to applicability) commits an offense if he knowingly fails to:

(1) register with the Pennsylvania State Police as required under 42 Pa.C.S. § 9799.15 (relating to period of registration), 9799.19 (relating to initial registration) or 9799.25 (relating to verification by sexual offenders and Pennsylvania State Police);

(2) verify his address or be photographed as required under 42 Pa.C.S. § 9799.15, 9799.19 or 9799.25; or

(3) provide accurate information when registering under 42 Pa.C.S. § 9799.15, 9799.19 or 9799.25.

(a.1) Transients.--An individual set forth in 42 Pa.C.S. § 9799.13 who is a transient commits an offense if he knowingly fails to:

(1) register with the Pennsylvania State Police as required under 42 Pa.C.S. §§ 9799.15, 9799.16(b)(6) (relating to registry) and 9799.25(a)(7);

(2) verify the information provided in 42 Pa.C.S. §§ 9799.15 and 9799.16(b)(6) or be photographed as required under 42 Pa.C.S. § 9799.15 or 9799.25;

(3) provide accurate information when registering under 42 Pa.C.S. § 9799.15, 9799.16(b)(6) or 9799.25.

(a.2) Counseling.--The following apply:

(1) An individual who is designated as a sexually violent predator or sexually violent delinquent child commits an offense if he knowingly fails to comply with 42 Pa.C.S. § 6404.2(g) (relating to duration of outpatient commitment and review) or 9799.36 (relating to counseling of sexually violent predators).

(2) An individual who is subject to a counseling requirement under a sex offender registration statute following conviction in another jurisdiction where the requirement is based on the commitment of an offense on or after December 20, 2012, for which the individual was convicted, commits an offense if the individual knowingly fails to comply with 42 Pa.C.S. § 9799.36.

(b) Grading for sexual offenders who must register for 15 years or who must register pursuant to 42 Pa.C.S. § 9799.13(7.1).--

(1) Except as set forth in paragraph (3), an individual who commits a violation of subsection (a)(1) or (2) commits a felony of the third degree.

(2) An individual who commits a violation of subsection (a)(1) or (2) and who has previously been convicted of an offense under subsection (a)(1) or (2) or (a.1)(1) or (2) or a similar offense commits a felony of the second degree.

(3) An individual who violates subsection (a)(3) commits a felony of the second degree.

(4) For the purposes of this subsection, an individual shall mean an individual that meets any of the following:

(i) Is a sexual offender subject to registration under 42 Pa.C.S. § 9799.13 and is required to register for a period of 15 years.

(ii) Is a sexual offender subject to registration under 42 Pa.C.S. § 9799.13(7.1).

(c) Grading for sexual offenders who must register for 25 years or life.--

(1) Except as set forth in paragraph (3), an individual subject to registration under 42 Pa.C.S. § 9799.13 and required to register for a period of 25 years or life who commits a violation of subsection (a)(1) or (2) commits a felony of the second degree.

(2) An individual subject to registration under 42 Pa.C.S. § 9799.13 and required to register for a period of 25 years or life who commits a violation of subsection (a)(1) or (2) and who has previously been convicted of an offense under subsection (a)(1) or (2) or (a.1)(1) or (2) or a similar offense commits a felony of the first degree.

(3) An individual subject to registration under 42 Pa.C.S. § 9799.13 and required to register for a period of 25 years or life who violates subsection (a)(3) commits a felony of the first degree.

(c.1) Grading for sexual offenders who are transients who must register for 15 years.--

(1) Except as set forth in paragraph (2) or (3), an individual commits a felony of the third degree if the individual violates subsection (a.1)(1) or (2).

(2) An individual commits a felony of the second degree if the individual violates subsection (a.1)(3).

(3) An individual commits a felony of the second degree if the individual violates subsection (a.1)(1) or (2) and has been previously convicted of an offense under subsection (a)(1) or (2) or (a.1)(1) or (2) or a similar offense.

(4) For the purposes of this subsection, an individual shall mean an individual that meets any of the following:

(i) Is a sexual offender subject to registration under 42 Pa.C.S. § 9799.13 and is a transient who must register for a period of 15 years.

(ii) Is a sexual offender subject to registration under 42 Pa.C.S. § 9799.13(7.1) and is a transient.

(c.2) Grading for sexual offenders who are transients who must register for 25 years or life.--

(1) Except as set forth in paragraph (2) or (3), an individual subject to registration under 42 Pa.C.S. § 9799.13 who is a transient who must register for a period of 25 years or life commits a felony of the second degree if the individual violates subsection (a.1)(1) or (2).

(2) An individual who is subject to registration under 42 Pa.C.S. § 9799.13 who is a transient who must register for a period of 25 years or life commits a felony of the first degree if the individual violates subsection (a.1)(3).

(3) An individual subject to registration under 42 Pa.C.S. § 9799.13 who is a transient who must register for a period of 25 years or life commits a felony of the first degree if the individual violates subsection (a.1)(1) or (2) and has been previously convicted of an offense under subsection (a)(1) or (2) or (a.1)(1) or (2) or a similar offense.

(c.3) **Grading for failure to comply with counseling requirements.**--An individual designated as a sexually violent predator or sexually violent delinquent child or an individual who is subject to a counseling requirement under a sex offender registration statute following conviction of a sexual offense on or after December 20, 2012, in another jurisdiction commits a misdemeanor of the first degree if the individual violates subsection (a.2).

(d) **Effect of notice.**--Neither failure on the part of the Pennsylvania State Police to send nor failure of a sexually violent predator or sexual offender to receive any notice or information pursuant to 42 Pa.C.S. § 9799.25 shall be a defense to a prosecution commenced against an individual arising from a violation of this section. The provisions of 42 Pa.C.S. §

9799.25 are not an element of an offense under this section.

(e) Arrests for violation.--

(1) A police officer shall have the same right of arrest without a warrant as in a felony whenever the police officer has probable cause to believe an individual has committed a violation of this section regardless of whether the violation occurred in the presence of the police officer.

(2) An individual arrested for a violation of this section shall be afforded a preliminary arraignment by the proper issuing authority without unnecessary delay. In no case may the individual be released from custody without first having appeared before the issuing authority.

(3) Prior to admitting an individual arrested for a violation of this section to bail, the issuing authority shall require all of the following:

(i) The individual must be fingerprinted and photographed in the manner required by 42 Pa.C.S. Ch. 97 Subch. H (relating to registration of sexual offenders).

(ii) The individual must provide the Pennsylvania State Police with all current or intended residences, all information concerning current or intended employment, including all employment locations, and all information concerning current or intended enrollment as a student. This subparagraph includes an individual who is a transient, in which case the individual must, in addition to other information required under this subparagraph, provide the information set forth in 42 Pa.C.S. § 9799.16(b)(6).

(iii) Law enforcement must make reasonable attempts to verify the information provided by the individual.

(e.1) Affirmative defense.--It is an affirmative defense for a prosecution under this section that the individual acted in accordance with a court order under 42 Pa.C.S. § 9799.15(a.2).

(f) Definitions.--As used in this section, the following words and phrases shall have the meanings given to them in this subsection unless the context clearly indicates otherwise:

"Sexual offender." The term shall have the meaning given to it in 42 Pa.C.S. § 9799.12 (relating to definitions).

"Sexually violent delinquent child." The term shall have the meaning given to it in 42 Pa.C.S. § 9799.12 (relating to definitions).

"Sexually violent predator." The term shall have the meaning given to it in 42 Pa.C.S. § 9799.12 (relating to definitions).

"Similar offense." An offense similar to an offense under either subsection (a)(1) or (2) under the laws of this Commonwealth, another jurisdiction or a foreign country or a military offense, as defined in 42 Pa.C.S. § 9799.12 (relating to definitions).

"Transient." The term shall have the meaning given to it in 42 Pa.C.S. § 9799.12 (relating to definitions).

(Dec. 20, 2011, P.L.446, No.111, eff. one year; July 5, 2012, P.L.880, No.91, eff. Dec. 20, 2012; Feb. 21, 2018, P.L.27, No.10, eff. imd.; June 12, 2018, P.L.140, No.29, eff. imd.)

2018 Amendments. Act 10 amended subsecs. (a.2)(2), (b)(4), (c.1)(4), (c.3) and (d) and added subsec. (e.1) and the def. of "sexual offender" in subsec. (f) and Act 29 reenacted subsecs. (a.2)(2), (b)(4), (c.1)(4), (c.3), (d), (e.1) and (f). Section 20(1) of Act 10 provided that the amendment of section 4915.1 shall apply to an individual who commits an offense on or after December 20, 2012. Section 21(1) of Act 29 provided that the reenactment or amendment of section 4915.1 shall apply to an individual who commits an offense on or after December 20, 2012.

2012 Amendment. Act 91 amended subsecs. (b) and (c.1).

2011 Amendment. Act 111 added section 4915.1.

Cross References. Section 4915.1 is referred to in sections 9122.1, 9122.3 of this title; sections 6404.2, 9718.4, 9799.15, 9799.21, 9799.25, 9799.36 of Title 42 (Judiciary and Judicial Procedure).

§ 4915.2. Failure to comply with 42 Pa.C.S. Ch. 97 Subch. I registration requirements.

(a) Offense defined.--An individual who is subject to registration under 42 Pa.C.S. § 9799.55(a), (a.1) or (b) (relating to registration) or who was subject to registration under former 42 Pa.C.S. § 9793 (relating to registration of certain offenders for ten years) commits an offense if the individual knowingly fails to:

(1) register with the Pennsylvania State Police as required under 42 Pa.C.S. § 9799.56 (relating to registration procedures and applicability);

(2) verify the individual's residence or be photographed as required under 42 Pa.C.S. §

9799.60 (relating to verification of residence); or

(3) provide accurate information when registering under 42 Pa.C.S. § 9799.56 or verifying a residence under 42 Pa.C.S. § 9799.60.

(a.1) Counseling.--The following apply:

(1) An individual who is designated as a sexually violent predator commits an offense if the individual knowingly fails to comply with 42 Pa.C.S. § 9799.70 (relating to counseling of sexually violent predators).

(2) An individual who is subject to a counseling requirement under a sex offender registration statute following conviction in another jurisdiction commits an offense if the individual knowingly fails to comply with that requirement, as provided in 42 Pa.C.S. § 9799.56(b)(4)(i).

(b) Grading for offenders who must register for 10 years.--

(1) (Reserved).

(2) Except as set forth in paragraph (3), an individual subject to registration under 42 Pa.C.S. § 9799.55(a) or (a.1) or former 42 Pa.C.S. § 9793 and required to register for a period of 10 years who commits a violation of subsection (a)(1) or (2) commits a felony of the third degree.

(3) An individual subject to registration under 42 Pa.C.S. § 9799.55(a) or (a.1) or former 42 Pa.C.S. § 9793 and required to register for a period of 10 years who commits a violation of subsection (a)(1) or (2) and who has previously been convicted of an offense under subsection (a)(1) or (2) or a similar offense commits a felony of the second degree.

(4) An individual subject to registration under 42 Pa.C.S. § 9799.55(a) or (a.1) or former 42 Pa.C.S. § 9793 and required to register for a period of 10 years who violates subsection (a)(3) commits a felony of the second degree.

(c) Grading for sexually violent predators and others with lifetime registration.--

(1) (Reserved).

(2) Except as set forth in paragraph (3), an individual subject to registration under 42 Pa.C.S. § 9799.55(b) or former 42 Pa.C.S. § 9793 and who is subject to lifetime registration who commits a violation of subsection (a)(1) or (2) commits a felony of the second degree.

(3) An individual subject to registration under 42 Pa.C.S. § 9799.55(b) or former 42 Pa.C.S. § 9793 and who is subject to lifetime registration who commits a violation of subsection (a)(1) or (2) and who has previously been convicted of an offense under subsection (a)(1) or (2) or a similar offense commits a felony of the first degree.

(4) An individual subject to registration under 42 Pa.C.S. § 9799.55(b) or former 42 Pa.C.S. § 9793 and who is subject to lifetime registration who violates subsection (a)(3) commits a felony of the first degree.

(c.1) Grading for failure to comply with counseling requirements.--An individual designated as a sexually violent predator or an individual who is subject to a counseling requirement under a sex offender registration statute following conviction in another jurisdiction who commits a violation of subsection (a.1) commits a misdemeanor of the first degree.

(d) Effect of notice.--Neither failure on the part of the Pennsylvania State Police to send nor failure of a sexually violent predator or offender to receive a notice or information under 42 Pa.C.S. § 9799.54(b) (relating to applicability) or 9799.60(a.1), (b.1) or (b.3) shall be a defense to a prosecution commenced against an individual arising from a violation of this section. The provisions of 42 Pa.C.S. §§ 9799.54(b) and 9799.60(a.1), (b.1) or (b.3) are not an element of an offense under this section.

(e) Arrests for violation.--

(1) A police officer shall have the same right of arrest without a warrant as in a felony whenever the police officer has probable cause to believe an individual has committed a violation of this section regardless of whether the violation occurred in the presence of the police officer.

(2) An individual arrested for a violation of this section shall be afforded a preliminary arraignment by the proper issuing authority without unnecessary delay. In no case may the individual be released from custody without first having appeared before the issuing authority.

(3) Prior to admitting an individual arrested for a violation of this section to bail, the issuing authority shall require all of the following:

(i) The individual must be fingerprinted and photographed in the manner required by 42 Pa.C.S. Ch. 97 Subch. I (relating to continued registration of sexual offenders).

(ii) The individual must provide the Pennsylvania State Police with all current or intended residences, all information concerning current or intended employment, including all employment locations, and all information concerning current or intended enrollment as a student. If the individual has a residence as defined in paragraph (2) of the definition of "residence" set forth in 42 Pa.C.S. § 9799.53 (relating to definitions), the individual must provide the Pennsylvania State Police with the information required under 42 Pa.C.S. § 9799.56(a)(2)(i)(A), (B) and (C).

(iii) Law enforcement must make reasonable attempts to verify the information provided by the individual.

(e.1) Affirmative defense.--It is an affirmative defense for any prosecution under this section that the individual acted in accordance with a court order under section 9799.59 (relating to exemption from certain notifications).

(f) Applicability.--This section applies to:

(1) An individual who committed an offense set forth in 42 Pa.C.S. § 9799.55 on or after April 22, 1996, but before December 20, 2012, and whose period of registration under 42 Pa.C.S. § 9799.55 has not expired.

(2) An individual who was required to register with the Pennsylvania State Police under a former sexual offender registration law of this Commonwealth on or after April 22, 1996, but before December 20, 2012, whose period of registration has not expired.

(3) An individual who, before February 21, 2018:

(i) commits an offense subject to 42 Pa.C.S. Ch. 97 Subch. H (relating to registration of sexual offenders); but

(ii) because of a judicial determination on or after February 21, 2018, of the invalidity of 42 Pa.C.S. Ch. 97 Subch. H, is not subject to registration as a sexual offender.

(g) Definitions.--As used in this section, the following words and phrases shall have the meanings given to them in this subsection unless the context clearly indicates otherwise:

"Sexually violent predator." As defined in 42 Pa.C.S. § 9799.53.

"Similar offense." An offense similar to an offense under either subsection (a)(1) or (2) under the laws of this Commonwealth, the United States or one of its territories or possessions, another state, the District of Columbia, the Commonwealth of Puerto Rico or a foreign nation.

(Feb. 21, 2018, P.L.27, No.10, eff. imd.; June 12, 2018, P.L.140, No.29, eff. imd.)

2018 Amendments. Act 10 added section 4915.2 and Act 29 reenacted and amended section 4915.2. See section 20(2) of Act 10 in the appendix to this title for special provisions relating to applicability. See section 21(2) of Act 29 in the appendix to this title for special provisions relating to applicability.

Cross References. Section 4915.2 is referred to in sections 9122.1, 9122.3 of this title; sections 9799.56, 9799.59, 9799.60 of Title 42 (Judiciary and Judicial Procedure).

SUBCHAPTER B
VICTIM AND WITNESS INTIMIDATION

Sec.
4951. Definitions.
4952. Intimidation of witnesses or victims.
4953. Retaliation against witness, victim or party.
4953.1. Retaliation against prosecutor or judicial official.
4954. Protective orders.
4954.1. Notice on protective order.
4955. Violation of orders.
4956. Pretrial release.
4957. Protection of employment of crime victims, family members of victims and witnesses.
4958. Intimidation, retaliation or obstruction in child abuse cases.

Enactment. Subchapter B was added December 4, 1980, P.L.1097, No.187, effective in 60 days.

Cross References. Subchapter B is referred to in sections 3016, 3502 of this title; section 3103 of Title 23 (Domestic Relations).

§ 4951. Definitions.

The following words and phrases when used in this subchapter shall have, unless the context clearly indicates otherwise, the meanings given to them in this section:

"Victim." Any person against whom any crime as defined under the laws of this State or of any other state or of the United States is being or has been perpetrated or attempted.

"Witness." Any person having knowledge of the existence or nonexistence of facts or information relating to any crime, including but not limited to those who have reported facts or information to any law enforcement officer, prosecuting official, attorney representing a criminal defendant or judge, those who have been served with a subpoena issued under the authority of this State or any other state or of the United States, and those who have given written or oral testimony in any criminal matter; or who would be believed by any reasonable person to be an individual described in this definition.

Cross References. Section 4951 is referred to in section 8127 of Title 42 (Judiciary and Judicial Procedure).

§ 4952. Intimidation of witnesses or victims.

(a) Offense defined.--A person commits an offense if, with the intent to or with the knowledge that his conduct will obstruct, impede, impair, prevent or interfere with the administration of criminal justice, he intimidates or attempts to intimidate any witness or victim to:

(1) Refrain from informing or reporting to any law enforcement officer, prosecuting official or judge concerning any information, document or thing relating to the commission of a crime.

(2) Give any false or misleading information or testimony relating to the commission of any crime to any law enforcement officer, prosecuting official or judge.

(3) Withhold any testimony, information, document or thing relating to the commission of a crime from any law enforcement officer, prosecuting official or judge.

(4) Give any false or misleading information or testimony or refrain from giving any testimony, information, document or thing, relating to the commission of a crime, to an attorney representing a criminal defendant.

(5) Elude, evade or ignore any request to appear or legal process summoning him to appear to testify or supply evidence.

(6) Absent himself from any proceeding or investigation to which he has been legally summoned.

(b) Grading.--

(1) The offense is a felony of the degree indicated in paragraphs (2) through (4) if:

(i) The actor employs force, violence or deception, or threatens to employ force or violence, upon the witness or victim or, with the requisite intent or knowledge upon any other person.

(ii) The actor offers any pecuniary or other benefit to the witness or victim or, with the requisite intent or knowledge, to any other person.

(iii) The actor's conduct is in furtherance of a conspiracy to intimidate a witness or victim.

(iv) The actor accepts, agrees or solicits another to accept any pecuniary or other benefit to intimidate a witness or victim.

(v) The actor has suffered any prior conviction for any violation of this section or any predecessor law hereto, or has been convicted, under any Federal statute or statute of any other state, of an act which would be a violation of this section if committed in this State.

(2) The offense is a felony of the first degree if a felony of the first degree or murder in the first or second degree was charged in the case in which the actor sought to influence or intimidate a witness or victim as specified in this subsection.

(3) The offense is a felony of the second degree if a felony of the second degree is the most serious offense charged in the case in which the actor sought to influence or intimidate a witness or victim as specified in this subsection.

(4) The offense is a felony of the third degree in any other case in which the actor sought to influence or intimidate a witness or victim as specified in this subsection.

(5) Otherwise the offense is a misdemeanor of the second degree.

(Dec. 10, 2001, P.L.855, No.90, eff. 60 days)

Cross References. Section 4952 is referred to in sections 4909, 4953, 4955, 4956, 5702, 5708, 6105 of this title; sections 5552, 5750 of Title 42 (Judiciary and Judicial Procedure); section 2303 of Title 44 (Law and Justice).

§ 4953. Retaliation against witness, victim or party.

(a) Offense defined.--A person commits an offense if he harms another by any unlawful act or engages in a course of conduct or repeatedly commits acts which threaten another in retaliation for anything lawfully done in the capacity of witness, victim or a party in a civil matter.

(b) Grading.--The offense is a felony of the third degree if the retaliation is accomplished by any of the means specified in section 4952(b)(1) through (5) (relating to intimidation of witnesses or victims). Otherwise the offense is a misdemeanor of the second degree.

(Dec. 20, 2000, P.L.837, No.117, eff. imd.)

Cross References. Section 4953 is referred to in sections 4955, 4956, 5702, 5708, 6105 of this title; section 5552 of Title 42 (Judiciary and Judicial Procedure); section 2303 of Title 44 (Law and Justice).

§ 4953.1. Retaliation against prosecutor or judicial official.

(a) Offense defined.--A person commits an offense if he harms or attempts to harm another or the tangible property of another by any unlawful act in retaliation for anything lawfully done in the official capacity of a prosecutor or judicial official.

(b) Grading.--The offense is a felony of the second degree if:

(1) The actor employs force, violence or deception or attempts or threatens to employ force, violence or deception upon the prosecutor or judicial official or, with the requisite intent or knowledge, upon any other person.

(2) The actor's conduct is in furtherance of a conspiracy to retaliate against a prosecutor or judicial official.

(3) The actor solicits another to or accepts or agrees to accept any pecuniary or other benefit to retaliate against a prosecutor or judicial official.

(4) The actor has suffered any prior conviction for any violation of this title or any predecessor law hereto or has been convicted under any Federal statute or statute of any other state of an act which would be a violation of this title if committed in this Commonwealth.

(5) The actor causes property damage or loss in excess of $1,000.

Otherwise, the offense is a misdemeanor of the first degree.

(c) Definitions.--As used in this section, the following words and phrases shall have the meanings given to them in this subsection:

"Judicial official." Any person who is a:

(1) judge of the court of common pleas;

(2) judge of the Commonwealth Court;

(3) judge of the Superior Court;

(4) justice of the Supreme Court;

(5) magisterial district judge;

(6) judge of the Pittsburgh Magistrate's Court;

(7) judge of the Philadelphia Municipal Court;

(8) judge of the Traffic Court of Philadelphia; or

(9) master appointed by a judge of a court of common pleas.

"Prosecutor." Any person who is:

(1) an Attorney General;

(2) a deputy attorney general;

(3) a district attorney; or

(4) an assistant district attorney.

(Dec. 21, 1998, P.L.1245, No.159, eff. 60 days; Nov. 30, 2004, P.L.1618, No.207, eff. 60 days)

2004 Amendment. Act 207 amended subsec. (c). See section 29 of Act 207 in the appendix to this title for special provisions relating to construction of law.

1998 Amendment. Act 159 added section 4953.1.

§ 4954. Protective orders.

Any court with jurisdiction over any criminal matter may, after a hearing and in its discretion, upon substantial evidence, which may include hearsay or the declaration of the prosecutor that a witness or victim has been intimidated or is reasonably likely to be intimidated, issue protective orders, including, but not limited to, the following:

(1) An order that a defendant not violate any provision of this subchapter or section 2709 (relating to harassment) or 2709.1 (relating to stalking).

(2) An order that a person other than the defendant, including, but not limited to, a subpoenaed witness, not violate any provision of this subchapter.

(3) An order that any person described in paragraph (1) or (2) maintain a prescribed geographic distance from any specified witness or victim.

(4) An order that any person described in paragraph (1) or (2) have no communication whatsoever with any specified witness or victim, except through an attorney under such reasonable restrictions as the court may impose.

(June 23, 1993, P.L.124, No.28, eff. imd.; Dec. 9, 2002, P.L.1759, No.218, eff. 60 days)

Cross References. Section 4954 is referred to in sections 2709.1, 4954.1, 4955, 4956 of this title; section 6711 of Title 23 (Domestic Relations); section 8127 of Title 42 (Judiciary and Judicial Procedure).

§ 4954.1. Notice on protective order.

All protective orders issued under section 4954 (relating to protective orders) shall contain in large print at the top of the order a notice that the witness or victim should immediately call the police if the defendant violates the protective order. The notice shall contain the telephone number of the police department where the victim or witness resides and where the victim or witness is employed.

(June 23, 1993, P.L.124, No.28, eff. imd.)

1993 Amendment. Act 28 added section 4954.1.

§ 4955. Violation of orders.

(a) Punishment.--Any person violating any order made pursuant to section 4954 (relating to protective orders) may be punished in any of the following ways:

(1) For any substantive offense described in this subchapter, where such violation of an order is a violation of any provision of this subchapter.

(2) As a contempt of the court making such order. No finding of contempt shall be a bar to prosecution for a substantive offense under section 2709 (relating to harassment), 2709.1 (relating to stalking), 4952 (relating to intimidation of witnesses or victims) or 4953 (relating to retaliation against witness or victim), but:

(i) any person so held in contempt shall be entitled to credit for any punishment imposed therein against any sentence imposed on conviction of said substantive offense; and

(ii) any conviction or acquittal for any substantive offense under this title shall be a bar to subsequent punishment for contempt arising out of the same act.

(3) By revocation of any form of pretrial release, or the forfeiture of bail and the issuance of a bench warrant for the defendant's arrest or remanding him to custody. Revocation may, after hearing and on substantial evidence, in the sound discretion of the court, be made whether the violation of order complained of has been committed by the defendant personally or was caused or encouraged to have been committed by the defendant.

(b) Arrest.--An arrest for a violation of an order issued under section 4954 may be without warrant upon probable cause whether or not the violation is committed in the presence of a law enforcement officer. The law enforcement officer may verify, if necessary, the existence of a protective order by telephone or radio communication with the appropriate police department.

(c) Arraignment.--Subsequent to an arrest, the defendant shall be taken without unnecessary delay before the court that issued the order. When that court is unavailable, the defendant shall be arraigned before a magisterial district judge or, in cities of the first class, a Philadelphia Municipal Court Judge, in accordance with the Pennsylvania Rules of Criminal Procedure.

(June 23, 1993, P.L.124, No.28, eff. imd.; Dec. 9, 2002, P.L.1759, No.218, eff. 60 days; Nov. 30, 2004, P.L.1618, No.207, eff. 60 days)

2004 Amendment. Act 207 amended subsec. (c). See section 29 of Act 207 in the appendix to this title for special provisions relating to construction of law.

2002 Amendment. Act 218 amended subsec. (a)(2).

Cross References. Section 4955 is referred to in section 4956 of this title.

§ 4956. Pretrial release.

(a) Conditions for pretrial release.-- Any pretrial release of any defendant whether on bail or under any other form of recognizance shall be deemed, as a matter of law, to include a condition that the defendant neither do, nor cause to be done, nor permit to be done on his behalf, any act proscribed by section 4952 (relating to intimidation of witnesses or victims) or 4953 (relating to retaliation against witness or victim) and any willful violation of said condition is subject to punishment as prescribed in section 4955(3) (relating to violation of orders) whether or not the defendant was the subject of an order under section 4954 (relating to protective orders).

(b) Notice of condition.--From and after the effective date of this subchapter, any receipt for any bail or bond given by the clerk of any court, by any court, by any surety or bondsman and any written promise to appear on one's own recognizance shall contain, in a conspicuous location, notice of this condition.

190

§ 4957. Protection of employment of crime victims, family members of victims and witnesses.

(a) General rule.--An employer shall not deprive an employee of his employment, seniority position or benefits, or threaten or otherwise coerce him with respect thereto, because the employee attends court by reason of being a victim of, or a witness to, a crime or a member of such victim's family. Nothing in this section shall be construed to require the employer to compensate the employee for employment time lost because of such court attendance.

(b) Penalty.--An employer who violates subsection (a) commits a summary offense.

(c) Civil remedy available.--If an employer penalizes an employee in violation of subsection (a), the employee may bring a civil action for recovery of wages and benefits lost as a result of the violation and for an order requiring the reinstatement of the employee. Damages recoverable shall not exceed wages and benefits actually lost. If he prevails, the employee shall be allowed a reasonable attorney fee fixed by the court.

(d) Definitions.--As used in this section, the following words and phrases shall have the meanings given to them in this subsection:

"Family." This term shall have the same meaning as in section 103 of the act of November 24, 1998 (P.L.882, No.111), known as the Crime Victims Act.

"Victim." This term shall have the same meaning as "direct victim" in section 103 of the act of November 24, 1998 (P.L.882, No.111), known as the Crime Victims Act.

(Oct. 22, 1986, P.L.1451, No.142, eff. 60 days; June 28, 2002, P.L.494, No.84, eff. 60 days)

2002 Amendment. Act 84 amended the section heading and subsec. (a) and added subsec. (d).

1986 Amendment. Act 142 added section 4957.

§ 4958. Intimidation, retaliation or obstruction in child abuse cases.

(a) Intimidation.--A person commits an offense if:

(1) The person has knowledge or intends that the person's conduct under paragraph (2) will obstruct, impede, impair, prevent or interfere with the making of a child abuse report or the conducting of an investigation into suspected child abuse under 23 Pa.C.S. Ch. 63 (relating to child protective services) or prosecuting a child abuse case.

(2) The person intimidates or attempts to intimidate any reporter, victim or witness to engage in any of the following actions:

(i) Refrain from making a report of suspected child abuse or not cause a report of suspected child abuse to be made.

(ii) Refrain from providing or withholding information, documentation, testimony or evidence to any person regarding a child abuse investigation or proceeding.

(iii) Give false or misleading information, documentation, testimony or evidence to any person regarding a child abuse investigation or proceeding.

(iv) Elude, evade or ignore any request or legal process summoning the reporter, victim or witness to appear to testify or supply evidence regarding a child abuse investigation or proceeding.

(v) Fail to appear at or participate in a child abuse proceeding or meeting involving a child abuse investigation to which the reporter, victim or witness has been legally summoned.

(b) Retaliation.--A person commits an offense if the person harms another person by any unlawful act or engages in a course of conduct or repeatedly commits acts which threaten another person in retaliation for anything that the other person has lawfully done in the capacity of a reporter, witness or victim of child abuse.

(b.1) Obstruction.--In addition to any other penalty provided by law, a person commits an offense if, with intent to prevent a public servant from investigating or prosecuting a report of child abuse under 23 Pa.C.S. Ch. 63, the person by any scheme or device or in any other manner obstructs, interferes with, impairs, impedes or perverts the investigation or prosecution of child abuse.

(c) Grading.--

(1) An offense under this section is a felony of the second degree if:

(i) The actor employs force, violence or deception or threatens to employ force, violence or deception upon the reporter, witness or victim or, with reckless intent or knowledge, upon any other person.

(ii) The actor offers pecuniary or other benefit to the reporter, witness or victim.

(iii) The actor's conduct is in furtherance of a conspiracy to intimidate or retaliate against the reporter, witness or victim.

(iv) The actor accepts, agrees or solicits another person to accept any pecuniary benefit to intimidate or retaliate against the reporter, witness or victim.

(v) The actor has suffered a prior conviction for a violation of this section or has been convicted under a Federal statute or statute of any other state of an act which would be a violation of this section if committed in this Commonwealth.

(2) An offense not otherwise addressed in paragraph (1) is a misdemeanor of the second degree.

(d) Definitions.--The following words and phrases when used in this section shall have the meanings given to them in this subsection unless the context clearly indicates otherwise:

"Child abuse." As defined in 23 Pa.C.S. § 6303(b.1) (relating to definitions).

"Mandated reporter." As defined in 23 Pa.C.S. § 6303(a).

"Public servant." As defined in section 4501 (relating to definitions).

"Reporter." A person, including a mandated reporter, having reasonable cause to suspect that a child under 18 years of age is a victim of child abuse.

(Dec. 18, 2013, P.L.1198, No.118, eff. Jan. 1, 2014)

2013 Amendment. Act 118 added section 4958.

Cross References. Section 4958 is referred to in sections 6311, 6335 of Title 23 (Domestic Relations); section 2303 of Title 44 (Law and Justice).

CHAPTER 51 OBSTRUCTING GOVERNMENTAL OPERATIONS

Subchapter
A. Definition of Offenses Generally
B. Escape
C. Criminal Gangs

Enactment. Chapter 51 was added December 6, 1972, P.L.1482, No.334, effective in six months.

Cross References. Chapter 51 is referred to in section 3016 of this title; section 5508.3 of Title 53 (Municipalities Generally); section 6017 of Title 64 (Public Authorities and Quasi-Public Corporations).

SUBCHAPTER A
DEFINITION OF OFFENSES
GENERALLY

Sec.
5101. Obstructing administration of law or other governmental function.
5102. Obstructing or impeding the administration of justice by picketing, etc.
5103. Unlawfully listening into deliberations of jury.
5103.1. Unlawful use of an audio or video device in court.
5104. Resisting arrest or other law enforcement.
5104.1. Disarming law enforcement officer.
5105. Hindering apprehension or prosecution.
5106. Failure to report injuries by firearm or criminal act.
5107. Aiding consummation of crime.
5108. Compounding.
5109. Barratry.
5110. Contempt of General Assembly.
5111. Dealing in proceeds of unlawful activities.
5112. Obstructing emergency services.

§ 5101. Obstructing administration of law or other governmental function.

A person commits a misdemeanor of the second degree if he intentionally obstructs, impairs or perverts the administration of law or other governmental function by force, violence, physical interference or obstacle, breach of official duty, or any other unlawful act, except that this section does not apply to flight by a person charged with crime, refusal to submit to arrest, failure to perform a legal duty other than an official duty, or any other means of avoiding compliance with law without affirmative interference with governmental functions.

Cross References. Section 5101 is referred to in section 5708 of this title; section 3132 of Title 27 (Environmental Resources; section 5552 of Title 42 (Judiciary and Judicial Procedure).

§ 5102. Obstructing or impeding the administration of justice by picketing, etc.

(a) Offense defined.--A person is guilty of a misdemeanor of the second degree if he intentionally interferes with, obstructs or impedes the administration of justice, or with the intent of influencing any judge, juror, witness or court officer in the discharge of his duty, pickets or parades in or near any building housing a court of this Commonwealth, or in or near a building or residence occupied by or used by such judge, juror, witness or court officer, or with such intent uses any sound-truck or similar device, or resorts to any other demonstration in or near any such building or residence.

(b) Exception.--Nothing in subsection (a) of this section shall interfere with or prevent the exercise by any court of this Commonwealth of its power to punish for contempt.

§ 5103. Unlawfully listening into deliberations of jury.

A person is guilty of a misdemeanor of the third degree if he, by any scheme or device, or in any manner, for any purpose, intentionally listens into the deliberations of any grand, petit, traverse, or special jury.

Cross References. Section 5103 is referred to in section 1515 of Title 42 (Judiciary and Judicial Procedure).

§ 5103.1. Unlawful use of an audio or video device in court.

(a) Offense defined.--A person commits an offense if the person in any manner and for any purpose uses or operates a device to capture, record, transmit or broadcast a photograph, video, motion picture or audio of a proceeding or person within a judicial facility or in an area adjacent to or immediately surrounding a judicial facility without the approval of the court or presiding judicial officer or except as provided by rules of court.

(b) Grading.--

(1) An offense under this section shall constitute a misdemeanor of the second degree.

(2) A second or subsequent offense shall constitute a misdemeanor of the first degree.

(c) Definition.--As used in this section, the term "judicial facility" means a courtroom, hearing room or judicial chambers used by the court to conduct trials or hearings or any other court-related business or any other room made available to interview witnesses. The term does not include the Pennsylvania State Capitol Building except for that portion of the Pennsylvania State Capitol Building designated by the Court Administrator of Pennsylvania, under the authority of the Supreme Court, as a judicial facility.

(Oct. 24, 2018, P.L.658, No.94, eff. 60 days)

2018 Amendment. Act 94 added section 5103.1.

§ 5104. Resisting arrest or other law enforcement.

A person commits a misdemeanor of the second degree if, with the intent of preventing a public servant from effecting a lawful arrest or discharging any other duty, the person creates a substantial risk of bodily injury to the public servant or anyone else, or employs means justifying or requiring substantial force to overcome the resistance.

§ 5104.1. Disarming law enforcement officer.

(a) Offense defined.--A person commits the offense of disarming a law enforcement officer if he:

(1) without lawful authorization, removes or attempts to remove a firearm, rifle, shotgun or weapon from the person of a law enforcement officer or corrections officer, or deprives a law enforcement officer or corrections officer of the use of a firearm, rifle, shotgun or weapon, when the officer is acting within the scope of the officer's duties; and

(2) has reasonable cause to know or knows that the individual is a law enforcement officer or corrections officer.

(b) Grading.--A violation of this section constitutes a felony of the third degree.

(July 5, 2005, P.L.76, No.30, eff. 60 days)

2005 Amendment. Act 30 added section 5104.1.

§ 5105. Hindering apprehension or prosecution.

(a) Offense defined.--A person commits an offense if, with intent to hinder the apprehension, prosecution, conviction or punishment of another for crime or violation of the terms of probation, parole, intermediate punishment or Accelerated Rehabilitative Disposition, he:

(1) harbors or conceals the other;

(2) provides or aids in providing a weapon, transportation, disguise or other means of avoiding apprehension or effecting escape;

(3) conceals or destroys evidence of the crime, or tampers with a witness, informant, document or other source of information, regardless of its admissibility in evidence;

(4) warns the other of impending discovery or apprehension, except that this paragraph does not apply to a warning given in connection with an effort to bring another into compliance with law; or

(5) provides false information to a law enforcement officer.

(b) Grading.--The offense is a felony of the third degree if the conduct which the actor knows has been charged or is liable to be charged against the person aided would constitute a felony of the first or second degree. Otherwise it is a misdemeanor of the second degree.

(Dec. 18, 1996, P.L.1074, No.160, eff. 60 days)

§ 5106. Failure to report injuries by firearm or criminal act.

(a) Offense defined.--Except as set forth in subsection (a.1), a physician, intern or resident, or any person conducting, managing or in charge of any hospital or pharmacy, or in charge of any ward or part of a hospital, to whom shall come or be brought any person:

(1) suffering from any wound or other injury inflicted by his own act or by the act of another which caused death or serious bodily injury, or inflicted by means of a deadly weapon as defined in section 2301 (relating to definitions); or

(2) upon whom injuries have been inflicted in violation of any penal law of this Commonwealth;

commits a summary offense if the reporting party fails to report such injuries immediately, both by telephone and in writing, to the chief of police or other head of the police department of the local government, or to the Pennsylvania State Police. The report shall state the name of the injured person, if known, the injured person's whereabouts and the character and extent of the person's injuries.

(a.1) Exception.--In cases of bodily injury as defined in section 2301 (relating to definitions), failure to report under subsection (a)(2) does not constitute an offense if all of the following apply:

(1) The victim is an adult and has suffered bodily injury.

(2) The injury was inflicted by an individual who:

(i) is the current or former spouse of the victim;

(ii) is a current or former sexual or intimate partner of the victim;

(iii) shares biological parenthood with the victim; or

(iv) is or has been living as a spouse of the victim.

(3) The victim has been informed:

(i) of the duty to report under subsection (a)(2); and

(ii) that the report under subsection (a)(2) cannot be made without the victim's consent.

(4) The victim does not consent to the report under subsection (a)(2).

(5) The victim has been provided with a referral to the appropriate victim service agency such as a domestic violence or sexual assault program.

(b) Immunity granted.--No physician or other person shall be subject to civil or criminal liability by reason of complying with this section.

(c) Physician-patient privilege unavailable.--In any judicial proceeding resulting from a report pursuant to this section, the physician-patient privilege shall not apply in respect to evidence regarding such injuries or the cause thereof. This subsection shall not apply where a report is not made pursuant to subsection (a.1).

(d) Reporting of crime encouraged.--Nothing in this chapter precludes a victim from reporting the crime that resulted in injury.

(e) Availability of information.--A physician or other individual may make available information concerning domestic violence or sexual assault to any individual subject to the provisions of this chapter.

(Dec. 9, 2002, P.L.1350, No.162, eff. 60 days)

§ 5107. Aiding consummation of crime.

(a) Offense defined.--A person commits an offense if he intentionally aids another to accomplish an unlawful object of a crime, as by safeguarding the proceeds thereof or converting the proceeds into negotiable funds.

(b) Grading.--The offense is a felony of the third degree if the principal offense was a felony of the first or second degree. Otherwise it is a misdemeanor of the second degree.

§ 5108. Compounding.

(a) Offense defined.--A person commits a misdemeanor of the second degree if he accepts or agrees to accept any pecuniary benefit in consideration of refraining from reporting to law enforcement authorities the commission or suspected commission of any offense or information relating to an offense.

(b) Defense.--It is a defense to prosecution under this section that the pecuniary benefit did not exceed an amount which the actor believed to be due as restitution or indemnification for harm caused by the offense.

§ 5109. Barratry.

A person is guilty of a misdemeanor of the third degree if he vexes others with unjust and vexatious suits.

§ 5110. Contempt of General Assembly.

A person is guilty of a misdemeanor of the third degree if he is disorderly or contemptuous in the presence of either branch of the General Assembly, or if he neglects or refuses to appear in the presence of either of such branches after having been duly served with a subpoena to so appear.

§ 5111. Dealing in proceeds of unlawful activities.

(a) Offense defined.--A person commits a felony of the first degree if the person conducts a financial transaction under any of the following circumstances:

(1) With knowledge that the property involved, including stolen or illegally obtained property, represents the proceeds of unlawful activity, the person acts with the intent to promote the carrying on of the unlawful activity.

(2) With knowledge that the property involved, including stolen or illegally obtained property, represents the proceeds of unlawful activity and that the transaction is designed in whole or in part to conceal or disguise the nature, location, source, ownership or control of the proceeds of unlawful activity.

(3) To avoid a transaction reporting requirement under State or Federal law.

(b) Penalty.--Upon conviction of a violation under subsection (a), a person shall be sentenced to a fine of the greater of $100,000 or twice the value of the property involved in the transaction or to imprisonment for not more than 20 years, or both.

(c) Civil penalty.--A person who conducts or attempts to conduct a transaction described in subsection (a) is liable to the Commonwealth for a civil penalty of the greater of:

(1) the value of the property, funds or monetary instruments involved in the transaction; or

(2) $10,000.

(d) Cumulative remedies.--Any proceedings under this section shall be in addition to any other criminal penalties or forfeitures authorized under the State law.

(e) Enforcement.--

(1) The Attorney General shall have the power and duty to institute proceedings to recover the civil penalty provided under subsection (c) against any person liable to the Commonwealth for such a penalty.

(2) The district attorneys of the several counties shall have authority to investigate and to institute criminal proceedings for any violation of subsection (a).

(3) In addition to the authority conferred upon the Attorney General by the act of October 15, 1980 (P.L.950, No.164), known as the Commonwealth Attorneys Act, the Attorney General shall have the authority to investigate and to institute criminal proceedings for any violation of subsection (a) or any series of related violations involving more than one county of the Commonwealth or involving any county of the Commonwealth and another state. No person charged with a violation of subsection (a) by the Attorney General shall have standing to challenge the authority of the Attorney General to investigate or prosecute the case, and, if any such challenge is made, the challenge shall be dismissed and no relief shall be available in the courts of the Commonwealth to the person making the challenge.

(4) Nothing contained in this subsection shall be construed to limit the regulatory or investigative authority of any department or agency of the Commonwealth whose functions might relate to persons, enterprises or matters falling within the scope of this section.

(e.1) Venue.--An offense under subsection (a) may be deemed to have been committed where any element of unlawful activity or of the offense under subsection (a) occurs.

(f) Definitions.--As used in this section, the following words and phrases shall have the meanings given to them in this subsection:

"Conducts." Includes initiating, concluding or participating in initiating or concluding a transaction.

"Financial institution." Any of the following:

(1) An insured bank as defined in section 3(h) of the Federal Deposit Insurance Act (64 Stat. 873, 12 U.S.C. § 1813(h)).

(2) A commercial bank or trust company.

(3) A private banker.

(4) An agency or bank of a foreign bank in this Commonwealth.

(5) An insured institution as defined in section 401(a) of the National Housing Act (48 Stat. 1246, 12 U.S.C. § 1724(a)).

(6) A thrift institution.

(7) A broker or dealer registered with the Securities and Exchange Commission under the Securities Exchange Act of 1934 (15 U.S.C. § 78a et seq.).

(8) A broker or dealer in securities or commodities.

(9) An investment banker or investment company.

(10) A currency exchange.

(11) An insurer, redeemer or cashier of travelers' checks, checks, money orders or similar instruments.

(12) An operator of a credit card system.

(13) An insurance company.

(14) A dealer in precious metals, stones or jewels.

(15) A pawnbroker.

(16) A loan or finance company.

(17) A travel agency.

(18) A licensed sender of money.

(19) A telegraph company.

(20) An agency of the Federal Government or of a state or local government carrying out a duty or power of a business described in this paragraph.

(21) Another business or agency carrying out a similar, related or substitute duty or power which the United States Secretary of the Treasury prescribes.

"Financial transaction." A transaction involving the movement of funds by wire or other means or involving one or more monetary instruments. The term includes any exchange of stolen or illegally obtained property for financial compensation or personal gain.

"Knowing that the property involved in a financial transaction represents the proceeds of unlawful activity." Knowing that the property involved in the transaction represents proceeds from some form, though not necessarily which form, of unlawful activity, regardless of whether or not the activity is specified in this section.

"Monetary instrument." Coin or currency of the United States or of any other country, traveler's checks, personal checks, bank checks, money orders, investment securities in bearer form or otherwise in such form that title thereto passes upon delivery and negotiable instruments in bearer form or otherwise in such form that title thereto passes upon delivery.

"Transaction." Includes a purchase, sale, loan, pledge, gift, transfer, delivery or other disposition. With respect to a financial institution, the term includes a deposit, withdrawal, transfer between accounts, exchange of currency, loan, extension of credit, purchase or sale of any stock, bond, certificate of deposit or other monetary instrument and any other payment, transfer or delivery by, through, or to a financial institution, by whatever means effected.

"Unlawful activity." Any activity graded a misdemeanor of the first degree or higher under Federal or State law.

(Dec. 22, 1989, P.L.770, No.108, eff. imd.; June 28, 2002, P.L.481, No.82, eff. 60 days; Oct. 25, 2012, P.L.1645, No.203, eff. 60 days)

2012 Amendment. Act 203 amended subsec. (a) and the def. of "financial transaction" in subsec. (f).

2002 Amendment. Act 82 amended subsec. (a) and added subsec. (e.1).

1989 Amendment. Act 108 added section 5111.

Cross References. Section 5111 is referred to in sections 911, 5708 of this title; section 5552 of Title 42 (Judiciary and Judicial Procedure).

§ 5112. Obstructing emergency services.

(a) Offense defined.--A person commits a misdemeanor of the third degree if he knowingly impedes, obstructs or interferes with emergency services personnel providing emergency medical services to an injured victim or performing rescue or firefighting activities.

(b) Definitions.--As used in this section, the following words and phrases shall have the meanings given to them in this subsection:

"Emergency medical services." The services utilized in responding to the needs of an individual for immediate medical care in order to prevent loss of life or the aggravation of physiological or psychological illness or injury.

"Emergency services personnel." A person, including a trained volunteer or a member of the armed forces of the United States or the National Guard, whose official or assigned responsibilities include performing or directly supporting the performance of emergency medical or rescue services or firefighting.

"Rescue." The act of extricating persons from entrapment or dangerous situations which pose the imminent threat of death or serious bodily injury.

(Dec. 21, 1998, P.L.1240, No.157, eff. 60 days)

1998 Amendment. Act 157 added section 5112.

SUBCHAPTER B
ESCAPE

Sec.
5121. Escape.
5122. Weapons or implements for escape.
5123. Contraband.
5124. Default in required appearance.
5125. Absconding witness.
5126. Flight to avoid apprehension, trial or punishment.

§ 5121. Escape.

(a) Escape.--A person commits an offense if he unlawfully removes himself from official detention or fails to return to official detention following temporary leave granted for a specific purpose or limited period.

(b) Permitting or facilitating escape.--A public servant concerned in detention commits an offense if he knowingly or recklessly permits an escape. Any person who knowingly causes or facilitates an escape commits an offense.

(c) Effect of legal irregularity in detention.--Irregularity in bringing about or maintaining detention, or lack of jurisdiction of the committing or detaining authority, shall not be a defense to prosecution under this section.

(d) Grading.--

(1) An offense under this section is a felony of the third degree where:

(i) the actor was:

(A) under arrest for or detained on a charge of felony;

(B) convicted of a crime; or

(C) found to be delinquent of an offense which, if committed by an adult, would be classified as a felony and the actor is at least 18 years of age at the time of the violation of this section;

(ii) the actor employs force, threat, deadly weapon or other dangerous instrumentality to effect the escape; or

(iii) a public servant concerned in detention of persons convicted of crime intentionally facilitates or permits an escape from a detention facility.

(2) Otherwise an offense under this section is a misdemeanor of the second degree.

(e) Definition.--As used in this section the phrase "official detention" means arrest, detention in any facility for custody of persons under charge or conviction of crime or alleged or found to be delinquent, detention for extradition or deportation, or any other detention for law enforcement purposes; but the phrase does not include supervision of probation or parole, or constraint incidental to release on bail.

(Sept. 27, 2014, P.L.2482, No.138, eff. 60 days)

2014 Amendment. Act 138 amended subsec. (d)(1)(i).

Cross References. Section 5121 is referred to in sections 5708, 6105 of this title; sections 9711, 9802 of Title 42 (Judiciary and Judicial Procedure); section 2303 of Title 44 (Law and Justice); sections 1162, 3513, 5006 of Title 61 (Prisons and Parole).

§ 5122. Weapons or implements for escape.

(a) Offenses defined.--

(1) Except as provided under 61 Pa.C.S. § 5902(e.1) (relating to contraband prohibited), a person commits a misdemeanor of the first degree if he unlawfully introduces within a detention facility, correctional institution or mental hospital, or unlawfully provides an inmate thereof with any weapon, tool, implement, or other thing which may be used for escape.

(2) An inmate commits a misdemeanor of the first degree if he unlawfully procures, makes or otherwise provides himself with, or unlawfully has in his possession or under his control, any weapon, tool, implement or other thing which may be used for escape.

(3) (Deleted by amendment).

(b) Definitions.--

(1) As used in this section, the word "unlawfully" means surreptitiously or contrary to law, regulation or order of the detaining authority.

(2) As used in this section, the word "weapon" means any implement readily capable of lethal use and shall include any firearm, ammunition, knife, dagger, razor, other cutting or stabbing implement or club, including any item which has been modified or adopted so that it can be used as a firearm, ammunition, knife, dagger, razor, other cutting or stabbing implement, or club. The word "firearm" includes an unloaded firearm and the unassembled components of a firearm.

(Dec. 10, 1974, P.L.910, No.300, eff. imd.; Dec. 15, 1999, P.L.915, No.59, eff. 60 days; Oct. 24, 2018, P.L.749, No.123, eff. 60 days)

2018 Amendment. Act 123 amended subsec. (a).

Cross References. Section 5122 is referred to in sections 6105, 9122.1, 9122.3 of this title; section 3513 of Title 61 (Prisons and Parole).

§ 5123. Contraband.

(a) **Controlled substance contraband to confined persons prohibited.**--A person commits a felony of the second degree if he sells, gives, transmits or furnishes to any convict in a prison, or inmate in a mental hospital, or gives away in or brings into any prison, mental hospital, or any building appurtenant thereto, or on the land granted to or owned or leased by the Commonwealth or county for the use and benefit of the prisoners or inmates, or puts in any place where it may be secured by a convict of a prison, inmate of a mental hospital, or employee thereof, any controlled substance included in Schedules I through V of the act of April 14, 1972 (P.L.233, No.64), known as The Controlled Substance, Drug, Device and Cosmetic Act, (except the ordinary hospital supply of the prison or mental hospital) without a written permit signed by the physician of such institution, specifying the quantity and quality of the substance which may be furnished to any convict, inmate, or employee in the prison or mental hospital, the name of the prisoner, inmate, or employee for whom, and the time when the same may be furnished, which permit shall be delivered to and kept by the warden or superintendent of the prison or mental hospital.

(a.1) **Mandatory minimum penalty.**-- Any person convicted of a violation of subsection (a) shall be sentenced to a minimum sentence of at least two years of total confinement, notwithstanding any other provision of this title or any other statute to the contrary. Nothing in this subsection shall prevent the sentencing court from imposing a sentence greater than that provided in this subsection, up to the maximum penalty prescribed by this title for a felony of the second degree. There shall be no authority in any court to impose on an offender to which this subsection is applicable any lesser sentence than provided for in subsection (a) or to place such offender on probation or to suspend sentence. Sentencing guidelines promulgated by the Pennsylvania Commission on Sentencing shall not supersede the mandatory sentences provided in this subsection. If a sentencing court refuses to apply this subsection where applicable, the Commonwealth shall have the right to appellate review of the action of the sentencing court. The appellate court shall vacate the sentence and remand the case to the sentencing court for imposition of a sentence in accordance with this subsection if it finds that the sentence was imposed in violation of this subsection.

(a.2) **Possession of controlled substance contraband by inmate prohibited.**--A prisoner or inmate commits a felony of the second degree if he unlawfully has in his possession or under his control any controlled substance in violation of section 13(a)(16) of The Controlled Substance, Drug, Device and Cosmetic Act. For purposes of this subsection, no amount shall be deemed de minimis.

(b) **Money to inmates prohibited.**--A person commits a misdemeanor of the third degree if he gives or furnishes money to any inmate confined in a State or county correctional institution, provided notice of this prohibition is adequately posted at the institution. A person may, however, deposit money with the superintendent, warden, or other authorized individual in charge of a State or county correctional institution for the benefit and use of an inmate confined therein, which shall be credited to the inmate's account and expended in accordance with the rules and regulations of the institution. The person making the deposit shall be provided with a written receipt for the amount deposited.

(c) Contraband other than controlled substance.--A person commits a misdemeanor of the first degree if he sells, gives or furnishes to any convict in a prison, or inmate in a mental hospital, or gives away in or brings into any prison, mental hospital, or any building appurtenant thereto, or on the land granted to or owned or leased by the Commonwealth or county for the use and benefit of the prisoners or inmates, or puts in any place where it may be secured by a convict of a prison, inmate of a mental hospital, or employee thereof, any kind of spirituous or fermented liquor, medicine or poison (except the ordinary hospital supply of the prison or mental hospital) without a written permit signed by the physician of such institution, specifying the quantity and quality of the substance which may be furnished to any convict, inmate or employee in the prison or mental hospital, the name of the prisoner, inmate or employee for whom, and the time when the same may be furnished, which permit shall be delivered to and kept by the warden or superintendent of the prison or mental hospital.

(c.1) Telecommunication devices to inmates prohibited.--A person commits a misdemeanor of the first degree if, without the written permission of superintendent, warden or otherwise authorized individual in charge of a correctional institution, prison, jail, detention facility or mental hospital, he sells, gives or furnishes to any inmate in a correctional institution, prison, jail, detention facility or mental hospital, or any building appurtenant thereto, or puts in any place where it may be obtained by an inmate of a correctional institution, prison, jail, detention facility or mental hospital, any telecommunication device.

(c.2) Possession of telecommunication devices by inmates prohibited.--An inmate in a correctional institution, prison, jail, detention facility or mental hospital, or any building appurtenant thereto, commits a misdemeanor of the first degree if he has in his possession any telecommunication device without the written permission of the superintendent, warden or otherwise authorized individual in charge of a correctional institution, prison, jail, detention facility or mental hospital.

(d) Drug-sniffing animals.--Any jail or prison may use dogs or other animals trained to sniff controlled substances or other contraband for such purposes in or on any part of the jail or prison at any time.

(e) Definitions.--As used in this section, the following words and phrases shall have the meanings given to them in this subsection:

"Inmate." A male or female offender who is committed to, under sentence to or confined in a penal or correctional institution.

"Telecommunication device." Any type of instrument, device, machine or equipment which is capable of transmitting telephonic, electronic, digital, cellular or radio communications or any part of such instrument, device, machine or equipment which is capable of facilitating the transmission of telephonic, electronic, digital, cellular or radio communications. The term shall include, but not be limited to, cellular phones, digital phones and modem equipment devices.

(June 23, 1978, P.L.498, No.77, eff. 60 days; Dec. 19, 1988, P.L.1275, No.158, eff. 60 days; Dec. 22, 1989, P.L.753, No.105, eff. 60 days; July 6, 1995, 1st Sp.Sess., P.L.1049, No.18, eff. 60 days; June 25, 1997, P.L.284, No.26, eff. 60 days; June 28, 2002, P.L.494, No.84, eff. 60 days)

2002 Amendment. Act 84 added subsecs. (c.1), (c.2) and (e).

1997 Amendment. Act 26 amended subsec. (a.2).

1995 Amendment. Act 18, 1st Sp.Sess., added subsecs. (a.1), (a.2) and (d).

1989 Amendment. Act 105 amended subsec. (a) and added subsec. (c).

Cross References. Section 5123 is referred to in section 3505 of this title; section 3513 of Title 61 (Prisons and Parole).

§ 5124. Default in required appearance.

(a) Offense defined.--A person set at liberty by court order, with or without bail, upon condition that he will subsequently appear at a specified time and place, commits a misdemeanor of the second degree if, without lawful excuse, he fails to appear at that time and place. The offense constitutes a felony of the third degree where the required appearance was to answer to a charge of felony, or for disposition of any such charge, and the actor took flight or went into hiding to avoid apprehension, trial or punishment.

(b) Exception.--Subsection (a) of this section does not apply to obligations to appear incident to release under suspended sentence or on probation or parole.

§ 5125. Absconding witness.

A person commits a misdemeanor of the third degree if, having been required by virtue of any legal process or otherwise to attend and testify in any prosecution for a crime before any court, judge, justice, or other judicial tribunal, or having been recognized or held to bail to attend as a witness on behalf of the Commonwealth or defendant, before any court having jurisdiction, to testify in any prosecution, he unlawfully and willfully conceals himself or absconds from this Commonwealth, or from the jurisdiction of such court, with intent to defeat the end of public justice, and refuses to appear as required by such legal process or otherwise.

§ 5126. Flight to avoid apprehension, trial or punishment.

(a) Offense defined.--A person who willfully conceals himself or moves or travels within or outside this Commonwealth with the intent to avoid apprehension, trial or punishment commits a felony of the third degree when the crime which he has been charged with or has been convicted of is a felony and commits a misdemeanor of the second degree when the crime which he has been charged with or has been convicted of is a misdemeanor.

(b) Exception.--Subsection (a) shall not apply to a person set at liberty by court order who fails to appear at the time or place specified in the order.

(May 31, 1990, P.L.219, No.47, eff. 60 days)

1990 Amendment. Act 47 added section 5126.

Cross References. Section 5126 is referred to in section 2303 of Title 44 (Law and Justice).

SUBCHAPTER C
CRIMINAL GANGS

Sec.
5131. Recruiting criminal gang members.

Enactment. Subchapter C was added October 25, 2012, P.L.1628, No.200, effective in 60 days.

§ 5131. Recruiting criminal gang members.

(a) Offense defined.--A person commits the offense of recruiting criminal gang members by:

(1) knowingly soliciting or otherwise causing or attempting to cause a person to participate or remain in a criminal gang;

(2) knowingly inflicting bodily injury as defined in section 2301 (relating to definitions) or using physical menace, force, threats or other intimidation causing or attempting to cause a person to participate or remain in a criminal gang; or

(3) knowingly inflicting serious bodily injury as defined in section 2301 on any person causing or attempting to cause a person to participate or remain in a criminal gang.

(b) Grading.--

(1) Except as provided under paragraph (2), the following shall apply:

(i) An offense under subsection (a)(1) is a misdemeanor of the second degree.

(ii) An offense under subsection (a)(2) is a misdemeanor of the first degree.

(iii) An offense under subsection (a)(3) is a felony of the third degree.

(2) A violation of this section shall be graded one degree higher than provided under paragraph (1) if the subject of the recruiting is under 16 years of age.

(c) Defenses.--It shall not be a defense to this offense that the subject of the recruiting did not join, participate or remain in a criminal gang.

(d) Liability for other violations of statutes.--This section shall not be construed to limit prosecution under any other provision of law.

(e) Definition.--As used in this section, the term "criminal gang" means a formal or informal ongoing organization, association or group, with or without an established hierarchy, that has as one of its primary activities the commission of criminal or delinquent acts and that consists of three or more persons.

Cross References. Section 5131 is referred to in section 9720.4 of Title 42 (Judiciary and Judicial Procedure); section 2303 of Title 44 (Law and Justice).

CHAPTER 53 ABUSE OF OFFICE

Enactment. Chapter 53 was added December 6, 1972, P.L.1482, No.334, effective in six months.

Cross References. Chapter 53 is referred to in section 5508.3 of Title 53 (Municipalities Generally); section 6017 of Title 64 (Public Authorities and Quasi-Public Corporations).

§ 5301. Official oppression.

A person acting or purporting to act in an official capacity or taking advantage of such actual or purported capacity commits a misdemeanor of the second degree if, knowing that his conduct is illegal, he:

(1) subjects another to arrest, detention, search, seizure, mistreatment, dispossession, assessment, lien or other infringement of personal or property rights; or

(2) denies or impedes another in the exercise or enjoyment of any right, privilege, power or immunity.

§ 5302. Speculating or wagering on official action or information.

A public servant commits a misdemeanor of the second degree if, in contemplation of official action by himself or by a governmental unit with which he is associated, or in reliance on information to which he has access in his official capacity and which has not been made public, he:

(1) acquires a pecuniary interest in any property, transaction or enterprise which may be affected by such information or official action;

(2) speculates or wagers on the basis of such information or official action; or

(3) aids another to do any of the foregoing.

§ 5303. Liability for reimbursement of costs for outside counsel.

(a) **General rule.**--A public official who is convicted of a felony or a misdemeanor under Federal law or under the laws of this Commonwealth shall be liable for and shall reimburse any public money expended by the Commonwealth to cover the costs incurred by an agency for outside counsel to defend the convicted public official in connection with a criminal investigation and prosecution of such public official.

(b) **Conviction in State court.**--When a public official is convicted of a felony or misdemeanor in State court, the court shall, in addition to the punishment prescribed for the offense, order the public official to reimburse any public money for which he is liable under subsection (a).

(c) **Conviction in Federal court.**--When a public official is convicted of a felony or misdemeanor in a Federal court, the Attorney General shall institute a civil action in Commonwealth Court to recover the public money for which the public official is liable under subsection (a).

(d) **Method of reimbursement.**--The court may order the public official to make reimbursement of public money in a lump sum, by monthly installments or according to such other schedule as the court may determine appropriate. The period of time during which the public official is ordered to make such reimbursement may exceed the maximum term of imprisonment to which the public official could have been sentenced for the crime of which he was convicted.

(e) **Status of reimbursement.**--Any reimbursement of public money ordered by the court under this section shall be a judgment in favor of the Commonwealth upon the public official or property of the public official ordered to make reimbursement. The Attorney General shall be responsible for enforcing such judgment in courts of competent jurisdiction in accordance with provisions of this title.

(f) **Disposition of funds.**--Any money reimbursed or recovered under this section shall be deposited in the fund from which the Commonwealth expended such public money.

(g) **Definitions.**--As used in this section, the following words and phrases shall have the meanings given to them in this subsection:

"Convicted." A finding or verdict of guilty, an admission of guilt or a plea of nolo contendere.

"Public money." Any money received by the Commonwealth or any agency of the Commonwealth through taxes imposed pursuant to the act of March 4, 1971 (P.L.6, No.2), known as the Tax Reform Code of 1971, and through fees, fines and penalties imposed pursuant to the laws of this Commonwealth.

"Public official." Any person who is required to file an annual statement of financial interests with the State Ethics Commission as a public official of the Commonwealth in accordance with the act of October 4, 1978 (P.L.883, No.170), referred to as the Public Official and Employee Ethics Law.

(July 11, 1996, P.L.552, No.98, eff. 60 days)

1996 Amendment. Act 98 added section 5303.

ARTICLE F OFFENSES AGAINST PUBLIC ORDER AND DECENCY

Chapter
55. Riot, Disorderly Conduct and Related Offenses
57. Wiretapping and Electronic Surveillance
59. Public Indecency

CHAPTER 55 RIOT, DISORDERLY CONDUCT AND RELATED OFFENSES

Subchapter
A. Definition of Offenses Generally
B. Cruelty to Animals

Enactment. Chapter 55 was added December 6, 1972, P.L.1482, No.334, effective in six months.
Cross References. Chapter 55 is referred to in section 2101 of Title 5 (Athletics and Sports)

SUBCHAPTER A
DEFINITION OF OFFENSES
GENERALLY

Sec.

5501. Riot.
5502. Failure of disorderly persons to disperse upon official order.
5503. Disorderly conduct.
5504. Harassment and stalking by communication or address (Repealed).
5505. Public drunkenness and similar misconduct.
5506. Loitering and prowling at night time.
5507. Obstructing highways and other public passages.
5508. Disrupting meetings and processions.
5509. Desecration, theft or sale of venerated objects.
5510. Abuse of corpse.
5511. Cruelty to animals (Repealed).
5511.1. Live animals as prizes prohibited (Repealed).
5511.2. Police animals (Repealed).
5511.3. Assault with a biological agent on animal, fowl or honey bees (Repealed).
5512. Lotteries, etc.
5513. Gambling devices, gambling, etc.
5514. Pool selling and bookmaking.
5515. Prohibiting of paramilitary training.
5516. Facsimile weapons of mass destruction.
5517. Unauthorized school bus entry.

Subchapter Heading. The heading of Subchapter A was added June 28, 2017, P.L.215, No.10, effective in 60 days.
§ 5501. Riot.
A person is guilty of riot, a felony of the third degree, if he participates with two or more others in a course of disorderly conduct:
(1) with intent to commit or facilitate the commission of a felony or misdemeanor;
(2) with intent to prevent or coerce official action; or
(3) when the actor or any other participant to the knowledge of the actor uses or plans to use a firearm or other deadly weapon.

Cross References. Section 5501 is referred to in section 6105 of this title; section 3304 of Title 5 (Athletics and Sports).
§ 5502. Failure of disorderly persons to disperse upon official order.
Where three or more persons are participating in a course of disorderly conduct which causes or may reasonably be expected to cause substantial harm or serious

inconvenience, annoyance or alarm, a peace officer or other public servant engaged in executing or enforcing the law may order the participants and others in the immediate vicinity to disperse. A person who refuses or knowingly fails to obey such an order commits a misdemeanor of the second degree.

§ 5503. Disorderly conduct.

(a) Offense defined.--A person is guilty of disorderly conduct if, with intent to cause public inconvenience, annoyance or alarm, or recklessly creating a risk thereof, he:

(1) engages in fighting or threatening, or in violent or tumultuous behavior;

(2) makes unreasonable noise;

(3) uses obscene language, or makes an obscene gesture; or

(4) creates a hazardous or physically offensive condition by any act which serves no legitimate purpose of the actor.

(b) Grading.--An offense under this section is a misdemeanor of the third degree if the intent of the actor is to cause substantial harm or serious inconvenience, or if he persists in disorderly conduct after reasonable warning or request to desist. Otherwise disorderly conduct is a summary offense.

(c) Definition.--As used in this section the word "public" means affecting or likely to affect persons in a place to which the public or a substantial group has access; among the places included are highways, transport facilities, schools, prisons, apartment houses, places of business or amusement, any neighborhood, or any premises which are open to the public.

Cross References. Section 5503 is referred to in section 3019 of this title; section 12432 of Title 11 (Cities); sections 3573, 6328, 8902 of Title 42 (Judiciary and Judicial Procedure).

§ 5504. Harassment and stalking by communication or address (Repealed).

2002 Repeal. Section 5504 was repealed December 9, 2002 (P.L.1759, No.218), effective in 60 days.

§ 5505. Public drunkenness and similar misconduct.

A person is guilty of a summary offense if he appears in any public place manifestly under the influence of alcohol or a controlled substance, as defined in the act of April 14, 1972 (P.L.233, No.64), known as The Controlled Substance, Drug, Device and Cosmetic Act, except those taken pursuant to the lawful order of a practitioner, as defined in The Controlled Substance, Drug, Device and Cosmetic Act, to the degree that he may endanger himself or other persons or property, or annoy persons in his vicinity. A person convicted of violating this section may be sentenced to pay a fine of not more than $500 for the first violation and not more than $1,000 for the second and each subsequent violation.

(June 18, 1999, P.L.67, No.8, eff. 60 days; Oct. 25, 2012, P.L.1663, No.205, eff. 60 days)

2012 Amendment. Section 2 of Act 205 provided that the amendment of section 5505 shall apply to offenses committed on or after the effective date of section 2.

Cross References. Section 5505 is referred to in sections 3573, 8902 of Title 42 (Judiciary and Judicial Procedure).

§ 5506. Loitering and prowling at night time.

Whoever at night time maliciously loiters or maliciously prowls around a dwelling house or any other place used wholly or in part for living or dwelling purposes, belonging to or occupied by another, is guilty of a misdemeanor of the third degree.

Cross References. Section 5506 is referred to in section 3019 of this title; section 6328 of Title 42 (Judiciary and Judicial Procedure).

§ 5507. Obstructing highways and other public passages.

(a) Obstructing.--A person, who, having no legal privilege to do so, intentionally or recklessly obstructs any highway, railroad track or public utility right-of-way, sidewalk, navigable waters, other public passage, whether alone or with others, commits a summary offense, or, in case he persists after warning by a law officer, a misdemeanor of the third degree. No person shall be deemed guilty of an offense under this subsection solely because of a gathering of persons to hear him speak or otherwise communicate, or solely because of being a member of such a gathering.

(b) Refusal to move on.--

(1) A person in a gathering commits a summary offense if he refuses to obey a reasonable official request or order to move:

(i) to prevent obstruction of a highway or other public passage; or

(ii) to maintain public safety by dispersing those gathered in dangerous proximity to a fire or other hazard.

(2) An order to move, addressed to a person whose speech or other lawful behavior attracts an obstructing audience, shall not be deemed reasonable if the obstruction can be readily remedied by police control of the size or location of the gathering.

(c) **Definition.**--As used in this section the word "obstructs" means renders impassable without unreasonable inconvenience or hazard.

Cross References. Section 5507 is referred to in sections 3019, 3065 of this title; section 8902 of Title 42 (Judiciary and Judicial Procedure).

§ 5508. Disrupting meetings and processions.

A person commits a misdemeanor of the third degree if, with intent to prevent or disrupt a lawful meeting, procession or gathering, he disturbs or interrupts it.

§ 5509. Desecration, theft or sale of venerated objects.

(a) **Offense defined.**--A person commits a misdemeanor of the second degree if he:

(1) intentionally desecrates any public monument or structure, or place of worship or burial;

(2) intentionally desecrates any other object of veneration by the public or a substantial segment thereof in any public place;

(3) sells, attempts to sell or removes with intent to sell a veteran's marker as described in section 1913 of the act of August 9, 1955 (P.L.323, No.130), known as The County Code. This paragraph shall not apply to the sale of veterans' markers authorized by statute; or

(4) intentionally receives, retains or disposes of a veteran's marker or item decorating a veteran's grave knowing that the item has been stolen, or believing that it has probably been stolen, unless it has been received, retained or disposed of with the intent to return it to the owner.

(a.1) **Historic burial lots and burial places.**--A person commits a misdemeanor of the first degree if the person intentionally desecrates a historic burial lot or historic burial place.

(b) **Definitions.**--As used in this section, the following words and phrases shall have the meanings given to them in this subsection:

"Desecrate." Defacing, damaging, polluting or otherwise physically mistreating in a way that the actor knows will outrage the sensibilities of persons likely to observe or discover the action.

"Historic burial lot." An individual burial site within a historic burial place.

"Historic burial place." A tract of land which has been:

(1) in existence as a burial ground for more than 100 years; or

(2) listed in or eligible for the National Register of Historic Places as determined by the Pennsylvania Historical and Museum Commission.

(May 4, 2001, P.L.3, No.3, eff. 60 days; Dec. 16, 2003, P.L.233, No.41, eff. 60 days; Oct. 9, 2008, P.L.1419, No.116, 60 days)

2008 Amendment. Section 2 of Act 116 provided that the amendment of section 5509 shall apply to offenses committed on or after the effective date of section 2.

2003 Amendment. Section 2 of Act 41 provided that the amendment of section 5509 shall apply to offenses committed on or after the effective date of Act 41.

Cross References. Section 5509 is referred to in section 3307 of this title.

§ 5510. Abuse of corpse.

Except as authorized by law, a person who treats a corpse in a way that he knows would outrage ordinary family sensibilities commits a misdemeanor of the second degree.

Cross References. Section 5510 is referred to in sections 9122.1, 9122.3 of this title; section 2303 of Title 44 (Law and Justice).

§ 5511. Cruelty to animals (Repealed).

2017 Repeal. Section 5511 was repealed June 28, 2017, P.L.215, No.10, effective in 60 days.

§ 5511.1. Live animals as prizes prohibited (Repealed).

2017 Repeal. Section 5511.1 was repealed June 28, 2017, P.L.215, No.10, effective in 60 days.

§ 5511.2. Police animals (Repealed).

2017 Repeal. Section 5511.2 was repealed June 28, 2017, P.L.215, No.10, effective in 60 days.

§ 5511.3. Assault with a biological agent on animal, fowl or honey bees (Repealed).

2017 Repeal. Section 5511.3 was repealed June 28, 2017, P.L.215, No.10, effective in 60 days.

§ 5512. Lotteries, etc.

(a) Status of activity.--All unlawful lotteries or numbers games are hereby declared to be common nuisances. Every transfer of property which shall be in pursuance of any unlawful lottery or numbers game is hereby declared to be invalid and void.

(b) Offense defined.--A person is guilty of a misdemeanor of the first degree if he:

(1) sets up, or maintains, any lottery or numbers game;

(2) manufactures or prints, or sells, exposes for sale or has in his possession with intent to sell any unlawful lottery or numbers ticket or share, or any writing, token or other device purporting or intending to entitle the holder or bearer, or any other person, to any prize to be drawn or obtained in any lottery, or numbers game; or

(3) publishes any advertisement of any lottery or numbers game.

(c) Status of purchaser.--The purchaser of any such ticket, or device, shall not be liable to any prosecution or penalty arising out of this crime, and shall in all respects be a competent witness to prove the offense.

(d) Definition.--As used in this section the term "unlawful" means not specifically authorized by law.

Cross References. Section 5512 is referred to in sections 911, 5708 of this title; section 341 of Title 4 (Amusements); section 3304 of Title 5 (Athletics and Sports); section 5552 of Title 42 (Judiciary and Judicial Procedure).

§ 5513. Gambling devices, gambling, etc.

(a) Offense defined.--A person is guilty of a misdemeanor of the first degree if he:

(1) intentionally or knowingly makes, assembles, sets up, maintains, sells, lends, leases, gives away, or offers for sale, loan, lease or gift, any punch board, drawing card, slot machine or any device to be used for gambling purposes, except playing cards;

(2) allows persons to collect and assemble for the purpose of unlawful gambling at any place under his control;

(3) solicits or invites any person to visit any unlawful gambling place for the purpose of gambling; or

(4) being the owner, tenant, lessee or occupant of any premises, knowingly permits or suffers the same, or any part thereof, to be used for the purpose of unlawful gambling.

(a.1) Electronic video monitor.--A person commits a misdemeanor of the first degree if he owns, operates, maintains, places into operation or has a financial interest in an electronic video monitor or business that owns, operates, maintains or places into operation or has a financial interest in an electronic video monitor:

(1) which is offered or made available to persons to play or participate in a simulated gambling program for direct or indirect consideration, including consideration associated with a related product, service or activity; and

(2) for which the person playing the simulated gambling program may become eligible for a cash or cash-equivalent prize, whether or not the eligibility for or value of the cash or cash-equivalent prize is determined by or has any relationship to the outcome of or play of the simulated gambling program.

(b) Confiscation of gambling devices.-- Any gambling device possessed or used in violation of the provisions of subsection (a) shall be seized and forfeited to the Commonwealth. The forfeiture shall be conducted in accordance with 42 Pa.C.S. §§ 5803 (relating to asset forfeiture), 5805 (relating to forfeiture procedure), 5806 (relating to motion for return of property), 5807 (relating to restrictions on use), 5807.1 (relating to prohibition on adoptive seizures) and 5808 (relating to exceptions).

(c) Antique slot machines.--

(1) A slot machine shall be established as an antique slot machine if the defendant shows by a preponderance of the evidence that it was manufactured at least 25 years before the current year and that it was not used or attempted to be used for any unlawful purposes. Notwithstanding subsection (b), no antique slot machine seized from any defendant shall be destroyed or otherwise altered until the defendant is given an opportunity to establish that the slot machine is an antique slot machine. After a final court determination that the slot machine is an antique slot machine, the slot machine shall be returned pursuant to the provisions of law providing for the return of property; otherwise, the slot machine shall be destroyed.

(2) It is the purpose of this subsection to protect the collection and restoration of antique slot machines not presently utilized for gambling purposes.

(d) Shipbuilding business.-- Notwithstanding any other provisions of this section, a person may construct, deliver, convert or repair a vessel that is equipped with gambling devices if all of the following conditions are satisfied:

(1) The work performed on the vessel is ordered by a customer who uses or possesses the vessel outside of this Commonwealth in a locality where the use or possession of the gambling devices on the vessel is lawful.

(2) The work performed on the vessel that is equipped with gambling devices is performed at a shipbuilding or repair yard located within a port facility under the jurisdiction of any port authority organized under the act of December 6, 1972 (P.L.1392, No.298), known as the Third Class City Port Authority Act.

(3) The person provides the Office of Attorney General, prior to the importation of the gambling devices into this Commonwealth, records that account for the gambling devices, including the identification number affixed to each gambling device by the manufacturer, and that identify the location where the gambling devices will be stored prior to the installation of the gambling devices on the vessel.

(4) The person stores the gambling devices at a secured location and permits any person authorized to enforce the gambling laws to inspect the location where the gambling devices are stored and records relating to the storage of the gambling devices.

(5) If the person removes used gambling devices from a vessel, the person shall provide the Office of Attorney General of Pennsylvania with an inventory of the used gambling devices prior to their removal from the vessel. The inventory shall include the identification number affixed to each gambling device by the manufacturer.

(6) The person submits documentation to the Office of Attorney General of Pennsylvania no later than 30 days after the date of delivery that the vessel equipped with gambling devices has been delivered to the customer who ordered the work performed on the vessel.

(7) The person does not sell a gambling device to any other person except to a customer who shall use or possess the gambling device outside of this Commonwealth in a locality where the use or possession of the gambling device is lawful. If a person sells a gambling device to such a customer, the person shall submit documentation to the Office of Attorney General of Pennsylvania no later than 30 days after the date of delivery that the gambling device has been delivered to the customer.

(e) Penalty.-- Any person who fails to provide records as provided in subsection (d) commits a summary offense.

(e.1) Construction.-- Nothing in this section shall be construed to prohibit any activity that is lawfully conducted under any of the following:

(1) The act of August 26, 1971 (P.L.351, No.91), known as the State Lottery Law.

(2) The act of July 10, 1981 (P.L.214, No.67), known as the Bingo Law.

(3) The act of December 19, 1988 (P.L.1262, No.156), known as the Local Option Small Games of Chance Act.

(4) 4 Pa.C.S. (relating to amusements).

(f) Definitions.-- The following words and phrases when used in this section shall have the meanings given to them in this subsection unless the context clearly indicates otherwise:

"Consideration associated with a related product, service or activity." Money or other value collected for a product, service or activity which is offered in any direct or indirect relationship to playing or participating in the simulated gambling program. The term includes consideration paid for computer time, Internet time, telephone calling cards and a sweepstakes entry.

"Electronic video monitor." An electronic device capable of showing moving or still images.

"Simulated gambling program." Any method intended to be used by a person interacting with an electronic video monitor in a business establishment that directly or indirectly implements the predetermination of sweepstakes cash or cash-equivalent prizes or otherwise connects the sweepstakes player or participant with the cash or cash-equivalent prize.

(July 1, 1978, P.L.572, No.103, eff. 30 days; July 11, 1996, P.L.552, No.98, eff. imd.; May 16, 2002, P.L.325, No.48, eff. 60 days; June 30, 2012, P.L.682, No.81, eff. imd.; June 29, 2017, P.L.247, No.13, eff. July 1, 2017)

2017 Amendment. Act 13 amended subsec. (b).

2012 Amendment. Act 81 amended subsec. (f) and added subsecs. (a.1) and (e.1).

2004 Partial Repeal. Section 1903(a)(2) of Title 4 (relating to amusements), which was added by Act 71 of 2004, provided that subsec. (a) is repealed insofar as it is inconsistent with Part II of Title 4.

2002 Amendment. Act 48 amended subsec. (c).

1996 Amendment. Act 98 added subsecs. (d), (e) and (f).

1981 Partial Repeal. Section 9 of the act of July 10, 1981 (P.L.214, No.67), known as the Bingo Law, repealed Title 18 to the extent that it is inconsistent with Act 67.

Cross References. Section 5513 is referred to in sections 911, 5708 of this title; sections 341, 1903 of Title 4 (Amusements); section 3304 of Title 5 (Athletics and Sports); sections 5552, 5803 of Title 42 (Judiciary and Judicial Procedure).

§ 5514. Pool selling and bookmaking.

A person is guilty of a misdemeanor of the first degree if he:

(1) engages in pool selling or bookmaking;

(2) occupies any place for the purpose of receiving, recording or registering bets or wagers, or of selling pools;

(3) receives, records, registers, forwards, or purports or pretends to forward, to another, any bet or wager upon the result of any political nomination, appointment or election, or upon any contest of any nature;

(4) becomes the custodian or depository, for gain or ward, of any property staked, wagered or pledged, or to be staked, wagered, or pledged upon any such result; or

(5) being the owner, lessee, or occupant of any premises, knowingly permits or suffers the same, to be used or occupied for any of such purposes.

Cross References. Section 5514 is referred to in sections 911, 5708 of this title; sections 341, 13C71 of Title 4 (Amusements); section 3304 of Title 5 (Athletics and Sports); section 5552 of Title 42 (Judiciary and Judicial Procedure).

§ 5515. Prohibiting of paramilitary training.

(a) Definitions.--As used in this section the following words and phrases shall have the meanings given to them in this subsection:

"Civil disorder." Any public disturbance involving acts of violence by assemblages of three or more persons, which causes an immediate danger of or results in damage or injury to the property or person of any other individual.

"Explosive or incendiary device." Includes:

(1) dynamite and all other forms of high explosives;

(2) any explosive bomb, grenade, missile or similar device; and

(3) any incendiary bomb or grenade, fire bomb or similar device, including any device which:

(i) consists of or includes a breakable container including a flammable liquid or compound and a wick composed of any material which, when ignited, is capable of igniting such flammable liquid or compound; and

(ii) can be carried or thrown by one individual acting alone.

"Firearm." Any weapon which is designed to or may readily be converted to expel any projectile by the action of an explosive; or the frame or receiver of any such weapon.

"Law enforcement officer." Any officer or employee of the United States, any state, any political subdivision of a state or the District of Columbia and such term shall specifically include, but shall not be limited to, members of the National Guard, as defined in 10 U.S.C. § 101(9), members of the organized militia of any state or territory of the United States, the Commonwealth of Puerto Rico or the District of Columbia, not included within the definition of National Guard as defined by 10 U.S.C. § 101(9) and members of the armed forces of the United States.

(b) Prohibited training.--

(1) Whoever teaches or demonstrates to any other person the use, application or making of any firearm, explosive or incendiary device or technique capable of causing injury or death to persons, knowing or having reason to know or intending that same will be unlawfully employed for use in, or in furtherance of, a civil disorder commits a misdemeanor of the first degree.

(2) Whoever assembles with one or more persons for the purpose of training with, practicing with or being instructed in the use of any firearm, explosive or incendiary device or

technique capable of causing injury or death to persons, said person intending to employ unlawfully the same for use in or in furtherance of a civil disorder commits a misdemeanor of the first degree.

(c) Exemptions.--Nothing contained in this section shall make unlawful any act of any law enforcement officer which is performed in the lawful performance of his official duties.

(d) Excluded activities.--Nothing contained in this section shall make unlawful any activity of the Game Commission, Fish and Boat Commission, or any law enforcement agency, or any hunting club, rifle club, rifle range, pistol range, shooting range or other program or individual instruction intended to teach the safe handling or use of firearms, archery equipment or other weapons or techniques employed in connection with lawful sports or other lawful activities.

(June 11, 1982, P.L.476, No.138, eff. 180 days; Mar. 19, 1992, P.L.18, No.7, eff. imd.)

1992 Amendment. Act 7 amended subsec. (d).

1982 Amendment. Act 138 added section 5515.

Cross References. Section 5515 is referred to in sections 4906, 6105, 6120, 9122.1, 9122.3 of this title; section 9720.6 of Title 42 (Judiciary and Judicial Procedure).

§ 5516. Facsimile weapons of mass destruction.

(a) Offense defined.--A person commits an offense if the person intentionally, knowingly or recklessly manufactures, sells, purchases, transports or causes another to transport, delivers or causes another to deliver, possesses or uses a facsimile weapon of mass destruction and by such action causes any of the following:

(1) Terrifying, intimidating, threatening or harassing an individual.

(2) Alarm or reaction on the part of any of the following:

(i) A public or volunteer organization that deals with emergencies involving danger to life or property.

(ii) A law enforcement organization.

(3) Serious public inconvenience not limited to the evacuation of a building, place of assembly or facility of public transportation.

(b) Grading.--An offense under this section is a felony of the third degree.

(b.1) Restitution.--A person convicted of violating this section shall, in addition to any other sentence imposed or restitution ordered under 42 Pa.C.S. § 9721(c) (relating to sentencing generally), be sentenced to pay restitution in an amount equal to the cost of the evacuation, including, but not limited to, fire and police response; emergency medical service or emergency preparedness response; and transportation of an individual from the building, place of assembly or facility.

(b.2) Preservation of private remedies.--No judgment or order of restitution shall debar a person, by appropriate action, to recover from the offender as otherwise provided by law, provided that any civil award shall be reduced by the amount paid under the criminal judgment.

(b.3) Enforcement.--

(1) In addition to the authority conferred upon the Attorney General under sections 205 and 206 of the act of October 15, 1980 (P.L.950, No.164), known as the Commonwealth Attorneys Act, the Attorney General has the authority to investigate and to institute criminal proceedings for a violation of this section committed:

(i) anywhere in this Commonwealth;

(ii) in different counties; or

(iii) in this Commonwealth and another jurisdiction.

(2) Each district attorney has the authority to investigate and to institute criminal proceedings for a violation of this section.

(b.4) Jurisdiction.--No person charged with a violation of this section shall have standing to challenge the authority of the Attorney General under subsection (g)(1). If a challenge is made in violation of this subsection, the challenge shall be dismissed, and no relief shall be available in the courts of this Commonwealth to the person making the challenge.

(c) Definitions.--As used in this section, the following words and phrases shall have the meanings given to them in this subsection:

"Facsimile biological agent." A material or substance which:

(1) resembles in appearance and external qualities a natural or genetically engineered pathogen, toxin, virus, bacteria, prion, fungus or microorganism which causes infections, disease or bodily harm; but

(2) does not have the capacity to cause infectious disease or bodily harm.

"Facsimile bomb." A device which:

(1) resembles in appearance and external qualities an explosive or incendiary device; but

(2) does not have the capability to cause an explosion or fire.

"Facsimile chemical agent." A material or substance which does not have the capacity to cause death or bodily harm but which resembles in appearance and external qualities any of the following:

(1) A nerve agent, including tabun (GA), sarin (GB), soman (GD), GF and VX.

(2) A choking agent, including phosgene (CG) and diphosgene (DP).

(3) A blood agent, including hydrogen cyanide (AC), cyanogen chloride (CK) and arsine (SA).

(4) A blister agent. This paragraph includes:

(i) Mustard (H).

(ii) Sulfur mustard (HD).

(iii) HN-1.

(iv) HN-2.

(v) Nitrogen mustard (HN-3).

(vi) An arsenical, such as lewisite (L).

(vii) An urticant, such as CX.

(viii) An incapacitating agent, such as B2.

(5) Any other chemical element or compound which causes death or bodily harm.

"Facsimile nuclear agent." A device, material or substance which:

(1) resembles in appearance and external qualities a radioactive material; but

(2) is not radioactive.

"Facsimile weapon of mass destruction." A facsimile biological agent, facsimile bomb, facsimile chemical agent or facsimile nuclear agent.

(Oct. 31, 1997, P.L.491, No.50, eff. 60 days; June 28, 2002, P.L.481, No.82, eff. 60 days)

Cross References. Section 5516 is referred to in sections 5708, 6105 of this title.

§ 5517. Unauthorized school bus entry.

(a) Offense defined.--A person who enters a school bus without prior authorization of the driver or a school official with intent to commit a crime or disrupt or interfere with the driver or a person who enters a school bus without prior authorization of the driver or a school official who refuses to disembark after being ordered to do so by the driver commits a misdemeanor of the third degree.

(b) Notice.--A school district may place a notice at the entrance of the school bus that warns against unauthorized entry.

(June 11, 1998, P.L.460, No.65, eff. 60 days)

1998 Amendment. Act 65 added section 5517.

SUBCHAPTER B
CRUELTY TO ANIMALS

Enactment. Subchapter B was added June 28, 2017, P.L.215, No.10, effective in 60 days.

Cross References. Subchapter B is referred to in sections 9318, 9323 of Title 3 (Agriculture); sections 3702, 3705, 3708, 3710, 3716 of Title 22 (Detectives and Private Police); section 2385 of Title 34 (Game and Wildlife); section 3573 of Title 42 (Judiciary and Judicial Procedure); section 2303 of Title 44 (Law and Justice).

§ 5531. Definitions.

The following words and phrases when used in this subchapter shall have the meanings given to them in this section unless the context clearly indicates otherwise:

"Accelerant detection dog." A dog that is trained for accelerant detection, commonly referred to as arson canines.

"Animal fighting." Fighting or baiting a bull, bear, dog, cock or other creature.

"Animal fighting paraphernalia." A device, implement, object or drug used or intended to be used for animal fighting, to train an animal for animal fighting or in furtherance of animal fighting. In determining whether an object is animal fighting paraphernalia, a court or other authority should consider the following:

(1) Statements by an owner or by an individual in control of the object concerning its use.

(2) A prior conviction under Federal or State law relating to animal fighting.

(3) The proximity of the object in time and space to the direct violation of this subchapter.

(4) Direct or circumstantial evidence of the intent of the accused to deliver the object to persons whom the accused knows or should reasonably know intends to use the object to facilitate a violation of this subchapter.

(5) Oral or written instructions provided with or in the vicinity of the object concerning the object's use.

(6) Descriptive materials accompanying the object which explain or depict the object's use.

(7) All other logically relevant factors.

"Audibly impaired." The inability to hear air conduction thresholds at an average of 40 decibels or greater in the better ear.

"Blind." Having a visual acuity of 20/200 or less in the better eye with correction or having a limitation of the field of vision such that the widest diameter of the visual field subtends an angular distance not greater than 20 degrees.

"Bodily injury." Impairment of physical condition or substantial pain.

"Bomb detection dog." A dog that is trained to locate a bomb or explosives by scent.

"Certified veterinary technician." As defined in section 3(13) of the act of December 27, 1974 (P.L.995, No.326), known as the Veterinary Medicine Practice Act.

"Conveyance." A truck, tractor, trailer or semitrailer, or a combination of these, propelled or drawn by mechanical power.

"Deaf." Totally impaired hearing or hearing with or without amplification which is so seriously impaired that the primary means of receiving spoken language is through other sensory input, including, but not limited to, lip reading, sign language, finger spelling or reading.

"Domestic animal." A dog, cat, equine animal, bovine animal, sheep, goat or porcine animal.

"Domestic fowl." An avis raised for food, hobby or sport.

"Equine animal." A member of the Equidae family, which includes horses, asses, mules, ponies and zebras.

"Humane society police officer." As defined in 22 Pa.C.S. § 3702 (relating to definitions).

"Licensed doctor of veterinary medicine." As defined in section 3(8) of the Veterinary Medicine Practice Act.

"Narcotic detection dog." A dog that is trained to locate narcotics by scent.

"Normal agricultural operation." Normal activities, practices and procedures that farmers adopt, use or engage in year after year in the production and preparation for market of poultry, livestock and their products in the production and harvesting of agricultural, agronomic, horticultural, silvicultural and aquicultural crops and commodities.

"Physically limited." Having limited ambulation, including, but not limited to, a temporary or permanent impairment or condition that causes an individual to use a wheelchair or walk with difficulty or insecurity, affects sight or hearing to the extent that an individual is insecure or exposed to danger, causes faulty coordination or reduces mobility, flexibility, coordination or perceptiveness.

"Police animal." An animal, including, but not limited to, dogs and horses, used by the Pennsylvania State Police, a police department created by a metropolitan transportation authority operating under 74 Pa.C.S. Ch. 17 (relating to metropolitan transportation authorities), a police department created under the act of April 6, 1956 (1955 P.L.1414, No.465), known as the Second Class County Port Authority Act, the Capitol Police, the Department of Corrections, a county facility or office or by a municipal police department, fire department, search and rescue unit or agency or handler under the supervision of the department, search and rescue unit or agency in the performance of the functions or duties of the department, search and rescue unit or agency, whether the animal is on duty or not on duty. The term shall include, but not be limited to, an accelerant detection dog, bomb detection dog, narcotic detection dog, search and rescue dog and tracking animal.

"Search and rescue dog." A dog that is trained to locate lost or missing persons, victims of natural or manmade disasters and human bodies.

"Serious bodily injury." Bodily injury that creates a substantial risk of death or causes serious, permanent disfigurement or protracted loss or impairment of the function of a bodily member or organ.

"Service, guide or support dog." A dog that is trained or is being trained to work or perform tasks for the benefit of an individual with a disability consistent with Federal and State law related to service animals.

"Torture." Any of the following acts directed toward or against an animal unless directed to be performed by a licensed doctor of veterinary medicine acting within the normal scope of practice:

(1) Breaking, severing or severely impairing limbs.

(2) Inflicting severe and prolonged pain from burning, crushing or wounding.

(3) Causing or allowing severe and prolonged pain through prolonged deprivation of food or sustenance without veterinary care.

"Tracking animal." An animal that is trained to track or used to pursue a missing person, escaped inmate or fleeing felon.

"Veterinary assistant." As defined in section 3(14) of the Veterinary Medicine Practice Act.

(Oct. 24, 2018, P.L.685, No.104, eff. 60 days)

2018 Amendment. Act 104 added the def. of "service, guide or support dog."

Cross References. Section 5531 is referred to in section 7325 of this title.

§ 5532. Neglect of animal.

(a) Offense defined.--A person commits an offense if the person fails to provide for the basic needs of each animal to which the person has a duty of care, whether belonging to himself or otherwise, including any of the following:

(1) Necessary sustenance and potable water.

(2) Access to clean and sanitary shelter and protection from the weather. The shelter must be sufficient to permit the animal to retain body heat and keep the animal dry.

(3) Necessary veterinary care.

(b) Grading.--

(1) Except as set forth in paragraph (2), a violation of this section is a summary offense.

(2) If the violation causes bodily injury to the animal or places the animal at imminent risk of serious bodily injury, a violation of this section is a misdemeanor of the third degree.

(Oct. 24, 2018, P.L.685, No.104, eff. 60 days)

2018 Amendment. Act 104 amended subsec. (a).

Cross References. Section 5532 is referred to in sections 5534, 5536, 5560 of this title.

§ 5533. Cruelty to animal.

(a) Offense defined.--A person commits an offense if the person intentionally, knowingly or recklessly illtreats, overloads, beats, abandons or abuses an animal.

(b) Grading.--

(1) Except as set forth in paragraph (2), a violation of this section is a summary offense.

(2) If the violation causes bodily injury to the animal or places the animal at imminent risk of serious bodily injury, a violation of this section is a misdemeanor of the second degree.

Cross References. Section 5533 is referred to in sections 5534, 5542, 5560, 9122.3 of this title.

§ 5534. Aggravated cruelty to animal.

(a) Offense defined.--A person commits an offense if the person intentionally or knowingly does any of the following:

(1) Tortures an animal.

(2) Violates section 5532 (relating to neglect of animal) or 5533 (relating to cruelty to animal) causing serious bodily injury to the animal or the death of the animal.

(b) Grading.--A violation of this section is a felony of the third degree.

Cross References. Section 5534 is referred to in section 5560 of this title.

§ 5535. Attack of service, guide or support dog.

(a) Offense defined.--A person commits a misdemeanor of the third degree if the person is the owner of a dog that kills, maims or disfigures a service, guide or support dog of an individual with a disability without provocation by the service, guide or support dog or the individual.

(b) Culpability.--A person commits an offense under this section only if the person:

(1) knew or should have known that the dog the person owns had a propensity to attack human beings or domestic animals without provocation; and

(2) knowingly or recklessly failed to restrain the dog or keep the dog in a contained, secure manner.

(c) Penalty.--A person convicted of violating this section shall be sentenced to pay a fine of not more than $5,000 and shall be ordered to make reparations for veterinary costs in treating the service, guide or support dog and, if necessary, the cost of obtaining and training a replacement service, guide or support dog.

(d) Civil penalty and restitution.--

(1) A person who is the owner of a dog that kills, maims or disfigures a service, guide or support dog of an individual with a disability shall be subject to paragraph (2) if both of the following apply:

(i) The owner knew the dog had a propensity to attack human beings or domestic animals.

(ii) The owner failed to restrain the dog or keep the dog in a contained, secure manner.

(2) A court of common pleas may impose any of the following upon a person who is the owner of a dog under paragraph (1):

(i) A civil penalty of up to $15,000.

(ii) Reparations for veterinary costs in treating the service, guide or support dog and, if necessary, the cost of retraining the dog or of obtaining and training a replacement service, guide or support dog.

(iii) Loss of income for the time the individual is unable to work due to the unavailability of the service, guide or support dog.

(Oct. 24, 2018, P.L.685, No.104, eff. 60 days)

§ 5536. Tethering of unattended dog.

(a) Presumptions.--

(1) Tethering an unattended dog out of doors for less than nine hours within a 24-hour period when all of the following conditions are present shall create a rebuttable presumption that a dog has not been the subject of neglect within the meaning of section 5532 (relating to neglect of animal):

(i) The tether is of a type commonly used for the size and breed of dog and is at least three times the length of the dog as measured from the tip of its nose to the base of its tail or 10 feet, whichever is longer.

(ii) The tether is secured to a well-fitted collar or harness by means of a swivel anchor, swivel latch or other mechanism designed to prevent the dog from becoming entangled.

(iii) The tethered dog has access to potable water and an area of shade that permits the dog to escape the direct rays of the sun.

(iv) The dog has not been tethered for longer than 30 minutes in temperatures above 90 or below 32 degrees Fahrenheit.

(2) The presence of any of the following conditions regarding tethering an unattended dog out of doors shall create a rebuttable presumption that a dog has been the subject of neglect within the meaning of section 5532:

(i) Excessive waste or excrement in the area where the dog is tethered.

(ii) Open sores or wounds on the dog's body.

(iii) The use of a tow or log chain, or a choke, pinch, prong or chain collar.

(b) Construction.--This section shall not be construed to prohibit any of the following:

(1) Tethering a dog while actively engaged in lawful hunting, exhibition, performance events or field training.

(2) Tethering a hunting, sporting or sledding dog breed where tethering is integral to the training, conditioning or purpose of the dog.

(3) Tethering a dog in compliance with the requirements of a camping or recreational area.

(4) Tethering a dog for a period of time, not to exceed one hour, reasonably necessary for the dog or person to complete a temporary task.

Cross References. Section 5536 is referred to in section 5560 of this title.

§ 5537. Selling or using disabled horse.

A person commits a summary offense if the person offers for sale or sells a horse, which by reason of debility, disease or lameness, or for other cause, could not be worked or used without violating the laws against cruelty to animals, or leads, rides, drives or transports any such horse for any purpose, except that of conveying the horse to the nearest available appropriate facility for humane keeping or destruction or for medical or surgical treatment.

§ 5538. Transporting animals in cruel manner.

(a) Offense defined.--A person commits a summary offense if the person carries, or causes or allows to be carried, in or upon any cart or other vehicle whatsoever an animal in a cruel or inhumane manner. The person taking the offender into custody may take charge of the animal and of the vehicle and the vehicle's contents, and deposit the same in a safe place of custody, and the necessary expenses that may be incurred for taking charge of and keeping the same, and sustaining the animal, shall be a lien thereon, to be paid before the same can lawfully be recovered, or the expenses or any part thereof remaining unpaid may be recovered by the person incurring the same from the owner of the animal in an action therefor.

(b) Exception.--For the purposes of this section, it shall not be deemed cruel or inhumane to transport live poultry in crates so long as not more than 15 pounds of live poultry are allocated to each cubic foot of space in the crate.

§ 5539. Transporting equine animals in cruel manner.

Notwithstanding any other provision of law, a person commits a summary offense for each equine animal if the person carries, or causes or allows to be carried, an equine animal in or upon a conveyance or other vehicle whatsoever with two or more levels stacked on top of one another. A person who violates this section on a second or subsequent occasion commits a misdemeanor of the third degree for each equine animal transported.

§ 5540. Hours of labor of animals.

(a) Offense defined.--A person commits a summary offense if the person leads, drives, rides or works or causes or permits another person to lead, drive, ride or work a horse, mule, ox or other animal, whether belonging to the person or in the person's possession or control, for more than 15 hours in a 24-hour period or more than 90 hours in one week.

(b) Construction.--Nothing in this section shall be construed to warrant a person leading, driving, riding or walking an animal for a period less than 15 hours, when doing so shall in any way violate the laws against cruelty to animals.

§ 5541. Cruelty to cow to enhance appearance of udder.

A person commits a summary offense if the person kneads or beats or pads the udder of a cow, or willfully allows it to go unmilked for a period of 24 hours or more, for the purpose of enhancing the appearance or size of the udder of the cow, or by a muzzle or any other device, prevents the cow's calf, if less than six weeks old, from obtaining nourishment, and thereby relieving the udder of the cow, for a period of 24 hours.

§ 5542. Animal mutilation and related offenses.

(a) Cropping of ear.--The following apply:

(1) A person commits an offense under section 5533 (relating to cruelty to animal) if the person crops, trims or cuts off, or causes or procures to be cropped, trimmed or cut off, the whole or part of the ear or ears of a dog.

(2) The provisions of this subchapter shall not prevent a licensed doctor of veterinary medicine from cropping, trimming or cutting off the whole or part of the ear or ears of a dog when the dog is anesthetized and shall not prevent a person from causing or procuring the cropping, trimming or cutting off of a dog's ear or ears by a licensed doctor of veterinary medicine.

(3) The possession by a person of a dog with an ear or ears cropped, trimmed or cut off and with the wound or incision site resulting therefrom unhealed, or any such dog being

found in the charge or custody of any person or confined upon the premises owned by or under the control of any person, shall be prima facie evidence of a violation by the person, except as provided for in this subsection.

(4) A person who procures the cropping, trimming or cutting off of the whole or part of an ear or ears of a dog shall record the procedure. The record shall include the name of the attending licensed doctor of veterinary medicine and the date and location at which the procedure was performed. The record shall be kept as long as the wound or incision site is unhealed and shall be transferred with the dog during that period of time.

(b) Debarking.--The following apply:

(1) A person commits an offense under section 5533 if the person debarks a dog by cutting, causing or procuring the cutting of its vocal cords or by altering, causing or procuring the alteration of a part of its resonance chamber.

(2) The provisions of this subchapter shall not prevent a licensed doctor of veterinary medicine from cutting the vocal cords or otherwise altering the resonance chamber of a dog when the dog is anesthetized and shall not prevent a person from causing or procuring a debarking procedure by a licensed doctor of veterinary medicine.

(3) The possession by a person of a dog with the vocal cords cut or the resonance chamber otherwise altered and with the wound or incision site resulting therefrom unhealed, or any such dog being found in the charge or custody of a person or confined upon the premises owned by or under the control of a person, shall be prima facie evidence of a violation by the person, except as provided in this subsection.

(4) A person who procures the cutting of vocal cords or the alteration of the resonance chamber of a dog shall record the procedure. The record shall include the name of the attending licensed doctor of veterinary medicine and the date and location at which the procedure was performed. The record shall be kept as long as the wound or incision site is unhealed and shall be transferred with the dog during that period of time.

(c) Docking of tail.--The following apply:

(1) A person commits an offense under section 5533 if the person docks, cuts off, causes or procures the docking or cutting off of the tail of a dog over five days old.

(2) The provisions of this subchapter shall not prevent a licensed doctor of veterinary medicine from docking, cutting off or cropping the whole or part of the tail of a dog when the dog is at least 12 weeks of age and the procedure is performed using general anesthesia and shall not prevent a person from causing or procuring the cutting off or docking of a tail of a dog by a licensed doctor of veterinary medicine as provided in this subsection.

(3) The provisions of this subchapter shall not prevent a licensed doctor of veterinary medicine from surgically removing, docking, cutting off or cropping the tail of a dog between five days and 12 weeks of age if, in the licensed doctor of veterinary medicine's professional judgment, the procedure is medically necessary for the health and welfare of the dog. If the procedure is performed, it shall be done in accordance with generally accepted standards of veterinary practice.

(4) The possession by a person of a dog with a tail cut off or docked and with the wound or incision site resulting therefrom unhealed, or any such dog being found in the charge or custody of any person or confined upon the premises owned by or under the control of any person, shall be prima facie evidence of a violation by the person, except as provided in this subsection.

(5) A person who procures the cutting off or docking of a tail of a dog shall record the procedure. The record shall include the name of the attending licensed doctor of veterinary medicine and the date and location at which the procedure was performed. The record shall be kept as long as the wound or incision site is unhealed and shall be transferred with the dog during that period of time.

(d) Surgical birth.--The following apply:

(1) A person commits an offense under section 5533 if the person surgically births or causes or procures a surgical birth.

(2) The provisions of this subchapter shall not prevent a licensed doctor of veterinary medicine from surgically birthing a dog when the dog is anesthetized and shall not prevent a person from causing or procuring a surgical birthing by a licensed doctor of veterinary medicine.

(3) The possession by a person of a dog with a wound or incision site resulting from a surgical birth unhealed, or any such dog being found in the charge or custody of a person or

confined upon the premises owned by or under the control of any person, shall be prima facie evidence of a violation by the person, except as provided in this subsection.

(4) A person who procures the surgical birth of a dog shall record the procedure. The record shall include the name of the attending licensed doctor of veterinary medicine and the date and location at which the procedure was performed. The record shall be kept as long as the wound or incision site is unhealed and shall be transferred with the dog during that period of time.

(5) This subsection shall not apply to personnel required to comply with standards to minimize pain to an animal set forth in section 2143(a)(3) of the Animal Welfare Act (Public Law 89-544, 7 U.S.C. § 2131 et seq.), trained in accordance with section 2143(d) of the Animal Welfare Act, who work in a federally registered research facility required to comply with the Animal Welfare Act under the guidance or oversight of a licensed doctor of veterinary medicine.

(e) **Dewclawing.**--The following apply:

(1) A person commits an offense under section 5533 if the person cuts off or causes or procures the cutting off of the dewclaw of a dog over five days old.

(2) The provisions of this subchapter shall not prevent a licensed doctor of veterinary medicine from cutting the dewclaw and shall not prevent a person from causing or procuring the procedure by a licensed doctor of veterinary medicine.

(3) The possession by a person of a dog with the dewclaw cut off and with the wound or incision site resulting therefrom unhealed, or any such dog being found in the charge or custody of a person or confined upon the premises owned by or under the control of a person, shall be prima facie evidence of a violation by the person, except as provided in this subsection.

(4) A person who procures the cutting off of the dewclaw of a dog shall record the procedure. The record shall include the name of the attending licensed doctor of veterinary medicine and the date and location at which the procedure was performed. The record shall be kept as long as the wound or incision site is unhealed and shall be transferred with the dog during that period of time.

(f) **Additional penalty.**--In addition to any other penalty provided by law, upon conviction for conduct described in this section, the court may order the convicted person to undergo a psychological or psychiatric evaluation and to undergo treatment at the convicted person's expense that the court determines to be appropriate after due consideration of the evaluation.

§ 5543. Animal fighting.

A person commits a felony of the third degree if the person:

(1) for amusement or gain, causes, allows or permits an animal to engage in animal fighting;

(2) receives compensation for the admission of another person to a place kept or used for animal fighting;

(3) owns, possesses, keeps, trains, promotes, purchases, steals or acquires in any manner or knowingly sells an animal for animal fighting;

(4) in any way knowingly encourages, aids or assists therein;

(5) wagers on the outcome of an animal fight;

(6) pays for admission to an animal fight or attends an animal fight as a spectator; or

(7) knowingly permits a place under the person's control or possession to be kept or used for animal fighting.

Cross References. Section 5543 is referred to in sections 5552, 5560 of this title.

§ 5544. Possession of animal fighting paraphernalia.

In addition to any other penalty provided by law, a person commits a misdemeanor of the third degree if the person knowingly owns or possesses animal fighting paraphernalia.

§ 5545. Killing homing pigeons.

A person commits a summary offense if the person shoots, maims or kills an antwerp or homing pigeon, either while on flight or at rest, or detains or entraps a pigeon which carries the name of the pigeon's owner.

§ 5546. Skinning of and selling or buying pelts of dogs and cats.

A person commits a summary offense if the person skins a dog or cat or offers for sale or exchange or offers to buy or exchange the pelt or pelts of a dog or cat.

§ 5547. Live animals as prizes prohibited.

(a) **General rule.**--No person shall give or offer to give away a live animal, except fish, as a prize in a drawing, lottery, contest, sweepstakes or other game. No person operating a drawing, lottery, contest, sweepstakes or other game shall sell or offer to sell a live animal, except fish, in conjunction with the operation of a drawing, lottery, contest, sweepstakes or other game.

(b) Regulating certain actions concerning fowl or rabbits.--No person shall sell, offer for sale, barter or give away baby chickens, ducklings or other fowl under one month of age or rabbits under two months of age as pets, toys, premiums or novelties or color, dye, stain or otherwise change the natural color of baby chickens, ducklings or other fowl or rabbits. This subsection shall not be construed to prohibit the sale or display of baby chickens, ducklings or other fowl or rabbits in proper facilities by persons engaged in the business of selling them for purposes of commercial breeding and raising.

(c) Exception.--

(1) This section shall not apply to a domestic animal given away or sold in connection with an agricultural, educational or vocational program sponsored or sanctioned by the Department of Agriculture.

(2) The Department of Agriculture shall promulgate the rules and regulations necessary to provide the conditions and requirements of live animal offerings under this subsection.

(d) Penalty.--A violation of this section constitutes a summary offense punishable by a fine of not more than $250.

§ 5548. Police animals.

(a) Illegal to taunt police animals.--It shall be unlawful for a person to intentionally or knowingly taunt, torment, tease, beat, kick or strike a police animal. A person who violates the provisions of this subsection commits a felony of the third degree.

(b) Illegal to torture police animals.--It shall be unlawful for a person to intentionally or knowingly torture, mutilate, injure, disable, poison or kill a police animal. A person who violates the provisions of this subsection commits a felony of the second degree.

(c) Restitution.--In a case in which a defendant is convicted of a violation of subsection (a) or (b), the defendant shall be ordered to make restitution to the agency or individual owning the animal for veterinary bills, for replacement costs of the animal if it is disabled or killed and for the salary of the animal's handler for the period of time the handler's services are lost to the agency.

§ 5549. Assault with a biological agent on animal, fowl or honey bees.

(a) Offense defined.--A person commits a felony of the second degree if the person intentionally, knowingly or maliciously exposes or causes to be exposed an animal, fowl or honey bees to a virus, bacteria, prion or other agent which causes infectious disease, including any of the following:

(1) Foot-and-mouth disease.

(2) Bovine spongiform encephalopathy (BSE), commonly known as mad cow disease.

(3) Avian influenza.

(4) Varroa mite.

(b) Restitution.--The person convicted of violating this section shall, in addition to any other sentence imposed, be sentenced to pay the owner of the afflicted animal, fowl or honey bees restitution in an amount equal to the cost of the financial damages incurred as a result of the offense, including the following:

(1) Value of afflicted animal, fowl or honey bees.

(2) Disposal of afflicted animal, fowl or honey bees.

(3) Testing for disease on existing animal.

(4) Cleanup and sanitization of property and buildings on and in which afflicted animals, fowl or honey bees were located.

(5) Liability insurance for cleanup and sanitization workers.

(6) Soil testing of property.

(7) Loss of revenue for the aggrieved owner of afflicted animal, fowl or honey bees.

(c) Exceptions.--The provisions of this section shall not apply to research or veterinarian services, including immunizations, vaccinations or other treatments administered during the normal scope of practice.

§ 5550. Fine and term of imprisonment for summary offense.

Unless otherwise specifically provided, a person convicted of a summary offense under this subchapter shall, upon conviction, be sentenced to pay a fine of not less than $50 nor more than $750 or imprisonment for not more than 90 days, or both.

§ 5551. Power to initiate criminal proceedings.

An agent of a society or association for the prevention of cruelty to animals, incorporated under the laws of this Commonwealth, shall have the same powers to initiate criminal proceedings provided for police officers by the Pennsylvania Rules of Criminal Procedure. An agent of a society or association for the prevention of cruelty to animals, incorporated under the laws of this Commonwealth, shall have standing to request a court of competent jurisdiction to enjoin a violation of this subchapter.

§ 5552. Seizure of animals kept or used for animal fighting.

A police officer or agent of a society or association for the prevention of cruelty to animals incorporated under the laws of this Commonwealth shall have power to seize an animal kept, used or intended to be used for animal fighting. When the seizure is made, the animal or animals seized shall not be deemed absolutely forfeited but shall be held by the officer or agent seizing the animal or animals until a conviction of a person is first obtained for a violation of section 5543 (relating to animal fighting) or forfeiture is obtained under the act of July 9, 2013 (P.L.263, No.50), known as the Costs of Care of Seized Animals Act. The officer or agent making the seizure shall make due return to the issuing authority of the number and kind of animals or creatures seized by the officer or agent. Where an animal is seized, the police officer or agent is authorized to provide the care that is reasonably necessary and, where an animal seized is found to be disabled, injured or diseased beyond reasonable hope of recovery, the police officer or agent is authorized to provide for the humane destruction of the animal. In addition to any other penalty provided by law, the authority imposing sentence upon a conviction for a violation of section 5543 shall order the forfeiture or surrender of an abused or neglected animal of the defendant to a society or association for the prevention of cruelty to animals duly incorporated under the laws of this Commonwealth and shall require that the owner pay the cost of the keeping, care and destruction of the animal.

§ 5553. Search warrants.

Where a violation of this subchapter is alleged, an issuing authority may, in compliance with the applicable provisions of the Pennsylvania Rules of Criminal Procedure, issue to a police officer or an agent of a society or association for the prevention of cruelty to animals duly incorporated under the laws of this Commonwealth a search warrant authorizing the search of a building or an enclosure in which a violation of this subchapter is occurring or has occurred and authorizing the seizure of evidence of the violation, including, but not limited to, the animals which were the subject of the violation. Where an animal seized is found to be neglected or starving, the police officer or agent is authorized to provide the care that is reasonably necessary and, where any animal seized is found to be disabled, injured or diseased beyond reasonable hope of recovery, the police officer or agent is authorized to provide for the humane destruction of the animal. The cost of the keeping, care and destruction of the animal shall be paid by the owner of the animal, and claims for the costs shall constitute a lien upon the animal. In addition to any other penalty provided by law, the authority imposing sentence upon a conviction for a violation of this subchapter may require that the owner pay the cost of the keeping, care and destruction of the animal. No search warrant shall be issued based upon an alleged violation of this subchapter which authorizes a police officer or agent or other person to enter upon or search premises where scientific research work is being conducted by or under the supervision of graduates of duly accredited scientific schools or where biological products are being produced for the care or prevention of disease.

§ 5554. Forfeiture.

(a) General rule.--Except as provided under subsection (b), in addition to any other penalty provided by law, the authority imposing sentence upon a conviction for a violation of this subchapter may order the forfeiture or surrender of an abused or neglected animal of the defendant to a society or association for the prevention of cruelty to animals duly incorporated under the laws of this Commonwealth.

(b) Forfeiture required for felony offense.--If the conviction under this subchapter is for an offense graded as a felony, the authority imposing sentence shall order forfeiture or surrender of an abused or neglected animal of the defendant to a society or association for the prevention of cruelty to animals duly incorporated under the laws of this Commonwealth.

§ 5555. Prohibition of ownership.

Notwithstanding any provision of law and in addition to any other penalty provided by law, the authority imposing sentence upon a conviction for a violation of this subchapter may order the prohibition or limitation of the defendant's ownership, possession, control or custody of animals or employment with the care of animals for a period of time not to exceed the statutory maximum term of imprisonment applicable to the offense for which sentence is being imposed. A humane society police officer, law enforcement officer or State dog warden shall have authority to ensure compliance with this section and may notify the local district attorney who may petition the court to remove animals kept in violation of this section.

§ 5556. Civil immunity for licensed doctors of veterinary medicine, technicians and assistants.

(a) General rule.--A licensed doctor of veterinary medicine, certified veterinary technician or veterinary assistant who reports, in good faith and in the normal course of business, a suspected violation of this subchapter to the proper authority shall not be liable for civil damages as a result of reporting the incident.

(b) Nonapplicability.--Subsection (a) shall not apply to an act or omission intentionally designed to harm or to an act or omission that constitutes gross negligence or willful, wanton or reckless conduct.

§ 5557. Civil immunity for humane society police officers.

(a) General rule.--A humane society police officer acting in good faith and within the scope of the authority provided under this subchapter shall not be liable for civil damages as a result of an act or omission in the course of an investigation or enforcement action.

(b) Nonapplicability.--Subsection (a) shall not apply to an act or omission intentionally designed to harm or to an act or omission that constitutes gross negligence or willful, wanton or reckless conduct.

§ 5558. Representation of humane society by attorney.

Upon prior authorization and approval by the district attorney of the county in which the proceeding is held, an association or agent may be represented in a proceeding under this subchapter by an attorney admitted to practice before the Supreme Court of Pennsylvania and in good standing. Attorney fees shall be borne by the humane society or association that is represented.

§ 5559. Construction of subchapter.

The provisions of this subchapter shall not supersede the act of December 7, 1982 (P.L.784, No.225), known as the Dog Law.

§ 5560. Exemption of normal agricultural operations.

Sections 5532 (relating to neglect of animal), 5533 (relating to cruelty to animal), 5534 (relating to aggravated cruelty to animal), 5536 (relating to tethering of unattended dog) and 5543 (relating to animal fighting) shall not apply to activity undertaken in a normal agricultural operation.

§ 5561. Nonapplicability of subchapter.

(a) Game law.--This subchapter shall not apply to, interfere with or hinder any activity which is authorized or permitted under 34 Pa.C.S. (relating to game) or the regulations promulgated under those laws.

(b) Exemptions.--The provisions of this subchapter shall not apply to the following:

(1) The killing of a dog or cat by the owner of that animal if it is accomplished in accordance with the act of December 22, 1983 (P.L.303, No.83), known as the Animal Destruction Method Authorization Law.

(2) The killing of an animal found pursuing, wounding or killing a domestic animal or domestic fowl.

(3) The killing of an animal or fowl under 34 Pa.C.S. §§ 2384 (relating to declaring dogs public nuisances) and 2385 (relating to destruction of dogs declared public nuisances) or regulations promulgated under 34 Pa.C.S. §§ 2384 and 2385.

(4) Reasonable activity that may be undertaken with vermin control or pest control.

(5) Shooting activities not otherwise prohibited under this subchapter.

(6) Conduct that is lawful under the laws of the United States or this Commonwealth relating to activities undertaken by a research facility that is one of the following:

(i) Registered and inspected under the Animal Welfare Act (Public Law 89-544, 7 U.S.C. § 2131 et seq.).

(ii) Subject to the Public Health Service Policy on Humane Care and Use of Laboratory Animals provided for under the Public Health Service Act (58 Stat. 682, 42 U.S.C. § 201 et seq.).

(iii) Subject to the provisions of 21 CFR Pt. 58 (relating to good laboratory practice for nonclinical laboratory studies) under the Federal Food, Drug, and Cosmetic Act (52 Stat.

1040, 21 U.S.C. § 301 et seq.) or the Public Health Service Act.

CHAPTER 57 WIRETAPPING AND ELECTRONIC SURVEILLANCE

Enactment. Present Chapter 57 was added October 4, 1978, P.L.831, No.164, effective in 60 days.

Prior Provisions. Former Chapter 57, which related to invasion of privacy, was added December 6, 1972, P.L.1482, No.334, and repealed October 4, 1978, P.L.831, No.164, effective in 60 days.

Cross References. Chapter 57 is referred to in section 1522 of Title 4 (Amusements); section 3575 of Title 42 (Judiciary and Judicial Procedure).

SUBCHAPTER A
GENERAL PROVISIONS

Subchapter Heading. The heading of Subchapter A was added October 21, 1988, P.L.1000, No.115, effective immediately.

§ 5701. Short title of chapter.

This chapter shall be known and may be cited as the "Wiretapping and Electronic Surveillance Control Act."

§ 5702. Definitions.

As used in this chapter, the following words and phrases shall have the meanings given to them in this section unless the context clearly indicates otherwise:

"Aggrieved person." A person who was a party to any intercepted wire, electronic or oral communication or a person against whom the interception was directed.

"Aural transfer." A transfer containing the human voice at any point between and including the point of origin and the point of reception.

"Communication common carrier." Any person engaged as a common carrier for hire, in intrastate, interstate or foreign communication by wire or radio or in intrastate, interstate or foreign radio transmission of energy; however, a person engaged in radio broadcasting shall not, while so engaged, be deemed a common carrier.

"Communication service." Any service which provides to users the ability to send or receive wire or electronic communications.

"Communication system." Any wire, radio, electromagnetic, photo-optical or photoelectronic facilities for the transmission of communications and any computer facilities or related electronic equipment for the electronic storage of such communications.

"Contents." As used with respect to any wire, electronic or oral communication, is any information concerning the substance, purport, or meaning of that communication.

"Court." The Superior Court. For the purposes of Subchapter C only, the term shall mean the court of common pleas.

"Crime of violence." Any of the following:

(1) Any of the following crimes:

(i) Murder in any degree as defined in section 2502(a), (b) or (c) (relating to murder).

(ii) Voluntary manslaughter as defined in section 2503 (relating to voluntary manslaughter), drug delivery resulting in death as defined in section 2506(a) (relating to drug delivery resulting in death), aggravated assault as defined in section 2702(a)(1) or (2) (relating to aggravated assault), kidnapping as defined in section 2901(a) or (a.1) (relating to kidnapping), rape as defined in section 3121(a), (c) or (d) (relating to rape), involuntary deviate sexual intercourse as defined in section 3123(a), (b) or (c) (relating to involuntary deviate sexual intercourse), sexual assault as defined in section 3124.1 (relating to sexual assault), aggravated indecent assault as defined in section 3125(a) or (b) (relating to aggravated indecent assault), incest as defined in section 4302(a) or (b) (relating to incest), arson as defined in section 3301(a) (relating to arson and related offenses), burglary as defined in section 3502(a)(1) (relating to burglary), robbery as defined in section 3701(a)(1)(i), (ii) or (iii) (relating to robbery) or robbery of a motor vehicle as defined in section 3702(a) (relating to robbery of a motor vehicle).

(iii) Intimidation of witness or victim as defined in section 4952(a) and (b) (relating to intimidation of witnesses or victims).

(iv) Retaliation against witness, victim or party as defined in section 4953(a) and (b) (relating to retaliation against witness, victim or party).

(v) Criminal attempt as defined in section 901(a) (relating to criminal attempt), criminal solicitation as defined in section 902(a) (relating to criminal solicitation) or criminal conspiracy as defined in section 903(a) (relating to criminal conspiracy) to commit any of the offenses specified in this definition.

(2) Any offense equivalent to an offense under paragraph (1) under the laws of this Commonwealth in effect at the time of the commission of that offense or under the laws of another jurisdiction.

"Electronic communication." Any transfer of signs, signals, writing, images, sounds, data or intelligence of any nature transmitted in whole or in part by a wire, radio, electromagnetic, photoelectronic or photo-optical system, except:

(1) (Deleted by amendment).

(2) Any wire or oral communication.

(3) Any communication made through a tone-only paging device.

(4) Any communication from a tracking device (as defined in this section).

"Electronic communication service." (Deleted by amendment).

"Electronic communication system." (Deleted by amendment).

"Electronic, mechanical or other device." Any device or apparatus, including, but not limited to, an induction coil or a telecommunication identification interception device, that can be used to intercept a wire, electronic or oral communication other than:

(1) Any telephone or telegraph instrument, equipment or facility, or any component thereof, furnished to the subscriber or user by a provider of wire or electronic communication service in the ordinary course of its business, or furnished by such subscriber or user for connection to the facilities of such service and used in the ordinary course of its business, or being used by a communication common carrier in the ordinary course of its business, or by an investigative or law enforcement officer in the ordinary course of his duties.

(2) A hearing aid or similar device being used to correct subnormal hearing to not better than normal.

(3) Equipment or devices used to conduct interceptions under section 5704(15) (relating to exceptions to prohibition of interception and disclosure of communications).

"Electronic storage."

(1) Any temporary, intermediate storage of a wire or electronic communication incidental to the electronic transmission thereof.

(2) Any storage of such a communication by an electronic communication service for purpose of backup protection of the communication.

"Home." The residence of a nonconsenting party to an interception, provided that access to the residence is not generally permitted to members of the public and the party has a reasonable expectation of privacy in the residence under the circumstances.

"In-progress trace." The determination of the origin of a telephonic communication to a known telephone during an interception.

"Intercept." Aural or other acquisition of the contents of any wire, electronic or oral communication through the use of any electronic, mechanical or other device. The term shall include the point at which the contents of the communication are monitored by investigative or law enforcement officers. The term shall not include the acquisition of the contents of a communication made through any electronic, mechanical or other device or telephone instrument to an investigative or law enforcement officer, or between a person and an investigative or law enforcement officer, where the investigative or law enforcement officer poses as an actual person who is the intended recipient of the communication, provided that the Attorney General, a deputy attorney general designated in writing by the Attorney General, a district attorney or an assistant district attorney designated in writing by a district attorney of the county wherein the investigative or law enforcement officer is to receive or make the communication has reviewed the facts and is satisfied that the communication involves suspected criminal activities and has given prior approval for the communication.

"Investigative or law enforcement officer." Any officer of the United States, of another state or political subdivision thereof or of the Commonwealth or political subdivision thereof, who is empowered by law to conduct investigations of or to make arrests for offenses enumerated in this chapter or an equivalent crime in another jurisdiction, and any attorney authorized by law to prosecute or participate in the prosecution of such offense.

"Judge." When referring to a judge authorized to receive applications for, and to enter, orders authorizing interceptions of wire, electronic or oral communications pursuant to Subchapter B (relating to wire, electronic or oral communication), any judge of the Superior Court.

"Mobile communications tracking information." Information generated by a communication common carrier or a communication service which indicates the location of an electronic device supported by the communication common carrier or communication service.

"One call system." A communication system established by users to provide a single telephone number for contractors or designers or any other person to call notifying users of the caller's intent to engage in demolition or excavation work.

"Oral communication." Any oral communication uttered by a person possessing an expectation that such communication is not subject to interception under circumstances justifying such expectation. The term does not include the following:

(1) An electronic communication.

(2) A communication made in the presence of a law enforcement officer on official duty who is in uniform or otherwise clearly identifiable as a law enforcement officer and who is using an electronic, mechanical or other device which has been approved under section 5706(b)(4) (relating to exceptions to prohibitions in possession, sale, distribution, manufacture or advertisement of electronic, mechanical or other devices) to intercept the communication in the course of law enforcement duties. As used in this paragraph only, "law enforcement officer" means a member of the Pennsylvania State Police, an individual employed as a police officer who

holds a current certificate under 53 Pa.C.S. Ch. 21 Subch. D (relating to municipal police education and training), a sheriff or a deputy sheriff.

"Organized crime."

(1) The unlawful activity of an association trafficking in illegal goods or services, including but not limited to, gambling, prostitution, loan sharking, controlled substances, labor racketeering, or other unlawful activities; or

(2) any continuing criminal conspiracy or other unlawful practice which has as its objective:

(i) large economic gain through fraudulent or coercive practices; or

(ii) improper governmental influence.

"Pen register." A device which is used to capture, record or decode electronic or other impulses which identify the numbers dialed or otherwise transmitted, with respect to wire or electronic communications, on the targeted telephone. The term includes a device which is used to record or decode electronic or other impulses which identify the existence of incoming and outgoing wire or electronic communications on the targeted telephone. The term does not include a device used by a provider or customer of a wire or electronic communication service for billing, or recording as an incident to billing, for communication service provided by the provider, or any device used by a provider, or customer of a wire communication service for cost accounting or other like purposes in the ordinary course of business.

"Person." Any employee, or agent of the United States or any state or political subdivision thereof, and any individual, partnership, association, joint stock company, trust or corporation.

"Readily accessible to the general public." As used with respect to a radio communication, that such communication is not:

(1) scrambled or encrypted;

(2) transmitted using modulation techniques of which the essential parameters have been withheld from the public with the intention of preserving the privacy of the communication;

(3) carried on a subscriber or other signal subsidiary to a radio transmission;

(4) transmitted over a communication system provided by a common carrier, unless

the communication is a tone-only paging system communication; or

(5) transmitted on frequencies allocated under 47 CFR Parts 25, 74D, E, F or 94, unless, in the case of a communication transmitted on a frequency allocated under Part 74 which is not exclusively allocated to broadcast auxiliary services, the communication is a two-way voice communication by radio.

"Remote computing service." The provision to the public of computer storage or processing services by means of an electronic communications system.

"Signed, written record." A memorialization of the contents of any wire, electronic or oral communication intercepted in accordance with this subchapter, including the name of the investigative or law enforcement officer who transcribed the record, kept in electronic, paper or any form. The signature of the transcribing officer shall not be required to be written, but may be electronic.

"State." Any state of the United States, the District of Columbia, the Commonwealth of Puerto Rico and any territory or possession of the United States.

"Suspected criminal activity." A particular offense that has been, is or is about to occur as set forth under section 5709(3)(ii) (relating to application for order), any communications to be intercepted as set forth under section 5709(3)(iii) or any of the criminal activity set forth under section 5709(3)(iv) establishing probable cause for the issuance of an order.

"Telecommunication identification interception device." Any equipment or device capable of intercepting any electronic communication which contains any electronic serial number, mobile identification number, personal identification number or other identification number assigned by a telecommunication service provider for activation or operation of a telecommunication device.

"Tracking device." An electronic or mechanical device which permits only the tracking of the movement of a person or object.

"Trap and trace device." A device which captures the incoming electronic or other impulses which identify the originating number of an instrument or device from which a wire or communication was transmitted. The term includes caller ID, deluxe caller ID or any other features available to ascertain the telephone number, location or subscriber information of a facility contacting the facility whose communications are to be intercepted.

"User." Any person or entity who:

(1) uses an electronic communication service; and

(2) is duly authorized by the provider of the service to engage in the use.

"Wire communication." Any aural transfer made in whole or in part through the use of facilities for the transmission of communication by wire, cable or other like connection between the point of origin and the point of reception, including the use of such a connection in a switching station, furnished or operated by a telephone, telegraph or radio company for hire as a communication common carrier.

(Dec. 23, 1981, P.L.593, No.175, eff. 60 days; Oct. 21, 1988, P.L.1000, No.115, eff. imd.; Feb. 18, 1998, P.L.102, No.19, eff. imd.; Dec. 9, 2002, P.L.1350, No.162, eff. 60 days; Oct. 25, 2012, P.L.1634, No.202, eff. 60 days; July 7, 2017, P.L.304, No.22, eff. 60 days)

2017 Amendment. Act 22 amended the def. of "oral communication."

2012 Amendment. Act 202 amended the defs. of "intercept," "trap and trace device" and "wire communication," added the defs. of "communication service," "communication system," "crime of violence," "mobile communications tracking information" and "signed, written record" and deleted the defs. of "electronic communication service" and "electronic communication system."

2002 Amendment. Act 162 added the def. of "suspected criminal activity."

1998 Amendment. Act 19 amended the defs. of "electronic communication," "electronic, mechanical or other device," "intercept," "investigative or law enforcement officer," "judge," "pen register" and "wire communication" and added the defs. of "home," "state" and "telecommunication identification interception device."

Cross References. Section 5702 is referred to in sections 911, 5706, 5903, 6321 of this title; section 901 of Title 34 (Game); section 67A07 of Title 42 (Judiciary and Judicial Procedure); sections 57A12, 57B02 of Title 53 (Municipalities Generally); section 2604.1 of Title 66 (Public Utilities).

SUBCHAPTER B
WIRE, ELECTRONIC OR ORAL
COMMUNICATION

Subchapter Heading. The heading of Subchapter B was added October 21, 1988, P.L.1000, No.115, effective immediately.

Cross References. Subchapter B is referred to in section 5702 of this title.

§ 5703. Interception, disclosure or use of wire, electronic or oral communications.

Except as otherwise provided in this chapter, a person is guilty of a felony of the third degree if he:

(1) intentionally intercepts, endeavors to intercept, or procures any other person to intercept or endeavor to intercept any wire, electronic or oral communication;

(2) intentionally discloses or endeavors to disclose to any other person the contents of any wire, electronic or oral communication, or evidence derived therefrom, knowing or having reason to know that the information was obtained through the interception of a wire, electronic or oral communication; or

(3) intentionally uses or endeavors to use the contents of any wire, electronic or oral communication, or evidence derived therefrom, knowing or having reason to know, that the information was obtained through the interception of a wire, electronic or oral communication.

(Oct. 21, 1988, P.L.1000, No.115, eff. imd.)

§ 5704. Exceptions to prohibition of interception and disclosure of communications.

It shall not be unlawful and no prior court approval shall be required under this chapter for:

(1) An operator of a switchboard, or an officer, agent or employee of a provider of wire or electronic communication service, whose facilities are used in the transmission of a wire communication, to intercept, disclose or use that communication in the normal course of his employment while engaged in any activity which is a necessary incident to the rendition of

his service or to the protection of the rights or property of the provider of wire or electronic communication service. However, no provider of wire or electronic communication service shall utilize service observing or random monitoring except for mechanical or service quality control checks.

(2) Any investigative or law enforcement officer or any person acting at the direction or request of an investigative or law enforcement officer to intercept a wire, electronic or oral communication involving suspected criminal activities, including, but not limited to, the crimes enumerated in section 5708 (relating to order authorizing interception of wire, electronic or oral communications), where:

(i) (Deleted by amendment).

(ii) one of the parties to the communication has given prior consent to such interception. However, no interception under this paragraph shall be made unless the Attorney General or a deputy attorney general designated in writing by the Attorney General, or the district attorney, or an assistant district attorney designated in writing by the district attorney, of the county wherein the interception is to be initiated, has reviewed the facts and is satisfied that the consent is voluntary and has given prior approval for the interception; however, such interception shall be subject to the recording and record keeping requirements of section 5714(a) (relating to recording of intercepted communications) and that the Attorney General, deputy attorney general, district attorney or assistant district attorney authorizing the interception shall be the custodian of recorded evidence obtained therefrom;

(iii) the investigative or law enforcement officer meets in person with a suspected felon and wears a concealed electronic or mechanical device capable of intercepting or recording oral communications. However, no interception under this subparagraph may be used in any criminal prosecution except for a prosecution involving harm done to the investigative or law enforcement officer. This subparagraph shall not be construed to limit the interception and disclosure authority provided for in this subchapter; or

(iv) the requirements of this subparagraph are met. If an oral interception otherwise authorized under this paragraph will take place in the home of a nonconsenting party, then, in addition to the requirements of subparagraph (ii), the interception shall not be conducted until an order is first obtained from the president judge, or his designee who shall also be a judge, of a court of common pleas, authorizing such in-home interception, based upon an affidavit by an investigative or law enforcement officer that establishes probable cause for the issuance of such an order. No such order or affidavit shall be required where probable cause and exigent circumstances exist. For the purposes of this paragraph, an oral interception shall be deemed to take place in the home of a nonconsenting party only if both the consenting and nonconsenting parties are physically present in the home at the time of the interception.

(3) Police and emergency communications systems to record telephone communications coming into and going out of the communications system of the Pennsylvania Emergency Management Agency or a police department, fire department or county emergency center, if:

(i) the telephones thereof are limited to the exclusive use of the communication system for administrative purposes and provided the communication system employs a periodic warning which indicates to the parties to the conversation that the call is being recorded;

(ii) all recordings made pursuant to this clause, all notes made therefrom, and all transcriptions thereof may be destroyed at any time, unless required with regard to a pending matter; and

(iii) at least one nonrecorded telephone line is made available for public use at the Pennsylvania Emergency Management Agency and at each police department, fire department or county emergency center.

(4) A person, to intercept a wire, electronic or oral communication, where all parties to the communication have given prior consent to such interception.

(5) Any investigative or law enforcement officer, or communication common carrier acting at the direction of an investigative or law enforcement officer or in the normal course of its business, to use a pen register, trap and trace device or telecommunication identification interception device as provided in Subchapter E (relating to pen registers, trap and trace devices and telecommunication identification interception devices).

(6) Personnel of any public utility to record telephone conversations with utility

customers or the general public relating to receiving and dispatching of emergency and service calls provided there is, during such recording, a periodic warning which indicates to the parties to the conversation that the call is being recorded.

(7) A user, or any officer, employee or agent of such user, to record telephone communications between himself and a contractor or designer, or any officer, employee or agent of such contractor or designer, pertaining to excavation or demolition work or other related matters, if the user or its agent indicates to the parties to the conversation that the call will be or is being recorded. As used in this paragraph, the terms "user," "contractor," "demolition work," "designer" and "excavation work" shall have the meanings given to them in the act of December 10, 1974 (P.L.852, No.287), referred to as the Underground Utility Line Protection Law; and a one call system shall be considered for this purpose to be an agent of any user which is a member thereof.

(8) A provider of electronic communication service to record the fact that a wire or electronic communication was initiated or completed in order to protect the provider, another provider furnishing service toward the completion of the wire or electronic communication, or a user of that service, from fraudulent, unlawful or abusive use of the service.

(9) A person or entity providing electronic communication service to the public to divulge the contents of any such communication:

(i) as otherwise authorized in this section or section 5717 (relating to investigative disclosure or use of contents of wire, electronic or oral communications or derivative evidence);

(ii) with the lawful consent of the originator or any addressee or intended recipient of the communication;

(iii) to a person employed or authorized, or whose facilities are used, to forward the communication to its destination; or

(iv) which were inadvertently obtained by the service provider and which appear to pertain to the commission of a crime, if such divulgence is made to a law enforcement agency.

A person or entity providing electronic communication service to the public shall not intentionally divulge the contents of any communication (other than one directed to the person or entity, or an agent thereof) while in transmission of that service to any person or entity other than an addressee or intended recipient of the communication or an agent of the addressee or intended recipient.

(10) Any person:

(i) to intercept or access an electronic communication made through an electronic communication system configured so that the electronic communication is readily accessible to the general public;

(ii) to intercept any radio communication which is transmitted:

(A) by a station for the use of the general public, or which relates to ships, aircraft, vehicles or persons in distress;

(B) by any governmental, law enforcement, civil defense, private land mobile or public safety communication system, including police and fire systems, readily accessible to the general public;

(C) by a station operating on an authorized frequency within the bands allocated to the amateur, citizens band or general mobile radio services; or

(D) by any marine or aeronautical communication system;

(iii) to engage in any conduct which:

(A) is prohibited by section 633 of the Communications Act of 1934 (48 Stat. 1105, 47 U.S.C. § 553); or

(B) is excepted from the application of section 705(a) of the Communications Act of 1934 (47 U.S.C. § 605(a)) by section 705(b) of that act (47 U.S.C. § 605(b)); or

(iv) to intercept any wire or electronic communication the transmission of which is causing harmful interference to any lawfully operating station, to the extent necessary to identify the source of the interference.

(11) Other users of the same frequency to intercept any radio communication made through a system which utilizes frequencies monitored by individuals engaged in the provisions or use of the system, if the communication is not scrambled or encrypted.

(12) Any investigative or law enforcement officer or any person acting at the direction or request of an investigative or law enforcement officer to intercept a wire or oral communication involving suspected criminal activities where the officer or the person is a party to the communication and there is reasonable cause to believe that:

(i) the other party to the communication is either:

(A) holding a hostage; or

(B) has barricaded himself and taken a position of confinement to avoid apprehension; and

(ii) that party:

(A) may resist with the use of weapons; or

(B) is threatening suicide or harm to himself or others.

(13) An investigative officer, a law enforcement officer or employees of the Department of Corrections for State correctional facilities to intercept, record, monitor or divulge any oral communication, electronic communication or wire communication from or to an inmate in a facility under the following conditions:

(i) The Department of Corrections shall adhere to the following procedures and restrictions when intercepting, recording, monitoring or divulging any oral communication, electronic communication or wire communication from or to an inmate in a State correctional facility as provided for by this paragraph:

(A) Before the implementation of this paragraph, all inmates of the facility shall be notified in writing that, as of the effective date of this paragraph, their oral communication, electronic communication or wire communication may be intercepted, recorded, monitored or divulged.

(B) Unless otherwise provided for in this paragraph, after intercepting or recording an oral communication, electronic communication or wire communication, only the superintendent, warden or a designee of the superintendent or warden or other chief administrative official or his or her designee, or law enforcement officers shall have access to that recording.

(C) The contents of an intercepted and recorded oral communication, electronic communication or wire communication shall be divulged only as is necessary to safeguard the orderly operation of the facility, in response to a court order or in the prosecution or investigation of any crime.

(ii) So as to safeguard the attorney-client privilege, the Department of Corrections shall not intercept, record, monitor or divulge an oral communication, electronic communication or wire communication between an inmate and an attorney.

(iii) Persons who are engaging in an oral communication, electronic communication or wire communication with an inmate shall be notified that the communication may be recorded or monitored. Notice may be provided by any means reasonably designed to inform the noninmate party of the recording or monitoring.

(iv) The Department of Corrections shall promulgate guidelines to implement the provisions of this paragraph for State correctional facilities.

(14) An investigative officer, a law enforcement officer or employees of a county correctional facility to intercept, record, monitor or divulge an oral communication, electronic communication or wire communication from or to an inmate in a facility under the following conditions:

(i) The county correctional facility shall adhere to the following procedures and restrictions when intercepting, recording, monitoring or divulging an oral communication, electronic communication or wire communication from or to an inmate in a county correctional facility as provided for by this paragraph:

(A) Before the implementation of this paragraph, all inmates of the facility shall be notified in writing that, as of the effective date of this paragraph, their oral communications, electronic communications or wire communications may be intercepted, recorded, monitored or divulged.

(B) Unless otherwise provided for in this paragraph, after intercepting or recording an oral communication, electronic communication or wire communication, only the superintendent, warden or a designee of the superintendent or warden or other chief administrative official or his or her designee, or law enforcement officers shall have access to that recording.

(C) The contents of an intercepted and recorded oral communication, electronic communication or wire communication shall be divulged only as is necessary to safeguard the orderly operation of the facility, in response to a court order or in the prosecution or investigation of any crime.

(ii) So as to safeguard the attorney-client privilege, the county correctional facility shall not intercept, record, monitor or divulge an oral communication, electronic communication or wire communication between an inmate and an attorney.

(iii) Persons who are engaging in an oral communication, electronic communication or wire communication with an inmate shall be notified that the communication may be recorded or monitored. Notice may be provided by any means reasonably designed to inform the noninmate party of the recording or monitoring.

(iv) The superintendent, warden or a designee of the superintendent or warden or other chief administrative official of the county correctional system shall promulgate guidelines to implement the provisions of this paragraph for county correctional facilities.

(15) The personnel of a business engaged in telephone marketing or telephone customer service by means of wire, oral or electronic communication to intercept such marketing or customer service communications where such interception is made for the sole purpose of training, quality control or monitoring by the business, provided that one party involved in the communications has consented to such intercept. Any communications recorded pursuant to this paragraph may only be used by the business for the purpose of training or quality control. Unless otherwise required by Federal or State law, communications recorded pursuant to this paragraph shall be destroyed within one year from the date of recording.

(16) (Deleted by amendment).

(17) Any victim, witness or private detective licensed under the act of August 21, 1953 (P.L.1273, No.361), known as The Private Detective Act of 1953, to intercept the contents of any wire, electronic or oral communication, if that person is under a reasonable suspicion that the intercepted party is committing, about to commit or has committed a crime of violence and there is reason to believe that evidence of the crime of violence may be obtained from the interception.

(18) A person to intercept oral communications for disciplinary or security purposes on a school bus or school vehicle, as those terms are defined in 75 Pa.C.S. § 102 (relating to definitions), if all of the following conditions are met:

(i) The school board has adopted a policy that authorizes audio interception on school buses or school vehicles for disciplinary or security purposes.

(ii) Each school year, the school board includes the policy in a student handbook and in any other publication of the school entity that sets forth the comprehensive rules, procedures and standards of conduct for the school entity.

(iii) The school board posts a notice that students may be audiotaped, which notice is clearly visible on each school bus or school vehicle that is furnished with audio-recording equipment.

(iv) The school entity posts a notice of the policy on the school entity's publicly accessible Internet website.

This paragraph shall not apply when a school bus or school vehicle is used for a purpose that is not school related.

(July 10, 1981, P.L.227, No.72, eff. 60 days; Dec. 23, 1981, P.L.593, No.175, eff. 60 days; Oct. 21, 1988, P.L.1000, No.115, eff. imd.; Sept. 26, 1995, 1st Sp.Sess., P.L.1056, No.20, eff. 60 days; Dec. 19, 1996, P.L.1458, No.186, eff. 60 days; Feb. 18, 1998, P.L.102, No.19, eff. imd.; June 11, 2002, P.L.367, No.52, eff. imd.; Oct. 25, 2012, P.L.1634, No.202, eff. 60 days; Feb. 4, 2014, P.L.21, No.9; June 23, 2016, P.L.392, No.56, eff. 60 days; July 7, 2017, P.L.304, No.22, eff. 60 days)

2017 Amendment. Act 22 amended pars. (13) and (14) and deleted par. (16).

2016 Amendment. Act 56 amended par. (18).

2014 Amendment. Act 9 amended par. (16) and added par. (18), effective in 60 days as to par. (16) and immediately as to the remainder of the section.

2012 Amendment. Act 202 amended pars. (2)(ii), (12)(ii), (13)(i)(B) and (14)(i)(B) and added par. (17).

1998 Amendment. Act 19 amended the intro. par. and pars. (2), (5) and (9) and added par. (15).

1996 Amendment. Act 186 amended par. (2) and added par. (14).

1995 Amendment. Act 20, 1st Sp.Sess., added par. (13).

Cross References. Section 5704 is referred to in sections 5702, 5706, 5717, 5720, 5721.1, 5742, 5747, 5749, 5782 of this title; section 901 of Title 30 (Fish); section 901 of Title 34 (Game).

§ 5705. Possession, sale, distribution, manufacture or advertisement of electronic, mechanical or other devices and telecommunication identification interception devices.

Except as otherwise specifically provided in section 5706 (relating to exceptions to prohibitions in possession, sale, distribution, manufacture or advertisement of electronic, mechanical or other devices), a person is guilty of a felony of the third degree if he does any of the following:

(1) Intentionally possesses an electronic, mechanical or other device, knowing or having reason to know that the design of such device renders it primarily useful for the purpose of the surreptitious interception of a wire, electronic or oral communication.

(2) Intentionally sells, transfers or distributes an electronic, mechanical or other device, knowing or having reason to know that the design of such device renders it primarily useful for the purpose of the surreptitious interception of a wire, electronic or oral communication.

(3) Intentionally manufactures or assembles an electronic, mechanical or other device, knowing or having reason to know that the design of such device renders it primarily useful for the purpose of the surreptitious interception of a wire, electronic or oral communication.

(4) Intentionally places in any newspaper, magazine, handbill, or other publication any advertisement of an electronic, mechanical or other device, knowing or having reason to know that the design of such device renders it primarily useful for the purpose of the surreptitious interception of a wire, electronic or oral communication or of an electronic, mechanical or other device where such advertisement promotes the use of such device for the purpose of the surreptitious interception of a wire, electronic or oral communication.

(5) Intentionally possesses a telecommunication identification interception device.

(Oct. 21, 1988, P.L.1000, No.115, eff. imd.; Oct. 25, 2012, P.L.1634, No.202, eff. 60 days)

2012 Amendment. Act 202 amended the section heading and added par. (5).

§ 5706. Exceptions to prohibitions in possession, sale, distribution, manufacture or advertisement of electronic, mechanical or other devices.

(a) Unlawful activities.--It shall not be unlawful under this chapter for:

(1) a provider of wire or electronic communication service or an officer, agent or employee of, or a person under contract with, such a provider, in the normal course of the business of providing the wire or electronic communication service; or

(2) a person under contract with the United States, the Commonwealth or a political subdivision thereof, a state or a political subdivision thereof, or an officer, agent or employee of the United States, the Commonwealth or a political subdivision thereof, or a state or a political subdivision thereof,

to possess, sell, distribute, manufacture, assemble or advertise an electronic, mechanical or other device, while acting in furtherance of the appropriate activities of the United States, the Commonwealth or a political subdivision thereof, a state or a political subdivision thereof or a provider of wire or electronic communication service.

(b) Responsibility.--

(1) Except as provided under paragraph (2), the Attorney General and the district attorney or their designees so designated in writing shall have the sole responsibility to buy, possess and loan any electronic, mechanical or other device which is to be used by investigative or law enforcement officers for purposes of interception as authorized under section 5704(2), (5) and (12) (relating to exceptions to prohibition of interception and disclosure of communications), 5712 (relating to issuance of order and effect), 5713 (relating to emergency situations) or 5713.1 (relating to emergency hostage and barricade situations).

(2) The division or bureau or section of the Pennsylvania State Police responsible for conducting the training in the technical aspects of wiretapping and electronic surveillance as required by section 5724 (relating to training) may buy and possess any electronic, mechanical or other device which is to be used by investigative or law enforcement officers for purposes of interception as authorized under section 5704(2), (5) and (12), 5712, 5713 or 5713.1 for the purpose of training. However, any electronic, mechanical or other device bought or possessed under this provision may be loaned to or used by investigative or law enforcement officers for purposes of interception as authorized under section

5704(2), (5) and (12), 5712, 5713 or 5713.1 only upon written approval by the Attorney General or a deputy attorney general designated in writing by the Attorney General or the district attorney or an assistant district attorney designated in writing by the district attorney of the county wherein the suspected criminal activity has been, is or is about to occur.

(3) With the permission of the Attorney General or a district attorney who has designated any supervising law enforcement officer for purposes of interceptions as authorized under section 5713.1, the law enforcement agency which employs the supervising law enforcement officer may buy, possess, loan or borrow any electronic, mechanical or other device which is to be used by investigative or law enforcement officers at the direction of the supervising law enforcement officer solely for the purpose of interception as authorized under sections 5704(12) and 5713.1.

(4) The Pennsylvania State Police shall annually establish equipment standards for any electronic, mechanical or other device which is to be used by law enforcement officers for purposes of recording a communication under circumstances within paragraph (2) of the definition of "oral communication" in section 5702 (relating to definitions). The equipment standards shall be published annually in the Pennsylvania Bulletin.

(5) The Pennsylvania State Police shall annually establish and publish standards in the Pennsylvania Bulletin for the secure onsite and off-site storage of an audio recording made in accordance with paragraph (4) or any accompanying video recording. The standards shall comply with the Federal Bureau of Investigation's Criminal Justice Information Services (CJIS) Security Policy.

(6) A vendor to law enforcement agencies which stores data related to audio recordings and video recordings shall, at a minimum, comply with the standards set forth by the Pennsylvania State Police under paragraphs (4) and (5). Law enforcement agencies under contract with a vendor for the storage of data before the effective date of this paragraph shall comply with paragraphs (4) and (5) and this paragraph upon expiration or renewal of the contract.

(Oct. 21, 1988, P.L.1000, No.115, eff. imd.; Feb. 18, 1998, P.L.102, No.19, eff. imd.; June 11, 2002, P.L.367, No.52, eff. imd.; Dec. 9, 2002, P.L.1350, No.162, eff. 60 days; July 7, 2017, P.L.304, No.22, eff. 60 days)

2017 Amendment. Act 22 amended subsec. (b).

Cross References. Section 5706 is referred to in sections 5702, 5705 of this title; section 901 of Title 34 (Game); section 67A07 of Title 42 (Judiciary and Judicial Procedure).

§ 5707. Seizure and forfeiture of electronic, mechanical or other devices.

Any electronic, mechanical or other device possessed, used, sent, distributed, manufactured, or assembled in violation of this chapter is hereby declared to be contraband and may be seized and forfeited to the Commonwealth in accordance with 42 Pa.C.S. §§ 5803 (relating to asset forfeiture), 5805 (relating to forfeiture procedure), 5806 (relating to motion for return of property), 5807 (relating to restrictions on use), 5807.1 (relating to prohibition on adoptive seizures) and 5808 (relating to exceptions).

(Oct. 21, 1988, P.L.1000, No.115, eff. imd.; June 29, 2017, P.L.247, No.13, eff. July 1, 2017)

Cross References. Section 5707 is referred to in section 5803 of Title 42 (Judiciary and Judicial Procedure).

§ 5708. Order authorizing interception of wire, electronic or oral communications.

The Attorney General, or, during the absence or incapacity of the Attorney General, a deputy attorney general designated in writing by the Attorney General, or the district attorney or, during the absence or incapacity of the district attorney, an assistant district attorney designated in writing by the district attorney of the county wherein the suspected criminal activity has been, is or is about to occur, may make written application to any Superior Court judge for an order authorizing the interception of a wire, electronic or oral communication by the investigative or law enforcement officers or agency having responsibility for an investigation involving suspected criminal activities when such interception may provide evidence of the commission of any of the following offenses, or may provide evidence aiding in the apprehension of the perpetrator or perpetrators of any of the following offenses:

(1) Under this title:

Section 911 (relating to corrupt organizations)

Section 2501 (relating to criminal homicide)

Section 2502 (relating to murder)

Section 2503 (relating to voluntary manslaughter)

Section 2702 (relating to aggravated assault)

Section 2706 (relating to terroristic threats)

Section 2709.1 (relating to stalking)

Section 2716 (relating to weapons of mass destruction)

Section 2901 (relating to kidnapping)

Section 3011 (relating to trafficking in individuals)

Section 3012 (relating to involuntary servitude)

Section 3121 (relating to rape)

Section 3123 (relating to involuntary deviate sexual intercourse)

Section 3124.1 (relating to sexual assault)

Section 3125 (relating to aggravated indecent assault)

Section 3301 (relating to arson and related offenses)

Section 3302 (relating to causing or risking catastrophe)

Section 3502 (relating to burglary)

Section 3701 (relating to robbery)

Section 3921 (relating to theft by unlawful taking or disposition)

Section 3922 (relating to theft by deception)

Section 3923 (relating to theft by extortion)

Section 4701 (relating to bribery in official and political matters)

Section 4702 (relating to threats and other improper influence in official and political matters)

Section 5512 (relating to lotteries, etc.)

Section 5513 (relating to gambling devices, gambling, etc.)

Section 5514 (relating to pool selling and bookmaking)

Section 5516 (relating to facsimile weapons of mass destruction)

Section 6318 (relating to unlawful contact with minor)

(2) Under this title, where such offense is dangerous to life, limb or property and punishable by imprisonment for more than one year:

Section 910 (relating to manufacture, distribution or possession of devices for theft of telecommunications services)

Section 2709(a)(4), (5), (6) or (7) (relating to harassment)

Section 3925 (relating to receiving stolen property)

Section 3926 (relating to theft of services)

Section 3927 (relating to theft by failure to make required disposition of funds received)

Section 3933 (relating to unlawful use of computer)

Section 4108 (relating to commercial bribery and breach of duty to act disinterestedly)

Section 4109 (relating to rigging publicly exhibited contest)

Section 4117 (relating to insurance fraud)

Section 4305 (relating to dealing in infant children)

Section 4902 (relating to perjury)

Section 4909 (relating to witness or informant taking bribe)

Section 4911 (relating to tampering with public records or information)

Section 4952 (relating to intimidation of witnesses or victims)

Section 4953 (relating to retaliation against witness or victim)

Section 5101 (relating to obstructing administration of law or other governmental function)

Section 5111 (relating to dealing in proceeds of unlawful activities)

Section 5121 (relating to escape)

Section 5902 (relating to prostitution and related offenses)

Section 5903 (relating to obscene and other sexual materials and performances)

Section 7313 (relating to buying or exchanging Federal Supplemental Nutrition Assistance Program (SNAP) benefit coupons, stamps, authorization cards or access devices)

(3) Under the act of March 4, 1971 (P.L.6, No.2), known as the Tax Reform Code of 1971, where such offense is dangerous to life, limb or property and punishable by imprisonment for more than one year:

Section 1272 (relating to sales of unstamped cigarettes)

Section 1273 (relating to possession of unstamped cigarettes)

Section 1274 (relating to counterfeiting)

(4) Any offense set forth under section 13(a) of the act of April 14, 1972 (P.L.233,

No.64), known as The Controlled Substance, Drug, Device and Cosmetic Act, not including the offense described in clause (31) of section 13(a).

(5) Any offense set forth under the act of November 15, 1972 (P.L.1227, No.272).

(6) Any conspiracy to commit any of the offenses set forth in this section.

(7) Under the act of November 24, 1998 (P.L.874, No.110), known as the Motor Vehicle Chop Shop and Illegally Obtained and Altered Property Act.

(Dec. 2, 1983, P.L.248, No.67, eff. imd.; Oct. 21, 1988, P.L.1000, No.115, eff. imd.; Feb. 2, 1990, P.L.4, No.3, eff. imd.; Feb. 18, 1998, P.L.102, No.19, eff. imd.; Dec. 21, 1998, P.L.1086, No.145, eff. 60 days; June 28, 2002, P.L.481, No.82, eff. 60 days; Nov. 20, 2002, P.L.1104, No.134, eff. 60 days; Dec. 9, 2002, P.L.1350, No.162, eff. 60 days; Dec. 9, 2002, P.L.1759, No.218, eff. 60 days; Nov. 9, 2006, P.L.1340, No.139, eff. 60 days; July 2, 2014, P.L.945, No.105, eff. 60 days; Oct. 24, 2018, P.L.1159, No.160, eff. 60 days)

2018 Amendment. Act 160 amended par. (2).

2014 Amendment. Act 105 amended par. (1).

2002 Amendments. Act 82 amended par. (1), Act 134 amended par. (1), Act 162 amended the entire section and Act 218 amended pars. (1) and (2). Act 162 overlooked the amendment by Act 134 and Act 218 overlooked the amendments by Acts 134 and 162, but the amendments do not conflict in substance and have been given effect in setting forth the text of section 5708.

Effective Date. After January 20, 2003, and before February 7, 2003, section 5708 will reflect only the amendment by Act 134, as follows:

§ 5708. Order authorizing interception of wire, electronic or oral communications.

The Attorney General, or, during the absence or incapacity of the Attorney General, a deputy attorney general designated in writing by the Attorney General, or the district attorney or, during the absence or incapacity of the district attorney, an assistant district attorney designated in writing by the district attorney of the county wherein the interception is to be made, may make written application to any Superior Court judge for an order authorizing the interception of a wire, electronic or oral

communication by the investigative or law enforcement officers or agency having responsibility for an investigation involving suspected criminal activities when such interception may provide evidence of the commission of any of the following offenses, or may provide evidence aiding in the apprehension of the perpetrator or perpetrators of any of the following offenses:

(1) Under this title:

Section 911 (relating to corrupt organizations)

Section 2501 (relating to criminal homicide)

Section 2502 (relating to murder)

Section 2503 (relating to voluntary manslaughter)

Section 2702 (relating to aggravated assault)

Section 2706 (relating to terroristic threats)

Section 2709(b) (relating to harassment and stalking)

Section 2716 (relating to weapons of mass destruction)

Section 2901 (relating to kidnapping)

Section 3121 (relating to rape)

Section 3123 (relating to involuntary deviate sexual intercourse)

Section 3124.1 (relating to sexual assault)

Section 3125 (relating to aggravated indecent assault)

Section 3301 (relating to arson and related offenses)

Section 3302 (relating to causing or risking catastrophe)

Section 3502 (relating to burglary)

Section 3701 (relating to robbery)

Section 3921 (relating to theft by unlawful taking or disposition)

Section 3922 (relating to theft by deception)

Section 3923 (relating to theft by extortion)

Section 4701 (relating to bribery in official and political matters)

Section 4702 (relating to threats and other improper influence in official and political matters)

Section 5512 (relating to lotteries, etc.)

Section 5513 (relating to gambling devices, gambling, etc.)

Section 5514 (relating to pool selling and bookmaking)

Section 5516 (relating to facsimile weapons of mass destruction)

Section 6318 (relating to unlawful contact with minor)

(2) Under this title, where such offense is dangerous to life, limb or property and punishable by imprisonment for more than one year:

Section 910 (relating to manufacture, distribution or possession of devices for theft of telecommunications services)

Section 3925 (relating to receiving stolen property)

Section 3926 (relating to theft of services)

Section 3927 (relating to theft by failure to make required disposition of funds received)

Section 3933 (relating to unlawful use of computer)

Section 4108 (relating to commercial bribery and breach of duty to act disinterestedly)

Section 4109 (relating to rigging publicly exhibited contest)

Section 4117 (relating to insurance fraud)

Section 4305 (relating to dealing in infant children)

Section 4902 (relating to perjury)

Section 4909 (relating to witness or informant taking bribe)

Section 4911 (relating to tampering with public records or information)

Section 4952 (relating to intimidation of witnesses or victims)

Section 4953 (relating to retaliation against witness or victim)

Section 5101 (relating to obstructing administration of law or other governmental function)

Section 5111 (relating to dealing in proceeds of unlawful activities)

Section 5121 (relating to escape)

Section 5504 (relating to harassment by communication or address)

Section 5902 (relating to prostitution and related offenses)

Section 5903 (relating to obscene and other sexual materials and performances)

Section 7313 (relating to buying or exchanging Federal food order coupons, stamps, authorization cards or access devices)

(3) Under the act of March 4, 1971 (P.L.6, No.2), known as the Tax Reform Code of 1971, where such offense is dangerous to life, limb or property and punishable by imprisonment for more than one year:

Section 1272 (relating to sales of unstamped cigarettes)

Section 1273 (relating to possession of unstamped cigarettes)

Section 1274 (relating to counterfeiting)

(4) Any offense set forth under section 13(a) of the act of April 14, 1972 (P.L.233, No.64), known as The Controlled Substance, Drug, Device and Cosmetic Act, not including the offense described in clause (31) of section 13(a).

(5) Any offense set forth under the act of November 15, 1972 (P.L.1227, No.272).

(6) Any conspiracy to commit any of the offenses set forth in this section.

(7) Under the act of November 24, 1998 (P.L.874, No.110), known as the Motor Vehicle Chop Shop and Illegally Obtained and Altered Property Act.

References in Text. The act of November 15, 1972 (P.L.1227, No.272), referred to in this section, amended the act of December 8, 1970 (P.L.874, No.276), known as The Pennsylvania Corrupt Organizations Act of 1970, which was repealed by the act of December 6, 1972 (P.L.1482, No.334). The subject matter is now contained in section 911 of Title 18.

Section 3933, referred to in this section, is repealed.

Section 5504, referred to in this section, is repealed.

The act of November 24, 1998 (P.L.874, No.110), known as the Vehicle Chop Shop and Illegally Obtained and Altered Property Act, referred to in paragraph (7), was repealed by the act of October 25, 2012 (P.L.1645, No.203). The subject matter is now contained in Chapter 77 of this title.

Cross References. Section 5708 is referred to in sections 5704, 5710, 5713, 5742 of this title.

§ 5709. Application for order.

Each application for an order of authorization to intercept a wire, electronic or oral communication shall be made in writing upon the personal oath or affirmation of the Attorney General or a district attorney of the county wherein the suspected criminal activity has been, is or is about to occur and shall contain all of the following:

(1) A statement of the authority of the applicant to make such application.

(2) A statement of the identity and qualifications of the investigative or law enforcement officers or agency for whom the

authority to intercept a wire, electronic or oral communication is sought.

(3) A sworn statement by the investigative or law enforcement officer who has knowledge of relevant information justifying the application, which shall include:

(i) The identity of the particular person, if known, committing the offense and whose communications are to be intercepted.

(ii) The details as to the particular offense that has been, is being, or is about to be committed.

(iii) The particular type of communication to be intercepted.

(iv) A showing that there is probable cause to believe that such communication will be communicated on the wire communication facility involved or at the particular place where the oral communication is to be intercepted.

(v) The character and location of the particular wire communication facility involved or the particular place where the oral communication is to be intercepted.

(vi) A statement of the period of time for which the interception is required to be maintained, and, if the character of the investigation is such that the authorization for interception should not automatically terminate when the described type of communication has been first obtained, a particular statement of facts establishing probable cause to believe that additional communications of the same type will occur thereafter.

(vii) A particular statement of facts showing that other normal investigative procedures with respect to the offense have been tried and have failed, or reasonably appear to be unlikely to succeed if tried or are too dangerous to employ.

(4) Where the application is for the renewal or extension of an order, a particular statement of facts showing the results thus far obtained from the interception, or a reasonable explanation of the failure to obtain such results.

(5) A complete statement of the facts concerning all previous applications, known to the applicant made to any court for authorization to intercept a wire, electronic or oral communication involving any of the same facilities or places specified in the application or involving any person whose communication is to be intercepted, and the action taken by the court on each such application.

(6) A proposed order of authorization for consideration by the judge.

(7) Such additional testimony or documentary evidence in support of the application as the judge may require.

(Oct. 21, 1988, P.L.1000, No.115, eff. imd.; Dec. 9, 2002, P.L.1350, No.162, eff. 60 days)

Cross References. Section 5709 is referred to in sections 5702, 5712.1, 5713.1 of this title.

§ 5710. Grounds for entry of order.

(a) Application.--Upon consideration of an application, the judge may enter an ex parte order, as requested or as modified, authorizing the interception of wire, electronic or oral communications anywhere within the Commonwealth, if the judge determines on the basis of the facts submitted by the applicant that there is probable cause for belief that all the following conditions exist:

(1) the person whose communications are to be intercepted is committing, has or had committed or is about to commit an offense as provided in section 5708 (relating to order authorizing interception of wire, electronic or oral communications);

(2) particular communications concerning such offense may be obtained through such interception;

(3) normal investigative procedures with respect to such offense have been tried and have failed or reasonably appear to be unlikely to succeed if tried or to be too dangerous to employ;

(4) the facility from which, or the place where, the wire, electronic or oral communications are to be intercepted, is, has been, or is about to be used, in connection with the commission of such offense, or is leased to, listed in the name of, or commonly used by, such person;

(5) the investigative or law enforcement officers or agency to be authorized to intercept the wire, electronic or oral communications are qualified by training and experience to execute the interception sought, and are certified under section 5724 (relating to training); and

(6) in the case of an application, other than a renewal or extension, for an order to intercept a communication of a person or on a facility which was the subject of a previous order authorizing interception, the application is based upon new evidence or information different from and in addition to the evidence or information offered to support the prior order,

regardless of whether such evidence was derived from prior interceptions or from other sources.

(b) Corroborative evidence.--As part of the consideration of an application in which there is no corroborative evidence offered, the judge may inquire in camera as to the identity of any informants or any other additional information concerning the basis upon which the investigative or law enforcement officer or agency has applied for the order of authorization which the judge finds relevant in order to determine if there is probable cause pursuant to this section.

(Oct. 21, 1988, P.L.1000, No.115, eff. imd.)

Cross References. Section 5710 is referred to in sections 5712, 5721.1 of this title.

§ 5711. Privileged communications.

No otherwise privileged communication intercepted in accordance with, or in violation of, the provisions of this chapter shall lose its privileged character.

§ 5712. Issuance of order and effect.

(a) Authorizing orders.--An order authorizing the interception of any wire, electronic or oral communication shall state the following:

(1) The identity of the investigative or law enforcement officers or agency to whom the authority to intercept wire, electronic or oral communications is given and the name and official identity of the person who made the application.

(2) The identity of, or a particular description of, the person, if known, whose communications are to be intercepted.

(3) The character and location of the particular communication facilities as to which, or the particular place of the communication as to which, authority to intercept is granted.

(4) A particular description of the type of the communication to be intercepted and a statement of the particular offense to which it relates.

(5) The period of time during which such interception is authorized, including a statement as to whether or not the interception shall automatically terminate when the described communication has been first obtained.

(b) Time limits.--No order entered under this section shall authorize the interception of any wire, electronic or oral communication for a period of time in excess of that necessary under the circumstances. Every order entered under this section shall require that such interception begin and terminate as soon as practicable and be conducted in such a manner as to minimize or eliminate the interception of such communications not otherwise subject to interception under this chapter by making reasonable efforts, whenever possible, to reduce the hours of interception authorized by said order. In the event the intercepted communication is in a code or foreign language and an expert in that code or foreign language is not reasonably available during the interception period, minimization may be accomplished as soon as practicable after such interception. No order entered under this section shall authorize the interception of wire, electronic or oral communications for any period exceeding 30 days. The 30-day period begins on the day on which the investigative or law enforcement officers or agency first begins to conduct an interception under the order, or ten days after the order is entered, whichever is earlier. Extensions or renewals of such an order may be granted for additional periods of not more than 30 days each. No extension or renewal shall be granted unless an application for it is made in accordance with this section, and the judge makes the findings required by section 5710 (relating to grounds for entry of order).

(c) Responsibility.--The order shall require the Attorney General or the district attorney, or their designees, to be responsible for the supervision of the interception.

(d) Progress reports.--Whenever an order authorizing an interception is entered, the order may require reports to be made to the judge who issued the order showing what progress has been made toward achievement of the authorized objective and the need for continued interception. The reports shall be made at such intervals as the judge may require.

(e) Final report.--Whenever an interception is authorized pursuant to this section, a complete written list of names of participants and evidence of offenses discovered, including those not stated in the application for order, shall be filed with the court as soon as practicable after the authorized interception is terminated.

(f) Assistance.--An order authorizing the interception of a wire, electronic or oral communication shall, upon request of the applicant, direct that a provider of communication service shall furnish the applicant forthwith all information, facilities and technical assistance necessary to accomplish the interception unobtrusively and with a minimum of interference with the services that such service provider is affording the person whose communications are to be intercepted. The obligation of a provider of communication service under such an order may include, but is not limited to, installation of a pen register or of a trap and trace device, providing caller ID, deluxe caller ID or any other features available to ascertain the telephone number, location or subscriber information of a facility contacting the facility whose communications are to be intercepted, disclosure of a record or other information otherwise available under section 5743 (relating to requirements for governmental access), including conducting an in-progress trace during an interception, provided that such obligation of a provider of communications service is technologically feasible. The order shall apply regardless of whether the electronic service provider is headquartered within this Commonwealth, if the interception is otherwise conducted within this Commonwealth as provided under this chapter. The order regarding disclosure of a record or other information otherwise available under section 5743 shall apply to all electronic service providers who service facilities which contact or are contacted by the facility whose communications are to be intercepted, regardless of whether the order specifically names any provider of communication service. The order may specify the period of time an electronic service provider has to furnish to the applicant who requests disclosure of a record or other information otherwise available under section 5743. Any provider of communication service furnishing such facilities or technical assistance shall be compensated therefor by the applicant for reasonable expenses incurred in providing the facilities or assistance. The service provider shall be immune from civil and criminal liability for any assistance rendered to the applicant pursuant to this section.

(g) **Entry by law enforcement officers.--** An order authorizing the interception of a wire, electronic or oral communication shall, if requested, authorize the entry of premises or facilities specified in subsection (a)(3), or premises necessary to obtain access to the premises or facilities specified in subsection (a)(3), by the law enforcement officers specified in subsection (a)(1), as often as necessary solely for the purposes of installing, maintaining or removing an electronic, mechanical or other device or devices provided that such entry is reasonably necessary to accomplish the purposes of this subchapter and provided that the judge who issues the order shall be notified of the time and method of each such entry prior to entry if practical and, in any case, within 48 hours of entry.

(Oct. 21, 1988, P.L.1000, No.115, eff. imd.; Feb. 18, 1998, P.L.102, No.19, eff. imd.; Oct. 25, 2012, P.L.1634, No.202, eff. 60 days)

2012 Amendment. Act 202 amended subsecs. (a) intro. par. and (f).

1998 Amendment. Act 19 amended subsecs. (e), (f) and (g).

Cross References. Section 5712 is referred to in sections 5706, 5712.1, 5713.1, 5721.1 of this title.

§ 5712.1. Target-specific orders.

(a) **Target-specific wiretaps.--** The requirements of sections 5712(a)(3) (relating to issuance of order and effect) and 5709(3)(iv) and (v) (relating to application for order) shall not apply if:

(1) In the case of an application with respect to the interception of an oral communication, all of the following apply:

(i) The application contains a full and complete statement as to why specification is not practical and identifies the person committing the offense and whose communications are to be intercepted.

(ii) The judge finds the specification is not practical.

(2) In the case of an application with respect to a wire or electronic communication, all of the following apply:

(i) The application identifies the person believed to be committing the offense and whose communications are to be intercepted and the applicant makes a showing that there is probable cause to believe that the person's actions could have the effect of thwarting interception by changing facilities or devices.

(ii) The judge finds that the purpose has been adequately shown.

(b) **Supplementary orders.--** Following the issuance of a target-specific wiretap order, the judge shall sign supplementary orders upon request and in a timely manner, authorizing the investigative or law enforcement officers or

235

agency to intercept additional communications devices or facilities upon a showing of reasonable suspicion that all of the following apply:

(1) The target of the original order has in fact changed communications devices or facilities or is presently using additional communications devices, communications facilities or places.

(2) The target of the original order is likely to use the specified communications device or facility for criminal purposes similar to or related to those specified in the original order.

(c) Application for supplementary orders.--An application for a supplementary order shall contain all of the following:

(1) The identity of the investigative or law enforcement officers or agency to whom the authority to intercept wire, electronic or oral communications is given and the name and official identity of the person who made the application.

(2) The identity of or a particular description of the person, if known, whose communications are to be intercepted.

(3) The period of time during which the interception is authorized, including a statement as to whether or not the interception shall automatically terminate when the described communication has been first obtained.

(4) A showing of reasonable suspicion that the target of the original order has in fact changed communications devices or facilities.

(5) A showing of reasonable suspicion that the target of the original order is likely to use the additional facility or device or place for criminal purposes similar to or related to those specified in the original order.

(d) Time limits.--A supplementary order shall not act as an extension of the time limit identified in section 5712(b).

(e) Responsibility.--The order shall require the Attorney General or the district attorney, or their designees, to be responsible for the supervision of the interception.

(f) Progress reports.--If an order authorizing an interception is entered, the order may require reports to be made to the judge who issued the order showing what progress has been made toward achievement of the authorized objective and the need for continued interception. The reports shall be made at intervals as the judge may require.

(g) Final report.--If an interception is authorized under this section, a complete written list of names of participants and evidence of offenses discovered, including those not stated in the application for order, shall be filed with the court as soon as practical after the authorized interception is terminated.

(h) Assistance.--

(1) An order authorizing the interception of a wire, electronic or oral communication shall, upon request of the applicant, direct that a provider of communication service furnish the applicant with all information, facilities and technical assistance necessary to accomplish the interception unobtrusively and with a minimum of interference with the services that the service provider is affording the person whose communications are to be intercepted.

(2) The obligation of a provider of communication service under an order may include installation of a pen register or trap and trace device and disclosure of a record or other information otherwise available under section 5743 (relating to requirements for governmental access), including conducting an in-progress trace during an interception, if the obligation of a provider of communications service is technologically feasible.

(3) A provider of communication service furnishing facilities or technical assistance shall be compensated by the applicant for reasonable expenses incurred in providing the facilities or assistance.

(4) A service provider shall be immune from civil and criminal liability for any assistance rendered to an applicant under this section.

(i) Entry by law enforcement officers.--An order authorizing the interception of a wire, electronic or oral communication shall, if requested, authorize the entry of premises or facilities specified under subsection (c)(3) or premises necessary to obtain access to the premises or facilities specified under subsection (c)(3) by law enforcement officers specified under subsection (c)(1) as often as necessary solely for the purposes of installing, maintaining or removing an electronic, mechanical or other device, if all of the following apply:

(1) The entry is reasonably necessary to accomplish the purposes of this subchapter.

(2) The judge who issues the order is notified of the time and method of each entry prior to entry within 48 hours of entry.

(Oct. 25, 2012, P.L.1634, No.202, eff. 60 days)

2012 Amendment. Act 202 added section 5712.1.

§ 5713. Emergency situations.

(a) Application.--Whenever, upon informal application by the Attorney General or a designated deputy attorney general authorized in writing by the Attorney General or a district attorney or an assistant district attorney authorized in writing by the district attorney of a county wherein the suspected criminal activity has been, is or is about to occur, a judge determines there are grounds upon which an order could be issued pursuant to this chapter, and that an emergency situation exists with respect to the investigation of an offense designated in section 5708 (relating to order authorizing interception of wire, electronic or oral communications), and involving conspiratorial activities characteristic of organized crime or a substantial danger to life or limb, dictating authorization for immediate interception of wire, electronic or oral communications before an application for an order could with due diligence be submitted to him and acted upon, the judge may grant oral approval for such interception without an order, conditioned upon the filing with him, within 48 hours thereafter, of an application for an order which, if granted, shall recite the oral approval and be retroactive to the time of such oral approval. Such interception shall immediately terminate when the communication sought is obtained or when the application for an order is denied, whichever is earlier. In the event no application for an order is made, the content of any wire, electronic or oral communication intercepted shall be treated as having been obtained in violation of this subchapter.

(b) Further proceedings.--In the event no application is made or an application pursuant to this section is denied, the court shall cause an inventory to be served as provided in section 5716 (relating to service of inventory and inspection of intercepted communications) and shall require the tape or other recording of the intercepted communication to be delivered to, and sealed by, the court. Such evidence shall be retained by the court in accordance with section 5714 (relating to recording of intercepted communications) and the same shall not be used or disclosed in any legal proceeding except in a civil action brought by an aggrieved person pursuant to section 5725 (relating to civil action for unlawful interception, disclosure or use of wire, electronic or oral communication) or as otherwise authorized by court order. In addition to other remedies and penalties provided by this chapter, failure to effect delivery of any such tape or other recording shall be punishable as contempt by the court directing such delivery. Evidence of oral authorization to intercept wire, electronic or oral communications shall be a defense to any charge against the investigating or law enforcement officer for engaging in unlawful interception.

(Oct. 21, 1988, P.L.1000, No.115, eff. imd.; Feb. 18, 1998, P.L.102, No.19, eff. imd.; Dec. 9, 2002, P.L.1350, No.162, eff. 60 days)

2002 Amendment. Act 162 amended subsec. (a).

Cross References. Section 5713 is referred to in sections 5706, 5713.1, 5716, 5721.1, 5747 of this title.

§ 5713.1. Emergency hostage and barricade situations.

(a) Designation.--The Attorney General or a district attorney may designate supervising law enforcement officers for the purpose of authorizing the interception of wire or oral communications as provided in this section.

(b) Procedure.--A supervising law enforcement officer who reasonably determines that an emergency situation exists that requires a wire or oral communication to be intercepted before an order authorizing such interception can, with due diligence, be obtained, and who determines that there are grounds upon which an order could be entered under this chapter to authorize such interception, may intercept such wire or oral communication. An application for an order approving the interception must be made by the supervising law enforcement officer in accordance with section 5709 (relating to application for order) within 48 hours after the interception has occurred or begins to occur. Interceptions pursuant to this section shall be conducted in accordance with the procedures of this subchapter. Upon request of the supervising law enforcement officer who determines to authorize interceptions of wire communications under this section, a provider of electronic communication service shall provide assistance and be compensated therefor as provided in section 5712(f) (relating to issuance of order and effect). In the absence of an order, such interception shall immediately terminate when the situation giving rise to the hostage or barricade situation ends or when the application for the order is denied, whichever is earlier. In the event such application for approval is denied or in any other case where the interception is terminated without an order having been issued, the contents of any wire or oral communication intercepted shall be treated as having been obtained in violation of this subchapter, and an inventory shall be served as provided in section 5716 (relating to service of inventory and inspection of intercepted communications). Thereafter, the supervising law enforcement officer shall follow the procedures set forth in section 5713(b) (relating to emergency situations).

(c) **Defense.**--A good faith reliance on the provisions of this section shall be a complete defense to any civil or criminal action brought under this subchapter or any other statute against any law enforcement officer or agency conducting any interceptions pursuant to this section as well as a provider of electronic communication service who is required to provide assistance in conducting such interceptions upon request of a supervising law enforcement officer.

(d) **Definitions.**--As used in this section, the following words and phrases shall have the meanings given to them in this subsection:

"Emergency situation." Any situation where:

(1) a person is holding a hostage and is threatening serious physical injury and may resist with the use of weapons; or

(2) a person has barricaded himself and taken a position of confinement to avoid apprehension and:

(i) has the ability to resist with the use of weapons; or

(ii) is threatening suicide or harm to himself or others.

"Supervising law enforcement officer."

(1) For designations by a district attorney, any law enforcement officer trained pursuant to section 5724 (relating to training) to carry out interceptions under this section who has attained the rank of lieutenant or higher in a law enforcement agency within the county or who is in charge of a county law enforcement agency.

(2) For designations by the Attorney General, any member of the Pennsylvania State Police trained pursuant to section 5724 to carry out interceptions under this section and designated by the Commissioner of the Pennsylvania State Police who:

(i) has attained the rank of lieutenant or higher; or

(ii) is in charge of a Pennsylvania State Police barracks.

(Oct. 21, 1988, P.L.1000, No.115, eff. imd.; Feb. 18, 1998, P.L.102, No.19, eff. imd.; Oct. 25, 2012, P.L.1634, No.202, eff. 60 days)

2012 Amendment. Act 202 amended subsec. (d).

1998 Amendment. Act 19 amended subsecs. (b) and (c).

1988 Amendment. Act 115 added section 5713.1.

Cross References. Section 5713.1 is referred to in sections 5706, 5716, 5721.1 of this title.

§ 5714. Recording of intercepted communications.

(a) **Recording and monitoring.**--Any wire, electronic or oral communication intercepted in accordance with this subchapter shall, if practicable, be recorded by tape or other comparable method. The recording shall be done in such a way as will protect it from editing or other alteration. Whenever an interception is being monitored, the monitor shall be an investigative or law enforcement officer certified under section 5724 (relating to training), and where practicable, keep a signed, written record which shall include the following:

(1) The date and hours of surveillance.

(2) The time and duration of each intercepted communication.

(3) The participant, if known, in each intercepted conversation.

(4) A summary of the content of each intercepted communication.

(b) **Sealing of recordings.**--Immediately upon the expiration of the order or extensions or renewals thereof, all monitor's records, tapes and other recordings shall be transferred to the judge issuing the order and sealed under his direction. Custody of the tapes, or other recordings shall be maintained wherever the court directs. They shall not be destroyed except upon an order of the court and in any event shall be kept for ten years. Duplicate tapes, or other recordings may be made for disclosure or use pursuant to section 5717 (relating to investigative disclosure or use of contents of wire, electronic or oral communications or derivative evidence). The presence of the seal provided by this section, or a satisfactory explanation for its absence, shall be a prerequisite for the disclosure of the contents of any wire, electronic or oral communication, or evidence derived therefrom, under section 5717(b).

(Oct. 21, 1988, P.L.1000, No.115, eff. imd.; Feb. 18, 1998, P.L.102, No.19, eff. imd.)

Cross References. Section 5714 is referred to in sections 5704, 5713, 5749, 5773 of this title.

§ 5715. Sealing of applications, orders and supporting papers.

Applications made, final reports, and orders granted pursuant to this subchapter and supporting papers and monitor's records shall be sealed by the court and shall be held in custody as the court shall direct and shall not be destroyed except on order of the court and in any event shall be kept for ten years. They may be disclosed only upon a showing of good cause before a court of competent jurisdiction except that any investigative or law enforcement officer may disclose such applications, orders and supporting papers and monitor's records to investigative or law enforcement officers of this or another state, any of its political subdivisions, or of the United States to the extent that such disclosure is appropriate to the proper performance of the official duties of the officer making or receiving the disclosure. In addition to any remedies and penalties provided by this subchapter, any violation of the provisions of this section may be punished as contempt of the court.

(Oct. 21, 1988, P.L.1000, No.115, eff. imd.; Feb. 18, 1998, P.L.102, No.19, eff. imd.)

§ 5716. Service of inventory and inspection of intercepted communications.

(a) Service of inventory.--Within a reasonable time but not later than 90 days after the termination of the period of the order or of extensions or renewals thereof, or the date of the denial of an order applied for under section 5713 (relating to emergency situations) or 5713.1 (relating to emergency hostage and barricade situations), the issuing or denying judge shall cause to be served on the persons named in the order, application, or final report an inventory which shall include the following:

(1) Notice of the entry of the order or the application for an order denied under section 5713 or 5713.1.

(2) The date of the entry of the order or the denial of an order applied for under section 5713 or 5713.1.

(3) The period of authorized or disapproved interception.

(4) The fact that during the period wire or oral communications were or were not intercepted.

(b) Postponement.--On an ex parte showing of good cause to the issuing or denying judge the service of the inventory required by this section may be postponed for a period of 30 days. Additional postponements may be granted for periods of not more than 30 days on an ex parte showing of good cause to the issuing or denying judge.

(c) Inspections.--The court, upon the filing of a motion, shall make available to such persons or their attorneys for inspection, the intercepted communications and monitor's records to which the movant was a participant and the applications and orders.

(Oct. 21, 1988, P.L.1000, No.115, eff. imd.)

Cross References. Section 5716 is referred to in sections 5713, 5713.1 of this title.

§ 5717. Investigative disclosure or use of contents of wire, electronic or oral communications or derivative evidence.

(a) Law enforcement personnel.--Any investigative or law enforcement officer who, under subsection (a.1), (b), (b.1) or (c), has obtained knowledge of the contents of any wire, electronic or oral communication, or evidence derived therefrom, may disclose such contents or evidence to another investigative or law enforcement officer to the extent that such disclosure is appropriate to the proper performance of the official duties of the officer making or receiving the disclosure.

(a.1) Use of information.--Any investigative or law enforcement officer who, by any means authorized by this subchapter, has obtained knowledge of the contents of any wire, electronic or oral communication or evidence derived therefrom may use such contents or evidence to the extent such use is appropriate to the proper performance of his official duties.

(b) Evidence.--Any person who by any means authorized by this chapter, has obtained knowledge of the contents of any wire, electronic or oral communication, or evidence derived therefrom, may disclose such contents or evidence to an investigative or law enforcement officer and may disclose such contents or evidence while giving testimony under oath or affirmation in any criminal proceeding in any court of this Commonwealth or of another state or of the United States or before any state or Federal grand jury or investigating grand jury.

(b.1) Criminal cases.--Any person who by means authorized by section 5704(17) (relating to exceptions to prohibition of interception and disclosure of communications) has obtained knowledge of the contents of any wire, electronic or oral communication, or evidence derived therefrom, may in addition to disclosures made under subsection (b) disclose such contents or evidence, on the condition that such disclosure is made for the purpose of providing exculpatory evidence in an open or closed criminal case.

(c) Otherwise authorized personnel.--

(1) Except as provided under paragraph (2), any person who, by any means authorized by the laws of another state or the Federal Government, has obtained knowledge of the contents of any wire, electronic or oral communication, or evidence derived from any wire, electronic or oral communication, may disclose the contents or evidence to an investigative or law enforcement officer and may disclose the contents or evidence where otherwise admissible while giving testimony under oath or affirmation in any proceeding in any court of this Commonwealth.

(2) The contents of a nonconsensual interception authorized by the laws of the Federal Government or another state shall not be admissible unless the interception was authorized by a court upon a finding of probable cause that the target of the surveillance is engaged or will engage in a violation of the criminal laws of the Federal Government or any state.

(Oct. 21, 1988, P.L.1000, No.115, eff. imd.; Feb. 18, 1998, P.L.102, No.19, eff. imd.; Oct. 25, 2012, P.L.1634, No.202, eff. 60 days)

2012 Amendment. Act 202 amended subsec. (a) and added subsecs. (b.1) and (c).

Cross References. Section 5717 is referred to in sections 5704, 5714, 5718, 5721.1, 5749 of this title.

§ 5718. Interception of communications relating to other offenses.

When an investigative or law enforcement officer, while engaged in court authorized interceptions of wire, electronic or oral communications in the manner authorized herein, intercepts wire, electronic or oral communications relating to offenses other than those specified in the order of authorization, the contents thereof, and evidence derived therefrom, may be disclosed or used as provided in section 5717(a) (relating to investigative disclosure or use of contents of wire, electronic or oral communications or derivative evidence). Such contents and evidence may be disclosed in testimony under oath or affirmation in any criminal proceeding in any court of this Commonwealth or of another state or of the United States or before any state or Federal grand jury when authorized by a judge who finds on subsequent application that the contents were otherwise intercepted in accordance with the provisions of this subchapter. Such application shall be made as soon as practicable.

(Oct. 21, 1988, P.L.1000, No.115, eff. imd.; Feb. 18, 1998, P.L.102, No.19, eff. imd.)

§ 5719. Unlawful use or disclosure of existence of order concerning intercepted communication.

Except as specifically authorized pursuant to this subchapter any person who willfully uses or discloses the existence of an order authorizing interception of a wire, electronic or oral communication is guilty of a misdemeanor of the second degree.

(Oct. 21, 1988, P.L.1000, No.115, eff. imd.; Feb. 18, 1998, P.L.102, No.19, eff. imd.)

§ 5720. Service of copy of order and application before disclosure of intercepted communication in trial, hearing or proceeding.

The contents of any wire, electronic or oral communication intercepted in accordance with the provisions of this subchapter, or evidence derived therefrom, shall not be disclosed in any trial, hearing, or other adversary proceeding before any court of the Commonwealth unless, not less than ten days before the trial, hearing or proceeding the parties to the action have been served with a copy of the order, the accompanying application and the final report under which the interception was authorized or, in the case of an interception under section 5704 (relating to exceptions to prohibition of interception and disclosure of communications), notice of the fact and nature of the interception. The service of inventory, order, application, and final report required by this section may be waived by the court only where it finds that the service is not feasible and that the parties will not be prejudiced by the failure to make the service.

(Oct. 21, 1988, P.L.1000, No.115, eff. imd.; Feb. 18, 1998, P.L.102, No.19, eff. imd.)

Suspension by Court Rule. Section 5720 was suspended by Pennsylvania Rule of Juvenile Court Procedure No. 800(14), amended February 12, 2010, insofar as it is inconsistent with Rule 340(B)(6) relating to pre-adjudicatory discovery and inspection.

Section 5720 was suspended by Pennsylvania Rule of Criminal Procedure No. 1101(5), adopted March 1, 2000, insofar as it is inconsistent with Rule No. 573 only insofar as section 5720 may delay disclosure to a defendant seeking discovery under Rule No. 573(B)(1)(g).

§ 5721. Suppression of contents of intercepted communication or derivative evidence (Repealed).

1998 Repeal. Section 5721 was repealed February 18, 1998 (P.L.102, No.19), effective immediately.

§ 5721.1. Evidentiary disclosure of contents of intercepted communication or derivative evidence.

(a) Disclosure in evidence generally.--

(1) Except as provided in paragraph (2), no person shall disclose the contents of any wire, electronic or oral communication, or evidence derived therefrom, in any proceeding in any court, board or agency of this Commonwealth.

(2) Any person who has obtained knowledge of the contents of any wire, electronic or oral communication, or evidence derived therefrom, which is properly subject to disclosure under section 5717 (relating to investigative disclosure or use of contents of wire, electronic or oral communications or derivative evidence) may also disclose such contents or evidence in any matter relating to any criminal, quasi-criminal, forfeiture, administrative enforcement or professional disciplinary proceedings in any court, board or agency of this Commonwealth or of another state or of the United States or before any state or Federal grand jury or investigating grand

jury. Once such disclosure has been made, then any person may disclose the contents or evidence in any such proceeding.

(3) Notwithstanding the provisions of paragraph (2), no disclosure in any such proceeding shall be made so long as any order excluding such contents or evidence pursuant to the provisions of subsection (b) is in effect.

(b) Motion to exclude.--Any aggrieved person who is a party to any proceeding in any court, board or agency of this Commonwealth may move to exclude the contents of any wire, electronic or oral communication, or evidence derived therefrom, on any of the following grounds:

(1) Unless intercepted pursuant to an exception set forth in section 5704 (relating to exceptions to prohibition of interception and disclosure of communications), the interception was made without prior procurement of an order of authorization under section 5712 (relating to issuance of order and effect) or an order of approval under section 5713(a) (relating to emergency situations) or 5713.1(b) (relating to emergency hostage and barricade situations).

(2) The order of authorization issued under section 5712 or the order of approval issued under section 5713(a) or 5713.1(b) was not supported by probable cause with respect to the matters set forth in section 5710(a)(1) and (2) (relating to grounds for entry of order).

(3) The order of authorization issued under section 5712 is materially insufficient on its face.

(4) The interception materially deviated from the requirements of the order of authorization.

(5) With respect to interceptions pursuant to section 5704(2), the consent to the interception was coerced by the Commonwealth.

(6) Where required pursuant to section 5704(2)(iv), the interception was made without prior procurement of a court order or without probable cause.

(c) Procedure.--

(1) The motion shall be made in accordance with the applicable rules of procedure governing such proceedings. The court, board or agency, upon the filing of such motion, shall make available to the movant or his counsel the intercepted communication and evidence derived therefrom.

(2) In considering a motion to exclude under subsection (b)(2), both the written application under section 5710(a) and all matters that were presented to the judge under section 5710(b) shall be admissible.

(3) The movant shall bear the burden of proving by a preponderance of the evidence the grounds for exclusion asserted under subsection (b)(3) and (4).

(4) With respect to exclusion claims under subsection (b)(1), (2) and (5), the respondent shall bear the burden of proof by a preponderance of the evidence.

(5) With respect to exclusion claims under subsection (b)(6), the movant shall have the initial burden of demonstrating by a preponderance of the evidence that the interception took place in his home. Once he meets this burden, the burden shall shift to the respondent to demonstrate by a preponderance of the evidence that the interception was in accordance with section 5704(2)(iv).

(6) Evidence shall not be deemed to have been derived from communications excludable under subsection (b) if the respondent can demonstrate by a preponderance of the evidence that the Commonwealth or the respondent had a basis independent of the excluded communication for discovering such evidence or that such evidence would have been inevitably discovered by the Commonwealth or the respondent absent the excluded communication.

(d) Appeal.--In addition to any other right of appeal, the Commonwealth shall have the right to appeal from an order granting a motion to exclude if the official to whom the order authorizing the intercept was granted shall certify to the court that the appeal is not taken for purposes of delay. The appeal shall be taken in accordance with the provisions of Title 42 (relating to judiciary and judicial procedure).

(e) Exclusiveness of remedies and sanctions.--The remedies and sanctions described in this subchapter with respect to the interception of wire, electronic or oral communications are the only judicial remedies and sanctions for nonconstitutional violations of this subchapter involving such communications.

(Feb. 18, 1998, P.L.102, No.19, eff. imd.)

1998 Amendment. Act 19 added section 5721.1.

Cross References. Section 5721.1 is referred to in section 5749 of this title.

§ 5722. Report by issuing or denying judge.

Within 30 days after the expiration of an order or an extension or renewal thereof entered under this subchapter or the denial of an order confirming verbal approval of interception, the issuing or denying judge shall make a report to the Administrative Office of Pennsylvania Courts stating the following:

(1) That an order, extension or renewal was applied for.

(2) The kind of order applied for.

(3) That the order was granted as applied for, was modified, or was denied.

(4) The period of the interceptions authorized by the order, and the number and duration of any extensions or renewals of the order.

(5) The offense specified in the order, or extension or renewal of an order.

(6) The name and official identity of the person making the application and of the investigative or law enforcement officer and agency for whom it was made.

(7) The character of the facilities from which or the place where the communications were to be intercepted.

(Oct. 21, 1988, P.L.1000, No.115, eff. imd.; Feb. 18, 1998, P.L.102, No.19, eff. imd.)

§ 5723. Annual reports and records of Attorney General and district attorneys.

(a) Judges.--In addition to reports required to be made by applicants pursuant to Title 18 U.S.C. § 2519, all judges who have issued orders pursuant to this title shall make annual reports on the operation of this chapter to the Administrative Office of Pennsylvania Courts. The reports by the judges shall contain the following information:

(1) The number of applications made.

(2) The number of orders issued.

(3) The effective periods of such orders.

(4) The number and duration of any renewals thereof.

(5) The crimes in connection with which the orders were sought.

(6) The names and official identity of the applicants.

(7) Such other and further particulars as the Administrative Office of Pennsylvania Courts may require.

(b) Attorney General.--In addition to reports required to be made by applicants pursuant to Title 18 U.S.C. § 2519, the Attorney General shall make annual reports on the operation of this chapter to the Administrative Office of Pennsylvania Courts and to the Judiciary Committees of the Senate and House of Representatives. The reports by the Attorney General shall contain the same information which must be reported pursuant to 18 U.S.C. § 2519(2).

(c) **District attorneys.**--Each district attorney shall annually provide to the Attorney General all of the foregoing information with respect to all applications authorized by that district attorney on forms prescribed by the Attorney General.

(d) **Other reports.**--The Chief Justice of the Supreme Court and the Attorney General shall annually report to the Governor and the General Assembly on such aspects of the operation of this chapter as they deem appropriate and make any recommendations they feel desirable as to legislative changes or improvements to effectuate the purposes of this chapter and to assure and protect individual rights.

(Oct. 21, 1988, P.L.1000, No.115, eff. imd.)

§ 5724. Training.

The Attorney General and the Commissioner of the Pennsylvania State Police shall establish a course of training in the legal and technical aspects of wiretapping and electronic surveillance as allowed or permitted by this subchapter, shall establish such regulations as they find necessary and proper for such training program and shall establish minimum standards for certification and periodic recertification of Commonwealth investigative or law enforcement officers as eligible to conduct wiretapping or electronic surveillance under this chapter. The Pennsylvania State Police shall charge each investigative or law enforcement officer who enrolls in this training program a reasonable enrollment fee to offset the costs of such training.

(Oct. 21, 1988, P.L.1000, No.115, eff. imd.; Feb. 18, 1998, P.L.102, No.19, eff. imd.)

Cross References. Section 5724 is referred to in sections 5706, 5710, 5713.1, 5714, 5749 of this title.

§ 5725. Civil action for unlawful interception, disclosure or use of wire, electronic or oral communication.

(a) **Cause of action.**--Any person whose wire, electronic or oral communication is intercepted, disclosed or used in violation of this chapter shall have a civil cause of action against any person who intercepts, discloses or uses or procures any other person to intercept, disclose or use, such communication; and shall be entitled to recover from any such person:

(1) Actual damages, but not less than liquidated damages computed at the rate of $100 a day for each day of violation, or $1,000, whichever is higher.

(2) Punitive damages.

(3) A reasonable attorney's fee and other litigation costs reasonably incurred.

(b) **Waiver of sovereign immunity.**--To the extent that the Commonwealth and any of its officers, officials or employees would be shielded from liability under this section by the doctrine of sovereign immunity, such immunity is hereby waived for the purposes of this section.

(c) **Defense.**--It is a defense to an action brought pursuant to subsection (a) that the actor acted in good faith reliance on a court order or the provisions of this chapter.

(July 10, 1981, P.L.228, No.73, eff. 60 days; Oct. 21, 1988, P.L.1000, No.115, eff. imd.)

Cross References. Section 5725 is referred to in section 5713 of this title.

§ 5726. Action for removal from office or employment.

(a) **Cause of action.**--Any aggrieved person shall have the right to bring an action in Commonwealth Court against any investigative or law enforcement officer, public official or public employee seeking the officer's, official's or employee's removal from office or employment on the grounds that the officer, official or employee has intentionally violated the provisions of this chapter. If the court shall conclude that such officer, official or employee has in fact intentionally violated the provisions of this chapter, the court shall order the dismissal or removal from office of said officer, official or employee.

(b) **Defense.**--It is a defense to an action brought pursuant to subsection (a) that the actor acted in good faith reliance on a court order or the provisions of this chapter.

(July 10, 1981, P.L.228, No.73, eff. 60 days)

§ 5727. Expiration (Repealed).

1988 Repeal. Section 5727 was repealed October 21, 1988 (P.L.1000, No.115), effective immediately.

§ 5728. Injunction against illegal interception.

Whenever it shall appear that any person is engaged or is about to engage in any act which constitutes or will constitute a felony violation of this subchapter, the Attorney General may initiate a civil action in the Commonwealth Court to enjoin the violation. The court shall proceed as soon as practicable to the hearing and determination of the action and may, at any time before final determination, enter a restraining order or prohibition, or take such other action, as is warranted to prevent a continuing and substantial injury to the Commonwealth or to any person or class of persons for whose protection the action is brought. A proceeding under this section is governed by the Pennsylvania Rules of Civil Procedure, except that, if a criminal complaint has been filed against the respondent, discovery is governed by the Pennsylvania Rules of Criminal Procedure.

(Oct. 21, 1988, P.L.1000, No.115, eff. imd.)

1988 Amendment. Act 115 added section 5728.

SUBCHAPTER C
STORED WIRE AND ELECTRONIC COMMUNICATIONS
AND TRANSACTIONAL RECORDS ACCESS

Enactment. Subchapter C was added October 21, 1988, P.L.1000, No.115, effective immediately.

§ 5741. Unlawful access to stored communications.

(a) Offense.--Except as provided in subsection (c), it is an offense to obtain, alter or prevent authorized access to a wire or electronic communication while it is in electronic storage by intentionally:

(1) accessing without authorization a facility through which an electronic communication service is provided; or

(2) exceeding the scope of one's authorization to access the facility.

(b) Penalty.--

(1) If the offense is committed for the purpose of commercial advantage, malicious destruction or damage, or private commercial gain, the offender shall be subject to:

(i) a fine of not more than $250,000 or imprisonment for not more than one year, or both, in the case of a first offense; or

(ii) a fine of not more than $250,000 or imprisonment for not more than two years, or both, for any subsequent offense.

(2) In any other case, the offender shall be subject to a fine of not more than $5,000 or imprisonment for not more than six months, or both.

(c) Exceptions.--Subsection (a) of this section does not apply with respect to conduct authorized:

(1) by the person or entity providing a wire or electronic communication service;

(2) by a user of that service with respect to a communication of or intended for that user; or

(3) in section 5743 (relating to requirements for governmental access) or 5744 (relating to backup preservation).

§ 5742. Disclosure of contents and records.

(a) Prohibitions.--Except as provided in subsection (b) and (c):

(1) A person or entity providing an electronic communication service to the public shall not knowingly divulge to any person or entity the contents of a communication while in electronic storage by that service:

(i) On behalf of, and received by means of electronic transmission from, or created by means of computer processing of communications received by means of electronic transmission from, a subscriber or customer of the service.

(ii) Solely for the purpose of providing storage or computer processing services to the subscriber or customer, if the provider is not authorized to access the contents of any such communication for the purpose of providing any services other than storage or computer processing.

(2) A person or entity providing remote computing service to the public shall not knowingly divulge to any person or entity the contents of any communication which is carried or maintained on that service:

(i) On behalf of, and received by means of electronic transmission from, or created by means of computer processing of communications received by means of electronic transmission from, a subscriber or customer of the service.

(ii) Solely for the purpose of providing storage or computer processing services to the subscriber or customer, if the provider is not authorized to access the contents of any such communication for the purpose of providing any services other than storage or computer processing.

(3) A person or entity providing an electronic communication service or remote computing service to the public shall not knowingly divulge a record or other information pertaining to a subscriber to, or customer of, the service.

(b) Exceptions.--A person or entity may divulge the contents of a communication:

(1) to an addressee or intended recipient of the communication or an agent of the addressee or intended recipient;

(2) as otherwise authorized in section 5704(1) (relating to prohibition of interception and disclosure of communications), 5708 (relating to order authorizing interception of wire, electronic or oral communications) or 5743 (relating to governmental access);

(3) with the lawful consent of the originator or an addressee or intended recipient of the communication, or the subscriber in the case of remote computing service;

(4) to a person employed or authorized or whose facilities are used to forward the communication to its destination;

(5) as may be necessarily incident to the rendition of the service or to the protection of the rights or property of the provider of the service; or

(6) to a law enforcement agency, if the contents:

(i) Were inadvertently obtained by the service provider.

(ii) Appear to pertain to the commission of a crime.

(c) Exceptions for disclosure of records or other information.--A person or entity may divulge a record or other information pertaining to a subscriber to, or customer of, the service if any of the following paragraphs apply:

(1) A record or other information may be divulged incident to any service or other business operation or to the protection of the rights or property of the provider.

(2) A record or other information may be divulged to any of the following:

(i) An investigative or law enforcement official as authorized in section 5743.

(ii) The subscriber or customer upon request.

(iii) A third party, upon receipt from the requester of adequate proof of lawful consent from the subscriber to, or customer of, the service to release the information to the third party.

(iv) A party to a legal proceeding, upon receipt from the party of a court order entered under subsection (c.1). This subparagraph does not apply to an investigative or law enforcement official authorized under section 5743.

(3) Notwithstanding paragraph (2), a record or other information may be divulged as authorized by a Commonwealth statute or as authorized by a Commonwealth regulatory agency with oversight over the person or entity.

(4) Subject to paragraph (2), a record or other information may be divulged as authorized by Federal law or as authorized by a Federal regulatory agency having oversight over the person or entity.

(c.1) Order for release of records.--

(1) An order to divulge a record or other information pertaining to a subscriber or customer under subsection (c)(2)(iv) must be approved by a court presiding over the proceeding in which a party seeks the record or other information.

(2) The order may be issued only after the subscriber or customer received notice from the party seeking the record or other information and was given an opportunity to be heard.

(3) The court may issue a preliminary order directing the provider to furnish the court

with the identity of or contact information for the subscriber or customer if the party does not possess this information.

(4) An order for disclosure of a record or other information shall be issued only if the party seeking disclosure demonstrates specific and articulable facts to show that there are reasonable grounds to believe that the record or other information sought is relevant and material to the proceeding. In making its determination, the court shall consider the totality of the circumstances, including input of the subscriber or customer, if any, and the likely impact of the provider.

(Oct. 9, 2008, P.L.1403, No.111, eff. imd.)

2008 Amendment. Act 111 amended the section heading and subsec. (a) intro. par. and added subsecs. (a)(3), (c) and (c.1).

Cross References. Section 5742 is referred to in section 5746 of this title.

§ 5743. Requirements for governmental access.

(a) **Contents of communications in electronic storage.**--Investigative or law enforcement officers may require the disclosure by a provider of communication service of the contents of a communication which is in electronic storage in a communication system for:

(1) One hundred eighty days or less only pursuant to a warrant issued under the Pennsylvania Rules of Criminal Procedure.

(2) More than 180 days by the means available under subsection (b).

(b) Contents of communications in a remote computing service.--

(1) Investigative or law enforcement officers may require a provider of remote computing service to disclose the contents of any communication to which this paragraph is made applicable by paragraph (2):

(i) without required notice to the subscriber or customer if the investigative or law enforcement officer obtains a warrant issued under the Pennsylvania Rules of Criminal Procedure; or

(ii) with prior notice from the investigative or law enforcement officer to the subscriber or customer if the investigative or law enforcement officer:

(A) uses an administrative subpoena authorized by a statute or a grand jury subpoena; or

(B) obtains a court order for the disclosure under subsection (d);

except that delayed notice may be given pursuant to section 5745 (relating to delayed notice).

(2) Paragraph (1) is applicable with respect to a communication which is held or maintained on that service:

(i) On behalf of and received by means of electronic transmission from, or created by means of computer processing of communications received by means of electronic transmission from, a subscriber or customer of the remote computing service.

(ii) Solely for the purpose of providing storage or computer processing services to the subscriber or customer, if the provider is not authorized to access the contents of any such communication for the purpose of providing any services other than storage or computer processing.

(c) Records concerning electronic communication service or remote computing service.--

(1) (Deleted by amendment).

(2) A provider of electronic communication service or remote computing service shall disclose a record or other information pertaining to a subscriber to or customer of the service, not including the contents of communications covered by subsection (a) or (b), to an investigative or law enforcement officer only when the investigative or law enforcement officer:

(i) uses an administrative subpoena authorized by a statute or a grand jury subpoena;

(ii) obtains a warrant issued under the Pennsylvania Rules of Criminal Procedure;

(iii) obtains a court order for the disclosure under subsection (d); or

(iv) has the consent of the subscriber or customer to the disclosure.

(3) An investigative or law enforcement officer receiving records or information under paragraph (2) is not required to provide notice to the customer or subscriber.

(d) **Requirements for court order.**--A court order for disclosure under subsection (b) or (c) shall be issued only if the investigative or law enforcement officer shows that there are specific and articulable facts showing that there are reasonable grounds to believe that the contents of a wire or electronic communication, or the records or other information sought, are

246

relevant and material to an ongoing criminal investigation. A court issuing an order pursuant to this section, on a motion made promptly by the service provider, may quash or modify the order if the information or records requested are unusually voluminous in nature or compliance with the order would otherwise cause an undue burden on the provider.

(e) No cause of action against a provider disclosing information under this subchapter.--No cause of action shall lie against any provider of wire or electronic communication service, its officers, employees, agents or other specified persons for providing information, facilities or assistance in accordance with the terms of a court order, warrant, subpoena or certification under this subchapter.

(Feb. 18, 1998, P.L.102, No.19, eff. imd.; Oct. 9, 2008, P.L.1403, No.111, eff. imd.; Oct. 25, 2012, P.L.1634, No.202, eff. 60 days)

2012 Amendment. Act 202 amended subsecs. (a) and (b).

2008 Amendment. Act 111 deleted subsec. (c)(1).

1998 Amendment. Act 19 amended subsecs. (d) and (e).

Cross References. Section 5743 is referred to in sections 5712, 5712.1, 5741, 5742, 5743.1, 5744, 5745, 5746, 5747 of this title.

§ 5743.1. Administrative subpoena.

(a) Authorization.--

(1) In an ongoing investigation that monitors or utilizes online services or other means of electronic communication to identify individuals engaged in an offense involving the sexual exploitation or abuse of children, the following shall apply:

(i) The following may issue in writing and cause to be served a subpoena requiring the production and testimony under subparagraph (ii):

(A) The Attorney General.

(B) A deputy attorney general designated in writing by the Attorney General.

(C) A district attorney.

(D) An assistant district attorney designated in writing by a district attorney.

(ii) A subpoena issued under subparagraph (i) may be issued to a provider of electronic communication service or remote computing service:

(A) requiring disclosure under section 5743(c)(2) (relating to requirements for governmental access) of a subscriber or customer's name, address, telephone or instrument number or other subscriber number or identity, including any temporarily assigned network address, which may be relevant to an authorized law enforcement inquiry; or

(B) requiring a custodian of the records of the provider to give testimony or affidavit concerning the production and authentication of the records or information.

(2) A subpoena under this section shall describe the information required to be produced and prescribe a return date within a reasonable period of time within which the information can be assembled and made available.

(3) If summoned to appear under paragraph (1)(ii)(B), a custodian of records subpoenaed under this section shall be paid the same fees and mileage that are paid to witnesses in the courts of this Commonwealth.

(4) Prior to the return date specified in the subpoena, the person or entity subpoenaed may, in the court of common pleas of the county in which the person or entity conducts business or resides, petition for an order modifying or setting aside the subpoena or for a prohibition of disclosure ordered by a court under paragraph (7).

(5) The following shall apply:

(i) Except as provided under subparagraph (ii), if no case or proceeding arises from the production of materials under this section within a reasonable time after the materials are produced, the agency to which the materials were delivered shall, upon written demand made by the person producing the materials, return the materials to the person.

(ii) This paragraph shall not apply if the production required was of copies rather than originals.

(6) A subpoena issued under paragraph (1) may require production as soon as possible.

(7) Without court approval, no person or entity may disclose to any other person or entity, other than to an attorney in order to obtain legal advice, the existence of the subpoena for a period of up to 90 days.

(8) A subpoena issued under this section may not require the production of anything that would be protected from production under the standards applicable to a subpoena for the production of documents issued by a court.

(b) Service.--The following shall apply:

(1) A subpoena issued under this section may be served by any person who is at least 18 years of age and is designated in the subpoena to serve it.

(2) Service upon a natural person may be made by personal delivery of the subpoena to the person.

(3) Service may be made upon a domestic or foreign corporation or upon a partnership or other unincorporated association which is subject to suit under a common name by delivering the subpoena to any of the following:

(i) An officer of the entity.

(ii) A managing or general agent of the entity.

(iii) An agent authorized by appointment or by law to receive service of process in this Commonwealth.

(4) The affidavit of the person serving the subpoena entered on a true copy of the subpoena by the person serving it shall be proof of service.

(c) Enforcement.--The following shall apply:

(1) The Attorney General or a district attorney, or a designee may invoke the aid of a court of common pleas within the following jurisdictions to compel compliance with the subpoena:

(i) The jurisdiction in which the investigation is being conducted.

(ii) The jurisdiction in which the subpoenaed person resides, conducts business or may be found.

(2) The court may issue an order requiring the subpoenaed person to appear before the Attorney General or a district attorney, or a designee to produce records or to give testimony concerning the production and authentication of the records. A failure to obey the order of the court may be punished by the court as contempt of court. All process may be served in a judicial district of the Commonwealth in which the person may be found.

(d) Immunity from civil liability.--Notwithstanding any State or local law, any person receiving a subpoena under this section who complies in good faith with the subpoena and produces the records sought shall not be liable in a court of this Commonwealth to a subscriber, customer or other person for the production or for the nondisclosure of that production to the subscriber, customer or person.

(e) Annual reports and records of Attorney General and district attorneys.--The following shall apply:

(1) On or before April 1 following the effective date of this section and annually thereafter, including the year following the expiration of this section, the Attorney General shall make a report on the operation of this section to the Judiciary Committee of the Senate and the Judiciary Committee of the House of Representatives. The reports by the Attorney General shall contain the following information for the previous calendar year:

(i) The number of administrative subpoenas issued.

(ii) The number of investigations for which an administrative subpoena was issued.

(iii) The number of court orders issued under subsections (a)(4) and (7) and (c)(2).

(iv) The number of arrests made and the type of charge filed in cases in which an administrative subpoena was issued.

(v) The number of cases in which an administrative subpoena was issued and in which no arrests or prosecutions resulted.

(2) On or before March 1 following the effective date of this section and annually thereafter, including the year following the expiration of this section, each district attorney shall provide to the Attorney General all of the information under paragraph (1) with respect to all administrative subpoenas issued by that district attorney on forms prescribed by the Attorney General.

(f) Expiration.--(Deleted by amendment).

(g) Definitions.--As used in this section, the following words and phrases shall have the meanings given to them in this subsection:

"Offense involving the sexual exploitation or abuse of children." An offense, including an attempt, conspiracy or solicitation involving any of the following, in which a victim is an individual who is under the age of 18 years:

(1) Chapter 29 (relating to kidnapping).

(2) Chapter 30 (relating to human trafficking).

(3) Chapter 31 (relating to sexual offenses).

(4) Section 6312 (relating to sexual abuse of children).

(5) Section 6318 (relating to unlawful contact with minor).

(6) Section 6320 (relating to sexual exploitation of children).

(Oct. 22, 2014, P.L.2522, No.151, eff. 60 days; Dec. 22, 2017, P.L.1218, No.67, eff. imd.)

2017 Amendment. Act 67 deleted subsec. (f).

2014 Amendment. Act 151 added section 5743.1.

§ 5744. Backup preservation.

(a) Backup preservation.--

(1) An investigative or law enforcement officer acting under section 5743(b)(2) (relating to requirements for governmental access) may include in its subpoena or court order a requirement that the service provider to whom the request is directed create a backup copy of the contents of the electronic communications sought in order to preserve those communications. Without notifying the subscriber or customer of the subpoena or court order, the service provider shall create the backup copy as soon as practicable, consistent with its regular business practices, and shall confirm to the investigative or law enforcement officer that the backup copy has been made. The backup copy shall be created within two business days after receipt by the service provider of the subpoena or court order.

(2) Notice to the subscriber or customer shall be made by the investigative or law enforcement officer within three days after receipt of confirmation that the backup copy has been made, unless the notice is delayed pursuant to section 5745(a) (relating to delayed notice).

(3) The service provider shall not destroy or permit the destruction of the backup copy until the later of:

(i) the delivery of the information; or

(ii) the resolution of all proceedings, including appeals of any proceeding, concerning the government's subpoena or court order.

(4) The service provider shall release the backup copy to the requesting investigative or law enforcement officer no sooner than 14 days after the officer's notice to the subscriber or customer if the service provider has not:

(i) received notice from the subscriber or customer that the subscriber or customer has challenged the officer's request; and

(ii) initiated proceedings to challenge the request of the officer.

(5) An investigative or law enforcement officer may seek to require the creation of a backup copy under paragraph (1) if in his sole discretion the officer determines that there is reason to believe that notification under section 5743 of the existence of the subpoena or court order may result in destruction of or tampering with evidence. This determination is not subject to challenge by the subscriber, customer or service provider.

(b) Customer challenges.--

(1) Within 14 days after notice by the investigative or law enforcement officer to the subscriber or customer under subsection (a)(2), the subscriber or customer may file a motion to quash the subpoena or vacate the court order, copies to be served upon the officer and written notice of the challenge to be given to the service provider. A motion to vacate a court order shall be filed in the court which issued the order. A motion to quash a subpoena shall be filed in the court which has authority to enforce the subpoena. The motion or application shall contain an affidavit or sworn statement:

(i) stating that the applicant is a customer of or subscriber to the service from which the contents of electronic communications maintained for the applicant have been sought; and

(ii) containing the applicant's reasons for believing that the records sought are not relevant to a legitimate investigative or law enforcement inquiry or that there has not been substantial compliance with the provisions of this subchapter in some other respect.

(2) Service shall be made under this section upon the investigative or law enforcement officer by delivering or mailing by registered or certified mail a copy of the papers to the person, office or department specified in the notice which the customer has received pursuant to this subchapter. For the purposes of this section, the term "delivery" has the meaning given that term in the Pennsylvania Rules of Civil Procedure.

(3) If the court finds that the customer has complied with paragraphs (1) and (2), the court shall order the investigative or law enforcement officer to file a sworn response, which may be filed in camera if the investigative or law enforcement officer includes in its response the reasons which make in camera review appropriate. If the court is unable to determine

the motion or application on the basis of the parties' initial allegations and responses, the court may conduct such additional proceedings as it deems appropriate. All such proceedings shall be completed and the motion or application decided as soon as practicable after the filing of the officer's response.

(4) If the court finds that the applicant is not the subscriber or customer for whom the communications sought by the investigative or law enforcement officer are maintained, or that there is reason to believe that the investigative or law enforcement inquiry is legitimate and that the communications sought are relevant to that inquiry, it shall deny the motion or application and order the process enforced. If the court finds that the applicant is the subscriber or customer for whom the communications sought by the governmental entity are maintained, and that there is not reason to believe that the communications sought are relevant to a legitimate investigative or law enforcement inquiry, or that there has not been substantial compliance with the provisions of this subchapter, it shall order the process quashed.

(5) A court order denying a motion or application under this section shall not be deemed a final order, and no interlocutory appeal may be taken therefrom. The Commonwealth or investigative or law enforcement officer shall have the right to appeal from an order granting a motion or application under this section.

(Feb. 18, 1998, P.L.102, No.19, eff. imd.)

1998 Amendment. Act 19 amended subsec. (b).

Cross References. Section 5744 is referred to in sections 5741, 5746 of this title.

§ 5745. Delayed notice.

(a) Delay of notification.--

(1) An investigative or law enforcement officer acting under section 5743(b) (relating to requirements for governmental access) may:

(i) where a court order is sought, include in the application a request for an order delaying the notification required under section 5743(b) for a period not to exceed 90 days, which request the court shall grant if it determines that there is reason to believe that notification of the existence of the court order may have an adverse result described in paragraph (2); or

(ii) where an administrative subpoena authorized by a statute or a grand jury subpoena is obtained, delay the notification required under section 5743(b) for a period not to exceed 90 days upon the execution of a written certification of a supervisory official that there is reason to believe that notification of the existence of the subpoena may have an adverse result described in paragraph (2).

(2) An adverse result for the purposes of paragraph (1) is:

(i) endangering the life or physical safety of an individual;

(ii) flight from prosecution;

(iii) destruction of or tampering with evidence;

(iv) intimidation of potential witnesses; or

(v) otherwise seriously jeopardizing an investigation or unduly delaying a trial.

(3) The investigative or law enforcement officer shall maintain a true copy of a certification under paragraph (1)(ii).

(4) Extensions of the delay of notification provided for in section 5743 of up to 90 days each may be granted by the court upon application or by certification by a supervisory official in the case of an administrative or grand jury subpoena.

(5) Upon expiration of the period of delay of notification under paragraph (1) or (4), the investigative or law enforcement officer shall serve upon, or deliver by registered or first class mail to, the customer or subscriber a copy of the process or request together with notice which:

(i) states with reasonable specificity the nature of the investigative or law enforcement inquiry; and

(ii) informs the customer or subscriber:

(A) that information maintained for the customer or subscriber by the service provider named in the process or request was supplied to or requested by the investigative or law enforcement officer and the date on which the supplying or request took place;

(B) that notification of the customer or subscriber was delayed;

(C) the identity of the investigative or law enforcement officer or the court which made the certification or determination pursuant to which that delay was made; and

(D) which provision of this subchapter authorizes the delay.

(6) As used in this subsection, the term "supervisory official" means the investigative

agent or assistant investigative agent in charge, or an equivalent, of an investigative or law enforcement agency's headquarters or regional office, or the chief prosecuting attorney or the first assistant prosecuting attorney, or an equivalent, of a prosecuting attorney's headquarters or regional office.

(b) Preclusion of notice to subject of governmental access.--An investigative or law enforcement officer acting under section 5743, when he is not required to notify the subscriber or customer under section 5743(b)(1), or to the extent that it may delay such notice pursuant to subsection (a), may apply to a court for an order commanding a provider of electronic communication service or remote computing service to whom a warrant, subpoena or court order is directed, not to notify any other person of the existence of the warrant, subpoena or court order for such period as the court deems appropriate. The court shall enter such an order if it determines that there is reason to believe that notification of the existence of the warrant, subpoena or court order will result in:

(1) endangering the life or physical safety of an individual;

(2) flight from prosecution;

(3) destruction of or tampering with evidence;

(4) intimidation of a potential witness; or

(5) otherwise seriously jeopardizing an investigation or unduly delaying a trial.

Cross References. Section 5745 is referred to in sections 5743, 5744 of this title.

§ 5746. Cost reimbursement.

(a) Payment.--Except as otherwise provided in subsection (c), an investigative or law enforcement officer obtaining the contents of communications, records or other information under section 5742 (relating to disclosure of contents and records), 5743 (relating to requirements for governmental access) or 5744 (relating to backup preservation) shall reimburse the person or entity assembling or providing the information for such costs as are reasonably necessary and which have been directly incurred in searching for, assembling, reproducing and otherwise providing the information. Reimbursable costs shall include any costs due to necessary disruption of normal operations of any electronic communication service or remote computing service in which the information may be stored.

(b) Amount.--The amount of the reimbursement provided for in subsection (a) shall be as mutually agreed upon by the investigative or law enforcement officer and the person or entity providing the information or, in the absence of agreement, shall be as determined by the court which issued the order for production of the information or the court before which a criminal prosecution relating to the information would be brought, if no court order was issued for production of the information.

(c) Applicability.--The requirement of subsection (a) does not apply with respect to records or other information maintained by a communication common carrier which relates to telephone toll records and telephone listings obtained under section 5743. The court may, however, order reimbursement as described in subsection (a) if the court determines the information required is unusually voluminous or otherwise caused an undue burden on the provider.

(d) Regulations.--The Attorney General shall promulgate regulations to implement this section.

(Oct. 9, 2008, P.L.1403, No.111, eff. imd.; Oct. 25, 2012, P.L.1634, No.202, eff. 60 days)

2012 Amendment. Act 202 added subsec. (d).

2008 Amendment. Act 111 amended subsec. (a).

§ 5747. Civil action.

(a) Cause of action.--Except as provided in subsection 5743(e) (relating to requirements for governmental access), any provider of electronic communication service, subscriber or customer aggrieved by any violation of this subchapter in which the conduct constituting the violation is engaged in with a knowing or intentional state of mind may, in a civil action, recover from the person or entity which engaged in the violation such relief as may be appropriate.

(b) Relief.--In a civil action under this section, appropriate relief shall include:

(1) such preliminary and other equitable or declaratory relief as may be appropriate;

(2) damages under subsection (c); and

(3) reasonable attorney fees and other litigation costs reasonably incurred.

(c) Damages.--The court may assess as damages in a civil action under this section the sum of the actual damages suffered by the plaintiff and any profits made by the violator as a result of the violation, but in no case shall a person entitled to recover receive less than the sum of $1,000.

(d) **Defense.**--A good faith reliance on:

(1) a court warrant or order, a grand jury subpoena, a legislative authorization or a statutory authorization;

(2) a request of an investigative or law enforcement officer under section 5713 (relating to emergency situations); or

(3) a good faith determination that section 5704(10) (relating to exceptions to prohibitions of interception and disclosure of communications) permitted the conduct complained of;

is a complete defense to any civil or criminal action brought under this subchapter or any other law.

(e) **Limitation.**--A civil action under this section may not be commenced later than two years after the date upon which the claimant first discovered or had a reasonable opportunity to discover the violation.

(Feb. 18, 1998, P.L.102, No.19, eff. imd.; Oct. 22, 2014, P.L.2522, No.151, eff. 60 days)

2014 Amendment. Act 151 amended subsec. (b).

1998 Amendment. Act 19 amended subsec. (d).

§ 5748. Exclusivity of remedies.

The remedies and sanctions described in this subchapter are the only judicial remedies and sanctions for nonconstitutional violations of this subchapter.

§ 5749. Retention of certain records.

(a) **Retention.**--The commander shall maintain all recordings of oral communications intercepted under section 5704(16) (relating to exceptions to prohibition of interception and disclosure of communications) for a minimum of 31 days after the date of the interception. All recordings made under section 5704(16) shall be recorded over or otherwise destroyed no later than 90 days after the date of the recording unless any of the following apply:

(1) The contents of the recording result in the issuance of a citation. Except as otherwise authorized under this subsection, any recording maintained under this paragraph shall be recorded over or destroyed no later than 90 days after the conclusion of the proceedings related to the citation. All recordings under this paragraph shall be maintained in accordance

with section 5714(a) (relating to recording of intercepted communications), except that monitors need not be certified under section 5724 (relating to training).

(2) The commander or a law enforcement officer on the recording believes that the contents of the recording or evidence derived from the recording may be necessary in a proceeding for which disclosure is authorized under section 5717 (relating to investigative disclosure or use of contents of wire, electronic or oral communications or derivative evidence) or 5721.1 (relating to evidentiary disclosure of contents of intercepted communication or derivative evidence) or in a civil proceeding. All recordings under this paragraph shall be maintained in accordance with section 5714(a), except that monitors need not be certified under section 5724.

(3) A criminal defendant who is a participant on the recording reasonably believes that the recording may be useful for its evidentiary value at some later time in a specific criminal proceeding and, no later than 30 days following the filing of criminal charges, provides written notice to the commander indicating a desire that the recording be maintained. The written notice must specify the date, time and location of the recording; the names of the parties involved; and, if known, the case docket number.

(4) An individual who is a participant on the recording intends to pursue a civil action or has already initiated a civil action and, no later than 30 days after the date of the recording, gives written notice to the commander indicating a desire that the recording be maintained. The written notice must specify the date, time and location of the recording; the names of the parties involved; and, if a civil action has been initiated, the case caption and docket number.

(5) The commander intends to use the recording for training purposes.

(b) **Disclosure.**--In addition to any disclosure authorized under sections 5717 and 5721.1, any recording maintained:

(1) Under subsection (a)(4) shall be disclosed pursuant to an order of court or as required by the Pennsylvania Rules of Civil Procedure or the Pennsylvania Rules of Evidence; and

(2) Under subsection (a)(5) shall be disclosed consistent with written consent

obtained from the law enforcement officer and all participants.

(c) Definitions.--As used in this section, the following words and phrases shall have the meanings given to them in this subsection:

"Commander." The:

(1) commissioner or a designee, if the recording at issue was made by a member of the Pennsylvania State Police; or

(2) chief or a designee of the law enforcement agency which made the recording at issue.

"Law enforcement officer." A member of the Pennsylvania State Police or an individual employed as a police officer who is required to be trained under 53 Pa.C.S. Ch. 21 Subch. D (relating to municipal police education and training).

(June 11, 2002, P.L.370, No.53, eff. imd.)

2002 Amendment. Act 53 added section 5749. Section 3 of Act 53 provided that section 5749 shall apply upon the enactment of a statute providing for the intercepting and recording of oral communications under 18 Pa.C.S. § 5704. Act 52 of 2002, effective June 11, 2002, added provisions relating to the intercepting and recording of oral communications under 18 Pa.C.S. § 5704.

References in Text. The reference to "commissioner" in par. (1) of the def. of "commander" in subsec. (c) probably should have been a reference to Commissioner of the Pennsylvania State Police.

Cross References. Section 5749 is referred to in section 5782 of this title.

SUBCHAPTER D
MOBILE TRACKING DEVICES

Sec.
5761. Mobile tracking devices.

Enactment. Subchapter D was added October 21, 1988, P.L.1000, No.115, effective immediately.

§ 5761. Mobile tracking devices.

(a) Authority to issue.--Orders for the installation and use of mobile tracking devices may be issued by a court of common pleas.

(b) Jurisdiction.--Orders permitted by this section may authorize the use of mobile tracking devices if the device is installed and monitored within this Commonwealth. The court issuing the order must have jurisdiction over the offense under investigation.

(c) Standard for issuance of order.--An order authorizing the use of one or more mobile tracking devices may be issued to an investigative or law enforcement officer by the court of common pleas upon written application. Each application shall be by written affidavit, signed and sworn to or affirmed before the court of common pleas. The affidavit shall:

(1) state the name and department, agency or address of the affiant;

(2) identify the vehicles, containers or items to which, in which or on which the mobile tracking device shall be attached or be placed, and the names of the owners or possessors of the vehicles, containers or items;

(3) state the jurisdictional area in which the vehicles, containers or items are expected to be found; and

(4) provide a statement setting forth all facts and circumstances which provide the applicant with probable cause that criminal activity has been, is or will be in progress and that the use of a mobile tracking device will yield information relevant to the investigation of the criminal activity.

(d) Notice.--The court of common pleas shall be notified in writing within 72 hours of the time the mobile tracking device has been activated in place on or within the vehicles, containers or items.

(e) Term of authorization.-- Authorization by the court of common pleas for the use of the mobile tracking device may continue for a period of 90 days from the placement of the device. An extension for an additional 90 days may be granted upon good cause shown.

(f) Removal of device.--Wherever practicable, the mobile tracking device shall be removed after the authorization period expires. If removal is not practicable, monitoring of the mobile tracking device shall cease at the expiration of the authorization order.

(g) Movement of device.--Movement of the tracking device within an area protected by a reasonable expectation of privacy shall not be monitored absent exigent circumstances or an order supported by probable cause that criminal activity has been, is or will be in progress in the protected area and that the use of a mobile tracking device in the protected area will yield information relevant to the investigation of the criminal activity.

(Oct. 9, 2008, P.L.1403, No.111, eff. imd.; Oct. 25, 2012, P.L.1634, No.202, eff. 60 days)

2012 Amendment. Act 202 amended subsecs. (b) and (c)(4).

SUBCHAPTER E
PEN REGISTERS, TRAP AND TRACE DEVICES
AND TELECOMMUNICATION IDENTIFICATION
INTERCEPTION DEVICES

Enactment. Subchapter E was added October 21, 1988, P.L.1000, No.115, effective immediately.
Subchapter Heading. The heading of Subchapter E was amended February 18, 1998, P.L.102, No.19, effective immediately.
Cross References. Subchapter E is referred to in section 5704 of this title.

§ 5771. General prohibition on use of certain devices and exception.

(a) General rule.--Except as provided in this section, no person may install or use a pen register or a trap and trace device or a telecommunication identification interception device without first obtaining a court order under section 5773 (relating to issuance of an order for use of certain devices).

(b) Exception.--The prohibition of subsection (a) does not apply with respect to the use of a pen register, a trap and trace device or a telecommunication identification interception device by a provider of electronic or wire communication service:

(1) relating to the operation, maintenance and testing of a wire or electronic communication service or to the protection of the rights or property of the provider, or to the protection of users of the service from abuse of service or unlawful use of service;

(2) to record the fact that a wire or electronic communication was initiated or completed in order to protect the provider, another provider furnishing service toward the completion of the wire communication or a user of the service from fraudulent, unlawful or abusive use of service; or

(3) with the consent of the user of the service.

(b.1) Limitation.--A government agency authorized to install and use a pen register under this chapter shall use technology reasonably available to it that restricts the recording or decoding of electronic or other impulses to the dialing and signaling information utilized in call processing.

(c) Penalty.--Whoever intentionally and knowingly violates subsection (a) is guilty of a misdemeanor of the third degree.

(Feb. 18, 1998, P.L.102, No.19, eff. imd.)

Cross References. Section 5771 is referred to in section 5773 of this title.

§ 5772. Application for an order for use of certain devices.

(a) Application.--The Attorney General or a deputy attorney general designated in writing by the Attorney General or a district attorney or an assistant district attorney designated in writing by the district attorney may make application for an order or an extension of an order under section 5773 (relating to issuance of an order for use of certain devices) authorizing or approving disclosure of mobile communications tracking information or, if necessary, the production and disclosure of mobile communications tracking information, the installation and use of a pen register, a trap and trace device or a telecommunication identification interception device under this subchapter, in writing, under oath or equivalent affirmation, to a court of common pleas having jurisdiction over the offense under investigation or to any Superior Court judge when an application for an order authorizing interception of communications is or has been made for the targeted telephone or another application for interception under this subchapter has been made involving the same investigation.

(b) Contents of application.--An application under subsection (a) shall include:

(1) The identity and authority of the attorney making the application and the identity of the investigative or law enforcement agency conducting the investigation.

(2) A certification by the applicant that the information likely to be obtained is relevant to an ongoing criminal investigation being conducted by that agency.

(3) An affidavit by an investigative or law enforcement officer which establishes probable cause for the issuance of an order or extension of an order under section 5773.

(Feb. 18, 1998, P.L.102, No.19, eff. imd.; Oct. 25, 2012, P.L.1634, No.202, eff. 60 days)

2012 Amendment. Act 202 amended subsec. (a).

1998 Amendment. Act 19 amended the section heading and subsec. (a).

Cross References. Section 5772 is referred to in section 5773 of this title.

§ 5773. Issuance of an order for use of certain devices.

(a) In general.--Upon an application made under section 5772 (relating to application for an order for use of certain devices), the court shall enter an ex parte order authorizing the disclosure of mobile communications tracking information, the installation and use of a pen register, a trap and trace device or a telecommunication identification interception device within this Commonwealth if the court finds that there is probable cause to believe that information relevant to an ongoing criminal investigation will be obtained by such installation and use on the targeted telephone. If exigent circumstances exist, the court may verbally authorize the disclosure of mobile communications tracking information, the installation and use of a pen register, a trap and trace device or a telecommunication identification interception device. The written order authorizing the disclosure must be entered within 72 hours of the court's verbal authorization.

(b) Contents of order.--An order issued under this section shall:

(1) Specify:

(i) That there is probable cause to believe that information relevant to an ongoing criminal investigation will be obtained from the targeted telephone.

(ii) The identity, if known, of the person to whom is leased or in whose name is listed the targeted telephone, or, in the case of the use of a telecommunication identification interception device, the identity, if known, of the person or persons using the targeted telephone.

(iii) The identity, if known, of the person who is the subject of the criminal investigation.

(iv) In the use of pen registers and trap and trace devices only, the physical location of the targeted telephone.

(v) A statement of the offense to which the information likely to be obtained by the pen register, trap and trace device or the telecommunication identification interception device relates.

(2) Direct, upon the request of the applicant, the furnishing of information, facilities and technical assistance necessary to accomplish the installation of the pen register under section 5771 (relating to general prohibition on use of certain devices and exception).

(3) In the case of a telecommunication identification interception device, direct that all interceptions be recorded and monitored in accordance with section 5714(a)(1) and (2) and (b) (relating to recording of intercepted communications).

(c) Time period and extensions.--

(1) An order issued under this section shall authorize the installation and use of a pen register, trap and trace device or a telecommunication identification interception device for a period not to exceed 60 days.

(2) Extensions of such an order may be granted but only upon an application for an order under section 5772 and upon the judicial finding required by subsection (a). The period of each extension shall be for a period not to exceed 30 days.

(d) Nondisclosure of existence of pen register, trap and trace device or a telecommunication identification interception device.--An order authorizing or approving the installation and use of a pen register, a trap and trace device or a telecommunication identification interception device shall direct that:

(1) The order be sealed until otherwise ordered by the court.

(2) The person owning or leasing the targeted telephone, or who has been ordered by the court to provide assistance to the applicant, not disclose the existence of the pen register, trap and trace device or telecommunication identification interception device or the

existence of the investigation to the listed subscriber, or to any other person, unless or until otherwise ordered by the court.

(Feb. 18, 1998, P.L.102, No.19, eff. imd.; Oct. 25, 2012, P.L.1634, No.202, eff. 60 days)

2012 Amendment. Act 202 amended subsecs. (a) and (c).

Cross References. Section 5773 is referred to in sections 5771, 5772, 5774 of this title.

§ 5774. Assistance in installation and use of certain devices.

(a) Pen register.--Upon the request of an applicant under this subchapter, a provider of wire or electronic communication service, landlord, custodian or other person shall forthwith provide all information, facilities and technical assistance necessary to accomplish the installation of the pen register unobtrusively and with a minimum of interference with the services that the person so ordered by the court accords the party with respect to whom the installation and use is to take place, if assistance is directed by a court order as provided in section 5773(b)(2) (relating to issuance of an order for use of certain devices).

(b) Trap and trace device.--Upon the request of an applicant under this subchapter, a provider of a wire or electronic communication service, landlord, custodian or other person shall install the device forthwith on the appropriate line and shall furnish all additional information, facilities and technical assistance, including installation and operation of the device unobtrusively and with a minimum of interference with the services that the person so ordered by the court accords the party with respect to whom the installation and use is to take place, if installation and assistance are directed by a court order as provided in section 5773. Unless otherwise ordered by the court, the results of the trap and trace device shall be furnished to the applicant designated in the court order at reasonable intervals during regular business hours for the duration of the order.

(c) Compensation.--A provider of wire or electronic communication service, landlord, custodian or other person who furnishes facilities or technical assistance pursuant to this section shall be reasonably compensated for reasonable expenses incurred in providing the facilities and assistance.

(d) No cause of action against a provider disclosing information under this subchapter.--No cause of action shall lie in any court against any provider of a wire or electronic communication service, its officers, employees, agents or other specified persons for providing information, facilities or assistance in accordance with the terms of a court order under this subchapter.

(e) Defense.--A good faith reliance on a court order or a statutory authorization is a complete defense against any civil or criminal action brought under this subchapter or any other law.

(Feb. 18, 1998, P.L.102, No.19, eff. imd.)

§ 5775. Reports concerning certain devices.

(a) Attorney General.--The Attorney General shall annually report to the Administrative Office of Pennsylvania Courts on the number of orders for pen registers, trap and trace devices and telecommunication identification interception devices applied for by investigative or law enforcement agencies of the Commonwealth or its political subdivisions.

(b) District attorney.--Each district attorney shall annually provide to the Attorney General information on the number of orders for pen registers, trap and trace devices and telecommunication identification interception devices applied for on forms prescribed by the Attorney General.

(Feb. 18, 1998, P.L.102, No.19, eff. imd.)

SUBCHAPTER F
MISCELLANEOUS

Sec.
5781. Expiration of chapter.
5782. Regulations.

Enactment. Subchapter F was added October 21, 1988, P.L.1000, No.115, effective immediately.

§ 5781. Expiration of chapter.

This chapter expires December 31, 2023, unless extended by statute.

(Dec. 12, 1994, P.L.1248, No.148, eff. imd.; Feb. 18, 1998, P.L.102, No.19, eff. imd.; Nov. 29, 2004, P.L.1349, No.173, eff. imd.; Oct. 9, 2008, P.L.1403, No.111, eff. imd.; Nov. 27, 2013, P.L.1147, No.102, eff. imd.; July 7, 2017, P.L.304, No.22, eff. 60 days)

§ 5782. Regulations.

The commissioner of the Pennsylvania State Police, in consultation with the Attorney General, shall promulgate regulations consistent with sections 5704(16) (relating to exceptions to prohibition of interception and disclosure of communications) and 5749 (relating to retention of certain records) setting forth procedures to be followed by law enforcement officers regarding the interception, maintenance and destruction of recordings made under section 5704(16).

(June 11, 2002, P.L.370, No.53, eff. imd.)

2002 Amendment. Act 53 added section 5782. Section 3 of Act 53 provided that section 5782 shall apply upon the enactment of a statute providing for the intercepting and recording of oral communications under 18 Pa.C.S. § 5704. Act 52 of 2002, effective June 11, 2002, added provisions relating to the intercepting and recording of oral communications under 18 Pa.C.S. § 5704.

CHAPTER 59 PUBLIC INDECENCY

Sec.
5901. Open lewdness.
5902. Prostitution and related offenses.
5903. Obscene and other sexual materials and performances.
5904. Public exhibition of insane or deformed person.

Enactment. Chapter 59 was added December 6, 1972, P.L.1482, No.334, effective in six months.

Cross References. Chapter 59 is referred to in sections 911, 3051 of this title; section 2101 of Title 5 (Athletics and Sports).

§ 5901. Open lewdness.

A person commits a misdemeanor of the third degree if he does any lewd act which he knows is likely to be observed by others who would be affronted or alarmed.

Cross References. Section 5901 is referred to in section 6318 of this title; section 3304 of Title 5 (Athletics and Sports); section 9718.1 of Title 42 (Judiciary and Judicial Procedure); sections 4503, 4601 of Title 61 (Prisons and Parole).

§ 5902. Prostitution and related offenses.

(a) Prostitution.--A person is guilty of prostitution if he or she:

(1) is an inmate of a house of prostitution or otherwise engages in sexual activity as a business; or

(2) loiters in or within view of any public place for the purpose of being hired to engage in sexual activity.

(a.1) Grading of offenses under subsection (a).--An offense under subsection (a) constitutes a:

(1) Misdemeanor of the third degree when the offense is a first or second offense.

(2) Misdemeanor of the second degree when the offense is a third offense.

(3) Misdemeanor of the first degree when the offense is a fourth or subsequent offense.

(4) Felony of the third degree if the person who committed the offense knew that he or she was human immunodeficiency virus (HIV) positive or manifesting acquired immune deficiency syndrome (AIDS).

(b) Promoting prostitution.--A person who knowingly promotes prostitution of another commits a misdemeanor or felony as provided in subsection (c) of this section. The following acts shall, without limitation of the foregoing, constitute promoting prostitution:

(1) owning, controlling, managing, supervising or otherwise keeping, alone or in association with others, a house of prostitution or a prostitution business;

(2) procuring an inmate for a house of prostitution or a place in a house of prostitution for one who would be an inmate;

(3) encouraging, inducing, or otherwise intentionally causing another to become or remain a prostitute;

(4) soliciting a person to patronize a prostitute;

(5) procuring a prostitute for a patron;

(6) transporting a person into or within this Commonwealth with intent to promote the engaging in prostitution by that person, or procuring or paying for transportation with that intent;

(7) leasing or otherwise permitting a place controlled by the actor, alone or in association with others, to be regularly used for prostitution or the promotion of prostitution, or failure to make reasonable effort to abate such use by ejecting the tenant, notifying law enforcement authorities, or other legally available means; or

(8) soliciting, receiving, or agreeing to receive any benefit for doing or agreeing to do anything forbidden by this subsection.

(b.1) Promoting prostitution of minor.-- A person who knowingly promotes prostitution of a minor commits a felony of the third degree. The following acts shall, without limitation of the foregoing, constitute promoting prostitution of a minor:

(1) owning, controlling, managing, supervising or otherwise keeping, alone or in association with others, a house of prostitution or a prostitution business in which a victim is a minor;

(2) procuring an inmate who is a minor for a house of prostitution or a place in a house of prostitution where a minor would be an inmate;

(3) encouraging, inducing or otherwise intentionally causing a minor to become or remain a prostitute;

(4) soliciting a minor to patronize a prostitute;

(5) procuring a prostitute who is a minor for a patron;

(6) transporting a minor into or within this Commonwealth with intent to promote the engaging in prostitution by that minor, or procuring or paying for transportation with that intent;

(7) leasing or otherwise permitting a place controlled by the actor, alone or in association with others, to be regularly used for prostitution of a minor or the promotion of prostitution of a minor, or failure to make reasonable effort to abate such use by ejecting the tenant, notifying law enforcement authorities or other legally available means; or

(8) soliciting, receiving or agreeing to receive any benefit for doing or agreeing to do anything forbidden by this subsection.

(c) Grading of offenses under subsection (b).--

(1) An offense under subsection (b) constitutes a felony of the third degree if:

(i) the offense falls within paragraphs (b)(1), (b)(2) or (b)(3);

(ii) the actor compels another to engage in or promote prostitution;

(iii) (Deleted by amendment);

(iv) the actor promotes prostitution of his spouse, child, ward or any person for whose care, protection or support he is responsible; or

(v) the person knowingly promoted prostitution of another who was HIV positive or infected with the AIDS virus.

(2) Otherwise the offense is a misdemeanor of the second degree.

(d) Living off prostitutes.-- A person, other than the prostitute or the prostitute's minor child or other legal dependent incapable of self-support, who is knowingly supported in whole or substantial part by the proceeds of prostitution is promoting prostitution in violation of subsection (b) of this section.

(e) Patronizing prostitutes.-- A person commits the offense of patronizing prostitutes if that person hires a prostitute or any other person to engage in sexual activity with him or her or if that person enters or remains in a house of prostitution for the purpose of engaging in sexual activity.

(e.1) Grading of offenses under subsection (e).--An offense under subsection (e) constitutes a:

(1) Misdemeanor of the third degree when the offense is a first or second offense.

(2) Misdemeanor of the second degree when the offense is a third offense.

(3) Misdemeanor of the first degree when the offense is a fourth or subsequent offense.

(4) Felony of the third degree if the person who committed the offense knew that he or she was human immunodeficiency virus (HIV) positive or manifesting acquired immune deficiency syndrome (AIDS).

(e.2) Publication of sentencing order.-- A court imposing a sentence for a second or subsequent offense committed under subsection (e) shall publish the sentencing order in a newspaper of general circulation in the judicial district in which the court sits, and the court costs imposed on the person sentenced shall include the cost of publishing the sentencing order.

(f) Definitions.-- As used in this section the following words and phrases shall have the meanings given to them in this subsection:

"House of prostitution." Any place where prostitution or promotion of prostitution is regularly carried on by one person under the control, management or supervision of another.

"Inmate." A person who engages in prostitution in or through the agency of a house of prostitution.

"Minor." An individual under 18 years of age.

"Public place." Any place to which the public or any substantial group thereof has access.

"Sexual activity." Includes homosexual and other deviate sexual relations.

(Oct. 4, 1978, P.L.909, No.173, eff. 60 days; Feb. 2, 1990, P.L.6, No.4, eff. 60 days; July 9, 1992, P.L.685, No.100, eff. 60 days; Mar. 31, 1995, 1st Sp.Sess., P.L.985, No.10, eff. 60 days; July 6, 1995, P.L.242, No.28, eff. 60 days; Dec. 20, 2000, P.L.973, No.134, eff. 60 days; Dec. 20, 2011, P.L.446, No.111, eff. 60 days)

Cross References. Section 5902 is referred to in sections 3013, 3019, 3064, 3065, 5708, 6318, 9122 of this title; section 3304 of Title 5 (Athletics and Sports); sections 5329, 6303, 6344 of Title 23 (Domestic Relations); sections 5552, 9718.1, 9799.14 of Title 42 (Judiciary and Judicial Procedure); section 2303 of Title 44 (Law and Justice); section 7122 of Title 61 (Prisons and Parole).

§ 5903. Obscene and other sexual materials and performances.

(a) Offenses defined.--No person, knowing the obscene character of the materials or performances involved, shall:

(1) display or cause or permit the display of any explicit sexual materials as defined in subsection (c) in or on any window, showcase, newsstand, display rack, billboard, display board, viewing screen, motion picture screen, marquee or similar place in such manner that the display is visible from any public street, highway, sidewalk, transportation facility or other public thoroughfare, or in any business or commercial establishment where minors, as a part of the general public or otherwise, are or will probably be exposed to view all or any part of such materials;

(2) sell, lend, distribute, transmit, exhibit, give away or show any obscene materials to any person 18 years of age or older or offer to sell, lend, distribute, transmit, exhibit or give away or show, or have in his possession with intent to sell, lend, distribute, transmit, exhibit or give away or show any obscene materials to any person 18 years of age or older, or knowingly advertise any obscene materials in any manner;

(3) (i) design, copy, draw, photograph, print, utter, publish or in any manner manufacture or prepare any obscene materials; or

(ii) design, copy, draw, photograph, print, utter, publish or in any manner manufacture or prepare any obscene materials in which a minor is depicted;

(4) (i) write, print, publish, utter or cause to be written, printed, published or uttered any advertisement or notice of any kind giving information, directly or indirectly, stating or purporting to state where, how, from whom, or by what means any obscene materials can be purchased, obtained or had; or

(ii) write, print, publish, utter or cause to be written, printed, published or uttered any advertisement or notice of any kind giving information, directly or indirectly, stating or purporting to state where, how, from whom or by what means any obscene materials can be purchased, obtained or had in which a minor is included;

(5) (i) produce, present or direct any obscene performance or participate in a portion thereof that is obscene or that contributes to its obscenity; or

(ii) produce, present or direct any obscene performance or participate in a portion thereof that is obscene or that contributes to its obscenity if a minor is included;

(6) hire, employ, use or permit any minor child to do or assist in doing any act or thing mentioned in this subsection;

(7) knowingly take or deliver in any manner any obscene material into a State correctional institution, county prison, regional prison facility or any other type of correctional facility;

(8) possess any obscene material while such person is an inmate of any State correctional institution, county prison, regional prison facility or any other type of correctional facility; or

(9) knowingly permit any obscene material to enter any State correctional institution, county prison, regional prison facility or any other type of correctional facility if such person is a prison guard or other employee of any correctional facility described in this paragraph.

(a.1) Dissemination of explicit sexual material via an electronic communication.-- No person, knowing the content of the advertisement to be explicit sexual materials as defined in subsection (c)(1) and (2), shall transmit or cause to be transmitted an unsolicited advertisement in an electronic communication as defined in section 5702 (relating to definitions) to one or more persons within this Commonwealth that contains explicit sexual materials as defined in subsection (c)(1) and (2) without including in the advertisement the term "ADV-ADULT" at the beginning of the subject line of the advertisement.

(b) Definitions.--As used in this section, the following words and phrases shall have the meanings given to them in this subsection:

"Community." For the purpose of applying the "contemporary community standards" in this section, community means the State.

"Knowing." As used in subsections (a) and (a.1), knowing means having general knowledge of, or reason to know or a belief or ground for belief which warrants further inspection or inquiry of, the character and content of any material or performance described therein which is reasonably susceptible of examination by the defendant.

"Material." Any literature, including any book, magazine, pamphlet, newspaper, storypaper, bumper sticker, comic book or writing; any figure, visual representation, or image, including any drawing, photograph, picture, videotape or motion picture.

"Minor." An individual under 18 years of age.

"Nude." Means showing the human male or female genitals, pubic area or buttocks with less than a fully opaque covering, or showing the female breast with less than a fully opaque covering of any portion thereof below the top of the nipple.

"Obscene." Any material or performance, if:

(1) the average person applying contemporary community standards would find that the subject matter taken as a whole appeals to the prurient interest;

(2) the subject matter depicts or describes in a patently offensive way, sexual conduct of a type described in this section; and

(3) the subject matter, taken as a whole, lacks serious literary, artistic, political, educational or scientific value.

"Performance." Means any play, dance or other live exhibition performed before an audience.

"Sadomasochistic abuse." Means, in a sexual context, flagellation or torture by or upon a person who is nude or clad in undergarments, a mask or in a bizarre costume or the condition of being fettered, bound or otherwise physically restrained on the part of one who is nude or so clothed.

"Sexual conduct." Patently offensive representations or descriptions of ultimate sexual acts, normal or perverted, actual or simulated, including sexual intercourse, anal or oral sodomy and sexual bestiality; and patently offensive representations or descriptions of masturbation, excretory functions, sadomasochistic abuse and lewd exhibition of the genitals.

"Subject line." The area of an electronic communication that contains a summary description of the content of the message.

"Transportation facility." Any conveyance, premises or place used for or in connection with public passenger transportation, whether by air, rail, motor vehicle or any other method, including aircraft, watercraft, railroad cars, buses, and air, boat, railroad and bus terminals and stations.

(c) Dissemination to minors.--No person shall knowingly disseminate by sale, loan or otherwise explicit sexual materials to a minor. "Explicit sexual materials," as used in this subsection, means materials which are obscene or:

(1) any picture, photograph, drawing, sculpture, motion picture film, videotape or similar visual representation or image of a person or portion of the human body which depicts nudity, sexual conduct, or sadomasochistic abuse and which is harmful to minors; or

(2) any book, pamphlet, magazine, printed matter however reproduced, or sound recording which contains any matter enumerated in paragraph (1), or explicit and detailed verbal descriptions or narrative accounts of sexual excitement, sexual conduct, or sadomasochistic abuse and which, taken as a whole, is harmful to minors.

(d) Admitting minor to show.--It shall be unlawful for any person knowingly to exhibit for monetary consideration to a minor or knowingly to sell to a minor an admission ticket or pass or knowingly to admit a minor for a monetary consideration to premises whereon there is exhibited, a motion picture show or other presentation or performance which, in whole or in part, depicts nudity, sexual conduct, or sadomasochistic abuse and which is harmful to minors, except that the foregoing shall not apply to any minor accompanied by his parent.

260

(e) Definitions.--As used in subsections (c) and (d) of this section:

(1) "Minor" (Deleted by amendment).

(2) "Nudity" means the showing of the human male or female genitals, pubic area, or buttocks with less than a fully opaque covering, or the showing of the female breast with less than a fully opaque covering of any portion thereof below the top of the nipple, or the depiction of covered male genitals in a discernibly turgid state.

(3) "Sexual conduct" means acts of masturbation, homosexuality, sexual intercourse, sexual bestiality or physical contact with a person's clothed or unclothed genitals, pubic area, buttocks or, if such person be a female, breast.

(4) "Sexual excitement" means the condition of human male or female genitals when in a state of sexual stimulation or arousal.

(5) "Sadomasochistic abuse" means flagellation or torture by or upon a person clad in undergarments, a mask or bizarre costume, or the condition of being fettered, bound or otherwise physically restrained on the part of one so clothed.

(6) "Harmful to minors" means that quality of any description or representation, in whatever form, of nudity, sexual conduct, sexual excitement, or sadomasochistic abuse, when it:

(i) predominantly appeals to the prurient, shameful, or morbid interest of minors; and

(ii) is patently offensive to prevailing standards in the adult community as a whole with respect to what is suitable material for minors; and

(iii) taken as a whole, lacks serious literary, artistic, political, educational or scientific value for minors.

(7) "Knowingly" means having general knowledge of, or reason to know, or a belief or ground for belief which warrants further inspection or inquiry of both:

(i) the character and content of any material or performance described herein which is reasonably susceptible of examination by the defendant; and

(ii) the age of the minor: Provided, however, That an honest mistake shall constitute an excuse from liability hereunder if the defendant made a reasonable bona fide attempt to ascertain the true age of such minor.

(f) Requiring sale as condition of business dealings.--No person shall knowingly require any distributor or retail seller as a condition to sale or delivery for resale or consignment of any literature, book, magazine, pamphlet, newspaper, storypaper, paper, comic book, writing, drawing, photograph, videotape, figure or image, or any written or printed matter, or any article or instrument to purchase or take by consignment for purposes of sale, resale or distribution any obscene literature, book, magazine, pamphlet, newspaper, storypaper, paper, comic book, writing, drawing, photograph, videotape, figure or image, or any written or printed matter of an obscene nature or any article or instrument of an obscene nature.

(g) Injunction.--The attorney for the Commonwealth may institute proceedings in equity in the court of common pleas of the county in which any person violates or clearly is about to violate this section for the purpose of enjoining such violation. The court shall issue an injunction only after written notice and hearing and only against the defendant to the action. The court shall hold a hearing within three days after demand by the attorney for the Commonwealth, one of which days must be a business day for the court, and a final decree shall be filed in the office of the prothonotary within 24 hours after the close of the hearing. A written memorandum supporting the decree shall be filed within five days of the filing of the decree. The attorney for the Commonwealth shall prove the elements of the violation beyond a reasonable doubt. The defendant shall have the right to trial by jury at the said hearing.

(h) Criminal prosecution.--

(1) Any person who violates subsection (a), (a.1) or (f) is guilty of a misdemeanor of the first degree. Violation of subsection (a) is a felony of the third degree if the offender has previously been convicted of a violation of subsection (a) or if the material was sold, distributed, prepared or published for the purpose of resale.

(2) Any person who violates subsection (c) or (d) is guilty of a felony of the third degree. Violation of subsection (c) or (d) is a felony of the second degree if the offender has previously been convicted of a violation of subsection (c) or (d).

(3) Findings made in an equity action shall not be binding in the criminal proceedings.

(i) Right to jury trial.--The right to trial by jury shall be preserved in all proceedings under this section.

(j) Exemptions.--Nothing in this section shall apply to any recognized historical society or museum accorded charitable status by the Federal Government, any county, city, borough, township or town library, any public library, any library of any school, college or university or any archive or library under the supervision and control of the Commonwealth or a political subdivision.

(k) Ordinances or resolutions.--Nothing in this chapter shall be construed to invalidate, supersede, repeal or preempt any ordinance or resolution of any political subdivision insofar as it is consistent with this chapter, and political subdivisions further retain the right to regulate any activities, displays, exhibitions or materials not specifically regulated by this chapter.

(l) Penalty for attempt to evade prosecution.--Any person who violates subsection (a.1) and attempts to avoid prosecution by knowingly including false or misleading information in the return address portion of the electronic communications such that the recipient would be unable to send a reply message to the original, authentic sender shall, in addition to any other penalty imposed, upon conviction, be sentenced to pay a fine of not less than $100 nor more than $500 per message or to imprisonment for not more than 90 days, or both, for a first offense and a fine of not less than $500 nor more than $1,000 or to imprisonment for not more than one year, or both, for a second or subsequent offense.

(m) Concurrent jurisdiction to prosecute.--The Attorney General shall have the concurrent prosecutorial jurisdiction with the district attorney for cases arising under subsection (a.1) and may refer to the district attorney, with the district attorney's consent, any violation or alleged violation of subsection (a.1) which may come to the Attorney General's attention.

(Nov. 5, 1977, P.L.221, No.68, eff. 60 days; Oct. 16, 1980, P.L.978, No.167, eff. 60 days; Dec. 19, 1990, P.L.1332, No.207, eff. imd.; June 18, 1998, P.L.534, No.76, eff. 60 days; June 13, 2000, P.L.130, No.25, eff. 60 days; Dec. 20, 2000, P.L.721, No.98, eff. imd.; Dec. 20, 2011, P.L.446, No.111, eff. 60 days)

2011 Amendment. Act 111 amended subsecs. (a)(3), (4) and (5) and (b) and deleted the def. of "minor" in subsec. (e)(1).

2000 Amendments. Act 25 amended subsecs. (a), (b) and (h)(1) and added subsecs. (a.1), (l) and (m) and Act 98 amended subsec. (h)(2). See the preamble to Acts 25 and 98 in the appendix to this title for special provisions relating to legislative findings and declarations. Section 3(1) of Act 98 provided that the amendment of section 5903 shall apply to offenses committed on or after the effective date of Act 98.

Cross References. Section 5903 is referred to in sections 3131, 3133, 5708, 6318, 9122 of this title; section 3304 of Title 5 (Athletics and Sports); section 4102 of Title 12 (Commerce and Trade); sections 5329, 6344 of Title 23 (Domestic Relations); section 9331 of Title 24 (Education); sections 9718.1, 9799.14 of Title 42 (Judiciary and Judicial Procedure); section 2303 of Title 44 (Law and Justice); section 7122 of Title 61 (Prisons and Parole); section 2905 of Title 66 (Public Utilities).

§ 5904. Public exhibition of insane or deformed person.

A person is guilty of a misdemeanor of the second degree if he exhibits in any place, for a pecuniary consideration or reward, any insane, idiotic or deformed person, or imbecile.

Cross References. Section 5904 is referred to in section 3304 of Title 5 (Athletics and Sports).

ARTICLE G
MISCELLANEOUS OFFENSES

Special Provisions in Appendix. See section 4 of Act 334 of 1972 in the appendix to this title for special provisions relating to the applicability of the Statutory Construction Act to this article.

CHAPTER 61 FIREARMS AND OTHER DANGEROUS ARTICLES

Subchapter
A. Uniform Firearms Act
B. Firearms Generally
C. Other Dangerous Articles
D. Straw Purchase Prevention Education Program

Enactment. Chapter 61 was added December 6, 1972, P.L.1482, No.334, effective in six months.

Special Provisions in Appendix. See the preamble to Act 66 of 2005 in the appendix to this title for special provisions relating to legislative findings and declarations.

Cross References. Chapter 61 is referred to in sections 9122.1, 9122.3 of this title; sections 6108, 6108.2, 6108.3 of Title 23 (Domestic Relations); sections 6307, 6308 of Title 42 (Judiciary and Judicial Procedure); sections 4503, 4601 of Title 61 (Prisons and Parole).

SUBCHAPTER A
UNIFORM FIREARMS ACT

Special Provisions in Appendix. See the preamble to Act 17 of the First Special Session of 1995 in the appendix to this title for special provisions relating to legislative purpose.

Cross References. Subchapter A is referred to in sections 6105, 6108.6 of Title 23 (Domestic Relations); section 2503 of Title 34 (Game).

§ 6101. Short title of subchapter.

This subchapter shall be known and may be cited as the Pennsylvania Uniform Firearms Act of 1995.

(June 13, 1995, 1st Sp.Sess., P.L.1024, No.17, eff. 120 days)

§ 6102. Definitions.

Subject to additional definitions contained in subsequent provisions of this subchapter which are applicable to specific provisions of this subchapter, the following words and phrases, when used in this subchapter shall have, unless the context clearly indicates otherwise, the meanings given to them in this section:

"Commissioner." The Commissioner of the Pennsylvania State Police.

"Commonwealth Photo Imaging Network." The computer network administered by the Commonwealth and used to record and store digital photographs of an individual's face and any scars, marks, tattoos or other unique features of the individual.

"Conviction." A conviction, a finding of guilty or the entering of a plea of guilty or nolo contendere, whether or not judgment of sentence has been imposed, as determined by the law of the jurisdiction in which the prosecution was held. The term does not include a conviction which has been expunged or overturned or for which an individual has been pardoned unless the pardon expressly provides that the individual may not possess or transport firearms.

"County treasurer." The county treasurer or, in home rule or optional plan counties, the person whose duties encompass those of a county treasurer.

"Crime punishable by imprisonment exceeding one year." The term does not include any of the following:

(1) Federal or State offenses pertaining to antitrust, unfair trade practices, restraints on trade or regulation of business.

(2) State offenses classified as misdemeanors and punishable by a term of imprisonment not to exceed two years.

"Firearm." Any pistol or revolver with a barrel length less than 15 inches, any shotgun with a barrel length less than 18 inches or any rifle with a barrel length less than 16 inches, or any pistol, revolver, rifle or shotgun with an overall length of less than 26 inches. The barrel length of a firearm shall be determined by measuring from the muzzle of the barrel to the face of the closed action, bolt or cylinder, whichever is applicable.

"Fund." The Firearm Ownership Fund established in section 6111.3 (relating to Firearm Ownership Fund).

"Law enforcement officer." Any person employed by any police department or organization of the Commonwealth or political subdivision thereof who is empowered to effect an arrest with or without warrant and who is authorized to carry a firearm in the performance of that person's duties.

"Loaded." A firearm is loaded if the firing chamber, the nondetachable magazine or, in the case of a revolver, any of the chambers of the cylinder contain ammunition capable of being fired. In the case of a firearm which utilizes a detachable magazine, the term shall mean a magazine suitable for use in said firearm which magazine contains such ammunition and has been inserted in the firearm or is in the same container or, where the container has multiple compartments, the same compartment thereof as the firearm. If the magazine is inserted into a pouch, holder, holster or other protective device that provides for a complete and secure enclosure of the ammunition, then the pouch, holder, holster or other protective device shall be deemed to be a separate compartment.

"Pennsylvania Sheriffs' Association." The State association of sheriffs authorized by the act of June 14, 1923 (P.L.774, No.305), entitled "An act authorizing the sheriffs of the several counties of this Commonwealth to organize themselves into a State Association, for the purpose of holding annual meetings, to secure more uniformity and cooperation in the conduct of their offices, and providing for the payment of certain expenses in connection with such meetings by the various counties."

"Safekeeping permit." As defined in 23 Pa.C.S. § 6102 (relating to definitions).

"Sheriff."

(1) Except as provided in paragraph (2), the sheriff of the county.

(2) In a city of the first class, the chief or head of the police department.

"State." When used in reference to different parts of the United States, includes the District of Columbia, the Commonwealth of Puerto Rico and territories and possessions of the United States.

(Dec. 19, 1988, P.L.1275, No.158, eff. 180 days; June 13, 1995, 1st Sp.Sess., P.L.1024, No.17, eff. 120 days; Nov. 22, 1995, P.L.621, No.66, eff. imd.; Nov. 10, 2005, P.L.335, No.66, eff. 180 days; June 28, 2011, P.L.48, No.10, eff. 60 days)

2011 Amendment. Act 10 amended the def. of "loaded." See the preamble to Act 10 in the appendix to this title for special provisions relating to legislative findings.

2005 Amendment. Act 66 added the defs. of "Commonwealth Photo Imaging Network," "Pennsylvania Sheriffs' Association," "safekeeping permit" and "state."

1995 Amendment. Act 66 added the defs. of "law enforcement officer" and "loaded."

Cross References. Section 6102 is referred to in sections 6105.1, 6106.1, 6111, 6111.1, 6113, 6121, 6141.1, 6142 of this title; section 5902 of Title 61 (Prisons and Parole).

§ 6103. Crimes committed with firearms.

If any person commits or attempts to commit a crime enumerated in section 6105 (relating to persons not to possess, use, manufacture, control, sell or transfer firearms) when armed with a firearm contrary to the provisions of this subchapter, that person may, in addition to the punishment provided for the crime, also be punished as provided by this subchapter.

(June 13, 1995, 1st Sp.Sess., P.L.1024, No.17, eff. 120 days)

§ 6104. Evidence of intent.

In the trial of a person for committing or attempting to commit a crime enumerated in section 6105 (relating to persons not to possess, use, manufacture, control, sell or transfer firearms), the fact that that person was armed with a firearm, used or attempted to be used, and had no license to carry the same, shall be evidence of that person's intention to commit the offense.

(June 13, 1995, 1st Sp.Sess., P.L.1024, No.17, eff. 120 days)

§ 6105. Persons not to possess, use, manufacture, control, sell or transfer firearms.

(a) Offense defined.--

(1) A person who has been convicted of an offense enumerated in subsection (b), within or without this Commonwealth, regardless of the length of sentence or whose conduct meets the criteria in subsection (c) shall not possess, use, control, sell, transfer or manufacture or obtain a license to possess, use, control, sell, transfer or manufacture a firearm in this Commonwealth.

(2) (i) Except as otherwise provided in this paragraph, a person who is prohibited from possessing, using, controlling, selling, transferring or manufacturing a firearm under paragraph (1) or subsection (b) or (c) shall have a reasonable period of time, not to exceed 60 days from the date of the imposition of the disability under this subsection, in which to sell or transfer that person's firearms to another eligible person who is not a member of the prohibited person's household.

(ii) This paragraph shall not apply to any person whose disability is imposed pursuant to subsection (c)(6).

(iii) A person whose disability is imposed pursuant to subsection (c)(9) shall relinquish any firearms and firearm licenses under that person's possession or control, as described in section 6105.2 (relating to relinquishment of firearms and firearm licenses by convicted persons).

(iv) A person whose disability is imposed pursuant to a protection from abuse order shall relinquish any firearms, other weapons, ammunition and firearm licenses under that person's possession or control, as described in 23 Pa.C.S. § 6108(a)(7) (relating to relief).

(a.1) Penalty.--

(1) Except as provided under paragraph (1.1), a person convicted of a felony enumerated under subsection (b) or a felony under the act of April 14, 1972 (P.L.233, No.64), known as The Controlled Substance, Drug, Device and Cosmetic Act, or any equivalent Federal statute or equivalent statute of any other state, who violates subsection (a) commits a felony of the second degree.

(1.1) The following shall apply:

(i) A person convicted of a felony enumerated under subsection (b) or a felony under The Controlled Substance, Drug, Device and Cosmetic Act, or any equivalent Federal statute or equivalent statute of any other state, who violates subsection (a) commits a felony of the first degree if:

(A) at the time of the commission of a violation of subsection (a), the person has previously been convicted of an offense under subsection (a); or

(B) at the time of the commission of a violation of subsection (a), the person was in physical possession or control of a firearm, whether visible, concealed about the person or within the person's reach.

(ii) The Pennsylvania Commission on Sentencing, under 42 Pa.C.S. § 2154 (relating to adoption of guidelines for sentencing), shall provide for a sentencing enhancement for a sentence imposed pursuant to this paragraph.

(2) A person who is the subject of an active final protection from abuse order issued pursuant to 23 Pa.C.S. § 6108, is the subject of any other active protection from abuse order issued pursuant to 23 Pa.C.S. § 6107(b) (relating to hearings), which provided for the relinquishment of firearms or other weapons or ammunition during the period of time the order is in effect, or is otherwise prohibited from possessing or acquiring a firearm under 18 U.S.C. § 922(g)(8) (relating to unlawful acts), commits a misdemeanor of the second degree if he intentionally or knowingly fails to relinquish a firearm or other weapon or ammunition to the sheriff or appropriate law enforcement agency as defined in 23 Pa.C.S. § 6102 (relating to definitions) as required by the order unless, in lieu of relinquishment, he provides an affidavit which lists the firearms or other weapons or ammunition to the sheriff in accordance with 23 Pa.C.S. § 6108(a)(7)(i)(B), 6108.2 (relating to relinquishment for consignment sale, lawful transfer or safekeeping) or 6108.3 (relating to relinquishment to third party for safekeeping).

(3) (i) A person commits a misdemeanor of the third degree if he intentionally or knowingly accepts possession of a firearm, other weapon or ammunition from another person he knows is the subject of an active final protection from abuse order issued pursuant to 23 Pa.C.S. § 6108 or an active protection from abuse order issued pursuant to 23 Pa.C.S. § 6107(b), which order provided for the relinquishment of the firearm, other weapon or ammunition during the period of time the order is in effect.

(ii) This paragraph shall not apply to:

(A) a third party who accepts possession of a firearm, other weapon or ammunition relinquished pursuant to 23 Pa.C.S. § 6108.3; or

(B) a dealer licensed pursuant to section 6113 (relating to licensing of dealers) or subsequent purchaser from a dealer licensed pursuant to section 6113, who accepts possession of a firearm, other weapon or ammunition relinquished pursuant to 23 Pa.C.S. § 6108.2.

(4) It shall be an affirmative defense to any prosecution under paragraph (3) that the person accepting possession of a firearm, other weapon or ammunition in violation of paragraph (3):

(i) notified the sheriff as soon as practicable that he has taken possession; and

(ii) relinquished possession of any firearm, other weapon or ammunition possessed in violation of paragraph (3) as directed by the sheriff.

(5) A person who has accepted possession of a firearm, other weapon or ammunition pursuant to 23 Pa.C.S. § 6108.3 commits a misdemeanor of the first degree if he intentionally or knowingly returns a firearm, other weapon or ammunition to a defendant or intentionally or knowingly allows a defendant to have access to the firearm, other weapon or ammunition prior to either of the following:

(i) The sheriff accepts return of the safekeeping permit issued to the party pursuant to 23 Pa.C.S. § 6108.3(d)(1)(i).

(ii) The issuance of a court order pursuant to subsection (f)(2) or 23 Pa.C.S. § 6108.1(b) (relating to return of relinquished firearms, other weapons and ammunition and additional relief) which modifies a valid protection from abuse order issued pursuant to 23 Pa.C.S. § 6108, which order provided for the relinquishment of the firearm, other weapon or ammunition by allowing the defendant to take possession of the firearm, other weapon or ammunition that had previously been ordered relinquished.

(b) Enumerated offenses.--The following offenses shall apply to subsection (a):

Section 908 (relating to prohibited offensive weapons).

Section 911 (relating to corrupt organizations).

Section 912 (relating to possession of weapon on school property).

Section 2502 (relating to murder).

Section 2503 (relating to voluntary manslaughter).

Section 2504 (relating to involuntary manslaughter) if the offense is based on the reckless use of a firearm.

Section 2702 (relating to aggravated assault).

Section 2703 (relating to assault by prisoner).

Section 2704 (relating to assault by life prisoner).

Section 2709.1 (relating to stalking).

Section 2716 (relating to weapons of mass destruction).

Section 2901 (relating to kidnapping).

Section 2902 (relating to unlawful restraint).

Section 2910 (relating to luring a child into a motor vehicle or structure).

Section 3121 (relating to rape).

Section 3123 (relating to involuntary deviate sexual intercourse).

Section 3125 (relating to aggravated indecent assault).

Section 3301 (relating to arson and related offenses).

Section 3302 (relating to causing or risking catastrophe).

Section 3502 (relating to burglary).

Section 3503 (relating to criminal trespass) if the offense is graded a felony of the second degree or higher.

Section 3701 (relating to robbery).

Section 3702 (relating to robbery of motor vehicle).

Section 3921 (relating to theft by unlawful taking or disposition) upon conviction of the second felony offense.

Section 3923 (relating to theft by extortion) when the offense is accompanied by threats of violence.

Section 3925 (relating to receiving stolen property) upon conviction of the second felony offense.

Section 4906 (relating to false reports to law enforcement authorities) if the fictitious report involved the theft of a firearm as provided in section 4906(c)(2).

Section 4912 (relating to impersonating a public servant) if the person is impersonating a law enforcement officer.

Section 4952 (relating to intimidation of witnesses or victims).

Section 4953 (relating to retaliation against witness, victim or party).

Section 5121 (relating to escape).

Section 5122 (relating to weapons or implements for escape).

Section 5501(3) (relating to riot).

Section 5515 (relating to prohibiting of paramilitary training).

Section 5516 (relating to facsimile weapons of mass destruction).

Section 6110.1 (relating to possession of firearm by minor).

Section 6301 (relating to corruption of minors).

Section 6302 (relating to sale or lease of weapons and explosives).

Any offense equivalent to any of the above-enumerated offenses under the prior laws of this Commonwealth or any offense equivalent to any of the above-enumerated offenses under the statutes of any other state or of the United States.

(c) Other persons.--In addition to any person who has been convicted of any offense listed under subsection (b), the following persons shall be subject to the prohibition of subsection (a):

(1) A person who is a fugitive from justice. This paragraph does not apply to an individual whose fugitive status is based upon a nonmoving or moving summary offense under Title 75 (relating to vehicles).

(2) A person who has been convicted of an offense under the act of April 14, 1972 (P.L.233, No.64), known as The Controlled Substance, Drug, Device and Cosmetic Act, or any equivalent Federal statute or equivalent statute of any other state, that may be punishable by a term of imprisonment exceeding two years.

(3) A person who has been convicted of driving under the influence of alcohol or controlled substance as provided in 75 Pa.C.S. § 3802 (relating to driving under influence of alcohol or controlled substance) or the former 75 Pa.C.S. § 3731, on three or more separate occasions within a five-year period. For the purposes of this paragraph only, the prohibition of subsection (a) shall only apply to transfers or purchases of firearms after the third conviction.

(4) A person who has been adjudicated as an incompetent or who has been involuntarily committed to a mental institution for inpatient care and treatment under section 302, 303 or 304 of the provisions of the act of July 9, 1976 (P.L.817, No.143), known as the Mental Health Procedures Act. This paragraph shall not apply to any proceeding under section 302 of the Mental Health Procedures Act unless the examining physician has issued a certification that inpatient care was necessary or that the person was committable.

(5) A person who, being an alien, is illegally or unlawfully in the United States.

(6) A person who is the subject of an active final protection from abuse order issued pursuant to 23 Pa.C.S. § 6108, is the subject of any other active protection from abuse order issued pursuant to 23 Pa.C.S. § 6107(b), which provided for the relinquishment of firearms during the period of time the order is in effect or is otherwise prohibited from possessing or acquiring a firearm under 18 U.S.C. § 922(g)(8). This prohibition shall terminate upon

the expiration or vacation of the order or portion thereof relating to the relinquishment of firearms.

(7) A person who was adjudicated delinquent by a court pursuant to 42 Pa.C.S. § 6341 (relating to adjudication) or under any equivalent Federal statute or statute of any other state as a result of conduct which if committed by an adult would constitute an offense under sections 2502, 2503, 2702, 2703 (relating to assault by prisoner), 2704, 2901, 3121, 3123, 3301, 3502, 3701 and 3923.

(8) A person who was adjudicated delinquent by a court pursuant to 42 Pa.C.S. § 6341 or under any equivalent Federal statute or statute of any other state as a result of conduct which if committed by an adult would constitute an offense enumerated in subsection (b) with the exception of those crimes set forth in paragraph (7). This prohibition shall terminate 15 years after the last applicable delinquent adjudication or upon the person reaching the age of 30, whichever is earlier.

(9) A person who is prohibited from possessing or acquiring a firearm under 18 U.S.C. § 922(g)(9). If the offense which resulted in the prohibition under 18 U.S.C. § 922(g)(9) was committed, as provided in 18 U.S.C. § 921(a)(33)(A)(ii) (relating to definitions), by a person in any of the following relationships:

(i) the current or former spouse, parent or guardian of the victim;

(ii) a person with whom the victim shares a child in common;

(iii) a person who cohabits with or has cohabited with the victim as a spouse, parent or guardian; or

(iv) a person similarly situated to a spouse, parent or guardian of the victim;

then the relationship need not be an element of the offense to meet the requirements of this paragraph.

(10) A person who has been convicted of an offense under subsection (a.1)(2). The prohibition shall terminate five years after the date of conviction, final release from confinement or final release from supervision, whichever is later.

(d) Exemption.--A person who has been convicted of a crime specified in subsection (a) or (b) or a person whose conduct meets the criteria in subsection (c)(1), (2), (5), (7) or (9) may make application to the court of common pleas of the county where the principal residence of the applicant is situated for relief from the disability imposed by this section upon the possession, transfer or control of a firearm. The court shall grant such relief if it determines that any of the following apply:

(1) The conviction has been vacated under circumstances where all appeals have been exhausted or where the right to appeal has expired.

(2) The conviction has been the subject of a full pardon by the Governor.

(3) Each of the following conditions is met:

(i) The Secretary of the Treasury of the United States has relieved the applicant of an applicable disability imposed by Federal law upon the possession, ownership or control of a firearm as a result of the applicant's prior conviction, except that the court may waive this condition if the court determines that the Congress of the United States has not appropriated sufficient funds to enable the Secretary of the Treasury to grant relief to applicants eligible for the relief.

(ii) A period of ten years, not including any time spent in incarceration, has elapsed since the most recent conviction of the applicant of a crime enumerated in subsection (b), a felony violation of The Controlled Substance, Drug, Device and Cosmetic Act or the offense which resulted in the prohibition under 18 U.S.C. § 922(g)(9).

(d.1) Concurrent jurisdiction to prosecute.--The following apply in a city of the first class where the Attorney General has operated a joint local-State firearm task force:

(1) In addition to the authority conferred upon the Attorney General by the act of October 15, 1980 (P.L.950, No.164), known as the Commonwealth Attorneys Act, the Attorney General shall have the authority to investigate and institute criminal proceedings for a violation of this section.

(2) No person charged with a violation of this section by the Attorney General shall have standing to challenge the authority of the Attorney General to prosecute the case, and, if any such challenge is made, the challenge shall be dismissed and no relief shall be available in the courts of this Commonwealth to the person making the challenge.

(3) This subsection shall not apply to any case instituted two years after the effective date of this subsection.

(e) Proceedings.--

(1) If a person convicted of an offense under subsection (a), (b) or (c)(1), (2), (5), (7) or (9) makes application to the court, a hearing shall be held in open court to determine whether the requirements of this section have been met. The commissioner and the district attorney of the county where the application is filed and any victim or survivor of a victim of the offense upon which the disability is based may be parties to the proceeding.

(2) Upon application to the court of common pleas pursuant to paragraph (1) by an applicant who is subject to the prohibition under subsection (c)(3), the court shall grant such relief if a period of ten years, not including any time spent in incarceration, has passed since the applicant's most recent conviction under subsection (c)(3).

(f) Other exemptions and proceedings.--

(1) Upon application to the court of common pleas under this subsection by an applicant subject to the prohibitions under subsection (c)(4), the court may grant such relief as it deems appropriate if the court determines that the applicant may possess a firearm without risk to the applicant or any other person.

(2) If application is made under this subsection for relief from the disability imposed under subsection (c)(6), notice of such application shall be given to the person who had petitioned for the protection from abuse order, and such person shall be a party to the proceedings. Notice of any court order or amendment to a court order restoring firearms possession or control shall be given to the person who had petitioned for the protection from abuse order, to the sheriff and to the Pennsylvania State Police. The application and any proceedings on the application shall comply with 23 Pa.C.S. Ch. 61 (relating to protection from abuse).

(3) All hearings conducted under this subsection shall be closed unless otherwise requested to be open by the applicant.

(4) (i) The owner of any seized or confiscated firearms or of any firearms ordered relinquished under 23 Pa.C.S. § 6108 shall be provided with a signed and dated written receipt by the appropriate law enforcement agency. This receipt shall include, but not limited to, a detailed identifying description indicating the serial number and condition of the firearm. In addition, the appropriate law enforcement agency shall be liable to the lawful owner of said confiscated, seized or relinquished firearm for any loss, damage or substantial decrease in value of said firearm that is a direct result of a lack of reasonable care by the appropriate law enforcement agency.

(ii) Firearms shall not be engraved or permanently marked in any manner, including, but not limited to, engraving of evidence or other identification numbers. Unless reasonable suspicion exists to believe that a particular firearm has been used in the commission of a crime, no firearm shall be test fired. Any reduction in the value of a firearm due to test firing, engraving or permanently marking in violation of this paragraph shall be considered damage, and the law enforcement agency shall be liable to the lawful owner of the firearm for the reduction in value caused by the test firing, engraving or permanently marking.

(iii) For purposes of this paragraph, the term "firearm" shall include any scope, sight, bipod, sling, light, magazine, clip, ammunition or other firearm accessory attached to or seized, confiscated or relinquished with a firearm.

(g) Other restrictions.--Nothing in this section shall exempt a person from a disability in relation to the possession or control of a firearm which is imposed as a condition of probation or parole or which is imposed pursuant to the provision of any law other than this section.

(h) License prohibition.--Any person who is prohibited from possessing, using, controlling, selling, purchasing, transferring or manufacturing any firearm under this section shall not be eligible for or permitted to obtain a license to carry a firearm under section 6109 (relating to licenses).

(i) Firearm.--As used in this section only, the term "firearm" shall include any weapons which are designed to or may readily be converted to expel any projectile by the action of an explosive or the frame or receiver of any such weapon.

(j) Copy of order to State Police.--If the court grants relief from the disabilities imposed under this section, a copy of the order shall be sent by the prothonotary within ten days of the entry of the order to the Pennsylvania State Police and shall include the name, date of birth and Social Security number of the individual.

(June 13, 1995, 1st Sp.Sess., P.L.1024, No.17, eff. 120 days; Nov. 22, 1995, P.L.621, No.66, eff. imd.; Apr. 22, 1997, P.L.73, No.5, eff. 60 days; June 18, 1998, P.L.503, No.70, eff. imd.; Dec. 3, 1998, P.L.933, No.121, eff. imd.; Dec. 15, 1999, P.L.915, No.59, eff. 60 days; June 28, 2002, P.L.481, No.82, eff. 60 days; Dec. 9, 2002, P.L.1759, No.218, eff. 60 days; Sept. 30, 2003, P.L.120, No.24, eff. Feb. 1, 2004; Nov. 10, 2005, P.L.335, No.66, eff. 180 days; Oct. 17, 2008, P.L.1628, No.131, eff. 60 days; Nov. 3, 2016, P.L.1052, No.134, eff. 60 days; Oct. 12, 2018, P.L.519, No.79, eff. 180 days; July 2, 2019, P.L.375, No.58, eff. 60 days)

2019 Amendment. Act 58 added subsec. (d.1).

2018 Amendment. Act 79 amended subsecs. (a)(2), (a.1)(2) and (3) and (c)(6) and (9) and added subsec. (c)(10). Act 79 shall apply to orders issued pursuant to 23 Pa.C.S. § 6108 on or after the effective date of section 11 of Act 79.

2016 Amendment. Act 134 amended subsec. (a.1)(1) and added (1.1).

2008 Amendment. Act 131 amended subsec. (b).

2005 Amendment. Act 66 amended subsecs. (a), (a.1), (c)(6), (d), (e)(1) and (f)(2) and (4) and added subsec. (c)(9).

2003 Amendment. Act 24 amended subsec. (c)(3).

1999 Amendment. Act 59 amended subsec. (c)(2) and added subsec. (a.1).

1998 Amendments. Act 70 amended subsec. (c)(4) and added subsec. (j) and Act 121 amended subsec. (c)(1).

1997 Amendment. Act 5 amended subsec. (f).

1995 Amendment. Act 66 amended subsecs. (a), (b), (c), (d) and (f).

Cross References. Section 6105 is referred to in sections 908.1, 6103, 6104, 6105.1, 6105.2, 6109, 6110.2, 6111, 6111.1, 6115, 6117, 6118, 6123, 6301 of this title; sections 6102, 6107, 6108, 6108.3, 6119 of Title 23 (Domestic Relations); sections 5802, 6308 of Title 42 (Judiciary and Judicial Procedure).

§ 6105.1. Restoration of firearm rights for offenses under prior laws of this Commonwealth.

(a) Restoration.--A person convicted of a disabling offense may make application to the court of common pleas in the county where the principal residence of the applicant is situated for restoration of firearms rights. The court shall grant restoration of firearms rights after a hearing in open court to determine whether the requirements of this section have been met unless:

(1) the applicant has been convicted of any other offense specified in section 6105(a) or (b) (relating to persons not to possess, use, manufacture, control, sell or transfer firearms) or the applicant's conduct meets the criteria in section 6105(c)(1), (2), (3), (4), (5), (6) or (7);

(2) the applicant has been convicted of any other crime punishable by imprisonment exceeding one year as defined in section 6102 (relating to definitions); or

(3) the applicant's character and reputation is such that the applicant would be likely to act in a manner dangerous to public safety.

(b) Notice and standing.--

(1) Notice of an application for restoration of firearms rights shall be provided to the Pennsylvania State Police, the district attorney of the county where the disabling offense occurred and the district attorney of the county where the application is filed. The district attorney of the county where the application is filed, the district attorney of the county where the disabling offense occurred and the Pennsylvania State Police may, at their option, be parties to the proceeding.

(2) Notwithstanding paragraph (1), the standing of the Pennsylvania State Police as a party to a proceeding under this section shall be limited to determinations of whether the offense meets the definition of the phrase "disabling offense" or whether the provisions of subsection (a)(1) and (2) have been satisfied.

(c) Copy of order to Pennsylvania State Police.--If the court grants restoration of firearms rights to an applicant, a copy of the order shall be sent by the prothonotary within ten days of the entry of the order to the district attorneys and the Pennsylvania State Police, Firearms Division, and shall include the name, date of birth and Social Security number of the applicant.

(d) Expungement and pardon.--A restoration of firearms rights under this section shall not result in the expungement of any criminal history record information nor will it constitute a gubernatorial pardon.

(e) Definitions.--As used in this section, the following words and phrases shall have the meanings given to them in this subsection:

270

"Disabling offense." A conviction for any offense which:

(1) resulted in a Federal firearms disability and is substantially similar to either an offense currently graded as a crime punishable by a term of imprisonment for not more than two years or conduct which no longer constitutes a violation of law; and

(2) was a violation of either of the following:

(i) the former act of May 1, 1929 (P.L.905, No.403), known as The Vehicle Code, or the former act of April 29, 1959 (P.L.58, No.32), known as The Vehicle Code; or

(ii) the former act of June 24, 1939 (P.L.872, No.375), known as the Penal Code.

The definition shall not include any offense which, if committed under contemporary standards, would constitute a misdemeanor of the second degree or greater under section 2701 (relating to simple assault) and was committed by a current or former spouse, parent or guardian of the victim, by a person with whom the victim shares a child in common, by a person who is cohabitating with or has cohabitated with the victim as a spouse, parent or guardian or by a person similarly situated to a spouse, parent or guardian of the victim.

"Restoration of firearms rights." Relieving any and all disabilities with respect to a person's right to own, possess, use, control, sell, purchase, transfer, manufacture, receive, ship or transport firearms, including any disabilities imposed pursuant to this subchapter. The phrase shall also mean the restoration of the right to vote, to hold public office and to serve on a jury.

(Dec. 9, 2002, P.L.1391, No.172, eff. imd.)

2002 Amendment. Act 172 added section 6105.1.

§ 6105.2. Relinquishment of firearms and firearm licenses by convicted persons.

(a) Procedure.--

(1) A person subject to a firearms disability pursuant to section 6105(c)(9) (relating to persons not to possess, use, manufacture, control, sell or transfer firearms) shall relinquish any firearms under the person's possession or control to the appropriate law enforcement agency of the municipality as described in subsection (b) or to a dealer as described in subsection (c).

(2) The court of conviction shall order the relinquishment, and the order shall be transmitted to the appropriate law enforcement agency of the municipality and to the sheriff of the county of which the person is a resident. The order shall contain a list of any firearm ordered relinquished.

(3) The person shall inform the court in what manner the person will relinquish the firearms.

(4) If the person is present in court at the time of the order, the person shall inform the court whether relinquishment will be made under subsection (b) or (c).

(b) Relinquishment to law enforcement agency.--

(1) Relinquishment to an appropriate law enforcement agency shall be made within a period not longer than 24 hours following conviction, except for cause shown, in which case the court shall specify the time for relinquishment of any or all of the person's firearms.

(2) In securing custody of the person's relinquished firearms, the law enforcement agency shall provide the person subject to the relinquishment order with a signed and dated written receipt, which shall include a detailed description of each firearm and its condition.

(3) As used in this subsection, the term "cause" shall be limited to facts relating to the inability of the person to retrieve a specific firearm within a period not longer than 24 hours due to the then-current location of the firearm.

(c) Relinquishment to dealer.--

(1) In lieu of relinquishment to the local law enforcement agency, the person subject to a court order may, within 24 hours or within the time ordered by the court upon cause being shown as in subsection (b), relinquish firearms to a dealer licensed pursuant to section 6113 (relating to licensing of dealers).

(2) The dealer may charge the person a reasonable fee for accepting relinquishment.

(3) The person shall obtain an affidavit from the dealer on a form prescribed by the Pennsylvania State Police, which shall include, at a minimum, the following:

(i) The caption of the case in which the person was convicted.

(ii) The name, address, date of birth and Social Security number of the person.

271

(iii) A list of the firearms, including the manufacturer, model and serial number.

(iv) The name and license number of the dealer licensed pursuant to section 6113 and the address of the licensed premises.

(v) An acknowledgment that the firearms will not be returned to the person, unless the person is no longer prohibited from possessing a firearm under Federal or State law, or sold or transferred to a person the dealer knows is a member of the defendant's household.

(vi) An acknowledgment that the firearms, if transferred, will be transferred in compliance with this chapter.

(4) Any person relinquishing a firearm pursuant to this subsection shall, within the specified time frame, provide to the appropriate law enforcement agency or the sheriff's office, or both, the affidavit required by this subsection and relinquish to the law enforcement agency any firearm ordered to be relinquished that is not specified in the affidavit.

(d) Notice of noncompliance.--

(1) If the person fails to relinquish any firearm within 24 hours or within the time ordered by the court upon cause being shown, the law enforcement agency shall, at a minimum, provide immediate notice to the court, the victim, the prosecutor and the sheriff.

(2) For purposes of this subsection, "victim" shall have the same meaning as "direct victim" in section 103 of the act of November 24, 1998 (P.L.882, No.111), known as the Crime Victims Act.

(e) Alternate relinquishment to dealer.--

(1) If the person relinquishes firearms to the appropriate law enforcement agency pursuant to subsection (b), the person may request that the appropriate law enforcement agency make one transfer of any such firearm to a dealer licensed pursuant to section 6113 within six months of relinquishment.

(2) If requesting a subsequent transfer, the person shall provide the appropriate law enforcement agency with the dealer affidavit described in subsection (c).

(3) The appropriate law enforcement agency shall make the transfer, if the person complies with this subsection, and may charge the person for any costs associated with making the transfer.

(f) Recordkeeping.--Any portion of an order or petition or other paper that includes a list of firearms ordered to be relinquished shall be kept in the files of the court as a permanent record and withheld from public inspection, except upon an order of the court granted upon cause shown, after redaction of information relating to the firearms, or, as necessary, by law enforcement and court personnel.

(g) Relinquishment of licenses.--

(1) A person convicted of a crime resulting in a firearm disability pursuant to section 6105(c)(9) shall also relinquish to the sheriff any firearm license issued under section 6106 (relating to firearms not to be carried without a license) or 6109 (relating to licenses) or 23 Pa.C.S. § 6108.3 (relating to relinquishment to third party for safekeeping).

(2) The provisions of subsections (a)(2) and (3), (b), (d) and (f) shall also apply to firearm licenses of the person.

(h) Penalty.--A person convicted of a crime resulting in a firearm disability pursuant to section 6105(c)(9) commits a misdemeanor of the second degree if the person intentionally or knowingly fails to relinquish a firearm or other weapon or ammunition to an appropriate law enforcement agency or a dealer in accordance with this section.

(i) Definition.--As used in this section, the term "firearm" means any weapon which is designed to or may readily be converted to expel any projectile by the action of an explosive or the frame or receiver of any such weapon.

(Oct. 12, 2018, P.L.519, No.79, eff. 180 days)

2018 Amendment. Act 79 added section 6105.2. Act 79 shall apply to orders issued pursuant to 23 Pa.C.S. § 6108 on or after the effective date of section 11 of Act 79.

Cross References. Section 6105.2 is referred to in section 6105 of this title.

§ 6106. Firearms not to be carried without a license.

(a) Offense defined.--

(1) Except as provided in paragraph (2), any person who carries a firearm in any vehicle or any person who carries a firearm concealed on or about his person, except in his place of abode or fixed place of business, without a valid and lawfully issued license under this chapter commits a felony of the third degree.

(2) A person who is otherwise eligible to possess a valid license under this chapter but carries a firearm in any vehicle or any person who carries a firearm concealed on or about his person, except in his place of abode or fixed

place of business, without a valid and lawfully issued license and has not committed any other criminal violation commits a misdemeanor of the first degree.

(b) **Exceptions.**--The provisions of subsection (a) shall not apply to:

(1) Constables, sheriffs, prison or jail wardens, or their deputies, policemen of this Commonwealth or its political subdivisions, or other law-enforcement officers.

(2) Members of the army, navy, marine corps, air force or coast guard of the United States or of the National Guard or organized reserves when on duty.

(3) The regularly enrolled members of any organization duly organized to purchase or receive such firearms from the United States or from this Commonwealth.

(4) Any persons engaged in target shooting with a firearm, if such persons are at or are going to or from their places of assembly or target practice and if, while going to or from their places of assembly or target practice, the firearm is not loaded.

(5) Officers or employees of the United States duly authorized to carry a concealed firearm.

(6) Agents, messengers and other employees of common carriers, banks, or business firms, whose duties require them to protect moneys, valuables and other property in the discharge of such duties.

(7) Any person engaged in the business of manufacturing, repairing, or dealing in firearms, or the agent or representative of any such person, having in his possession, using or carrying a firearm in the usual or ordinary course of such business.

(8) Any person while carrying a firearm which is not loaded and is in a secure wrapper from the place of purchase to his home or place of business, or to a place of repair, sale or appraisal or back to his home or place of business, or in moving from one place of abode or business to another or from his home to a vacation or recreational home or dwelling or back, or to recover stolen property under section 6111.1(b)(4) (relating to Pennsylvania State Police), or to a place of instruction intended to teach the safe handling, use or maintenance of firearms or back or to a location to which the person has been directed to relinquish firearms under 23 Pa.C.S. § 6108 (relating to relief) or back upon return of the relinquished firearm or to a licensed dealer's place of business for relinquishment pursuant to 23 Pa.C.S. § 6108.2 (relating to relinquishment for consignment sale, lawful transfer or safekeeping) or back upon return of the relinquished firearm or to a location for safekeeping pursuant to 23 Pa.C.S. § 6108.3 (relating to relinquishment to third party for safekeeping) or back upon return of the relinquished firearm.

(9) Persons licensed to hunt, take furbearers or fish in this Commonwealth, if such persons are actually hunting, taking furbearers or fishing as permitted by such license, or are going to the places where they desire to hunt, take furbearers or fish or returning from such places.

(10) Persons training dogs, if such persons are actually training dogs during the regular training season.

(11) Any person while carrying a firearm in any vehicle, which person possesses a valid and lawfully issued license for that firearm which has been issued under the laws of the United States or any other state.

(12) A person who has a lawfully issued license to carry a firearm pursuant to section 6109 (relating to licenses) and that said license expired within six months prior to the date of arrest and that the individual is otherwise eligible for renewal of the license.

(13) Any person who is otherwise eligible to possess a firearm under this chapter and who is operating a motor vehicle which is registered in the person's name or the name of a spouse or parent and which contains a firearm for which a valid license has been issued pursuant to section 6109 to the spouse or parent owning the firearm.

(14) A person lawfully engaged in the interstate transportation of a firearm as defined under 18 U.S.C. § 921(a)(3) (relating to definitions) in compliance with 18 U.S.C. § 926A (relating to interstate transportation of firearms).

(15) Any person who possesses a valid and lawfully issued license or permit to carry a firearm which has been issued under the laws of another state, regardless of whether a reciprocity agreement exists between the Commonwealth and the state under section 6109(k), provided:

(i) The state provides a reciprocal privilege for individuals licensed to carry firearms under section 6109.

(ii) The Attorney General has determined that the firearm laws of the state are similar to the firearm laws of this Commonwealth.

(16) Any person holding a license in accordance with section 6109(f)(3).

(c) Sportsman's firearm permit.--

(1) Before any exception shall be granted under paragraph (b)(9) or (10) of this section to any person 18 years of age or older licensed to hunt, trap or fish or who has been issued a permit relating to hunting dogs, such person shall, at the time of securing his hunting, furtaking or fishing license or any time after such license has been issued, secure a sportsman's firearm permit from the county treasurer. The sportsman's firearm permit shall be issued immediately and be valid throughout this Commonwealth for a period of five years from the date of issue for any legal firearm, when carried in conjunction with a valid hunting, furtaking or fishing license or permit relating to hunting dogs. The sportsman's firearm permit shall be in triplicate on a form to be furnished by the Pennsylvania State Police. The original permit shall be delivered to the person, and the first copy thereof, within seven days, shall be forwarded to the Commissioner of the Pennsylvania State Police by the county treasurer. The second copy shall be retained by the county treasurer for a period of two years from the date of expiration. The county treasurer shall be entitled to collect a fee of not more than $6 for each such permit issued, which shall include the cost of any official form. The Pennsylvania State Police may recover from the county treasurer the cost of any such form, but may not charge more than $1 for each official permit form furnished to the county treasurer.

(2) Any person who sells or attempts to sell a sportsman's firearm permit for a fee in excess of that amount fixed under this subsection commits a summary offense.

(d) **Revocation of registration.**--Any registration of a firearm under subsection (c) of this section may be revoked by the county treasurer who issued it, upon written notice to the holder thereof.

(e) Definitions.--

(1) For purposes of subsection (b)(3), (4), (5), (7) and (8), the term "firearm" shall include any weapon which is designed to or may readily be converted to expel any projectile by the action of an explosive or the frame or receiver of the weapon.

(2) As used in this section, the phrase "place of instruction" shall include any hunting club, rifle club, rifle range, pistol range, shooting range, the premises of a licensed firearms dealer or a lawful gun show or meet.

(Oct. 12, 1973, P.L.283, No.81, eff. June 6, 1973; July 8, 1986, P.L.442, No.93, eff. July 1, 1987; Dec. 19, 1988, P.L.1275, No.158, eff. 180 days; Nov. 22, 1995, P.L.621, No.66, eff. imd.; Apr. 22, 1997, P.L.73, No.5, eff. 60 days; Dec. 20, 2000, P.L.728, No.101, eff. 60 days; Nov. 10, 2005, P.L.335, No.66, eff. 180 days; Oct. 17, 2008, P.L.1628, No.131, eff. 60 days)

2008 Amendment. Act 131 added subsec. (b)(16).

2005 Amendment. Act 66 amended subsec. (b) and added subsec. (e).

1997 Amendment. Act 5 amended subsecs. (a) and (b).

1988 Amendment. Act 158 amended subsecs. (b)(4) and (c).

Cross References. Section 6106 is referred to in sections 913, 6105.2, 6106.1, 6107, 6108, 6109, 6118, 6122 of this title; section 6108 of Title 23 (Domestic Relations).

§ 6106.1. Carrying loaded weapons other than firearms.

(a) **General rule.**--Except as provided in Title 34 (relating to game), no person shall carry a loaded pistol, revolver, shotgun or rifle, other than a firearm as defined in section 6102 (relating to definitions), in any vehicle. The provisions of this section shall not apply to persons excepted from the requirement of a license to carry firearms under section 6106(b)(1), (2), (5) or (6) (relating to firearms not to be carried without a license) nor shall the provisions of this section be construed to permit persons to carry firearms in a vehicle where such conduct is prohibited by section 6106.

(b) **Penalty.**--A person who violates the provisions of this section commits a summary offense.

(Dec. 7, 1989, P.L.607, No.68, eff. 60 days; June 13, 1995, 1st Sp.Sess., P.L.1024, No.17, eff. 120 days)

§ 6107. Prohibited conduct during emergency.

(a) **General rule.**--No person shall carry a firearm upon the public streets or upon any public property during an emergency proclaimed by a State or municipal governmental executive unless that person is:

(1) Actively engaged in a defense of that person's life or property from peril or threat.

(2) Licensed to carry firearms under section 6109 (relating to licenses) or is exempt from licensing under section 6106(b) (relating to firearms not to be carried without a license).

(b) Seizure, taking and confiscation.-- Except as otherwise provided under subsection (a) and notwithstanding the provisions of 35 Pa.C.S. Ch. 73 (relating to Commonwealth services) or any other provision of law to the contrary, no firearm, accessory or ammunition may be seized, taken or confiscated during an emergency unless the seizure, taking or confiscation would be authorized absent the emergency.

(c) Definitions.--As used in this section, the following words and phrases shall have the meanings given to them in this subsection:

"Accessory." Any scope, sight, bipod, sling, light, magazine, clip or other related item that is attached to or necessary for the operation of a firearm.

"Firearm." The term includes any weapon that is designed to or may readily be converted to expel any projectile by the action of an explosive or the frame or receiver of any weapon.

(June 13, 1995, 1st Sp.Sess., P.L.1024, No.17, eff. 120 days; Oct. 17, 2008, P.L.1628, No.131, eff. 60 days)

§ 6108. Carrying firearms on public streets or public property in Philadelphia.

No person shall carry a firearm, rifle or shotgun at any time upon the public streets or upon any public property in a city of the first class unless:

(1) such person is licensed to carry a firearm; or

(2) such person is exempt from licensing under section 6106(b) of this title (relating to firearms not to be carried without a license).

Cross References. Section 6108 is referred to in section 6109 of this title.

§ 6109. Licenses.

(a) Purpose of license.--A license to carry a firearm shall be for the purpose of carrying a firearm concealed on or about one's person or in a vehicle throughout this Commonwealth.

(b) Place of application.--An individual who is 21 years of age or older may apply to a sheriff for a license to carry a firearm concealed on or about his person or in a vehicle within this Commonwealth. If the applicant is a resident of this Commonwealth, he shall make application with the sheriff of the county in which he resides or, if a resident of a city of the first class, with the chief of police of that city.

(c) Form of application and content.-- The application for a license to carry a firearm shall be uniform throughout this Commonwealth and shall be on a form prescribed by the Pennsylvania State Police. The form may contain provisions, not exceeding one page, to assure compliance with this section. Issuing authorities shall use only the application form prescribed by the Pennsylvania State Police. One of the following reasons for obtaining a firearm license shall be set forth in the application: self-defense, employment, hunting and fishing, target shooting, gun collecting or another proper reason. The application form shall be dated and signed by the applicant and shall contain the following statement:

I have never been convicted of a crime that prohibits me from possessing or acquiring a firearm under Federal or State law. I am of sound mind and have never been committed to a mental institution. I hereby certify that the statements contained herein are true and correct to the best of my knowledge and belief. I understand that, if I knowingly make any false statements herein, I am subject to penalties prescribed by law. I authorize the sheriff, or his designee, or, in the case of first class cities, the chief or head of the police department, or his designee, to inspect only those records or documents relevant to information required for this application. If I am issued a license and knowingly become ineligible to legally possess or acquire firearms, I will promptly notify the sheriff of the county in which I reside or, if I reside in a city of the first class, the chief of police of that city.

(d) Sheriff to conduct investigation.-- The sheriff to whom the application is made shall:

(1) investigate the applicant's record of criminal conviction;

(2) investigate whether or not the applicant is under indictment for or has ever been convicted of a crime punishable by imprisonment exceeding one year;

(3) investigate whether the applicant's character and reputation are such that the applicant will not be likely to act in a manner dangerous to public safety;

(4) investigate whether the applicant would be precluded from receiving a license under subsection (e)(1) or section 6105(h) (relating to persons not to possess, use, manufacture, control, sell or transfer firearms); and

(5) conduct a criminal background, juvenile delinquency and mental health check following the procedures set forth in section 6111 (relating to sale or transfer of firearms), receive a unique approval number for that inquiry and record the date and number on the application.

(e) Issuance of license.--

(1) A license to carry a firearm shall be for the purpose of carrying a firearm concealed on or about one's person or in a vehicle and shall be issued if, after an investigation not to exceed 45 days, it appears that the applicant is an individual concerning whom no good cause exists to deny the license. A license shall not be issued to any of the following:

(i) An individual whose character and reputation is such that the individual would be likely to act in a manner dangerous to public safety.

(ii) An individual who has been convicted of an offense under the act of April 14, 1972 (P.L.233, No.64), known as The Controlled Substance, Drug, Device and Cosmetic Act.

(iii) An individual convicted of a crime enumerated in section 6105.

(iv) An individual who, within the past ten years, has been adjudicated delinquent for a crime enumerated in section 6105 or for an offense under The Controlled Substance, Drug, Device and Cosmetic Act.

(v) An individual who is not of sound mind or who has ever been committed to a mental institution.

(vi) An individual who is addicted to or is an unlawful user of marijuana or a stimulant, depressant or narcotic drug.

(vii) An individual who is a habitual drunkard.

(viii) An individual who is charged with or has been convicted of a crime punishable by imprisonment for a term exceeding one year except as provided for in section 6123 (relating to waiver of disability or pardons).

(ix) A resident of another state who does not possess a current license or permit or similar document to carry a firearm issued by that state if a license is provided for by the laws of that state, as published annually in the Federal Register by the Bureau of Alcohol, Tobacco and Firearms of the Department of the Treasury under 18 U.S.C. § 921(a)(19) (relating to definitions).

(x) An alien who is illegally in the United States.

(xi) An individual who has been discharged from the armed forces of the United States under dishonorable conditions.

(xii) An individual who is a fugitive from justice. This subparagraph does not apply to an individual whose fugitive status is based upon nonmoving or moving summary offense under Title 75 (relating to vehicles).

(xiii) An individual who is otherwise prohibited from possessing, using, manufacturing, controlling, purchasing, selling or transferring a firearm as provided by section 6105.

(xiv) An individual who is prohibited from possessing or acquiring a firearm under the statutes of the United States.

(2) (Deleted by amendment).

(3) The license to carry a firearm shall be designed to be uniform throughout this Commonwealth and shall be in a form prescribed by the Pennsylvania State Police. The license shall bear the following:

(i) The name, address, date of birth, race, sex, citizenship, height, weight, color of hair, color of eyes and signature of the licensee.

(ii) The signature of the sheriff issuing the license.

(iii) A license number of which the first two numbers shall be a county location code followed by numbers issued in numerical sequence.

(iv) The point-of-contact telephone number designated by the Pennsylvania State Police under subsection (l).

(v) The reason for issuance.

(vi) The period of validation.

(4) The sheriff shall require a photograph of the licensee on the license. The photograph shall be in a form compatible with the Commonwealth Photo Imaging Network.

(5) The original license shall be issued to the applicant. The first copy of the license shall be forwarded to the Pennsylvania State Police within seven days of the date of issue. The second copy shall be retained by the issuing authority for a period of seven years. Except pursuant to court order, both copies and the application shall, at the end of the seven-year

period, be destroyed unless the license has been renewed within the seven-year period.

(f) Term of license.--

(1) A license to carry a firearm issued under subsection (e) shall be valid throughout this Commonwealth for a period of five years unless extended under paragraph (3) or sooner revoked.

(2) At least 60 days prior to the expiration of each license, the issuing sheriff shall send to the licensee an application for renewal of license. Failure to receive a renewal application shall not relieve a licensee from the responsibility to renew the license.

(3) Notwithstanding paragraph (1) or any other provision of law to the contrary, a license to carry a firearm that is held by a member of the United States Armed Forces or the Pennsylvania National Guard on Federal active duty and deployed overseas that is scheduled to expire during the period of deployment shall be extended until 90 days after the end of the deployment.

(4) Possession of a license, together with a copy of the person's military orders showing the dates of overseas deployment, including the date that the overseas deployment ends, shall constitute, during the extension period specified in paragraph (3), a defense to any charge filed pursuant to section 6106 (relating to firearms not to be carried without a license) or 6108 (relating to carrying firearms on public streets or public property in Philadelphia).

(g) **Grant or denial of license.**--Upon the receipt of an application for a license to carry a firearm, the sheriff shall, within 45 days, issue or refuse to issue a license on the basis of the investigation under subsection (d) and the accuracy of the information contained in the application. If the sheriff refuses to issue a license, the sheriff shall notify the applicant in writing of the refusal and the specific reasons. The notice shall be sent by certified mail to the applicant at the address set forth in the application.

(h) Fee.--

(1) In addition to fees described in paragraphs (2)(ii) and (3), the fee for a license to carry a firearm is $19. This includes all of the following:

(i) A renewal notice processing fee of $1.50.

(ii) An administrative fee of $5 under section 14(2) of the act of July 6, 1984

(P.L.614, No.127), known as the Sheriff Fee Act.

(2) (Expired).

(3) An additional fee of $1 shall be paid by the applicant for a license to carry a firearm and shall be remitted by the sheriff to the Firearms License Validation System Account, which is hereby established as a special restricted receipt account within the General Fund of the State Treasury. The account shall be used for purposes under subsection (l). Moneys credited to the account and any investment income accrued are hereby appropriated on a continuing basis to the Pennsylvania State Police.

(4) No fee other than that provided by this subsection or the Sheriff Fee Act may be assessed by the sheriff for the performance of any background check made pursuant to this act.

(5) The fee is payable to the sheriff to whom the application is submitted and is payable at the time of application for the license.

(6) Except for the administrative fee of $5 under section 14(2) of the Sheriff Fee Act, all other fees shall be refunded if the application is denied but shall not be refunded if a license is issued and subsequently revoked.

(7) A person who sells or attempts to sell a license to carry a firearm for a fee in excess of the amounts fixed under this subsection commits a summary offense.

(i) **Revocation.**--A license to carry firearms may be revoked by the issuing authority for good cause. A license to carry firearms shall be revoked by the issuing authority for any reason stated in subsection (e)(1) which occurs during the term of the permit. Notice of revocation shall be in writing and shall state the specific reason for revocation. Notice shall be sent by certified mail to the individual whose license is revoked, and, at that time, notice shall also be provided to the Pennsylvania State Police by electronic means, including e-mail or facsimile transmission, that the license is no longer valid. An individual whose license is revoked shall surrender the license to the issuing authority within five days of receipt of the notice. An individual whose license is revoked may appeal to the court of common pleas for the judicial district in which the individual resides. An individual who violates this section commits a summary offense.

(i.1) Notice to sheriff.--Notwithstanding any statute to the contrary:

(1) Upon conviction of a person for a crime specified in section 6105(a) or (b) or upon conviction of a person for a crime punishable by imprisonment exceeding one year or upon a determination that the conduct of a person meets the criteria specified in section 6105(c)(1), (2), (3), (5), (6) or (9), the court shall determine if the defendant has a license to carry firearms issued pursuant to this section. If the defendant has such a license, the court shall notify the sheriff of the county in which that person resides, on a form developed by the Pennsylvania State Police, of the identity of the person and the nature of the crime or conduct which resulted in the notification. The notification shall be transmitted by the judge within seven days of the conviction or determination.

(2) Upon adjudication that a person is incompetent or upon the involuntary commitment of a person to a mental institution for inpatient care and treatment under the act of July 9, 1976 (P.L.817, No.143), known as the Mental Health Procedures Act, or upon involuntary treatment of a person as described under section 6105(c)(4), the judge of the court of common pleas, mental health review officer or county mental health and mental retardation administrator shall notify the sheriff of the county in which that person resides, on a form developed by the Pennsylvania State Police, of the identity of the person who has been adjudicated, committed or treated and the nature of the adjudication, commitment or treatment. The notification shall be transmitted by the judge, mental health review officer or county mental health and mental retardation administrator within seven days of the adjudication, commitment or treatment.

(j) Immunity.--A sheriff who complies in good faith with this section shall be immune from liability resulting or arising from the action or misconduct with a firearm committed by any individual to whom a license to carry a firearm has been issued.

(k) Reciprocity.--

(1) The Attorney General shall have the power and duty to enter into reciprocity agreements with other states providing for the mutual recognition of a license to carry a firearm issued by the Commonwealth and a license or permit to carry a firearm issued by the other state. To carry out this duty, the Attorney General is authorized to negotiate reciprocity agreements and grant recognition of a license or permit to carry a firearm issued by another state.

(2) The Attorney General shall report to the General Assembly within 180 days of the effective date of this paragraph and annually thereafter concerning the agreements which have been consummated under this subsection.

(l) Firearms License Validation System.--

(1) The Pennsylvania State Police shall establish a nationwide toll-free telephone number, known as the Firearms License Validation System, which shall be operational seven days a week, 24 hours per day, for the purpose of responding to law enforcement inquiries regarding the validity of any Pennsylvania license to carry a firearm.

(2) Notwithstanding any other law regarding the confidentiality of information, inquiries to the Firearms License Validation System regarding the validity of any Pennsylvania license to carry a firearm may only be made by law enforcement personnel acting within the scope of their official duties.

(3) Law enforcement personnel outside this Commonwealth shall provide their originating agency identifier number and the license number of the license to carry a firearm which is the subject of the inquiry.

(4) Responses to inquiries by law enforcement personnel outside this Commonwealth shall be limited to the name of the licensee, the validity of the license and any information which may be provided to a criminal justice agency pursuant to Chapter 91 (relating to criminal history record information).

(m) Inquiries.--

(1) The Attorney General shall, not later than one year after the effective date of this subsection and not less than once annually, contact in writing the appropriate authorities in any other state which does not have a current reciprocity agreement with the Commonwealth to determine if:

(i) the state will negotiate a reciprocity agreement;

(ii) a licensee may carry a concealed firearm in the state; or

(iii) a licensee may apply for a license or permit to carry a firearm issued by the state.

(2) The Attorney General shall maintain a current list of those states which have a reciprocity agreement with the Commonwealth,

those states which allow licensees to carry a concealed firearm and those states which allow licensees to apply for a license or permit to carry a firearm. This list shall be posted on the Internet, provided to the Pennsylvania State Police and made available to the public upon request.

(m.1) Temporary emergency licenses.--

(1) A person seeking a temporary emergency license to carry a concealed firearm shall submit to the sheriff of the county in which the person resides all of the following:

(i) Evidence of imminent danger to the person or the person's minor child. For purposes of this subparagraph, the term "minor" shall have the same meaning as provided in 1 Pa.C.S. § 1991 (relating to definitions).

(ii) A sworn affidavit that contains the information required on an application for a license to carry a firearm and attesting that the person is 21 years of age or older, is not prohibited from owning firearms under section 6105 (relating to persons not to possess, use, manufacture, control, sell or transfer firearms) or any other Federal or State law and is not currently subject to a protection from abuse order or a protection order issued by a court of another state.

(iii) In addition to the provisions of subsection (h), a temporary emergency license fee established by the Commissioner of the Pennsylvania State Police for an amount that does not exceed the actual cost of conducting the criminal background check or $10, whichever is less.

(iv) An application for a license to carry a firearm on the form prescribed pursuant to subsection (c).

(2) Upon receipt of the items required under paragraph (1), the sheriff immediately shall conduct a criminal history, juvenile delinquency and mental health record check of the applicant pursuant to section 6105. Immediately upon receipt of the results of the records check, the sheriff shall review the information and shall determine whether the applicant meets the criteria set forth in this subsection. If the sheriff determines that the applicant has met all of the criteria, the sheriff shall immediately issue the applicant a temporary emergency license to carry a concealed firearm.

(3) If the sheriff refuses to issue a temporary emergency license, the sheriff shall specify the grounds for the denial in a written

notice to the applicant. The applicant may appeal the denial or challenge criminal records check results that were the basis of the denial, if applicable, in the same manner as a denial of a license to carry a firearm under this section.

(4) A temporary emergency license issued under this subsection shall be valid for 45 days and may not be renewed. A person who has been issued a temporary emergency license under this subsection shall not be issued another temporary emergency license unless at least five years have expired since the issuance of the prior temporary emergency license. During the 45 days the temporary emergency license is valid, the sheriff shall conduct an additional investigation of the person for the purposes of determining whether the person may be issued a license pursuant to this section. If, during the course of this investigation, the sheriff discovers any information that would have prohibited the issuance of a license pursuant to this section, the sheriff shall be authorized to revoke the temporary emergency license as provided in subsection (i).

(5) The temporary emergency license issued pursuant to this section shall be consistent with the form prescribed in subsection (e)(3), (4) and (5). In addition to the information provided in those paragraphs, the temporary emergency license shall be clearly marked "Temporary."

(6) A person who holds a temporary emergency license to carry a firearm shall have the same rights to carry a firearm as a person issued a license to carry a firearm under this section. A licensee under this subsection shall be subject to all other duties, restrictions and penalties under this section, including revocation pursuant to subsection (i).

(7) A sheriff who issues a temporary emergency license to carry a firearm shall retain, for the entire period during which the temporary emergency license is in effect, the evidence of imminent danger that the applicant submitted to the sheriff that was the basis for the license, or a copy of the evidence, as appropriate.

(8) A person applying for a temporary emergency license shall complete the application required pursuant to subsection (c) and shall provide at the time of application the information required in paragraph (1).

(9) Prior to the expiration of a temporary emergency license, if the sheriff has determined pursuant to investigation that the person issued

a temporary emergency license is not disqualified and if the temporary emergency license has not been revoked pursuant to subsection (i), the sheriff shall issue a license pursuant to this section that is effective for the balance of the five-year period from the date of the issuance of the temporary emergency license. Records and all other information, duties and obligations regarding such licenses shall be applicable as otherwise provided in this section.

(10) As used in this subsection, the term "evidence of imminent danger" means:

(i) a written document prepared by the Attorney General, a district attorney, a chief law enforcement officer, judicial officer or their designees describing the facts that give a person reasonable cause to fear a criminal attack upon the person or the person's minor child. For the purposes of this subparagraph, the term "chief law enforcement officer" shall have the same meaning as provided in 42 Pa.C.S. § 8951 (relating to definitions) and "judicial officer" shall have the same meaning as provided in 42 Pa.C.S. § 102 (relating to definitions).

(ii) a police report.

(m.2) Inconsistent provisions.-- Notwithstanding the provisions of section 7506 (relating to violation of rules regarding conduct on Commonwealth property), 75 Pa.C.S. § 7727 (relating to additional limitations on operation) or the act of June 28, 1995 (P.L.89, No.18), known as the Conservation and Natural Resources Act, and regulations promulgated under that act, a firearm may be carried as provided in subsection (a) by:

(1) a law enforcement officer whose current identification as a law enforcement officer shall be construed as a valid license to carry a firearm; or

(2) any licensee.

(m.3) Construction.--Nothing in this section shall be construed to:

(1) Permit the hunting or harvesting of any wildlife with a firearm or ammunition not otherwise permitted by 34 Pa.C.S. (relating to game).

(2) Authorize any Commonwealth agency to regulate the possession of firearms in any manner inconsistent with the provisions of this title.

(n) Definition.--As used in this section, the term "licensee" means an individual who is licensed to carry a firearm under this section.

(Apr. 17, 1986, P.L.82, No.28, eff. Jan. 1, 1987; Dec. 19, 1988, P.L.1275, No.158, eff. 180 days; June 13, 1995, 1st Sp.Sess., P.L.1024, No.17, eff. 120 days; Nov. 22, 1995, P.L.621, No.66, eff. imd.; Apr. 22, 1997, P.L.73, No.5, eff. 60 days; June 18, 1998, P.L.503, No.70, eff. imd.; Nov. 10, 2005, P.L.335, No.66; Oct. 17, 2008, P.L.1628, No.131, eff. 60 days; June 28, 2011, P.L.48, No.10, eff. 60 days)

2011 Amendment. Act 10 amended subsec. (m.3). See the preamble to Act 10 in the appendix to this title for special provisions relating to legislative findings.

2011 Expiration. Subsec. (h)(2) expired May 9, 2011. See Act 66 of 2005.

2008 Amendment. Act 131 amended subsec. (f)(1) and added subsecs. (f)(3) and (4), (m.1), (m.2) and (m.3).

2005 Amendment. Act 66 amended subsecs. (c), (d), (e), (h), (i) and (k) and added subsecs. (i.1), (l), (m) and (n). Section 14 of Act 66 provided that the Pennsylvania Commission on Crime and Delinquency shall submit a report to the General Assembly three years after the effective date of section 14 on the progress of the Firearms License to Carry Modernization Account. See section 15 of Act 66 in the appendix to this title for special provisions relating to effective date.

1997 Amendment. Act 5 amended subsec. (a).

1995 Amendment. Act 66 amended subsecs. (a), (f) and (h).

Cross References. Section 6109 is referred to in sections 913, 6105, 6105.2, 6106, 6107, 6111, 6115, 6124 of this title; section 6108 of Title 23 (Domestic Relations); sections 2325, 2525 of Title 34 (Game).

§ 6110. Persons to whom delivery shall not be made (Repealed).

1995 Repeal. Section 6110 was repealed June 13, 1995 (1st Sp.Sess., P.L.1024, No.17), effective in 120 days.

§ 6110.1. Possession of firearm by minor.

(a) Firearm.--Except as provided in subsection (b), a person under 18 years of age shall not possess or transport a firearm anywhere in this Commonwealth.

(b) Exception.--Subsection (a) shall not apply to a person under 18 years of age:

(1) who is under the supervision of a parent, grandparent, legal guardian or an adult

acting with the expressed consent of the minor's custodial parent or legal guardian and the minor is engaged in lawful activity, including safety training, lawful target shooting, engaging in an organized competition involving the use of a firearm or the firearm is unloaded and the minor is transporting it for a lawful purpose; or

(2) who is lawfully hunting or trapping in accordance with 34 Pa.C.S. (relating to game).

(c) Responsibility of adult.--Any person who knowingly and intentionally delivers or provides to the minor a firearm in violation of subsection (a) commits a felony of the third degree.

(d) Forfeiture.--Any firearm in the possession of a person under 18 years of age in violation of this section shall be promptly seized by the arresting law enforcement officer and upon conviction or adjudication of delinquency shall be forfeited or, if stolen, returned to the lawful owner.

(June 13, 1995, 1st Sp.Sess., P.L.1024, No.17, eff. 120 days; Nov. 22, 1995, P.L.621, No.66, eff. imd.)

1995 Amendments. Act 17, 1st Sp.Sess., added section 6110.1 and Act 66 amended subsec. (b).

Cross References. Section 6110.1 is referred to in sections 6105, 6115 of this title.

§ 6110.2. Possession of firearm with altered manufacturer's number.

(a) General rule.--No person shall possess a firearm which has had the manufacturer's number integral to the frame or receiver altered, changed, removed or obliterated.

(b) Penalty.--A person who violates this section commits a felony of the second degree.

(c) Definition.--As used in this section, the term "firearm" shall have the same meaning as that term is defined in section 6105(i) (relating to persons not to possess, use, manufacture, control, sell or transfer firearms), except that the term shall not include antique firearms as defined in section 6118 (relating to antique firearms).

(Dec. 15, 1999, P.L.915, No.59, eff. 60 days; Oct. 17, 2008, P.L.1628, No.131, eff. 60 days)

§ 6111. Sale or transfer of firearms.

(a) Time and manner of delivery.--

(1) Except as provided in paragraph (2), no seller shall deliver a firearm to the purchaser or transferee thereof until 48 hours shall have elapsed from the time of the application for the purchase thereof, and, when delivered, the firearm shall be securely wrapped and shall be unloaded.

(2) Thirty days after publication in the Pennsylvania Bulletin that the Instantaneous Criminal History Records Check System has been established in accordance with the Brady Handgun Violence Prevention Act (Public Law 103-159, 18 U.S.C. § 921 et seq.), no seller shall deliver a firearm to the purchaser thereof until the provisions of this section have been satisfied, and, when delivered, the firearm shall be securely wrapped and shall be unloaded.

(b) Duty of seller.--No licensed importer, licensed manufacturer or licensed dealer shall sell or deliver any firearm to another person, other than a licensed importer, licensed manufacturer, licensed dealer or licensed collector, until the conditions of subsection (a) have been satisfied and until he has:

(1) For purposes of a firearm as defined in section 6102 (relating to definitions), obtained a completed application/record of sale from the potential buyer or transferee to be filled out in triplicate, the original copy to be sent to the Pennsylvania State Police, postmarked via first class mail, within 14 days of the sale, one copy to be retained by the licensed importer, licensed manufacturer or licensed dealer for a period of 20 years and one copy to be provided to the purchaser or transferee. The form of this application/record of sale shall be no more than one page in length and shall be promulgated by the Pennsylvania State Police and provided by the licensed importer, licensed manufacturer or licensed dealer. The application/record of sale shall include the name, address, birthdate, gender, race, physical description and Social Security number of the purchaser or transferee, the date of the application and the caliber, length of barrel, make, model and manufacturer's number of the firearm to be purchased or transferred. The application/record of sale shall also contain the following question:

Are you the actual buyer of the firearm(s), as defined under 18 Pa.C.S. § 6102 (relating to definitions), listed on this application/record of sale? Warning: You are not the actual buyer if you are acquiring the firearm(s) on behalf of another person, unless you are legitimately acquiring the firearm as a gift for any of the following individuals who are legally eligible to own a firearm:

(1) spouse;

(2) parent;

(3) child;

(4) grandparent; or

(5) grandchild.

(1.1) On the date of publication in the Pennsylvania Bulletin of a notice by the Pennsylvania State Police that the instantaneous records check has been implemented, all of the following shall apply:

(i) In the event of an electronic failure under section 6111.1(b)(2) (relating to Pennsylvania State Police) for purposes of a firearm which exceeds the barrel and related lengths set forth in section 6102, obtained a completed application/record of sale from the potential buyer or transferee to be filled out in triplicate, the original copy to be sent to the Pennsylvania State Police, postmarked via first class mail, within 14 days of sale, one copy to be retained by the licensed importer, licensed manufacturer or licensed dealer for a period of 20 years and one copy to be provided to the purchaser or transferee.

(ii) The form of the application/record of sale shall be no more than one page in length and shall be promulgated by the Pennsylvania State Police and provided by the licensed importer, licensed manufacturer or licensed dealer.

(iii) For purposes of conducting the criminal history, juvenile delinquency and mental health records background check which shall be completed within ten days of receipt of the information from the dealer, the application/record of sale shall include the name, address, birthdate, gender, race, physical description and Social Security number of the purchaser or transferee and the date of application.

(iv) No information regarding the type of firearm need be included other than an indication that the firearm exceeds the barrel lengths set forth in section 6102.

(v) Unless it has been discovered pursuant to a criminal history, juvenile delinquency and mental health records background check that the potential purchaser or transferee is prohibited from possessing a firearm pursuant to section 6105 (relating to persons not to possess, use, manufacture, control, sell or transfer firearms), no information on the application/record of sale provided pursuant to this subsection shall be retained as precluded by section 6111.4 (relating to registration of firearms) by the Pennsylvania State Police either through retention of the application/record of sale or by entering the information onto a computer, and, further, an application/record of sale received by the Pennsylvania State Police pursuant to this subsection shall be destroyed within 72 hours of the completion of the criminal history, juvenile delinquency and mental health records background check.

(1.2) Fees collected under paragraph (3) and section 6111.2 (relating to firearm sales surcharge) shall be transmitted to the Pennsylvania State Police within 14 days of collection.

(1.3) In addition to the criminal penalty under section 6119 (relating to violation penalty), any person who knowingly and intentionally maintains or fails to destroy any information submitted to the Pennsylvania State Police for purposes of a background check pursuant to paragraphs (1.1) and (1.4) or violates section 6111.4 shall be subject to a civil penalty of $250 per violation, entry or failure to destroy.

(1.4) Following implementation of the instantaneous records check by the Pennsylvania State Police on or before December 1, 1998, no application/record of sale shall be completed for the purchase or transfer of a firearm which exceeds the barrel lengths set forth in section 6102. A statement shall be submitted by the dealer to the Pennsylvania State Police, postmarked via first class mail, within 14 days of the sale, containing the number of firearms sold which exceed the barrel and related lengths set forth in section 6102, the amount of surcharge and other fees remitted and a list of the unique approval numbers given pursuant to paragraph (4), together with a statement that the background checks have been performed on the firearms contained in the statement. The form of the statement relating to performance of background checks shall be promulgated by the Pennsylvania State Police.

(2) Inspected photoidentification of the potential purchaser or transferee, including, but not limited to, a driver's license, official Pennsylvania photoidentification card or official government photoidentification card. In the case of a potential buyer or transferee who is a member of a recognized religious sect or community whose tenets forbid or discourage the taking of photographs of members of that

sect or community, a seller shall accept a valid-without-photo driver's license or a combination of documents, as prescribed by the Pennsylvania State Police, containing the applicant's name, address, date of birth and the signature of the applicant.

(3) Requested by means of a telephone call that the Pennsylvania State Police conduct a criminal history, juvenile delinquency history and a mental health record check. The purchaser and the licensed dealer shall provide such information as is necessary to accurately identify the purchaser. The requester shall be charged a fee equivalent to the cost of providing the service but not to exceed $2 per buyer or transferee.

(4) Received a unique approval number for that inquiry from the Pennsylvania State Police and recorded the date and the number on the application/record of sale form.

(5) Issued a receipt containing the information from paragraph (4), including the unique approval number of the purchaser. This receipt shall be prima facie evidence of the purchaser's or transferee's compliance with the provisions of this section.

(6) Unless it has been discovered pursuant to a criminal history, juvenile delinquency and mental health records background check that the potential purchaser or transferee is prohibited from possessing a firearm pursuant to section 6105, no information received via telephone following the implementation of the instantaneous background check system from a purchaser or transferee who has received a unique approval number shall be retained by the Pennsylvania State Police.

(7) For purposes of the enforcement of 18 U.S.C. § 922(d)(9), (g)(1) and (s)(1) (relating to unlawful acts), in the event the criminal history or juvenile delinquency background check indicates a conviction for a misdemeanor that the Pennsylvania State Police cannot determine is or is not related to an act of domestic violence, the Pennsylvania State Police shall issue a temporary delay of the approval of the purchase or transfer. During the temporary delay, the Pennsylvania State Police shall conduct a review or investigation of the conviction with courts, local police departments, district attorneys and other law enforcement or related institutions as necessary to determine whether or not the misdemeanor conviction involved an act of domestic violence. The Pennsylvania State Police shall

conduct the review or investigation as expeditiously as possible. No firearm may be transferred by the dealer to the purchaser who is the subject of the investigation during the temporary delay. The Pennsylvania State Police shall notify the dealer of the termination of the temporary delay and either deny the sale or provide the unique approval number under paragraph (4).

(c) Duty of other persons.--Any person who is not a licensed importer, manufacturer or dealer and who desires to sell or transfer a firearm to another unlicensed person shall do so only upon the place of business of a licensed importer, manufacturer, dealer or county sheriff's office, the latter of whom shall follow the procedure set forth in this section as if he were the seller of the firearm. The provisions of this section shall not apply to transfers between spouses or to transfers between a parent and child or to transfers between grandparent and grandchild.

(d) Defense.--Compliance with the provisions of this section shall be a defense to any criminal complaint under the laws of this Commonwealth or other claim or cause of action under this chapter arising from the sale or transfer of any firearm.

(d.1) Concurrent jurisdiction to prosecute.--The following apply in a city of the first class where the Attorney General has operated a joint local-State firearm task force:

(1) In addition to the authority conferred upon the Attorney General by the act of October 15, 1980 (P.L.950, No.164), known as the Commonwealth Attorneys Act, the Attorney General shall have the authority to investigate and institute criminal proceedings for a violation of this section.

(2) No person charged with a violation of this section by the Attorney General shall have standing to challenge the authority of the Attorney General to prosecute the case, and, if any such challenge is made, the challenge shall be dismissed and no relief shall be available in the courts of this Commonwealth to the person making the challenge.

(3) This subsection shall not apply to any case instituted two years after the effective date of this subsection.

(e) Nonapplicability of section.--This section shall not apply to the following:

(1) Any firearm manufactured on or before 1898.

(2) Any firearm with a matchlock, flintlock or percussion cap type of ignition system.

(3) Any replica of any firearm described in paragraph (1) if the replica:

(i) is not designed or redesigned to use rimfire or conventional center fire fixed ammunition; or

(ii) uses rimfire or conventional center fire fixed ammunition which is no longer manufactured in the United States and which is not readily available in the ordinary channels of commercial trade.

(f) Application of section.--

(1) For the purposes of this section only, except as provided by paragraph (2), "firearm" shall mean any weapon which is designed to or may readily be converted to expel any projectile by the action of an explosive or the frame or receiver of any such weapon.

(2) The provisions contained in subsections (a) and (c) shall only apply to pistols or revolvers with a barrel length of less than 15 inches, any shotgun with a barrel length of less than 18 inches, any rifle with a barrel length of less than 16 inches or any firearm with an overall length of less than 26 inches.

(3) The provisions contained in subsection (a) shall not apply to any law enforcement officer whose current identification as a law enforcement officer shall be construed as a valid license to carry a firearm or any person who possesses a valid license to carry a firearm under section 6109 (relating to licenses).

(4) (i) The provisions of subsection (a) shall not apply to any person who presents to the seller or transferor a written statement issued by the official described in subparagraph (iii) during the ten-day period ending on the date of the most recent proposal of such transfer or sale by the transferee or purchaser stating that the transferee or purchaser requires access to a firearm because of a threat to the life of the transferee or purchaser or any member of the household of that transferee or purchaser.

(ii) The issuing official shall notify the applicant's local police authority that such a statement has been issued. In counties of the first class the chief of police shall notify the police station or substation closest to the applicant's residence.

(iii) The statement issued under subparagraph (ii) shall be issued by the district attorney, or his designee, of the county of residence if the transferee or purchaser resides in a municipality where there is no chief of police. Otherwise, the statement shall be issued by the chief of police in the municipality in which the purchaser or transferee resides.

(g) Penalties.--

(1) Any person, licensed dealer, licensed manufacturer or licensed importer who knowingly or intentionally sells, delivers or transfers a firearm in violation of this section commits a misdemeanor of the second degree.

(2) Any person, licensed dealer, licensed manufacturer or licensed importer who knowingly or intentionally sells, delivers or transfers a firearm under circumstances intended to provide a firearm to any person, purchaser or transferee who is unqualified or ineligible to control, possess or use a firearm under this chapter commits a felony of the third degree and shall in addition be subject to revocation of the license to sell firearms for a period of three years.

(3) Any person, licensed dealer, licensed manufacturer or licensed importer who knowingly and intentionally requests a criminal history, juvenile delinquency or mental health record check or other confidential information from the Pennsylvania State Police under this chapter for any purpose other than compliance with this chapter or knowingly and intentionally disseminates any criminal history, juvenile delinquency or mental health record or other confidential information to any person other than the subject of the information commits a felony of the third degree.

(3.1) Any person, licensed dealer, licensed manufacturer or licensed importer who knowingly and intentionally obtains or furnishes information collected or maintained pursuant to section 6109 for any purpose other than compliance with this chapter or who knowingly or intentionally disseminates, publishes or otherwise makes available such information to any person other than the subject of the information commits a felony of the third degree.

(4) Any person, purchaser or transferee commits a felony of the third degree if, in connection with the purchase, delivery or transfer of a firearm under this chapter, he knowingly and intentionally:

(i) makes any materially false oral statement;

(ii) makes any materially false written statement, including a statement on any form promulgated by Federal or State agencies; or

(iii) willfully furnishes or exhibits any false identification intended or likely to deceive the seller, licensed dealer or licensed manufacturer.

(5) Notwithstanding section 306 (relating to liability for conduct of another; complicity) or any other statute to the contrary, any person, licensed importer, licensed dealer or licensed manufacturer who knowingly and intentionally sells, delivers or transfers a firearm in violation of this chapter who has reason to believe that the firearm is intended to be used in the commission of a crime or attempt to commit a crime shall be criminally liable for such crime or attempted crime.

(6) Notwithstanding any act or statute to the contrary, any person, licensed importer, licensed manufacturer or licensed dealer who knowingly and intentionally sells or delivers a firearm in violation of this chapter who has reason to believe that the firearm is intended to be used in the commission of a crime or attempt to commit a crime shall be liable in the amount of the civil judgment for injuries suffered by any person so injured by such crime or attempted crime.

(h) Subsequent violation penalty.--

(1) A second or subsequent violation of this section shall be a felony of the second degree. A person who at the time of sentencing has been convicted of another offense under this section shall be sentenced to a mandatory minimum sentence of imprisonment of five years. A second or subsequent offense shall also result in permanent revocation of any license to sell, import or manufacture a firearm.

(2) Notice of the applicability of this subsection to the defendant and reasonable notice of the Commonwealth's intention to proceed under this section shall be provided prior to trial. The applicability of this section shall be determined at sentencing. The court shall consider evidence presented at trial, shall afford the Commonwealth and the defendant an opportunity to present necessary additional evidence and shall determine by a preponderance of the evidence if this section is applicable.

(3) There shall be no authority for a court to impose on a defendant to which this subsection is applicable a lesser sentence than provided for in paragraph (1), to place the defendant on probation or to suspend sentence. Nothing in this section shall prevent the sentencing court from imposing a sentence greater than that provided in this section. Sentencing guidelines promulgated by the Pennsylvania Commission on Sentencing shall not supersede the mandatory sentences provided in this section.

(4) If a sentencing court refuses to apply this subsection where applicable, the Commonwealth shall have the right to appellate review of the action of the sentencing court. The appellate court shall vacate the sentence and remand the case to the sentencing court for imposition of a sentence in accordance with this section if it finds that the sentence was imposed in violation of this subsection.

(5) For the purposes of this subsection, a person shall be deemed to have been convicted of another offense under this section whether or not judgment of sentence has been imposed for that violation.

(i) Confidentiality.--All information provided by the potential purchaser, transferee or applicant, including, but not limited to, the potential purchaser, transferee or applicant's name or identity, furnished by a potential purchaser or transferee under this section or any applicant for a license to carry a firearm as provided by section 6109 shall be confidential and not subject to public disclosure. In addition to any other sanction or penalty imposed by this chapter, any person, licensed dealer, State or local governmental agency or department that violates this subsection shall be liable in civil damages in the amount of $1,000 per occurrence or three times the actual damages incurred as a result of the violation, whichever is greater, as well as reasonable attorney fees.

(j) Exemption.--

(1) The provisions of subsections (a) and (b) shall not apply to:

(i) sales between Federal firearms licensees; or

(ii) the purchase of firearms by a chief law enforcement officer or his designee, for the official use of law enforcement officers.

(2) For the purposes of this subsection, the term "chief law enforcement officer" shall include the Commissioner of the Pennsylvania State Police, the chief or head of a police department, a county sheriff or any equivalent law enforcement official.

(June 13, 1995, 1st Sp.Sess., P.L.1024, No.17, eff. 120 days; Nov. 22, 1995, P.L.621,

No.66; Apr. 22, 1997, P.L.73, No.5; June 18, 1998, P.L.503, No.70, eff. imd.; Dec. 3, 1998, P.L.933, No.121, eff. imd.; Dec. 15, 1999, P.L.915, No.59, eff. 60 days; Dec. 20, 2000, P.L.728, No.101, eff. 60 days; Oct. 17, 2008, P.L.1628, No.131, eff. 60 days; Oct. 25, 2012, P.L.1626, No.199, eff. 60 days; July 2, 2019, P.L.375, No.58, eff. 60 days)

2019 Amendment. Act 58 added subsec. (d.1).

2012 Amendment. Act 199 amended subsec. (h).

2008 Amendment. Act 131 amended subsecs. (b)(1), (g)(4) and (j).

2000 Amendment. Act 101 amended subsec. (j).

1998 Amendments. Act 70 amended subsecs. (b)(1.1) intro. par. and (i), (1.4) and (3) and (g)(3) and added subsecs. (b)(7) and (g)(3.1) and Act 121 amended subsec. (b)(1.4). Act 121 overlooked the amendment by Act 70, but the amendments do not conflict in substance (except for the date, as to which Act 121 has been given effect) and have both been given effect in setting forth the text of subsec. (b)(1.4).

1997 Amendment. Act 5 amended the entire section, effective immediately as to subsec. (b)(1.1) and 60 days as to the remainder of the section.

Cross References. Section 6111 is referred to in sections 6109, 6111.1, 6111.2, 6111.3, 6113 of this title; section 6108.3 of Title 23 (Domestic Relations); section 5552 of Title 42 (Judiciary and Judicial Procedure).

§ 6111.1. Pennsylvania State Police.

(a) Administration.--The Pennsylvania State Police shall have the responsibility to administer the provisions of this chapter.

(b) Duty of Pennsylvania State Police.--

(1) Upon receipt of a request for a criminal history, juvenile delinquency history and mental health record check of the potential purchaser or transferee, the Pennsylvania State Police shall immediately during the licensee's call or by return call forthwith:

(i) review the Pennsylvania State Police criminal history and fingerprint records to determine if the potential purchaser or transferee is prohibited from receipt or possession of a firearm under Federal or State law;

(ii) review the juvenile delinquency and mental health records of the Pennsylvania State Police to determine whether the potential purchaser or transferee is prohibited from receipt or possession of a firearm under Federal or State law; and

(iii) inform the licensee making the inquiry either:

(A) that the potential purchase or transfer is prohibited; or

(B) provide the licensee with a unique approval number.

(2) In the event of electronic failure, scheduled computer downtime or similar event beyond the control of the Pennsylvania State Police, the Pennsylvania State Police shall immediately notify the requesting licensee of the reason for and estimated length of the delay. If the failure or event lasts for a period exceeding 48 hours, the dealer shall not be subject to any penalty for completing a transaction absent the completion of an instantaneous records check for the remainder of the failure or similar event, but the dealer shall obtain a completed application/record of sale following the provisions of section 6111(b)(1) and (1.1) (relating to sale or transfer of firearms) as if an instantaneous records check has not been established for any sale or transfer of a firearm for the purpose of a subsequent background check.

(3) The Pennsylvania State Police shall fully comply, execute and enforce the directives of this section as follows:

(i) The instantaneous background check for firearms as defined in section 6102 (relating to definitions) shall begin on July 1, 1998.

(ii) The instantaneous background check for firearms that exceed the barrel lengths set forth in section 6102 shall begin on the later of:

(A) the date of publication of the notice under section 6111(a)(2); or

(B) December 31, 1998.

(4) The Pennsylvania State Police and any local law enforcement agency shall make all reasonable efforts to determine the lawful owner of any firearm confiscated or recovered by the Pennsylvania State Police or any local law enforcement agency and return said firearm to its lawful owner if the owner is not otherwise prohibited from possessing the firearm. When a court of law has determined that the Pennsylvania State Police or any local law enforcement agency have failed to exercise the duty under this subsection, reasonable attorney fees shall be awarded to any lawful owner of

said firearm who has sought judicial enforcement of this subsection.

(c) Establish a telephone number.--The Pennsylvania State Police shall establish a telephone number which shall be operational seven days a week between the hours of 8 a.m. and 10 p.m. local time for purposes of responding to inquiries as described in this section from licensed manufacturers, licensed importers and licensed dealers. The Pennsylvania State Police shall employ and train such personnel as are necessary to administer expeditiously the provisions of this section.

(d) Distribution.--The Pennsylvania State Police shall provide, without charge, summaries of uniform firearm laws and firearm safety brochures pursuant to section 6125 (relating to distribution of uniform firearm laws and firearm safety brochures).

(e) Challenge to records.--

(1) Any person who is denied the right to receive, sell, transfer, possess, carry, manufacture or purchase a firearm as a result of the procedures established by this section may challenge the accuracy of that person's criminal history, juvenile delinquency history or mental health record pursuant to a denial by the instantaneous records check by submitting a challenge to the Pennsylvania State Police within 30 days from the date of the denial.

(2) The Pennsylvania State Police shall conduct a review of the accuracy of the information forming the basis for the denial and shall have the burden of proving the accuracy of the record. Within 20 days after receiving a challenge, the Pennsylvania State Police shall notify the challenger of the basis for the denial, including, but not limited to, the jurisdiction and docket number of any relevant court decision and provide the challenger an opportunity to provide additional information for the purposes of the review. The Pennsylvania State Police shall communicate its final decision to the challenger within 60 days of the receipt of the challenge. The decision of the Pennsylvania State Police shall include all information which formed a basis for the decision.

(3) If the challenge is ruled invalid, the person shall have the right to appeal the decision to the Attorney General within 30 days of the decision. The Attorney General shall conduct a hearing de novo in accordance with

the Administrative Agency Law. The burden of proof shall be upon the Commonwealth.

(4) The decision of the Attorney General may be appealed to the Commonwealth Court by an aggrieved party.

(f) Notification of mental health adjudication, treatment, commitment, drug use or addiction.--

(1) Notwithstanding any statute to the contrary, judges of the courts of common pleas shall notify the Pennsylvania State Police, on a form developed by the Pennsylvania State Police, of:

(i) the identity of any individual who has been adjudicated as an incompetent or as a mental defective or who has been involuntarily committed to a mental institution under the act of July 9, 1976 (P.L.817, No.143), known as the Mental Health Procedures Act, or who has been involuntarily treated as described in section 6105(c)(4) (relating to persons not to possess, use, manufacture, control, sell or transfer firearms) or as described in 18 U.S.C. § 922(g)(4) (relating to unlawful acts) and its implementing Federal regulations; and

(ii) any finding of fact or court order related to any person described in 18 U.S.C. § 922(g)(3).

(2) The notification shall be transmitted by the judge to the Pennsylvania State Police within seven days of the adjudication, commitment or treatment.

(3) Notwithstanding any law to the contrary, the Pennsylvania State Police may disclose, electronically or otherwise, to the United States Attorney General or a designee, any record relevant to a determination of whether a person is disqualified from possessing or receiving a firearm under 18 U.S.C. § 922 (g)(3) or (4) or an applicable state statute.

(g) Review by court.--

(1) Upon receipt of a copy of the order of a court of competent jurisdiction which vacates a final order or an involuntary certification issued by a mental health review officer, the Pennsylvania State Police shall expunge all records of the involuntary treatment received under subsection (f).

(2) A person who is involuntarily committed pursuant to section 302 of the Mental Health Procedures Act may petition the court to review the sufficiency of the evidence upon which the commitment was based. If the court determines that the evidence upon which

the involuntary commitment was based was insufficient, the court shall order that the record of the commitment submitted to the Pennsylvania State Police be expunged. A petition filed under this subsection shall toll the 60-day period set forth under section 6105(a)(2).

(3) The Pennsylvania State Police shall expunge all records of an involuntary commitment of an individual who is discharged from a mental health facility based upon the initial review by the physician occurring within two hours of arrival under section 302(b) of the Mental Health Procedures Act and the physician's determination that no severe mental disability existed pursuant to section 302(b) of the Mental Health Procedures Act. The physician shall provide signed confirmation of the determination of the lack of severe mental disability following the initial examination under section 302(b) of the Mental Health Procedures Act to the Pennsylvania State Police.

(h) Juvenile registry.--

(1) The contents of law enforcement records and files compiled under 42 Pa.C.S. § 6308 (relating to law enforcement records) concerning a child shall not be disclosed to the public except if the child is 14 years of age or older at the time of the alleged conduct and if any of the following apply:

(i) The child has been adjudicated delinquent by a court as a result of an act or acts which constitute any offense enumerated in section 6105.

(ii) A petition alleging delinquency has been filed by a law enforcement agency alleging that the child has committed an act or acts which constitute an offense enumerated in section 6105 and the child previously has been adjudicated delinquent by a court as a result of an act or acts which included the elements of one of such crimes.

(2) Notwithstanding any provision of this subsection, the contents of law enforcement records and files concerning any child adjudicated delinquent for the commission of any criminal activity described in paragraph (1) shall be recorded in the registry of the Pennsylvania State Police for the limited purposes of this chapter.

(i) Reports.--The Pennsylvania State Police shall annually compile and report to the General Assembly, on or before December 31, the following information for the previous year:

(1) number of firearm sales, including the types of firearms;

(2) number of applications for sale of firearms denied, number of challenges of the denials and number of final reversals of initial denials;

(3) summary of the Pennsylvania State Police's activities, including the average time taken to complete a criminal history, juvenile delinquency history or mental health record check; and

(4) uniform crime reporting statistics compiled by the Pennsylvania State Police based on the National Incident-based Reporting System.

(j) Other criminal information.--The Pennsylvania State Police shall be authorized to obtain any crime statistics necessary for the purposes of this chapter from any local law enforcement agency.

(j.1) Delinquency and mental health records.--The provisions of this section which relate to juvenile delinquency and mental health records checks shall be applicable when the data has been made available to the Pennsylvania State Police but not later than October 11, 1999.

(j.2) Records check.--The provisions of this section which relate to the instantaneous records check conducted by telephone shall be applicable 30 days following notice by the Pennsylvania State Police pursuant to section 6111(a)(2).

(j.3) Immunity.--The Pennsylvania State Police and its employees shall be immune from actions for damages for the use of a firearm by a purchaser or for the unlawful transfer of a firearm by a dealer unless the act of the Pennsylvania State Police or its employees constitutes a crime, actual fraud, actual malice or willful misconduct.

(k) Definitions.--As used in this section, the following words and phrases shall have the meanings given to them in this subsection:

"Firearm." The term shall have the same meaning as in section 6111.2 (relating to firearm sales surcharge).

"Physician." Any licensed psychiatrist or clinical psychologist as defined in the act of July 9, 1976 (P.L.817, No.143), known as the Mental Health Procedures Act.

(June 13, 1995, 1st Sp.Sess., P.L.1024, No.17, eff. 120 days; Nov. 22, 1995, P.L.621, No.66, eff. imd.; Apr. 22, 1997, P.L.73, No.5, eff. 60 days; June 18, 1998, P.L.503, No.70, eff. imd.; Dec. 3, 1998, P.L.933, No.121, eff. imd.; Oct. 17, 2008, P.L.1628, No.131; Nov. 6, 2014, P.L.2921, No.192, eff. 60 days)

2016 Unconstitutionality. Act 192 of 2014 was declared unconstitutional. Leach v. Commonwealth, 141 A.3d 426 (Pa. 2016). The Legislative Reference Bureau effectuated the 2016 unconstitutionality.

2014 Amendment. Act 192 amended subsecs. (f)(3) and (g)(1) and (3).

2008 Amendment. Act 131 amended subsecs. (b)(4), (e) and (f), effective immediately as to subsec. (e) and 60 days as to the remainder of the section.

1998 Amendments. Act 70 amended subsecs. (b)(3) and (e) and added subsec. (j.3) and Act 121 amended subsec. (b)(3). Act 121 overlooked the amendment by Act 70, but the amendments do not conflict in substance (except for the date, as to which Act 121 has been given effect) and have both been given effect in setting forth the text of subsec. (b)(3).

1997 Amendment. Act 5 amended subsecs. (b)(2) and (k).

1995 Amendments. Act 17, 1st Sp.Sess., added section 6111.1 and Act 66 amended subsecs. (b), (d), (e), (f), (g), (h) and (i) and added subsecs. (j.1) and (j.2).

Cross References. Section 6111.1 is referred to in sections 6106, 6111 of this title.

§ 6111.2. Firearm sales surcharge.

(a) Surcharge imposed.--There is hereby imposed on each sale of a firearm subject to tax under Article II of the act of March 4, 1971 (P.L.6, No.2), known as the Tax Reform Code of 1971, an additional surcharge of $3. This shall be referred to as the Firearm Sale Surcharge. All moneys received from this surcharge shall be deposited in the Firearm Instant Records Check Fund.

(b) Increases or decreases.--Five years from the effective date of this subsection, and every five years thereafter, the Pennsylvania State Police shall provide such information as necessary to the Legislative Budget and Finance Committee for the purpose of reviewing the need to increase or decrease the instant check fee. The committee shall issue a report of its findings and recommendations to the General Assembly for a statutory change in the fee.

(c) Revenue sources.--Funds received under the provisions of this section and section 6111(b)(3) (relating to sale or transfer of firearms), as estimated and certified by the Secretary of Revenue, shall be deposited within five days of the end of each quarter into the fund.

(d) Definition.--As used in this section only, the term "firearm" shall mean any weapon which is designed to or may readily be converted to expel any projectile by the action of an explosion or the frame or receiver of any such weapon.

(June 13, 1995, 1st Sp.Sess., P.L.1024, No.17, eff. 120 days; Nov. 22, 1995, P.L.621, No.66, eff. imd.)

References in Text. The Firearm Instant Records Check Fund, referred to in subsec. (a), is now the Firearm Records Check Fund.

Cross References. Section 6111.2 is referred to in sections 6111, 6111.1, 6111.3 of this title.

§ 6111.3. Firearm Records Check Fund.

(a) Establishment.--The Firearm Records Check Fund is hereby established as a restricted account in the State Treasury, separate and apart from all other public money or funds of the Commonwealth, to be appropriated annually by the General Assembly, for use in carrying out the provisions of section 6111 (relating to firearm ownership). The moneys in the fund on June 1, 1998, are hereby appropriated to the Pennsylvania State Police.

(b) Source.--The source of the fund shall be moneys collected and transferred under section 6111.2 (relating to firearm sales surcharge) and moneys collected and transferred under section 6111(b)(3).

(June 13, 1995, 1st Sp.Sess., P.L.1024, No.17, eff. 120 days; Nov. 22, 1995, P.L.621, No.66, eff. imd.; June 18, 1998, P.L.503, No.70, eff. imd.)

1998 Amendment. Act 70 amended the section heading and subsec. (a).

1995 Amendments. Act 17, 1st Sp.Sess., added section 6111.3 and Act 66 amended the section heading.

Cross References. Section 6111.3 is referred to in section 6102 of this title.

§ 6111.4. Registration of firearms.

Notwithstanding any section of this chapter to the contrary, nothing in this chapter shall be construed to allow any government or law enforcement agency or any agent thereof to create, maintain or operate any registry of firearm ownership within this Commonwealth.

For the purposes of this section only, the term "firearm" shall include any weapon that is designed to or may readily be converted to expel any projectile by the action of an explosive or the frame or receiver of any such weapon.

(June 13, 1995, 1st Sp.Sess., P.L.1024, No.17, eff. 120 days)

1995 Amendment. Act 17, 1st Sp.Sess., added section 6111.4.

Cross References. Section 6111.4 is referred to in section 6111 of this title.

§ 6111.5. Rules and regulations.

The Pennsylvania State Police shall in the manner provided by law promulgate the rules and regulations necessary to carry out this chapter, including regulations to ensure the identity, confidentiality and security of all records and data provided pursuant hereto.

(June 13, 1995, 1st Sp.Sess., P.L.1024, No.17, eff. 120 days)

1995 Amendment. Act 17, 1st Sp.Sess., added section 6111.5.

§ 6112. Retail dealer required to be licensed.

No retail dealer shall sell, or otherwise transfer or expose for sale or transfer, or have in his possession with intent to sell or transfer, any firearm as defined in section 6113(d) (relating to licensing of dealers) without being licensed as provided in this chapter.

(June 13, 1995, 1st Sp.Sess., P.L.1024, No.17, eff. 120 days; Apr. 22, 1997, P.L.73, No.5, eff. 60 days)

Cross References. Section 6112 is referred to in section 6113 of this title.

§ 6113. Licensing of dealers.

(a) General rule.--The chief or head of any police force or police department of a city, and, elsewhere, the sheriff of the county, shall grant to reputable applicants licenses, in form prescribed by the Pennsylvania State Police, effective for three years from date of issue, permitting the licensee to sell firearms direct to the consumer, subject to the following conditions in addition to those specified in section 6111 (relating to sale or transfer of firearms), for breach of any of which the license shall be forfeited and the licensee subject to punishment as provided in this subchapter:

(1) The business shall be carried on only upon the premises designated in the license or at a lawful gun show or meet.

(2) The license, or a copy thereof, certified by the issuing authority, shall be displayed on the premises where it can easily be read.

(3) No firearm shall be sold in violation of any provision of this subchapter.

(4) No firearm shall be sold under any circumstances unless the purchaser is personally known to the seller or shall present clear evidence of the purchaser's identity.

(5) A true record in triplicate shall be made of every firearm sold, in a book kept for the purpose, the form of which may be prescribed by the Pennsylvania State Police, and shall be personally signed by the purchaser and by the person effecting the sale, each in the presence of the other, and shall contain the information required by section 6111. The record shall be maintained by the licensee for a period of 20 years.

(6) No firearm as defined in section 6102 (relating to definitions) shall be displayed in any part of any premises where it can readily be seen from the outside. In the event that the Commissioner of the Pennsylvania State Police shall find a clear and present danger to public safety within this Commonwealth or any area thereof, firearms shall be stored and safeguarded pursuant to regulations to be established by the Pennsylvania State Police by the licensee during the hours when the licensee is closed for business.

(7) The dealer shall possess all applicable current revenue licenses.

(b) Fee.--The fee for issuing said license shall be $30, which fee shall be paid into the county treasury.

(c) Revocation.--Any license granted under subsection (a) of this section may be revoked for cause by the person issuing the same, upon written notice to the holder thereof.

(d) Definitions.--For the purposes of this section and section 6112 (relating to retail dealer required to be licensed) only unless otherwise specifically provided, the term "firearm" shall include any weapon that is designed to or may readily be converted to expel any projectile by the action of an explosive or the frame or receiver of any such weapon.

(June 13, 1995, 1st Sp.Sess., P.L.1024, No.17, eff. 120 days; Nov. 22, 1995, P.L.621,

No.66, eff. imd.; June 18, 1998, P.L.503, No.70, eff. imd.)

1998 Amendment. Act 70 amended subsecs. (a)(5) and (d).
1995 Amendment. Act 66 amended subsec. (a).
Cross References. Section 6113 is referred to in sections 6105, 6105.2, 6112 of this title; section 6108.2 of Title 23 (Domestic Relations).

§ 6114. Judicial review.

The action of the chief of police, sheriff, county treasurer or other officer under this subchapter shall be subject to judicial review in the manner and within the time provided by 2 Pa.C.S. Ch. 7 Subch. B (relating to judicial review of local agency action). A judgment sustaining a refusal to grant a license shall not bar, after one year, a new application; nor shall a judgment in favor of the petitioner prevent the defendant from thereafter revoking or refusing to renew such license for any proper cause which may thereafter occur. The court shall have full power to dispose of all costs.

(June 13, 1995, 1st Sp.Sess., P.L.1024, No.17, eff. 120 days)

§ 6115. Loans on, or lending or giving firearms prohibited.

(a) Offense defined.--No person shall make any loan secured by mortgage, deposit or pledge of a firearm, nor, except as provided in subsection (b), shall any person lend or give a firearm to another or otherwise deliver a firearm contrary to the provisions of this subchapter.

(b) Exception.--

(1) Subsection (a) shall not apply if any of the following apply:

(i) The person who receives the firearm is licensed to carry a firearm under section 6109 (relating to licenses).

(ii) The person who receives the firearm is exempt from licensing.

(iii) The person who receives the firearm is engaged in a hunter safety program certified by the Pennsylvania Game Commission or a firearm training program or competition sanctioned or approved by the National Rifle Association.

(iv) The person who receives the firearm meets all of the following:

(A) Is under 18 years of age.

(B) Pursuant to section 6110.1 (relating to possession of firearm by minor) is under the supervision, guidance and instruction of a responsible individual who:

(I) is 21 years of age or older; and

(II) is not prohibited from owning or possessing a firearm under section 6105 (relating to persons not to possess, use, manufacture, control, sell or transfer firearms).

(v) The person who receives the firearm is lawfully hunting or trapping and is in compliance with the provisions of Title 34 (relating to game).

(vi) A bank or other chartered lending institution is able to adequately secure firearms in its possession.

(2) Nothing in this section shall be construed to prohibit the transfer of a firearm under 20 Pa.C.S. Ch. 21 (relating to intestate succession) or by bequest if the individual receiving the firearm is not precluded from owning or possessing a firearm under section 6105.

(3) Nothing in this section shall be construed to prohibit the loaning or giving of a firearm to another in one's dwelling or place of business if the firearm is retained within the dwelling or place of business.

(4) Nothing in this section shall prohibit the relinquishment of firearms to a third party in accordance with 23 Pa.C.S. § 6108.3 (relating to relinquishment to third party for safekeeping).

(June 13, 1995, 1st Sp.Sess., P.L.1024, No.17, eff. 120 days; Nov. 10, 2005, P.L.335, No.66, eff. 180 days)

2005 Amendment. Act 66 added subsec. (b)(4).
Cross References. Section 6115 is referred to in section 6108.3 of Title 23 (Domestic Relations).

§ 6116. False evidence of identity.

In addition to any other penalty provided in this chapter, the furnishing of false information or offering false evidence of identity is a violation of section 4904 (relating to unsworn falsification to authorities).

(Dec. 19, 1988, P.L.1275, No.158, eff. 180 days; June 13, 1995, 1st Sp.Sess., P.L.1024, No.17, eff. 120 days)

§ 6117. Altering or obliterating marks of identification.

(a) Offense defined.--No person shall change, alter, remove, or obliterate the manufacturer's number integral to the frame or receiver of any firearm which shall have the same meaning as provided in section 6105 (relating to persons not to possess, use, manufacture, control, sell or transfer firearms).

(b) Presumption.--(Deleted by amendment).

(c) Penalty.--A violation of this section constitutes a felony of the second degree.

(d) Appellate review.--(Deleted by amendment).

(June 13, 1995, 1st Sp.Sess., P.L.1024, No.17, eff. 120 days; Nov. 22, 1995, P.L.621, No.66, eff. imd.; Oct. 17, 2008, P.L.1628, No.131, eff. 60 days)

§ 6118. Antique firearms.

(a) General rule.--This subchapter shall not apply to antique firearms.

(b) Exception.--Subsection (a) shall not apply to the extent that such antique firearms, reproductions or replicas of firearms are concealed weapons as provided in section 6106 (relating to firearms not be carried without a license), nor shall it apply to the provisions of section 6105 (relating to persons not to possess, use, manufacture, control, sell or transfer firearms) if such antique firearms, reproductions or replicas of firearms are suitable for use.

(c) Definition.--As used in this section, the term "antique firearm" means:

(1) Any firearm with a matchlock, flintlock or percussion cap type of ignition system.

(2) Any firearm manufactured on or before 1898.

(3) Any replica of any firearm described in paragraph (2) if such replica:

(i) is not designed or redesigned for using rimfire or conventional center fire fixed ammunition; or

(ii) uses rimfire or conventional center fire fixed ammunition which is no longer manufactured in the United States and which is not readily available in the ordinary channels of commercial trade.

(July 16, 1979, P.L.116, No.47, eff. 60 days; Dec. 20, 1983, P.L.291, No.78, eff. imd.; June 13, 1995, 1st Sp.Sess., P.L.1024, No.17, eff. 120 days; Nov. 22, 1995, P.L.621, No.66, eff. imd.)

Cross References. Section 6118 is referred to in sections 6110.2, 6142 of this title.

§ 6119. Violation penalty.

Except as otherwise specifically provided, an offense under this subchapter constitutes a misdemeanor of the first degree.

(Dec. 7, 1989, P.L.607, No.68, eff. 60 days)

Cross References. Section 6119 is referred to in section 6111 of this title.

§ 6120. Limitation on the regulation of firearms and ammunition.

(a) General rule.--No county, municipality or township may in any manner regulate the lawful ownership, possession, transfer or transportation of firearms, ammunition or ammunition components when carried or transported for purposes not prohibited by the laws of this Commonwealth.

(a.1) No right of action.--

(1) No political subdivision may bring or maintain an action at law or in equity against any firearms or ammunition manufacturer, trade association or dealer for damages, abatement, injunctive relief or any other relief or remedy resulting from or relating to either the lawful design or manufacture of firearms or ammunition or the lawful marketing or sale of firearms or ammunition to the public.

(2) Nothing in this subsection shall be construed to prohibit a political subdivision from bringing or maintaining an action against a firearms or ammunition manufacturer or dealer for breach of contract or warranty as to firearms or ammunition purchased by the political subdivision.

(a.2) Relief.--(Unconstitutional).

(a.3) Reasonable expenses.-- (Unconstitutional).

(b) Definitions.--As used in this section, the following words and phrases shall have the meanings given to them in this subsection:

"Dealer." The term shall include any person engaged in the business of selling at wholesale or retail a firearm or ammunition.

"Firearms." This term shall have the meaning given to it in section 5515 (relating to prohibiting of paramilitary training) but shall not include air rifles as that term is defined in section 6304 (relating to sale and use of air rifles).

"Person adversely affected." (Unconstitutional).

"Political subdivision." The term shall include any home rule charter municipality, county, city, borough, incorporated town, township or school district.

"Reasonable expenses." (Unconstitutional).

(Oct. 18, 1974, P.L.768, No.260, eff. imd.; Dec. 19, 1988, P.L.1275, No.158, eff. 180 days; Oct. 4, 1994, P.L.571, No.84, eff. 60 days; Dec. 15, 1999, P.L.915, No.59, eff. imd.; Nov. 6, 2014, P.L.2921, No.192, eff. 60 days)

2016 Unconstitutionality. Act 192 of 2014 was declared unconstitutional. Leach v. Commonwealth, 141 A.3d 426 (Pa. 2016). The Legislative Reference Bureau effectuated the 2016 unconstitutionality.

2014 Amendment. Act 192 amended subsec. (b) and added subsecs. (a.2) and (a.3).

§ 6121. Certain bullets prohibited.

(a) Offense defined.--It is unlawful for any person to possess, use or attempt to use a KTW teflon-coated bullet or other armor-piercing ammunition while committing or attempting to commit a crime of violence as defined in section 6102 (relating to definitions).

(b) Grading.--An offense under this section constitutes a felony of the third degree.

(c) Sentencing.--Any person who is convicted in any court of this Commonwealth of a crime of violence and who uses or carries, in the commission of that crime, a firearm loaded with KTW ammunition or any person who violates this section shall, in addition to the punishment provided for the commission of the crime, be sentenced to a term of imprisonment for not less than five years. Notwithstanding any other provision of law, the court shall not suspend the sentence of any person convicted of a crime subject to this subsection nor place him on probation nor shall the term of imprisonment run concurrently with any other term of imprisonment including that imposed for the crime in which the KTW ammunition was being used or carried. No person sentenced under this subsection shall be eligible for parole.

(d) Definition.--As used in this section the term "armor-piercing ammunition" means ammunition which, when or if fired from any firearm as defined in section 6102 that is used or attempted to be used in violation of subsection (a) under the test procedure of the National Institute of Law Enforcement and Criminal Justice Standard for the Ballistics Resistance of Police Body Armor promulgated December 1978, is determined to be capable of penetrating bullet-resistant apparel or body armor meeting the requirements of Type IIA of Standard NILECJ-STD-0101.01 as formulated by the United States Department of Justice and published in December of 1978.

(Dec. 21, 1984, P.L.1210, No.230, eff. imd.)

1984 Amendment. Act 230 added section 6121.

§ 6122. Proof of license and exception.

(a) General rule.--When carrying a firearm concealed on or about one's person or in a vehicle, an individual licensed to carry a firearm shall, upon lawful demand of a law enforcement officer, produce the license for inspection. Failure to produce such license either at the time of arrest or at the preliminary hearing shall create a rebuttable presumption of nonlicensure.

(b) Exception.--An individual carrying a firearm on or about his person or in a vehicle and claiming an exception under section 6106(b) (relating to firearms not to be carried without a license) shall, upon lawful demand of a law enforcement officer, produce satisfactory evidence of qualification for exception.

(Dec. 19, 1988, P.L.1275, No.158, eff. 180 days; Apr. 22, 1997, P.L.73, No.5, eff. 60 days)

1997 Amendment. Act 5 amended subsec. (a).

1988 Amendment. Act 158 added section 6122.

§ 6123. Waiver of disability or pardons.

A waiver of disability from Federal authorities as provided for in 18 U.S.C. § 925 (relating to exceptions; relief from disabilities), a full pardon from the Governor or an overturning of a conviction shall remove any corresponding disability under this subchapter except the disability under section 6105 (relating to persons not to possess, use, manufacture, control, sell or transfer firearms).

(Dec. 19, 1988, P.L.1275, No.158, eff. 180 days; Nov. 22, 1995, P.L.621, No.66, eff. imd.)

Cross References. Section 6123 is referred to in section 6109 of this title.

§ 6124. Administrative regulations.

The commissioner may establish form specifications and regulations, consistent with section 6109(c) (relating to licenses), with respect to uniform forms control, including the following:

(1) License to carry firearms.
(2) Firearm registration.
(3) Dealer's license.
(4) Application for purchase of a firearm.
(5) Record of sale of firearms.
(Dec. 19, 1988, P.L.1275, No.158, eff. 180 days)

1988 Amendment. Act 158 added section 6124.

§ 6125. Distribution of uniform firearm laws and firearm safety brochures.

It shall be the duty of the Pennsylvania State Police beginning January 1, 1996, to distribute to every licensed firearm dealer in this Commonwealth firearms safety brochures at no cost to the dealer. The brochures shall be written by the Pennsylvania State Police, with the cooperation of the Pennsylvania Game Commission, and shall include a summary of the major provisions of this subchapter, including, but not limited to, the duties of the sellers and purchasers and the transferees of firearms. The brochure or a copy thereof shall be provided without charge to each purchaser.
(June 13, 1995, 1st Sp.Sess., P.L.1024, No.17, eff. 120 days; Nov. 22, 1995, P.L.621, No.66, eff. imd.)

Cross References. Section 6125 is referred to in section 6111.1 of this title.

§ 6126. Firearms Background Check Advisory Committee (Expired).

2002 Expiration. Section 6126 expired November 30, 2002. See Act 101 of 2001.

§ 6127. Firearm tracing.

(a) Illegal possession.--Upon confiscating or recovering a firearm from the possession of anyone who is not permitted by Federal or State law to possess a firearm, a local law enforcement agency shall use the best available information, including a firearms trace where necessary, to determine how and from where the person gained possession of the firearm.

(b) Tracing.--Local law enforcement shall use the National Tracing Center of the Federal Bureau of Alcohol, Tobacco, Firearms and Explosives in complying with subsection (a).

(c) Notification.--Local law enforcement agencies shall advise the Pennsylvania State Police of all firearms that are recovered in accordance with this section.

(July 17, 2007, P.L.139, No.41, eff. 60 days; Oct. 17, 2008, P.L.1628, No.131, eff. 60 days)

2008 Amendment. Act 131 amended subsec. (a).
2007 Amendment. Act 41 added section 6127.

§ 6128. Abandonment of firearms, weapons or ammunition.

(a) General rule.--Firearms, weapons or ammunition which are itemized on a list required under 23 Pa.C.S. § 6108(a)(7)(v) (relating to relief) or the possession or acquisition of which is prohibited under 18 U.S.C. § 922(g)(9) (relating to unlawful acts) and relinquished into or otherwise coming into the custody of a police department, Pennsylvania State Police, coroner, medical examiner, district attorney, sheriff or licensed dealer shall be deemed abandoned when:

(1) Relinquished by its lawful owner pursuant to court order or executed warrant, and no written request to return or otherwise dispose of the firearms, weapons or ammunition is made by the lawful owner or the lawful owner's attorney or duly appointed representative after a period of one year from the date an order of relinquishment or seizure has expired.

(2) Found, discovered or otherwise passed into the custody of the police department, Pennsylvania State Police, coroner, medical examiner, district attorney, sheriff or licensed dealer and no owner can be determined after a documented search of the database of firearms sales maintained by the Pennsylvania State Police is made at the time the firearms come into the custody of the police department, coroner, medical examiner, district attorney, sheriff or licensed dealer and is again made one year from the date of the first documented search.

(b) Methods of disposal.--If firearms, weapons or ammunition are deemed abandoned under subsection (a), the custodian may dispose of the firearms, weapons or ammunition by:

(1) Arranging for the sale of the firearms, weapons or ammunition to a federally licensed firearms dealer by sealed bid with proceeds of the sale to be retained by the custodian.

(2) Arranging for the lawful and complete destruction of the firearms, weapons or ammunition. Firearms, weapons or ammunition that cannot lawfully be sold to a federally

licensed firearms dealer in this Commonwealth shall be destroyed.

(c) **Limitation.**--A custodian may not dispose of firearms, weapons or ammunition deemed abandoned under subsection (a)(1) without first notifying the person who relinquished the firearms, weapons or ammunition. If the person who relinquished the firearms, weapons or ammunition fails to respond within 20 days to the notice, the custodian may proceed with disposal of the firearms, weapons or ammunition. Notification shall be by certified mail to:

(1) an address where the person relinquishing the firearms, weapons or ammunition is now known by the custodian to reside;

(2) the last known address of the person relinquishing the firearms, weapons or ammunition;

(3) the address of the person relinquishing the firearms, weapons or ammunition which was provided at the time of relinquishment; or

(4) the address of the person relinquishing the firearms, weapons or ammunition which is found after searching the available sources of address data maintained in the Commonwealth's databases of motor vehicle registration, motor vehicle driver licensing, occupational and professional licensure, corrections facilities and public assistance.

(d) **Illegal seizure.**--A custodian who sells or destroys seized firearms, weapons or ammunition with pending or unresolved evidentiary challenges to the legality of the seizure shall be liable to the lawful owner of the illegally seized firearms, weapons or ammunition for the actual value of the illegally seized firearms, weapons or ammunition plus reasonable attorney fees. Actual value shall be determined by the owner, who shall be required to obtain an estimate of value from a private third-party licensed firearms dealer.

(e) **Public inspection.**--A portion of an order or petition or other paper which includes a list of firearms or other weapons or ammunition in possession of a custodian under this section shall be withheld from public inspection except:

(1) upon an order of a court granted upon cause shown;

(2) as necessary, by law enforcement and court personnel; or

(3) after redaction of information listing firearms, other weapons or ammunition.

(f) **Definitions.**--As used in this section, the following words and phrases shall have the meanings given to them in this subsection unless the context clearly indicates otherwise:

"Custodian." A police department, Pennsylvania State Police, coroner, medical examiner, district attorney, sheriff or licensed dealer into whose custody firearms, weapons or ammunition has passed.

"Firearm." Any weapon which is designed to or may readily be converted to expel any projectile by the action of an explosive or the frame or receiver of any such weapon.

(Oct. 12, 2018, P.L.519, No.79, eff. 180 days)

2018 Amendment. Act 79 added section 6128. Act 79 shall apply to orders issued pursuant to 23 Pa.C.S. § 6108 on or after the effective date of section 11 of Act 79.

Cross References. Section 6128 is referred to in sections 6108, 6108.1 of Title 23 (Domestic Relations).

SUBCHAPTER B
FIREARMS GENERALLY

Sec.
6141. Purchase of firearms in contiguous states (Repealed).
6141.1. Purchase of rifles and shotguns outside this Commonwealth.
6142. Locking device for firearms.
§ 6141. Purchase of firearms in contiguous states (Repealed).

1997 Repeal. Section 6141 was repealed April 22, 1997 (P.L.73, No.5), effective in 60 days.

§ 6141.1. Purchase of rifles and shotguns outside this Commonwealth.

Nothing in this chapter shall be construed to prohibit a person in this Commonwealth who may lawfully purchase, possess, use, control, sell, transfer or manufacture a firearm which exceeds the barrel and related lengths set forth in section 6102 (relating to definitions) from lawfully purchasing or otherwise obtaining such a firearm in a jurisdiction outside this Commonwealth.

(Apr. 22, 1997, P.L.73, No.5, eff. 60 days)

1997 Amendment. Act 5 added section 6141.1.

§ 6142. Locking device for firearms.

(a) Offense defined.--It shall be unlawful for any licensee to sell, deliver or transfer any firearm as defined in section 6102 (relating to definitions), other than an antique firearm as defined in section 6118 (relating to antique firearms), to any other person, other than another licensee, unless the transferee is provided with or purchases a locking device for that firearm or the design of the firearm incorporates a locking device.

(b) Exceptions.--Firearms for transfer to or possession by any law enforcement officer employed by any Federal, State or local government entity or rail police employed and certified by a rail carrier as a police officer are not subject to the provisions of this section.

(c) Penalties.--A violation of the provisions of this section shall be a summary offense.

(d) Good faith compliance.--A licensee who in good faith complies with this section shall not be civilly liable as a result of such compliance with this section, except for any acts or omissions intentionally designed to harm or for grossly negligent acts or omissions which result in harm.

(e) Admissibility of evidence.--A transferee's purchase or receipt of a locking device in conjunction with the purchase of a firearm pursuant to this section shall not be admissible as evidence in any civil action brought against the transferee.

(f) Definitions.--As used in this section, the following words and phrases shall have the meanings given to them in this subsection:

"Licensee." Any licensed manufacturer, importer or dealer of firearms.

"Locking device." Either of the following:

(1) a device that, when installed on a firearm, is designed to prevent the firearm from being operated without first deactivating the device; or

(2) a device that is incorporated into the design of a firearm and that is designed to prevent the operation of the firearm by anyone not having access to the device.

(Dec. 15, 1999, P.L.915, No.59, eff. 60 days)

1999 Amendment. Act 59 added section 6142.

Cross References. Section 6142 is referred to in section 6108.3 of Title 23 (Domestic Relations).

SUBCHAPTER C
OTHER DANGEROUS ARTICLES

Sec.
6161. Carrying explosives on conveyances.
6162. Shipping explosives.

§ 6161. Carrying explosives on conveyances.

(a) Offense defined.--A person is guilty of a misdemeanor of the second degree if he enters into or upon any railroad train, locomotive, tender or car thereof, or into or upon any automobile or other conveyance used for the carrying of freight or passengers, having in his custody or about his person any nitroglycerine or other explosive, other than as freight regularly shipped as such.

(b) Powers of crew.--The conductor or person having charge and control of any railroad train, coach, or other conveyance for the carriage of freight or passengers, may arrest any person found violating the provisions of this section and detain such person until reaching some place, where such person may be delivered to a constable or other police authority.

(c) Venue.--It shall be lawful to prosecute such offenders in any county through which said public conveyance passes, without reference to the place where such offenders were arrested.

§ 6162. Shipping explosives.

(a) Offense defined.--A person is guilty of a misdemeanor of the third degree if he knowingly delivers, or causes to be delivered to any transportation company, or to any person engaged in the business of transportation, any explosive material adapted for blasting, or for any other purpose for which such articles may be used, under any false or deceptive invoice or description, or without informing the carrier at or before the time when such delivery is made, of the true nature of the same, and without having the keg, barrel, can or package containing the same plainly marked with the name of the explosive material therein contained, together with the word "dangerous."

(b) Damages.--Any person convicted of an offense under this section shall, in addition to any other penalty, be responsible for all damages to persons or property directly or indirectly resulting from the explosion of any such article.

(c) **Opening of suspected containers.--** Any person engaged in the business of transportation, upon affidavit made of the fact that any container tendered for transportation, not in compliance with the provisions of this section is believed to contain explosive material, may require such container to be opened, and refuse to receive any such container unless such requirement is complied with.

(d) **Disposition of explosives.--** If such container is opened and found to contain any explosive material, the container and its contents shall be forthwith removed to any lawful place for the storing of explosives. After conviction of the offender, or after three months from such removal, the container, with its contents, shall be sold at public sale, after the expiration of ten days from notice of the time and place of such sale, published in one newspaper in the county where such seizure shall have been made. The proceeds of such sale, after deducting therefrom the expenses of removal, storage, advertisement and sale, shall be paid into the treasury of the county.

SUBCHAPTER D
STRAW PURCHASE PREVENTION
EDUCATION PROGRAM

Enactment. Subchapter D was added October 17, 2008, P.L.1628, No.131, effective 60 days.

§ 6181. Scope of subchapter.

This subchapter provides for the establishment of the Straw Purchase Prevention Education Program within the Office of Attorney General.

§ 6182. Legislative findings and declarations.

The General Assembly finds and declares that:

(1) The illegal purchase of firearms throughout this Commonwealth is a threat to public safety and security.

(2) Urban areas are experiencing increased violence as a result of criminal misuse of firearms. Stemming the flow of these illegal firearms through straw purchases will help to curb the crime rate throughout this Commonwealth and increase public safety.

(3) Educating the public that illegally purchasing a firearm for someone otherwise prohibited from possessing one is a serious crime and punishable under Federal law by ten years' imprisonment advances public safety.

(4) Committed to educating firearms dealers and the general public, the National Shooting Sports Foundation, in partnership with the Bureau of Alcohol, Tobacco, Firearms and Explosives, in July 2000 created the "Don't Lie for the Other Guy Program."

(5) The "Don't Lie for the Other Guy Program" was developed to raise public awareness that it is a serious crime to purchase a firearm for someone who cannot legally do so and to educate firearms dealers on how to better detect and deter potential straw purchases. The campaign delivers the message that anyone attempting an illegal firearm purchase faces a stiff Federal penalty.

(6) The "Don't Lie for the Other Guy Program" is vital to educating federally licensed firearms dealers and their employees on how to recognize and deter the illegal purchase of firearms through straw purchases. This program is an important tool for the Bureau of Alcohol, Tobacco, Firearms and Explosives to pursue its mission of preventing terrorism, reducing violent crime and protecting the public.

(7) The nationally recognized "Don't Lie for the Other Guy Program" has been endorsed by United States attorneys throughout the nation, various law enforcement agencies, the Bureau of Alcohol, Tobacco, Firearms and Explosives and the Department of Justice.

(8) It is in the best interest of this Commonwealth to establish a straw purchase prevention education program within the Office of Attorney General to provide resources and direct grant money to the "Don't Lie for the

Other Guy Program" and similar programs that offer straw purchase prevention education.

§ 6183. Definitions.

The following words and phrases when used in this subchapter shall have the meanings given to them in this section unless the context clearly indicates otherwise:

"Fund." The Straw Purchase Prevention Education Fund established in section 6186 (relating to Straw Purchase Prevention Education Fund).

"Program." The Straw Purchase Prevention Education Program established in section 6184 (relating to Straw Purchase Prevention Education Program).

§ 6184. Straw Purchase Prevention Education Program.

(a) Establishment.--The Straw Purchase Prevention Education Program is established and shall provide resources and direct grant money to underwrite the cost of implementing an educational and public service outreach program in the community.

(b) Outreach.--The educational and public service outreach program shall inform individuals of the illegal nature of purchasing a firearm for an individual prohibited from owning firearms. The outreach program shall be developed by a not-for-profit organization which:

(1) Is a national trade association representing the shooting, hunting and firearm industry.

(2) Has a membership consisting of firearm manufacturers, firearm distributors, firearm retailers, publishers and sportsmen's organizations.

(3) Has been in existence for at least 45 years prior to the effective date of this section.

(c) Priority of grants.--Grants shall be prioritized based on the highest incidence of firearm violence in a county of this Commonwealth.

Cross References. Section 6184 is referred to in sections 6183, 6185 of this title.

§ 6185. Powers and duties of Attorney General.

In addition to any other powers and duties, the Attorney General of the Commonwealth shall:

(1) Establish a grant program to provide moneys from the fund pursuant to section 6184 (relating to Straw Purchase Prevention Education Program).

(2) Promulgate rules and regulations to carry out the provisions of this subchapter.

§ 6186. Straw Purchase Prevention Education Fund.

(a) Establishment.--The Straw Purchase Prevention Education Fund is hereby established in the State Treasury as a restricted account. The fund shall consist of funds appropriated by the General Assembly.

(b) Continuing appropriation.--All moneys in the fund and the interest accruing thereon are hereby appropriated to the Office of Attorney General on a continuing basis to carry out the provisions of this subchapter.

Cross References. Section 6186 is referred to in section 6183 of this title.

§ 6187. Transfer for initial funding.

The sum of $100,000 is hereby transferred from the General Fund to the Straw Purchase Prevention Education Fund for expenditure during the fiscal year July 1, 2009, to June 30, 2010, to carry out the provisions of this subchapter.

CHAPTER 63 MINORS

Enactment. Chapter 63 was added December 6, 1972, P.L.1482, No.334, effective in six months.

Cross References. Chapter 63 is referred to in section 2101 of Title 5 (Athletics and Sports).

§ 6301. Corruption of minors.

(a) Offense defined.--

(1) (i) Except as provided in subparagraph (ii), whoever, being of the age of 18 years and upwards, by any act corrupts or tends to corrupt the morals of any minor less than 18 years of age, or who aids, abets, entices or encourages any such minor in the commission of any crime, or who knowingly assists or encourages such minor in violating his or her parole or any order of court, commits a misdemeanor of the first degree.

(ii) Whoever, being of the age of 18 years and upwards, by any course of conduct in violation of Chapter 31 (relating to sexual offenses) corrupts or tends to corrupt the morals of any minor less than 18 years of age, or who aids, abets, entices or encourages any such minor in the commission of an offense under Chapter 31 commits a felony of the third degree.

(2) Any person who knowingly aids, abets, entices or encourages a minor younger than 18 years of age to commit truancy commits a summary offense. Any person who violates this paragraph within one year of the date of a first conviction under this section commits a misdemeanor of the third degree. A conviction under this paragraph shall not, however, constitute a prohibition under section 6105 (relating to persons not to possess, use, manufacture, control, sell or transfer firearms).

(b) **Adjudication of delinquency unnecessary.**--A conviction under the provisions of this section may be had whether or not the jurisdiction of any juvenile court has attached or shall thereafter attach to such minor or whether or not such minor has been adjudicated a delinquent or shall thereafter be adjudicated a delinquent.

(c) **Presumptions.**--In trials and hearings upon charges of violating the provisions of this section, knowledge of the minor's age and of the court's orders and decrees concerning such minor shall be presumed in the absence of proof to the contrary.

(d) Mistake as to age.--

(1) Whenever in this section the criminality of conduct depends upon the corruption of a minor whose actual age is under 16 years, it is no defense that the actor did not know the age of the minor or reasonably believed the minor to be older than 18 years.

(2) Whenever in this section the criminality of conduct depends upon the corruption of a minor whose actual age is 16 years or more but less than 18 years, it is a defense for the actor to prove by a preponderance of the evidence that he reasonably believed the minor to be 18 years or older.

(July 1, 1978, P.L.573, No.104, eff. 60 days; July 11, 1996, P.L.552, No.98, eff. 60 days; Oct. 7, 2010, P.L.482, No.69, eff. 60 days)

2010 Amendment. Act 69 amended subsec. (a)(1).

1996 Amendment. Act 98 amended subsec. (a).

1978 Amendment. Act 104 added present section 6301. Former section 6301, relating to the same subject matter, was repealed November 28, 1973, P.L.341, No.117.

Cross References. Section 6301 is referred to in sections 3104, 6105, 9122.1,

9122.3 of this title; section 3304 of Title 5 (Athletics and Sports); sections 5329, 6344 of Title 23 (Domestic Relations); sections 5552, 5985.1, 5993, 62A03, 9718.1, 9799.13, 9799.14 of Title 42 (Judiciary and Judicial Procedure).

§ 6302. Sale or lease of weapons and explosives.

(a) Offense defined.--A person is guilty of a misdemeanor of the first degree if he sells or causes to be sold or leases to any person under 18 years of age any deadly weapon, cartridge, gunpowder, or other similar dangerous explosive substance.

(b) Exception.--The provisions of subsection (a) shall not prohibit hunting by minors under 18 years of age permitted under Title 34 (relating to game).

(July 8, 1986, P.L.442, No.93, eff. July 1, 1987)

Cross References. Section 6302 is referred to in section 6105 of this title.

§ 6303. Sale of starter pistols.

(a) Offense defined.--A person is guilty of a misdemeanor of the first degree if he sells, causes to be sold, gives or furnishes to any person under the age of 18 years, or if he, being under the age of 18 years, purchases, accepts, receives or possesses, any pistol commonly referred to as "starter pistol" specially designed to receive and discharge blank cartridges only or similar pistol.

(b) Exception.--Nothing in this section shall prohibit the use of starter pistols for the purpose of starting or officiating at athletic events, use in dramatic productions, or other similar events.

§ 6304. Sale and use of air rifles.

(a) Sale or transfer of air rifles.--

(1) It shall be unlawful for any dealer to sell, lend, rent, give, or otherwise transfer an air rifle to any person under the age of 18 years, where the dealer knows, or has reasonable cause to believe, the person to be under 18 years of age, or where such dealer has failed to make reasonable inquiry relative to the age of such person, and such person is under 18 years of age.

(2) It shall be unlawful for any person to sell, give, lend, or otherwise transfer any air rifle to any person under 18 years of age, except where the relationship of parent and child, guardian and ward or adult instructor and pupil exists between such person and the person under 18 years of age.

(b) Carrying or discharging air rifles.--

(1) It shall be unlawful for any person under 18 years of age to carry any air rifle on the highways or public lands unless accompanied by an adult, except that a person under 18 years of age may carry such rifle unloaded in a suitable case or securely wrapped.

(2) It shall be unlawful for any person to discharge any air rifle from or across any highway or public land or any public place, except on a properly constructed target range.

(c) Exceptions.--

(1) Nothing in this section shall make it unlawful for any person under 18 years of age to have in his possession any air rifle, if it is:

(i) kept within his domicile;

(ii) used by the person under 18 years of age and he is a duly enrolled member of any club, team or society organized for educational purposes and maintaining as part of its facilities or having written permission to use an indoor or outdoor rifle range under the supervision, guidance and instruction of a responsible adult, and then only, if said air rifle is actually being used in connection with the activities of said club, team or society under the supervision of a responsible adult; or

(iii) used in or on any private grounds or residence under circumstances when such air rifle can be fired, discharged or operated in such a manner as not to endanger persons or property, and then only, if it is used in such manner as to prevent the projectile from transversing any grounds or space outside the limits of such grounds or residence.

(2) Nothing in this section shall prohibit sales of air rifles:

(i) By wholesale dealers or jobbers.

(ii) To be shipped out of this Commonwealth.

(iii) To be used at a target range operated in accordance with paragraph (1) of this subsection or by members of the armed services of the United States or veterans' organizations.

(d) Seizure.--Any law enforcement officer may seize, take, remove or cause to be removed, at the expense of the owner, all air rifles used or offered for sale in violation of this section.

(e) No preemption.--The provisions of any ordinance enacted by any political subdivision which impose greater restrictions or limitations in respect to the sale and purchase, use or possession of air rifles, than is imposed by this section, shall not be invalidated or affected by this section.

(f) Grading.--Any dealer violating the provisions of paragraph (a)(1) of this section shall be guilty of a misdemeanor of the third degree. Any person violating any other provision of this section shall be guilty of a summary offense.

(g) Definitions.--As used in this section the following words and phrases shall have the meanings given to them in this subsection:

"Air rifle." Any air gun, air pistol, spring gun, spring pistol, B-B gun, or any implement that is not a firearm, which impels a pellet of any kind with a force that can reasonably be expected to cause bodily harm. The term does not include a paintball gun or paintball marker as defined in section 2707.2 (relating to paintball guns and paintball markers).

"Dealer." Any person engaged in the business of selling at retail or renting any air rifles.

 (Dec. 22, 2005, P.L.449, No.85, eff. 60 days)

2005 Amendment. Act 85 amended subsec. (g).

Cross References. Section 6304 is referred to in section 6120 of this title.

§ 6305. Sale of tobacco products.

(a) Offense defined.--Except as set forth in subsection (f), a person is guilty of a summary offense if the person:

(1) sells a tobacco product to any minor;

(2) furnishes, by purchase, gift or other means, a tobacco product to a minor;

(3) (Deleted by amendment).

(4) locates or places a vending machine containing a tobacco product in a location accessible to minors;

(5) displays or offers a cigarette for sale out of a pack of cigarettes; or

(6) displays or offers for sale tobacco products in any manner which enables an individual other than the retailer or an employee of the retailer to physically handle tobacco products prior to purchase unless the tobacco products are located within the line of sight or under the control of a cashier or other employee during business hours, except that this paragraph shall not apply to retail stores which derive 75% or more of sales revenues from tobacco products.

(a.1) Purchase.--A minor is guilty of a summary offense if the minor:

(1) purchases or attempts to purchase a tobacco product; or

(2) knowingly falsely represents himself to be at least 21 years of age or if the minor is a member of the active or reserve components of any branch or unit of the armed forces of the United States or a veteran who received an honorable discharge from any branch or unit of the active or reserve components of the armed forces of the United States, at least 18 years of age to a person for the purpose of purchasing or receiving a tobacco product.

(b) Penalty.--

(1) Except as set forth in paragraph (2), a person that violates subsection (a) shall be sentenced as follows:

(i) for a first offense, to pay a fine of not less than $100 nor more than $250;

(ii) for a second offense, to pay a fine of not less than $250 nor more than $500; or

(iii) for a third or subsequent offense, to pay a fine of not less than $500 nor more than $1,000.

(2) A retailer that violates subsection (a) shall be sentenced as follows:

(i) for a first offense, to pay a fine of not less than $100 nor more than $500;

(ii) for a second offense, to pay a fine of not less than $500 nor more than $1,000;

(iii) for a third offense, to pay a fine of not less than $1,000 nor more than $3,000; or

(iv) for a fourth or subsequent offense, to pay a fine of not less than $3,000 nor more than $5,000.

(3) A minor who violates subsection (a.1) shall be sentenced to any or all of the following:

(i) not more than 75 hours of community service;

(ii) complete a tobacco use prevention and cessation program approved by the Department of Health; or

(iii) a fine not to exceed $200.

(iv) (Deleted by amendment).

(c) Notification.--

(1) Upon issuing or filing a citation charging a violation of subsection (a.1), the affiant shall notify the parent or guardian of the minor charged.

(2) Upon imposing a sentence under subsection (b)(1) or (2), a court shall notify the department of the violation committed by the person if the person is a retailer or an employee of a retailer and the person committed the

violation in the course of the person's employment.

(d) Nature of offense.--

(1) An offense under subsection (a.1) shall not be a criminal offense of record, shall not be reportable as a criminal act and shall not be placed on the criminal record of the offender. The failure of a minor to comply with a sentence under subsection (b)(3) shall not constitute a delinquent act under 42 Pa.C.S. Ch. 63 (relating to juvenile matters).

(2) A record of participation in an adjudication alternative program under subsection (e) shall be maintained for purposes of determining subsequent eligibility for such a program.

(3) Except as provided in subsection (f)(1), a retailer is liable for the acts of its agents as permitted by section 307 (relating to liability of organizations and certain related persons).

(e) Preadjudication disposition.--If a person is charged with violating this section, the court may admit the offender to the adjudication alternative program as authorized in 42 Pa.C.S. § 1520 (relating to adjudication alternative program) or any other preadjudication disposition if the offender has not previously received a preadjudication disposition for violating this section. Accelerated Rehabilitative Disposition or any other preadjudication alternative for a violation of subsection (a) shall be considered an offense for the purposes of imposing criminal penalties under subsection (b)(1) and (2).

(f) Exceptions.--

(1) The following affirmative defense is available:

(i) It is an affirmative defense for a retailer to an offense under subsection (a)(1) and (2) that, prior to the date of the alleged violation, the retailer has complied with all of the following:

(A) adopted and implemented a written policy against selling tobacco products to minors which includes:

(I) a requirement that an employee ask an individual who appears to be 25 years of age or younger for a valid photoidentification as proof of age prior to making a sale of tobacco products;

(II) a list of all types of acceptable photoidentification;

(III) a list of factors to be examined in the photoidentification, including photo likeness,

birth date, expiration date, bumps, tears or other damage and signature;

(IV) a requirement that, if the photoidentification is missing any of the items listed in subclause (III), it is not valid and cannot be accepted as proof of age for the sale of tobacco products. A second photoidentification may be required to make the sale of tobacco products, with questions referred to the manager; and

(V) a disciplinary policy which includes employee counseling and suspension for failure to require valid photoidentification and dismissal for repeat improper sales.

(B) informed all employees selling tobacco products through an established training program of the applicable Federal and State laws regarding the sale of tobacco products to minors;

(C) documented employee training indicating that all employees selling tobacco products have been informed of and understand the written policy referred to in clause (A);

(D) trained all employees selling tobacco products to verify that the purchaser is at least 21 years of age or if the minor is a member of the active or reserve components of any branch or unit of the armed forces of the United States or a veteran who received an honorable discharge from any branch or unit of the active or reserve components of the armed forces of the United States, at least 18 years of age before selling tobacco products;

(E) conspicuously posted a notice that selling tobacco products to a minor is illegal, that the purchase of tobacco products by a minor is illegal and that a violator is subject to penalties; and

(F) established and implemented disciplinary sanctions for noncompliance with the policy under clause (A).

(ii) An affirmative defense under this paragraph must be proved by a preponderance of the evidence.

(iii) An affirmative defense under this paragraph may be used by a retailer no more than three times at each retail location during any 24-month period.

(2) No more than one violation of subsection (a) per person arises out of separate incidents which take place in a 24-hour period.

(3) It is not a violation of subsection (a.1)(1) for a minor to purchase or attempt to purchase a tobacco product if all of the following apply:

(i) The minor is at least 14 years of age.

(ii) The minor is an employee, volunteer or an intern with:

(A) a State or local law enforcement agency;

(B) the Department of Health or a primary contractor pursuant to Chapter 7 of the act of June 26, 2001 (P.L.755, No.77), known as the Tobacco Settlement Act;

(C) a single county authority created pursuant to the act of April 14, 1972 (P.L.221, No.63), known as the Pennsylvania Drug and Alcohol Abuse Control Act;

(D) a county or municipal health department; or

(E) a retailer.

(iii) The minor is acting within the scope of assigned duties as part of an authorized investigation, compliance check under subsection (g) or retailer-organized self-compliance check.

(iv) A minor shall not use or consume a tobacco product.

(g) Compliance checks.--This subsection shall apply to compliance checks conducted by the Department of Health, a primary contractor pursuant to Chapter 7 of the Tobacco Settlement Act, a single county authority created pursuant to the Pennsylvania Drug and Alcohol Abuse Control Act or a county or municipal health department for the purpose of conducting retailer education, assessing compliance with Federal or State law and enforcing the provisions of this section. Compliance checks shall be conducted, at a minimum, in accordance with all of the following:

(1) Compliance checks shall only be conducted in consultation with the Department of Health and the law enforcement agency providing primary police services to the municipality where the compliance check is being conducted.

(2) A minor participating in a compliance check must be at least 14 years of age, complete a course of training approved by the Department of Health and furnish the Department of Health with a signed, written parental consent agreement allowing the minor to participate in the compliance check.

(3) A retailer that is found to be in compliance with this section during a compliance check shall be notified in writing of the compliance check and the determination of compliance.

(4) Compliance checks conducted under this subsection shall be in a manner consistent with this subsection and the regulations as promulgated by the Department of Health.

(5) The Department of Health, a primary contractor pursuant to Chapter 7 of the Tobacco Settlement Act, a single county authority created pursuant to the Pennsylvania Drug and Alcohol Abuse Control Act or a county or municipal health department shall conduct a compliance check under this subsection no more than once every 30 days at any one retail location. This paragraph shall not preclude the law enforcement agency providing primary police services to the municipality in which the retail store is located from otherwise enforcing this section.

(6) Individuals participating in compliance checks under this subsection shall not be deemed employees under the act of July 23, 1970 (P.L.563, No.195), known as the Public Employe Relations Act, nor shall participating individuals be considered policemen under the act of June 24, 1968 (P.L.237, No.111), referred to as the Policemen and Firemen Collective Bargaining Act.

(h) Administrative action.--

(1) Upon receiving notice, in accordance with subsection (c) or otherwise, of a third conviction of a retailer during any 24-month period, the department may, after an opportunity for a hearing, suspend the retailer's cigarette license for up to 30 days. The department, in a hearing held pursuant to this paragraph, has jurisdiction only to determine whether or not the retailer was convicted of a violation of subsection (a). The introduction of a certified copy of a conviction for a violation of subsection (a) shall be sufficient evidence for the suspension of the cigarette license.

(2) Upon receiving notice, in accordance with subsection (c) or otherwise, of a fourth conviction of a retailer during any 24-month period, the department may, after an opportunity for a hearing, revoke the retailer's cigarette license for up to 60 days. The department, in a hearing held under this paragraph, has jurisdiction only to determine whether or not the retailer was convicted of a violation of subsection (a). The introduction of a certified copy of a conviction for a violation of subsection (a) shall be sufficient evidence for the revocation of the cigarette license.

(i) Enforcement.--An employee of the Department of Health, a single county authority created pursuant to the Pennsylvania Drug and Alcohol Abuse Control Act, a county or municipal health department or a primary contractor pursuant to Chapter 7 of the Tobacco Settlement Act may institute a proceeding to enforce the provisions of this section in accordance with any means authorized by the Rules of Criminal Procedure. The enforcement authority granted pursuant to this subsection may not be delegated.

(j) **Other penalties.**--Notwithstanding any other law to the contrary, prosecution or conviction under this section shall not constitute a bar to any prosecution, penalty or administrative action under any other applicable statutory provision.

(k) **Definitions.**--As used in this section, the following words and phrases shall have the meanings given to them in this subsection:

"**Cigarette.**" A roll for smoking made wholly or in part of tobacco, irrespective of size or shape and whether or not the tobacco is flavored, adulterated or mixed with any other ingredient, the wrapper or cover of which is made of paper or other substance or material except tobacco. The term does not include a cigar.

"**Cigarette license.**" A license issued under section 203-A or 213-A of the act of April 9, 1929 (P.L.343, No.176), known as The Fiscal Code.

"**Department.**" The Department of Revenue of the Commonwealth.

"**Electronic cigarette.**" An electronic device that delivers nicotine or other substances through vaporization and inhalation.

"**Electronic nicotine delivery system**" or "**ENDS.**" A product or device used, intended for use or designed for the purpose of ingesting a nicotine product. The term includes an electronic cigarette.

"**Minor.**" As follows:

(1) Except as provided under paragraph (2), an individual under 21 years of age.

(2) A member of the active or reserve components of any branch or unit of the armed forces of the United States under 18 years of age or a veteran who received an honorable discharge from any branch or unit of the active or reserve components of the armed forces of the United States under 18 years of age.

"**Nicotine product.**" A product that contains or consists of nicotine in a form that can be ingested by chewing, smoking, inhaling or any other means.

"**Pack of cigarettes.**" As defined in section 1201 of the act of March 4, 1971 (P.L.6, No.2), known as the Tax Reform Code of 1971.

"**Pipe tobacco.**" Any product containing tobacco made primarily for individual consumption that is intended to be smoked using tobacco paraphernalia.

"**Retailer.**" A person licensed under section 203-A or 213-A of the act of April 9, 1929 (P.L.343, No.176), known as The Fiscal Code, or other lawful retailer of other tobacco products.

"**Smokeless tobacco.**" Any product containing finely cut, ground, powdered, blended or leaf tobacco made primarily for individual consumption that is intended to be placed in the oral or nasal cavity and not intended to be smoked. The term includes, but is not limited to, chewing tobacco, dipping tobacco and snuff.

"Tobacco product." As follows:

(1) The term includes:

(i) Any product containing, made or derived from tobacco or nicotine that is intended for human consumption, whether smoked, heated, chewed, absorbed, dissolved, inhaled, snorted, sniffed or ingested by any other means, including, but not limited to, a cigarette, a cigar, a little cigar, chewing tobacco, pipe tobacco, snuff and snus.

(ii) Any electronic device that delivers nicotine or another substance to a person inhaling from the device, including, but not limited to, electronic nicotine delivery systems, an electronic cigarette, a cigar, a pipe and a hookah.

(iii) Any product containing, made or derived from either:

(A) Tobacco, whether in its natural or synthetic form; or

(B) Nicotine, whether in its natural or synthetic form, which is regulated by the United States Food and Drug Administration as a deemed tobacco product.

(iv) Any component, part or accessory of the product or electronic device under subparagraphs (i), (ii) and (iii), whether or not sold separately.

(2) The term does not include:

(i) A product that has been approved by the United States Food and Drug Administration for sale as a tobacco cessation product or for other therapeutic purposes where the product is marketed and sold solely for such approved purpose, so long as the product is not inhaled.

(ii) A device under paragraph (1)(ii) or (iii) if sold by a dispensary licensed under the act of April 17, 2016 (P.L.84, No.16), known as the Medical Marijuana Act.

"Tobacco vending machine." A mechanical or electrical device from which one or more tobacco products are dispensed for a consideration.

(Feb. 14, 1990, P.L.54, No.7, eff. imd.; July 10, 2002, P.L.789, No.112, eff. 30 days; Oct. 24, 2018, P.L.659, No.95, eff. 180 days; Nov. 27, 2019, P.L.669, No.93, eff. 60 days; Nov. 27, 2019, P.L.759, No.111, eff. July 1, 2020)

2019 Amendments. Act 93 amended the heading and subsecs. (a)(4) and (k) and Act 111 amended the heading and subsecs. (a)(4), (a.1), (f)(1)(i)(D) and (k). Act 111 overlooked the amendment by Act 93, but the amendments do not conflict in substance and have both been given effect in setting forth the text of section 6305.

2018 Amendment. Act 95 amended subsec. (b)(3).

2002 Amendment. Section 4 of Act 112 provided that Act 112 shall apply to offenses committed on or after the effective date of Act 112.

Cross References. Section 6305 is referred to in section 301 of Title 53 (Municipalities Generally).

§ 6306. Furnishing cigarettes or cigarette papers (Repealed).

2002 Repeal. Section 6306 was repealed July 10, 2002 (P.L.789, No.112), effective in 30 days.

§ 6306.1. Use of tobacco products in schools prohibited.

(a) Pupils.--A pupil commits a summary offense if the pupil possesses or uses a tobacco product:

(1) in a school building;

(2) on a school bus or other vehicle owned by, leased by or under the control of a school district; or

(3) on school property owned by, leased by or under the control of a school district.

(a.1) Other persons.--

(1) Any person, other than a pupil, commits a summary offense if the person uses a tobacco product:

(i) in a school building;

(ii) on a school bus or other vehicle owned by, leased by or under the control of a school district; or

(iii) on school property owned by, leased by or under the control of a school district.

(2) The board of school directors may designate certain areas on property owned by, leased by or under the control of the school district where tobacco product use by persons other than pupils is permitted. The areas must be no less than 50 feet from school buildings, stadiums or bleachers.

(a.2) Policy.--

(1) The board of school directors shall establish a policy to enforce the prohibition of tobacco product use under this section and may further establish policy relating to tobacco product use at school-sponsored events that are held off school premises.

(2) The board of school directors shall notify employees, pupils and parents of the policy developed in accordance with paragraph (1) by publishing the information in a student handbook and parent newsletter and on posters or other efficient means.

(b) Grading.--A pupil who commits an offense under this section shall be subject to prosecution initiated by the local school district and shall, upon conviction, be sentenced to pay a fine of not more than $50 for the benefit of the school district in which such offending pupil resides and to pay court costs. When a pupil is charged with violating subsection (a), the court may admit the offender to an adjudication alternative as authorized under 42 Pa.C.S. § 1520 (relating to adjudication alternative program) in lieu of imposing the fine.

(c) Nature of offense.--A summary offense under this section shall not be a criminal offense of record, shall not be reportable as a criminal act and shall not be placed on the criminal record of the offending school-age person if any such record exists.

(c.1) Preemption.--This section preempts any municipal ordinance or school board regulation to the contrary.

(d) Definitions.--As used in this section, the following words and phrases shall have the meanings given to them in this subsection:

"Electronic cigarette." An electronic device that delivers nicotine or other substances through vaporization and inhalation.

"**Electronic nicotine delivery system**" or "**ENDS.**" A product or device used, intended for use or designed for the purpose of ingesting a nicotine product. The term includes an electronic cigarette.

"**Nicotine product.**" A product that contains or consists of nicotine in a form that can be ingested by chewing, smoking, inhaling or any other means.

"**Pupil.**" A person between the ages of 6 and 21 years who is enrolled in school.

"**School.**" A school operated by a joint board, board of directors or school board where pupils are enrolled in compliance with Article XIII of the act of March 10, 1949 (P.L.30, No.14), known as the Public School Code of 1949, including a career and technical school, charter school and intermediate unit.

"Tobacco product." As follows:

(1) The term includes:

(i) Any product containing, made or derived from tobacco or nicotine that is intended for human consumption, whether smoked, heated, chewed, absorbed, dissolved, inhaled, snorted, sniffed or ingested by any other means, including, but not limited to, a cigarette, a cigar, a little cigar, chewing tobacco, pipe tobacco, snuff and snus.

(ii) Any electronic device that delivers nicotine or another substance to a person inhaling from the device, including, but not limited to, electronic nicotine delivery systems, an electronic cigarette, a cigar, a pipe and a hookah.

(iii) Any product containing, made or derived from either:

(A) Tobacco, whether in its natural or synthetic form; or

(B) Nicotine, whether in its natural or synthetic form, which is regulated by the United States Food and Drug Administration as a deemed tobacco product.

(iv) Any component, part or accessory of the product or electronic device under subparagraphs (i), (ii) and (iii), whether or not sold separately.

(2) The term does not include:

(i) A product that has been approved by the United States Food and Drug Administration for sale as a tobacco cessation product or for other therapeutic purposes where the product is marketed and sold solely for such approved purpose, so long as the product is not inhaled.

(ii) A device under paragraph (1)(ii) or (iii) if sold by a dispensary licensed under the act of April 17, 2016 (P.L.84, No.16), known as the Medical Marijuana Act.

(Dec. 4, 1996, P.L.902, No.145, eff. 60 days; Nov. 27, 2019, P.L.669, No.93, eff. 60 days; Nov. 27, 2019, P.L.759, No.111, eff. July 1, 2020)

2019 Amendments. Act 93 amended the heading and subsecs. (a) and (d) and added subsecs. (a.1), (a.2) and (c.1) and Act 111 amended the heading and subsecs. (a) and (d) and added subsecs. (a.1), (a.2) and (c.1). Act 111 overlooked the amendment by Act 93, but the amendments do not conflict in substance and have both been given effect in setting forth the text of section 6306.1.

1996 Amendment. Act 145 added section 6306.1.

§ 6307. Misrepresentation of age to secure liquor or malt or brewed beverages.

(a) Offense defined.--A person is guilty of a summary offense for a first violation and a misdemeanor of the third degree for any subsequent violations if he, being under the age of 21 years, knowingly and falsely represents himself to be 21 years of age or older to any licensed dealer, distributor or other person, for the purpose of procuring or having furnished to him, any liquor or malt or brewed beverages.

(b) Minimum penalty.--A person who is convicted of violating subsection (a) may be sentenced to pay a fine of not more than $500 for subsequent violations. No court shall have the authority to suspend any sentence as defined in this section.

(c) Adjudication of delinquency.--In addition to any other disposition authorized by law, a person adjudicated delinquent under subsection (a) may be ordered to pay a fine not exceeding $500 for an adjudication of delinquency.

(d) Preadjudication disposition.--

(1) When a person is charged with violating subsection (a), the court may admit the offender to an adjudication alternative program under 42 Pa.C.S. § 1520 (relating to adjudication alternative program) or to any other preadjudication disposition, if the offender has not previously received a preadjudication disposition for violating subsection (a).

(2) The use of a preadjudication disposition shall be considered a first or

subsequent offense, whichever is applicable, for the purpose of further adjudication under this section or under section 6310.4.

(Mar. 25, 1988, P.L.262, No.31, eff. 60 days; Oct. 24, 2018, P.L.659, No.95, eff. 180 days)

2018 Amendment. Act 95 amended subsec. (b).

Cross References. Section 6307 is referred to in sections 6310.5, 6310.6, 6313 of this title; section 1532 of Title 75 (Vehicles).

§ 6308. Purchase, consumption, possession or transportation of liquor or malt or brewed beverages.

(a) Offense defined.--A person commits a summary offense if he, being less than 21 years of age, attempts to purchase, purchases, consumes, possesses or knowingly and intentionally transports any liquor or malt or brewed beverages, as defined in section 6310.6 (relating to definitions). For the purposes of this section, it shall not be a defense that the liquor or malt or brewed beverage was consumed in a jurisdiction other than the jurisdiction where the citation for underage drinking was issued.

(b) Penalty.--A person convicted of violating subsection (a) may be sentenced to pay a fine of not more than $500 for the first violation and not more than $1,000 for the second and each subsequent violation.

(c) Preadjudication disposition.--

(1) When a person is charged with violating subsection (a), the magisterial district judge may admit the offender to the adjudication alternative as authorized in 42 Pa.C.S. § 1520 (relating to adjudication alternative program) or any other preadjudication disposition if the offender has not previously received a preadjudication disposition for violating subsection (a).

(2) The use of a preadjudication disposition shall be considered a first or subsequent offense, whichever is applicable, for the purpose of further adjudication under this section or under section 6310.4.

(d) Notification.--The police department making an arrest for a suspected violation of subsection (a) shall so notify the parents or guardian of the minor charged.

(e) Exception for compliance checks.--(Repealed).

(f) Exception for person seeking medical attention for another.--(Repealed).

(Apr. 28, 1978, P.L.202, No.53, eff. 60 days; Mar. 25, 1988, P.L.262, No.31, eff. 60 days; Mar. 17, 2000, P.L.11, No.4, eff. 60 days; Dec. 3, 2002, P.L.1144, No.141, eff. 60 days; Nov. 30, 2004, P.L.1618, No.207, eff. 60 days; July 7, 2011, P.L.288, No.66, eff. 60 days; Oct. 25, 2012, P.L.1663, No.205, eff. 60 days; Dec. 22, 2017, P.L.1237, No.75, eff. imd.; Oct. 19, 2018, P.L.535, No.80, eff. 30 days; Oct. 24, 2018, P.L.659, No.95, eff. 180 days)

2018 Amendments. Act 80 repealed subsec. (f) and Act 95 amended subsec. (b). Act 80 of 2018 shall be referred to as the "Timothy J. Piazza Antihazing Law."

2017 Amendment. Act 75 repealed subsec. (e) and section 2 of Act 141 of 2002.

2012 Amendment. Section 2 of Act 205 provided that the amendment shall apply to offenses committed on or after the effective date of section 2.

2007 Amendment. Section 2 of Act 141 of 2002 was amended by Act 75 of 2007, amending the expiration date of subsec. (e) to December 31, 2017.

2004 Amendment. Act 207 amended subsec. (c)(1). See section 29 of Act 207 in the appendix to this title for special provisions relating to construction of law.

2002 Amendment. Act 141 added subsec. (e). Section 2 of Act 141 provided that subsec. (e) shall expire December 31, 2007, unless sooner reauthorized by the General Assembly.

2000 Amendment. Act 4 amended subsec. (a).

Cross References. Section 6308 is referred to in sections 2810, 6308.1, 6310.5, 6310.6, 6313, 9122, 9123 of this title; sections 1518, 3905 of Title 4 (Amusements); sections 3573, 8902 of Title 42 (Judiciary and Judicial Procedure); sections 1532, 1553 of Title 75 (Vehicles).

§ 6308.1. Safe harbor for violation of section 6308(a).

(a) Immunity for the individual seeking medical attention for another.--An individual shall not be prosecuted for an offense under section 6308(a) (relating to purchase, consumption, possession or transportation of liquor or malt or brewed beverages) if the individual can establish all of the following:

(1) A law enforcement officer first became aware of the individual's violation of section 6308(a) because the individual placed a 911 call or contacted campus security, police or

emergency services, based on a reasonable belief that another individual was in need of immediate medical attention to prevent death or serious bodily injury.

(2) The individual reasonably believed the individual was the first individual to make a 911 call or contact campus security, police or emergency services and report that the other individual needed immediate medical attention to prevent death or serious bodily injury.

(3) The individual provided the individual's own name to the 911 operator or equivalent campus security officer, police or emergency services personnel.

(4) The individual remained with the other individual needing medical assistance until a campus security officer, police or emergency services personnel arrived and the need for the individual's presence ended.

(b) Immunity for the individual needing medical attention.--An individual needing medical attention shall be immune under this section from prosecution for an offense under section 6308(a) if another individual reported the incident and remained with the individual needing medical attention and is entitled to immunity under this section.

(c) Limitations.--The immunity described under this section shall be limited as follows:

(1) This section may not bar prosecuting a person for an offense under section 6308(a) if a law enforcement officer learns of the offense prior to and independent of the action of seeking or obtaining emergency assistance as described in subsection (a).

(2) This section shall not interfere with or prevent the investigation, arrest, charging or prosecution of an individual for a crime other than an offense under section 6308(a).

(3) This section shall not bar the admissibility of evidence in connection with the investigation and prosecution for a crime other than an offense under section 6308(a).

(4) This section shall not bar the admissibility of evidence in connection with the investigation and prosecution of a crime with regard to another defendant who does not independently qualify for immunity under this section.

(d) Good faith immunity.--In addition to any other applicable immunity or limitation on civil liability, a law enforcement officer, campus security officer or prosecuting attorney who, acting in good faith, charges a person who

is thereafter determined to be entitled to immunity under this section shall not be subject to civil liability for the filing of the charges.

(e) Definitions.--As used in this section, the following words and phrases shall have the meanings given to them in this subsection unless the context clearly indicates otherwise:

"911 system." A system, including enhanced 911 service and a wireless e-911 system, that permits a person dialing 911 by telephone to be connected to a public safety answering point, via normal telephone facilities, for the reporting of police, fire, medical or other emergency situations.

"Campus security officer." An employee of an institution of higher education charged with maintaining the safety and security of the property of the institution and persons on the property.

"Emergency services personnel." Individuals, including a trained volunteer or a member of the armed forces of the United States or the National Guard, whose official or assigned responsibilities include performing or directly supporting the performance of emergency medical and rescue services or firefighting.

"Law enforcement officer." A person who by virtue of the person's office or public employment is vested by law with a duty to maintain public order or to make arrests for offenses, whether that duty extends to all offenses or is limited to specific offenses, or a person on active State duty under 51 Pa.C.S. § 508 (relating to active duty for emergency).

(Oct. 19, 2018, P.L.535, No.80, eff. 30 days)

2018 Amendment. Act 80 added section 6308.1. Act 80 of 2018 shall be referred to as the "Timothy J. Piazza Antihazing Law."

§ 6309. Representing that minor is of age.

(a) Offense defined.--A person is guilty of a misdemeanor of the third degree if he knowingly, willfully, and falsely represents to any licensed dealer, or other person, any minor to be of full age, for the purpose of inducing any such licensed dealer or other person, to sell or furnish any liquor or malt or brewed beverages, as defined in section 6310.6 (relating to definitions), to the minor.

(b) Minimum penalty.--In addition to any other penalty imposed pursuant to this title or other statute, a person committing an offense under this section shall be sentenced to pay a fine of not less than $300. There shall be no authority in any court to impose on an offender any lesser sentence than the minimum sentence mandated by this subsection. In no case shall the sentence exceed the maximum sentence prescribed by law. No court shall have the authority to suspend any sentence as defined in this section.

(Mar. 25, 1988, P.L.262, No.31, eff. 60 days)

Cross References. Section 6309 is referred to in section 6310.6 of this title.

§ 6310. Inducement of minors to buy liquor or malt or brewed beverages.

(a) Offense defined.--A person is guilty of a misdemeanor of the third degree if he hires or requests or induces any minor to purchase, or offer to purchase, liquor or malt or brewed beverages, as defined in section 6310.6 (relating to definitions), from a duly licensed dealer for any purpose.

(b) Minimum penalty.--In addition to any other penalty imposed pursuant to this title or other statute, a person convicted of an offense under this section shall be sentenced to pay a fine of not less than $300. There shall be no authority in any court to impose on an offender any lesser sentence than the minimum sentence mandated by this subsection. Nothing in this section shall prevent the sentencing court from imposing a sentence greater than the minimum sentence mandated in this subsection. In no case shall the sentence exceed the maximum sentence prescribed by law. No court shall have the authority to suspend any sentence as defined in this section.

(c) Exception for compliance checks.--(Repealed).

(Mar. 25, 1988, P.L.262, No.31, eff. 60 days; Dec. 3, 2002, P.L.1144, No.141, eff. 60 days; Dec. 22, 2017, P.L.1237, No.75, eff. imd.)

2017 Amendment. Act 75 repealed subsec. (c) and section 2 of Act 141 of 2002.

2007 Amendment. Section 2 of Act 141 of 2002 was amended by Act 75 of 2007, amending the expiration date of subsec. (c) to December 31, 2017.

2002 Amendment. Section 2 of Act 141 provided that subsec. (c) shall expire December 31, 2007, unless sooner reauthorized by the General Assembly.

Cross References. Section 6310 is referred to in section 6310.6 of this title.

§ 6310.1. Selling or furnishing liquor or malt or brewed beverages to minors.

(a) Offense defined.--Except as provided in subsection (b), a person commits a misdemeanor of the third degree if he intentionally and knowingly sells or intentionally and knowingly furnishes, or purchases with the intent to sell or furnish, any liquor or malt or brewed beverages to a person who is less than 21 years of age.

(b) Exceptions.--The provisions of this section shall not apply to any religious service or ceremony which may be conducted in a private home or a place of worship where the amount of wine served does not exceed the amount reasonably, customarily and traditionally required as an integral part of the service or ceremony.

(c) Minimum penalty.--In addition to any other penalty imposed pursuant to this title or other statute, a person who is convicted of violating subsection (a) shall be sentenced to pay a fine of not less than $1,000 for the first violation and a fine of $2,500 for each subsequent violation. There shall be no authority in any court to impose on an offender any lesser sentence than the minimum sentence mandated by this subsection. No court shall have the authority to suspend any sentence as defined in this section. Nothing in this section shall prevent the sentencing court from imposing a sentence greater than the minimum sentence mandated in this subsection. In no case shall the sentence exceed the maximum sentence prescribed by law.

(Mar. 25, 1988, P.L.262, No.31, eff. 60 days)

1988 Amendment. Act 31 added section 6310.1.

Cross References. Section 6310.1 is referred to in section 6310.6 of this title.

§ 6310.2. Manufacture or sale of false identification card.

(a) Offense defined.--A person commits a misdemeanor of the second degree if he intentionally, knowingly or recklessly manufactures, makes, alters, sells or attempts to sell an identification card falsely representing the identity, birth date or age of another.

(b) Minimum penalty.--In addition to any other penalty imposed pursuant to this title or any other statute, a person who is convicted of violating subsection (a) shall be sentenced to pay a fine of not less than $1,000 for the first violation and a fine of not less than $2,500 for each subsequent violation. There shall be no authority in any court to impose on an offender any lesser sentence than the minimum sentence mandated by this subsection. In no case shall the sentence exceed the maximum sentence prescribed by law. No court shall have the authority to suspend any sentence as defined in this section.

(c) Adjudication of delinquency.--In addition to any other disposition authorized by law, a person adjudicated delinquent under subsection (a) shall be ordered to pay a fine of $500 for the first adjudication of delinquency and a fine of $1,000 for each subsequent adjudication of delinquency.

(Mar. 25, 1988, P.L.262, No.31, eff. 60 days)

1988 Amendment. Act 31 added section 6310.2.

Cross References. Section 6310.2 is referred to in section 6310.6 of this title.

§ 6310.3. Carrying a false identification card.

(a) Offense defined.--A person commits a summary offense for a first violation and a misdemeanor of the third degree for any subsequent violation if he, being under 21 years of age, possesses an identification card falsely identifying that person by name, age, date of birth or photograph as being 21 years of age or older or obtains or attempts to obtain liquor or malt or brewed beverages by using the identification card of another or by using an identification card that has not been lawfully issued to or in the name of that person who possesses the card.

(b) Minimum penalty.--A person who is convicted of violating subsection (a) shall be sentenced to pay a fine of not more than $500 for the second and subsequent violations. No court shall have the authority to suspend any sentence as defined in this section.

(c) Adjudication of delinquency.--In addition to any other disposition authorized by law, a person adjudicated delinquent under subsection (a) may be ordered to pay a fine not exceeding $500 for an adjudication of delinquency.

(d) Preadjudication disposition.--

(1) When a person is charged with violating subsection (a), the court may admit the offender to the adjudication alternative as authorized in 42 Pa.C.S. § 1520 (relating to adjudication alternative program) or any other preadjudication disposition if the offender has not previously received a preadjudication disposition for violating subsection (a).

(2) The use of a preadjudication disposition shall be considered a first or subsequent offense, whichever is applicable, for the purpose of further adjudication under this section or under section 6310.4.

(e) Notification.--The police department making an arrest for a suspected violation of subsection (a) shall so notify the parents or guardian of the minor charged.

(Mar. 25, 1988, P.L.262, No.31, eff. 60 days; Oct. 24, 2018, P.L.659, No.95, eff. 180 days)

2018 Amendment. Act 95 amended subsec. (b).

1988 Amendment. Act 31 added section 6310.3.

Cross References. Section 6310.3 is referred to in sections 6310.5, 6310.6, 6313 of this title; section 1532 of Title 75 (Vehicles).

§ 6310.4. Restriction of operating privileges (Repealed).

2018 Repeal. Section 6310.4 was repealed October 24, 2018, P.L.659, No.95, effective in 180 days.

§ 6310.5. Predisposition evaluation.

(a) General rule.--If an individual is convicted, adjudicated delinquent or offered preadjudication disposition for a violation of section 6307 (relating to misrepresentation of age to secure liquor or malt or brewed beverages), 6308 (relating to purchase, consumption, possession or transportation of liquor or malt or brewed beverages) or 6310.3 (relating to carrying a false identification card), the following shall apply:

(1) For a first violation of any of the preceding offenses, the court may, in addition to other requirements, require the individual to be evaluated prior to an adjudication of delinquency, sentencing or receiving preadjudication disposition.

(2) For a subsequent violation of any of the preceding offenses, the court shall, in addition to other requirements, require the individual to be evaluated prior to sentencing or receiving preadjudication disposition.

(3) Evaluation under this subsection may consist of evaluation techniques if deemed appropriate by the court to determine the extent of the individual's involvement with alcohol.

(b) **Program of education, intervention and counseling.**--Based on the results of the evaluation authorized under subsection (a) and any additional information, the court may require that the person successfully complete a prescribed program of education, intervention or counseling approved by the Department of Health.

(c) **Costs.**--Costs of any and all requirements applied under this section shall be in addition to any other penalty required or allowed by law and shall be the responsibility of the person upon whom the requirement is placed.

(Mar. 25, 1988, P.L.262, No.31, eff. 60 days)

1988 Amendment. Act 31 added section 6310.5.

§ 6310.6. Definitions.

The following words and phrases when used in sections 6307 (relating to misrepresentation of age to secure liquor or malt or brewed beverages) through 6310.3 (relating to carrying a false identification card) shall have the meanings given to them in this section unless the context clearly indicates otherwise:

"Furnish." To supply, give or provide to, or allow a minor to possess on premises or property owned or controlled by the person charged.

"Identification card." A driver's license, a Department of Transportation nondriver's identification card or a card issued by the Pennsylvania Liquor Control Board for the purpose of identifying a person desiring liquor or malt or brewed beverages, a card which falsely purports to be any of the foregoing, or any card, paper or document which falsely identifies the person by name, photograph, age or date of birth as being 21 years of age or older.

"Liquor." Includes any alcoholic, spirituous, vinous, fermented or other alcoholic beverage, or combination of liquors and mixed liquor a part of which is spirituous, vinous, fermented or otherwise alcoholic, including all drinks or drinkable liquids, preparations or mixtures and reused, recovered or redistilled denatured alcohol usable or taxable for beverage purposes which contain more than 0.50% of alcohol by volume, except pure ethyl alcohol and malt or brewed beverages.

"Malt or brewed beverages." Any beer, lager beer, ale, porter or similar fermented malt beverage containing 0.50% or more of alcohol by volume, by whatever name such beverage may be called.

(Mar. 25, 1988, P.L.262, No.31, eff. 60 days)

1988 Amendment. Act 31 added section 6310.6.

Cross References. Section 6310.6 is referred to in sections 6308, 6309, 6310 of this title.

§ 6310.7. Selling or furnishing nonalcoholic beverages to persons under 21 years of age.

(a) **Offense defined.**--A person commits a summary offense if he intentionally and knowingly sells or furnishes nonalcoholic beverages to any person under 21 years of age.

(b) **Definitions.**--As used in this section, the term "nonalcoholic beverage" means any beverage intended to be marketed or sold as nonalcoholic beer, wine or liquor having some alcohol content but does not contain more than 0.5% alcohol by volume.

(Dec. 12, 1994, P.L.1248, No.148, eff. 60 days)

1994 Amendment. Act 148 added section 6310.7. See the preamble to Act 148 in the appendix to this title for special provisions relating to legislative findings and declarations.

§ 6311. Tattooing and body piercing.

(a) **Tattooing.**--A person commits an offense if he tattoos any person under the age of 18 years without the parent or guardian of such person giving consent for the tattooing of the person and being present at the time of the tattooing of the person.

(b) **Body piercing.**--A person commits an offense if for compensation he punctures a part of the body of any person under the age of 18 years with the intent to create a permanent hole for cosmetic purposes without the parent or guardian of such person giving consent for the piercing of the person and being present at the time of the piercing of the person.

(c) **Grading.**--A person who commits an offense under this section shall be guilty of a misdemeanor of the third degree for the first offense. A person who commits a second or subsequent offense under this section within one year of the preceding offense commits a misdemeanor of the second degree.

(May 21, 2004, P.L.232, No.36, eff. 60 days)

§ 6312. Sexual abuse of children.

(a) **Definition.**--(Deleted by amendment).

(b) Photographing, videotaping, depicting on computer or filming sexual acts.--

(1) Any person who causes or knowingly permits a child under the age of 18 years to engage in a prohibited sexual act or in the simulation of such act commits an offense if such person knows, has reason to know or intends that such act may be photographed, videotaped, depicted on computer or filmed.

(2) Any person who knowingly photographs, videotapes, depicts on computer or films a child under the age of 18 years engaging in a prohibited sexual act or in the simulation of such an act commits an offense.

(c) **Dissemination of photographs, videotapes, computer depictions and films.**--Any person who knowingly sells, distributes, delivers, disseminates, transfers, displays or exhibits to others, or who possesses for the purpose of sale, distribution, delivery, dissemination, transfer, display or exhibition to others, any book, magazine, pamphlet, slide, photograph, film, videotape, computer depiction or other material depicting a child under the age of 18 years engaging in a prohibited sexual act or in the simulation of such act commits an offense.

(d) **Child pornography.**--Any person who intentionally views or knowingly possesses or controls any book, magazine, pamphlet, slide, photograph, film, videotape, computer depiction or other material depicting a child under the age of 18 years engaging in a prohibited sexual act or in the simulation of such act commits an offense.

(d.1) **Grading.**--The offenses shall be graded as follows:

(1) Except as provided in paragraph (3), an offense under subsection (b) is a felony of the second degree.

(2) (i) Except as provided in paragraph (3), a first offense under subsection (c) or (d) is a felony of the third degree.

(ii) A second or subsequent offense under subsection (c) or (d) is a felony of the second degree.

(3) When a person commits an offense graded under paragraph (1) or (2)(i) and

indecent contact with the child as defined in section 3101 (relating to definitions) is depicted, the grading of the offense shall be one grade higher than the grade specified in paragraph (1) or (2)(i).

(e) **Evidence of age.**--In the event a person involved in a prohibited sexual act is alleged to be a child under the age of 18 years, competent expert testimony shall be sufficient to establish the age of said person.

(e.1) **Mistake as to age.**--Under subsection (b) only, it is no defense that the defendant did not know the age of the child. Neither a misrepresentation of age by the child nor a bona fide belief that the person is over the specified age shall be a defense.

(f) **Exceptions.**--This section does not apply to any of the following:

(1) Any material that is viewed, possessed, controlled, brought or caused to be brought into this Commonwealth, or presented, for a bona fide educational, scientific, governmental or judicial purpose.

(2) Conduct prohibited under section 6321 (relating to transmission of sexually explicit images by minor), unless the conduct is specifically excluded by section 6321(d).

(3) An individual under 18 years of age who knowingly views, photographs, videotapes, depicts on a computer or films or possesses or intentionally views a visual depiction as defined in section 6321 of himself alone in a state of nudity as defined in section 6321.

(f.1) Criminal action.--

(1) A district attorney shall have the authority to investigate and to institute criminal proceedings for any violation of this section.

(2) In addition to the authority conferred upon the Attorney General by the act of October 15, 1980 (P.L.950, No.164), known as the Commonwealth Attorneys Act, the Attorney General shall have the authority to investigate and to institute criminal proceedings for any violation of this section or any series of violations of this section involving more than one county of this Commonwealth or involving any county of this Commonwealth and another state. No person charged with a violation of this section by the Attorney General shall have standing to challenge the authority of the Attorney General to investigate or prosecute the case, and, if any such challenge is made, the challenge shall be dismissed and no relief shall be available in the courts of this

Commonwealth to the person making the challenge.

(g) **Definitions.**--As used in this section, the following words and phrases shall have the meanings given to them in this subsection:

"**Intentionally views.**" The deliberate, purposeful, voluntary viewing of material depicting a child under 18 years of age engaging in a prohibited sexual act or in the simulation of such act. The term shall not include the accidental or inadvertent viewing of such material.

"**Prohibited sexual act.**" Sexual intercourse as defined in section 3101 (relating to definitions), masturbation, sadism, masochism, bestiality, fellatio, cunnilingus, lewd exhibition of the genitals or nudity if such nudity is depicted for the purpose of sexual stimulation or gratification of any person who might view such depiction.

(Oct. 26, 1977, P.L.212, No.62, eff. 60 days; Dec. 19, 1988, P.L.1275, No.158, eff. 60 days; Mar. 31, 1995, 1st Sp.Sess., P.L.985, No.10, eff. 60 days; Nov. 20, 2002, P.L.1104, No.134, eff. 60 days; July 14, 2009, P.L.63, No.15, eff. 60 days; Oct. 7, 2010, P.L.482, No.69, eff. 60 days; Oct. 25, 2012, P.L.1623, No.198, eff. 60 days; Dec. 18, 2013, P.L.1163, No.105, eff. Jan. 1, 2014)

2013 Amendment. Act 105 amended subsecs. (b), (c) and (d) and added subsec. (d.1).

2012 Amendment. Act 198 amended subsec. (f).

2010 Amendment. Act 69 added subsec. (f.1).

2009 Amendment. Act 15 amended subsecs. (d) hdg. and (1) and (f), added subsec. (g) and deleted subsec. (a).

Cross References. Section 6312 is referred to in sections 3051, 3104, 3131, 5743.1, 6318, 6321, 7621, 7626, 7627 of this title; section 3304 of Title 5 (Athletics and Sports); section 2106 of Title 20 (Decedents, Estates and Fiduciaries); sections 5329, 6303, 6344, 6702 of Title 23 (Domestic Relations); sections 5551, 5552, 5985.1, 5993, 62A03, 6302, 9718.1, 9720.5, 9730.3, 9799.14 of Title 42 (Judiciary and Judicial Procedure).

§ 6313. Special information.

(a) **General rule.**--At the time of conviction or admission to a preadjudication disposition for a violation of section 6307 (relating to misrepresentation of age to secure liquor or malt or brewed beverages), 6308 (relating to purchase, consumption, possession or transportation of liquor or malt or brewed beverages) or 6310.3 (relating to carrying a false identification card), the court shall provide to the Department of Transportation, in such form as prescribed by the department, the name of the offender, the offender's date of birth, the disposition of the case and the duration of any license suspension.

(b) **Availability.**--Information under this section shall be available to law enforcement agencies and the judicial system for the purpose of determining whether the offender has a prior record of violation of the offenses listed in subsection (a).

(Mar. 25, 1988, P.L.262, No.31, eff. 60 days)

1988 Amendment. Act 31 added section 6313.

§ 6314. Sentencing and penalties for trafficking drugs to minors.

(a) **General rule.**--A person over 18 years of age who is convicted in any court of this Commonwealth of a violation of section 13(a)(14) or (30) of the act of April 14, 1972 (P.L.233, No.64), known as The Controlled Substance, Drug, Device and Cosmetic Act, shall, if the delivery or possession with intent to deliver of the controlled substance was to a minor, be sentenced to a minimum sentence of at least one year total confinement, notwithstanding any other provision of this title or other statute to the contrary.

(b) **Additional penalties.**--In addition to the mandatory minimum sentence set forth in subsection (a), the person shall be sentenced to an additional minimum sentence of at least two years total confinement, notwithstanding any other provision of this title or other statute to the contrary, if the person did any of the following:

(1) Committed the offense with the intent to promote the habitual use of the controlled substance.

(2) Intended to engage the minor in the trafficking, transportation, delivery, manufacturing, sale or conveyance.

(3) Committed the offense within 1,000 feet of the real property on which is located a public, private or parochial school or a college or university.

(4) Committed the offense on a school bus or within 500 feet of a school bus stop.

(c) Proof at sentencing.--The provisions of this section shall not be an element of the crime. Notice of the applicability of this section to the defendant shall not be required prior to conviction, but reasonable notice of the Commonwealth's intention to proceed under this section shall be provided after conviction and before sentencing. The applicability of this section shall be determined at sentencing. The court shall consider evidence presented at trial, shall afford the Commonwealth and the defendant an opportunity to present necessary additional evidence, and shall determine, by a preponderance of the evidence, if this section is applicable.

(d) Authority of court in sentencing.-- There shall be no authority for a court to impose on a defendant to which this section is applicable a lesser sentence than provided for in subsection (a), to place the defendant on probation or to suspend sentence. Nothing in this section shall prevent the sentencing court from imposing a sentence greater than that provided in this section. Sentencing guidelines promulgated by the Pennsylvania Commission on Sentencing shall not supersede the mandatory sentences provided in this section. Disposition under section 17 or 18 of The Controlled Substance, Drug, Device and Cosmetic Act shall not be available to a defendant to which this section applies.

(e) Appeal by Commonwealth.--If a sentencing court refuses to apply this section where applicable, the Commonwealth shall have the right to appellate review of the action of the sentencing court. The appellate court shall vacate the sentence and remand the case to the sentencing court for imposition of a sentence in accordance with this section if it finds that the sentence was imposed in violation of this section.

(f) Forfeiture.--Assets against which a petition seeking forfeiture has been filed and is pending or against which the Commonwealth has indicated an intention to file a petition seeking forfeiture shall not be subject to a fine under this section.

(g) Definition.--As used in this section, the term "minor" means an individual under 18 years of age.

(Mar. 25, 1988, P.L.262, No.31, eff. July 1, 1988; May 9, 1997, P.L.142, No.8, eff. 60 days; June 29, 2017, P.L.247, No.13, eff. July 1, 2017)

2017 Amendment. Act 13 amended subsec. (f).

1997 Amendment. Act 8 amended subsec. (b).

1988 Amendment. Act 31 added section 6314.

Cross References. Section 6314 is referred to in section 6317 of this title.

§ 6315. Selling or furnishing butane to minors.

(a) Offense defined.--A person commits a summary offense if he knowingly sells or knowingly furnishes or purchases with the intent to sell or furnish butane to a person who is less than 18 years of age, except where the relationship of parent and child, guardian and ward or adult instructor and pupil exists between such person and the person who is less than 18 years of age.

(b) Penalty.--A person who is convicted of violating subsection (a) shall be sentenced to pay a fine of not less than $250 for the first violation and a fine of $500 for each subsequent violation.

(c) Definition.--As used in this section, the term "butane" means any product which contains 90% by weight or more of n-butane, isobutane or both. It does not include products which contain n-butane, isobutane or both as a secondary component, or within the formulation as a solvent or propellant.

(Nov. 22, 1995, P.L.621, No.66, eff. 60 days)

1995 Amendment. Act 66 added section 6315.

§ 6316. Selling or furnishing certain stimulants to minors.

(a) Offense defined.--A person commits a summary offense if he knowingly sells or purchases with the intent to sell ephedrine to a person who is less than 18 years of age.

(b) Penalty.--A person who is convicted of violating subsection (a) shall be sentenced to pay a fine of not less than $250 nor more than $500 for the first violation and a fine of $500 for each subsequent violation.

(c) Definitions.--As used in this section, the following words and phrases shall have the meanings given to them in this subsection:

"Ephedrine."

(1) Except as provided in paragraph (2), any product that contains any quantity of ephedrine, a salt of ephedrine, an optical isomer

of ephedrine or a salt of an optical isomer of ephedrine.

(2) The term does not include a product containing ephedrine if it may lawfully be sold over the counter without a prescription under the Federal Food, Drug, and Cosmetic Act (52 Stat. 1040, 21 U.S.C. § 301 et seq.); is labeled and marketed in a manner consistent with the pertinent OTC Tentative Final or Final Monograph; is manufactured and distributed for legitimate medicinal use in a manner that reduces or eliminates the likelihood of abuse; and as described as follows:

(i) Solid oral dosage forms, including soft gelatin caplets, that combine active ingredients in the following ranges for each dosage unit:

(A) Theophylline (100-130 mg), ephedrine (12.5-24 mg).

(B) Theophylline (60-100 mg), ephedrine (12.5-24 mg), guaifenesin (200-400 mg).

(C) Ephedrine (12.5-25 mg), guaifenesin (200-400 mg).

(D) Phenobarbital (not greater than 8 mg) in combination with the ingredients of clause (A) or (B).

(ii) Liquid oral dosage forms that combine active ingredients in the following ranges for each 5 ml dose:

(A) Theophylline (not greater than 45 mg), ephedrine (not greater than 36 mg), guaifenesin (not greater than 100 mg), phenobarbital (not greater than 12 mg).

(B) Phenylephephrine (not greater than 5 mg), ephedrine (not greater than 5 mg), chlorpheniramine (not greater than 2 mg), dextromethorphan (not greater than 10 mg), ammonium Cl (not greater than 40 mg), ipecac fluid extract (not greater than 0.005 ml).

(iii) Anorectal preparations containing less than 5% ephedrine.

(iv) Any liquid compound, mixture or preparation containing 0.5% or less of ephedrine.

(May 9, 1997, P.L.142, No.8, eff. 60 days)

1997 Amendment. Act 8 added section 6316. See the preamble to Act 8 in the appendix to this title for special provisions relating to legislative findings and declarations.

§ 6317. Drug-free school zones.

(a) General rule.--A person 18 years of age or older who is convicted in any court of this Commonwealth of a violation of section 13(a)(14) or (30) of the act of April 14, 1972 (P.L.233, No.64), known as The Controlled Substance, Drug, Device and Cosmetic Act, shall, if the delivery or possession with intent to deliver of the controlled substance occurred within 1,000 feet of the real property on which is located a public, private or parochial school or a college or university or within 250 feet of the real property on which is located a recreation center or playground or on a school bus, be sentenced to a minimum sentence of at least two years of total confinement, notwithstanding any other provision of this title, The Controlled Substance, Drug, Device and Cosmetic Act or other statute to the contrary. The maximum term of imprisonment shall be four years for any offense:

(1) subject to this section; and

(2) for which The Controlled Substance, Drug, Device and Cosmetic Act provides for a maximum term of imprisonment of less than four years.

If the sentencing court finds that the delivery or possession with intent to deliver was to an individual under 18 years of age, then this section shall not be applicable and the offense shall be subject to section 6314 (relating to sentencing and penalties for trafficking drugs to minors).

(b) Proof at sentencing.--The provisions of this section shall not be an element of the crime. Notice of the applicability of this section to the defendant shall not be required prior to conviction, but reasonable notice of the Commonwealth's intention to proceed under this section shall be provided after conviction and before sentencing. The applicability of this section shall be determined at sentencing. The court shall consider evidence presented at trial, shall afford the Commonwealth and the defendant an opportunity to present necessary additional evidence and shall determine by a preponderance of the evidence if this section is applicable.

(c) Authority of court in sentencing.--There shall be no authority for a court to impose on a defendant to which this section is applicable a lesser sentence than provided for in subsection (a), to place the defendant on probation or to suspend sentence. Nothing in this section shall prevent the sentencing court from imposing a sentence greater than that provided in this section. Sentencing guidelines promulgated by the Pennsylvania Commission on Sentencing shall not supersede the mandatory sentences provided in this section.

Disposition under section 17 or 18 of The Controlled Substance, Drug, Device and Cosmetic Act shall not be available to a defendant to which this section applies.

(d) Appeal by Commonwealth.--If a sentencing court refuses to apply this section where applicable, the Commonwealth shall have the right to appellate review of the action of the sentencing court. The appellate court shall vacate the sentence and remand the case to the sentencing court for imposition of a sentence in accordance with this section if it finds that the sentence was imposed in violation of this section.

(June 25, 1997, P.L.284, No.26, eff. 60 days)

1997 Amendment. Act 26 added section 6317. Section 5 of Act 26 provided that the addition of section 6317 shall apply to all offenses occuring on or after the effective date of Act 26.

§ 6318. Unlawful contact with minor.

(a) Offense defined.--A person commits an offense if he is intentionally in contact with a minor, or a law enforcement officer acting in the performance of his duties who has assumed the identity of a minor, for the purpose of engaging in an activity prohibited under any of the following, and either the person initiating the contact or the person being contacted is within this Commonwealth:

(1) Any of the offenses enumerated in Chapter 31 (relating to sexual offenses).

(2) Open lewdness as defined in section 5901 (relating to open lewdness).

(3) Prostitution as defined in section 5902 (relating to prostitution and related offenses).

(4) Obscene and other sexual materials and performances as defined in section 5903 (relating to obscene and other sexual materials and performances).

(5) Sexual abuse of children as defined in section 6312 (relating to sexual abuse of children).

(6) Sexual exploitation of children as defined in section 6320 (relating to sexual exploitation of children).

(b) Grading.--A violation of subsection (a) is:

(1) an offense of the same grade and degree as the most serious underlying offense in subsection (a) for which the defendant contacted the minor; or

(2) a felony of the third degree;

whichever is greater.

(b.1) Concurrent jurisdiction to prosecute.--The Attorney General shall have concurrent prosecutorial jurisdiction with the district attorney for violations under this section and any crime arising out of the activity prohibited by this section when the person charged with a violation of this section contacts a minor through the use of a computer, computer system or computer network. No person charged with a violation of this section by the Attorney General shall have standing to challenge the authority of the Attorney General to prosecute the case, and, if any such challenge is made, the challenge shall be dismissed and no relief shall be available in the courts of this Commonwealth to the person making the challenge.

(c) Definitions.--As used in this section, the following words and phrases shall have the meanings given to them in this subsection:

"Computer." An electronic, magnetic, optical, hydraulic, organic or other high-speed data processing device or system which performs logic, arithmetic or memory functions and includes all input, output, processing, storage, software or communication facilities which are connected or related to the device in a computer system or computer network.

"Computer network." The interconnection of two or more computers through the usage of satellite, microwave, line or other communication medium.

"Computer system." A set of related, connected or unconnected computer equipment, devices and software.

"Contacts." Direct or indirect contact or communication by any means, method or device, including contact or communication in person or through an agent or agency, through any print medium, the mails, a common carrier or communication common carrier, any electronic communication system and any telecommunications, wire, computer or radio communications device or system.

"Minor." An individual under 18 years of age.

(Dec. 19, 1997, P.L.615, No.62, eff. imd.; Nov. 20, 2002, P.L.1104, No.134, eff. 60 days; Dec. 9, 2002, P.L.1391, No.172, eff. 60 days; Nov. 29, 2006, P.L.1567, No.178, eff. Jan. 1, 2007)

2006 Amendment. See the preamble to Act 178 in the appendix to this title for special provisions relating to legislative intent.

Cross References. Section 6318 is referred to in sections 3104, 5708, 5743.1 of this title; sections 5329, 6303, 6702 of Title 23 (Domestic Relations); sections 5985.1, 5993, 62A03, 9718.1, 9799.14 of Title 42 (Judiciary and Judicial Procedure).

§ 6319. Solicitation of minors to traffic drugs.

(a) Offense defined.--A person 18 years of age or older commits a felony of the second degree if he solicits a person who is less than 18 years of age to engage in a violation of section 13(a)(14) or (30) of the act of April 14, 1972 (P.L.233, No.64), known as The Controlled Substance, Drug, Device and Cosmetic Act, or delivers or conspires to deliver a controlled substance to such a person, intending, knowing or having reason to know that the person intends to engage in such a violation with the controlled substance.

(b) Drug-free school zone.--A person violating subsection (a) commits a felony of the first degree if he intends, knows or has reason to know that the person under 18 years of age intends to violate section 13(a)(14) or (30) of The Controlled Substance, Drug, Device and Cosmetic Act in a drug-free school zone.

(c) Definition.--As used in this section, the term "drug-free school zone" means the area within 1,000 feet of the real property on which is located a public, private or parochial school or a college or university. The term also includes a school bus or the area within 500 feet of a school bus stop.

 (Mar. 24, 1998, P.L.228, No.40, eff. 60 days)

1998 Amendment. Act 40 added section 6319.

§ 6320. Sexual exploitation of children.

(a) Offense defined.--A person commits the offense of sexual exploitation of children if he procures for another person a child under 18 years of age for the purpose of sexual exploitation.

(b) Penalty.--An offense under this section is a felony of the second degree.

(c) Definitions.--As used in this section, the following words and phrases shall have the meanings given to them in this subsection:

"Procure." To obtain or make available for sexual exploitation.

"Sexual exploitation." Actual or simulated sexual activity or nudity arranged for the purpose of sexual stimulation or gratification of any person.

(May 10, 2000, P.L.41, No.14, eff. 60 days)

2000 Amendment. Act 14 added section 6320.

Cross References. Section 6320 is referred to in sections 3104, 5743.1, 6318 of this title; sections 5329, 6303, 6702 of Title 23 (Domestic Relations); sections 5552, 5985.1, 5993, 62A03, 9718.1, 9799.14 of Title 42 (Judiciary and Judicial Procedure).

§ 6321. Transmission of sexually explicit images by minor.

(a) Summary offense.--Except as provided in section 6312 (relating to sexual abuse of children), a minor commits a summary offense when the minor:

(1) Knowingly transmits, distributes, publishes or disseminates an electronic communication containing a sexually explicit image of himself.

(2) Knowingly possesses or knowingly views a sexually explicit image of a minor who is 12 years of age or older.

(b) Misdemeanor of the third degree.--Except as provided in section 6312, a minor commits a misdemeanor of the third degree when the minor knowingly transmits, distributes, publishes or disseminates an electronic communication containing a sexually explicit image of another minor who is 12 years of age or older.

(c) Misdemeanor of the second degree.--Except as provided in section 6312, a minor commits a misdemeanor of the second degree when, with the intent to coerce, intimidate, torment, harass or otherwise cause emotional distress to another minor, the minor:

(1) makes a visual depiction of any minor in a state of nudity without the knowledge and consent of the depicted minor; or

(2) transmits, distributes, publishes or disseminates a visual depiction of any minor in a state of nudity without the knowledge and consent of the depicted minor.

(d) Application of section.--This section shall not apply to the following:

(1) Conduct that involves images that depict sexual intercourse, deviate sexual intercourse or penetration, however slight, of

317

the genitals or anus of a minor, masturbation, sadism, masochism or bestiality.

(2) Conduct that involves a sexually explicit image of a minor if the image was taken, made, used or intended to be used for or in furtherance of a commercial purpose.

(e) **Forfeiture.**--Any electronic communication device used in violation of this section shall be subject to forfeiture to the Commonwealth, and no property right shall exist in it.

(f) **Diversionary program.**--The magisterial district judge or any judicial authority with jurisdiction over the violation shall give first consideration to referring a person charged with a violation of subsection (a) to a diversionary program under 42 Pa.C.S. § 1520 (relating to adjudication alternative program) and the Pennsylvania Rules of Criminal Procedure. As part of the diversionary program, the magisterial district judge or any judicial authority with jurisdiction over the violation may order the person to participate in an educational program which includes the legal and nonlegal consequences of sharing sexually explicit images. If the person successfully completes the diversionary program, the person's records of the charge of violating subsection (a) shall be expunged as provided for under Pa.R.C.P. No.320 (relating to expungement upon successful completion of ARD program).

(g) **Definitions.**--As used in this section, the following words and phrases shall have the meanings given to them in this subsection unless the context clearly indicates otherwise:

"Disseminate." To cause or make an electronic or actual communication from one person, place or electronic communication device to two or more other persons, places or electronic communication devices.

"Distribute." To deliver or pass out.

"Electronic communication." As defined in section 5702 (relating to definitions).

"Knowingly possesses." The deliberate, purposeful, voluntary possession of a sexually explicit image of another minor who is 12 years of age or older. The term shall not include the accidental or inadvertent possession of such an image.

"Knowingly views." The deliberate, purposeful, voluntary viewing of a sexually explicit image of another minor who is 12 years of age or older. The term shall not include the

accidental or inadvertent viewing of such an image.

"Minor." An individual under 18 years of age.

"Nudity." The showing of the human male or female genitals, pubic area or buttocks with less than a fully opaque covering, the showing of the female breast with less than a fully opaque covering of any portion thereof below the top of the nipple or the depiction of covered male genitals in a discernibly turgid state.

"Publish." To issue for distribution.

"Sexually explicit image." A lewd or lascivious visual depiction of a minor's genitals, pubic area, breast or buttocks or nudity, if such nudity is depicted for the purpose of sexual stimulation or gratification of any person who might view such nudity.

"Transmit." To cause or make an electronic communication from one person, place or electronic communication device to only one other person, place or electronic communication device.

"Visual depiction." A representation by picture, including, but not limited to, a photograph, videotape, film or computer image.

(Oct. 25, 2012, P.L.1623, No.198, eff. 60 days)

2012 Amendment. Act 198 added section 6321.

Cross References. Section 6321 is referred to in sections 3131, 6312 of this title.

§ 6322. Access of minors to dextromethorphan.

(a) Offenses defined.--

(1) A person commits a summary offense if he knowingly sells or purchases with the intent to sell a finished drug product containing any quantity of dextromethorphan to a person who is less than 18 years of age.

(2) A person commits a summary offense if he falsely represents himself to be 18 years of age or older to another for the purpose of procuring a finished drug product containing any quantity of dextromethorphan.

(b) **Proof of age requirements.**--A person making a retail sale of a finished drug product containing any quantity of dextromethorphan shall obtain proof of age from the purchaser before completing the sale unless the purchaser's outward appearance is such that a person would reasonably presume the purchaser to be at least 25 years of age.

(c) Penalty.--A person who is convicted of violating subsection (a) shall be sentenced to pay a fine of not less than $250 nor more than $500 for the first violation and a fine of $500 for each subsequent violation.

(d) Exception.--This section does not apply to a medication containing dextromethorphan that is sold pursuant to a valid prescription.

(e) Preemption.--This section shall be construed to preempt any ordinance regulating the sale, distribution, receipt or possession of dextromethorphan enacted by any political subdivision, and dextromethorphan is not subject to further regulation by political subdivisions.

(f) Definitions.--As used in this section, the following words and phrases shall have the meanings given to them in this subsection unless the context clearly indicates otherwise:

"Finished drug product." A drug legally marketed under the Federal Food, Drug, and Cosmetic Act (52 Stat. 1040, 21 U.S.C. § 301 et seq.) that is in finished dosage form.

"Proof of age." A document issued by a governmental agency that contains a description or photograph of a person and gives the person's date of birth, including a passport, military identification card or driver's license.

(Oct. 24, 2018, P.L.727, No.116, eff. 60 days)

2018 Amendment. Act 116 added section 6322.

CHAPTER 65
NUISANCES

Sec.
6501. Scattering rubbish.
6502. Refrigerators and iceboxes.
6503. Posting advertisements on property of another.
6504. Public nuisances.
6505. Discarding television sets and tubes.

Enactment. Chapter 65 was added December 6, 1972, P.L.1482, No.334, effective in six months.

§ 6501. Scattering rubbish.

(a) Offense defined.--A person is guilty of an offense if he:

(1) causes any waste paper, sweepings, ashes, household waste, glass, metal, refuse or rubbish, or any dangerous or detrimental substance to be deposited into or upon any road, street, highway, alley or railroad right-of-way, or upon the land of another or into the waters of this Commonwealth;

(2) interferes with, scatters, or disturbs the contents of any receptacle containing ashes, garbage, household waste, or rubbish; or

(3) is the owner or operator, or an agent of either, of a trash, garbage or debris collection vehicle, including private automobiles and small trucks, or any other type of vehicles used to collect or transport trash, garbage or debris, who knowingly causes to be deposited or deposits the vehicle's load or any part thereof upon any road, street, highway, alley or railroad right-of-way, or upon the land of another or into the waters of this Commonwealth.

(b) Penalty.--

(1) A person who violates subsection (a)(1) or (2) is guilty of a summary offense for the first offense and upon conviction thereof shall be sentenced to pay a fine of not less than $50 nor more than $300 and be required to pick up litter or illegally dumped trash for not less than five nor more than 30 hours to be completed within six months, or to imprisonment for not more than 90 days, or both.

(2) A person who violates subsection (a)(1) or (2) is guilty of a misdemeanor of the third degree for the second and subsequent offense and upon conviction thereof shall be sentenced to pay a fine of not less than $300 nor more than $1,000. The person also may be sentenced to imprisonment or be required to pick up litter or illegally dumped trash for not less than 30 nor more than 100 hours to be completed within one year.

(3) A person who violates subsection (a)(3) is guilty of a misdemeanor of the second degree for the first offense and upon conviction thereof shall be sentenced to pay a fine of not less than $500 nor more than $5,000. The person also may be sentenced to imprisonment or to performing a community service for a period not to exceed two years.

(4) A person who violates subsection (a)(3) is guilty of a misdemeanor of the first degree for the second or subsequent offense and upon conviction thereof shall be sentenced to pay a fine of not less than $1,000 nor more than $10,000. The person also may be sentenced to

imprisonment or to performing a community service for a period not to exceed five years.

(5) Any vehicle, equipment or conveyance, including any private automobile and small truck, used for the transportation or disposal of trash, garbage or debris in the commission of a second or subsequent offense under subsection (a)(3) may be deemed contraband and forfeited in accordance with 42 Pa.C.S. §§ 5803 (relating to asset forfeiture), 5805 (relating to forfeiture procedure), 5806 (relating to motion for return of property), 5807 (relating to restrictions on use), 5807.1 (relating to prohibition on adoptive seizures) and 5808 (relating to exceptions).

(c) **Arrest powers.**--A police officer shall have the same right of arrest without a warrant as in a felony whenever the officer has probable cause to believe the defendant has violated subsection (a)(3), although the offense did not take place in the officer's presence. A police officer may not make a warrantless arrest pursuant to this section without first observing recent evidence of a subsection (a)(3) offense or other corroborative evidence.

(d) **Forfeiture.**--(Deleted by amendment).

(e) **Responsibility for costs.**--The operator, owner or agent of any vehicle, equipment or conveyance, including private automobiles and small trucks, forfeited under this section shall be responsible for any costs incurred in properly disposing of waste in the vehicle, equipment or conveyance.

(f) **Exception.**--Subsection (a)(3) does not apply to the lawful depositing of waste at any site regulated by the Department of Environmental Resources.

(g) **Other available rights and remedies.**--The proceedings specified in this section shall not, in any way, limit the right of the Commonwealth to exercise any rights or remedies otherwise provided by law.

(Mar. 22, 1974, P.L.207, No.42; Apr. 28, 1978, P.L.202, No.53, eff. 60 days; Mar. 25, 1988, P.L.262, No.31, eff. imd.; May 31, 1990, P.L.219, No.47, eff. 60 days; June 29, 2017, P.L.247, No.13, eff. July 1, 2017; June 28, 2018, P.L.429, No.62, eff. 6 mos.)

2018 Amendment. Act 62 amended subsec. (b)(1) and (2).

2017 Amendment. Act 13 amended subsec. (b)(5) and deleted subsec. (d).

1990 Amendment. Section 3 of Act 47 provided that the amendment shall apply to all offenses committed on or after the effective date of Act 47.

References in Text. The Department of Environmental Resources, referred to in subsec. (f), was abolished by Act 18 of 1995. Its functions were transferred to the Department of Conservation and Natural Resources and the Department of Environmental Protection.

Cross References. Section 6501 is referred to in sections 3573, 5803 of Title 42 (Judiciary and Judicial Procedure); sections 3329, 3742.1 of Title 75 (Vehicles).

§ 6502. Refrigerators and iceboxes.

(a) **Offense defined.**--A person is guilty of a summary offense if he discards or abandons in any place accessible to children any refrigerator or icebox having a capacity of 1.5 cubic feet or more with an attached lid or door, or being the owner, lessee or manager of any place accessible to children knowingly permits an abandoned or discarded refrigerator, icebox or chest to remain there with an attached lid or door.

(b) **Effect of violation.**--A violation of this section shall not in itself render a person guilty of manslaughter, assault or other crime against a person who may suffer death or injury from entrapment in an icebox or refrigerator.

§ 6503. Posting advertisements on property of another.

(a) **Offense defined.**--A person is guilty of a summary offense if he pastes, paints, brands or stamps or in any manner whatsoever places upon or attaches to any building, fence, bridge, gate, outbuilding or other object, upon the grounds of any charitable, educational or penal institution of the Commonwealth, or upon any property belonging to the Commonwealth government, any political subdivision, or municipal or local authority, any written, printed, painted or other advertisement, bill, notice, sign or poster, or pastes, paints, brands, stamps or in any manner whatsoever places upon, or attaches to any building, fence, bridge, gate, outbuilding or property of another, whether within or without the limits of a highway, any written, printed, painted or other advertisement, bill, notice, sign, card or poster, without first having obtained the written consent of the owner, or tenant lawfully in possession or occupancy thereof.

(b) **Exception.**--Subsection (a) of this section shall not prevent the posting or placing of any notice required by law or order of court, nor to prevent the posting or placing of any notice particularly concerning or pertaining to premises upon which the same is so posted or placed.

§ 6504. Public nuisances.

Whoever erects, sets up, establishes, maintains, keeps or continues, or causes to be erected, set up, established, maintained, kept or continued, any public or common nuisance is guilty of a misdemeanor of the second degree. Where the nuisance is in existence at the time of the conviction and sentence, the court, in its discretion, may direct either the defendant or the sheriff of the county at the expense of the defendant to abate the same.

§ 6505. Discarding television sets and tubes.

(a) Offense defined.--A person is guilty of a summary offense if he discards or abandons in any place accessible to the public any television picture tube or television set containing any picture tube which has not been neutralized to eliminate the danger of implosion, or if the owner, lessee, manager or person in possession of any place accessible to the public knowingly permits an abandoned or discarded television picture tube or a set containing such a tube to remain in such place without the tube having been neutralized to eliminate the danger of implosion.

(b) Other responsibility.--A violation of this section shall not in itself render a person guilty of manslaughter, assault or other crime against a person who may suffer death or injury from implosion of a television picture tube.

(June 4, 1976, P.L.153, No.74)

1976 Amendment. Act 74 added section 6505.

CHAPTER 67 PROPRIETARY AND OFFICIAL RIGHTS

Sec.
6701. Wearing of uniforms and insignia and misrepresentation of military service or honors.
6702. Sale of veterans' flowers.
6703. Dealing in military decorations.
6704. Fraud on association having grand lodge.
6705. Use of containers bearing owner's name (Repealed).
6706. Use or possession of stamped containers (Repealed).
6707. False registration of domestic animals.
6708. Retention of library property after notice to return.
6709. Use of union labels.
6710. Unauthorized use of registered insignia.
6711. Retention of military property after notice to return.
6712. Use of carts, cases, trays, baskets, boxes and other containers.

Enactment. Chapter 67 was added December 6, 1972, P.L.1482, No.334, effective in six months.

§ 6701. Wearing of uniforms and insignia and misrepresentation of military service or honors.

(a) Wearing of uniforms and insignia.-- A person is guilty of a summary offense if, without authority, he:

(1) wears or displays the uniform, decoration, insignia or other distinctive emblem of any branch of the armed forces of the United States or of any of the several states, or of any association, for the purpose of obtaining aid or profit, or while soliciting contributions or subscriptions; or

(2) wears an honorable discharge button issued or authorized by the United States.

(b) Misrepresentation of military service or honors.--A person commits a misdemeanor of the third degree if, with intent to obtain money, property or other benefit, the person fraudulently holds himself out to be any of the following:

(1) A member or veteran of any branch of the armed forces of the United States or of any of the several states.

(2) The recipient of any decoration or medal authorized by the Congress of the United States for the armed forces of the United States or any of the service medals or any decoration awarded to members of the armed forces of the United States or of any of the several states.

(c) Deposit of fines.--Notwithstanding any other provision of this title or other law to the contrary, the full amount of each fine collected under this section shall be deposited into the Veterans' Trust Fund under 51 Pa.C.S. § 1721 (relating to Veterans' Trust Fund).

(June 27, 2017, P.L.214, No.9, eff. 60 days; July 2, 2019, P.L.393, No.62, eff. 60 days)

2019 Amendment. Act 62 added subsec. (c).

Cross References. Section 6701 is referred to in section 1721 of Title 51 (Military Affairs).

§ 6702. Sale of veterans' flowers.

A person is guilty of a summary offense if, without authority, he sells, or offers for sale, the labeled artificial flowers, or any imitation thereof, of any bona fide war veterans' organization, or affiliate thereof.

§ 6703. Dealing in military decorations.

A person is guilty of a misdemeanor of the third degree if, without authority, he purchases, sells, or offers for sale, or accepts as a pledge or pawn, any medal, insignia or decoration granted by the United States for service in the armed forces.

§ 6704. Fraud on association having grand lodge.

A person is guilty of a summary offense if, without the authority of the grand lodge described in this section, he:

(1) fraudulently uses, in any manner, the name or title of any secret fraternal association, which has had a grand lodge having jurisdiction in this Commonwealth for at least ten years;

(2) imitates such name or title with intent to deceive;

(3) wears or uses any insignia of such association with intent to deceive;

(4) publishes or distributes, in any manner, any written or printed matter soliciting applications for membership in such secret fraternal association, or any alleged association claiming to be known by such title, or by a title in imitation or resemblance of such title; or

(5) sells or gives or offers to sell or give any information as to how any alleged degree, secret work or secret of such fraternal association or of any alleged association, claiming to be known by such title, or by a title in imitation or resemblance of such title may be obtained.

§ 6705. Use of containers bearing owner's name (Repealed).

1987 Repeal. Section 6705 was repealed July 9, 1987 (P.L.215, No.37), effective in 90 days.

§ 6706. Use or possession of stamped containers (Repealed).

1987 Repeal. Section 6706 was repealed July 9, 1987 (P.L.215, No.37), effective in 90 days.

§ 6707. False registration of domestic animals.

A person is guilty of a misdemeanor of the third degree if he, by any false pretense, obtains from any club, association, society or company for improving the breed of domestic animals the registration or transfer of registration, of any animal in its herd, or other register, or knowingly gives a false pedigree of any animal.

§ 6708. Retention of library property after notice to return.

(a) Offense defined.--A person is guilty of a summary offense if he retains any book, pamphlet, magazine, newspaper, manuscript, map or other property belonging in, or to, or on deposit with, any library open to the public or any part thereof, for a period exceeding 30 days after such library has given written notice to return the same.

(b) Disposition of fine.--Any fine imposed under this section shall be paid over by the magistrate imposing such fine to the library instituting the prosecution, and costs of prosecution.

(c) Form of notice.--Such notice may be given by personal service upon the borrower, or by the mailing of a registered or certified letter to the address of the borrower on file with said library. The notice shall recite this section, and shall contain a demand that the property be returned.

Cross References. Section 6708 is referred to in section 9376 of Title 24 (Education).

§ 6709. Use of union labels.

A person commits a misdemeanor of the third degree if, without the authority of the labor union or unions interested, such person:

(1) uses any union label registered under Chapter 13 of Title 54 (relating to insignia);

(2) uses any such union label on goods which are not the product of the members of the union or unions owning such label; or

(3) sells or offers for sale any goods knowing that such goods bear a union label whose use on such goods is not authorized by the union or unions owning such label.

(Dec. 16, 1982, P.L.1309, No.295, eff. 90 days)

1982 Amendment. Act 295 added section 6709.

§ 6710. Unauthorized use of registered insignia.

A person commits a summary offense if, without authority, such person knowingly wears, exhibits, displays or uses, for any purpose, any insignia registered under Chapter 13 of Title 54 (relating to insignia).

(Dec. 16, 1982, P.L.1309, No.295, eff. 90 days)

1982 Amendment. Act 295 added section 6710.

§ 6711. Retention of military property after notice to return.

(a) Offense defined.--A person who fails to return any military property, equipment, identification papers or other items belonging to the armed forces of the United States, any reserve component, element or component thereof, or the Pennsylvania military forces, after having been given proper notice to return the property or equipment, commits a summary offense.

(b) Form of notice.--Notice to return military property, equipment, identification papers or other items to the armed forces of the United States, any reserve component, element or component thereof, or the Pennsylvania military forces, may be given by personal notice upon the person in possession of the property or by mailing a registered or certified letter to the person's last known address. The notice shall recite this section and contain a demand that the property be returned or, if it has been lost or destroyed, that restitution be paid as provided in subsection (c).

(c) Restitution to avoid prosecution.--A person may avoid prosecution under this section by returning the property or making restitution to the responsible official of the armed forces of the United States or the Pennsylvania military forces, as applicable, prior to the date of the hearing before the magisterial district judge, municipal court judge or other official authorized to conduct the hearing.

(Dec. 11, 1986, P.L.1517, No.164, eff. 60 days; Nov. 30, 2004, P.L.1618, No.207, eff. 60 days)

2004 Amendment. Act 207 amended subsec. (c). See section 29 of Act 207 in the appendix to this title for special provisions relating to construction of law.

1986 Amendment. Act 164 added section 6711.

§ 6712. Use of carts, cases, trays, baskets, boxes and other containers.

(a) General rule.--A person owning shopping carts, laundry carts or containers may adopt and use a name or mark on the carts or containers and may register the same pursuant to 54 Pa.C.S. Ch. 15 (relating to reusable marked articles and receptacles).

(b) Prohibited uses of containers.--A person may not do any of the following:

(1) Use for any purpose, when not on the premises of the owner or an adjacent parking area, a container of another which is identified with or by any name or mark unless the use is authorized by the owner.

(2) Sell, or offer for sale, a container of another which is identified with or by a name or mark unless the sale is authorized by the owner.

(3) Deface, obliterate, destroy, cover up or otherwise remove or conceal a name or mark on a container of another without the written consent of the owner.

(c) Presumption of possession.--Any person who is in possession of any shopping cart, laundry cart or container which has a name or mark and is not on the premises of the owner or an adjacent parking area shall be presumed to be in possession of stolen property.

(d) Transportation of containers; bill of lading.--It shall be unlawful for any common carrier or private carrier for hire, except those engaged in the transporting of dairy products, eggs and poultry to and from farms where they are produced, to receive or transport any container marked with a name or mark unless the carrier has in his possession a bill of lading or invoice therefor.

(e) Unlawful removal of containers.--It is a violation of this section for any person to remove a container from the premises, parking area or any other area of any processor, distributor or retail establishment, or from any delivery vehicle, unless legally authorized to do so, if:

(1) The container is marked on at least one side with a name or mark.

(2) A notice to the public, warning that use by any person other than the owner is

punishable by law, is visibly displayed on the container.

(f) Illegal use of shopping carts and laundry carts.--It is a violation of this section:

(1) To remove any shopping cart or laundry cart from the premises or parking area of a retail establishment with intent to temporarily or permanently deprive the owner of the cart, or the retailer, of possession of the cart.

(2) To remove a shopping cart or laundry cart, without written authorization from the owner of the cart, from the premises or parking area of any retail establishment.

(3) To possess, without the written permission of the owner or retailer in lawful possession thereof, any shopping cart or laundry cart off the premises or parking lot of the retailer whose name or mark appears thereon.

(4) To remove, obliterate or alter any serial number, name or mark affixed to a shopping cart or laundry cart.

(g) **Deposits.**--The requiring, taking or accepting of any deposit, upon delivery of a container, shopping cart or laundry cart, shall not be deemed a sale thereof, optional or otherwise.

(h) **Penalty.**--A person who violates this section commits a summary offense and shall, upon conviction, be sentenced to pay a fine not exceeding $300 or to imprisonment for not more than 90 days. Each violation shall constitute a separate offense.

(i) **Scope of section.**--This section shall not apply to the owner of a shopping cart, laundry cart or container, or to a customer or any other person who has written consent from the owner of a shopping cart, laundry cart or container, or from a retailer, in lawful possession thereof, to remove it from the premises or the parking area of the retail establishment. For the purposes of this section, the term "written consent" includes tokens and other indicia of consent which may be established by the owner of the carts or the retailer.

(j) **Definitions.**--As used in this section, the following words and phrases shall have the meanings given to them in this subsection:

"Bakery basket." A wire or plastic container which holds bread or other baked goods and is used by a distributor or retailer, or his agent, as a means to transport, store or carry bakery products.

"Bakery tray." A wire or plastic container which holds bread or other baked goods and is used by a distributor or retailer, or his agent, as a means to transport, store or carry bakery products.

"Container." A bakery basket, bakery tray, dairy case, egg basket, poultry box or any other container used to transport, store or carry any product.

"Dairy case." A wire or plastic container which holds 16 quarts or more of beverage and is used by distributors or retailers, or their agents, as a means to transport, store or carry dairy products.

"Egg basket." Any permanent type of container which contains four dozen or more shell eggs and is used by distributors or retailers, or their agents, as a means to transport, store or carry eggs.

"Laundry cart." A basket which is mounted on wheels and used in a coin-operated laundry or drycleaning establishment by a customer or an attendant for the purpose of transporting laundry and laundry supplies.

"Name" or "mark." Any permanently affixed or permanently stamped name or mark which is used for the purpose of identifying the owner of shopping carts, laundry carts, dairy cases, egg baskets, poultry boxes, bakery trays or bakery boxes.

"Parking area." A lot or other property provided by a retail establishment for the use of customers to park automobiles or other vehicles while doing business in that establishment.

"Poultry box." Any permanent type of container which is used by processors, distributors, retailers or food service establishments, or their agents, as a means to transport, store or carry poultry.

"Shopping cart." A basket which is mounted on wheels, or a similar device, generally used in a retail establishment by a customer for the purpose of transporting goods of any kind.

(July 9, 1987, P.L.215, No.37, eff. 90 days)

1987 Amendment. Act 37 added section 6712.

CHAPTER 69 PUBLIC UTILITIES

Enactment. Chapter 69 was added December 6, 1972, P.L.1482, No.334, effective in six months.

§ 6901. Extension of water line.

A person is guilty of a misdemeanor of the third degree if he, without first securing a permit from the water company or municipality or municipal authority supplying such person with water, shall convey, or permit or procure another to convey, any part of such water by means of pipe, hose or other conduit to any building, residence or structure beyond the limits of the tract occupied by such person.

§ 6902. Willful obstruction of emergency telephone calls.

(a) Offense defined.--A person is guilty of a summary offense if he willfully refuses to relinquish immediately a party line when informed that the line is needed for an emergency call to a fire department or police department or for medical aid or ambulance service, or if he secures the use of a party line by falsely stating that the line is needed for an emergency call.

(b) Notice to public.--Every telephone directory distributed to the members of the general public in this Commonwealth, or in any portion thereof, which lists the calling numbers of telephones of any telephone exchange located in this Commonwealth, shall contain a notice which explains the offense provided for in this section. The notice shall be printed in type which is not smaller than the smallest other type on the same page, and to be preceded by the word "warning" printed in type at least as large as the largest type on the same page. The provisions of this subsection shall not apply to those directories distributed solely for business advertising purposes commonly known as classified directories. Any person, providing telephone service which distributes, or causes to be distributed, in this Commonwealth copies of a telephone directory violating the provisions of this subsection, shall be guilty of a summary offense.

(c) Definitions.--As used in this section the following words and phrases shall have the meanings given to them in this subsection:

"Emergency." A situation in which property or human life are in jeopardy and the prompt summoning of aid is essential.

"Party line." A subscriber's line telephone circuit, consisting of two or more main telephone stations connected therewith each station with a distinctive ring or telephone number.

§ 6903. Railroad employee abandoning train.

A person is guilty of a summary offense if he, being a locomotive engineer or other railroad employee engaged in any strike, or with a view to incite others to such strike or in furtherance of any combination or preconcerted arrangement with any other person to bring about a strike, abandons the locomotive engine in his charge, when attached either to a passenger or freight train, at any place other than the scheduled or otherwise appointed destination of such train, or refuses or neglects to continue to discharge his duty, or to proceed with said train to the place of destination.

§ 6904. Interfering with railroad employee.

A person is guilty of a summary offense if he, in aid or furtherance of the objects of any strike upon any railroad, interferes with, molests or obstructs any locomotive engineer or other railroad employee engaged in the discharge and performance of his duty as such.

§ 6905. Nails and other hard substances attached to utility poles.

(a) Offense defined.--A person is guilty of a summary offense if he drives a nail or tack or attaches any metal or hard substance to or into any pole of any public utility pole line.

(b) Exceptions.--Subsection (a) of this section does not apply to:

(1) the public utility or its licensee using the poles from affixing its metal or other

markers or from otherwise using the poles in its public service; or

(2) the erecting traffic signs and other signs similar thereto by a municipality when authorized by statute or by the owner of such poles.

§ 6906. Erection of crossing signboards.

(a) Offense defined.--A person is guilty of a summary offense if he erects or maintains any device or sign in the form of railway-crossing signboards on or near any of the public highways of this Commonwealth, or if he permits such a device or sign to remain on or near the public highways of this Commonwealth, unless such sign or device is erected under a permit from the Department of Transportation, which shall approve the location, construction, and design of such sign or device.

(b) Exception.--The provisions of subsection (a) of this section shall not apply to crossing signboards erected or maintained by any railroad or railway company.

§ 6907. Obstructing public crossings.

It shall be a summary offense for any railroad to obstruct or block up the passage of any crossings of a highway, or obstruct such crossings, with its rolling stock. If any engineer, or any member of the train crew, or other agent of any such railroad, shall obstruct or block up such crossings, he shall be guilty of a summary offense.

§ 6908. Obstructing private crossings.

It shall be a summary offense for any railroad to continue to obstruct or block up the passage of any private crossing, wherever any private road or crossing-place may be necessary to enable the occupant or occupants of land or farms to pass over the railroad with livestock, wagons and implements of husbandry, after the railroad shall have received at least 15 minutes verbal notice to remove its rolling stock, or other obstructions from any such private road or crossing-place.

§ 6909. Lights obstructing view of signals.

It shall be a summary offense to locate, maintain, or allow to remain, any light in such a place or manner that such light interferes with the view of any railroad signal to an extent which causes danger in the operation of trains.

§ 6910. Unauthorized sale or transfer of tickets.

(a) Sale of tickets.--A person, not possessed of authority, is guilty of a misdemeanor of the third degree if he sells, barters, or transfers, for any consideration whatever, the whole or any part of any ticket or tickets, passes, or other evidences of the title of the holder to travel on any public conveyance, whether the same be situated, operated, or owned within or without the limits of this Commonwealth.

(b) Disposition by passenger.--Every person, being a passenger for hire, to whom has been issued a nontransferable ticket valid in full or part payment of fare for passage upon any public conveyance operated upon the same or any other line or route, or any person into whose possession any such ticket may come, who shall sell, barter, give away, or otherwise transfer the same, and every person who shall offer for passage any such ticket which was not issued to any person so offering it, is guilty of a summary offense.

CHAPTER 71
SPORTS AND AMUSEMENTS

Enactment. Chapter 71 was added December 6, 1972, P.L.1482, No.334, effective in six months.

§ 7101. Fraudulent entry of horses in race.

A person is guilty of a summary offense if he enters or causes to be entered for competition, or competes for any purse, prize, premium, stake or sweepstake, offered or given by any agricultural or other society, association, or person, any horse, mare or gelding, colt or filly, under an assumed name, or out of its proper class, when such prize, purse, premium, stake or sweepstake is to be decided by a contest, in running, trotting or pacing races.

§ 7102. Administering drugs to race horses.

A person is guilty of a misdemeanor of the first degree if he administers drugs or stimulants with the intent to affect the speed of horses in races where there is a monetary award offered.

Cross References. Section 7102 is referred to in sections 9318, 9323 of Title 3 (Agriculture).

§ 7103. Horse racing.

(a) Offense defined.--A person is guilty of a misdemeanor of the third degree if he races, runs, paces or trots any horse, mare or gelding for money, goods or other valuable things, or contributes or collects any money, goods or valuable things to make up a purse therefor, or prints or causes to be printed, sets up or causes to be set up any advertisement mentioning the time and place for the running, pacing or trotting of any horses, mares or geldings, or knowingly suffers any such advertisement to be attached to his property or to remain on his property.

(b) Wagers void.--All wagers and bets laid on any such race shall be null and void, and money, goods and valuable things lost on any such race, or the value thereof, may be recovered from the winner by action of assumpsit.

(c) Exceptions.--Nothing contained in this section shall be construed as applying to racing at exhibitions of agricultural societies and associations, nor to trials of speed in any incorporated driving park, nor to races given by regularly incorporated trotting or thoroughbred racing associations, nor to races conducted pursuant to other applicable provisions of law.

§ 7104. Fortune telling.

(a) Offense defined.--A person is guilty of a misdemeanor of the third degree if he pretends for gain or lucre, to tell fortunes or predict future events, by cards, tokens, the inspection of the head or hands of any person, or by the age of anyone, or by consulting the movements of the heavenly bodies, or in any other manner, or for gain or lucre, pretends to effect any purpose by spells, charms, necromancy, or incantation, or advises the taking or administering of what are commonly called love powders or potions, or prepares the same to be taken or administered, or publishes by card, circular, sign, newspaper or other means that he can predict future events, or for gain or lucre, pretends to enable anyone to get or to recover stolen property, or to tell where lost property is, or to stop bad luck, or to give good luck, or to put bad luck on a person or animal, or to stop or injure the business or health of a person or shorten his life, or to give success in business, enterprise, speculation, and games of chance, or to win the affection of a person, or to make one person marry another, or to induce a person to make or alter a will, or to tell where money or other property is hidden, or to tell where to dig for treasure, or to make a person to dispose of property in favor of another.

(b) Advertising as evidence.--Any publication contrary to this section may be given in evidence to sustain the indictment.

(c) Competency of witnesses.--Any person whose fortune may have been told shall be a competent witness against the person charged with violating this section.

§ 7105. Pool and billiard rooms.

A person is guilty of a summary offense if he, being a licensed keeper, proprietor, owner or superintendent of any public poolroom or billiard room except as otherwise provided in this section for cities of the first class, permits such place to remain open on Sunday or between the hours of one o'clock antemeridian and six o'clock antemeridian of any secular day, or knowingly allows or permits any person under the age of 18 years to be present in any public poolroom or billiard room, or if he, being a licensed keeper, proprietor, owner or superintendent of any public poolroom or billiard room having at least six tables, in a city of the first class, permits such place to remain open on Sunday, except between the hours of one o'clock postmeridian and ten o'clock postmeridian, or knowingly allows or permits any person under the age of 16 years to be present in any such public poolroom or billiard room.

§ 7106. Theater operators to require proof of age.

Every person who operates a motion picture theater, when showing a motion picture rated as being suitable for viewing for adults only, shall not sell to a minor under 16 years of age an admission ticket or pass, or shall not admit such minor for a monetary consideration to the theater wherein the motion picture is exhibited, unless such minor is accompanied by his parent. Whoever violates the provisions of this section is guilty of a summary offense.

§ 7107. Unlawful actions by athlete agents.

(a) Offense defined.--An athlete agent shall not do any of the following:

(1) Enter into an oral or written agent contract or professional sport services contract with a student athlete before the student athlete's eligibility for collegiate athletics expires.

(2) Give, offer or promise anything of value to a student athlete, to his parent or guardian or to any member of the student athlete's immediate family before the student athlete's eligibility for collegiate athletics expires.

(3) Enter into an oral or written agreement whereby the athlete agent gives, offers or promises anything of value to an employee of an institution of higher education in return for the referral of a student athlete by that employee.

(b) Penalty.--An athlete agent who violates subsection (a) commits a misdemeanor of the first degree and shall, upon conviction, be sentenced to pay a fine of not more than $10,000 or an amount equal to three times the amount given, offered or promised as an inducement as described in subsection (a)(2) or three times the value of the agreement entered into as described in subsection (a)(3), whichever is greater, or imprisonment for not more than one year, or both.

(c) Definitions.--As used in this section, the following words and phrases shall have the meanings given to them in this subsection:

"Agent contract." Any contract or agreement pursuant to which a person authorizes or empowers an athlete agent to negotiate or solicit on behalf of the person with one or more professional sport teams for the employment of the person by a professional sport team or to negotiate or solicit on behalf of the person for the employment of the person as a professional athlete.

"Athlete agent." A person who, directly or indirectly, recruits or solicits a person to enter into an agent contract or professional sport services contract, or who procures, offers, promises or attempts to obtain employment for a person with a professional sport team or as a professional athlete.

"Institution of higher education." A public or private college or university, including a community college.

"Person." An individual, sole proprietorship, partnership, association, corporation or other legal entity.

"Professional sport services contract." A contract or agreement pursuant to which a person is employed or agrees to render services as a player on a professional sport team or as a professional athlete.

"Student athlete." A student enrolled in an institution of higher education who, while a student at the institution in which enrolled, is eligible to participate in any intercollegiate sporting event or contest in a particular sport and may have athletic eligibility remaining in that particular sport.

"Value." Anything of value shall be any payment, loan, gift, good, service, expense of any kind or the promise of any of these for the future, regardless of the monetary worth of any of these items.

(Dec. 21, 1988, P.L.1896, No.187, eff. 60 days)

1988 Amendment. Act 187 added section 7107.

Cross References. Section 7107 is referred to in sections 3304, 3307, 3314, 3315 of Title 5 (Athletics and Sports).

CHAPTER 73 TRADE AND COMMERCE

Subchapter
A. Definition of Offenses Generally
B. Sunday Trading

Enactment. Chapter 73 was added December 6, 1972, P.L.1482, No.334, effective in six months.

SUBCHAPTER A
DEFINITION OF OFFENSES GENERALLY

§ 7301. Distribution of samples of medicine, dyes, etc.

(a) Offense defined.--A person is guilty of a summary offense if he distributes or deposits any package, parcel, or sample of any medicine, dye, ink, or polishing compounds, in any form of preparation, upon the ground, sidewalks, porches, yards, or into or under doors or windows so that children may get possession of or secure the same.

(b) Exception.--Nothing contained in this section shall prohibit such distribution to adult persons only.

§ 7302. Sale and labeling of solidified alcohol.

(a) Sale.--A person commits a misdemeanor of the second degree if he manufactures, sells, or offers or exposes for sale, or has in his possession with intent to distribute or sell, for use as a heating fuel any mixture or preparation of solidified alcohol which contains more than 4% methyl or wood alcohol.

(b) Labeling.--A person commits a misdemeanor of the first degree if he manufactures, sells, or offers or exposes for sale, or has in his possession with intent to distribute or sell, any mixture or preparation of solidified alcohol which does not have the methyl alcohol content or wood alcohol content permanently embossed upon each individual container along with the manufacturer's name. In addition, each individual container shall have a label warning against the internal use of solidified alcohol including that it may cause blindness or death.

(Apr. 14, 1983, P.L.1, No.1, eff. 180 days)

§ 7303. Sale or illegal use of certain solvents and noxious substances.

(a) Offense defined.--No person shall, for the purpose of causing a condition of intoxication, inebriation, excitement, stupefaction, or the dulling of his brain or nervous system, intentionally smell or inhale the fumes from any noxious substance or substance containing a solvent having the property of releasing toxic vapors or fumes.

(b) Exception.--Subsection (a) of this section shall not apply to the inhalation of any anesthesia for medical or dental purposes.

(c) Possession prohibited.--No person shall, for the purpose of violating subsection (a) of this section, use, or possess for the purpose of so using, any noxious substance or substance containing a solvent having the property of releasing toxic vapors or fumes.

(d) Sale prohibited.--No person shall sell at retail, or offer to sell, to any other person any tube or other container of any noxious substance or substance containing a solvent having the property of releasing toxic vapors or fumes, if he has reasonable cause to suspect that the product sold, or offered for sale, will be used for the purpose set forth in subsection (a) of this section.

(e) Grading.--Any person who violates any provision of this section shall be guilty of a misdemeanor of the third degree.

(f) Definition.--As used in this section, the phrase "any noxious substance or substance containing a solvent having the property of releasing toxic vapors or fumes" shall mean any substance containing one or more of the following chemical compounds: acetone, acetate, benzene, butyl alcohol, cyclohexyl nitrite, ethyl alcohol, ethylene dichloride, gaseous or liquid fluorocarbons, isopropyl alcohol, methyl alcohol, methyl ethyl ketone, nitrous oxide, pentachlorophenol, petroleum ether, or toluene.

(Dec. 19, 1997, P.L.615, No.62, eff. imd.; Dec. 20, 2000, P.L.831, No.116, eff. 60 days)

Cross References. Section 7303 is referred to in section 5502 of Title 30 (Fish); section 3802 of Title 75 (Vehicles).

§ 7304. Illegal sale or use of certain fire extinguishers.

(a) Use prohibited.--It shall be unlawful for any building used for private, public or parochial school purposes, or any bus being used for the transportation of school children, to be equipped with or to have available for use a fire extinguisher containing carbon tetrachloride, and any person having immediate control over such buildings or buses, who permits them to be so equipped or to have such fire extinguishers available for use therein, is guilty of a summary offense.

(b) Sale prohibited.--Whoever sells any portable fire extinguisher containing carbon tetrachloride, chlorobromomethane, or methyl bromide, knowing it is intended for use in a single or multiple family dwelling or a hospital, rest-home, school, theater or other building generally open to the public, is guilty of a summary offense.

§ 7305. Sale of gasoline in glass container.

A person is guilty of a summary offense if he sells gasoline in a glass container.

§ 7306. Incendiary devices.

(a) Offense defined.--A person is guilty of a misdemeanor of the first degree if he owns, manufactures, sells, transfers, uses or possesses any incendiary device or similar device or parts thereof, including but not limited to a "molotov cocktail."

(b) Exception.--The provisions of subsection (a) of this section shall not apply to authorized personnel of the United States, the Commonwealth or any political subdivision, who use incendiary devices as part of their duties.

(c) Definition.--As used in this section the phrase "incendiary device" means any inflammable liquid enclosed in a readily breakable container that can be equipped with an igniter of any type.

§ 7307. Out-of-state convict made goods.

A person is guilty of a misdemeanor of the second degree if he sells or exchanges on the open market any goods, wares or merchandise prepared, wholly or in part, or manufactured by convicts or prisoners of other states, except convicts or prisoners on parole or probation.

§ 7308. Unlawful advertising of insurance business.

(a) Offense defined.--A person is guilty of a misdemeanor of the second degree if he publishes or prints in any newspaper, magazine, periodical, circular, letter, pamphlet, or in any other manner, or publishes by radio or television broadcasting, any advertisement or other notice, either directly or indirectly, setting forth the advantages of, or soliciting business for, any insurance company, association, society, exchange or person which has not been authorized to do business in this Commonwealth, or accepts for publication or printing in any newspaper, magazine or other periodical, or for radio or television broadcasting, any advertisement or other notice, either directly or indirectly, setting forth the advantages of or soliciting business for any insurance company, association, exchange or person, unless such newspaper, magazine or other periodical, or the radio or television broadcasting company has in its possession a true and attested or photostatic copy of a certificate of authority from the Insurance Department to the effect that the insurance company, association, society, exchange or person named therein is authorized to do business in this Commonwealth.

(b) Issue of certificate.--Such certificates shall be issued by the Insurance Department to any person applying therefor.

§ 7309. Unlawful coercion in contracting insurance.

(a) Offense defined.--A person is guilty of a misdemeanor of the first degree if he, being engaged in the business of financing the purchase of real or personal property or of lending money on the security of real or personal property, requires, as a condition precedent to financing the purchase of such property, or to lending money upon the security of a mortgage thereon, or as a condition prerequisite for the renewal or extension of any such loan or mortgage, or for the performance of any other act in connection therewith, that the person for whom such purchase is to be financed, or to whom the money is to be loaned, or for whom such extension, renewal or other act is to be granted or performed, shall negotiate through a particular insurance company, agent or broker, any policy of insurance or renewal thereof covering such property, or, with the exception of a group creditor policy, any policy covering the life or health of such person.

(b) Exception.--This section shall prevent any person from approving or disapproving the insurance company selected to underwrite such insurance.

(c) Penalty.--A person other than individuals or the responsible officers, agents or employees of a corporation, partnership or association, who commits an offense under this section shall be sentenced to pay a fine not exceeding $1,000.

§ 7310. Furnishing free insurance as inducement for purchases.

(a) Offense defined.--A person is guilty of a misdemeanor of the third degree if he, being a manufacturer, broker, wholesaler, retailer or agent of any manufacturer, broker, wholesaler or retailer, offers any policy of insurance free of cost as an inducement to any person to purchase any real or personal property.

(b) Exception.--The provisions of this section shall not affect the right of any person who, in connection with a sale of property or services or any credit transaction, shall have, retain or acquire an insurable interest in any subject of insurance, related to such sale or transaction, including person or property or risk pertaining thereto, to procure and maintain insurance embracing any or all insurable interests in such subject, or to agree to do so, and neither such insurance nor the procurement or maintaining thereof or agreement to procure or maintain the same shall be construed to be an inducement to purchase.

§ 7311. Unlawful collection agency practices.

(a) Assignments of claims.--It is lawful for a collection agency, for the purpose of collecting or enforcing the payment thereof, to take an assignment of any such claim from a creditor, if all of the following apply:

(1) The assignment between the creditors and collection agency is in writing.

(2) The original agreement between the creditor and debtor does not prohibit assignments.

(3) The collection agency complies with the act of December 17, 1968 (P.L.1224, No.387), known as the Unfair Trade Practices and Consumer Protection Law, and with the regulations promulgated under that act.

(b) Appearance for creditor.--It is unlawful for a collection agency to appear for or represent a creditor in any manner whatsoever, but a collection agency, pursuant to subsection (a), may bring legal action on claims assigned to it and not be in violation of subsection (c) if the agency appears by an attorney.

(b.1) Unfair or deceptive collection methods.--It is unlawful for a collector to collect any amount, including any interest, fee, charge or expense incidental to the principal obligation, unless such amount is expressly provided in the agreement creating the debt or is permitted by law.

(c) Furnishing legal services.--It is unlawful for a collection agency to furnish, or offer to furnish legal services, directly or indirectly, or to offer to render or furnish such services within or without this Commonwealth. The forwarding of a claim by a collection agency to an attorney at law, for the purpose of collection, shall not constitute furnishing legal service for the purposes of this subsection.

(d) Services for debtor.--It is unlawful for a collection agency to act for, represent or undertake to render services for any debtor with regard to the proposed settlement or adjustment of the affairs of such debtor, whether such compromise, settlement, or adjustment be made through legal proceedings or otherwise, or to demand, ask for, or receive any compensation for services in connection with the settlement or collection of any claim except from the creditor for whom it has rendered lawful services.

(e) Running for attorneys.--It is unlawful for a collection agency to solicit employment for any attorney at law, whether practicing in this Commonwealth or elsewhere, or to receive from or divide with any such attorney at law any portion of any fee received by such attorney at law. This subsection does not prohibit the established custom of sharing commissions at a commonly accepted rate upon collection of claims between a collection agency and an attorney at law.

(f) Coercion or intimidation.--

(1) It is unlawful for a collection agency to coerce or intimidate any debtor by delivering or mailing any paper or document simulating, or intending to simulate, a summons, warrant, writ, or court process as a means for the collection of a claim, or to threaten legal proceedings against any debtor.

(2) Paragraph (1) of this subsection shall not prohibit:

(i) A collection agency from informing a debtor that if a claim is not paid, it will be referred to an attorney at law for such action as he may deem necessary, without naming a specific attorney.

(ii) A magisterial district judge from sending out notices to debtors before the institution of suit.

(g) Grading.--Whoever violates any of the provisions of this section is guilty of a misdemeanor of the third degree.

(h) Definitions.--As used in this section the following words and phrases shall have the meanings given to them in this subsection:

"Claim." Includes any claim, demand, account, note, or any other chose in action or liability of any kind whatsoever.

"Collection agency." A person, other than an attorney at law duly admitted to practice in any court of record in this Commonwealth, who, as a business, enforces, collects, settles, adjusts, or compromises claims, or holds himself out, or offers, as a business, to enforce, collect, settle, adjust, or compromise claims.

"Creditor." Includes a person having or asserting such a claim.

"Debtor." Includes any person against whom a claim is asserted.

(Dec. 19, 1990, P.L.1451, No.219, eff. imd.; Nov. 30, 2004, P.L.1618, No.207, eff. 60 days)

2004 Amendment. Act 207 amended subsec. (f)(2). See section 29 of Act 207 in the appendix to this title for special provisions relating to construction of law.

1990 Amendment. Act 219 amended subsecs. (a) and (b) and added subsec. (b.1).

§ 7312. Debt pooling.

(a) Offense defined.--Any person engaged in the business of debt pooling shall be guilty of a misdemeanor of the third degree.

(b) Exceptions.--Subsection (a) of this section shall not apply to:

(1) Any person who is admitted to practice before the Supreme Court of Pennsylvania or any court of common pleas of this Commonwealth or any partnership or professional corporation all of the members or shareholders of which are so admitted.

(2) Better business bureaus, legal aid societies or welfare agencies who act without compensation or profit on behalf of debtors as debt adjusters or debt poolers.

(3) Organizations in the business of debt adjusting or debt pooling that are exempt from taxation under section 501(c)(3) of the Internal Revenue Code of 1986 (Public Law 99-514, 26 U.S.C. § 501(c)(3)) or any successor provisions thereof.

(c) Definitions.--As used in this section the following words and phrases shall have the meanings given to them in this subsection:

"Creditor." A person to whom a debt or obligation is owed from another whether such is payable in installments or otherwise.

"Debtor." A person who owes an obligation or debt to another whether such is repayable in installments or otherwise.

"Debt pooling." The making of a contract, express or implied, with a debtor or debtors whereby the debtor agrees to pay a sum of money periodically or otherwise to another person for the purpose of having such other person distribute the same among certain specified creditors in accordance with a plan agreed upon, or to be agreed upon, and whereby such other person shall receive a consideration for any such services rendered, or to be rendered, in connection therewith.

(Dec. 18, 2007, P.L.462, No.70, eff. imd.)

2007 Amendment. Act 70 amended subsec. (b).

§ 7313. Buying or exchanging Federal Supplemental Nutrition Assistance Program (SNAP) benefit coupons, stamps, authorization cards or access devices.

(a) Offense defined.--A person commits the offense of buying or exchanging Federal SNAP benefit coupons, stamps, authorization cards or access devices if he, not being authorized to do so by the United States Department of Agriculture, buys or exchanges Federal SNAP benefit coupons, stamps, authorization cards or access devices for currency, or if he accepts or causes to be accepted Federal SNAP benefit coupons, stamps, authorization cards or access devices in exchange for any merchandise or article except food, as defined by the United States Department of Agriculture, or Federal SNAP benefit coupons, stamps, authorization cards or access devices in exchange for merchandise or articles, not defined by the United States Department of Agriculture to be surplus foods.

(b) Grading.--A person who violates this section commits a felony of the third degree if the amount involved is $1,000 or more. If the amount involved is less than $1,000, the person commits a misdemeanor of the first degree. Amounts involved in buying or exchanging Federal SNAP benefit coupons, stamps, authorization cards or access devices committed pursuant to one scheme or course of conduct, whether from the same person or several persons, shall be aggregated in determining the grade of the offense.

(c) Definitions.--As used in this section, the following words and phrases shall have the meanings given to them in this subsection:

"Access device." The Pennsylvania ACCESS card or electronic benefit transfer card.

"Authorization card." The paper authorization to participate that a person signs and then exchanges for the designated amount of food coupons at a bank.

"SNAP benefit." The value of supplemental nutrition assistance provided to a household for the purchase of eligible foods as defined in 7 CFR 271.2 (relating to definitions).

(Nov. 22, 1995, P.L.621, No.66, eff. 60 days; Oct. 24, 2018, P.L.1159, No.160, eff. 60 days)

Cross References. Section 7313 is referred to in section 5708 of this title.

§ 7314. Fraudulent traffic in Supplemental Nutrition Assistance Program (SNAP) benefits.

(a) Offense defined.--A person commits the offense of fraudulent traffic in SNAP benefits if he, whether acting for himself or for another, directly or indirectly, furnishes or delivers to any person money, merchandise, or anything other than food, on or in exchange for a SNAP benefit, or furnishes or delivers food on or in exchange for a SNAP benefit to any person, other than the original recipient of the SNAP benefit, or in quantities or for prices other than those itemized on the SNAP benefit at the time the food is furnished or delivered.

(a.1) Grading.--

(1) A person who violates this section commits:

(i) A felony of the second degree if the amount involved is $2,500 or more.

(ii) A felony of the third degree if the amount involved is $1,000 or more, but less than $2,500.

(iii) A misdemeanor of the first degree if the amount involved is less than $1,000.

(2) Amounts involved in fraudulent traffic in SNAP benefits committed pursuant to one scheme or course of conduct, whether from the same person or several persons, shall be aggregated in determining the grade of the offense.

(b) Additional penalty.--In addition to the penalties otherwise prescribed and any restitution ordered, the defendant shall also be ordered to pay to the agency which shall have issued such SNAP benefit, not less than two times, but not more than three times the amount of restitution ordered.

(b.1) Referral.--If the defendant is commercially licensed by the Commonwealth or one of its political subdivisions, the Office of State Inspector General may refer a violation of this section to the licensing entity for action by the licensing entity as provided under law.

(c) Exception.--Subsection (a) of this section shall not apply to the negotiation of a SNAP benefit after food to the full amount of the SNAP benefit shall have been furnished thereon to the original recipient of the SNAP benefit.

(d) Definition.--As used in this section, the term "SNAP benefit" means the value of supplemental nutrition assistance provided to a household for the purchase of eligible food as defined in 7 CFR 271.2 (relating to definitions).

(Nov. 22, 1995, P.L.621, No.66, eff. 60 days; Oct. 24, 2018, P.L.1159, No.160, eff. 60 days)

Cross References. Section 7314 is referred to in section 531 of Title 62 (Procurement).

§ 7315. Unauthorized disposition of donated food commodities.

A person is guilty of a summary offense if he, whether acting for himself or for another, directly or indirectly willfully makes any unauthorized disposition of any food commodity donated under any program of the Federal Government or if he, not being an authorized recipient thereof, willfully converts to his own use or benefit any such food commodity.

§ 7316. Keeping bucket-shop.

(a) Offense defined.--A person is guilty of a misdemeanor of the third degree if he keeps, or causes to be kept, any bucket-shop, or assists in the keeping of any bucket-shop.

(b) Corporate penalty.--If a corporation is convicted, its charter shall be forfeited by a proceeding in quo warranto, instituted either at the relation of the Attorney General or the district attorney.

(c) Second offense.--The continuance of the establishment after the first conviction shall be deemed a second offense.

(d) Evidence required.--It shall not be necessary, in order to convict any person of keeping a bucket-shop, or causing one to be kept, to show that such person has entered into any contract, agreement, trade, or transaction of the nature of a "bucket-shop" as defined in this section; but it shall be sufficient to show that such person has offered to make such a contract, agreement, trade, or transaction, whether the contract, agreement, trade, or transaction was accepted or not. Proof of a single instance wherein any person or another on his behalf, has made or offered to make any such contract, agreement, trade, or transaction, shall be conclusive that the place wherein the same was made is a bucket-shop.

(e) Definition.--As used in this section "bucket-shop" means a place where contracts, agreements, trades, or transactions respecting the sale or purchase of stocks, bonds, securities, grains, provisions or other commodities are made or offered to be made, to be closed, adjusted or settled upon the basis of public market quotations on a board of trade or exchange, but without a bona fide transaction on such board of trade or exchange.

Cross References. Section 7316 is referred to in sections 7317, 7318, 7319 of this title.

§ 7317. Accessories in conduct of bucket-shop.

(a) Offense defined.--A person is guilty of a misdemeanor of the third degree if he transmits or communicates by telegraph, telephone, wireless, telegraphy, express, mail, or otherwise or if he receives, exhibits, or displays, in any manner, any statement or quotation of the prices of any property, mentioned in section 7316(e) of this title (relating to definition of bucket-shop), with a view of entering into any contract, agreement, trade, or transaction, or offering to enter into any contract, agreement, trade, or transaction, or with a view of aiding others to enter or offer to enter into any such contract, agreement, trade, or transaction, of the nature described in the definition of "bucket-shop."

(b) Corporate penalty.--If a corporation is convicted, its charter shall be forfeited by a proceeding in quo warranto, instituted either at the relation of the Attorney General or the district attorney.

§ 7318. Maintaining of premises in which bucket-shop operated.

(a) Offense defined.--A person is guilty of a misdemeanor of the third degree if he knowingly permits a bucket-shop, as defined in section 7316(e) of this title (relating to definition of bucket-shop) to be maintained or operated in any premises owned, leased, controlled, or operated by him.

(b) Fine a lien.--Any fine imposed under this section shall be a lien upon the premises, in or on which the bucket-shop shall be maintained and operated.

§ 7319. Bucket-shop contracts.

(a) Status of contracts.--All contracts, agreements, trades, or transactions of the nature of a bucket-shop as defined in section 7316(e) of this title (relating to definition of bucket-shop), are hereby declared gambling, and criminal acts, and null and void.

(b) Offense defined.--A person is guilty of a misdemeanor of the third degree if he shall enter into the same, whether for himself or as agent or broker of any person.

§ 7320. Attaching advertisement without consent of publisher.

A person is guilty of a summary offense if he places or affixes or inserts, or causes to be placed or affixed or inserted, any advertisement, notice, circular, pamphlet, card, handbill, book, booklet, or other printed notice of any kind, on or in or to any newspaper, magazine, periodical, or book, when such newspaper, magazine, periodical, or book is in the possession of the owner, or publisher thereof, or in the possession of any news dealer, distributor, or carrier, or of any agent or servant of such owner or publisher, without the consent of the owner or publisher.

§ 7321. Lie detector tests.

(a) Offense defined.--A person is guilty of a misdemeanor of the second degree if he requires as a condition for employment or continuation of employment that an employee or other individual shall take a polygraph test or any form of a mechanical or electrical lie detector test.

(b) Exception.--The provisions of subsection (a) of this section shall not apply to employees or other individuals in the field of public law enforcement or who dispense or have access to narcotics or dangerous drugs.

§ 7322. Demanding property to secure employment.

A person is guilty of a misdemeanor of the third degree if he, being an officer or employee of any employer of labor, solicits, demands or receives, directly or indirectly, from any person any money or other valuable thing, for the purpose, actual or alleged, of either obtaining for such person employment in the service of said employer or of the continuing of such person in employment.

§ 7323. Discrimination on account of uniform.

A person is guilty of a misdemeanor of the second degree if, being the proprietor, manager, or employee of a theatre, hotel, restaurant, or other place of public entertainment or amusement, he discriminates against any person wearing the uniform of the armed forces of the United States, because of that uniform.

§ 7324. Unlawful sale of dissertations, theses and term papers.

(a) Definitions.--As used in this section:

(1) "Assignment" means any specific written, recorded, pictorial, artistic, or other academic task that is intended for submission to any university, academy, school or other educational institution which is chartered, incorporated, licensed, registered or supervised by the Commonwealth, in fulfillment of the requirements of a degree, diploma, certificate or course of study at any such institution.

(2) "Prepare" means to create, write, or in any way produce in whole or substantial part, a term paper, thesis, dissertation, essay, report or other written, recorded, pictorial, artistic or other assignment for a fee.

(b) Sale of assistance to student.--No person shall sell or offer for sale to any student enrolled in a university, college, academy, school or other educational institution within the Commonwealth of Pennsylvania any assistance in the preparation, research or writing of a dissertation, thesis, term paper, essay, report or other written assignment knowing, or under the circumstances having reason to know, that said assignment is intended for submission either in whole or substantial part under said student's name to such educational institution in fulfillment of the requirements for a degree, diploma, certificate or course of study.

(c) Sale or distribution of assignment to student.--No person shall sell or offer for distribution any dissertation, thesis, term paper, essay, report or other written assignment to any student enrolled in a university, college, academy, school or any other institution within the Commonwealth of Pennsylvania knowing, or under the circumstances having reason to know, that said assignment is intended for submission either in whole or substantial part under said student's name to such educational institution in fulfillment of the requirement for a degree, diploma, certificate or course of study.

(d) Sale or distribution for sale to student.--No person shall sell or offer for distribution any dissertation, thesis, term paper, essay, report or other written assignment to any person who, sells or offers for sale any such dissertation, thesis, term paper, essay, report or other written assignment to any student enrolled in a university, college, academy, school or other educational institution within the Commonwealth of Pennsylvania knowing, or under the circumstances having reason to know, that said assignment is intended for submission either in whole or substantial part under said student's name to such educational institution in fulfillment of the requirements for a degree, diploma, certificate or course of study.

(e) Authorized activities and services.--Nothing herein contained shall prevent such educational institution or any member of its faculty or staff, from offering courses, instruction, counseling or tutoring for research or writing as part of a curriculum or other program conducted by such educational institution. Nor shall this section prevent any educational institution or any member of its faculty or staff from authorizing students to use statistical, computer, or any other services which may be required or permitted by such educational institution in the preparation, research or writing of a dissertation, thesis, term paper, essay, report or other written assignment. Nor shall this section prevent tutorial assistance rendered by other persons which does not include the preparation, research or writing of a dissertation, thesis, term paper, essay, report or other written assignment knowing, or under the circumstances having reason to know, that said assignment is intended for submission either in whole or substantial part under said student's name to such educational institution in fulfillment of the requirements for a degree, diploma, certificate or course of study. Nor shall any person be prevented by the provisions of this section from rendering services for a fee which shall be limited to the typing, transcription or reproduction of a manuscript.

(f) Authorized sale of copyrighted material.--Nothing contained within this section shall prevent any person from selling or offering for sale a publication or other written material which shall have been registered under the United States Laws of Copyright: Provided, however, That the owner of such copyright shall have given his authorization or approval for such sale: And, provided further, That said person shall not know or under the circumstances have reason to know that said assignment is intended for submission either in whole, or substantial part, under a student's name as a dissertation, thesis, term paper, essay, report or other written assignment to such educational institution within the Commonwealth of Pennsylvania in fulfillment of the requirements for a degree, diploma, certificate or course of study.

(g) Grading.--Any person who violates the provisions of this section shall be guilty of a misdemeanor of the third degree.

(h) Injunction.--Whenever there shall be a violation of this section an application also may be made by the Attorney General in the name of the people of the Commonwealth of Pennsylvania to a court having jurisdiction to issue an injunction, and upon notice to the defendant of not less than five days, to enjoin and restrain the continuance of such violation; and if it shall appear to the satisfaction of the court or justice that the defendant has, in fact, violated this section, an injunction may be issued by such court, enjoining and restraining any further violation, without requiring proof that any person has, in fact, been injured or damaged thereby. In connection with any such proposed application, the Attorney General is authorized to take proof and make a determination of the relevant facts and to issue subpoenas in accordance with the laws and rules of civil procedure.

(July 27, 1973, P.L.226, No.58, eff. imd.)

1973 Amendment. Act 58 added section 7324.

§ 7325. Discrimination on account of service, guide or support dog or other aid animal.

(a) Offense defined.--A person is guilty of a summary offense if he, being the proprietor, manager or employee of a theatre, hotel, restaurant or other place of public accommodation, entertainment or amusement, refuses, withholds or denies any person, who is using a service, guide or support dog or other aid animal to assist an individual with a disability or who is training a service, guide or support dog or other aid animal for an individual with a disability, the use of or access to any accommodation, advantage, facility or privilege of such theatre, hotel, restaurant or other place of public entertainment or amusement.

(b) Definition.--As used in this section, the term "service, guide or support dog" shall have the same meaning given it under section 5531 (relating to definitions).

(Dec. 18, 1980, P.L.1251, No.227, eff. 60 days; May 12, 1982, P.L.416, No.121, eff. imd.; May 31, 1990, P.L.219, No.47, eff. 60 days; Oct. 18, 2000, P.L.605, No.80, eff. 60 days; Oct. 24, 2018, P.L.685, No.104, eff. 60 days)

§ 7326. Disclosure of confidential tax information.

(a) Offense defined.--A person commits a misdemeanor of the third degree if he discloses, except to authorized persons for official governmental purposes, any tax information that is:

(1) designated as confidential by a statute or ordinance of a city of the second class; and

(2) obtained by him in conjunction with any declaration, return, audit, hearing or

verification required or authorized by statute or ordinance.

(b) Exception.--Subsection (a) shall not apply where disclosure is required by law or by court order.

(c) Definition.--As used in this section, the term "person" includes, but is not limited to, a current or former officer or employee of the Commonwealth or any of its political subdivisions and any other individual who has access to confidential tax information.

(Dec. 19, 1990, P.L.1332, No.207, eff. imd.; Dec. 19, 1990, P.L.1451, No.219, eff. imd.)

1990 Amendments. Acts 207 and 219 added section 7326. The amendments by Acts 207 and 219 are identical.

§ 7327. Storage, consumption and sale of alcoholic beverages on unlicensed business premises.

(a) Storage.--A person commits a summary offense if he stores or permits storage by others of liquor or malt or brewed beverages for the purpose of consumption between the hours of 2 a.m. and 8 a.m. on business premises owned, operated, leased or controlled by such person which are not licensed under the act of April 12, 1951 (P.L.90, No.21), known as the Liquor Code.

(b) Consumption.--A person commits a summary offense if he allows another to consume liquor or malt or brewed beverages, after payment of an entry fee, cover charge or membership fee, between the hours of 2 a.m. and 8 a.m. on business premises owned, operated, leased or controlled by such person which are not licensed under the Liquor Code.

(c) Sale.--A person commits a summary offense if he sells or offers to sell any liquor or malt or brewed beverages between the hours of 2 a.m. and 8 a.m. on business premises owned, operated, leased or controlled by such person which are not licensed under the Liquor Code.

(Dec. 19, 1990, P.L.1451, No.219, eff. imd.)

1990 Amendment. Act 219 added section 7327.

§ 7328. Operation of certain establishments prohibited without local option.

(a) Offense defined.--A person commits a misdemeanor of the third degree if that person operates an establishment commonly referred to as a bottle club in a municipality or part of a split municipality where the operation of such establishments has been disapproved by the voters in accordance with subsection (b). The provisions of this subsection shall not apply to the first 30-day time period following the adoption of the disapproval referendum under subsection (b).

(b) Local option; election to be held.--

(1) In any municipality or any part of a municipality where such municipality is split so that each part is separated by another municipality, an election may be held on the date of the primary election immediately preceding any general or municipal election, but not more than once in four years, to determine the will of the electors with respect to prohibiting the operation, within the limits of the municipality or part of a split municipality, of establishments commonly referred to as bottle clubs. Where an election shall have been held at the primary election preceding a general or municipal election in any year, another election may be held under the provisions of this subsection at the primary election occurring the fourth year after such prior election. Whenever electors equal to at least 25% of the highest vote cast for any office in the municipality or part of a split municipality at the last preceding general election shall file a petition with the county board of elections of the county, or the governing body of the municipality adopts by majority vote a resolution to place the question on the ballot and a copy of the resolution is filed with the board of elections of the county, for a referendum on the question of prohibiting the operation of establishments commonly referred to as bottle clubs, the said county board of elections shall cause a question to be placed on the ballot or on the voting machine board and submitted at the primary election immediately preceding the general or municipal election. The question shall be in the following form:

Do you favor the prohibition of the operation of establishments, commonly referred to as bottle clubs in   of   ?

(2) In the case of a tie vote, the status quo shall obtain. If a majority of the electors voting on the question votes "yes," then an establishment commonly referred to as a bottle club shall not be operated in the municipality or part of a split municipality after 30 days from the certification of the vote on the question, but, if a majority of the electors voting on the question votes "no," then the operation of these

establishments shall be permitted in the municipality or part of a split municipality unless and until at a later election a majority of the voting electors votes "yes" on the question.

(3) Proceedings under this subsection shall be in accordance with the provisions of the act of June 3, 1937 (P.L.1333, No.320), known as the Pennsylvania Election Code.

(c) **Definition.**--As used in this section, the term "bottle club" means an establishment operated for profit or pecuniary gain, which admits patrons upon the payment of a fee, has a capacity for the assemblage of 20 or more persons, and in which alcoholic liquors, alcohol or malt or brewed beverages are not legally sold but where alcoholic liquors, alcohol or malt or brewed beverages are either provided by the operator or agents or employees of the operator for consumption on the premises or are brought into or kept at the establishment by the patrons or persons assembling there for use and consumption. The term shall not include a licensee under the act of April 12, 1951 (P.L.90, No.21), known as the Liquor Code, or any organization as set forth in section 6 of the act of December 19, 1990 (P.L.1200, No.202), known as the Solicitation of Funds for Charitable Purposes Act.

(Nov. 22, 1995, P.L.621, No.66, eff. imd.)

1995 Amendment. Act 66 added section 7328.

§ 7329. Prohibition of certain types of entertainment on bottle club premises.

(a) **Offense defined.**--No bottle club operator or servants, agents or employees of the same shall knowingly permit on premises used as a bottle club or in any place operated in connection therewith any lewd, immoral or improper entertainment.

(b) **Penalty for violation.**--Any person who violates subsection (a) commits a summary offense.

(c) **Definitions.**--As used in this section, the following words and phrases shall have the meanings given to them in this subsection:

"Bottle club." An establishment operated for profit or pecuniary gain, which has a capacity for the assemblage of 20 or more persons and in which alcoholic liquors, alcohol or malt or brewed beverages are not legally sold but where alcoholic liquors, alcohol or malt or brewed beverages are either provided by the operator or agents or employees of the operator for consumption on the premises or are brought into or kept at the establishment by the patrons or persons assembling there for use and consumption. The term shall not include a licensee under the act of April 12, 1951 (P.L.90, No.21), known as the Liquor Code, or any organization as set forth in section 6 of the act of December 19, 1990 (P.L.1200, No.202), known as the Solicitation of Funds for Charitable Purposes Act.

"Lewd, immoral or improper entertainment." Includes, but is not limited to, the following acts of conduct:

(1) Acts or simulated acts of sexual intercourse, masturbation, sodomy, bestiality, oral copulation, flagellation or excretion or any sexual acts which are prohibited by law.

(2) Any person being touched, caressed or fondled on the buttocks, anus, vulva, genitals or female breasts. This paragraph includes simulation.

(3) Scenes wherein a person displays or exposes to view any portion of the pubic area, anus, cleft of the buttocks, vulva, genitals or any portion of the female breast directly or laterally below the top of the areola. This paragraph includes simulation.

(4) Scenes wherein artificial devices or inanimate objects are employed to portray any of the prohibited activities described in paragraph (1), (2) or (3).

(5) Employment or use of any person in the sale and service of alcoholic beverages while such person is unclothed or in such attire, costume or clothing as to expose to view any portion of the anatomy described in paragraph (3).

(6) Employment or use of the services of a person while the person is unclothed or in such attire as to expose to view any portion of the anatomy described in paragraph (3).

(7) Permitting any person on the premises to touch, caress or fondle the buttocks, anus, vulva, genitals or female breasts of any other person.

(8) Permitting any person on the premises while such person is unclothed or in such attire as to expose to view any portion of the anatomy described in paragraph (3).

(9) Permitting any person to wear or use any device or covering exposed to view which simulates the human buttocks, anus, vulva, genitals or female breasts.

(10) Permitting any person to show, display or exhibit on the premises any film, still picture, electronic reproduction or any other

visual reproduction or image the content of which primarily depicts graphic sexual acts as described in paragraphs (1) and (4).

(Feb. 23, 1996, P.L.17, No.7, eff. 60 days; Dec. 18, 1996, P.L.1074, No.160, eff. 60 days)

1996 Amendments. Act 7 added section 7329 and Act 160 amended subsec. (c).

§ 7330. Internet child pornography (Repealed).

2002 Repeal. Section 7330 was repealed December 16, 2002 (P.L.1953, No.226), effective in 60 days.

§ 7331. Unlicensed mortgage loan business.

A person that operates without a license in violation of 7 Pa.C.S. § 6111 (relating to license requirements) commits a felony of the third degree.

(July 8, 2008, P.L.796, No.56, eff. 120 days)

2008 Amendment. Act 56 added section 7331.

SUBCHAPTER B
SUNDAY TRADING

Sec.
7361. Worldly employment or business.
7362. Trading in motor vehicles and trailers (Repealed).
7363. Selling certain personal property.
7364. Selling or otherwise dealing in fresh meats, produce and groceries.
7365. Trading in motor vehicles and trailers.

Constitutionality. Subchapter B (§§ 7361 - 7364) was declared unconstitutional on October 5, 1978, by the Supreme Court of Pennsylvania in Kroger Co. v. O'Hara Township, 481 Pa. 101, 392 A.2d 266 (1978).

§ 7361. Worldly employment or business.
(a) Offense defined.--A person is guilty of a summary offense if he does or performs any worldly employment or business whatsoever on Sunday (works of necessity, charity and wholesome recreation excepted).
(b) Exception.--Subsection (a) of this section shall not prohibit:
(1) The dressing of victuals in private families, bake-houses, lodginghouses, inns and

other houses of entertainment for the use of sojourners, travellers or strangers.
(2) The sale of newspapers.
(3) Watermen from landing their passengers, or ferrymen from carrying over the water travellers.
(4) Work in connection with the rendering of service by a public utility as defined in the Public Utility Law.
(5) Persons removing with their families.
(6) The delivery of milk or the necessaries of life, before nine o'clock antemeridian, nor after five o'clock postmeridian.
(7) The production and performance of drama and civic light opera for an admission charge by nonprofit corporations in cities of the second class, between the hours of two o'clock postmeridian and 12 o'clock midnight.
(8) The conducting, staging, managing, operating, performing or engaging in basketball, ice shows and ice hockey for an admission charge in cities of the first and second class, between the hours of two o'clock postmeridian and 12 o'clock midnight.
(c) Definition.--As used in this section "wholesome recreation" means golf, tennis, boating, swimming, bowling, basketball, picnicking, shooting at inanimate targets and similar healthful or recreational exercises and activities.

(Apr. 28, 1978, P.L.202, No.53, eff. 60 days)

1978 Repeal. Act 53 repealed the last sentence of subsec. (a). The repealed provisions have been deleted from the text.
Constitutionality. Section 7361 was declared unconstitutional on October 5, 1978, by the Supreme Court of Pennsylvania in Kroger Co. v. O'Hara Township, 481 Pa. 101, 392 A.2d 266 (1978).
References in Text. The Public Utility Law, referred to in subsection (b), was repealed by the act of July 1, 1978 (P.L.598, No.116). The subject matter is now contained in Part I of Title 66 (Public Utilities).
Cross References. Section 7361 is referred to in section 3571 of Title 42 (Judiciary and Judicial Procedure).
§ 7362. Trading in motor vehicles and trailers (Repealed).

1979 Repeal. Section 7362 was repealed December 7, 1979 (P.L.487, No.103), effective in 60 days. The subject matter is now contained in section 7365 of this title.

Constitutionality. Section 7362 was declared unconstitutional on October 5, 1978, by the Supreme Court of Pennsylvania in Kroger Co. v. O'Hara Township, 481 Pa. 101, 392 A.2d 266 (1978).

§ 7363. Selling certain personal property.

(a) Offense defined.--A person is guilty of a summary offense if he engages on Sunday in the business of selling, or sells or offers for sale, on such day, at retail, clothing and wearing apparel, clothing accessories, furniture, housewares, home, business or office furnishings, household, business or office appliances, hardware, tools, paints, building and lumber supply materials, jewelry, silverware, watches, clocks, luggage, musical instruments and recordings, or toys.

(b) Separate offenses.--Each separate sale or offer to sell shall constitute a separate offense.

(c) Exceptions.--

(1) Subsection (a) of this section shall not apply to novelties, souvenirs and antiques.

(2) No individual who by reason of his religious conviction observes a day other than Sunday as his day of rest and actually refrains from labor or secular business on that day shall be prohibited from selling on Sunday in a business establishment which is closed on such other day the articles specified in subsection (a) of this section.

(d) Limitation of action.--Information charging violations of this section shall be brought within 72 hours after the commission of the alleged offense and not thereafter.

(e) Repeated offense penalty.--A person who commits a second or any subsequent offense within one year after conviction for the first offense shall be sentenced to pay a fine of not exceeding $200.

(f) Definitions.--As used in this section the following words and phrases shall have the meanings given to them in this subsection:

"A day other than Sunday." Any consecutive 24 hour period.

"Antique." An item over 100 years old, or ethnographic objects made in traditional aboriginal styles and made at least 50 years prior to their sale.

Constitutionality. Section 7363 was declared unconstitutional on October 5, 1978, by the Supreme Court of Pennsylvania in

Kroger Co. v. O'Hara Township, 481 Pa. 101, 392 A.2d 266 (1978).

§ 7364. Selling or otherwise dealing in fresh meats, produce and groceries.

(a) Offense defined.--A person is guilty of a summary offense if he engages in the business of selling or otherwise dealing at retail in fresh meats, produce and groceries on Sunday.

(b) Separate offenses.--Each separate sale, or offer to sell, shall constitute a separate offense.

(c) Exceptions.--Subsection (a) of this section shall not apply to any retail establishment:

(1) employing less than ten persons;

(2) where fresh meats, produce and groceries are offered so sold by the proprietor or members of his immediate family; or

(3) where food is prepared on the premises for human consumption.

(d) Limitation of action.--Information charging violations of this section shall be brought within 72 hours after the commission of the alleged offense and not thereafter.

(e) Repeated offense penalty.--A person who commits a second or any subsequent offense within one year after conviction for the first offense shall be sentenced to pay a fine not exceeding $200.

Constitutionality. Section 7364 was declared unconstitutional on October 5, 1978, by the Supreme Court of Pennsylvania in Kroger Co. v. O'Hara Township, 481 Pa. 101, 392 A.2d 266 (1978).

§ 7365. Trading in motor vehicles and trailers.

(a) Offense defined.--A person is guilty of a summary offense if he engages in the business of buying, selling, exchanging, trading, or otherwise dealing in new or used motor vehicles or trailers, on Sunday.

(b) Repeated offense penalty.--A person who commits a second or any subsequent offense within one year after conviction for the first offense, shall be sentenced to pay a fine not exceeding $200.

(c) Definitions.--As used in this section the following words and phrases shall have the meanings given to them in this subsection:

"Motor vehicle." Every self-propelled device in, upon or by which any person or property is or may be transported or drawn on a public highway.

"Trailer." Every vehicle, without motor power, designed to carry property or passengers or designed and used exclusively for living quarters wholly on its own structure, and to be drawn by a motor vehicle.
(Dec. 7, 1979, P.L.487, No.103, eff. 60 days)

1979 Amendment. Act 103 added section 7365.

2011 Partial Repeal. Section 5(2) of Act 65 provided that section 7365 is repealed insofar as it relates to motorcycles.

CHAPTER 75 OTHER OFFENSES

Sec.
7501. Removal of mobile home to evade tax.
7502. Failure of mobile home court operator to make reports.
7503. Interest of certain architects and engineers in public work contracts.
7504. Appointment of special policemen.
7505. Violation of governmental rules regarding traffic.
7506. Violation of rules regarding conduct on Commonwealth property.
7507. Breach of privacy by using a psychological-stress evaluator, an audio-stress monitor or a similar device without consent.
7507.1. Invasion of privacy.
7508. Drug trafficking sentencing and penalties.
7508.1. Substance Abuse Education and Demand Reduction Fund.
7508.2. Operation of methamphetamine laboratory.
7509. Furnishing drug-free urine.
7510. Municipal housing code avoidance (Repealed).
7511. Control of alarm devices and automatic dialing devices.
7512. Criminal use of communication facility.
7513. Restriction on alcoholic beverages (Repealed).
7514. Operating a motor vehicle not equipped with ignition interlock (Repealed).
7515. Contingent compensation.
7516. Greyhound racing and simulcasting.
7517. Commemorative service demonstration activities.

Enactment. Chapter 75 was added December 6, 1972, P.L.1482, No.334, effective in six months.

§ 7501. Removal of mobile home to evade tax.

A person is guilty of a summary offense if he, being the titled owner of a mobile home or house trailer which is subject to a tax, and having received an official tax notice levying such tax thereon, thereafter for the purpose of evading the payment of such tax, removes such mobile home or house trailer from the political subdivision levying such tax.

§ 7502. Failure of mobile home court operator to make reports.

A person is guilty of a summary offense if he, being an operator of a mobile home or house trailer court, shall fail to submit to the tax assessor of the political subdivision, in which such court is located, after written notice to do so, such report or reports as are required by law to be submitted by an operator to such tax assessor.

§ 7503. Interest of certain architects and engineers in public work contracts.

(a) **Offense defined.**--A person is guilty of a misdemeanor of the third degree if he, being an architect or engineer, in the employ of the Commonwealth, or any political subdivision thereof, and engaged in the preparation of plans, specifications, or estimates, bids on any public work at any letting of such work in this Commonwealth; or if he, being an officer of the Commonwealth, or any political subdivision thereof, charged with the duty of letting any public work, awards a contract to any such architect or engineer; or if he, being any such architect or engineer, is in any way interested in any contract for public work, or receives any remuneration or gratuity from any person interested in such contract.

(b) **Forfeiture of office.**--A person who commits an offense under this section shall, in addition to the penalty prescribed herein, forfeit his office.

§ 7504. Appointment of special policemen.

(a) **Offense defined.**--A person is guilty of a misdemeanor of the third degree if he, having authority to do so, appoints as a special deputy, or policeman, to preserve the public peace and prevent or quell public disturbances, any person who is not a citizen of this Commonwealth.

(b) Exception.--Subsection (a) of this section shall not apply to policemen, constables or specials appointed by municipalities for municipal purposes.

(c) Organization penalty.--If any corporation, company or association is convicted under this section, it shall be sentenced to pay a fine not exceeding $5,000.

§ 7505. Violation of governmental rules regarding traffic.

Each Commonwealth agency shall promulgate rules and regulations governing all vehicular traffic at those Commonwealth facilities situated upon property of the Commonwealth which are within the exclusive jurisdiction of such agency including but not limited to regulations governing the parking of vehicles upon such property. Whoever violates any of the rules and regulations promulgated pursuant to this section governing the parking of vehicles shall, upon conviction in a summary proceeding, be sentenced to pay a fine not exceeding $5. Whoever violates any of the rules and regulations promulgated pursuant to this section governing the movement of traffic or the operation of vehicles shall, upon conviction in a summary proceeding, be sentenced to pay a fine not exceeding $15.

Cross References. Section 7505 is referred to in section 7506 of this title.

§ 7506. Violation of rules regarding conduct on Commonwealth property.

(a) Promulgation of rules and regulations.--The Department of Environmental Resources, Pennsylvania Game Commission and Pennsylvania Historical and Museum Commission may promulgate rules and regulations governing conduct, other than conduct regulated in section 7505 (relating to violation of governmental rules regarding traffic), on Commonwealth property within the jurisdiction of that agency. Such rules and regulations shall be reasonably related to the preservation and protection of such property for its specified or intended use, or to promote the welfare, safety or protection of those persons using such property, shall be consistent with existing law and shall be posted in a manner reasonable likely to come to the attention of persons using such property.

(b) Violation penalty.--A person who violates any of the rules and regulations promulgated pursuant to this section is guilty of a summary offense.

(July 1, 1978, P.L.564, No.97, eff. imd.; July 8, 1986, P.L.442, No.93, eff. July 1, 1987)

1996 Partial Repeal. Section 18 of Act 49 of 1996 provided that section 7506 is repealed insofar as it is inconsistent with Act 49.

Department of Conservation and Natural Resources. Section 313(e) of Act 18 of 1995, which created the Department of Conservation and Natural Resources and renamed the Department of Environmental Resources as the Department of Environmental Protection, provided that the Department of Conservation and Natural Resources shall exercise the powers and duties vested in the Department of Environmental Resources by section 7506.

Cross References. Section 7506 is referred to in section 6109 of this title.

§ 7507. Breach of privacy by using a psychological-stress evaluator, an audio-stress monitor or a similar device without consent.

A person commits a misdemeanor of the second degree if he uses a psychological-stress evaluator, an audio-stress monitor or a similar device which measures voice waves or tonal inflections to judge the truth or falsity of oral statements without the consent of the person whose statement is being tested.

(Oct. 4, 1978, P.L.976, No.194, eff. imd.)

1978 Amendment. Act 194 added section 7507.

§ 7507.1. Invasion of privacy.

(a) Offense defined.--Except as set forth in subsection (d), a person commits the offense of invasion of privacy if he, for the purpose of arousing or gratifying the sexual desire of any person, knowingly does any of the following:

(1) Views, photographs, videotapes, electronically depicts, films or otherwise records another person without that person's knowledge and consent while that person is in a state of full or partial nudity and is in a place where that person would have a reasonable expectation of privacy.

(2) Photographs, videotapes, electronically depicts, films or otherwise records or personally views the intimate parts, whether or not covered by clothing, of another

person without that person's knowledge and consent and which intimate parts that person does not intend to be visible by normal public observation.

(3) Transfers or transmits an image obtained in violation of paragraph (1) or (2) by live or recorded telephone message, electronic mail or the Internet or by any other transfer of the medium on which the image is stored.

(a.1) Separate violations.--A separate violation of this section shall occur:

(1) for each victim of an offense under subsection (a) under the same or similar circumstances pursuant to one scheme or course of conduct whether at the same or different times; or

(2) if a person is a victim of an offense under subsection (a) on more than one occasion during a separate course of conduct either individually or otherwise.

(b) Grading.--Invasion of privacy is a misdemeanor of the second degree if there is more than one violation. Otherwise, a violation of this section is a misdemeanor of the third degree.

(c) Commencement of prosecution.-- Notwithstanding the provisions of 42 Pa.C.S. Ch. 55 Subch. C (relating to criminal proceedings), a prosecution under this section must be commenced within the following periods of limitation:

(1) two years from the date the offense occurred; or

(2) if the victim did not realize at the time that there was an offense, within three years of the time the victim first learns of the offense.

(d) Exceptions.--Subsection (a) shall not apply if the conduct proscribed by subsection (a) is done by any of the following:

(1) Law enforcement officers during a lawful criminal investigation.

(2) Law enforcement officers or by personnel of the Department of Corrections or a local correctional facility, prison or jail for security purposes or during investigation of alleged misconduct by a person in the custody of the department or local authorities.

(e) Definitions.--As used in this section, the following words and phrases shall have the meanings given to them in this subsection:

"Full or partial nudity." Display of all or any part of the human genitals or pubic area or buttocks, or any part of the nipple of the breast of any female person, with less than a fully opaque covering.

"Intimate part." Any part of:

(1) the human genitals, pubic area or buttocks; and

(2) the nipple of a female breast.

"Photographs" or "films." Making any photograph, motion picture film, videotape or any other recording or transmission of the image of a person.

"Place where a person would have a reasonable expectation of privacy." A location where a reasonable person would believe that he could disrobe in privacy without being concerned that his undressing was being viewed, photographed or filmed by another.

"Views." Looking upon another person with the unaided eye or with any device designed or intended to improve visual acuity.

(Mar. 24, 1998, P.L.215, No.38, eff. 60 days; Nov. 16, 2005, P.L.378, No.69, eff. 60 days)

Cross References. Section 7507.1 is referred to in sections 8317, 9799.13, 9799.14 of Title 42 (Judiciary and Judicial Procedure).

§ 7508. Drug trafficking sentencing and penalties.

(a) General rule.--Notwithstanding any other provisions of this or any other act to the contrary, the following provisions shall apply:

(1) A person who is convicted of violating section 13(a)(14), (30) or (37) of the act of April 14, 1972 (P.L.233, No.64), known as The Controlled Substance, Drug, Device and Cosmetic Act, where the controlled substance is marijuana shall, upon conviction, be sentenced to a mandatory minimum term of imprisonment and a fine as set forth in this subsection:

(i) when the amount of marijuana involved is at least two pounds, but less than ten pounds, or at least ten live plants but less than 21 live plants; one year in prison and a fine of $5,000 or such larger amount as is sufficient to exhaust the assets utilized in and the proceeds from the illegal activity; however, if at the time of sentencing the defendant has been convicted of another drug trafficking offense: two years in prison and a fine of $10,000 or such larger amount as is sufficient to exhaust the assets utilized in and the proceeds from the illegal activity;

(ii) when the amount of marijuana involved is at least ten pounds, but less than 50 pounds, or at least 21 live plants but less than 51 live plants; three years in prison and a fine of $15,000 or such larger amount as is

343

sufficient to exhaust the assets utilized in and the proceeds from the illegal activity; however, if at the time of sentencing the defendant has been convicted of another drug trafficking offense: four years in prison and a fine of $30,000 or such larger amount as is sufficient to exhaust the assets utilized in and the proceeds from the illegal activity; and

(iii) when the amount of marijuana involved is at least 50 pounds, or at least 51 live plants; five years in prison and a fine of $50,000 or such larger amount as is sufficient to exhaust the assets utilized in and the proceeds from the illegal activity.

(2) A person who is convicted of violating section 13(a)(14), (30) or (37) of The Controlled Substance, Drug, Device and Cosmetic Act where the controlled substance or a mixture containing it is classified in Schedule I or Schedule II under section 4 of that act and is a narcotic drug shall, upon conviction, be sentenced to a mandatory minimum term of imprisonment and a fine as set forth in this subsection:

(i) when the aggregate weight of the compound or mixture containing the substance involved is at least 2.0 grams and less than ten grams; two years in prison and a fine of $5,000 or such larger amount as is sufficient to exhaust the assets utilized in and the proceeds from the illegal activity; however, if at the time of sentencing the defendant has been convicted of another drug trafficking offense: three years in prison and $10,000 or such larger amount as is sufficient to exhaust the assets utilized in and the proceeds from the illegal activity;

(ii) when the aggregate weight of the compound or mixture containing the substance involved is at least ten grams and less than 100 grams; three years in prison and a fine of $15,000 or such larger amount as is sufficient to exhaust the assets utilized in and the proceeds from the illegal activity; however, if at the time of sentencing the defendant has been convicted of another drug trafficking offense: five years in prison and $30,000 or such larger amount as is sufficient to exhaust the assets utilized in and the proceeds from the illegal activity; and

(iii) when the aggregate weight of the compound or mixture containing the substance involved is at least 100 grams; five years in prison and a fine of $25,000 or such larger amount as is sufficient to exhaust the assets utilized in and the proceeds from the illegal

activity; however, if at the time of sentencing the defendant has been convicted of another drug trafficking offense: seven years in prison and $50,000 or such larger amount as is sufficient to exhaust the assets utilized in and the proceeds from the illegal activity.

(3) A person who is convicted of violating section 13(a)(14), (30) or (37) of The Controlled Substance, Drug, Device and Cosmetic Act where the controlled substance is coca leaves or is any salt, compound, derivative or preparation of coca leaves or is any salt, compound, derivative or preparation which is chemically equivalent or identical with any of these substances or is any mixture containing any of these substances except decocainized coca leaves or extracts of coca leaves which (extracts) do not contain cocaine or ecgonine shall, upon conviction, be sentenced to a mandatory minimum term of imprisonment and a fine as set forth in this subsection:

(i) when the aggregate weight of the compound or mixture containing the substance involved is at least 2.0 grams and less than ten grams; one year in prison and a fine of $5,000 or such larger amount as is sufficient to exhaust the assets utilized in and the proceeds from the illegal activity; however, if at the time of sentencing the defendant has been convicted of another drug trafficking offense: three years in prison and $10,000 or such larger amount as is sufficient to exhaust the assets utilized in and the proceeds from the illegal activity;

(ii) when the aggregate weight of the compound or mixture containing the substance involved is at least ten grams and less than 100 grams; three years in prison and a fine of $15,000 or such larger amount as is sufficient to exhaust the assets utilized in and the proceeds from the illegal activity; however, if at the time of sentencing the defendant has been convicted of another drug trafficking offense: five years in prison and $30,000 or such larger amount as is sufficient to exhaust the assets utilized in and the proceeds from the illegal activity; and

(iii) when the aggregate weight of the compound or mixture of the substance involved is at least 100 grams; four years in prison and a fine of $25,000 or such larger amount as is sufficient to exhaust the assets utilized in and the proceeds from the illegal activity; however, if at the time of sentencing the defendant has been convicted of another drug trafficking offense: seven years in prison and $50,000 or such larger amount as is sufficient to exhaust the assets utilized in and the proceeds from the illegal activity.

(4) A person who is convicted of violating section 13(a)(14), (30) or (37) of The Controlled Substance, Drug, Device and Cosmetic Act where the controlled substance is methamphetamine or phencyclidine or is a salt, isomer or salt of an isomer of methamphetamine or phencyclidine or is a mixture containing methamphetamine or phencyclidine, containing a salt of methamphetamine or phencyclidine, containing an isomer of methamphetamine or phencyclidine, containing a salt of an isomer of methamphetamine or phencyclidine shall, upon conviction, be sentenced to a mandatory minimum term of imprisonment and a fine as set forth in this subsection:

(i) when the aggregate weight of the compound or mixture containing the substance involved is at least five grams and less than ten grams; three years in prison and a fine of $15,000 or such larger amount as is sufficient to exhaust the assets utilized in and the proceeds from the illegal activity; however, if at the time of sentencing the defendant has been convicted of another drug trafficking offense: five years in prison and $30,000 or such larger amount as is sufficient to exhaust the assets utilized in and the proceeds from the illegal activity;

(ii) when the aggregate weight of the compound or mixture containing the substance involved is at least ten grams and less than 100 grams; four years in prison and a fine of $25,000 or such larger amount as is sufficient to exhaust the assets utilized in and the proceeds from the illegal activity; however, if at the time of sentencing the defendant has been convicted of another drug trafficking offense: seven years in prison and $50,000 or such larger amount as is sufficient to exhaust the assets utilized in and the proceeds from the illegal activity; and

(iii) when the aggregate weight of the compound or mixture containing the substance involved is at least 100 grams; five years in prison and a fine of $50,000 or such larger amount as is sufficient to exhaust the assets utilized in and the proceeds from the illegal activity; however, if at the time of sentencing the defendant has been convicted of another drug trafficking offense: eight years in prison and $50,000 or such larger amount as is

sufficient to exhaust the assets utilized in and the proceeds from the illegal activity.

(5) A person who is convicted of violating section 13(a)(14), (30) or (37) of The Controlled Substance, Drug, Device and Cosmetic Act, and who, in the course of the offense, manufactures, delivers, brings into this Commonwealth or possesses with intent to manufacture or deliver amphetamine or any salt, optical isomer, or salt of an optical isomer, or a mixture containing any such substances shall, when the aggregate weight of the compound or mixture containing the substance involved is at least five grams, be sentenced to two and one-half years in prison and a fine of $15,000 or such larger amount as is sufficient to exhaust the assets utilized in and the proceeds from the illegal activity; however, if at the time of sentencing the defendant has been convicted of another drug trafficking offense: be sentenced to five years in prison and $30,000 or such larger amount as is sufficient to exhaust the assets utilized in and the proceeds from the illegal activity.

(6) A person who is convicted of violating section 13(a)(14), (30) or (37) of The Controlled Substance, Drug, Device and Cosmetic Act where the controlled substance is methaqualone shall, upon conviction, be sentenced to a mandatory minimum term of imprisonment and a fine as set forth in this subsection:

(i) when the aggregate weight of the compound or mixture containing the substance involved is at least 50 tablets, capsules, caplets or other dosage units, or 25 grams and less than 200 tablets, capsules, caplets or other dosage units, or 100 grams; one year in prison and a fine of $2,500 or such larger amount as is sufficient to exhaust the assets utilized in and the proceeds from the illegal activity; however, if at the time of sentencing the defendant has been convicted of another drug trafficking offense: three years in prison and $5,000 or such larger amount as is sufficient to exhaust the assets utilized in and the proceeds from the illegal activity; and

(ii) when the aggregate weight of the compound or mixture containing the substance involved is at least 200 tablets, capsules, caplets or other dosage units, or more than 100 grams; two and one-half years in prison and a fine of $15,000 or such larger amount as is sufficient to exhaust the assets utilized in and the proceeds from the illegal activity; however, if at the time of sentencing the defendant has been convicted of another drug trafficking offense: five years in prison and $30,000 or such larger amount as is sufficient to exhaust the assets utilized in and the proceeds from the illegal activity.

(7) A person who is convicted of violating section 13(a)(14), (30) or (37) of The Controlled Substance, Drug, Device and Cosmetic Act where the controlled substance or a mixture containing it is heroin shall, upon conviction, be sentenced as set forth in this paragraph:

(i) when the aggregate weight of the compound or mixture containing the heroin involved is at least 1.0 gram but less than 5.0 grams the sentence shall be a mandatory minimum term of two years in prison and a fine of $5,000 or such larger amount as is sufficient to exhaust the assets utilized in and the proceeds from the illegal activity; however, if at the time of sentencing the defendant has been convicted of another drug trafficking offense: a mandatory minimum term of three years in prison and $10,000 or such larger amount as is sufficient to exhaust the assets utilized in and the proceeds from the illegal activity;

(ii) when the aggregate weight of the compound or mixture containing the heroin involved is at least 5.0 grams but less than 50 grams: a mandatory minimum term of three years in prison and a fine of $15,000 or such larger amount as is sufficient to exhaust the assets utilized in and the proceeds from the illegal activity; however, if at the time of sentencing the defendant has been convicted of another drug trafficking offense: a mandatory minimum term of five years in prison and $30,000 or such larger amount as is sufficient to exhaust the assets utilized in and the proceeds from the illegal activity; and

(iii) when the aggregate weight of the compound or mixture containing the heroin involved is 50 grams or greater: a mandatory minimum term of five years in prison and a fine of $25,000 or such larger amount as is sufficient to exhaust the assets utilized in and the proceeds from the illegal activity; however, if at the time of sentencing the defendant has been convicted of another drug trafficking offense: a mandatory minimum term of seven years in prison and $50,000 or such larger amount as is sufficient to exhaust the assets utilized in and the proceeds from the illegal activity.

(8) A person who is convicted of violating section 13(a)(12), (14) or (30) of The Controlled Substance, Drug, Device and Cosmetic Act where the controlled substance or a mixture containing it is 3,4-methylenedioxyamphetamine (MDA); 3,4-methylenedioxymethamphetamine (MDMA); 5-methoxy-3,4-methylenedioxyamphetamine (MMDA); 3,4-methylenedioxy-N-ethylamphetamine; N-hydroxy-3,4-methylenedioxyamphetamine; or their salts, isomers and salts of isomers, whenever the existence of such salts, isomers and salts of isomers is possible within the specific chemical designation, shall, upon conviction, be sentenced as set forth in this paragraph:

(i) When the aggregate weight of the compound or mixture containing the substance involved is at least 50 tablets, capsules, caplets or other dosage units, or 15 grams and less than 100 tablets, capsules, caplets or other dosage units, or less than 30 grams, the person is guilty of a felony and, upon conviction thereof, shall be sentenced to imprisonment not exceeding five years or to pay a fine not exceeding $15,000, or both.

(ii) When the aggregate weight of the compound or mixture containing the substance involved is at least 100 tablets, capsules, caplets or other dosage units, or 30 grams and less than 1,000 tablets, capsules, caplets or other dosage units, or less than 300 grams, the person is guilty of a felony and, upon conviction thereof, shall be sentenced to imprisonment not exceeding ten years or to pay a fine not exceeding $100,000, or both.

(iii) When the aggregate weight of the compound or mixture containing the substance involved is at least 1,000 tablets, capsules, caplets or other dosage units, or 300 grams, the person is guilty of a felony and, upon conviction thereof, shall be sentenced to imprisonment not exceeding 15 years or to pay a fine not exceeding $250,000, or both.

(a.1) Previous conviction.--For purposes of this section, it shall be deemed that a defendant has been convicted of another drug trafficking offense when the defendant has been convicted of another offense under section 13(a)(14), (30) or (37) of The Controlled Substance, Drug, Device and Cosmetic Act, or of a similar offense under any statute of any state or the United States, whether or not judgment of sentence has been imposed concerning that offense.

(b) Proof of sentencing.--Provisions of this section shall not be an element of the crime. Notice of the applicability of this section to the defendant shall not be required prior to conviction, but reasonable notice of the Commonwealth's intention to proceed under this section shall be provided after conviction and before sentencing. The applicability of this section shall be determined at sentencing. The court shall consider evidence presented at trial, shall afford the Commonwealth and the defendant an opportunity to present necessary additional evidence and shall determine, by a preponderance of the evidence, if this section is applicable.

(c) Mandatory sentencing.--There shall be no authority in any court to impose on an offender to which this section is applicable a lesser sentence than provided for herein or to place the offender on probation, parole or work release or to suspend sentence. Nothing in this section shall prevent the sentencing court from imposing a sentence greater than provided herein. Sentencing guidelines promulgated by the Pennsylvania Commission on Sentencing shall not supersede the mandatory sentences provided herein. Disposition under section 17 or 18 of The Controlled Substance, Drug, Device and Cosmetic Act shall not be available to a defendant to which this section applies.

(d) Appellate review.--If a sentencing court refuses to apply this section where applicable, the Commonwealth shall have the right to appellate review of the action of the sentencing court. The appellate court shall vacate the sentence and remand the case to the sentencing court for imposition of a sentence in accordance with this section if it finds that the sentence was imposed in violation of this section.

(e) Forfeiture.--Assets against which a petition seeking forfeiture has been filed and is pending or against which the Commonwealth has indicated an intention to file a petition seeking forfeiture shall not be subject to a fine. Nothing in this section shall prevent a fine from being imposed on assets which have been subject to an unsuccessful forfeiture petition.

(f) Growing plants.--When the controlled substance is marijuana in the form of growing plants and the number of plants is nine or less, weighing may be accomplished by law enforcement officials utilizing any certified scale convenient to the place of arrest for the purpose of determining the weight of the growing marijuana plant. The aggregate weight of the plant is to include the whole plant including the root system if possible. The weight is not to include any substance not a part of the growing plant.

(Mar. 25, 1988, P.L.262, No.31, eff. July 1, 1988; Dec. 19, 1990, P.L.1451, No.219, eff. imd.; June 22, 2000, P.L.345, No.41, eff. 60 days; Dec. 9, 2002, P.L.1439, No.183, eff. 60 days; June 10, 2003, P.L.10, No.4, eff. imd.; July 5, 2012, P.L.1050, No.122, eff. July 1, 2013; June 29, 2017, P.L.247, No.13, eff. July 1, 2017)

2017 Amendment. Act 13 amended subsec. (e).

2012 Amendment. Act 122 amended subsec. (c).

2003 Amendment. Act 4 amended subsec. (a)(8).

2000 Amendment. Act 41 added subsec. (a)(7).

Cross References. Section 7508 is referred to in sections 704, 706 of Title 3 (Agriculture); sections 9711, 9712.1 of Title 42 (Judiciary and Judicial Procedure); sections 3903, 4103, 4503 of Title 61 (Prisons and Parole).

§ 7508.1. Substance Abuse Education and Demand Reduction Fund.

(a) Establishment.--The Substance Abuse Education and Demand Reduction Fund is hereby established as an account in the State Treasury. This fund shall be administered by the Pennsylvania Commission on Crime and Delinquency and shall be comprised of costs imposed and collected in accordance with the provisions of this section. All moneys in the fund and the interest accruing thereon are hereby appropriated, upon approval of the Governor, to the commission to carry out the provisions of this section.

(b) Imposition.--Unless the court finds that undue hardship would result, a mandatory cost of $100, which shall be in addition to any other costs imposed pursuant to statutory authority, shall automatically be assessed on any individual convicted, adjudicated delinquent or granted Accelerated Rehabilitative Disposition or any individual who pleads guilty or nolo contendere for a violation of the act of April 14, 1972 (P.L.233, No.64), known as The Controlled Substance, Drug, Device and Cosmetic Act, or a violation of 75 Pa.C.S. § 3802 (relating to driving under influence of alcohol or controlled substance).

(c) Additional assessment.--In addition to the assessment required by subsection (b), a person convicted of or adjudicated delinquent for a violation of 75 Pa.C.S. § 3802 shall be assessed $200 where the amount of alcohol by weight in the blood of the person is equal to or greater than 0.16% at the time a chemical test is performed on a sample of the person's breath, blood or urine. For the purposes of this subsection, the sample of the person's blood, breath or urine shall be taken within two hours after the person is placed under arrest.

(d) Collection.--Costs imposed under this section shall be collected in accordance with local court rules by the clerk of courts in the county where the violation has occurred. Of the amount collected, 50% shall remain in that county to be used for substance abuse treatment or prevention programs and the remaining 50% shall be deposited into the Substance Abuse Education and Demand Reduction Fund established under this section.

(e) Application.--All costs provided for in this section shall be in addition to and not in lieu of any fine authorized by law or required to be imposed under the act of November 24, 1998 (P.L.882, No.111), known as the Crime Victims Act, or any other law. Nothing in this section shall be construed to affect, suspend or diminish any other criminal sanction, penalty or property forfeiture permitted by law.

(f) Grants.--Notwithstanding any other provision of law, the commission shall, upon written application and subsequent approval, use moneys received under this section to annually award grants to approved applicants in the following manner:

(1) (i) Subject to the provisions of subparagraph (ii), 45% of grant moneys deposited into the fund each fiscal year shall be made available to nonprofit organizations to provide research-based approaches to prevention, intervention, training, treatment and education services to reduce substance abuse or to provide resources to assist families in assessing the services. Nonprofit organizations may jointly apply for grant moneys with a local government unit but shall not be required to do so.

(ii) (A) Up to 20% of grant moneys available under subparagraph (i) may be used to:

(I) Assist in the start-up of victim impact panel programs under 75 Pa.C.S. § 3804(f.1) (relating to penalties).

(II) Study the impact outcome and benefits of victim impact panels within this Commonwealth, including the impact of victim impact panels on driving under the influence recidivism and their impact on the well-being of participating victims.

(III) Provide assistance for the ongoing operation of victim impact panels.

(B) An applicant for a grant under this subparagraph may be an entity other than a nonprofit organization.

(2) Twenty percent of grant moneys deposited into the fund each fiscal year shall be made available to eligible organizations to educate youth, caregivers of youth and employers about the dangers of substance abuse and to increase the awareness of the benefits of a drug-free Pennsylvania through media-related efforts that may include public service announcements, public awareness campaigns and media literacy.

(3) Twenty percent of grant moneys deposited into the fund each fiscal year shall be made available to eligible organizations to educate employers, unions and employees about the dangers of substance abuse in the workplace and provide comprehensive drug-free workplace programs and technical resources for businesses, including, but not limited to, training for working parents to keep their children drug free.

(4) Ten percent of the grant moneys deposited into the fund each fiscal year shall be transferred annually to the Community Drug Abuse Prevention Grant Program within the Office of Attorney General.

(g) Administration.--The commission shall develop guidelines and procedures necessary to implement the grant program. The commission shall equitably distribute grant moneys to approved applicants under subsection (f)(1) and eligible organizations under subsection (f)(2) and (3). Each fiscal year the commission shall make available grant moneys equaling, except for funds to be transferred under subsection (f)(4) and administrative funds as provided for in this subsection, the balance of moneys deposited into the fund as of June 30 of the previous fiscal year. No more than 5% of total moneys deposited in the fund during a fiscal year may be used by the commission to administer the provisions of this section.

(h) Other initiatives.--Funds disbursed under this section shall not supplant Federal, State or local funds that would have otherwise been made available for substance abuse prevention, education, support, treatment and outreach initiatives.

(i) Definitions.--As used in this section, the following words and phrases shall have the meanings given to them in this subsection:

"Commission." The Pennsylvania Commission on Crime and Delinquency.

"Eligible organization." A Statewide organization that meets all of the following requirements:

(1) Possesses five or more consecutive years of experience carrying out substance abuse education and demand reduction or substance abuse treatment programs.

(2) Maintains a drug-free workplace policy.

(3) Has as its purpose the reduction of substance abuse.

"Fund." The Substance Abuse Education and Demand Reduction Fund established by this section.

(Dec. 9, 2002, P.L.1539, No.198, eff. 60 days; Sept. 30, 2003, P.L.120, No.24, eff. Feb. 1, 2004; May 11, 2006, P.L.155, No.36, eff. imd.)

2006 Amendment. Act 36 amended subsecs. (f), (g) and (i). See the preamble to Act 36 in the appendix to this title for special provisions relating to legislative findings and declarations.

2003 Amendment. Act 24 amended subsecs. (b) and (c).

2002 Amendment. Act 198 added section 7508.1.

§ 7508.2. Operation of methamphetamine laboratory.

(a) Offense defined.--A person commits the offense of operating a methamphetamine laboratory if the person knowingly causes a chemical reaction involving ephedrine, pseudoephedrine or phenylpropanolamine, or any other precursor or reagent substance under section 13.1 of the act of April 14, 1972 (P.L.233, No.64), known as The Controlled Substance, Drug, Device and Cosmetic Act, for the purpose of manufacturing methamphetamine or preparing a precursor or reagent substance for the manufacture of methamphetamine.

(b) Grading.--

(1) Except as provided in paragraph (2), an offense under this subsection constitutes a felony of the second degree and is also subject to section 1110 (relating to restitution for cleanup of clandestine laboratories).

(2) A person who violates subsection (a) commits a felony of the first degree if the chemical reaction occurs within 1,000 feet of the real property on which is located a public, private or parochial school, a college or university or a nursery school or day care center, or within 250 feet of the real property on which is located a recreation center or playground. The person shall also be subject to section 1110.

(c) Applicability.--

(1) This section does not apply to the manufacturing operation of a licensed pharmaceutical company in the normal course of business.

(2) Nothing in this section shall be construed to preclude a prosecution for the same or similar activity under The Controlled Substance, Drug, Device and Cosmetic Act.

(d) Definitions.--As used in this section, the following words and phrases shall have the meanings given to them in this subsection unless the context clearly indicates otherwise:

"Manufacture." The term shall have the same meaning given to the term in section 2(b) of the act of April 14, 1972 (P.L.233, No.64), known as The Controlled Substance, Drug, Device and Cosmetic Act.

(Apr. 29, 2010, P.L.174, No.18, eff. 60 days)

2010 Amendment. Act 18 added section 7508.2.

Cross References. Section 7508.2 is referred to in section 6303 of Title 23 (Domestic Relations).

§ 7509. Furnishing drug-free urine.

(a) Unlawful sale or attempt.--A person commits a misdemeanor of the third degree if he offers for sale, sells, causes to be sold or gives drug-free urine for the purpose of or with the intent or knowledge that the urine will be used for evading or causing deceitful results in a test for the presence of drugs.

(b) Use or attempt.--A person commits a misdemeanor of the third degree if he uses or attempts to use drug-free urine as provided in subsection (a) for the purpose of evading or causing deceitful results in a test for the presence of drugs.

(Nov. 26, 1997, P.L.500, No.52, eff. 60 days)

1997 Amendment. Act 52 added section 7509.

§ 7510. Municipal housing code avoidance (Repealed).

2015 Repeal. Section 7510 was repealed July 10, 2015 (P.L.162, No.34), effective in 60 days.

§ 7511. Control of alarm devices and automatic dialing devices.

(a) Automatic dialing devices.--A person may not attach or use an automatic dialing device without doing all of the following:

(1) Providing the disclosure under subsection (b).

(2) Obtaining prior written approval from a public safety agency to use the automatic dialing device to alert the public safety agency of an alarm condition. The public safety agency shall not be responsible for any costs for the installation and maintenance of any dedicated telephone line or equipment associated with the alarm termination.

(b) Disclosure.--A person seeking approval under subsection (a) shall disclose the telephone number of a person to be contacted if the automatic dialing device is activated and all relevant facts concerning the design and layout of the premises to be protected by the automatic dialing device. The person shall inform the public safety agency of any change in the information required by this subsection as soon as practicable.

(c) False alarms prohibited.--

(1) A person that owns, uses or possesses an alarm device or automatic dialing device may not, after causing or permitting three false alarms to occur in a consecutive 12-month period, cause or permit a subsequent false alarm to occur in the same consecutive 12-month period. A person that violates this paragraph commits a summary offense and shall, upon conviction, be sentenced to pay a fine of not more than $300.

(2) Venue for prosecution of an offense under this subsection shall lie at any of the following places:

(i) Where the alarm originated.

(ii) Where the alarm was received by the:

(A) public service agency; or

(B) third person designated to notify the public service agency.

(3) Notwithstanding 42 Pa.C.S. § 3733 (relating to deposits into account) or any other law, the disposition of fines shall be as follows:

(i) The fine shall be paid to the municipality if all of the following apply:

(A) The public safety agency which responded to the false alarm serves the municipality.

(B) The prosecution is initiated by the public safety agency under clause (A) or by the municipality.

(ii) The full amount of the fine shall be paid to the Commonwealth if all of the following apply:

(A) The Pennsylvania State Police is the public safety agency which responded to the false alarm.

(B) The prosecution is initiated by the Pennsylvania State Police.

(C) There is no prosecution under subparagraph (i).

(d) Suspension or revocation of approval.--The public safety agency may refuse, revoke or suspend the approval granted under subsection (a) if the public safety agency determines any of the following:

(1) The request for approval contains a statement of material fact which is false.

(2) The person failed to comply with this section.

(3) The person violated subsection (c).

(e) Local regulation of installers.--

(1) General rule.--Except as set forth in paragraph (2), nothing in this section shall prohibit a municipality from requiring any individual who installs or inspects alarm devices in such municipality to acquire a license, meet educational requirements or pass an examination relating to competence to perform such installations. Nothing in this section shall preclude municipalities from doing any of the following:

(i) Denying or revoking local permits for failure to comply with local ordinances.

(ii) Levying lawful taxes and fees.

(iii) Requiring the purchase of a business privilege license.

(2) Limitation.--A municipality may not require a licensed electrical contractor to acquire a separate or additional license or certification to install or inspect alarm devices if the electrical contractor is licensed by the municipality and has passed an examination in the National Electrical Code, a similar code or local electrical code and has at least two years' experience as an electrical contractor.

(f) Definitions.--As used in this section, the following words and phrases shall have the meanings given to them in this subsection:

"Alarm." A communication to a public safety agency indicating that a crime, fire or other emergency warranting immediate action by that public safety agency has occurred or is occurring.

"Alarm device." A device designed to automatically transmit an alarm:

(1) directly to a public safety agency; or

(2) to a person that is instructed to notify the public safety agency of the alarm.

"Automatic dialing device." A device which is interconnected to a telephone line and preprogrammed to transmit the coded signal of an alarm to a dedicated telephone trunk line or to dial a predetermined telephone number to an alarm to a public safety agency.

"Dedicated telephone trunk line." A telephone line or lines which serve a public safety agency which is dedicated to receiving transmissions from an automatic dialing device.

"False alarm." The activation of an alarm device to which a public safety agency responds when a crime, fire or other emergency has not occurred.

"Person." An individual, corporation, partnership, incorporated association or other similar entity.

"Public safety agency." The Pennsylvania State Police or any municipal police or fire department.

(June 18, 1998, P.L.503, No.70, eff. 60 days; Dec. 21, 1998, P.L.1103, No.149, eff. 60 days)

1998 Amendments. Act 70 added section 7511 and Act 149 amended subsec. (e).

Cross References. Section 7511 is referred to in section 304 of Title 53 (Municipalities Generally).

§ 7512. Criminal use of communication facility.

(a) Offense defined.--A person commits a felony of the third degree if that person uses a communication facility to commit, cause or facilitate the commission or the attempt thereof of any crime which constitutes a felony under this title or under the act of April 14, 1972

(P.L.233, No.64), known as The Controlled Substance, Drug, Device and Cosmetic Act. Every instance where the communication facility is utilized constitutes a separate offense under this section.

(b) Penalty.--A person who violates this section shall, upon conviction, be sentenced to pay a fine of not more than $15,000 or to imprisonment for not more than seven years, or both.

(c) Definition.--As used in this section, the term "communication facility" means a public or private instrumentality used or useful in the transmission of signs, signals, writing, images, sounds, data or intelligence of any nature transmitted in whole or in part, including, but not limited to, telephone, wire, radio, electromagnetic, photoelectronic or photo-optical systems or the mail.

(Dec. 21, 1998, P.L.1240, No.157, eff. 60 days)

1998 Amendment. Act 157 added section 7512.

§ 7513. Restriction on alcoholic beverages (Repealed).

2003 Repeal. Section 7513 was repealed September 30, 2003 (P.L.120, No.24), effective February 1, 2004. Section 21(1) of Act 24 provided that the repeal of section 7513 shall not affect offenses committed prior to February 1, 2004.

§ 7514. Operating a motor vehicle not equipped with ignition interlock (Repealed).

2003 Repeal. Section 7514 was repealed September 30, 2003, (P.L.120, No.24), effective February 1, 2004. Section 21(2) of Act 24 provided that the repeal of section 7514 shall not affect offenses committed prior to February 1, 2004, or civil and administrative penalties imposed as a result of those offenses. Section 21(3) of Act 24 provided that an individual sentenced under section 7514 shall be subject to administrative and civil sanctions in effect on January 31, 2004. The subject matter is now contained in Chapter 38 of Title 75 (Vehicles).

§ 7515. Contingent compensation.

(a) Offense defined.--

(1) No person may compensate or incur an obligation to compensate any person to engage in lobbying for compensation

contingent in whole or in part upon the passage, defeat, approval or veto of legislation.

(2) No person may engage or agree to engage in lobbying for compensation contingent in whole or in part upon the passage, defeat, approval or veto of legislation.

(b) Penalty.--Any person who violates this section commits a misdemeanor of the third degree.

(c) Definition.--As used in this section, the term "lobbying" means an effort to influence State legislative action for economic consideration.

(Dec. 9, 2002, P.L.1391, No.172, eff. imd.)

2002 Amendment. Act 172 added section 7515.

Cross References. Section 7515 is referred to in section 13A11 of Title 65 (Public Officers).

§ 7516. Greyhound racing and simulcasting.

(a) Racing.--A person who holds, conducts or operates a greyhound race for public exhibition in this Commonwealth for monetary remuneration commits a misdemeanor of the first degree.

(b) Simulcasting.--

(1) A person shall not transmit or receive interstate or intrastate simulcasting of a greyhound race in this Commonwealth for monetary remuneration.

(2) A court of common pleas may impose a civil penalty of up to $10,000 upon any person who violates this subsection.

(May 21, 2004, P.L.232, No.36, eff. 60 days; July 7, 2011, P.L.210, No.32, eff. 60 days)

§ 7517. Commemorative service demonstration activities.

(a) Legislative intent.--The General Assembly finds and declares that:

(1) Families have a substantial interest in organizing and attending commemorative services for deceased relatives.

(2) The interests of families in privately and peacefully mourning the loss of deceased relatives are violated when commemorative services are targeted for picketing and other public demonstrations.

(3) Picketing of commemorative services causes emotional disturbance and distress to grieving families who participate in commemorative services.

(4) Full opportunity exists under the terms and provisions of this section for the exercise of freedom of speech and other constitutional rights at times other than within one hour prior to, during and one hour following the commemorative services.

(b) Offense defined.--A person commits a misdemeanor of the third degree if the person engages in demonstration activities within 500 feet of any cemetery, mortuary, church or other location being utilized for the purposes of a commemorative service within one hour prior to, during and one hour following the commemorative service.

(c) Definitions.--As used in this section, the following words and phrases shall have the meanings given to them in this subsection:

"Commemorative service." An event involving the gathering of individuals who assemble:

(1) At a cemetery or other location during the burial, funeral, ceremony or memorial service of a specific deceased person to mourn or honor the deceased person or to pay respect to the family of the deceased person.

(2) In a building during the viewing, visitation, burial, funeral, ceremony or memorial service of a specific deceased person to mourn or honor the deceased person or to pay respect to the family of the deceased person.

(3) To participate in a procession to a cemetery, building or other location in which a viewing, visitation, burial, funeral, ceremony or memorial service of a specific deceased person is to be conducted to mourn or honor the deceased person or to pay respect to the family of the deceased person.

"Demonstration activities." Any of the following:

(1) Any picketing or similar conduct.

(2) Any oration, speech or use of sound amplification equipment or device or similar conduct that is not part of a commemorative service.

(3) The display of any placard, sign, banner, flag or similar device, unless such display is part of a commemorative service.

(4) The distribution of any handbill, pamphlet, leaflet or other written or printed matter, other than a program distributed as part of a commemorative service.

(June 30, 2006, P.L.288, No.63, eff. 60 days)

2006 Amendment. Act 63 added section 7517.

Cross References. Section 7517 is referred to in section 8320 of Title 42 (Judiciary and Judicial Procedure).

CHAPTER 76 COMPUTER OFFENSES

Subchapter
A. General Provisions
B. Hacking and Similar Offenses
C. Internet Child Pornography
D. Unlawful Use of Computers
E. Electronic Mail

Enactment. Chapter 76 was added December 16, 2002, P.L.1953, No.226, effective in 60 days.
Cross References. Chapter 76 is referred to in section 3575 of Title 42 (Judiciary and Judicial Procedure).

SUBCHAPTER A
GENERAL PROVISIONS

§ 7601. Definitions.

The following words and phrases when used in this chapter shall have the meanings given to them in this section unless the context clearly indicates otherwise:

"Access." To intercept, instruct, communicate with, store data in, retrieve data from or otherwise make use of any resources of a computer, computer system, computer network or database.

"Computer." An electronic, magnetic, optical, hydraulic, organic or other high-speed data processing device or system which performs logic, arithmetic or memory functions and includes all input, output, processing, storage, software or communication facilities which are connected or related to the device in a system or network.

"Computer data." A representation of information, knowledge, facts, concepts or instructions which is being prepared or has been prepared and is intended to be processed, is being processed or has been processed in a computer or computer network and may be in any form, whether readable only by a computer or only by a human or by either, including, but not limited to, computer printouts, magnetic storage media, punched card or stored internally in the memory of the computer.

"Computer network." The interconnection of two or more computers through the usage of satellite, microwave, line or other communication medium.

"Computer operation." Arithmetic, logical, monitoring, storage or retrieval functions and any combination thereof, including, but not limited to, communication with, storage of data to or retrieval of data from any device or human hand manipulation of electronic or magnetic impulses. In reference to a particular computer, the term also includes any function for which that computer was generally designed.

"Computer program." An ordered set of instructions or statements and related data that, when automatically executed in actual or modified form in a computer system, causes it to perform specified functions.

"Computer software." A set of computer programs, procedures or associated documentation concerned with the operation of a computer system.

"Computer system." A set of related, connected or unconnected computer equipment, devices and software.

"Computer virus." A computer program copied to, created on or installed to a computer, computer network, computer program, computer software or computer system without the informed consent of the owner of the computer, computer network, computer program, computer software or computer system that may replicate itself and that causes or can cause unauthorized activities within or by the computer, computer network, computer program, computer software or computer system.

"Database." A representation of information, knowledge, facts, concepts or instructions which are being prepared or processed or have been prepared or processed in a formalized manner and are intended for use in a computer, computer system or computer network, including, but not limited to, computer printouts, magnetic storage media, punched cards or data stored internally in the memory of the computer.

"Denial-of-service attack." An explicit attempt to prevent legitimate users of a service from using that service, including, but not limited to:

(1) flooding a network, thereby preventing legitimate network traffic;

(2) disrupting connections between two computers, thereby preventing access to a service;

(3) preventing a particular person from accessing a service; or

(4) disrupting service to a specific computer system or person.

"Deprive." To withhold property of another permanently or for so extended a period as to appropriate a major portion of its economic value, or with intent to restore only upon payment of reward or other compensation, or to dispose of the property so as to make it unlikely that the owner will recover it.

"Economic value." The market value of property or an instrument which creates, releases, discharges or otherwise affects a valuable legal right, privilege or obligation at the time and place of the crime or, if such cannot be satisfactorily ascertained, the cost of replacement of the property or instrument within a reasonable time after the crime.

"Electronic mail service provider." A person who is an intermediary in sending or receiving electronic mail or who provides to end-users of electronic mail services the ability to send or receive electronic mail.

"Electronic mail transmission information." Information used to identify the origin or destination of a transmission or to aid in its routing, including information recorded as part of electronic mail whether or not such information is displayed initially to the user upon receipt of electronic mail, that purports to represent the information used to identify the origin or destination of a transmission or to aid in its routing.

"Established business relationship." A prior or existing relationship formed by a voluntary two-way communication initiated by a person or entity and a recipient with or without an exchange of consideration, on the basis of an inquiry, application purchase or transaction by the recipient regarding products or services offered by such persons or entity. In regard to an inquiry, the person or entity shall obtain the consent of a recipient beyond the initial inquiry. An established business relationship does not exist if the recipient requests to be removed from the distribution lists of an initiator.

"Fax." The transmission of the facsimile of a document through a connection with a telephone or computer network.

"Financial instrument." Includes, but is not limited to, any check, draft, warrant, money order, note, certificate of deposit, letter of credit, bill of exchange, credit or debit card, transaction authorization mechanism, marketable security or any computer system representation thereof.

"Internet service provider." A person who furnishes a service that enables users to access content, information, electronic mail or other services offered over the Internet.

"Person." Any individual, corporation, partnership, association, organization or entity capable of holding a legal or beneficial interest in property.

"Property." Includes, but is not limited to, financial instruments, computer software and programs in either machine or human readable form, and anything of value, tangible or intangible.

"Telecommunication device." Any type of instrument, device, machine or equipment which is capable of transmitting, acquiring, decrypting or receiving any telephonic, electronic, data, Internet access, audio, video, microwave or radio transmissions, signals, communications or services, including the receipt, acquisition, transmission or decryption of all such communications, transmissions, signals or services over any cable television, telephone, satellite, microwave, radio or wireless distribution system or facility, or any part, accessory or component thereof, including any computer circuit, security module, smart card, software, computer chip, electronic mechanism or other component, accessory or part which is capable of facilitating the transmission, decryption, acquisition or reception of all such communications transmissions, signals or services.

"Wireless advertisement." The initiation of a telephone call or a message capable of providing text, graphic or image messages by a commercial mobile service provider, unlicensed wireless services provider or common carrier wireless exchange access service provider for the purpose of marketing goods or services. The term does not include a call or message to a person with that person's prior express invitation or permission or to a person with whom the caller has an established business relationship.

"World Wide Web." Includes, but is not limited to, a computer server-based file archive accessible over the Internet, using a hypertext transfer protocol, file transfer or other similar protocols.

§ 7602. Jurisdiction.

An offense under this chapter may be deemed to have been committed either at the place where conduct constituting an element of the offense occurred or at the place where the result which is an element of the offense occurred within this Commonwealth in accordance with section 102 (relating to territorial applicability). It shall be no defense to a violation of this chapter that some of the acts constituting the offense occurred outside of this Commonwealth.

§ 7603. Restitution.

Upon conviction of an offense under section 7611 (relating to unlawful use of computer and other computer crimes), 7612 (relating to disruption of service) or 7616 (relating to distribution of computer virus), the sentence shall include an order for restitution to the victim for:

(1) the cost of repairing or replacing the affected computer, computer system, computer network, computer software, computer program, computer database, World Wide Web site or telecommunication device;

(2) lost profits for the period that the computer, computer system, computer network, computer software, computer program, computer database, World Wide Web site or telecommunication device is not usable; or

(3) the cost of replacing or restoring the data lost or damaged as a result of a violation of section 7611, 7612 or 7616.

§ 7604. Concurrent jurisdiction.

The Attorney General shall have concurrent prosecutorial jurisdiction with the county district attorney for violations of this chapter. No person charged with a violation of this section by the Attorney General shall have standing to challenge the authority of the Attorney General to prosecute the case, and, if any such challenge is made, the challenge shall be dismissed and no relief shall be available in the courts of this Commonwealth to the person making the challenge.

§ 7605. Defense.

It is a defense to an action brought pursuant to Subchapter B (relating to hacking and similar offenses) that the actor:

(1) was entitled by law or contract to engage in the conduct constituting the offense; or

(2) reasonably believed that he had the authorization or permission of the owner, lessee, licensee, authorized holder, authorized possessor or agent of the computer, computer network, computer software, computer system, database or telecommunication device or that the owner or authorized holder would have authorized or provided permission to engage in the conduct constituting the offense. As used in this section, the term "authorization" includes express or implied consent, including by trade usage, course of dealing, course of performance or commercial programming practices.

§ 7606. Construction.

Nothing in Subchapter B (relating to hacking and similar offenses) shall be construed to interfere with or prohibit terms or conditions in a contract or license related to a computer, computer network, computer software, computer system, database or telecommunication device or software or hardware designed to allow a computer, computer network, computer software, computer system, database or telecommunications device to operate in the ordinary course of a lawful business or that is designed to allow an owner or authorized holder of information to protect data information or rights in it.

SUBCHAPTER B
HACKING AND SIMILAR OFFENSES

Cross References. Subchapter B is referred to in sections 7605, 7606 of this title.

§ 7611. Unlawful use of computer and other computer crimes.

(a) Offense defined.--A person commits the offense of unlawful use of a computer if he:

(1) accesses or exceeds authorization to access, alters, damages or destroys any computer, computer system, computer network, computer software, computer program, computer database, World Wide Web site or telecommunication device or any part thereof with the intent to interrupt the normal functioning of a person or to devise or execute any scheme or artifice to defraud or deceive or control property or services by means of false or fraudulent pretenses, representations or promises;

(2) intentionally and without authorization accesses or exceeds authorization to access, alters, interferes with the operation of, damages or destroys any computer, computer system, computer network, computer software, computer program, computer database, World Wide Web site or telecommunication device or any part thereof; or

(3) intentionally or knowingly and without authorization gives or publishes a password, identifying code, personal identification number or other confidential information about a computer, computer system, computer network, computer database, World Wide Web site or telecommunication device.

(b) Grading.--An offense under this section shall constitute a felony of the third degree.

(c) Prosecution not prohibited.-- Prosecution for an offense under this section shall not prohibit prosecution under any other section of this title.

Cross References. Section 7611 is referred to in section 7603 of this title.

§ 7612. Disruption of service.

(a) Offense defined.--A person commits an offense if he intentionally or knowingly engages in a scheme or artifice, including, but not limited to, a denial of service attack upon any computer, computer system, computer network, computer software, computer program, computer server, computer database, World Wide Web site or telecommunication device or any part thereof that is designed to block, impede or deny the access of information or initiation or completion of any sale or transaction by users of that computer, computer system, computer network, computer software, computer program, computer server or database or any part thereof.

(b) Grading.--An offense under this section shall constitute a felony of the third degree.

Cross References. Section 7612 is referred to in section 7603 of this title.

§ 7613. Computer theft.

(a) Offense defined.--A person commits an offense if he unlawfully accesses or exceeds his authorization to access any data from a computer, computer system or computer network or takes or copies any supporting documentation whether existing or residing internal or external to a computer, computer system or computer network of another with the intent to deprive him thereof.

(b) Grading.--An offense under this section shall constitute a felony of the third degree.

§ 7614. Unlawful duplication.

(a) Offense defined.--A person commits the offense of unlawful duplication if he makes or causes to be made an unauthorized copy, in any form, including, but not limited to, any printed or electronic form of computer data, computer programs or computer software residing in, communicated by or produced by a computer or computer network.

(b) Grading.--An offense under subsection (a) shall be graded as follows:

(1) An offense under this section shall constitute a felony of the third degree.

(2) If the economic value of the duplicated material is greater than $2,500, the grading of the offense shall be one grade higher than specified in paragraph (1).

§ 7615. Computer trespass.

(a) Offense defined.--A person commits the offense of computer trespass if he knowingly and without authority or in excess of given authority uses a computer or computer network with the intent to:

(1) temporarily or permanently remove computer data, computer programs or computer software from a computer or computer network;

(2) cause a computer to malfunction, regardless of the amount of time the malfunction persists;

(3) alter or erase any computer data, computer programs or computer software;

(4) effect the creation or alteration of a financial instrument or of an electronic transfer of funds; or

(5) cause physical injury to the property of another.

(b) Grading.--An offense under this section shall constitute a felony of the third degree.

§ 7616. Distribution of computer virus.

(a) Offense defined.--A person commits an offense if the person intentionally or knowingly sells, gives or otherwise distributes or possesses with the intent to sell, give or distribute computer software or a computer program that is designed or has the capability to:

(1) prevent, impede, control, delay or disrupt the normal operation or use of a computer, computer program, computer software, computer system, computer network, computer database, World Wide Web site or telecommunication device; or

(2) degrade, disable, damage or destroy the performance of a computer, computer program, computer software, computer system, computer network, computer database, World Wide Web site or telecommunication device or any combination thereof.

(b) Grading.--An offense under this section shall constitute a felony of the third degree.

Cross References. Section 7616 is referred to in section 7603 of this title.

SUBCHAPTER C
INTERNET CHILD PORNOGRAPHY

Cross References. Subchapter C is referred to in sections 4503, 4601 of Title 61 (Prisons and Parole).

§ 7621. Definitions.

The following words and phrases when used in this subchapter shall have the meanings given to them in this section unless the context clearly indicates otherwise:

"Child pornography." As described in section 6312 (relating to sexual abuse of children).

"Internet." The myriad of computer and telecommunications facilities, including equipment and operating software, which comprise the interconnected worldwide network of networks that employ the transmission control protocol/Internet protocol or any predecessor or successor protocols to such protocol to communicate information of all kinds by wire or radio.

"Internet service provider." A person who provides a service that enables users to access content, information, electronic mail or other services offered over the Internet.

§ 7622. Duty of Internet service provider.

An Internet service provider shall remove or disable access to child pornography items residing on or accessible through its service in a manner accessible to persons located within this Commonwealth within five business days of when the Internet service provider is notified by the Attorney General pursuant to section 7628 (relating to notification procedure) that child pornography items reside on or are accessible through its service.

Cross References. Section 7622 is referred to in section 7624 of this title.

§ 7623. Protection of privacy.

Nothing in this subchapter may be construed as imposing a duty on an Internet service provider to actively monitor its service or affirmatively seek evidence of illegal activity on its service.

§ 7624. Penalty.

Notwithstanding any other provision of law to the contrary, any Internet service provider who violates section 7622 (relating to duty of Internet service provider) commits:

(1) A misdemeanor of the third degree for a first offense punishable by a fine of $5,000.

(2) A misdemeanor of the second degree for a second offense punishable by a fine of $20,000.

357

(3) A felony of the third degree for a third or subsequent offense punishable by a fine of $30,000 and imprisonment for a maximum of seven years.

§ 7625. Jurisdiction for prosecution.

The Attorney General shall have concurrent prosecutorial jurisdiction with the county district attorney for violations of this subchapter. No person charged with a violation of this subchapter by the Attorney General shall have standing to challenge the authority of the Attorney General to prosecute the case. If a challenge is made, the challenge shall be dismissed and no relief shall be available in the courts of this Commonwealth to the person making the challenge.

§ 7626. Application for order to remove or disable items.

An application for an order of authorization to remove or disable items residing on or accessible through an Internet service provider's service shall be made to the court of common pleas having jurisdiction in writing upon the personal oath or affirmation of the Attorney General or a district attorney of the county wherein the items have been discovered and, if available, shall contain all of the following information:

(1) A statement of the authority of the applicant to make the application.

(2) A statement of the identity of the investigative or law enforcement officer that has, in the official scope of that officer's duties, discovered the child pornography items.

(3) A statement by the investigative or law enforcement officer who has knowledge of relevant information justifying the application.

(4) The Uniform Resource Locator providing access to the items.

(5) The identity of the Internet service provider used by the law enforcement officer.

(6) A showing that there is probable cause to believe that the items constitute a violation of section 6312 (relating to sexual abuse of children).

(7) A proposed order of authorization for consideration by the judge.

(8) Contact information for the Office of Attorney General, including the name, address and telephone number of any deputy or agent authorized by the Attorney General to submit notification.

(9) Additional testimony or documentary evidence in support of the application as the judge may require.

Cross References. Section 7626 is referred to in section 7628 of this title.

§ 7627. Order to remove or disable certain items from Internet service provider's service.

Upon consideration of an application, the court may enter an order, including an ex parte order as requested, advising the Attorney General or a district attorney that the items constitute probable cause evidence of a violation of section 6312 (relating to sexual abuse of children) and that such items shall be removed or disabled from the Internet service provider's service. The court may include such other information in the order as the court deems relevant and necessary.

Cross References. Section 7627 is referred to in section 7628 of this title.

§ 7628. Notification procedure.

(a) Duty of Attorney General.--The Attorney General shall have exclusive jurisdiction to notify Internet service providers under this subchapter. The Attorney General shall initiate notification under this subchapter if requested in writing by a district attorney who has provided the Attorney General with a copy of an application made under section 7626 (relating to application to remove or disable items) and a copy of the order issued under section 7627 (relating to order to remove or disable certain items from Internet service provider's service) or upon the issuance of an order based upon an application filed by the Attorney General.

(b) Timely notification.--For purposes of this section, an Internet service provider or the person designated by the Internet service provider as provided for in section 7629 (relating to designated agent) shall be notified in writing by the Attorney General within three business days of the Attorney General's receipt of an order.

(c) Contents.--The notice shall include the following information:

(1) A copy of the application made under section 7626.

(2) A copy of the court order issued under section 7627.

(3) Notification that the Internet service provider must remove or disable the items residing on or accessible through its service within five business days of the date of receipt of the notification.

(4) Contact information for the Office of Attorney General, including the name, address and telephone number of any deputy or agent authorized by the Attorney General to submit notification pursuant to this subsection.

Cross References. Section 7628 is referred to in sections 7622, 7629 of this title.

§ 7629. Designated agent.

An Internet service provider may designate an agent to receive notification provided under section 7628 (relating to notification procedure).

Cross References. Section 7629 is referred to in section 7628 of this title.

§ 7630. Report to General Assembly.

The Attorney General shall make an annual report to the chairman and minority chairman of the Judiciary Committee of the Senate and to the chairman and minority chairman of the Judiciary Committee of the House of Representatives providing information on the number of notifications issued and the prosecutions made under this subchapter and making any recommendations for amendatory language.

SUBCHAPTER D
UNLAWFUL USE OF COMPUTERS

Sec.
7641. Computer-assisted remote harvesting of animals.

Subchapter Heading. The heading of Subchapter D was amended November 1, 2005, P.L.329, No.63, effective in 60 days.

§ 7641. Computer-assisted remote harvesting of animals.

(a) **Offense defined.**--A person who engages in computer-assisted remote harvesting of an animal or provides or operates a facility for another person to engage in computer-assisted remote harvesting of an animal commits a misdemeanor of the third degree.

(b) **Definitions.**--As used in this section, "computer-assisted remote harvesting of an animal" means the use of a computer or software to control remotely the aiming and discharge of any implement that allows a person who is not physically present at the location of that implement to harvest an animal located in this Commonwealth. The term does

not include such use at an establishment as defined under section 2 of the act of July 9, 1968 (P.L.304, No.151), known as the Pennsylvania Meat and Poultry Hygiene Law of 1968.

(Nov. 1, 2005, P.L.329, No.63, eff. 60 days)

2005 Amendment. Act 63 added section 7641.

SUBCHAPTER E
ELECTRONIC MAIL

Sec.
7661. Unlawful transmission of electronic mail.

§ 7661. Unlawful transmission of electronic mail.

(a) **Offense defined.**--A person commits the offense of unlawful transmission of electronic mail if he:

(1) Uses a computer or computer network without authority and with the intent to falsify or forge electronic mail transmission information or other routine information in any manner in connection with the transmission of unsolicited electronic mail through or into the computer network of an electronic mail service provider, Internet service provider or its subscribers.

(2) Sells, gives or otherwise distributes or possesses with the intent to sell, give or distribute computer software which:

(i) is primarily designed or produced for the purpose of facilitating or enabling the falsification of electronic mail transmission information or other routing information;

(ii) has only limited commercially significant purpose or use other than to facilitate or to enable the falsification of electronic mail transmission information or other routing information; or

(iii) is marketed by that person or another person acting in concert with that person with that person's knowledge for the use in facilitating or enabling the falsification of electronic mail transmission information or other routing information.

(b) Grading.--

(1) Except as provided in paragraphs (2) and (3), unlawful transmission of electronic mail is a misdemeanor of the third degree punishable by a fine of not more than $2,500.

(2) If there is damage to the property of another valued at $2,500 or more caused by that person's reckless disregard for the consequences of his act in violation of this section, unlawful transmission of electronic mail is a misdemeanor of the first degree punishable by a fine of not more than $10,000.

(3) If there is damage to the property of another valued at $2,500 or more caused by that person's malicious act in violation of this section, unlawful transmission of electronic mail is a felony of the third degree punishable by a fine of not more than $15,000.

(c) **Rights preserved.**--Nothing in this section shall be construed to:

(1) Establish any liability by reason of terms or conditions adopted by or technical measures implemented by an electronic mail service provider or Internet service provider doing business in this Commonwealth to prevent the transmission of unsolicited electronic mail in violation of this section.

(2) Interfere with or prohibit terms or conditions in a contract or license related to computers, computer data, computer networks, computer operations, computer programs, computer services or computer software.

(d) **Definitions.**--As used in this section, the term "electronic mail" shall include facsimiles and wireless advertisements in addition to other electronic mail.

CHAPTER 77 VEHICLE CHOP SHOP AND ILLEGALLY OBTAINED AND ALTERED PROPERTY

Enactment. Chapter 77 was added October 25, 2012, P.L.1645, No.203, effective in 60 days.

Continuation of Prior Law. Section 5 of Act 203 of 2012 provided that Chapter 77 is a continuation of the former act of November 24, 1998 (P.L.874, No.110), known as the Motor Vehicle Chop Shop and Illegally Obtained and Altered Property Act.

§ 7701. Definitions.

The following words and phrases when used in this chapter shall have the meanings given to them in this section unless the context clearly indicates otherwise:

"Chop shop." A building, lot or other premises where one or more persons engage in altering, destroying, disassembling, dismantling, reassembling, storing or possessing a vehicle or vehicle part known to be illegally obtained by theft, fraud or conspiracy to defraud in order to either:

(1) alter, counterfeit, deface, destroy, disguise, falsify, forge, obliterate or remove the identification, including, but not limited to, the vehicle identification number of the vehicle or vehicle part, in order to misrepresent the identity of the vehicle or vehicle part or to prevent the identification of the vehicle or vehicle part; or

(2) sell or dispose of the vehicle or vehicle part.

"Person." A natural person, firm, copartnership, association or cooperation.

"Semitrailer." A trailer so constructed that some part of its weight rests upon or is carried by the towing vehicle.

"Trailer." A vehicle designed to be towed by a motor vehicle.

"Vehicle." Every device in, upon or by which any person or property is or may be transported or drawn upon a highway, except devices used exclusively upon rails or tracks. The term does not include a self-propelled wheelchair or an electrical mobility device operated by and designed for the exclusive use of a person with a mobility-related disability.

"Vehicle identification number." A combination of numerals or letters, or both, which a manufacturer of a vehicle assigns to a vehicle for identification purposes or, in the absence of a manufacturer assigned number, which the Department of Transportation assigns to a vehicle for identification purposes.

§ 7702. Owning, operating or conducting a chop shop.

Any person who knowingly:

(1) owns, operates or conducts a chop shop; or

(2) transports, sells, transfers, purchases or receives any vehicle or vehicle part that was illegally obtained either to or from a chop shop

commits a felony of the second degree and, upon conviction, shall be sentenced to imprisonment for not more than ten years or a fine of not more than $100,000, or both.

Cross References. Section 7702 is referred to in sections 7705, 7706 of this title.

§ 7703. Alteration or destruction of vehicle identification number.

Any person who alters, counterfeits, defaces, destroys, disguises, falsifies, forges, obliterates or removes a vehicle identification number with the intent to conceal or misrepresent the identity or prevent the identification of a vehicle or vehicle part commits a felony of the third degree and, upon conviction, shall be sentenced to imprisonment for not more than seven years or a fine of not more than $50,000, or both.

§ 7704. Disposition of vehicle or vehicle part with altered vehicle identification number.

Any person who purchases, receives, disposes, sells, transfers or possesses a vehicle or vehicle part with knowledge that the vehicle identification number of the vehicle or vehicle part has been altered, counterfeited, defaced, destroyed, disguised, falsified, forged, obliterated or removed and with the intent to conceal or misrepresent the identity or prevent the identification of a vehicle or vehicle part commits a felony of the third degree and, upon conviction, shall be sentenced to imprisonment for not more than seven years or a fine of not more than $50,000, or both.

§ 7705. Exceptions.

(a) Scrap processor.--The provisions of section 7702 (relating to owning, operating or conducting a chop shop) shall not apply to a scrap processor who, in the normal legal course of business and in good faith, processes a vehicle or vehicle part by crushing, compacting or other similar methods, provided that any vehicle identification number is not removed from the vehicle or vehicle part prior to or during any such processing.

(b) Repair of vehicle.--The provisions of section 7702 shall not be construed to prohibit the removal of a vehicle identification number plate from a vehicle part that is damaged when:

(1) The removal is necessary for proper repair or matching identification of a replacement vehicle part.

(2) The proper matching vehicle identification number plate is immediately and properly secured to the repaired or replacement part.

§ 7706. Presumptions.

(a) Vehicles.--Any person or persons who transport, sell, transfer, purchase, possess or receive any vehicle or vehicle part upon which the vehicle identification number has been altered, counterfeited, defaced, destroyed, disguised, falsified, forged, obliterated or removed or who fails to keep, possess or produce the records required to be kept, possessed or produced for the vehicle or vehicle part under 75 Pa.C.S. § 6308 (relating to investigation by police officers) shall be prima facie evidence under section 7702 (relating to owning, operating or conducting a chop shop) of that person's or persons' knowledge that the vehicle or vehicle part was illegally obtained.

(b) Police report.--A police report which indicates that a vehicle or vehicle part was reported to police to be in a stolen status at the time it was possessed shall be prima facie evidence that the vehicle or vehicle part was possessed without permission of the owner.

§ 7707. Loss of property rights to Commonwealth.

(a) Forfeitures generally.--The following shall be subject to forfeiture to the Commonwealth, and no property right shall exist in them:

(1) Any tool, implement or instrumentality, including, but not limited to, a vehicle or vehicle part used or possessed in connection with any violation of this chapter.

(2) All materials, products and equipment of any kind which are used or intended for use in violation of this chapter.

(3) All books, records, microfilm, tapes and data which are used or intended for use in violation of this chapter.

(4) All money, negotiable instruments, securities or other things of value used or intended to be used to facilitate any violation of this chapter and all proceeds traceable to any transactions in violation of this chapter.

(5) All real property used or intended to be used to facilitate any violation of this chapter, including structures or other

improvements thereon and including any right, title and interest in the whole or any lot or tract of land and any appurtenances or improvements which are used or intended to be used in any manner or part to commit or to facilitate the commission of a violation of this chapter.

(a.1) Conduct of forfeiture.--Forfeiture of property shall be authorized for a violation of this chapter and conducted in accordance with 42 Pa.C.S. §§ 5803 (relating to asset forfeiture), 5805 (relating to forfeiture procedure), 5806 (relating to motion for return of property), 5807 (relating to restrictions on use), 5807.1 (relating to prohibition on adoptive seizures) and 5808 (relating to exceptions).

(b) Exceptions.--(Deleted by amendment).

(c) Process and seizure.--(Deleted by amendment).

(d) Seizure without process.--(Deleted by amendment).

(e) Custody of property.--(Deleted by amendment).

(f) Use of property held in custody.--(Deleted by amendment).

(g) Use of cash, property or proceeds of property.--(Deleted by amendment).

(h) Distribution of property among law enforcement authorities.--(Deleted by amendment).

(i) Annual audit of forfeited property.--(Deleted by amendment).

(j) Annual report; confidential information regarding property.--(Deleted by amendment).

(k) Proceeds and appropriations.--(Deleted by amendment).

(June 29, 2017, P.L.247, No.13, eff. July 1, 2017)

Cross References. Section 7707 is referred to in section 5803 of Title 42 (Judiciary and Judicial Procedure).

§ 7708. Procedure with respect to seized property subject to liens and rights of lienholders (Repealed).

2017 Repeal. Section 7708 was repealed June 29, 2017, P.L.247, No.13, effective July 1, 2017.

PART III
MISCELLANEOUS PROVISIONS

Chapter
91. Criminal History Record Information
92. Conflicts of Interest
93. Independent Counsel (Repealed)
94. Crime Victims
95. Independent Counsel

Enactment. Part III was added July 16, 1979, P.L.116, No.47, effective January 1, 1980.

CHAPTER 91 CRIMINAL HISTORY RECORD INFORMATION

Subchapter
A. General Provisions
B. Completeness and Accuracy
C. Dissemination of Criminal History Record Information
D. Security
E. Audit
F. Individual Right of Access and Review
G. Responsibility of Attorney General
H. Public Notice
I. Sanctions

Enactment. Chapter 91 was added July 16, 1979, P.L.116, No.47, effective January 1, 1980.

Cross References. Chapter 91 is referred to in section 6109 of this title; sections 1202, 1317.2, 1317.3, 1517, 1801, 3509, 3904 of Title 4 (Amusements); sections 8616, 8660 of Title 20 (Decedents, Estates and Fiduciaries); sections 3705, 3714 of Title 22 (Detectives and Private Police); section 6344 of Title 23 (Domestic Relations); section 925 of Title 34 (Game); section 7713 of Title 35 (Health and Safety); sections 1904, 6309, 9799.27, 9799.28, 9799.62, 9799.63, 9799.68 of Title 42 (Judiciary and Judicial Procedure); section 702 of Title 54 (Names); section 327 of Title 57 (Notaries Public).

SUBCHAPTER A
GENERAL PROVISIONS

§ 9101. Short title of chapter.

This chapter shall be known and may be cited as the "Criminal History Record Information Act."

§ 9102. Definitions.

The following words and phrases when used in this chapter shall have the meanings given to them in this section unless the context clearly indicates otherwise:

"Administration of criminal justice." The activities directly concerned with the prevention, control or reduction of crime, the apprehension, detention, pretrial release, post-trial release, prosecution, adjudication, correctional supervision or rehabilitation of accused persons or criminal offenders; criminal identification activities; or the collection, storage dissemination or usage of criminal history record information.

"Audit." The process of reviewing compliance with applicable Federal and State laws and regulations related to the privacy and security of criminal history record information.

"Automated systems." A computer or other internally programmed device capable of automatically accepting and processing data, including computer programs, data communication links, input and output data and data storage devices.

"Central repository." The central location for the collection, compilation, maintenance and dissemination of criminal history record information by the Pennsylvania State Police.

"Criminal history record information." Information collected by criminal justice agencies concerning individuals, and arising from the initiation of a criminal proceeding, consisting of identifiable descriptions, dates and notations of arrests, indictments, informations or other formal criminal charges and any dispositions arising therefrom. The term does not include intelligence information, investigative information or treatment information, including medical and psychological information, or information and records specified in section 9104 (relating to scope).

"Criminal justice agency." Any court, including the minor judiciary, with criminal jurisdiction or any other governmental agency, or subunit thereof, created by statute or by the State or Federal constitutions, specifically authorized to perform as its principal function the administration of criminal justice, and which allocates a substantial portion of its annual budget to such function. Criminal justice agencies include, but are not limited to: organized State and municipal police departments, local detention facilities, county, regional and State correctional facilities, probation agencies, district or prosecuting attorneys, parole boards, pardon boards, the facilities and administrative offices of the Department of Public Welfare that provide care, guidance and control to adjudicated delinquents, and such agencies or subunits thereof, as are declared by the Attorney General to be criminal justice agencies as determined by a review of applicable statutes and the State and Federal Constitutions or both.

"Disposition." Information indicating that criminal proceedings have been concluded, including information disclosing that police have elected not to refer a matter for prosecution, that a prosecuting authority has elected not to commence criminal proceedings or that a grand jury has failed to indict and disclosing the nature of the termination of the proceedings; or information disclosing that proceedings have been indefinitely postponed and also disclosing the reason for such postponement. Dispositions of criminal proceedings in the Commonwealth shall include, but not be limited to, acquittal, acquittal by reason of insanity, pretrial probation or diversion, charge dismissed, guilty plea, nolle prosequi, no information filed, nolo contendere plea, convicted, abatement, discharge under rules of the Pennsylvania Rules of Criminal Procedure, demurrer sustained, pardoned, sentence commuted, mistrial-defendant discharged, discharge from probation or parole or correctional supervision.

"Dissemination." The oral or written transmission or disclosure of criminal history record information to individuals or agencies other than the criminal justice agency which maintains the information.

"Expunge."

(1) To remove information so that there is no trace or indication that such information existed;

(2) to eliminate all identifiers which may be used to trace the identity of an individual, allowing remaining data to be used for statistical purposes; or

(3) maintenance of certain information required or authorized under the provisions of section 9122(c) (relating to expungement), when an individual has successfully completed the conditions of any pretrial or posttrial diversion or probation program.

"Intelligence information." Information concerning the habits, practices, characteristics, possessions, associations or financial status of any individual compiled in an effort to anticipate, prevent, monitor, investigate or prosecute criminal activity. Notwithstanding the definition of "treatment information" contained in this section, intelligence information may include information on prescribing, dispensing, selling, obtaining or using a controlled substance as defined in the act of April 14, 1972 (P.L.233, No.64), known as The Controlled Substance, Drug, Device and Cosmetic Act.

"Investigative information." Information assembled as a result of the performance of any inquiry, formal or informal, into a criminal incident or an allegation of criminal wrongdoing and may include modus operandi information.

"Police blotter." A chronological listing of arrests, usually documented contemporaneous with the incident, which may include, but is not limited to, the name and address of the individual charged and the alleged offenses.

"Repository." Any location in which criminal history record information is collected, compiled, maintained and disseminated by a criminal justice agency.

"Treatment information." Information concerning medical, psychiatric, psychological or other rehabilitative treatment provided, suggested or prescribed for any individual charged with or convicted of a crime.

(Dec. 14, 1979, P.L.556, No.127, eff. imd.; June 11, 1982, P.L.476, No.138, eff. 180 days; Dec. 19, 1990, P.L.1332, No.207, eff. imd.; Nov. 29, 2004, P.L.1349, No.173, eff. 60 days)

2004 Amendment. Act 173 amended the def. of "criminal justice agency."

1990 Amendment. Act 207 amended the defs. of "intelligence information" and "treatment information."

1982 Amendment. Act 138 amended the defs. of "criminal justice agency," "expunge" and "intelligence information" and added the def. of "police blotter."

1979 Amendment. Act 127 amended the def. of "criminal history record information," added the defs. of "automated systems," "intelligence information," "investigative information" and "treatment information" and deleted the def. of "secondary dissemination."

References in Text. The Department of Public Welfare, referred to in this section, was redesignated as the Department of Human Services by Act 132 of 2014.

Cross References. Section 9102 is referred to in section 6108.7 of Title 23 (Domestic Relations); section 6309 of Title 42 (Judiciary and Judicial Procedure); section 2303 of Title 44 (Law and Justice); section 2162 of Title 53 (Municipalities Generally).

§ 9103. Applicability.

This chapter shall apply to persons within this Commonwealth and to any agency of the Commonwealth or its political subdivisions which collects, maintains, disseminates or receives criminal history record information.

§ 9104. Scope.

(a) General rule.--Except for the provisions of Subchapter B (relating to completeness and accuracy), Subchapter D (relating to security) and Subchapter F (relating to individual right of access and review), nothing in this chapter shall be construed to apply to:

(1) Original records of entry compiled chronologically, including, but not limited to, police blotters and press releases that contain criminal history record information and are disseminated contemporaneous with the incident.

(2) Any documents, records or indices prepared or maintained by or filed in any court of this Commonwealth, including but not limited to the minor judiciary.

(3) Posters, announcements, or lists for identifying or apprehending fugitives or wanted persons.

(4) Announcements of executive clemency.

(b) Court dockets, police blotters and press releases.--Court dockets, police blotters and press releases and information contained therein shall, for the purpose of this chapter, be considered public records.

(c) Substitutes for court dockets.-- Where court dockets are not maintained any reasonable substitute containing that information traditionally available in court dockets shall, for the purpose of this chapter, be considered public records.

(d) Certain disclosures authorized.-- Nothing in this chapter shall prohibit a criminal justice agency from disclosing an individual's prior criminal activity to an individual or agency if the information disclosed is based on records set forth in subsection (a).

(e) Noncriminal justice agencies.-- Information collected by noncriminal justice agencies and individuals from the sources identified in this section shall not be considered criminal history record information.

(Dec. 14, 1979, P.L.556, No.127, eff. imd.; June 11, 1982, P.L.476, No.138, eff. 180 days)

1982 Amendment. Act 138 amended subsecs. (a) and (b).

1979 Amendment. Act 127 deleted subsec. (d) and relettered subsec. (e) to (d) and subsec. (f) to (e).

Cross References. Section 9104 is referred to in sections 9102, 9122 of this title.

§ 9105. Other criminal justice information.

Nothing in this chapter shall be construed to apply to information concerning juveniles, except as provided in section 9123 (relating to juvenile records), unless they have been adjudicated as adults, nor shall it apply to intelligence information, investigative information, treatment information, including medical and psychiatric information, caution indicator information, modus operandi information, wanted persons information, stolen property information, missing persons information, employment history information, personal history information, nor presentence investigation information. Criminal history record information maintained as a part of these records shall not be disseminated unless in compliance with the provisions of this chapter.

Cross References. Section 9105 is referred to in section 9123 of this title; section

6309 of Title 42 (Judiciary and Judicial Procedure).

§ 9106. Information in central repository or automated systems.

(a) General rule.--Intelligence information, investigative information and treatment information shall not be collected in the central repository. This prohibition shall not preclude the collection in the central repository of names, words, numbers, phrases or other similar index keys to serve as indices to investigative reports.

(b) Collection of protected information.--

(1) Intelligence information may be placed in an automated or electronic criminal justice system only if the following apply:

(i) The criminal justice agency has reasonable suspicion of criminal activity.

(ii) Access to the intelligence information contained in the automated or electronic criminal justice system is restricted to the authorized employees of the criminal justice agency and cannot be accessed by any other individuals inside or outside of the agency.

(iii) The intelligence information is related to criminal activity that would give rise to prosecution for a State offense graded a misdemeanor or felony, or for a Federal offense for which the penalty is imprisonment for more than one year. Intelligence information shall be categorized based upon subject matter.

(iv) The intelligence information is not collected in violation of State law.

(2) Intelligence information may not be collected or maintained in an automated or electronic criminal justice system concerning participation in a political, religious or social organization, or in the organization or support of any nonviolent demonstration, assembly, protest, rally or similar form of public speech, unless there is a reasonable suspicion that the participation by the subject of the information is related to criminal activity or prison rule violation.

(3) Investigative information and treatment information contained in files of any criminal justice agency may be placed within an automated or electronic criminal justice information system, provided that access to the investigative information and treatment information contained in the automated or electronic criminal justice information system is restricted to authorized employees of that agency and cannot be accessed by individuals outside of the agency.

(c) Dissemination of protected information.--

(1) Intelligence information may be placed within an automated or electronic criminal justice information system and disseminated only if the following apply:

(i) The information is reliable as determined by an authorized intelligence officer.

(ii) The department, agency or individual requesting the information is a criminal justice agency which has policies and procedures adopted by the Office of Attorney General in consultation with the Pennsylvania State Police which are consistent with this act and include:

(A) Designation of an intelligence officer or officers by the head of the criminal justice agency or his designee.

(B) Adoption of administrative, technical and physical safeguards, including audit trails, to insure against unauthorized access and against intentional or unintentional damages.

(C) Labeling information to indicate levels of sensitivity and levels of confidence in the information.

(iii) The information is requested in connection with the duties of the criminal justice agency requesting the information, and the request for information is based upon a name, fingerprints, modus operandi, genetic typing, voice print or other identifying characteristic.

(2) If an intelligence officer of a disseminating agency is notified that intelligence information which has been previously disseminated to another criminal justice agency is materially misleading, obsolete or otherwise unreliable, the information shall be corrected and the recipient agency notified of the change within a reasonable period of time.

(3) Criminal justice agencies shall establish retention schedules for intelligence information. Intelligence information shall be purged under the following conditions:

(i) The data is no longer relevant or necessary to the goals and objectives of the criminal justice agency.

(ii) The data has become obsolete, making it unreliable for present purposes and the utility of updating the data would be worthless.

(iii) The data cannot be utilized for strategic or tactical intelligence studies.

(4) Investigative and treatment information shall not be disseminated to any department, agency or individual unless the department, agency or individual requesting the information is a criminal justice agency which requests the information in connection with its duties, and the request is based upon a name, fingerprints, modus operandi, genetic typing, voice print or other identifying characteristic.

(5) Each municipal police department accessing automated information shall file a copy of its procedures with the Pennsylvania State Police for approval. Such plan shall be reviewed within 60 days.

(6) Each district attorney accessing automated information shall file a copy of its procedures with the Office of Attorney General for approval. Such plan shall be reviewed within 60 days.

(d) Secondary dissemination prohibited.--A criminal justice agency which possesses information protected by this section, but which is not the source of the information, shall not disseminate or disclose the information to another criminal justice agency but shall refer the requesting agency to the agency which was the source of the information. This prohibition shall not apply if the agency receiving the information is investigating or prosecuting a criminal incident in conjunction with the agency possessing the information. Agencies receiving information protected by this section assume the same level of responsibility for the security of such information as the agency which was the source of the information.

(e) Notations of the record.--Criminal justice agencies maintaining intelligence information, investigative information or treatment information must enter, as a permanent part of an individual's information file, a listing of all persons and agencies to whom they have disseminated that particular information, the date of the dissemination and the purpose for which the information was disseminated. This listing shall be maintained separate from the record itself.

(f) Security requirements.--Every criminal justice agency collecting, storing or disseminating intelligence information, investigative information or treatment information shall insure the confidentiality and security of such information by providing that, wherever such information is maintained, a criminal justice agency must:

(1) institute procedures to reasonably protect any repository from theft, fire, sabotage, flood, wind or other natural or manmade disasters;

(2) select, supervise and train all personnel authorized to have access to intelligence information, investigative information or treatment information;

(3) insure that, where computerized data processing is employed, the equipment utilized for maintaining intelligence information, investigative information or treatment information is dedicated solely to purposes related to the administration of criminal justice or, if the equipment is not used solely for the administration of criminal justice, the criminal justice agency is accorded equal management participation in computer operations used to maintain the intelligence information, investigative information or treatment information.

(g) Penalties.--Any person, including any agency or organization, who violates the provisions of this section shall be subject to the administrative penalties provided in section 9181 (relating to general administrative sanctions) and the civil penalties provided in section 9183 (relating to civil actions) in addition to any other civil or criminal penalty provided by law.

(Dec. 14, 1979, P.L.556, No.127, eff. imd.; Dec. 19, 1990, P.L.1332, No.207, eff. 60 days)

Cross References. Section 9106 is referred to in section 9141 of this title.

SUBCHAPTER B
COMPLETENESS AND ACCURACY

Cross References. Subchapter B is referred to in section 9104 of this title.

§ 9111. Duties of criminal justice agencies.

It shall be the duty of every criminal justice agency within the Commonwealth to maintain complete and accurate criminal history record information and to report such information at such times and in such manner as required by the provisions of this chapter or other applicable statutes.

§ 9112. Mandatory fingerprinting.

(a) General rule.--Fingerprints of all persons arrested for a felony, misdemeanor or summary offense which becomes a misdemeanor on a second arrest after conviction of that summary offense, shall be taken by the arresting authority, and within 48 hours of the arrest, shall be forwarded to, and in a manner and such a form as provided by, the central repository.

(b) Other cases.--

(1) Where private complaints for a felony or misdemeanor result in a conviction, the court of proper jurisdiction shall order the defendant to submit for fingerprinting by the municipal police of the jurisdiction in which the offense was allegedly committed or in the absence of a police department, the State Police. Fingerprints so obtained shall, within 48 hours, be forwarded to the central repository in a manner and in such form as may be provided by the central repository.

(2) Where defendants named in police complaints are proceeded against by summons, or for offenses under section 3929 (relating to retail theft), the court of proper jurisdiction shall order the defendant to submit within five days of such order for fingerprinting by the municipal police of the jurisdiction in which the offense allegedly was committed or, in the absence of a police department, the State Police. Fingerprints so obtained shall, within 48 hours, be forwarded to the central repository in a manner and in such form as may be provided by the central repository.

(c) Transmittal of information.--The central repository shall transmit the criminal history record information to the criminal justice agency which submitted a complete, accurate and classifiable fingerprint card.

(Dec. 14, 1979, P.L.556, No.127, eff. imd.; June 11, 1982, P.L.476, No.138, eff. 180 days)

Cross References. Section 9112 is referred to in section 6309 of Title 42 (Judiciary and Judicial Procedure).

§ 9113. Disposition reporting by criminal justice agencies.

(a) Reports of dispositions required.-- All criminal justice agencies, including but not limited to, courts, county, regional and State correctional institutions and parole and probation agencies, shall collect and submit reports of dispositions occurring within their respective agencies for criminal history record information, within 90 days of the date of such disposition to the central repository as provided for in this section.

(b) Courts.--Courts shall collect and submit criminal court dispositions as required by the Administrative Office of Pennsylvania Courts.

(c) Correctional institutions.--County, regional and State correctional institutions shall collect and submit information regarding the admission, release and length of sentence of individuals sentenced to local and county institutions as required by the Bureau of Correction.

(d) Probation and parole offices.-- County probation and parole offices shall collect and submit information relating to the length of time and charges for which an individual is placed under and released from the jurisdiction of such agency as required by the Pennsylvania Board of Probation and Parole.

(e) State agencies.--The Administrative Office of Pennsylvania Courts, the Bureau of Correction, the Pennsylvania Board of Probation and Parole and the Pennsylvania Board of Pardons shall collect and submit to the central repository such information necessary to maintain complete and accurate criminal history record information. Each State agency listed in this subsection shall submit to the central repository any reports of dispositions occurring within their respective agencies and such information reported from county and local criminal justice agencies.

References in Text. The Bureau of Correction, referred to in subsecs. (c) and (e), is now the Department of Corrections.

Cross References. Section 9113 is referred to in section 6309 of Title 42 (Judiciary and Judicial Procedure).

§ 9114. Correction of inaccurate information.

Within 15 days of the detection of inaccurate data in a criminal history record, regardless of the manner of discovery, the criminal justice agency which reported the information shall comply with the following procedures to effect correction:

(1) Correct its own records.

(2) Notify all recipients, including the central repository, of the inaccurate data and the required correction.

SUBCHAPTER C
DISSEMINATION OF CRIMINAL HISTORY
RECORD INFORMATION

§ 9121. General regulations.

(a) Dissemination to criminal justice agencies.--Criminal history record information maintained by any criminal justice agency shall be disseminated without charge to any criminal justice agency or to any noncriminal justice agency that is providing a service for which a criminal justice agency is responsible.

(b) Dissemination to noncriminal justice agencies and individuals.--Criminal history record information shall be disseminated by a State or local police department to any individual or noncriminal justice agency only upon request. The following apply:

(1) A fee may be charged by a State or local police department for each request for criminal history record information by an individual or noncriminal justice agency, except that no fee shall be charged to an individual who makes the request in order to apply to become a volunteer with an affiliate of Big Brothers of America or Big Sisters of America or with a rape crisis center or domestic violence program.

(2) Except as provided for in subsections (b.1) and (b.2), before a State or local police department disseminates criminal history record information to an individual or noncriminal justice agency, it shall extract from the record the following:

(i) All notations of arrests, indictments or other information relating to the initiation of criminal proceedings where:

(A) three years have elapsed from the date of arrest;

(B) no disposition is indicated in the record; and

(C) nothing in the record indicates that proceedings seeking conviction remain pending.

(ii) All information relating to a conviction and the arrest, indictment or other information leading thereto, which is the subject of a court order for limited access as provided in section 9122.1 (relating to petition for limited access).

(iii) All information relating to a conviction or nonconviction final disposition and the arrest, indictment or other information leading to the arrest or indictment which is subject to a court order for limited access as provided for in section 9122.2 (relating to clean slate limited access).

(3) A court or the Administrative Office of Pennsylvania Courts may not disseminate to an individual, a noncriminal justice agency or an Internet website any information which is the subject of a court order for limited access as provided in section 9122.1 or 9122.2.

(b.1) Exception.--Subsection (b)(1) and (2) shall not apply if the request is made by a county children and youth agency or the Department of Human Services in the performance of duties relating to children and youth under the act of June 24, 1937 (P.L.2017, No.396), known as the County Institution District Law, section 2168 of the act of August 9, 1955 (P.L.323, No.130), known as The County Code, the act of June 13, 1967 (P.L.31, No.21), known as the Human Services Code, 23 Pa.C.S. Ch. 63 (relating to child protective services) or 42 Pa.C.S. Ch. 63 (relating to juvenile matters).

(b.2) Additional exceptions.--

(1) Subsection (b)(2)(ii) and (iii) shall not apply if the request is made under a court order:

(i) In a case brought under 23 Pa.C.S. Ch. 53 (relating to child custody) or 61 (relating to protection from abuse).

(ii) By an employer against whom a claim of civil liability has been brought as described under section 9122.6 (relating to employer immunity from liability) for purposes of defending against a claim of civil liability.

(2) Subsection (b)(2) shall not apply:

(i) To the verification of information provided by an applicant if Federal law, including rules and regulations promulgated by a self-regulatory organization that has been created under Federal law, requires the consideration of an applicant's criminal history for purposes of employment.

(ii) To the verification of information provided to the Supreme Court, or an entity of the Supreme Court, in its capacity to govern the practice, procedure and conduct of all courts, the admission to the bar, the practice of law, the administration of all courts and supervision of all officers of the judicial branch.

(c) Data required to be kept.--Any criminal justice agency which disseminates criminal history record information must indicate to the recipient that the information disseminated is only that information contained in its own file, the date of the last entry, and that a summary of the Statewide criminal history record information may be obtained from the central repository.

(d) Extracting from the record.--When criminal history record information is maintained by a criminal justice agency in records containing investigative information, intelligence information, treatment information or other nonpublic information, the agency may extract and disseminate only the criminal history record information if the dissemination is to be made to a noncriminal justice agency or individual.

(e) Dissemination procedures.--Criminal justice agencies may establish reasonable procedures for the dissemination of criminal history record information.

(f) Notations on record.--Repositories must enter as a permanent part of an individual's criminal history record information file, a listing of all persons and agencies to whom they have disseminated that particular criminal history record information and the date and purpose for which the information was disseminated. Such listing shall be maintained separate from the record itself.

(Dec. 14, 1979, P.L.556, No.127, eff. imd.; June 11, 1982, P.L.476, No.138, eff. 180 days; July 2, 1996, P.L.480, No.76, eff. 60 days; Dec. 21, 1998, P.L.1103, No.149, eff. 60 days; Oct. 28, 2002, P.L.888, No.129, eff. imd.; Feb. 16, 2016, P.L.10, No.5, eff. 270 days; June 28, 2018, P.L.402, No.56, eff. 365 days)

2018 Amendment. Act 56 amended subsecs. (b) intro. par., (b)(2) and (3), (b.1) and (b.2). See Act 56 in the appendix to this title for special provisions relating to findings and declarations.

2002 Amendment. Act 129 amended subsec. (b).

1996 Amendment. Act 76 amended subsec. (b) and added subsec. (b.1).

1982 Amendment. Act 138 amended subsecs. (a) and (b).

References in Text. The Department of Public Welfare, referred to in this section, was redesignated as the Department of Human Services by Act 132 of 2014.

The short title of the act of June 13, 1967 (P.L.31, No.21), known as the Public Welfare Code, referred to in subsection (b)(1), was amended by the act of December 28, 2015 (P.L.500, No.92). The amended short title is now the Human Services Code.

Cross References. Section 9121 is referred to in sections 9122.1, 9122.2, 9122.3, 9122.5 of this title; sections 314, 1206, 3305 of Title 4 (Amusements); section 3705 of Title 22 (Detectives and Private Police); section 6344 of Title 23 (Domestic Relations); sections 2161, 6309 of Title 42 (Judiciary and Judicial Procedure).

§ 9122. Expungement.

(a) Specific proceedings.--Criminal history record information shall be expunged in a specific criminal proceeding when:

(1) no disposition has been received or, upon request for criminal history record information, no disposition has been recorded in the repository within 18 months after the date of arrest and the court of proper jurisdiction certifies to the director of the repository that no disposition is available and no action is pending. Expungement shall not occur until the certification from the court is received and the director of the repository authorizes such expungement;

(2) a court order requires that such nonconviction data be expunged; or

(3) a person 21 years of age or older who has been convicted of a violation of section 6308 (relating to purchase, consumption, possession or transportation of liquor or malt or brewed beverages), which occurred on or after the day the person attained 18 years of age, petitions the court of common pleas in the county where the conviction occurred seeking expungement and the person has satisfied all terms and conditions of the sentence imposed for the violation, including any suspension of operating privileges imposed pursuant to

section 6310.4 (relating to restriction of operating privileges). Upon review of the petition, the court shall order the expungement of all criminal history record information and all administrative records of the Department of Transportation relating to said conviction.

(b) Generally.--Criminal history record information may be expunged when:

(1) An individual who is the subject of the information reaches 70 years of age and has been free of arrest or prosecution for ten years following final release from confinement or supervision.

(2) An individual who is the subject of the information has been dead for three years.

(3) (i) An individual who is the subject of the information petitions the court for the expungement of a summary offense and has been free of arrest or prosecution for five years following the conviction for that offense.

(ii) Expungement under this paragraph shall only be permitted for a conviction of a summary offense.

(b.1) Prohibition.--A court shall not have the authority to order expungement of the defendant's arrest record where the defendant was placed on Accelerated Rehabilitative Disposition for a violation of any offense set forth in any of the following where the victim is under 18 years of age:

Section 3121 (relating to rape).

Section 3122.1 (relating to statutory sexual assault).

Section 3123 (relating to involuntary deviate sexual intercourse).

Section 3124.1 (relating to sexual assault).

Section 3125 (relating to aggravated indecent assault).

Section 3126 (relating to indecent assault).

Section 3127 (relating to indecent exposure).

Section 5902(b) (relating to prostitution and related offenses).

Section 5903 (relating to obscene and other sexual materials and performances).

(c) Maintenance of certain information required or authorized.--Notwithstanding any other provision of this chapter, the prosecuting attorney and the central repository shall, and the court may, maintain a list of the names and other criminal history record information of persons whose records are required by law or court rule to be expunged where the individual has successfully completed the conditions of any pretrial or post-trial diversion or probation program or where the court has ordered expungement under this section. Such information shall be used solely for the purposes of determining subsequent eligibility for such programs, identifying persons in criminal investigations or determining the grading of subsequent offenses. Such information shall be made available to any court or law enforcement agency upon request.

(d) Notice of expungement.--Notice of expungement shall promptly be submitted to the central repository which shall notify all criminal justice agencies which have received the criminal history record information to be expunged.

(e) Public records.--Public records listed in section 9104(a) (relating to scope) shall not be expunged.

(f) District attorney's notice.--The court shall give ten days prior notice to the district attorney of the county where the original charge was filed of any applications for expungement under the provisions of subsection (a)(2).

(June 11, 1982, P.L.476, No.138, eff. 180 days; Oct. 16, 1996, P.L.715, No.128, eff. 60 days; Apr. 22, 1997, P.L.73, No.5, eff. 60 days; Nov. 29, 2004, P.L.1349, No.173, eff. 60 days Nov. 26, 2008, P.L.1670, No.134, eff. 60 days; Oct. 25, 2012, P.L.1655, No.204, eff. 60 days)

2012 Amendment. Act 204 amended subsecs. (a)(3) and (d).

2008 Amendment. Act 134 amended subsecs. (b), (b.1) and (c).

2004 Amendment. Act 173 amended subsec. (a).

1982 Amendment. Act 138 amended subsec. (f).

References in Text. 18 Pa.C.S. § 6310.4, referred to in subsec. (a)(3), was repealed by the act of October 24, 2018 (P.L.659, No.95).

Cross References. Section 9122 is referred to in sections 3019, 9102 of this title; section 1725.7 of Title 42 (Judiciary and Judicial Procedure).

§ 9122.1. Petition for limited access.

(a) General rule.--Subject to the exceptions in subsection (b) and notwithstanding any other provision of this chapter, upon petition of a person who has been free from conviction for a period of 10 years for an offense punishable by one or more years in prison and has completed each court-ordered financial obligation of the sentence, the court of common pleas in the jurisdiction where a conviction occurred may enter an order that criminal history record information maintained by a criminal justice agency pertaining to a qualifying misdemeanor or an ungraded offense which carries a maximum penalty of no more than five years be disseminated only to a criminal justice agency or as provided in section 9121(b.1) and (b.2) (relating to general regulations).

(1) (Deleted by amendment).

(2) (Deleted by amendment).

(b) Exceptions.--An order for limited access under this section shall not be granted for any of the following:

(1) A conviction for an offense punishable by more than two years in prison which is any of the following or an attempt, conspiracy or solicitation to commit any of the following:

(i) An offense under Article B of Part II (relating to offenses involving danger to the person).

(ii) An offense under Article D of Part II (relating to offenses against the family).

(iii) An offense under Chapter 61 (relating to firearms and other dangerous articles).

(iv) An offense specified in 42 Pa.C.S. §§ 9799.14 (relating to sexual offenses and tier system) and 9799.55 (relating to registration).

(v) An offense under section 6301(a)(1) (relating to corruption of minors).

(2) An individual who meets any of the following:

(i) Has been convicted of murder, a felony of the first degree or an offense punishable by imprisonment of 20 or more years.

(ii) Has been convicted within the previous 20 years of:

(A) a felony or an offense punishable by imprisonment of seven or more years involving:

(I) an offense under Article B of Part II;

(II) an offense under Article D of Part II;

(III) an offense under Chapter 61; or

(IV) an offense specified in 42 Pa.C.S. §§ 9799.14 and 9799.55; or

(B) four or more offenses punishable by imprisonment of two or more years.

(iii) Has, within the previous 15 years, been convicted of:

(A) two or more offenses punishable by more than two years in prison; or

(B) any of the following:

(I) An offense under section 3127 (relating to indecent exposure).

(II) An offense under section 3129 (relating to sexual intercourse with animal).

(III) An offense under section 4915.1 (relating to failure to comply with registration requirements) or 4915.2 (relating to failure to comply with 42 Pa.C.S. Ch. 97 Subch. I registration requirements).

(IV) An offense under section 5122 (relating to weapons or implements for escape).

(V) An offense under section 5510 (relating to abuse of corpse).

(VI) An offense under section 5515 (relating to prohibiting of paramilitary training).

(3) (Deleted by amendment).

(4) (Deleted by amendment).

(5) (Deleted by amendment).

(6) (Deleted by amendment).

(7) (Deleted by amendment).

(8) (Deleted by amendment).

(9) (Deleted by amendment).

(c) Notice to district attorney.--The court shall provide notice of the filing of a petition under subsection (a) to the district attorney within 10 days. Within 30 days of receipt of notice, the district attorney may file objections to the petition. If no objection is timely filed, the court may grant the petition without further hearing if the requirements of this section have been met.

(d) Notice to central repository.--Notice of an order for limited access shall promptly be submitted to the central repository which shall notify all criminal justice agencies which have received criminal history record information related to such conviction that access to such criminal history record has been limited by order of the court.

(Feb. 16, 2016, P.L.10, No.5, eff. 270 days; June 28, 2018, P.L.402, No.56, eff. 180 days)

2018 Amendment. Act 56 amended the section heading and subsecs. (a) and (b). See section 4(2) of Act 56 in the appendix to this title for special provisions relating to applicability. See Act 56 in the appendix to this title for special provisions relating to findings and declarations.

2016 Amendment. Act 5 added section 9122.1.

Cross References. Section 9122.1 is referred to in sections 9121, 9122.3, 9122.5, 9122.6 of this title; section 1725.7 of Title 42 (Judiciary and Judicial Procedure).

§ 9122.2. Clean slate limited access.

(a) General rule.--The following shall be subject to limited access:

(1) Subject to the exceptions under section 9122.3 (relating to exceptions) or if a court has vacated an order for limited access under section 9122.4 (relating to order to vacate order for limited access), criminal history record information pertaining to a conviction of a misdemeanor of the second degree, a misdemeanor of the third degree or a misdemeanor offense punishable by imprisonment of no more than two years if a person has been free for 10 years from conviction for any offense punishable by imprisonment of one or more years and if completion of each court-ordered financial obligation of the sentence has occurred.

(2) Criminal history record information pertaining to charges which resulted in a final disposition other than a conviction.

(3) Criminal history record information pertaining to a conviction for a summary offense when 10 years have elapsed since entry of the judgment of conviction and completion of all court-ordered financial obligations of the sentence has occurred.

(b) Procedures.--

(1) On a monthly basis, the Administrative Office of Pennsylvania Courts shall transmit to the Pennsylvania State Police central repository the record of any conviction eligible for limited access under subsection (a)(1).

(2) The Administrative Office of Pennsylvania Courts shall transmit to the Pennsylvania State Police repository:

(i) The record of charges subject to limited access under subsection (a)(2) within 30 days after entry of the disposition and payment of each court-ordered obligation.

(ii) The record of any conviction under subsection (a)(3) within 30 days after the record becomes subject to limited access.

(3) If the Pennsylvania State Police central repository determines through a validation process that a record transmitted is not eligible for limited access relief under subsection (a) or does not match data held in the repository, the Pennsylvania State Police shall notify the Administrative Office of Pennsylvania Courts of this determination within 30 days of receiving the information.

(4) Upon the expiration of the 30-day period, the Administrative Office of Pennsylvania Courts shall remove from the list of eligible records any record for which the Administrative Office of Pennsylvania Courts received a notification of ineligibility or nonmatch with repository data.

(5) Each court of common pleas shall issue monthly an order for limited access for any record in its judicial district for which no notification of ineligibility was received by the Administrative Office of Pennsylvania Courts.

(c) Limitation on release of records.--A criminal history record that is the subject of an order for limited access under this section shall be made available to a noncriminal justice agency only as provided for in section 9121(b), (b.1) and (b.2) (relating to general regulations).

(June 28, 2018, P.L.402, No.56, eff. 365 days)

2018 Amendment. Act 56 added section 9122.2. See section 4(1) of Act 56 in the appendix to this title for special provisions relating to applicability. See Act 56 in the appendix to this title for special provisions relating to findings and declarations.

Cross References. Section 9122.2 is referred to in sections 9121, 9122.3, 9122.4, 9122.5, 9122.6 of this title.

§ 9122.3. Exceptions.

(a) Limited access not applicable.-- Limited access to records under section 9122.2(a)(1) (relating to clean slate limited access) shall not be granted for any of the following:

(1) A conviction for any of the following or an attempt, conspiracy or solicitation to commit any of the following:

(i) An offense under Article B of Part II (relating to offenses involving danger to the person).

(ii) An offense under Article D of Part II (relating to offenses against the family).

(iii) An offense under Chapter 61 (relating to firearms and other dangerous articles).

(iv) An offense specified under 42 Pa.C.S. §§ 9799.14 (relating to sexual offenses and tier system) and 9799.55 (relating to registration).

(v) An offense under section 5533 (relating to cruelty to animal).

(vi) An offense under section 6301 (relating to corruption of minors).

(2) An individual who at any time has been convicted of:

(i) A felony.

(ii) Two or more offenses punishable by imprisonment of more than two years.

(iii) Four or more offenses punishable by imprisonment of one or more years.

(iv) An offense under the following:

(A) Section 3127 (relating to indecent exposure).

(B) Section 3129 (relating to sexual intercourse with animal).

(C) Section 4915.1 (relating to failure to comply with registration requirements) or 4915.2 (relating to failure to comply with 42 Pa.C.S. Ch. 97 Subch. I registration requirements).

(D) Section 5122 (relating to weapons or implements for escape).

(E) Section 5510 (relating to abuse of corpse).

(F) Section 5515 (relating to prohibiting of paramilitary training).

(b) Limited access to same case.-- Limited access under this section shall not apply to an otherwise qualifying conviction if a conviction for an offense punishable by imprisonment of five or more years or an offense enumerated in subsection (a) arose out of the same case.

(c) Filing.--Nothing in this section shall preclude the filing of a petition for limited access under section 9122.1 (relating to petition for limited access) if limited access is available under that section.

(June 28, 2018, P.L.402, No.56, eff. 365 days)

2018 Amendment. Act 56 added section 9122.3. See Act 56 in the appendix to this title for special provisions relating to findings and declarations.

Cross References. Section 9122.3 is referred to in section 9122.2 of this title.

§ 9122.4. Order to vacate order for limited access.

(a) General rule.--Upon petition of the prosecuting attorney to the court where a conviction occurred, and with notice to the defendant and opportunity to be heard, the court shall vacate an order for limited access granted under section 9122.2 (relating to clean slate limited access) if the court determines that the order was erroneously entered and not in accordance with section 9122.2.

(b) Conviction.--Upon conviction of a misdemeanor or felony offense and motion of the prosecuting attorney, the court shall enter an order vacating any prior order for limited access pertaining to a record of the defendant, except under section 9122.2(a)(2).

(c) Transmission to repository.--An order under subsection (a) or (b) shall be transmitted to the central repository of the Pennsylvania State Police.

(June 28, 2018, P.L.402, No.56, eff. 365 days)

2018 Amendment. Act 56 added section 9122.4. See Act 56 in the appendix to this title for special provisions relating to findings and declarations.

Cross References. Section 9122.4 is referred to in section 9122.2 of this title.

§ 9122.5. Effects of expunged records and records subject to limited access.

(a) Disclosure.--

(1) Except if requested or required by a criminal justice agency, or if disclosure to noncriminal justice agencies is authorized or required by section 9121(b.1) and (b.2) (relating to general regulations), an individual may not be required or requested to disclose information about the individual's criminal history record that has been expunged or provided limited access under section 9122.1 (relating to petition for limited access) or 9122.2 (relating to clean slate limited access). An individual required or requested to provide information in violation of this section may respond as if the offense did not occur.

(2) This subsection shall not apply if Federal law, including rules and regulations promulgated by a self-regulatory organization that has been created under Federal law, requires the consideration of an applicant's criminal history for purposes of employment.

(b) Disqualification by law.--An expunged record or a record subject to limited access under section 9122.1 or 9122.2 may not be considered a conviction that would prohibit the employment of a person under any law of this Commonwealth or under Federal laws that prohibit employment based on State convictions to the extent permitted by Federal law.

(June 28, 2018, P.L.402, No.56, eff. 365 days)

2018 Amendment. Act 56 added section 9122.5. See Act 56 in the appendix to this title for special provisions relating to findings and declarations.

§ 9122.6. Employer immunity from liability.

An employer who employs or otherwise engages an individual whose criminal history record has been expunged or to which limited access has been applied under section 9122.1 (relating to petition for limited access) or 9122.2 (relating to clean slate limited access) shall be immune from liability for any claim arising out of the misconduct of the individual, if the misconduct relates to the portion of the criminal history record that has been expunged or provided limited access.

(June 28, 2018, P.L.402, No.56, eff. 365 days)

2018 Amendment. Act 56 added section 9122.6. See Act 56 in the appendix to this title for special provisions relating to findings and declarations.

Cross References. Section 9122.6 is referred to in section 9121 of this title.

§ 9123. Juvenile records.

(a) Expungement of juvenile records.-- Notwithstanding the provisions of section 9105 (relating to other criminal justice information) and except as provided under subsection (a.1), expungement of records of juvenile delinquency cases and cases involving summary offenses committed while the individual was under 18 years of age, wherever kept or retained, shall occur after 30 days' notice to the district attorney whenever the court upon its own motion or upon the motion of a child or the parents or guardian finds:

(1) a complaint is filed which is not substantiated or the petition which is filed as a result of a complaint is dismissed by the court;

(1.1) a written allegation is filed which was not approved for prosecution;

(1.2) six months have elapsed since the individual successfully completed an informal adjustment and no proceeding seeking adjudication or conviction is pending;

(2) six months have elapsed since the final discharge of the person from supervision under a consent decree or diversion program, including a program under 42 Pa.C.S. § 1520 (relating to adjudication alternative program) and no proceeding seeking adjudication or conviction is pending;

374

(2.1) the individual is 18 years of age or older and six months have elapsed since the individual has satisfied all terms and conditions of the sentence imposed following a conviction for a summary offense, with the exception of a violation of section 6308 (relating to purchase, consumption, possession or transportation of liquor or malt or brewed beverages), committed while the individual was under 18 years of age and, since satisfying all terms and conditions of the sentence, the individual has not been convicted of a felony, misdemeanor or adjudicated delinquent and no proceeding is pending to seek such conviction and adjudication;

(2.2) the individual is 18 years of age or older and has been convicted of a violation of section 6308 which occurred while the individual was under 18 years of age and six months have elapsed since the individual has satisfied all terms and conditions of the sentence imposed for the violation, including any suspension of operating privileges imposed under section 6310.4 (relating to restriction of operating privileges). Expungement shall include all criminal history record information and all administrative records of the Department of Transportation relating to the conviction;

(3) five years have elapsed since the final discharge of the person from commitment, placement, probation or any other disposition and referral and since such final discharge, the person has not been convicted of a felony, misdemeanor or adjudicated delinquent and no proceeding is pending seeking such conviction or adjudication; or

(4) the attorney for the Commonwealth consents to the expungement and a court orders the expungement after giving consideration to the following factors:

(i) the type of offense;

(ii) the individual's age, history of employment, criminal activity and drug or alcohol problems;

(iii) adverse consequences that the individual may suffer if the records are not expunged; and

(iv) whether retention of the record is required for purposes of protection of the public safety.

(a.1) Exceptions.--Subsection (a) shall not apply if any of the following apply:

(1) The individual meets all of the following:

(i) Was 14 years of age or older at the time the individual committed an offense which, if committed by an adult, would be classified as:

(A) An offense under section 3121 (relating to rape), 3123 (relating to involuntary deviate sexual intercourse) or 3125 (relating to aggravated indecent assault).

(B) An attempt, solicitation or conspiracy to commit an offense under section 3121, 3123 or 3125.

(ii) Was adjudicated delinquent for the offense under subparagraph (i).

(2) Upon cause shown.

(b) Notice to prosecuting attorney.--The court shall give notice of the applications for the expungement of juvenile records to the prosecuting attorney.

(c) Dependent children.--All records of children alleged to be or adjudicated dependent may be expunged upon court order after the child is 21 years of age or older.

(Dec. 14, 1979, P.L.556, No.127, eff. imd.; June 11, 1982, P.L.476, No.138, eff. 180 days; Dec. 11, 1986, P.L.1517, No.164, eff. 60 days; Mar. 15, 1995, 1st Sp.Sess., P.L.978, No.7, eff. 60 days; July 5, 2012, P.L.880, No.91, eff. Dec. 20, 2012; Oct. 25, 2012, P.L.1655, No.204, eff. 60 days; Sept. 27, 2014, P.L.2482, No.138, eff. 60 days)

2014 Amendment. Act 138 amended subsec. (a)(2.1).

2012 Amendments. Act 91 amended subsec. (a) intro. par. and added subsec. (a.1) and Act 204 amended subsec. (a).

References in Text. 18 Pa.C.S. § 6310.4, referred to in subsec. (a)(2.2), was repealed by the act of October 24, 2018 (P.L.659, No.95).

Cross References. Section 9123 is referred to in sections 2709, 9105 of this title; section 6328 of Title 42 (Judiciary and Judicial Procedure).

§ 9124. Use of records by licensing agencies.

(a) State agencies.--Except as provided by this chapter, a board, commission or department of the Commonwealth, when determining eligibility for licensing, certification, registration or permission to engage in a trade, profession or occupation, may consider convictions of the applicant of crimes but the convictions shall not preclude the issuance of a license, certificate, registration or permit.

(b) Prohibited use of information.--The following information shall not be used in consideration of an application for a license, certificate, registration or permit:

(1) Records of arrest if there is no conviction of a crime based on the arrest.

(2) Convictions which have been annulled or expunged.

(3) Convictions of a summary offense.

(4) Convictions for which the individual has received a pardon from the Governor.

(5) Convictions which do not relate to the applicant's suitability for the license, certificate, registration or permit.

(c) State action authorized.--Boards, commissions or departments of the Commonwealth authorized to license, certify, register or permit the practice of trades, occupations or professions may refuse to grant or renew, or may suspend or revoke any license, certificate, registration or permit for the following causes:

(1) Where the applicant has been convicted of a felony.

(2) Where the applicant has been convicted of a misdemeanor which relates to the trade, occupation or profession for which the license, certificate, registration or permit is sought.

(d) Notice.--The board, commission or department shall notify the individual in writing of the reasons for a decision which prohibits the applicant from practicing the trade, occupation or profession if such decision is based in whole or part on conviction of any crime.

(Dec. 14, 1979, P.L.556, No.127, eff. imd.)

1979 Amendment. Act 127 amended subsec. (b).

Cross References. Section 9124 is referred to in section 1310 of Title 4 (Amusements).

§ 9125. Use of records for employment.

(a) General rule.--Whenever an employer is in receipt of information which is part of an employment applicant's criminal history record information file, it may use that information for the purpose of deciding whether or not to hire the applicant, only in accordance with this section.

(b) Use of information.--Felony and misdemeanor convictions may be considered by the employer only to the extent to which they relate to the applicant's suitability for employment in the position for which he has applied.

(c) Notice.--The employer shall notify in writing the applicant if the decision not to hire the applicant is based in whole or in part on criminal history record information.

(Dec. 14, 1979, P.L.556, No.127, eff. imd.; June 11, 1982, P.L.476, No.138, eff. 180 days)

1982 Amendment. Act 138 amended subsec. (b).

SUBCHAPTER D
SECURITY

Sec.
9131. Security requirements for repositories.

Cross References. Subchapter D is referred to in section 9104 of this title.

§ 9131. Security requirements for repositories.

Every criminal justice agency collecting, storing or disseminating criminal history record information shall ensure the confidentiality and security of criminal history record information by providing that wherever such information is maintained, a criminal justice agency must:

(1) Institute procedures to reasonably protect any repository from theft, fire, sabotage, flood, wind or other natural or man-made disasters.

(2) Select, supervise and train all personnel authorized to have access to criminal history record information.

(3) Ensure that, where computerized data processing is employed, the equipment utilized for maintaining criminal history record information is solely dedicated to purposes related to the administration of criminal justice, or, if the equipment is not used solely for the administration of criminal justice, the criminal justice agency shall be accorded equal management participation in computer operations used to maintain the criminal history record information.

(June 11, 1982, P.L.476, No.138, eff. 180 days)

SUBCHAPTER E
AUDIT

§ 9141. Audits.

(a) Audit required.--

(1) The Attorney General shall conduct annual audits of the central repository and of a representative sample of all repositories. The Office of Attorney General shall conduct a review of State criminal justice agencies' automated policies and procedures established pursuant to section 9106 (relating to information in central repository or automated systems) to ensure that the provisions of this chapter are upheld within two years of the effective date of this act.

(2) The Pennsylvania State Police shall conduct an annual audit of at least 5% of all municipal police department plans, policies or procedures which are implemented pursuant to section 9106(c) to ensure that the provisions of this chapter are upheld. The first such audit shall be conducted within two years of the effective date of this act. A copy of the audit shall be submitted to the Attorney General.

(b) Access to records.--Persons conducting the audit shall be provided access to all records, reports and listings required to conduct an audit of criminal history record information, and all persons with access to such information or authorized to receive such information shall cooperate with and provide information requested.

(c) Contents of audit.--The audit shall contain a report of deficiencies and recommendations for the correction of such deficiencies. Upon the completion of every audit, the audited agency shall carry out the recommendations within a reasonable period of time unless the audit report is appealed to the Attorney General and the appeal is upheld.

(d) Modification of recommendations.-- The Attorney General shall have the power to modify the corrective measures recommended by the audit.

(Dec. 19, 1990, P.L.1332, No.207, eff. imd.)

§ 9142. Quality control.

Each repository shall establish effective procedures, in compliance with rules and regulations promulgated by the Attorney General, for the completeness and accuracy of criminal history record information.

§ 9143. Regulations.

It shall be the duty and responsibility of the Attorney General, in consultation with the Pennsylvania State Police, to adopt rules and regulations pursuant to this act. The Office of Attorney General, in consultation with the Pennsylvania State Police, shall have the power and authority to promulgate, adopt, publish and use guidelines for the implementation of this act for a period of one year immediately following the effective date of this section pending adoption of final rules and regulations.

(Dec. 19, 1990, P.L.1332, No.207, eff. imd.)

1990 Amendment. Act 207 added section 9143.

SUBCHAPTER F
INDIVIDUAL RIGHT OF ACCESS
AND REVIEW

Cross References. Subchapter F is referred to in section 9104 of this title.

§ 9151. Right to access and review.

(a) General rule.--Any individual or his legal representative has the right to review, challenge, correct and appeal the accuracy and completeness of his criminal history record information.

(b) Prisoners.--Persons incarcerated in correctional facilities and institutions may authorize a correctional employee to obtain a copy of their criminal history record information for the purpose of review, challenge and appeal.

§ 9152. Procedure.

(a) Rules and regulations.--The Attorney General in cooperation with appropriate criminal justice agencies shall promulgate rules and regulations to implement this section and shall establish reasonable fees.

(b) Requests for information.--Any individual requesting to review his or her own criminal history record information shall submit proper identification to the criminal justice agency which maintains his or her record. Proper identification shall be determined by the officials of the repository where the request is made. If criminal history record information exists the individual may review a copy of such information without undue delay for the purpose of review and challenge.

(c) Challenge of accuracy.--The individual may challenge the accuracy of his or her criminal history record information by specifying which portion of the record is incorrect and what the correct version should be. Failure to challenge any portion of the record in existence at that time will place the burden of proving the inaccuracy of any part subsequently challenged upon the individual. Information subsequently added to such record shall also be subject to review, challenge, correction or appeal.

(d) Review of challenge.--All criminal justice agencies shall have 60 days to conduct a review of any challenge and shall have the burden of proving the accuracy of the record. The decision on the challenge shall include all information, including, but not limited to, the jurisdiction and docket number of any relevant court decision which formed a basis for the decision. If the challenge is deemed valid, the appropriate officials must ensure that:

(1) The criminal history record information is corrected.

(2) A certified and corrected copy of the criminal history record information is provided to the individual.

(3) Prior erroneous criminal history record information disseminated to criminal justice agencies shall be destroyed or returned and replaced with corrected information.

(4) The individual is supplied with the names of those noncriminal justice agencies and individuals which have received erroneous criminal history record information.

(e) Appeals.--

(1) If the challenge is ruled invalid, an individual has the right to appeal the decision to the Attorney General within 30 days of notification of the decision by the criminal justice agency.

(2) The Attorney General shall conduct a hearing de novo in accordance with the Administrative Agency Law. The burden of proof shall be upon the party bearing the burden of proof on the challenge.

(3) The decision of the Attorney General may be appealed to the Commonwealth Court by an aggrieved individual.

(Oct. 17, 2008, P.L.1628, No.131, eff. imd.)

2008 Amendment. Act 131 amended subsecs. (d) and (e).

§ 9153. Individual rights on access and review.

Any individual exercising his or her right to access and review under the provisions of this subchapter shall be informed when criminal history record information is made available that he or she is under no obligation to divulge such information to any person or agency.

SUBCHAPTER G
RESPONSIBILITY OF ATTORNEY GENERAL

Sec.
9161. Duties of the Attorney General.
§ 9161. Duties of the Attorney General.
The Attorney General shall have the power and authority to:

(1) Establish rules and regulations for criminal history record information with respect to security, completeness, accuracy, individual access and review, quality control and audits of repositories.

(2) Establish the maximum fees which may be charged for the costs of reproducing criminal history record information for individual access and review for research or statistical purposes and for access by noncriminal justice agencies and individuals.

(3) Make investigations concerning all matters touching the administration and enforcement of this chapter and the rules and regulations promulgated thereunder.

(4) Institute civil proceedings for violations of this chapter and the rules and regulations adopted thereunder.

(5) Conduct annual audits of the central repository and of a representative sample of all repositories within the Commonwealth, collecting, compiling, maintaining and disseminating criminal history record information.

(6) Appoint such employees and agents as it may deem necessary.

(June 11, 1982, P.L.476, No.138, eff. 180 days)

SUBCHAPTER H
PUBLIC NOTICE

Sec.
9171. Requirements of repositories relating to public notice.
§ 9171. Requirements of repositories relating to public notice.
Repositories maintaining criminal history record information shall inform the public and post in a public place, notice of the existence, purpose, use and accessibility of the criminal history record information they maintain and the requirements of the repository for identification on individual access and review.

SUBCHAPTER I
SANCTIONS

Sec.
9181. General administrative sanctions.
9182. Criminal penalties (Deleted by amendment).
9183. Civil actions.
§ 9181. General administrative sanctions.
Any person, including any agency or organization, who violates the provisions of this chapter or any regulations or rules promulgated under it may:
(1) Be denied access to specified criminal history record information for such period of time as the Attorney General deems appropriate.
(2) Be subject to civil penalties or other remedies as provided for in this chapter.
(3) In the case of an employee of any agency who violates any provision of this chapter, be administratively disciplined by discharge, suspension, reduction in grade, transfer or other formal disciplinary action as the agency deems appropriate.
(June 11, 1982, P.L.476, No.138, eff. 180 days)

Cross References. Section 9181 is referred to in section 9106 of this title.
§ 9182. Criminal penalties (Deleted by amendment).

1979 Amendment. Section 9182 was deleted by amendment December 14, 1979 (P.L.556, No.127), effective immediately.
§ 9183. Civil actions.

(a) Injunctions.--The Attorney General or any other individual or agency may institute an action in a court of proper jurisdiction against any person, agency or organization to enjoin any criminal justice agency, noncriminal justice agency, organization or individual violating the provisions of this chapter or to compel such agency, organization or person to comply with the provisions of this chapter.
(b) Action for damages.--
(1) Any person aggrieved by a violation of the provisions of this chapter or of the rules and regulations promulgated under this chapter, shall have the substantive right to bring an action for damages by reason of such violation in a court of competent jurisdiction.
(2) A person found by the court to have been aggrieved by a violation of this chapter or the rules or regulations promulgated under this chapter, shall be entitled to actual and real damages of not less than $100 for each violation and to reasonable costs of litigation and attorney's fees. Exemplary and punitive damages of not less than $1,000 nor more than $10,000 shall be imposed for any violation of this chapter, or the rules or regulations adopted under this chapter, found to be willful.

Cross References. Section 9183 is referred to in section 9106 of this title.

CHAPTER 92 CONFLICTS OF INTEREST

Sec.
9201. Procedures.

Enactment. Chapter 92 was added November 3, 2016, P.L.1016, No.131, effective in 60 days.
§ 9201. Procedures.
If a district attorney requests that the Attorney General exercise the power to prosecute in a county criminal court or juvenile delinquency court under section 205(a)(3) of the act of October 15, 1980 (P.L.950, No.164), known as the Commonwealth Attorneys Act, and the Attorney General declines to accept or act on the request, the following shall apply:
(1) The district attorney may refer the matter to a district attorney of a contiguous county who has sufficient resources and has no

conflict of interest in representing the Commonwealth.

(2) If the district attorneys of the contiguous counties decline to accept the referral for any reason, the referring district attorney may refer the matter to a district attorney of a noncontiguous county.

(3) A district attorney who has accepted a case under paragraph (1) or (2) and a deputy or assistant district attorney on the district attorney's staff shall have the same authority to investigate and prosecute as the district attorney who referred the matter.

CHAPTER 93 INDEPENDENT COUNSEL (Repealed)

2016 Repeal. Chapter 93 (Subchapters A - D) was added February 18, 1998, P.L.102, No.19 and repealed November 3, 2016, P.L.1016, No.131, effective in 60 days. The subject matter is now contained in Chapter 95 of this title.

CHAPTER 94 CRIME VICTIMS

Sec.
9401. Definitions.
9402. Office of Victim Advocate.

Enactment. Chapter 94 was added October 25, 2012, P.L.1655, No.204, effective in 60 days.

§ 9401. Definitions.
The following words and phrases when used in this chapter shall have the meanings given to them in this section unless the context clearly indicates otherwise:

"Crime Victims Act." The act of November 24, 1998 (P.L.882, No.111), known as the Crime Victims Act.

"Office of Victim Advocate." The Office of Victim Advocate established under section 302 of the act of November 24, 1998 (P.L.882, No.111), known as the Crimes Victims Act.

§ 9402. Office of Victim Advocate.
The Office of Victim Advocate has the power and duty to represent and advocate for the interests of individual crime victims in accordance with section 302 of the Crime Victims Act, and advocate for the interests of crime victims generally, including the victims of crimes committed by juveniles.

CHAPTER 95 INDEPENDENT COUNSEL

Subchapter
A. Preliminary Provisions
B. General Provisions
C. Authority and Duties of Independent Counsel

Enactment. Chapter 95 was added November 3, 2016, P.L.1016, No.131, effective in 60 days.

SUBCHAPTER A
PRELIMINARY PROVISIONS

Sec.
9501. Scope of chapter.
9502. Definitions.
9503. Administrative expenses.
§ 9501. Scope of chapter.
This chapter relates to independent counsel authorization.

§ 9502. Definitions.
The following words and phrases when used in this chapter shall have the meanings given to them in this section unless the context clearly indicates otherwise:

"Grounds to investigate." Information which would lead a reasonable person to suspect that a crime is being or has been committed.

"Independent counsel." A person appointed by the panel upon the request of a special investigative counsel.

"Panel." The Special Independent Prosecutor's Panel established under this chapter.

"Requesting judge." A president judge of a court of common pleas, or a judge of an intermediate court sitting in the court's original jurisdiction, who applies for the appointment of a special investigative counsel to investigate a contempt of court.

"Special investigative counsel." A person appointed by the panel to conduct a preliminary investigation under this chapter.

§ 9503. Administrative expenses.

All expenses attributable to the appointment of either a special investigative counsel or an independent counsel shall be paid from the annual appropriation for the Office of Attorney General's general government operations.

SUBCHAPTER B
GENERAL PROVISIONS

Sec.
9511. Organization of panel.
9512. Preliminary investigation.
9513. Conduct of preliminary investigation.
9514. Determination that further investigation not warranted.
9515. Determination that further investigation is warranted.
9516. Contents of application.
9517. Duties of panel.
9518. Disclosure of information.

§ 9511. Organization of panel.

(a) Composition and selection.--The Special Independent Prosecutor's Panel shall be composed of one judge of the Superior Court and two judges, which may include senior judges, of the courts of common pleas of the Commonwealth. The members of the panel shall be chosen by lot. The procedure shall be determined and supervised by the Court Administrator of Pennsylvania in the Administrative Office of Pennsylvania Courts. The Administrative Office of Pennsylvania Courts shall disclose to the public the membership of the panel and publish the membership on its publicly accessible Internet website and in the Pennsylvania Bulletin.

(b) Term of members.--Each member of the panel shall hold office for a term of three years. Judges who are members of the panel and are required to retire under section 16 of Article V of the Constitution of Pennsylvania shall also vacate their positions on the panel unless assigned under Pa.R.J.A. No. 701 (relating to assignment of judges to courts), No. 702 (relating to divisional assignments of judges), No. 703 (relating to reports of judges), No. 704 (relating to judicial leave), No. 705 (relating to seniority of judges) or No. 706

(relating to determination or selection of Chief Justice and president and administrative judges). A judge who is otherwise removed or suspended from office shall automatically forfeit the position held by that judge on the panel.

(c) Vacancies.--Any vacancy on the panel shall be filled only for the remainder of the three-year period in which the vacancy occurs and in the same manner as initial assignments to the panel were made.

(d) Decisions by majority vote.--All decisions of the panel shall be by majority vote of the members.

(e) Clerk.--The Prothonotary of the Superior Court shall serve as the clerk of the panel and shall provide services as are needed by the panel.

(f) Restriction.--A member of the panel who participated in a function conferred on the panel under this chapter involving an independent counsel shall not be eligible to participate in any judicial or disciplinary proceeding concerning a matter which involves the independent counsel and which involves the exercise of the independent counsel's official duties, notwithstanding whether the independent counsel is still serving in that office.

§ 9512. Preliminary investigation.

(a) Covered persons.--The panel, upon the petition of a district attorney, shall appoint a special investigative counsel to conduct a preliminary investigation in accordance with this chapter whenever the panel receives information from a district attorney sufficient to constitute grounds to investigate whether any person described in subsection (b) may have committed an offense which is classified higher than a summary offense in the district attorney's county. If a district attorney receives information that any person described in subsection (b) may have committed an offense which is classified higher than a summary offense in a county other than the district attorney's county, the district attorney shall refer the information to the district attorney of that county.

(a.1) Special investigative counsel.--The panel, upon the petition of the requesting judge, shall appoint a special investigative counsel to conduct a preliminary investigation in accordance with this chapter whenever the panel receives information from a requesting judge sufficient to constitute grounds to investigate criminal contempt of court as described in subsection (d).

(b) Applicability.--The persons referred to in subsection (a) shall be as follows:

(1) The Attorney General.

(1.1) A deputy Attorney General or an individual working in the Office of Attorney General who is defined as a "public employee" under 65 Pa.C.S. § 1102 (relating to definitions) acting in concert with the Attorney General to commit an offense which is classified higher than a summary offense.

(2) Any individual who leaves any office or position described in paragraph (1) or (1.1) during the incumbency of the Attorney General with or under whom the individual served in the office or position, plus one year after the incumbency, but not longer than a period of three years after the individual leaves the office or position. This paragraph shall only apply to an individual described in paragraph (1.1) who may have acted in concert with an individual described in paragraph (1) to commit an offense which is classified higher than a summary offense.

(3) Any individual who held an office or position described in paragraph (1) or (1.1) during the incumbency of one Attorney General and who continued to hold the office or position for not more than 90 days into the term of the next Attorney General, during the one-year period after the individual leaves the office or position. This paragraph shall only apply to an individual described in paragraph (1.1) who may have acted in concert with an individual described in paragraph (1) to commit an offense which is classified higher than a summary offense.

(4) The chairman and treasurer of the principal campaign committee seeking the election or reelection of the Attorney General, and any officer of that committee exercising authority at the State level, during the incumbency of the elected Attorney General. This paragraph shall only apply to an individual described in paragraph (1.1) who may have acted in concert with an individual described in paragraph (1) to commit an offense which is classified higher than a summary offense.

(b.1) Petition for special investigative counsel.--A district attorney, at his or her discretion, may petition the panel to appoint special investigative counsel, if the district attorney with appropriate jurisdiction receives information that any person described in subsection (b)(1.1), (2), (3) or (4) may have committed an offense which is classified higher than a summary offense regardless of whether or not the individual acted in concert with a person described in subsection (b)(1).

(c) Examination of information to determine need for preliminary investigation.--In determining under subsection (a) whether grounds to investigate exist, a district attorney shall consider only the specificity of the information received and the credibility of the source of the information. A district attorney shall determine whether grounds to investigate exist no later than 90 days after the information is first received. If within that 90-day period a district attorney determines that the information is not specific or is not from a credible source, then a district attorney shall close the matter. If within that 90-day period a district attorney determines that the information is specific and from a credible source, the district attorney shall, upon making that determination, petition the panel to appoint a special investigative counsel to commence a preliminary investigation with respect to that information. If a district attorney is unable to determine within that 90-day period whether the information is specific and from a credible source, the district attorney shall at the end of that 90-day period petition the panel to appoint a special investigative counsel to commence a preliminary investigation with respect to that information. If a special investigative counsel is appointed, the special investigative counsel may only accept the appointment when the appointment would not conflict with the rules governing professional conduct.

(d) Requesting judge's application.--A requesting judge, on his own or at the request of another judge, may apply to the panel for appointment of a special investigative counsel upon a certification that there are reasonable grounds to believe that:

(1) there has been a criminal contempt of court;

(2) investigation by a prosecutor may be necessary to address a breach in the sanctity of court proceedings; and

(3) the prosecutor with statutory authority to conduct the investigation has or is likely to have a conflict of interest.

(e) Compensation.--A special investigative counsel appointed under this chapter shall receive compensation at the per diem rate equal to the annual rate of basic pay payable to the Attorney General. A special investigative counsel shall be entitled to the payment of travel expenses.

Cross References. Section 9512 is referred to in section 9517 of this title.

§ 9513. Conduct of preliminary investigation.

(a) In general.--A preliminary investigation conducted under this chapter shall be of matters as the special investigative counsel considers appropriate in order to make a determination under section 9514 (relating to determination that further investigation not warranted) or 9515 (relating to determination that further investigation is warranted) of whether further investigation is warranted with respect to each potential violation or allegation of a violation of criminal law. The special investigative counsel shall make the determination no later than 90 days after the preliminary investigation is commenced. The special investigative counsel shall promptly notify the panel of the date of the commencement of the preliminary investigation.

(b) Limited authority of special investigative counsel.--

(1) In conducting preliminary investigations under this chapter, the special investigative counsel shall have no authority to convene grand juries, plea bargain, grant immunity or issue subpoenas.

(2) The special investigative counsel shall not base a determination under this chapter that information with respect to a violation of criminal law by a person is not specific and from a credible source upon a determination that the person lacked the state of mind required for the violation of criminal law. The special investigative counsel shall not base a determination under this chapter that there are no reasonable grounds to believe that further investigation is warranted upon a determination that the person lacked the state of mind required for the violation of criminal law involved unless there is clear and convincing evidence that the person lacked the required state of mind.

(c) Extension of time for preliminary investigation.--The special investigative counsel may apply to the panel for a single extension, for a period of no more than 60 days, of the 90-day period referred to in subsection (a). The panel may, upon a showing of good cause, grant the extension.

Cross References. Section 9513 is referred to in section 9515 of this title.

§ 9514. Determination that further investigation not warranted.

(a) Notification of panel.--If the special investigative counsel, upon completion of a preliminary investigation under this chapter, determines that there are no reasonable grounds to believe that further investigation is warranted, the special investigative counsel shall promptly so notify the panel.

(b) Form of notification.--The notification shall contain a summary of the information received, a summary of the results of the preliminary investigation and all materials collected as part of the preliminary investigation. The summaries shall be confidential and not subject to public disclosure. The summaries shall be considered an exception for the purposes of section 708(b)(16) of the act of February 14, 2008 (P.L.6, No.3), known as the Right-to-Know Law.

Cross References. Section 9514 is referred to in sections 9513, 9515 of this title.

§ 9515. Determination that further investigation is warranted.

(a) Application for appointment of independent counsel.--The special investigative counsel shall apply to the panel for the appointment of an independent counsel if the special investigative counsel, upon completion of a preliminary investigation under this chapter, determines that there are reasonable grounds to believe that further investigation is warranted.

(a.1) Review by panel.--The panel shall review and consider appointing independent counsel if the 90-day period referred to in section 9513(a) (relating to conduct of preliminary investigation) and any extension granted under section 9513(c) have elapsed and the special investigative counsel has not filed a notification with the panel under section 9514(a) (relating to determination that further investigation not warranted).

(b) Receipt of additional information.-- If, after submitting a notification under section 9514(a), the special investigative counsel receives additional information sufficient to constitute grounds to investigate the matters to which the notification related, the special investigative counsel shall:

(1) Conduct an additional preliminary investigation as the special investigative counsel considers appropriate for a period of no more than 90 days after the date on which the additional information is received.

(2) Otherwise comply with the provisions of this subchapter with respect to the additional preliminary investigation to the same extent as any other preliminary investigation under this chapter.

Cross References. Section 9515 is referred to in section 9513 of this title.

§ 9516. Contents of application.

Any application for the appointment of an independent counsel under this chapter shall contain sufficient information to assist the panel in selecting an independent counsel and in defining that independent counsel's prosecutorial jurisdiction so that the independent counsel has adequate authority to fully investigate and prosecute the subject matter and all matters related to that subject matter.

Cross References. Section 9516 is referred to in section 9518 of this title.

§ 9517. Duties of panel.

(a) Appointment and jurisdiction of independent counsel.--

(1) Upon receipt of an application, the panel shall appoint an appropriate independent counsel and shall define that independent counsel's prosecutorial jurisdiction. The appointment shall occur no later than 30 days after the receipt of the application.

(2) The panel shall appoint as independent counsel an individual who has appropriate experience and who will conduct the investigation and any prosecution in a prompt, responsible and cost-effective manner. The panel shall seek to appoint as independent counsel an individual who will serve to the extent necessary to complete the investigation and any prosecution without undue delay. The panel may not appoint as an independent counsel any person who holds any office of profit or trust with the Commonwealth. A person who is serving as a special investigative counsel may not be appointed or serve as an independent counsel in the matter for which the person had been appointed to investigate as special investigative counsel. If an independent

counsel is appointed, the independent counsel may only accept the appointment when the appointment would not conflict with the rules governing professional conduct.

(3) In defining the independent counsel's prosecutorial jurisdiction, the panel shall assure that the independent counsel has adequate authority to fully investigate and prosecute the subject matter with respect to which the special investigative counsel has requested the appointment of the independent counsel and all matters related to that subject matter. Jurisdiction shall also include the authority to investigate and prosecute an offense classified higher than a summary offense or a contempt of court which may arise out of the investigation with respect to which the special investigative counsel's request was made.

(4) The panel shall disclose the identity of the independent counsel upon appointment.

(b) Expansion of jurisdiction.--

(1) The panel upon the request of a district attorney or a requesting judge may expand the prosecutorial jurisdiction of an independent counsel. The expansion may be in lieu of the appointment of another independent counsel.

(2) If the independent counsel discovers or receives information about possible violations of criminal law by persons as provided in section 9512 (relating to preliminary investigation) which are not covered by the prosecutorial jurisdiction of the independent counsel, the independent counsel may submit the information to a district attorney. In accordance with this subchapter, a district attorney shall petition the panel to appoint a special investigative counsel to conduct a preliminary investigation of the information, except that the preliminary investigation shall not exceed 30 days from the date the information is received. In making the determinations required by this subchapter, the special investigative counsel shall give great weight to any recommendations of the independent counsel.

(3) If the special investigative counsel determines, after according great weight to the recommendations of the independent counsel, that there are no reasonable grounds to believe that further investigation is warranted, the special investigative counsel shall promptly notify the panel.

(4) The panel shall expand the jurisdiction of the appropriate independent counsel to

include the matters involved or shall appoint another independent counsel to investigate the matters if:

(i) the special investigative counsel determines that there are reasonable grounds to believe that further investigation is warranted; or

(ii) the 30-day period referred to in paragraph (2) elapses without a notification to the panel that no further investigation is warranted.

(5) If the independent counsel discovers or receives information about possible violations of criminal law by persons other than those provided for in section 9512 and which are not covered by the prosecutorial jurisdiction of the independent counsel and a request for expansion under this subsection has not been made by a district attorney or a requesting judge or the request for expansion under this subsection has been denied by the panel, the independent counsel shall submit the information to the appropriate law enforcement authority.

(c) **Return for further explanation.--** Upon receipt of a notification under this subchapter that there are no reasonable grounds to believe that further investigation is warranted with respect to information received under this chapter, the panel shall have no authority to overrule this determination but may return the matter to the special investigative counsel for further explanation of the reasons for the determination.

(d) **Vacancies.--**If a vacancy in office arises by reason of the resignation, death or removal of an independent counsel, the panel shall appoint an independent counsel to complete the work of the independent counsel whose resignation, death or removal caused the vacancy, except that, in the case of a vacancy arising by reason of the removal of an independent counsel, the panel may appoint an acting independent counsel to serve until any judicial review of the removal is completed.

§ 9518. Disclosure of information.

Except as otherwise provided in this chapter, no officer or employee of the office of special investigative counsel or the office of independent counsel may, without leave of the panel, disclose to any individual outside the office of special investigative counsel or office of independent counsel any notification, application or any other document, material or memorandum supplied to the panel under this chapter, including an application submitted under section 9516 (relating to contents of application) or the identity of a special investigative counsel or independent counsel. Nothing in this chapter shall be construed as authorizing the withholding of information from the General Assembly unless the panel determines that disclosure of the information would not be in the best interest of justice.

SUBCHAPTER C
AUTHORITY AND DUTIES OF
INDEPENDENT COUNSEL

§ 9531. Authorities.

Notwithstanding any other provision of law, an independent counsel appointed under this chapter shall have, with respect to all matters in the independent counsel's prosecutorial jurisdiction established under this chapter, full power and independent authority to exercise all investigative and prosecutorial functions and powers of the Office of Attorney General, the Attorney General and any other officer or employee of the Office of Attorney General. Investigative and prosecutorial functions and powers shall include, but are not limited to:

(1) Conducting proceedings before grand juries and other investigations.

(2) Participating in court proceedings and engaging in any litigation, including civil and criminal matters, that the independent counsel considers necessary.

(3) Appealing any decision of a court in any case or proceeding in which the independent counsel participates in an official capacity.

(4) Reviewing all documentary evidence available from any source.

(5) Determining whether to contest the assertion of any testimonial privilege.

(6) Receiving appropriate security clearances and, if necessary, contesting in court, including, where appropriate, participating in an in camera proceeding, any claim of privilege or attempt to withhold evidence on grounds of security.

(7) Making applications to any State court for a grant of immunity to any witness, consistent with applicable statutory requirements, or for warrants, subpoenas or other court orders and exercising the authority vested in the Attorney General or a district attorney.

(8) Inspecting, obtaining or using the original or a copy of any tax return in accordance with applicable statutes and regulations.

(9) Initiating and conducting prosecutions in any court of competent jurisdiction, framing and signing indictments, filing information and handling all aspects of any case in the name of the Commonwealth.

(10) Consulting with the district attorney for the county in which any violation of law with respect to which the independent counsel is appointed was alleged to have occurred.

§ 9532. Compensation and travel expenses.

An independent counsel appointed under this chapter shall receive compensation at the per diem rate equal to the annual rate of basic pay payable to the Attorney General. An independent counsel and persons appointed under section 9533 (relating to additional personnel) shall be entitled to the payment of travel expenses.

Cross References. Section 9532 is referred to in section 9543 of this title.

§ 9533. Additional personnel.

For the purposes of carrying out the duties of the office of independent counsel, the independent counsel may appoint, fix the compensation and assign the duties of the employees the independent counsel considers necessary, including, but not limited to, investigators, attorneys and necessary experts to assist with the criminal investigation. The positions of these employees are exempted from the competitive service. Employees shall be compensated at levels not to exceed those payable for comparable positions in the Office of Attorney General.

Cross References. Section 9533 is referred to in sections 9532, 9538, 9539, 9543 of this title.

§ 9534. Assistance of Pennsylvania State Police.

An independent counsel may request assistance from the Pennsylvania State Police in carrying out the functions of the independent counsel, and the Pennsylvania State Police shall provide that assistance, which may include the use of the resources and personnel necessary to perform the independent counsel's duties.

§ 9535. Referral of other matters to independent counsel.

An independent counsel may petition the panel to refer to the independent counsel matters related to the independent counsel's prosecutorial jurisdiction, and the panel may refer these matters.

Cross References. Section 9535 is referred to in section 9545 of this title.

§ 9536. Dismissal of matters.

The independent counsel shall have full authority to dismiss matters within the independent counsel's prosecutorial jurisdiction at any subsequent time before prosecution.

§ 9537. Reports by independent counsel.

(a) Required reports.--An independent counsel shall:

(1) File with the panel, with respect to the six-month period beginning on the date of appointment and with respect to each six-month period thereafter until the office of that independent counsel terminates, a report which identifies and details all actual expenses, summarizes all other expenses incurred by that office during the six-month period with respect to which the report is filed and estimates future expenses of that office.

(2) Before the termination of the independent counsel's office under section 9543(b) (relating to removal of independent counsel and termination of office), file a final

report with the panel, setting forth fully and completely a description of all prosecutions. All other information shall be confidential and not subject to public disclosure.

(a.1) Subject to requirements.-- Individuals serving as an independent counsel and persons employed by or serving an independent counsel shall be subject to the requirements of the following acts:

(1) The act of July 19, 1957 (P.L.1017, No.451), known as the State Adverse Interest Act.

(2) The provisions of 65 Pa.C.S. Ch. 11 (relating to ethics standards and financial disclosure).

(b) Disclosure of information in reports.--The panel may release to the General Assembly, the Governor, the State Treasurer, the public or any appropriate person the portions of a report made under this section as the panel considers appropriate. The panel shall make any orders as are appropriate to protect the rights of any individual named in the report and to prevent undue interference with any pending prosecution. The panel may make any portion of a final report filed under subsection (a)(2) available to any individual named in the report for the purposes of receiving within a time limit set by the panel any comments or factual information that the individual may submit. The comments and factual information, in whole or in part, may in the discretion of the panel be included as an appendix to the final report.

Cross References. Section 9537 is referred to in sections 9542, 9543 of this title.

§ 9538. Independence from Office of Attorney General.

Each independent counsel appointed under this chapter and the persons appointed by that independent counsel under section 9533 (relating to additional personnel) are separate from and independent of the Office of Attorney General.

§ 9539. Standards of conduct.

(a) Restrictions on employment while independent counsel and appointees are serving.--During the period in which an independent counsel is serving under this chapter, the independent counsel and any person associated with a firm with which the independent counsel is associated may not represent in any matter any person involved in any investigation or prosecution under this chapter. During the period in which any person appointed by an independent counsel under section 9533 (relating to additional personnel) is serving in the office of independent counsel, the person may not represent in any matter any person involved in any investigation or prosecution under this chapter.

(b) Postemployment restrictions on independent counsel and appointees.--

(1) Each independent counsel and each person appointed by that independent counsel under section 9533 may not for three years following the termination of service under this chapter of that independent counsel or appointed person, as the case may be, represent any person in any matter if that individual was the subject of an investigation or prosecution conducted by that independent counsel under this chapter.

(2) Each independent counsel and each person appointed by that independent counsel under section 9533 may not for one year following the termination of service under this chapter of that independent counsel or appointed person, as the case may be, represent any person in any matter involving any investigation or prosecution under this chapter.

(c) One-year ban on representation by members of firms of independent counsel.-- Any person who is associated with a firm with which an independent counsel is associated or becomes associated after termination of service of that independent counsel under this chapter may not for one year following the termination represent any person in any matter involving any investigation or prosecution under this chapter.

(d) Definitions.--As used in this section, the following words and phrases shall have the meanings given to them in this subsection:

"Associated with a firm." A person who is an officer, director, partner or other member or employee of a law firm.

"Firm." A law firm, whether organized as a partnership or corporation.

§ 9540. Custody of records of independent counsel.

(a) Transfer of records.--Upon termination of the office of independent counsel, that independent counsel shall transfer to the Bureau of the Pennsylvania State Archives of the Pennsylvania Historical and Museum Commission all records which have been created or received by that office. Before this transfer, the independent counsel shall clearly identify which of these records are subject to the Pennsylvania Rules of Criminal Procedure as grand jury materials.

(b) Maintenance, use and disposal of records.--Records transferred to the Bureau of the Pennsylvania State Archives under this section shall be maintained, used and disposed of as provided by law.

§ 9541. Cost controls and administrative support.

(a) Cost controls.--An independent counsel shall:

(1) Conduct all activities with due regard for expense.

(2) Authorize only reasonable and lawful expenditures.

(3) Promptly upon taking office assign to a specific employee the duty of certifying that expenditures of the independent counsel are reasonable and made in accordance with law.

(b) Office of Administration policies.--An independent counsel shall comply with the established policies of the Office of Administration of the Governor respecting expenditures of funds, except to the extent that compliance would be inconsistent with the purposes of this chapter.

§ 9542. Legislative oversight.

(a) Oversight of conduct of independent counsel.--An independent counsel appointed under this chapter shall submit to the General Assembly a report detailing all funds expended as required under section 9537(a)(1) (relating to reports by independent counsel) and shall submit annually a report on the activities of the independent counsel, including a description of the progress of any investigation or prosecution conducted by the independent counsel. The report may omit any matter that in the judgment of the independent counsel should be kept confidential but shall provide information adequate to justify the expenditures that the office of the independent counsel has made.

(b) Information relating to impeachment.--An independent counsel shall advise the House of Representatives of any substantial and credible information which the independent counsel receives in carrying out the independent counsel's responsibilities under this chapter that may constitute grounds for an impeachment. Nothing in this chapter shall prevent the General Assembly or either house thereof from obtaining information in the course of an impeachment proceeding.

§ 9543. Removal of independent counsel and termination of office.

(a) Removal, report on removal and termination.--

(1) An independent counsel appointed under this chapter may be removed from office only by the personal action of the panel and only for good cause, physical disability, mental incapacity or any other condition that substantially impairs the performance of the independent counsel's duties. For purposes of this paragraph, the term "good cause" includes violations of any ethical rules governing the independent counsel, the Attorney General or district attorneys.

(2) If an independent counsel is removed from office, the panel shall promptly submit to the Judiciary Committee of the Senate and the Judiciary Committee of the House of Representatives a report specifying the facts found and the ultimate grounds for the removal. The committees may make available to the public the report, except that each committee may, if necessary to protect the rights of any individual named in the report or to prevent undue interference with any pending prosecution, postpone or refrain from publishing any or all of the report. The panel may release any or all of the report in accordance with section 9537(b) (relating to reports by independent counsel).

(3) An independent counsel removed from office may obtain judicial review of the removal in a civil action commenced in the Commonwealth Court. The independent counsel may be reinstated or granted other appropriate relief by order of the Commonwealth Court. A member of the panel may not hear or determine the civil action or any appeal of a decision in the civil action.

(b) Termination of office.--

(1) An office of independent counsel shall terminate when the independent counsel:

(i) notifies the panel that the investigation of all matters within the prosecutorial jurisdiction of the independent counsel or accepted by the independent counsel, and any resulting prosecutions, have been completed; and

(ii) files a final report in compliance with section 9537.

(2) The panel shall determine on its own motion whether termination is appropriate under this subsection no later than two years after the appointment of an independent counsel

or the reported expenditures of the independent counsel, including personnel costs under sections 9532 (relating to compensation and travel expenses) and 9533 (relating to additional personnel), have reached $2,000,000, whichever occurs first, and at the end of each succeeding one-year period.

Cross References. Section 9543 is referred to in section 9537 of this title.

§ 9544. Audits.

By December 31 of each year, an independent counsel shall prepare a statement of expenditures for the fiscal year that ended on the immediately preceding June 30. An independent counsel whose office is terminated prior to the end of the fiscal year shall prepare a statement of expenditures within 90 days of the date on which the office is terminated. The Auditor General shall audit each statement and report the results of each audit to the appropriate committees of the General Assembly no later than March 31 of the year following the submission of the statement.

§ 9545. Relationship with Office of Attorney General.

Whenever a matter is in the prosecutorial jurisdiction of an independent counsel or has been accepted by an independent counsel under section 9535 (relating to referral of other matters to independent counsel), the Office of Attorney General, the Attorney General, all other officers and employees of the Office of Attorney General and any district attorney shall suspend all investigations and proceedings regarding that matter and shall turn over to the independent counsel all materials, files and other data relating to that matter.

§ 9546. Venue.

The proper venue for all prosecutions conducted by the independent counsel shall be determined in accordance with the Pennsylvania Rules of Criminal Procedure, except that for the purposes of convenience and fairness, the panel may set the venue in any other county on its own motion or at the request of the independent counsel or on petition of the defendant.

APPENDIX TO TITLE 18
CRIMES AND OFFENSES

Supplementary Provisions of Amendatory Statutes

1972, DECEMBER 6, P.L.1482, NO.334

§ 2. Offenses committed prior to June 6, 1973.

Title 18 of the Pennsylvania Consolidated Statutes (relating to crimes and offenses), as added by this act, does not apply to offenses committed prior to the effective date of this act and prosecutions for such offenses shall be governed by the prior law, which is continued in effect for that purpose, as if this act were not in force. For the purposes of this section, an offense was committed prior to the effective date of this act if any of the elements of the offense occurred prior thereto.

§ 3. Severability.

If any provision of this act or the application thereof to any person or circumstances is held invalid, such invalidity shall not affect other provisions or applications of the act which can be given effect without the invalid provision or application, and to this end the provisions of this act are declared to be severable.

§ 4. Applicability of Statutory Construction Act.

Sections 72 and 94 of the Statutory Construction Act shall not be applicable to any provision of Title 18 of the Pennsylvania Consolidated Statutes (relating to crimes and offenses) as added by this act, except Article G (relating to miscellaneous offenses) of Part II (relating to definition of specific offenses).

References in Text. The Statutory Construction Act of 1937, referred to in text, was repealed December 6, 1972, P.L.1339, No.290, effective immediately, and the former provisions of sections 72 and 94 are now contained in sections 1952 and 1974, respectively, of Title 1 (General Provisions).

§ 6. Effective date.

This act shall take effect January 1, 1972, or six months from the date of final enactment, whichever is later.

Effective Date. The effective date of Act 334 was June 6, 1973.

1974, MARCH 26, P.L.213, NO.46

§ 5. Severability.

If any subparagraph, paragraph, or subsection of section 2502 of the "Crimes Code," as amended by this act, or any other provision of this act or the application thereof to any person or circumstances is held invalid, such invalidity shall not affect other subparagraphs, paragraphs, subsections, provisions or applications of the act which can be given effect without the invalid subparagraph, paragraph, subsection, provision or application, and to this end the provisions of this act are declared to be severable.

1976, DECEMBER 2, P.L.1230, NO.272

§ 2. Severability.

The provisions of this act shall not affect any act done, liability incurred or right accrued or vested, or affect any suit or prosecution pending or to be instituted to enforce any right or penalty or punish any offense under the authority of any act or part thereof repealed in this act.

Explanatory Note. Act 272 amended section 3929 of Title 18.

1978, NOVEMBER 26, P.L.1316, NO.319

Explanatory Note. The provisions of Act 319 of 1978 which were formerly contained in this appendix are now contained in the appendix to Title 42 (Judiciary and Judicial Procedure).

1982, JUNE 18, P.L.537, NO.154

§ 2. Right of action for injunction, damages or other relief.

(a) General rule.--Any person who incurs injury to his person or damage or loss to his property as a result of conduct described in 18 Pa.C.S. § 2710 (relating to ethnic intimidation) or 18 Pa.C.S. § 3307 (relating to institutional vandalism) shall have a right of action against the actor for injunction, damages or other appropriate civil or equitable relief. In any such action the issue of whether the defendant engaged in the conduct alleged shall be determined according to the burden of proof used in other civil actions for similar relief.

(b) Damages and expenses recoverable.--The plaintiff in an action under this section may recover:

(1) General and special damages, including damages for emotional distress.

(2) Punitive damages.

(3) Reasonable attorneys fees and costs.

1989, NOVEMBER 17, P.L.592, NO.64

§ 6. Severability.

The provisions of this act are severable. If any word, phrase or provision of this act or its application to any person or circumstance is held invalid, the invalidity shall not affect any other word, phrase or provision or application of this act which can be given effect without the invalid word, phrase, provision or application.

Explanatory Note. Act 64 added or amended the defs. of "fertilization," "gestational age," "pregnancy" and "unborn child" in section 3203 and added or amended sections 3204(c) and (d), 3205(a) and (c), 3206(f)(1), 3208(a), 3208.1, 3209, 3210, 3211, 3212(b), 3214(a), 3215(b), 3216, 3217, 3218(a), 3220 and 4302 of Title 18.

§ 7. Publication of forms and materials.

The Department of Health shall create the forms required by 18 Pa.C.S. §§ 3209(d) and 3214(a) within 30 days after the effective date of this act and shall cause to be published, within 60 days after the effective date of this act, the printed materials described in 18 Pa.C.S. § 3208(a).

§ 8. Applicability of reporting and distribution requirements.

No provision of this act requiring the reporting of information on forms published by the Department of Health, or requiring the distribution of printed materials published by the Department of Health pursuant to 18 Pa.C.S. § 3208, shall be applicable until ten days after the requisite forms are first created and printed materials are first published by the

Department of Health or until the effective date of this act, whichever is later.

§ 9. Effective date.
This act shall take effect as follows:
(1) The provisions of 18 Pa.C.S. §§ 3209(d) and 3214(a) requiring the Department of Health to create forms and of 18 Pa.C.S. § 3208(a) requiring the department to publish certain information shall take effect immediately.
(2) The remainder of this act shall take effect in 60 days.

1994, APRIL 21, P.L.130, NO.16

Preamble
The General Assembly finds and declares as follows:
(1) For the health, safety and welfare of the residents of this Commonwealth, the laws designed to deter the defacement of public and private property through the use of aerosol spray-paint cans, broad-tipped indelible markers and other marking devices should be strengthened.
(2) Where appropriate, the court should require those who commit acts of defacement to restore the damaged property to its original condition.

Explanatory Note. Act 16 amended section 3307 of Title 18.

1994, APRIL 21, P.L.131, NO.17

Preamble
The General Assembly finds and declares as follows:
(1) For the health, safety and welfare of the residents of this Commonwealth, the laws designed to deter the defacement of public and private property through the use of aerosol spray-paint cans, broad-tipped indelible markers and other marking devices should be strengthened.
(2) Where appropriate, the court should require those who commit acts of defacement to restore the damaged property to its original condition.

Explanatory Note. Act 17 amended section 3304 of Title 18 and added section 9720 of Title 42.

1994, DECEMBER 12, P.L.1248, NO.148

Preamble
The General Assembly finds and declares as follows:
The youth of Pennsylvania are the greatest resource of this Commonwealth and the Commonwealth finds that the protection of minors from the possible abuse of alcohol is of great importance.
The Commonwealth seeks to prevent minors from using alcoholic products. Nonalcoholic beer, wine and liquor contain amounts of alcohol and often taste, look and smell like legitimate alcoholic products. Therefore, the Commonwealth has a purpose in the restriction of sales of these products to minors.
Nonalcoholic beverages are made for those who want to enjoy the taste of alcohol without the effects of alcohol and should never be intended to introduce the youth of this Commonwealth to drinking beer, wine or liquor.

Explanatory Note. Act 148 amended or added sections 5781 and 6310.7 of Title 18.

1995, JUNE 13, 1ST SP.SESS., P.L.1024, NO.17

Preamble
The General Assembly hereby declares that the purpose of this act is to provide support to law enforcement in the area of crime prevention and control, that it is not the purpose of this act to place any undue or unnecessary restrictions or burdens on law-abiding citizens with respect to the acquisition, possession, transfer, transportation or use of firearms, rifles or shotguns for personal protection, hunting, target shooting, employment or any other lawful activity, and that this act is not intended to discourage or restrict the private ownership and use of firearms by law-abiding citizens for lawful purposes or to provide for the imposition by rules or regulations of any procedures or requirements other than those necessary to implement and effectuate the provisions of this

act. The General Assembly hereby recognizes and declares its support of the fundamental constitutional right of Commonwealth citizens to bear arms in defense of themselves and this Commonwealth.

Explanatory Note. Act 17 amended, added or repealed sections 913, 6101, 6102, 6103, 6104, 6105, 6106.1, 6107, 6109, 6110, 6110.1, 6111, 6111.1, 6111.2, 6111.3, 6111.4, 6111.5, 6112, 6113, 6114, 6115, 6116, 6117, 6118 and 6125 of Title 18 and sections 6308 and 9712 of Title 42 (Judiciary and Judicial Procedure).

1995, OCTOBER 11, 1ST SP.SESS., P.L.1058, NO.21

§ 5. Projected increases in State prison population.

Within 180 days of the effective date of this act, the Pennsylvania Commission on Sentencing shall, for the purpose of advising the General Assembly concerning future prison construction expenditures, publish projected increases in the State prison population resulting from implementation of this act.

Explanatory Note. Act 21 amended section 1103 of Title 18 and sections 6335, 9712, 9713 and 9714 of Title 42.

1997, MAY 9, P.L.142, NO.8

Preamble
The General Assembly finds and declares as follows:

(1) That look-alike or act-alike drugs are those drugs which are regularly marketed as stimulants or weight-loss aids and in their appearance look and in their effect act upon the body like illegal stimulants containing amphetamines.

(2) That look-alike or act-alike drugs are composed of various forms of ephedrine.

(3) That these look-alike or act-alike drugs are readily available to the public, regardless of age.

(4) That many children employ the use of look-alike or act-alike drugs as a starter drug prior to the use of illegal controlled substances.

Explanatory Note. Act 8 amended or added sections 6314 and 6316 of Title 18.

2000, JUNE 13, P.L.130, NO.25

Preamble
The General Assembly finds and declares as follows:

(1) The Internet is an increasingly valuable medium for communication and the dissemination and collection of information.

(2) The children of this Commonwealth utilize the Internet for entertainment, education and commerce.

(3) Many children in this Commonwealth have access to electronic mail accounts through their parents' accounts, shared accounts or their own personal accounts.

(4) Increasingly advertisers use the Internet to market explicit sexual materials to millions of users of the Internet.

(5) One of the frequently used vehicles for the marketing of explicit sexual materials via the Internet is unsolicited electronic mail messages.

(6) These unsolicited explicit sexual advertisements are sent to computers in Commonwealth households allowing children to view or have access to pornographic materials.

(7) Although there are an increasing number of Internet filtering software titles that parents can use to block access to obscene World Wide Web sites, these filtering software titles are ineffective against explicit sexual material that is sent via electronic mail.

(8) There is no universal method of identifying electronic mail messages that market explicit sexual materials.

(9) Despite the best efforts of parents to protect their children from explicit sexual material via electronic mail messages, they are unable to do so because there is no method by which they can separate and filter out inappropriate messages from appropriate messages.

(10) The Commonwealth has a compelling interest in protecting children from explicit sexual material.

(11) In doing so, government must enact a narrowly tailored remedy to avoid interfering with the growth or accessibility of this important medium and with the rights of adult users of the Internet under the first amendment

to the Constitution of the United States and section 7 of Article I of the Constitution of Pennsylvania.

(12) This act empowers parents to decide what type of messages are inappropriate for their children and effectively block those messages from their children's electronic mail accounts.

(13) This act does not restrict or prevent the sending of unsolicited explicit sexual electronic advertisements to any and all prospective recipients as long as an appropriate warning accompanies such advertisements.

Explanatory Note. Act 25 amended section 5903 of Title 18.

2000, DECEMBER 20, P.L.721, NO.98

Preamble

It is the intent of the General Assembly to protect our most vulnerable and precious citizens, the Commonwealth's children, from the ravages of sexual abuse. Because sexual crimes committed against children are among the most heinous imaginable, the General Assembly declares it to be in the public interest to enact this act.

Explanatory Note. Act 98 amended sections 2902, 2903 and 5903 of Title 18 and added section 9718.1 of Title 42.

2002, DECEMBER 9, P.L.1759, NO.218

§ 9. References to section 2709.

(1) Except as otherwise provided for in paragraph (2), any reference in any act or part of an act to 18 Pa.C.S. § 2709 without specification as to subsection (a) or (b) of that section shall be deemed to include a reference to 18 Pa.C.S. § 2709.1 as if fully set forth in that act or part of that act.

(2) Any reference in any act or part of an act to 18 Pa.C.S. § 2709(b) shall be deemed a reference to 18 Pa.C.S. § 2709.1 as if fully set forth in that act or part of that act.

Explanatory Note. Act 218 amended, added or repealed sections 2709, 2709.1, 2710, 2711, 4954, 4955, 5504, 5708 and 6105 of Title 18.

§ 10. References to section 5504.

(1) Except as otherwise provided for in paragraph (2) or (3), any reference in any act or part of an act to 18 Pa.C.S. § 5504 without specification as to subsection (a) or (a.1) of that section shall be deemed a reference to 18 Pa.C.S. §§ 2709(a)(4), (5), (6) and (7) and 2709.1 as if fully set forth in that act or part of that act.

(2) Any reference in any act or part of an act to 18 Pa.C.S. § 5504(a) shall be deemed a reference to 18 Pa.C.S. § 2709(a)(4), (5), (6) and (7) as if fully set forth in that act or part of that act.

(3) Any reference in any act or part of an act to 18 Pa.C.S. § 5504(a.1) shall be deemed a reference to 18 Pa.C.S. § 2709.1 as if fully set forth in that act or part of that act.

2003, SEPTEMBER 30, P.L.120, NO.24

§ 21. Applicability.
The following shall apply:
* * *
(5) The following apply to offenses committed before February 1, 2004:

(i) Except as set forth in subparagraph (ii) or (iii), this act shall not affect an offense committed before February 1, 2004, or any criminal, civil and administrative penalty assessed as a result of that offense.

(ii) Subparagraph (i) does not apply if a provision added or amended by this act specifies application to an offense committed before February 1, 2004, or to any criminal, civil or administrative penalty assessed as a result of that offense.

(iii) Subparagraph (i) does not apply to the following provisions:

(A) The amendment of 42 Pa.C.S. § 7003(5) in section 3 of this act.

(B) The amendment of 75 Pa.C.S. § 1516(c) and (d).

(C) The amendment of 75 Pa.C.S. § 1534(b).

(D) The amendment of 75 Pa.C.S. § 1547(d) in section 9.1 of this act.

(E) The amendment of 75 Pa.C.S. § 3731(a)(4)(i) and (a.1)(1)(i) in section 13 of this act.

Explanatory Note. Act 24 amended or repealed sections 6105, 7508.1, 7513 and 7514 of Title 18.

2004, NOVEMBER 30, P.L.1618, NO.207

§ 28. Applicability.

This act shall apply as follows:

(1) Except as otherwise provided in paragraph (2), any and all references in any other law to a "district justice" or "justice of the peace" shall be deemed to be references to a magisterial district judge.

(2) Paragraph (1) shall not apply to the provisions of 71 Pa.C.S.

Explanatory Note. Act 207 amended sections 103, 913, 1106, 2702, 3929, 3929.1, 4953.1, 4955, 6308, 6711 and 7311 of Title 18.

§ 29. Construction of law.

Nothing in this act shall be construed or deemed to provide magisterial district judges with retirement benefits or rights that are different from those available to district justices or justices of the peace immediately prior to the effective date of this act. Nothing in this act shall be construed or deemed to provide senior magisterial district judges with retirement benefits or rights that are different from those available to senior district justices immediately prior to the effective date of this act.

2005, NOVEMBER 10, P.L.335, NO.66

Preamble

The General Assembly finds and declares as follows:

(1) The provisions of 23 Pa.C.S. Ch. 61 (relating to protection from abuse) are necessary and proper in that they further the Commonwealth's compelling State interest to protect victims of domestic violence from abuse.

(2) The Second Amendment to the Constitution of the United States and section 21 of Article I of the Constitution of Pennsylvania recognize a fundamental right to keep and bear arms.

(3) The limitation of firearm rights for the duration of a protection from abuse order as authorized by 23 Pa.C.S. Ch. 61 is a reasonable regulation, a valid exercise of the police power of the Commonwealth and furthers the compelling State interest to protect victims from abuse.

(4) As provided in 23 Pa.C.S. Ch. 61, a court may impose limitations on firearm rights prohibiting someone who has engaged in domestic violence from possessing firearms when the court deems it appropriate to do so in order to protect a victim.

Explanatory Note. Act 66 amended or added sections 6102, 6105, 6106, 6109 and 6115 of Title 18 and sections 6102, 6103, 6104, 6105, 6106, 6107, 6108, 6108.1, 6108.2, 6108.3, 6108.4, 6108.5, 6110, 6113, 6113.1, 6114, 6117, 6119, 6120, 6121 and 6122 of Title 23.

§ 15. Effective date.

This act shall take effect as follows:

(1) The addition or amendment of 18 Pa.C.S. § 6109(e)(3) introductory paragraph, (i), (ii), (v) and (vi) shall take effect in 90 days.

(2) The addition or amendment of 18 Pa.C.S. § 6109(e)(3)(iii), (iv) and (4) shall take effect upon publication of the notice under 18 Pa.C.S. § 6109(h)(2) or five years and 60 days, whichever is first.

(3) This section shall take effect immediately.

(4) The remainder of this act shall take effect in 180 days.

2006, MAY 11, P.L.155, NO.36

Preamble

The General Assembly finds and declares as follows:

(1) Driving under the influence of alcohol or a controlled substance is a crime with thousands of victims in this Commonwealth.

(2) Evidence exists that victim impact panels are effective in reducing offender recidivism and restoring balance to victims' lives in driving under the influence cases.

(3) The purpose of this act is to recognize the value of victim impact panels at reducing offender recidivism and addressing victims' issues, to encourage counties to implement the panels and to establish a coordinating committee to provide standardized guidance for the panels.

Explanatory Note. Act 36 amended section 7508.1 of Title 18 and sections 3802 and 3804 of Title 75.

2006, NOVEMBER 29, P.L.1567, NO.178

Preamble

The General Assembly hereby declares its intention to enact versions of Jessica's Law and Megan's Law in this Commonwealth.

Explanatory Note. Act 178 amended or added section 3130, Subchapter C of Chapter 31 and sections 4915 and 6138 of Title 18 and sections 9718, 9718.2, 9718.3, 9795.1, 9795.2, 9798.3 and 9799.2 of Title 42.

2011, JUNE 28, P.L.48, NO.10

Preamble
The General Assembly finds that:
(1) It is proper for law-abiding people to protect themselves, their families and others from intruders and attackers without fear of prosecution or civil action for acting in defense of themselves and others.
(2) The Castle Doctrine is a common law doctrine of ancient origins which declares that a home is a person's castle.
(3) Section 21 of Article I of the Constitution of Pennsylvania guarantees that the "right of the citizens to bear arms in defense of themselves and the State shall not be questioned."
(4) Persons residing in or visiting this Commonwealth have a right to expect to remain unmolested within their homes or vehicles.
(5) No person should be required to surrender his or her personal safety to a criminal, nor should a person be required to needlessly retreat in the face of intrusion or attack outside the person's home or vehicle.

Explanatory Note. Act 10 amended or added sections 501, 505, 506, 3903, 6102 and 6109 of Title 18 and section 8340.2 of Title 42.

2014, JULY 2, P.L.945, NO.105

§ 9. Application of law.
Applicability is as follows:
(1) The addition of 18 Pa.C.S. Ch. 30 shall apply to offenses committed on or after the effective date of this section.
(2) Section 2 (repeal of 18 Pa.C.S. §§ 3001, 3002, 3003 and 3004) of this act shall not affect the validity of a prosecution initiated under the repealed sections.

Explanatory Note. Act 105 amended, added or repealed section 911, Chapter 30 and section 5708 of Title 18 and sections 4415, 4436, 5552, 5945.3, 9720.2, 9738 and 9799.14 of Title 42.

2015, NOVEMBER 4, P.L.224, NO.59

Preamble
The General Assembly finds and declares that it is the legislative intent in enacting this act:
to deter and prohibit an individual who is involved with matters relating to labor relations from engaging in harassment, stalking and threats to use weapons of mass destruction, as set forth in this act; and
not to modify or repeal an otherwise legal right that an individual who is involved with matters relating to labor relations may otherwise have.

Explanatory Note. Act 59 amended sections 2709, 2709.1 and 2715 of Title 18.

2018, FEBRUARY 21, P.L.27, NO.10

§ 20. Applicability.
This act applies as follows:
* * *
(2) The addition of 18 Pa.C.S. § 4915.2 and 42 Pa.C.S. Ch. 97 Subch. I shall apply to:
(i) An individual who committed an offense set forth in 42 Pa.C.S. § 9799.55 on or after April 22, 1996, but before December 20, 2012, and whose period of registration as set forth in 42 Pa.C.S. § 9799.55 has not expired.
(ii) An individual required to register with the Pennsylvania State Police under a former sexual offender registration law of this Commonwealth as set forth in 42 Pa.C.S. § 9799.55(a)(1)(i), (b)(2) and (4).

(iii) An individual who, before or after the effective date of this paragraph:

(A) commits an offense subject to 42 Pa.C.S. Subch. H; but

(B) because of a judicial determination on or after the effective date of this section of the invalidity of 42 Pa.C.S. Subch. H, is not subject to registration as a sexual offender.

Explanatory Note. Act 10 amended or added sections 3130, 3141, 4915.1 and 4915.2 of Title 18, sections 2511, 6303, 6338.1 and 6707 of Title 23 and sections 9718.1, 9718.5, 9799.10, 9799.11, 9799.12, 9799.13, 9799.14, 9799.15, 9799.16, 9799.19, 9799.23, 9799.25, 9799.26, 9799.31, 9799.32, 9799.34, 9799.36, 9799.38, 9799.39, 9799.42 and Subchapter I of Chapter 97 of Title 42.

2018, JUNE 12, P.L.140, NO.29

§ 21. Applicability.
This act shall apply as follows:
* * *

(2) The reenactment or amendment of 18 Pa.C.S. § 4915.2 and 42 Pa.C.S. Ch. 97 Subch. I shall apply to:

(i) An individual who committed an offense set forth in 42 Pa.C.S. § 9799.55 on or after April 22, 1996, but before December 20, 2012, and whose period of registration as set forth in 42 Pa.C.S. § 9799.55 has not expired.

(ii) An individual required to register with the Pennsylvania State Police under a former sexual offender registration law of this Commonwealth as set forth in 42 Pa.C.S. § 9799.55(a)(1)(i), (b)(2) and (4).

(iii) Before or after February 21, 2018, an individual who:

(A) commits an offense subject to 42 Pa.C.S. Ch. 97 Subch. H; but

(B) because of a judicial determination on or after February 21, 2018 of the invalidity of 42 Pa.C.S. Ch. 97 Subch. H, is not subject to registration as a sexual offender.

Explanatory Note. Act 29 amended or reenacted sections 3130, 3141, 4915.1 and 4915.2 of Title 18, sections 2511, 6303, 6338.1 and 6707 of Title 23 and sections 9718.1, 9799.10, 9799.11, 9799.12, 9799.13, 9799.14, 9799.15, 9799.16, 9799.19, 9799.23, 9799.25, 9799.26, 9799.31, 9799.32, 9799.34, 9799.36,

9799.38, 9799.39, 9799.42 and Subchapter I of Chapter 97 of Title 42.

2018, JUNE 28, P.L.402, NO.56

Preamble
The General Assembly finds and declares as follows:

(1) Individuals with charges not leading to convictions may be inherently harmed by the maintenance of that record and have a constitutional presumption of innocence.

(2) Individuals convicted of crimes in this Commonwealth should serve their sentences as ordered by the courts of this Commonwealth.

(3) After less violent individuals convicted of crimes have served their sentences and remained crime free long enough to demonstrate rehabilitation, the individuals' access to employment, housing, education and other necessities of life should be fully restored.

(4) Criminal justice agencies need access to all criminal history record information in order to effectively carry out the agencies' duties to protect the public.

(5) The Commonwealth shall provide a clean slate remedy, as set forth under this act, to:

(i) Create a strong incentive for avoidance of recidivism by offenders.

(ii) Provide hope for the alleviation of the hardships of having a criminal record by offenders who are trying to rehabilitate themselves.

(iii) Save the Commonwealth money that must be spent in the administration of criminal justice when offenders recidivate.

(iv) Ensure appropriate access to criminal history information by criminal justice agencies.

(6) The clean slate remedy should be implemented without cost to the former offender of filing a petition with a court.

Explanatory Note. Act 56 amended or added sections 9121, 9122.1, 9122.2, 9122.3, 9122.4, 9122.5, 9122.6 of Title 18 and sections 6307, 6308 of Title 42.

§ 4. Applicability.
The following shall apply:

(1) The Pennsylvania State Police and the Administrative Office of Pennsylvania Courts shall identify and complete the processing of

records that are eligible, on the effective date of this paragraph, for limited access under 18 Pa.C.S. § 9122.2, within 365 days following the effective date of this paragraph.

(2) A petition for limited access under 18 Pa.C.S. § 9122.1 may be filed beginning 180 days after the effective date of this paragraph.

2018, OCTOBER 19, P.L.535, NO.80

§ 6. Continuation of prior law.

The addition of 18 Pa.C.S. Ch. 28 is a continuation of the act of December 15, 1986 (P.L.1595, No.175), known as the Antihazing Law. Except as otherwise provided in 18 Pa.C.S. Ch. 28, all activities and duties initiated under the Antihazing Law shall continue and remain in full force and effect and may be completed under 18 Pa.C.S. Ch. 28. Orders, regulations, rules and decisions which were made under the Antihazing Law and which are in effect on the effective date of this section shall remain in full force and effect until revoked, vacated or modified under 18 Pa.C.S. Ch. 28. Prosecutions and policies entered into under the Antihazing Law are not affected nor impaired by the repeal of the Antihazing Law.

Explanatory Note. Act 80 amended, added or repealed Chapter 28 and sections 6308 and 6308.1 of Title 18 and section 5803 of Title 42.

Made in the USA
Middletown, DE
11 June 2021